Bible Prophecy Secrets

Unlocking the Ancient Mystery of Daniel's 70 Weeks that was Sealed Until the Time of the End

Abraham Ojeda

Bible Prophecy Secrets: Unlocking the Ancient Mystery of Daniel's 70 Weeks that was Sealed Until the Time of the End

Second Edition 2024 - Revised, Expanded, and Updated

First Edition Published in 2023

Kingdom Secrets LLC
1942 Broadway St. STE 314C
Boulder, CO, 80302, US

https://www.kingdom-secrets.com

For permission requests, speaking inquiries, and bulk order purchase options, email abraham@kingdom-secrets.com.

Print ISBN: 979-8-9916555-0-7
Ebook ISBN: 979-8-9916555-9-0

Cover Design: Jorfran David S. and Abraham Ojeda
Illustrations: Abraham Ojeda, Jorfran David S., and Glenn Barbosa

Printed in the United States of America.

"…To you has been given to know the secrets of the kingdom of God…"

— Luke 8:10 (TLV)

Contents

Secret Five

How to Overcome These Evil Days with Faith

Preface to the 2nd Edition

The purpose of this expanded version of *Bible Prophecy Secrets* is to provide the most definitive and up-to-date work that explains the 70 Weeks of Daniel prophecy in its entirety. Once this prophecy is properly unlocked, nearly all of the Bible's prophetic Scriptures make sense and can be further reckoned into God's specific timeline of the final 49-year cycle of mankind's history that we are currently living through. Rather than being in a place of constantly guessing, any student who has understood the full context and message of Daniel chapter 9 will be able to proceed calmly and triumphantly into the chaotic future of the coming Great Tribulation period.

To date, the vast multitude of Christian authors and leaders are continuing to promote the completely erroneous 490-year interpretation of the 70 Weeks prophecy. Mind you, this is an interpretation that has been promoted since roughly the third century AD. By continuing to push this lie, people are placing themselves under the dangerous condemnation of being false teachers, albeit some do have good intentions. It is my hope that with this updated second edition, a great revival can still take place—an outpouring of the profound truth within God's Word coupled with a renewed respect and love for His Torah (Genesis to Deuteronomy), a love which is absolutely essential for *any* attempt at understanding end-times prophecy.

If I could do it all over again and release the first and original edition exactly as it was written, I would have no choice. Back in early 2023 when the first edition was published, I was not sure exactly what was to happen on September 22, 2023—the prophesied date of the abomination of desolation spoken of by Daniel the prophet and further explained by Jesus in the Gospels. To be more exact, the first edition maintained a strong emphasis on the words of Daniel 12:11 where we are given the exact number of the 1290 day count. This verse was carefully interpreted to be the number of days from March 11, 2020 (the taking away of the "tamid" or "daily life" with the Covid-19 pandemic declaration) to September 22, 2023 (the abomination of desolation). My interpretation of Scripture further maintained that the aforementioned date would be the exact moment in time when Jesus warned His people in Judea to flee when they see the abomination of desolation and to brace themselves for a time more disastrous than even Noah's Flood (see Mat. 24:21).

Preface to the 2nd Edition

Being one of the very few believers to understand the gravity of this prophetic situation together with the immense warnings given by Jesus in the Gospels, I had no choice but to warn as many as I could about September 22, 2023 as being the likely beginning of the Great Tribulation, lest there be blood on my hands for remaining silent. I had mentioned many times in the Overcome Babylon podcast that I could be wrong about this assertion; and Elohim is my witness that I was never so presumptuous as to state "Thus says the Lord" when speaking of my findings, though people falsely accused me of such foolish behavior. Looking back on the first edition, I believe that my only shortcoming was that I did not incessantly state a similar disclaimer that I could be wrong about when the Great Tribulation begins.

As you will find out in this updated edition, I do not believe I was wrong *at all* about September 22, 2023 being directly connected to the prophecy of the abomination of desolation, as it is my conclusion that this was the precise date that Iran "set up" one or more nuclear weapons that will be used to unleash the Great Tribulation very soon. The key words of Daniel 12:11 are the words "set up", and I failed to connect this understanding to Zechariah 5:11 and the "set there" of the flying missile (scroll) in the land of Shinar (Iran). I will explain to you all of these connected scriptures, evidence, and real-world events that all intersected before and shortly after September 22, 2023 to easily arrive at this conclusion; and this information is precisely why this second edition was necessary to produce. The world will soon see that the Great Tribulation will begin with devastating attacks on 1948 Israel and more specifically, Jerusalem; and as these events unfold, this book will be your go-to guide for fully understanding all of the things the our loving Father intended for His people to know. This book will provide clear and quantifiable outcomes of the major prophetic events of human history that are to unfold within the next twenty years, and especially in the next ten.

By God's grace, get ready to overcome the darkest days of humanity's existence, and may *Bible Prophecy Secrets* assist you in navigating all of the madness that is about to unfold.

Your brother in this spiritual war,
Abraham Ojeda

PS: Every marriage begins with a date,
Every date begins with a first impression,
And every first impression begins with an introduction.

Preface to the 2nd Edition

If your first impression of Jesus has been polluted by the mainstream churches and their politically correct and effeminate pulpits, then in reality, you have never actually had a first impression of Jesus after all, because the vast majority of religious institutions are not actually capable of introducing Someone that they have never personally met.

Having not been to church since 2016, I can testify to the fact that I only found my life's calling, purpose, and profound fulfillment outside of the four prison walls of a religious organization.

Church, Bible college, and seminary have miserably failed us, as you will fully realize in this book.

And it's now time to rise up and meet Jesus, if perhaps for the first time ever, in the most humble atmosphere of privacy and intimacy—where there is no artificial pressure of an "altar call," laced with emotionally manipulative music and the glaring eyes of churchgoers whose boisterous opinions regarding your personal life with God hold far too much destructive influence.

Yes.

It is within this very moment that Jesus—the Elohim (God) of Genesis chapter one—the Author of Life has arrived at this exact intersection of space and time, as if to provide the proverbial tap on the shoulder, standing at the door of your heart and knocking.

For it is time to simply say, "Yes, Lord Jesus… I am here. Reveal Yourself to Me. I want to know You for who You really are, and not who they say You are. I want to know You for real. I am ready to know the Truth, and I want the Truth to set me free. I want the evil and sin of my life, whatever that is and whatever it looks like—You know—to be a thing of the past. Forgive me, and cleanse me of all unrighteousness. Amen."

That's it.

It's not the word count that matters but the deep, profound, and reckless abandonment of one's preconceived notions that creates a new world of possibilities within your heart and mind.

Preface to the 2nd Edition

A world of possibilities to see God for who He really is and experience a radically different "narrow road" than the nonsense that has been portrayed by unregenerate and degenerate men disguised as "leaders" in pulpits.

It's time to be sincere in the eyes of Almighty God, for nothing is hidden from His view, and attempting to deceive Him is impossible. Let anything less than pure, undefiled sincerity be left behind, and let the altar of falsehood belong to those who walk in the stubbornness of their hearts while thinking themselves blessed and holy.

Why This Book Is Different

Bible Prophecy Secrets will show you how to think for yourself and apply principles that you can take with you for the rest of your life. This work is an exercise in biblical mastery.

What you are going to discover within the pages of this book is a deep love, pursuit, and showcase of the truth. You are going to hear me repeat many times that the best commentary on the Bible is the Bible itself. The problem is that most people lose sight of the importance of the languages—Hebrew and Greek—in which the Text was originally written.

When seeking for the absolute truth, it's far less important what has been translated into English (or German, Spanish, French, etc.), and it is of utmost importance to know what the original words of the Text actually mean. Not only that, but the Hebrew language came first!

So, what language do you think we are going to focus on like crazy?

In the spirit of honoring the original Hebrew God-breathed Text in which the 70 Weeks prophecy of Daniel was originally given, I will be regularly using *Yeshua* instead of the modern English equivalent, *Jesus,* even though I personally use both names in everyday life. I will also make an effort to include the tetragrammaton name of God as *Yehovah* instead of the inaccurate English replacement word, *LORD*. I will also sometimes use *Elohim* instead of the modern English equivalent, *God.*

The 70 weeks of Daniel will also be the central theme of this book. In order to begin to understand Daniel, you must put on the mind of a Hebrew man living in the 6th century BC. This was a man that practiced the Laws of God and was considered among the three most righteous men of all time alongside Noah and Job (Eze.14:14). Using a concordance (Hebrew and Greek word-study tool) to extract the original meanings isn't a suggestion, it's a law of interpretation. We'll talk more about the Three Laws of Interpretation later.

Over the years, there have been many cash-grab books and presentations that have flooded the end times marketplace. Books with very little Scriptural backing have been hitting the bestsellers lists on Amazon, and even though they end up being wrong, nobody ever gets a refund. Since Covid and the events of 2020, there have been so many teachers and commentators of biblical end times prophecy popping up all over the place. Tik-Tok and YouTube are getting flooded with content about Revelation, the mark of the beast, and the antichrist. It seems like everyone has just a slightly different "spin" on an idea and then go on to create a whole platform and brand from which to monetize their idea.

It is unsettling to think about how people are going to have to answer for their misguided, inaccurate, and outright false teachings of Scripture. From Moses to Revelation, we are told that there are consequences for adding to or taking away from the Word of God (Deu. 12:32, Rev. 22:18,19). James even warns us that teachers will receive a stricter judgment (Jas. 3:1).

I understand these things.

I am not ignorant of what the Bible plainly warns.

But when was the last time you heard all those preachers out there put their own feet to the fire and admit these truths to you? There is a cancer of Bible interpretation out there where people boldly state their own opinions as facts; and you won't see that here. I will honestly tell you when something is my opinion. I will also show you where the Bible speaks for itself.

This book is about much more than prophecy and the 70 weeks of Daniel. *Bible Prophecy Secrets* will give you a solid foundation for biblical interpretation that will equip you to draw close to God and experience His power in your life like you never could have imagined.

Get ready.

Introduction

Before unpacking any of the treasure found in the Scriptures, I have a question for you. Do you want to be obedient to God?

The truth is that you and I today are explicitly commanded to know and understand the prophecy of the 70 weeks of Daniel. Here's what the Text says:

"…consider the matter, and understand the vision…"
(Daniel 9:23 NKJV)

"Know therefore and understand…"
(Daniel 9:25)

"…none of the wicked shall understand, but the wise shall understand."
(Daniel 12:10)

Figure 0.1: God's Command To Us. We are told at the end of the book of Daniel that the prophecy was "sealed till the time of the end" (Dan. 12:9). We are the final generation to whom this commandment of understanding was explicitly given, and it's time to walk into a place of obedience.

When the angelic messenger was saying these words, he wasn't actually telling Daniel to understand the vision. Daniel couldn't. He *tried* but simply could not understand. However, Daniel was obedient to write down what was said to him because the command was for those of us living in the time of the end that I will prove to you is *right now*.

The truth is that seminaries, church leaders, and religious institutions of all kinds have utterly failed us. They lied to us. And it's now time to open up this prophecy with a fresh understanding. Now that we are at the time of the end, we must look at this prophecy like a studious Berean from the book of Acts and unseal its truths, before it's too late to take action. *The time for spiritual preparation is right now.*

Please hear me out.

We are running out of time. There are events unfolding right at this moment that are truly horrifying. World War III, vaccine injuries, new pandemics, monetary inflation—the list goes on and on.

But what if I told you that in the midst of all the noise and distractions, there is a truly urgent event that is about to unfold, yet hardly anyone is talking about it? This event has to do with the abomination of desolation that has been prophesied by Daniel the prophet and again repeated by Yeshua in Matthew, Mark, and Luke. When our Master repeats something three times, I think we should really be paying attention, don't you? Before we explore the heart of the Text, I know what you might be thinking:

> "But, no man knows the day or the hour…"
> "You sound like a date-setting false prophet…"

Let me start by saying that I don't claim to be a prophet. I am simply a watchman and a practitioner of the Word. Now, let's talk about Yeshua's words. The reality is that He was talking about a very specific event when He said "no man knows the day or the hour". He was talking about His return to earth. He was *not* talking about prophecies like the abomination of desolation. Why else would Daniel have been given exact—and I mean exact—numbers that pertain to this particular event? Just take a look for yourself at what is written at the very end of the book of Daniel.

11 "And from the time *that* the daily *sacrifice* is taken away, and the abomination of desolation is set up, *there shall be* one thousand two hundred and ninety days.
12 "Blessed *is* he who waits, and comes to the one thousand three hundred and thirty-five days.
(Dan. 12:11,12)

Why would Daniel have recorded such specific days for us if it's utterly pointless information because "no man knows the day or the hour"? The answer to this question will both amaze and humble you.

Introduction

WHAT IS MYSTERY BABYLON?

In early 2022, I launched my website and podcast called Overcome Babylon, out of which this book has been born. This simple act of being obedient to the calling of God on my life has changed me forever, and I encourage you to be faithful to His calling, whatever that may look like. For me, it was sitting inside of my truck, grabbing a microphone, and recording deep studies through the Word of God that had been on my heart for years.

Figure 0.2: The Overcome Babylon Logo. The pyramid represents the Freemasons, Illuminati, and other secret societies that have seduced the masses into serving the Mystery Babylon system. The sword of God's Word (Eph. 6:17) stabs through the "all-seeing eye" of the satanic New World Order, causing it to bleed a slow, painful death.

Throughout the podcast and this book, I talk about Babylon and Mystery Babylon quite a bit. This spiritual metaphor is based on this passage from Revelation 17:3-5:

3 "So he carried me away in the Spirit into the wilderness. And I saw a woman sitting on a scarlet beast *which was* full of names of blasphemy, having seven heads and ten horns.
4 "The woman was arrayed in purple and scarlet, and adorned with gold and precious stones and pearls, having in her hand a golden cup full of abominations and the filthiness of her fornication.
5 "And on her forehead a name *was* written:
MYSTERY, BABYLON THE GREAT, THE MOTHER OF HARLOTS AND OF THE ABOMINATIONS OF THE EARTH."

When you see me referring to Mystery Babylon, I'm not talking about the literal kingdom that conquered Judah in 586 BC. I'm talking about the spiritual system of darkness that has existed for quite a long time now. We are also told that this system currently ruling over the earth is a "great city" in these words of John: "And the woman whom you saw is that great city which reigns over the kings of the earth" (Rev. 17:18).

Introduction

Many people speculate about where this *great city* might be. The majority say it's the Vatican. Some say it's Washington D.C., or maybe it's the City of London. Many others say it is New York City. The problem is that anyone can make the Bible say whatever they want it to, but what does it actually tell us? Well, it turns out that these words of Rev. 11:7-8 give us the exact answer within the context of a future event where the "two witnesses" are killed:

7 "When they finish their testimony, the beast that ascends out of the bottomless pit will make war against them, overcome them, and kill them.
8 "And their dead bodies *will lie* in the street of the great city which spiritually is called Sodom and Egypt, where also our Lord was crucified."

The obvious question for us to ask is where was Yeshua crucified? We are told that He was on the cross on Golgotha which is immediately outside the city of Jerusalem. Therefore, Jerusalem is Mystery Babylon the Great, that Great City which has been ruling over all the kings of the earth during the last days of mankind. It is also spiritually Sodom and Egypt—a place of great wickedness and bondage. The identity of "Sodom" is plainly evident. Tel-Aviv together with Jerusalem host some of the largest annual gay pride festivals in the entire Middle East and indeed, the world, recently boasting a 150,000-person march during the 25th anniversary event of 2023.[1] In light of Revelation's description, the words from Psalm 74:4 must also be carefully considered, where the Psalmist declares, "Your enemies roar in the midst of Your meeting place; They set up their banners *for* signs." As will be thoroughly discussed in this book, an enemy has possessed the land of Israel in these last days, and they are easily recognizable simply by looking at their signs. In other words, we must pay attention to the symbolism, banners, and insignia that completely reveal the true identity of Mystery Babylon.

Regarding Egyptian symbolism, have you ever paid attention to the symbolism used throughout the building of the highest court in Israel? This Supreme Court building was not a taxpayer-funded project democratically instituted by the people of 1948 Israel. Rather, this building was donated by a member of arguably the most powerful banking cartel in the world today—the Rothschild family. It was actually the Jewish woman Dorothy de Rothschild that donated this building to the Israeli government in the late 1960s.[2] The official website of the Supreme Court allows you to take a virtual tour through the various rooms and hallways of the court, and there is one particular webpage called "The Symbols" that explains the significance of a particular tablet with nine symbols hanging on a wall as one enters the administration wing.[3] Right in the center of this tablet is a pyramid. Of course, this isn't the only pyramid you will find. There is a giant copper-clad pyramid that projects outward from a prominent courtyard, and this pyramid is equipped with a circular window of an all-seeing-eye, just like you would see on a greenback dollar bill or any variety of Freemason or occult objects. This pyramid is a focal point of the entire Supreme Court building and is the most distinguishable feature of the entire architecture. In attempting to downplay the sinister nature of this pyramid, the official Supreme Court website states the following:

> "In Egyptian culture the pyramid symbolizes the concept of eternity, as it was the Pharaoh's eternal resting place after his death. According to the architects, the pyramid and the library are not only intended to serve our generation but to be a place where justice is dispensed in perpetuity."[4]

In other words, they are saying that the pyramid is a symbol of eternal justice being administered for the people. If by *justice* they meant the establishment of a Zionist new world order under the direction of foreign gods, then certainly this sign of the pyramid starts making more sense. The book of Revelation already predicted nearly 2,000 years ago that Mystery Babylon would be full of Egyptian symbolism and false gods—a description that would be impossible to perfectly predict apart from the divine authorship of the Holy Spirit.

However, this city will soon be destroyed by an alliance of ten kings as expressly declared within the words of Revelation 17:16 and further explained throughout Revelation 18. I will later show you that this is most certainly referring to the BRICS alliance of nations. Once this great city is judged and burned with fire, we are commanded to rejoice over her once God avenges His people as explicitly stated in Revelation 18:20. Because many people do not understand what the Bible plainly tells us about Mystery Babylon, many Christians, Messianics, and followers of Jesus will, sadly, be found weeping and mourning like the wicked when they should actually be celebrating with the "holy apostles and prophets" (Rev. 18:20) once Jerusalem is burned. The inevitable end of the current Western establishment headquartered in Jerusalem will be witnessed very soon, and you must understand which side of history you will fall under—on God's side with His rejoicing holy apostles and prophets, or with the weeping kings, merchants, and wicked men who lived luxuriously with Mystery Babylon.

Now please, don't get me wrong. I am not anti-Jewish. I have Jewish friends and have great respect for the land of Israel.

The problem is that 1948 Israel has its *deep state* just like any country.

Introduction

What do I mean by "deep state"? I am talking about the unelected, unaccountable elites hidden behind the veil of government that rule and enslave the people but without the people even being aware of their existence. These elites (most of them wealthy bankers and secret society families) create their agendas behind closed doors and use various non-governmental organizations (NGOs) in order to push their power on the masses.

Revelation tells us that Jerusalem is in fact the headquarters that has been responsible for all of this behavior worldwide from the time when the book of Revelation was first given to John until now. Jerusalem is the center and focal point of the history of the "synagogue of satan" that Jesus warned us about (Rev. 2:9, 3:9). It is a spiritual, economic, and military power; and throughout this book, we will focus on all three of these aspects of Mystery Babylon as they pertain to end times prophecy and Daniel.

The bottom line is that there is a dangerous and pervasive group-think mindset (as George Orwell calls it in *1984*) or "hive" mentality about the 70 weeks of Daniel that has been pushed within all of the major religions and their institutions. They all teach the same interpretation. They all repeat the same misguided lie. We are told in Revelation that it is in fact Mystery Babylon in Jerusalem that is responsible for all abominations and false doctrines worldwide. It is this spiritual Mystery Babylon system within all seminaries and establishments of biblical education that has been pushing the same interpretation of the 70 weeks of Daniel for many centuries now, and everyone has bought into it without even questioning it.

Take heed to the words of Daniel!

It's time for us to overcome this spiritual darkness together once and for all and shine like the stars forever:

"Those who are wise shall shine
Like the brightness of the firmament,
And those who turn many to righteousness
Like the stars forever and ever."
(Dan. 12:3)

Think about the power and outright beauty of that promise. Make no mistake, that's a promise in Dan. 12:3. It's a promise straight from the throne of our Father. As you go through these amazing words of prophecy with me line-by-line, please share this message with other people. Let's do our part to help others be wise and understand this prophecy so that they, too, might shine like the brightness of the firmament and like the stars forever. Let's teach others so that they can take their rightful place in the Kingdom of Heaven.

Secret I:

Unlocking the Truth of Daniel's 70 Weeks Prophecy

"And he said, 'Go your way, Daniel, for the words are closed up and sealed till the time of the end.'"

- *Daniel 12:9*

Chapter 1
Sealed Until the Time of the End

Let's get started by taking a look at the 70 weeks prophecy of Daniel chapter 9, which is the foundation of this entire book. Unless otherwise noted, I will continue to use the New King James Version since this is the translation I am the most familiar with and also because the English wording used in this prophecy is reasonably accurate to the Hebrew.

24 "Seventy weeks are determined
For your people and for your holy city,
To finish the transgression,
To make an end of sins,
To make reconciliation for iniquity,
To bring in everlasting righteousness,
To seal up vision and prophecy,
And to anoint the Most Holy.
25 "Know therefore and understand,
That from the going forth of the command
To restore and build Jerusalem
Until Messiah the Prince,
There shall be seven weeks and sixty-two weeks;
The street shall be built again, and the wall,
Even in troublesome times.
26 "And after the sixty-two weeks
Messiah shall be cut off, but not for Himself;
And the people of the prince who is to come
Shall destroy the city and the sanctuary.
The end of it *shall be* with a flood,
And till the end of the war desolations are determined.
27 "Then he shall confirm a covenant with many for one week;
But in the middle of the week
He shall bring an end to sacrifice and offering.
And on the wing of abominations shall be one who makes
    desolate,
Even until the consummation, which is determined,

Is poured out on the desolate."
(Dan. 9:24-27)

Merely reading these words fails to bring any level of satisfaction because they were meant to be diligently studied. If this is your first time looking at these words of prophecy, then you are in for a real treat within the pages of this book. If you have attempted to understand this prophecy in the past, you most likely heard the voices of many people echoing their man-made interpretations within your head as you simply read the prophecy at face value. I know what you are going through because I have been there myself. It can feel like a smothering or drowning sensation when you have the words of other people clouding your perception of the Bible. It is as if an invisible prison has been placed over your mind, and the first step to emphatically breaking free and thinking for yourself is to identify the problem. Consciously recognize what is happening within your mind so that you can finally break new ground in your comprehension of the Bible as a whole. I encourage you to maintain an open mind and be ready to be thoroughly challenged in regard to any preconceived notions that you may have about what the 70 weeks prophecy is truly talking about. I assure you that the diligent study presented in this book will allow you to step into a place of full consciousness concerning all of end-times prophecy.

Let me also start by saying that this book isn't what you think it is.

Yes, I am going to uncover what the 70 weeks prophecy of Daniel is actually talking about. I am going to show you the mysteries of God hidden from the foundation of the world and now revealed to us in these last days. But this book is much deeper than that.

This book is a formula.

I will show you how to apply very specific principles of Bible interpretation that if you choose to apply strictly in your own walk will radically and fundamentally change your life forever. Why do I say this with such authority? Because that's what the Word tells us. It simply *cannot and does not return void* but "shall prosper in the thing for which I sent it" (Isa. 55:11). However, I will tell you what *does* return void and worthless; and those are the man-made interpretations of Scripture that are disconnected from the foundation of the Truth.

THE PROPHECY HAS BEEN SEALED

The number one problem we as believers face is when church leaders present their own opinions as facts, and Bible facts as opinions. Here's what I mean by that.

Too many Bible teachers out there will authoritatively say something like "this is what the Bible says" as a statement of fact when in reality, it is a subjective opinion. Conversely, they will also present the Truth of the Bible as if it were a subjective opinion that doesn't really mean what it says or say what it means.

To make matters worse, church leaders have a take-it-or-leave-it approach to Scripture. They get upset if you disagree with their opinions. They don't like to be challenged. They'll kick you out of their fellowship if you find truths in the Bible that are different from the "statement of faith" on their website and literature. It's no wonder, then, that the vast majority of Bible believers have never had the kind of breakthrough understanding of prophecy that you will be experiencing in the pages of this book.

It is absolutely mind blowing that all of the Mystery Babylon institutions, churches, and seminaries have been teaching an identical interpretation of the 70 weeks of Daniel chapter 9 since the beginning of the 3rd century AD,[1] yet we are explicitly and undeniably told in the Text that this prophecy was *sealed until the time of the end.* This statement doesn't show up just once, but two times as recorded in Dan. 12:4 and 12:9:

4 "But you, Daniel, shut up the words, and seal the book until the time of the end; many shall run to and fro, and knowledge shall increase."
9 "And he said, 'Go *your way,* Daniel, for the words *are* closed up and sealed till the time of the end.'"

The angelic messenger that was sent to Daniel made it crystal clear that this message would be unable to be understood until the last days. So, let me ask the obvious question here: is God true and every man a liar, or is it the other way around? I'm not confused about the authority of the Bible, and you shouldn't be either.

Figure 1.1: The prophecy was written in code. We are told multiple times that Daniel recorded his book in such a way that it was "sealed". It is rather ridiculous that people have been promoting the same interpretation of the 490-years since the 3rd century AD when only our last-days generation would be able to understand the prophecy.

MODERN INTERPRETATIONS OF THE 70 WEEKS

Let's now take a quick moment to address the age old point of view and put it to the test. Here is how everyone under the sun teaches that the 70 weeks prophecy that you just read should be interpreted:

7 Years per Week x 70 Weeks = 490 Years Total

In other words, people have been saying that all end-times prophecy must fit into a 490-year period of time. Again, let me emphasize that this interpretation has been pushed since the 3rd century AD in order to promote the specific idea that this prophecy was mostly speaking of the first coming of Christ. There are some major problems that will become glaringly obvious as we unpack them together.

First, just stop and think about the four Gospels that we have. Look at all of the things Yeshua said about Himself and the various fulfillments of prophecy sprinkled throughout the texts of the Gospels. Now let me ask the obvious question. How many times do you see either Yeshua Himself or the author of a particular Gospel mention the book of Daniel?

Well, it is actually only mentioned three times—once in Matthew 24, Mark 13, and Luke 21, respectively. However, each time that Daniel is mentioned, Yeshua was warning about the abomination of desolation. He absolutely never under any circumstance whatsoever says something like:

Bible Prophecy Secrets

"Now is the word spoken of by Daniel the prophet concerning Me fulfilled, for the Son of Man must be cut off after the sixty-two weeks and raised up."

Yeshua absolutely *never* said this, yet every religion teaches what I just fabricated out of thin air as if it's part of the four Gospels.

Now I want you to examine the rest of the New Testament and see what these writers said about the book of Daniel. Do you see a major red flag? Absolutely none of the other writers ever speak of the book of Daniel at all, with *maybe* the minor exception of Revelation in which there is some overlap of abstract concepts.

My point is that none of the writers reference, quote, or point to Daniel chapter 9 at all in order to prove that the first coming of the Messiah in the first century AD was either a partial or complete fulfillment of the 70 weeks prophecy. Think about all of the various letters that Paul wrote. Out of the 27 books of the New Testament, he wrote 13 of them. He talked about all kinds of mysteries and quoted multitudes of prophets and passages from the Old Testament to give his readers understanding. Yet, Paul himself (as educated and eloquent as he was) never used Daniel 9 and the 70 weeks as authority or proof to write about the first coming of the Messiah.

With what I have just pointed out to you, it's really not necessary to go down the rabbit hole of understanding exactly *why* the 490-year interpretation has been pushed. It's really the same old thing we have been seeing in recent times. People desperately want to have an explanation for absolutely everything in the Bible, and cults are very notorious for this practice. Being humble enough to say *"I don't know"* is a rare practice amongst the leadership of Judeo-Christian religions. Some want to write books for fame and fortune. Others love the power trip that comes with a captive audience and speaking from stages.

The first century apostles and writers were a completely different breed. Even though many of them saw Yeshua's face, talked with Him, ate lunch together with Him, and heard the words directly out of His mouth, these believers did something that is completely radical according to today's standards. They chose to remain silent when the Bible was not clear to them.

Let that sink in for a moment.

Think of the humility of these people. This is the true reason why the writers of the New Testament did not speak at all about the 70 weeks of Daniel. It was not the time of the end yet, and they didn't understand it. Therefore, the Holy Spirit *did not* breathe inspiration into them so that they could write things down to explain the prophecy.

It's really that simple.

Just to get a clear picture of all the primary doctrines currently being taught, let's take a look at some of the major camps of religion and their views on the 70 weeks of Daniel chapter 9. I will be referring back to these diagrams in later chapters.

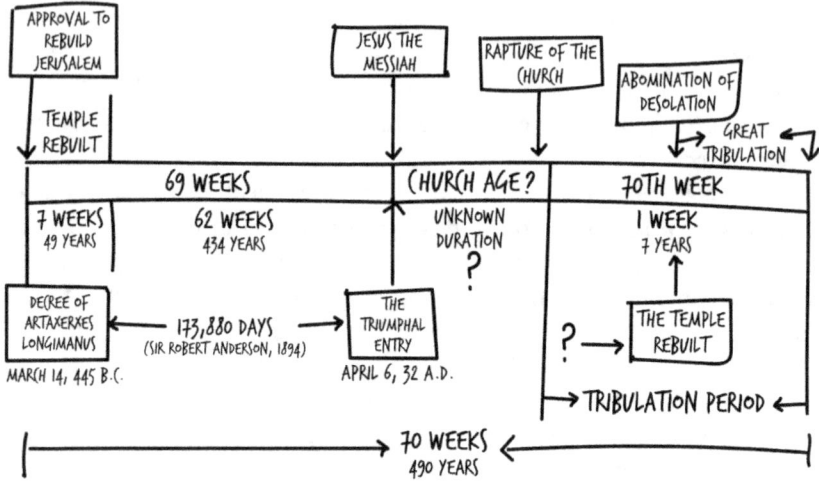

Figure 1.2: Evangelical, Protestant Christian Point of View. The idea here is that the rebuilding of the second temple in Jerusalem under Nehemiah begins the clock. There is then a gap after the death and resurrection of Jesus. This is referred to as the *gap theory,* and it has now lasted almost 2,000 years. The clock will then restart at some unknown time in the future to finish the final seven year period, or seventieth week, of Daniel. After the 70th week is complete, there is to be a millennial kingdom according to this viewpoint.

This chart represents a very large camp of people. Baptists, Pentecostals, Calvinists, Non-denominational—the belief here arguably represents the majority of Christians. In fact, this is the camp that I personally belonged to for the longest time. In recent times, this viewpoint became widely popularized by a Scottish Presbyterian author named Sir Robert Anderson with his 1894 book *The Coming Prince.* He calculated the first 69 weeks of the prophecy to be a period of 173,880 days, which is equivalent to 7 times 69 prophetic years of 360 days each.[2] According to Anderson, these 69 weeks took place from the decree of Artaxerxes on March 14, 445 BC to the triumphal entry of Jesus on April 6, AD 32.

However, there are disagreements as to when the clock starts. Though it is widely understood that Cyrus the Great initiated the return of Judah back to Jerusalem, the exact year that Artaxerxes Longimanus showed favor towards Nehemiah his cupbearer is debated. Nehemiah 2:1 tells us that it was the 20th year of the reign of Artaxerxes when Nehemiah received favor, and Robert Anderson's decision to declare 445 BC as the beginning of the prophetic clock was based on various calculations. Without getting too lost in all of the details, the main idea is that the 70 weeks prophecy supposedly began with the rebuilding of Jerusalem under the leadership of Nehemiah. The first sixty nine weeks, or 483 years, were then completed once the crucifixion of Christ took place, since Christians view Jesus as the only possible fulfillment of Dan. 9:26 where it speaks of an "anointed" (commonly translated as "messiah") being "cut off" (we will explore this verse in much greater detail later on).

The clock then suddenly stops. Without offering a proper explanation, this mainstream Christian doctrine of the 70 weeks prophecy goes on to assert that a gap theory is a vital part of God's prophetic time clock because we will not know when the seventieth week, or final seven-year period, of Daniel's prophecy will begin in the future. Proponents of this idea then go on to quote passages from the Gospels where Jesus states that "no man knows the day or the hour" of His return as being proof that a gap is part of the 70 weeks time-line. This argument is a blatantly dishonest handling of the Text, since Jesus only spoke explicitly of His return to Earth as being the day and hour which no man knows (Mar. 13:32, Mat. 24:36). As of the time of this writing, the unexplainable gap of the popular 490-year interpretation has now lasted roughly 1992 years from AD 32 (Anderson's assumed date of the crucifixion) to 2024.

As you will see in the next diagrams, the Jehovah's Witnesses and Seventh Day Adventists do not agree with the year 445 BC to begin the prophetic clock. In fact, they don't even agree with each other as to the specific year that the prophecy begins. Regardless of the nuances, mainstream Christians believe that Jesus has everything to do with the 70 weeks prophecy, and after His work on the cross was finished, the massive gap in the timeline commonly called the Church Age will continue until perhaps a rapture event (pretribula-tional rapture) or the rebuilding of a Jewish temple in Jerusalem initiates the future seventieth week of Daniel. We will explore the pre-trib rapture and these other related ideas later after first establishing the proper biblical foun-dation of the 70 weeks prophecy.

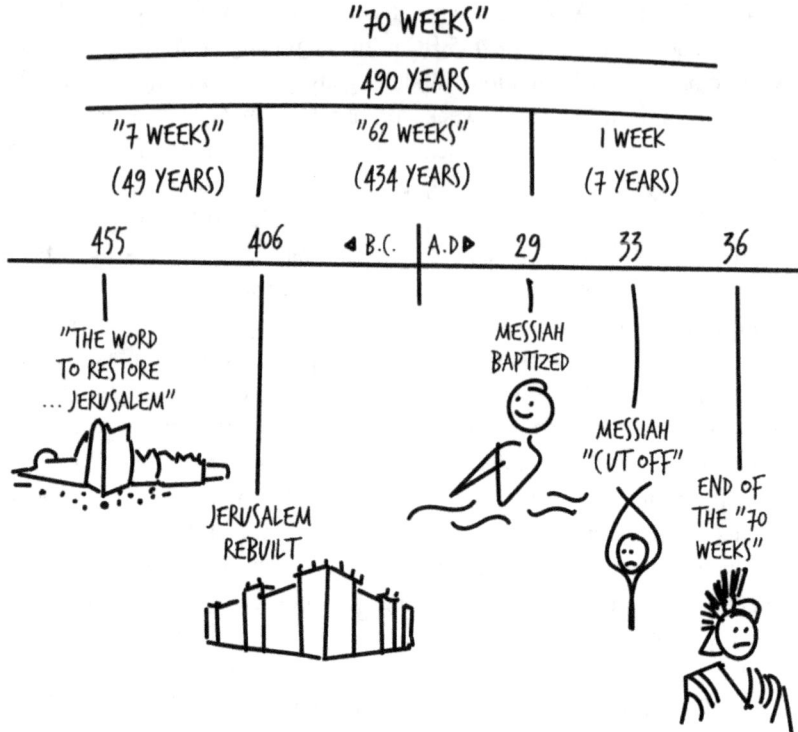

Figure 1.3: Jehovah's Witnesses (JW) and Traditional Catholic Viewpoints.
Rather than having a futurist, or future fulfillment, point of view like the
one mainstream Christianity holds, the JW and Catholic viewpoint is a
historicist, or purely historical, interpretation whereby the entire 70 weeks
prophecy was already fulfilled in the first century AD.

I have discovered through my research and conversations with members of
the Jehovah's Witnesses organization that they believe in a completely historical fulfillment of the 70 weeks of Daniel; and this illustration is based off of
the one found on their official website.[3]

The interpretation here also emphasizes the rebuilding of the walls of
Jerusalem while asserting that 455 BC was the 20th year of the reign of Artaxerxes when Nehemiah also received favor. In other words, the starting date is
ten years prior to the 445 BC date held by mainstream Christianity. This
different starting date might seem trivial at first glance, but it provides the
needed space to fit the additional seven-year period of the seventieth week of
Daniel into the timeline. If they had also declared the year 445 BC to be the
starting point of the prophecy, they would not be able to arrive at this historicist interpretation. Like the other interpretations of the 70 weeks, this point of

view is exclusively Messianic with a sole emphasis on the first coming of Christ. For example, when Daniel 9:24 says that 70 weeks are determined "to anoint the most holy", this is interpreted as referring to the calling of the 12 Apostles, which are said to have been recipients of miraculous power at Pentecost—a power that no other believers were privileged to experience like these founders of the New Testament church. However, this teaching false into disagreement with the plain words of Jesus, where He said, "And these signs will follow those who believe: In My name they will cast out demons; they will speak with new tongues; they will take up serpents; and if they drink anything deadly, it will by no means hurt them; they will lay hands on the sick, and they will recover" (Mark 16:17,18). Jesus never said that only the 12 Apostles would be recipients of the miraculous power of the Holy Spirit. That is why Paul, who was *not* one of the twelve, was endowed with the Holy Spirit in a remarkable way. Though absent from the vast majority of cold, dead religious organizations, this same power of the Holy Spirit continues to be available amongst believers to this very day.

The JW's final week of Daniel is said to have taken place from AD 29 right when Jesus was baptized to AD 36. They say that He was "cut off" in the middle of this seven year period which was the year AD 33. According to this historicist point of view, Daniel 9:27 is used to say that Jesus also brought a complete end to "sacrifice and offering" in the middle of this same seven-year period, but this teaching fails to recognize that early believers like Paul still attended the Temple in Jerusalem *after* the resurrection of Christ in order to voluntarily offer animal sacrifices as recorded in Acts 21:26. Ezekiel 40:5 also introduces the coming Temple in the city of the New Jerusalem, and animal sacrifices are once again instituted in this future Temple as recorded in Ezekiel 46, further making the aforementioned Messianic interpretation of Daniel 9:27 completely inconsistent with Scripture. Finally, no valid explanation is offered as to why the year AD 36 makes sense as a definitive stopping point according to the Scriptures. This final year is only selected out of the necessity to force the Messianic interpretation into the timeline.

I went ahead and mixed the Catholic church into this camp as well because they certainly do not fall into the Seventh Day Adventist camp, but they aren't completely in the mainstream Christian camp, either. Though the Catholics have varying positions, the traditionally held to viewpoint is that of a complete fulfillment of the 70 weeks in the past with Jesus the Messiah as the key component of the prophecy.[4]

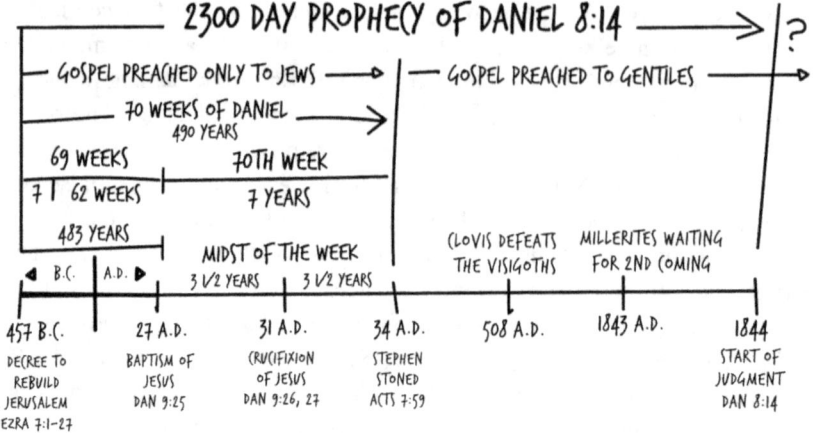

Figure 1.4: The Seventh Day Adventists (SDA) Interpretation. This interpretation borrows a verse from Daniel 8:14 speaking of the "two thousand three hundred evening-mornings" and then invents the idea that these 2,300 evening-mornings must be symbolic of prophetic years. Therefore, the 2,300-year prophecy of the SDA spans across quite a length of time from 457 BC all the way to AD 1844.

Boasting over 22 million members worldwide and 97,811 churches,[5] the SDA organization's influence is far greater than many realize. There are also various offshoots of the SDA such as the Worldwide Church of God originally started by Herbert W. Armstrong; and therefore, these beliefs apply to a large number of subgroups. Once again, we see inconsistencies between the three primary religious interpretations examined. In this case, the 20th year of Artaxerxes is now stated to be 457 BC by the SDA, and the baptism of Jesus is claimed to be AD 27. Recall that the JW organization declared these dates to be 455 BC and AD 26, respectively. Mainstream Christians have typically reckoned the starting point of the timeline to be 445 BC as opposed to 457 or 455 BC due to the influence of Sir Robert Anderson's work. As you can see, the ultra-popular Messianic interpretation of Daniel's 70 weeks prophecy is not so straightforward after all. With so much disagreement, it might seem like a hopeless endeavor to place any confidence in the 20th year of Artaxerxes as the starting point of the timeline. Thankfully, you will see that the true meaning of the 70 weeks prophecy is entirely different from these popular ideas presented so far. In fact, we can achieve extreme and perfect accuracy once the true meaning of the word *weeks* is understood.

Regarding the SDA viewpoint, the belief here is very similar to the Catholics and JW in that the entire 70 weeks prophecy was fulfilled in the past; but there is an interesting twist that involves the founding group of the

SDA called the Millerites. This group falsely predicted the second coming of Christ to be October 22, 1844 because their prophetic time clock of 2300 "years" began in 457 BC.[6,7] When this false prophecy did not occur and Christ did not appear in 1844, the event was labeled the Great Disappointment, and a major split in the early Adventist community occurred. Those who still wanted to have community and fellowship continued to call themselves *Adventists* and simply restructured their doctrinal beliefs to support the idea that something did in fact take place in 1844, but it was the beginning of judgment that was only visible in the heavenly realm.[8] How convenient, right? Surprisingly, the early SDA community continued to expand resiliently under the leadership of James White and particularly his wife, Ellen G. White, who received numerous "special revelations" and authored a large number of books to carry the relatively new religious movement forward.

Going back to Figure 1.4, notice that there is a question mark to the right of the 2300-Day prophecy arrow because it is not clear what exactly the SDA expect to take place beyond the year 1844. By declaring an end to two major prophecies—the 70 weeks and the 2300 evening-mornings—the SDA have shut their eyes and ears to some of the biggest events of the last days—events that will undoubtedly shock you as we uncover them together in this book. We will talk more about the "two thousand three hundred" of Daniel 8:14 in greater detail, and I will prove to you that the prophecy is in fact describing a specific number of days and *not* years based on careful handling of the Hebrew language.

Now that we have understood the three primary interpretations of the 70 weeks, it is important to point out that this is not an all-inclusive list. Some religions do not have a strong stance on this prophecy and vary greatly in their opinions. Other organizations like the Mormon Church (Latter Day Saints) do not have an official stance on the 70 weeks of Daniel, and most of their members are completely unaware of this prophecy's existence.

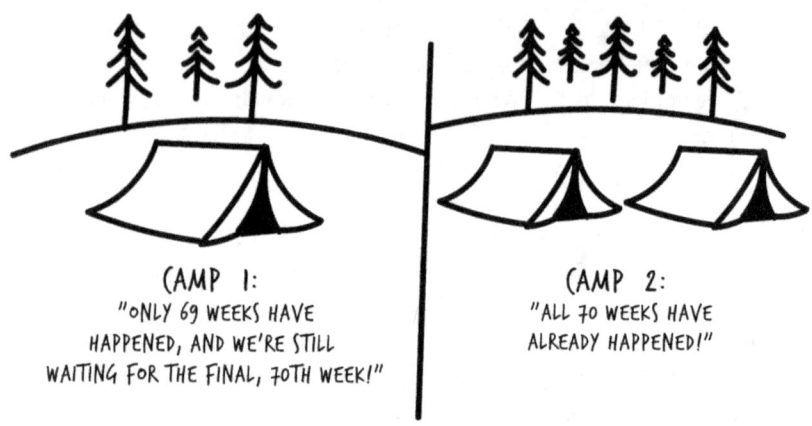

Figure 1.5: The Two Camps of Thought. All currently accepted interpretations of the 70 weeks of Daniel fall into two simple categories.

What it all really boils down to is that there are two camps of thought. People either believe that all of the 70 weeks already happened at some point in the past, or people believe that 69 weeks have been fulfilled and there is just one week left that will take place at a completely unknown time in the future. Regardless of the specifics, everyone thinks that this prophecy has something to do with a 490-year period of time. Everyone also assumes this prophecy *must* be talking about Jesus the Messiah and cannot possibly be referring to anything else.

Now you have a good idea of what the vast majority of religions are currently teaching and have been teaching for a long time. As I have already alluded to, we are now about to dive into the heart of what makes this book different from any other end times book you have ever read.

THE THREE LAWS OF INTERPRETATION

There are fundamental rules that will be applied consistently and methodically as we go through this prophecy together. These are the same rules that John, Peter, Paul, and all of the apostles used when they wrote their letters to different congregations around the world. These are the same principles of Bible interpretation that, if applied relentlessly, will guarantee that we will never, ever twist the Word of God to our own destruction like we are warned about in 2 Peter 3:16. I can't tell you how blessed and profound my walk has been with God since applying these exact same rules in my life that I am now about to show you. Not only will you discover a deeper, more meaningful and prosperous relationship with our Father, but you will begin to have the mind of Christ spoken of in Philippians 2:5—a mind of humility that does not seek recognition from and agreement with men, but a mind of obedience that seeks only the Truth that proceeds from the mouth of Yehovah. In other words, this book probably isn't what you were expecting. I am not going to simply give you the fish, but I am going to equip you with the skills so you can go catch fish for yourself. So, here they are:

Figure: 1.6: The Three Laws of Biblical Interpretation: 1. Law of First Mention; 2. Law of Definitions; 3. Law of Context

Notice that I am calling these "Laws", which is a rather bold claim. We are commanded in Deuteronomy 12:32 that we are not to add to or take away from the Word. But at the same time, we have received God's Holy Spirit, who Yeshua referred to as our Teacher (Jhn. 14:26); and through the born-again experience of belief we are able to interpret not just the exact letter of the Law but the Spirit of the Law that's behind the letters (Rom. 7:6). It is within this precise intersection that these three Laws can be discovered.

I can tell you based on the past 17 years of being a believer that failure to apply these methods of biblical interpretation will result in making the Bible say whatever imagination of the heart comes to mind. I've heard numerous evangelicals say that they rely on "feeling the presence of God" in order to decide whether or not certain teachings are true. Many mormons refer to this phenomenon as the "burning in the bosom." Don't get me wrong. Feelings aren't bad or evil in and of themselves because God gave them to us. But we don't use feelings as a primary tool for Bible interpretation. That's just *not* how it works. Destructive cults, wolves in sheep's clothing, and all false teachers have one thing in common. They will always be found breaking these three rules. Always. That's why I refer to them as *Laws*. These three unwritten Laws, like scales of justice, must be constantly used to weigh out words, verses, and passages of Scripture so that the absolute truth can be found. In order for something to be *truth*, it must be balanced and found in agreement with the whole of God's Word. This book will clearly demonstrate this process through a variety of case studies, with some of them being the most difficult prophecy studies of the entire Bible.

Law of First Mention

The original Text of the Bible has been preserved as Hebrew in the Old Testament and Greek in the New Testament. Because the Hebrew Scriptures came first they determine all (and I mean 100%) of Scripture interpretation from cover to cover. If there is a concept in the Greek that seems to contradict the Hebrew Scriptures, it is not the Greek words in question that contradict the Hebrew. It is only your understanding that is faulty, and you have to go back to the Hebrew to make the proper connections.

That's the first part of this law.

The second part of this law of interpretation is that when a Hebrew word appears in the Text for the very first time, then that usage of the word is extremely important for understanding the meaning that the Holy Spirit breathed for that word throughout the rest of the Text.

Law of Definitions

In order to understand the meaning of a verse or a passage, the definitions of each and every single word should be looked up in order to fully and completely understand what is being said. Again, we don't care what we in our 21st century mind and vocabulary believe the words to say. Instead, what do the words actually mean? What is the originally intended meaning in the Text?

We are commanded that we should not live by bread alone but by every word that proceeds from the mouth of Yehovah (Deu. 8:3). How in the world can you and I actually live this way if we don't bother to understand the true meaning found in the Text? We must constantly be going back to the original Hebrew and Greek tongues, for this necessity was actually prophesied by Isaiah in the 8th century BC:

9 To whom will he teach knowledge, and to whom will he explain the message? Those who are weaned from the milk, those taken from the breast?
10 For it is precept upon precept, precept upon precept, line upon line, line upon line, here a little, there a little.
11 For by people of strange lips **and with a foreign tongue** the LORD will speak to this people
(Isa. 28:9-11 ESV) [emphasis added]

This prophetic declaration would not have made sense to Isaiah's audience in those days but instead applies to you and I today. We must always investigate the foreign tongues of the Bible, and for many centuries, this was not an easy task for God's people. Thanks to the work of James Strong who published his Exhaustive Concordance of the Bible in 1890, students now have an index to be able to easily find Hebrew, Aramaic, and Greek words throughout the Bible. This work is kind of like the Rosetta Stone of deciphering the Bible. Known as the "Strong's numbers", Strong assigned a numerical value to every single original language word in the King James Version of the Bible. This advancement allowed students to take the power of interpretation back into their own hands rather than relying exclusively on a translator or a translation. Strong's numbers clearly show how a given original language word was translated into an equivalent English word, giving readers the ability to locate the exact places in which the same ancient word is used in order to discern the original meanings. Students now have much needed insight into the inevitable mistakes and misunderstandings throughout modern translations using the lens of the concordance. Again, it is not the original Word of God that is inaccurate, but it is only faulty understandings that cause problems. We will be discovering several of these misunderstandings in this book, so make sure to verify the information presented by getting access to a Strong's Concordance if you don't have one already.

One of the best free resources containing an easy-to-use Strong's Concordance is Blue Letter Bible (BLB),[9] but there are others like Logos and e-Sword that are also free and friendly to use. These online resources also have smartphone apps to make studying the Word even easier. I like BLB because you can get a CD copy of the entire website for a donation of any amount and load it on your computer offline as the internet gets increasingly censored and even disrupted in the future. BLB also makes interlinear studies and comparisons very easy. If you are not familiar with the term *interlinear,* it simply refers to the idea that the English can be studied directly alongside (or in line) with the Hebrew or Greek. The BLB uses the Westminster Leningrad Codex (WLC), which is a digital version of the Leningrad Codex, an ancient manuscript of the Hebrew Masoretic Text. This WLC is the default manuscript for studying the Old Testament, which is why I highly recommend BLB. The Masoretic is the gold standard of the Hebrew scriptures while the Textus Receptus is the best manuscript of the Greek New Testament. Some will argue that studying the Septuagint—a Greek translation of the Old Testament—is needed in order to understand the original Hebrew language. This approach never made any sense to me. Why use a Greek translation of the Old Testament to understand Hebrew concepts when we can simply go back directly to the Hebrew itself using the Masoretic Text? I will not be using the Septuagint at all within the analysis of this book.

No matter what you decide on in terms of a concordance tool, just pick one resource, stick with it, and consistently go back to the original Hebrew Masoretic and Greek Textus Receptus manuscripts.

Law of Context

The first part of this Law is that you must remove yourself and your cultural understandings from your ability to interpret Scripture. What do I mean by *"remove yourself"?* I am talking about throwing away your biases. Leave your religious baggage at the front door. Walk into this place of interpreting Scripture with fresh eyes to see what it actually says, rather than what you want it to say or what you were told it says. We absolutely cannot think about and interpret Scripture according to the customs and practices of modern Western belief systems.

For years I sat listening to pastors and preachers in the pulpit of the Christian college I attended, and they would *primarily* teach the Bible with funny jokes, personal stories, and modern day metaphors in a laughable attempt to present the truth of the Word of God.

We won't be playing games like that here.

Our primary methods of interpretation will be far removed from the people-pleasing, mass market approach you've seen in the mega churches. What you'll find here is that the more you study and practice what the Hebrew Scriptures teach, the more you will understand *all* of the cultural nuances of the New Testament because the people, places, and events of Yeshua's day mostly took place amongst Torah observant Hebrew people.

Think about that carefully.

Now, the second part of Context is simple. For whatever verse or passage is in question, you must look at the verses before it and after it in order to understand the proper context. Again, you can't simply look at the English only. You have to also apply our other laws to those verses as well. Once you have applied the laws of first mention and definitions, then you can better understand the context of what has been translated in English. Tools like BLB also make it easy to see every place that a specific word in question is used throughout the Bible. There are so many times that I have gained immense clarity and understanding by comparing different passages that use the same word I'm seeking to understand.

It may seem like a lot of work, but the more you practice these laws, the more you will begin to deeply know the Text, and more importantly, the Author of the Text. Just look at what Psalm 138:2 (NKJV) says:

"I will worship toward Your holy temple,
And praise Your name
For Your lovingkindness and Your truth;
For You have magnified Your word above all Your name."

Did you see the significance of what is being said here? God's Word is elevated above His own name! What you will discover after applying these laws is something special that very few people ever achieve in this life. You will begin to hide His words in your heart so that you might not sin against Him, and you will live in the fullness and abundance that Yeshua promised to those who follow Him (Ps. 119:11, Jhn. 10:10).

One day you will wake up, read the Word, and make remarkable connections without even looking at the concordance.

This power that comes with understanding the original languages cannot be overstated. That's why I have dedicated an entire program centered around this subject called Kingdom Secrets Academy. We live in a time of extreme biblical illiteracy. Rightly dividing the Word of Truth has become a lost art, and that's why so many people no longer know what it's like to experience intimacy with God on a daily basis. People cannot and will not experience the fullness of God's plans for them if a lot of what they believe originates from misunderstandings and false applications of the Word. For more information on how you can walk completely into the truth of the Word and become the living sacrifice that you were truly meant to be, visit https://www.kingdom-secrets.com/academy.

3 GOLDEN RULES FOR UNDERSTANDING THE 70 WEEKS

Before we can even touch this prophecy, we must wholeheartedly accept three important principles concerning authority. The truth is that these principles are necessary to understand the entire Bible, not just the 70 weeks prophecy. Again, this book is a case study of legitimate, life-changing Bible interpretation methods.

When it comes to the topic of *prophecy* in particular, people get really crazy. The majority of false religions fundamentally grow out of a unique spin on prophecy. Because of the nature of this subject, people feel like they can throw logic out of the window. They feel like they can make prophecy say whatever they want it to say. They feel like they have more permission than usual to destroy and misrepresent the truth. With that said, here are three golden rules we must understand about authority and prophecy:

1. The Bible is the Word of God (not man's imagination).

I have already shown you how God's Word is elevated above His own name. Paul tells us another radical and often misunderstood truth in 2 Timothy 3:16, when he states, "All Scripture *is* given by inspiration of God, and *is* profitable for doctrine, for reproof, for correction, for instruction in righteousness." Go look up the word *inspiration* in the Greek language, and you will find that it means *divinely breathed* by the Holy Spirit. I'm telling you that this verse is misunderstood by 99% of people because they ignore the fact that Paul's letters were not considered "Bible" at the exact moment when he wrote these words. He was specifically referring to Moses and the Prophets. He was specifically referring to the accounts recorded in the Gospels. Those were the things that had been God-breathed and recorded as Scripture at the time when he was writing this letter to his disciple, Timothy. Paul was absolutely not proclaiming that his words were Scripture because he wasn't arrogant like that.

Now, don't get me wrong!

Paul's letters are inspired by the Holy Spirit because it is obvious that he was called by Yeshua to do miraculous works and teach sound doctrine as recorded in the book of Acts. All I am stating here is that we are to place utmost importance on the Hebrew Scriptures and all of Yeshua's Words in order to understand the 70 weeks of Daniel. That's *exactly* what Paul was proclaiming to Timothy.

2. The Bible is Absolute Truth, and there are no errors.

Of all the translations I have looked at, the Tree of Life Version shows us this truth most powerfully in 1 Samuel 15:29 where Samuel the prophet states: "Moreover, the Eternal Glory of Israel does not lie or change His mind. For He is not human that He should change His mind."

This verse doesn't need an explanation. It's really that simple. Before we move on to dissecting the 70 weeks prophecy, you and I agree that 100% of the words found inside of the Bible are God-breathed, and therefore, there are no contradictions, no lies, no errors, and no problems.

If there is an *apparent* contradiction in the Scriptures (and trust me, there are a number of instances), then it is our understanding that is faulty, not the Word of God. The three laws of interpretation must be faithfully applied, and when they are, you will know the truth, and the truth will set you free.

3. We have inherited lies from our fathers and also from the theological echo-chambers of seminaries and churches.

I didn't choose to be born during this period of history, and neither did you. At one point or another, we felt God's presence. We felt His Holy Spirit.

We felt Him calling to us.

We felt convicted of our sin and desired to live a life of true purpose, so we said *yes* to Him. We said *yes* to Jesus being the God of our lives. And when we answered His calling, we began looking for answers. Like growing children, we sought out leadership and environments to help us grow and mature. We sought out counsel. We sought community and churches to attend.

Please understand that there is nothing fundamentally wrong with this sequence of events I have just described because we all go through it. We just have a major inheritance problem, which is exactly what Jeremiah the prophet foretold:

> "O LORD, my strength and my fortress,
> My refuge in the day of affliction,
> The Gentiles shall come to You
> From the ends of the earth and say,
> 'Surely our fathers have inherited lies,
> Worthlessness and unprofitable *things.'*"
> (Jer. 16:19 NKJV)

We have inherited *nothing but lies* from the modern day religious establishment, and it's time to unlearn those lies. You might be thinking *well, that's a little too harsh.* Remember, I didn't write the Bible. It's not my book; I am simply called to proclaim it's truth. When it says "lies" and "worthlessness", then that's what it means. This is the spiritual condition that is ruining our society right now, and you must understand this spiritual reality in order to address it and actually overcome it.

THE BACKSTORY (CONTEXT) OF THE 70 WEEKS

Now, let's begin to get into the Context of this prophecy in order to unlock all of its truths. First, who exactly is this man, Daniel?

Daniel was a Hebrew man taken captive to Babylon after the Southern Kingdom of Israel fell in 586 BC. We are told that Daniel is specifically from the Tribe of Judah (Dan 1:6). Because of his wisdom and ability to interpret King Nebuchadnezzar's dream as a young man, Daniel was elevated to a high political position in the kingdom of Babylon. During his time as an exile, Daniel discovered something one day. He was able to figure out one of the prophecies of Jeremiah the prophet (see Dan 9:2). Here's what he figured out:

"And this whole land shall be a desolation and an astonishment, and these nations shall serve the king of Babylon seventy years."
(Jer. 25:11)

He figured out that Jerusalem (the capital city of the Southern Kingdom) would be desolate for 70 years, and it cut him to the heart. He then immediately proceeded to ask for the forgiveness of the sins of his people with fasting, sackcloth, and ashes. Now, pay very close attention to the wording of his prayer, especially in Dan 9:4,5,11 which I will include here:

4 ..."O Lord, great and awesome God, who keeps His covenant and mercy with those who love Him, and with those who keep His commandments,
5 "we have sinned and committed iniquity, we have done wickedly and rebelled, even by departing from Your precepts and Your judgments.
11 "Yes, all Israel has transgressed Your law, and has departed so as not to obey Your voice; therefore the curse and the oath written in the Law of Moses the servant of God have been poured out on us, because we have sinned against Him."

Remember, you already agreed with me that the Bible is the truth, God's words, and that He doesn't change his mind. Because of this truth, we can begin to understand one extremely important point about why Daniel is praying the way that he is praying in the beginning of chapter 9 before he receives the prophecy.

Don't skip ahead!

Understanding *sin* and the consequences of disobeying God are absolutely critical in decoding the 70 weeks of Daniel prophecy. Again, let me emphasize the importance of his prayer. Failure to understand what Daniel is saying at the beginning of chapter 9 will set us up for even more failure—kind of like building a house on top of a crumbling foundation. It won't work!

So, what was Daniel confessing? What exactly is sin?

There are plenty of places to find a definition, but my favorite is within these words of John: "Whoever commits sin also commits lawlessness, and sin is lawlessness" (1Jhn 3:4). Now that we understand how the English language defines sin, it is necessary to truly understand the Greek language.

So, what is lawlessness? If you look up this word *lawlessness* in John's letter, here's what you find in the Greek:

Strong's G458:
ἀνομία
"anomia"[10]

This is the same word (anomia, or lawlessness) that is used in the very frightening "depart from Me" verse of Matthew 7:23 where Jesus stated: "And then I will declare to them, 'I never knew you; depart from Me, you who practice lawlessness!'" (Mat. 7:23).

If sin is lawlessness, as John told us, and lawlessness is a translation of the Greek word *anomia*, then here's the equation we are looking at:

$$sin = lawlessness = anomia$$

Once you understand the math here, then you can easily conclude that sin is breaking of the laws of God, whether one is ignorant of the law, or if someone knows full well the law of God and chooses to disobey it anyway. And, because God does not change His mind, this definition of sin is the same in the Old Testament, New Testament, and beyond. Sin will always be the disobedience of a direct or written command of God, including all of the words written inside of the Law (Torah in Hebrew). Now let's go back to Daniel 9:11, where Daniel prays: "Yes, all Israel has transgressed Your law, and has departed so as not to obey Your voice; therefore the curse and the oath written in the Law of Moses the servant of God have been poured out on us, because we have sinned against Him." So, again, I know I just mentioned it. But where exactly can this "law" and the "curse" and "oath" that Daniel is talking about be found? Well, let's start by taking a look at what the word "law" means in Dan. 9:11:

Strong's H8451:
תּוֹרָה
"Torah"[11]

The English translation of "Torah" is "law", which is actually a poor translation of this Hebrew concept. *Instructions* fits the translation much more accurately for *Torah* in the majority of places it is used due the narrative of Genesis through Deuteronomy being primarily filled with case studies and lessons of both holy and unholy conduct. Daniel's use of the phrase "Law of

Moses" is simply a reference to these first five books of the Bible that are commonly attributed to Moses as being the author. Even Yeshua made reference to this fact numerous times such as Mark 12:26 where He specifically refers to the Law as "the book of Moses." If you are not familiar with the words *Decalogue* or *Pentateuch* they are also just fancy words referring to the first five books of the Torah that were written by Moses (Genesis to Deuteronomy).

Instructions for farming; justice; cleansing a home from mold poisoning; taking the seventh day off from monetary gain every week; renting your neighbors tool; differentiating between clean foods and unclean non-foods—all of these instructions and more are there for us to follow, to this very day, and they are found in the Torah. Observing God's Holy Days of Passover, Pentecost, the Feast of Trumpets, and more are also expressly found in the Torah and are to be upheld by His peculiar people. Even though it is commonly referred to as the Law of Moses, the distinction must be made that the Torah is actually the Law of God, since He is the only and true source of the wisdom of the Torah, rather than the man Moses. Most believers today foolishly say that following the Law of Moses is a yoke of bondage due to grave misunderstandings of Paul's letters, particularly his angry letter to the Judiazed Galatains (Gal. 5:1). Always remember that rabbinical Judaism and all of its man-made written and oral traditions represent the fundamental religion of Mystery Babylon (Jerusalem). This system of religion is solely responsible for the great persecution that took place amongst the followers of Christ in Jerusalem as recorded in Acts 8:1, and that is why Paul wrote so strongly against the teachings of Judaism and its false "laws" of men. However, referring to God's actual Law as a yoke of bondage is quite an egregious offense that far too many have committed under the deceitful banner of mainstream Christianity. Failure to follow God's instructions is considered "sin" and "lawlessness" by the Creator, and there's no escaping this fact.

As a side note, Yeshua extends the definition of Torah to also include not only His own words but also all the other books of the Old Testament, specifically the Prophets and the Psalms (see Mat. 5:17 and Luke 24:44). For example, look how He quotes Psalm 82:6 and refers to it as *law:* "Jesus answered them, 'Is it not written in your law, *I said, You are gods*?'" (John 10:34). Therefore, the God's instructions should be understood as being the Tanakh (Hebrew Bible) together with the Gospels and the Revelation of Jesus, since these are the direct words of Chirst Himself. That is not to say that the various letters and epistles of the New Testament are to be neglected, however. They are certainly inspired commentaries of God's instructions.

Now that you understand the concept of *sin,* you can more clearly understand what Daniel was going through before he received the 70 weeks vision. He was interceding for the people, asking for forgiveness, *and only then* does he receive one of the most important messages of the entire Bible in the verses that follow.

Question: Are you broken over your personal sin and the sin of your country?

The USA and Western nations have descended into total lawlessness (Torah-lessness), and you are about to learn about the ultimate consequences of this spiritual decline that Daniel already witnessed in a vision roughly 2,600 years ago.

Chapter 2
The Hidden Meanings of "Shabua" and Daniel's "People"

Moving forward, each chapter of this book will be dedicated to explaining an entire verse of the 70 weeks prophecy. By the time we reach Chapter 6, and the abomination of desolation, we will have finished unlocking the entire prophecy. This chapter will begin with Dan. 9:24, which I will now include below:

"Seventy weeks are determined
For your people and for your holy city,
To finish the transgression,
To make an end of sins,
To make reconciliation for iniquity,
To bring in everlasting righteousness,
To seal up vision and prophecy,
And to anoint the Most Holy."

Before we get started, can I let you in on a little secret?

You don't have to read, write, or speak Hebrew in order to understand the original meanings found in the Masoretic Hebrew Text. You don't need to go to a seminary for years, spend multiple five figures on a fancy degree, jump through other educational hoops, or travel to the land of Israel to be qualified enough to interpret Scripture.

Notice that I said *qualified*.

Sure, some of those things can absolutely help to understand Scripture. But those things don't actually qualify a person.

The reason we are in such a spiritual decline as a society is because we have been indoctrinated from an early age to think that gathering knowledge of a subject is the same thing as actually learning by applying the subject with the goal of eventually achieving mastery of the subject. We get an A or B on the test, and we think we've got it pretty much all figured out. What you are going to find inside the pages of this book is something quite different from knowledge alone.

The unsealing of this prophecy has only been possible through the actual practice of all the Words that proceed out of the mouth of Yehovah. So, as we go through this prophecy, remember that learning is good, and practicing the Word is even better; but achieving mastery is the only way to *know and understand* all of the mysteries of the Bible. Mastery is the place where you have practiced hiding so many words of the Text in your heart that the Holy Spirit can actually bring all things to your remembrance and direct you into new places of spiritual awakening.

I've done the work. I've proven what I am about to show you. Now it's your turn.

Like I already mentioned in the last chapter, there are tons of free resources out there to use to break down the meanings of the Hebrew words of Daniel chapter 9. To me, Blue Letter Bible (BLB) has the easiest interface, it's free, and I just like the ability to click on any verse that I want and the Hebrew (or Greek) just pops out of the screen at me on a line-by-line basis. This is the resource I will be mostly using throughout this book. Let us begin by looking at the first and most important phrase "seventy weeks are determined".

שָׁבֻעִים שִׁבְעִים נֶחְתַּךְ

Figure 2.1: "Seventy Weeks Are Determined". Remember to read Hebrew from right to left. The literal reading of this phrase is "weeks seventy are determined" or transliterated as "shabuim shibim nekhtak".

Let's take a look at what the BLB shows us when examining each word in the very first line.

"Shibim" is the first word we will look at. Again, we will be using the Law of Definitions in which we examine every single Hebrew word in this prophecy. Here it's obvious that this word simply is the numerical value of 70. If you are using BLB, it's very clear when you click on Strong's H7657 and read through the information for this word and the Bible verses where it is used. No problem. Easy.

Before looking at the very next word "weeks", let's just skip over to the last word. Seventy weeks are "determined". This word "nekh-tak" is derived from the root word חָתַךְ which is Strong's H2852 (khaw-thak') and according to BLB is "a primitive root; properly, to cut off, i.e. (figuratively) to decree:—determine."[1] So, we can say that 70 weeks until *cut off* happens. We will revisit this idea later.

Notice the next word *weeks* which is Strong's H7620. Used exactly as it is found within this sentence in Daniel 9:24, it is pronounced "sha-boo'eem", but the root word from which this word is derived is pronounced "shabua." The former word is simply the plural form of *shabua* that indicates *more than one*. Of course, we are told that there are 70 of these measures of "shabua", whatever they are.

This is where the fun begins.

The Translation of *shabua* into the English word *weeks* is intellectual murder, yet almost *every* translation of the Bible does this. Look, it's not the translators' fault. And it's not your fault either. If you're like me, you've sat in church services and maybe even college level Bible courses that taught you about the concept of weeks, sevens, or some variation of that theme, without questioning or even considering an alternative idea. As I have already alluded to, there's a very obvious reason for this group-think, echo-chamber interpretation of the word *shabua* that we've inherited for hundreds of years now. I now direct your attention to these words of Daniel 12:4,8-9:

4 "But you, Daniel, shut up the words, and seal the book until the time of the end; many shall run to and fro, and knowledge shall increase.
8 "Although I heard, I did not understand. Then I said, 'My lord, what shall be the end of these things?'
9 "And he said, 'Go your way, Daniel, for the words are closed up and sealed till the time of the end.'"

Not even Daniel, a man who was greatly beloved by God; a man about whom the Bible says *nothing* evil or wrong; the direct recipient of multiple visions and who was gifted in the interpretation of dreams; a man that was not harmed after he was wrongfully thrown into a pit with lions—not even Daniel understood the 70 shabuim prophecy. It all has to do with the fact that we are explicitly told that this information was sealed until the time of the end and that Daniel shut up the words. It was written in code *on purpose!*

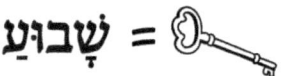

Figure 2.2: Shabua. This Hebrew root word *shabua* is the key to unlocking the entire prophecy of the 70 weeks of Daniel.

THE DEEPER MEANING OF THE WORD "SHABUA"

Like I already showed you, every major religion has interpreted *shabua* to mean the number *seven*. Going back to our law of first mention, we should look to see the first places in the Bible where the word *seven* or this concept is used. The very first place is Genesis 2:2 where we see Elohim resting on the seventh day as an example for mankind to follow. The word translated as *seventh* is pronounced "sheh-bee-ee" (Strong's H7637). We also see another word translated as *seven* or *sevenfold* throughout the Scriptures, and this word is pronounced "sheh-bah" (Strong's H7651). Daniel—a natively Hebrew-speaking man—deliberately chose *not* to use either of these words in his prophecy.

I now bring your attention back to the Strong's Concordance entry for "shabua" (Strong's H7620). Notice the "Outline of Biblical Usage" section in Blue Letter Bible.[2] Yes, like we have already mentioned, this word has been translated as a period of seven days or years, or a week.

But notice something really special here.

This word *shabua* is used in the Bible to describe the Feast of Weeks (Feast of Shabua). This holiday is also known as the Feast of Oaths. Chances are you know very little about this special Feast if you are like how I was when I first started studying the Bible. You probably are not aware of the significance, and you have probably never practiced observing this Feast. God commands his people to observe this Feast every single year at the specifically appointed time, forever. It is a perpetual, everlasting commandment; and this Feast happens to contain one of the first secrets that unlocks the entire Daniel prophecy. Let me show you how understanding this concept changes everything.

So, what exactly is the Feast of Shabua, or more correctly stated with regard to Hebrew grammar, the Feast of Shabuot?

In order to answer this question, we must first go back to the Exodus when the command to observe this Feast was first given. First, we need to establish a little context. The nation of Israel had just observed the *Feast of Passover* ("Pesach" in Hebrew) in the land of Egypt after seeing intense plagues come upon the Pharaoh and all his people because the Israelites were being released from slavery by God Himself. It was exactly 50 days later that they arrived at Mount Sinai at the exact appointed time of the *Feast of Pentecost* ("Shabuot" in the Masoretic Hebrew Text; "Shavout" in modern Hebrew). Later in the New Testament we learn that Shabuot (Pentecost) was the time when the Holy Spirit was poured on the believers after the resurrection of the Messiah. This feast always takes place during the time of the wheat harvest in the land of Canaan. It symbolizes the time of the marriage covenant between the mixed multitude of Israelites that came out from Egypt and Yehovah (יְהֹוָה) Himself. This marriage covenant took place at Mount Sinai.

It is during this special time of Shabuot that the Torah (literally "Instruction") is given to mankind on two tablets in Exodus 24. The first time Moses went up to Mount Sinai, he stayed there 40 days and nights. But the Israelites grew faithless and impatient and foolishly made a golden calf to worship. Upon his return, Moses threw down the two tablets (breaking them) and dealt with the sin of the people. He was commanded to go up again to Mount Sinai for 40 days and nights in order to make two new tablets to replace the original ones that he broke.

It is at this moment in history where we learn about the rich meaning of the word *shabua* in Exodus 34. Let's take a closer look at Exodus 34:18,22-23 which is where we see the Feast of Shabuot mentioned for the first time in the Bible:

18 "The Feast of Unleavened Bread you shall keep. Seven days you shall eat unleavened bread, as I commanded you, in the appointed time of the month of Abib; for in the month of Abib you came out from Egypt.
22 "And you shall observe the Feast of Weeks, of the firstfruits of wheat harvest, and the Feast of Ingathering at the year's end.
23 "Three times in the year all your men shall appear before the Lord, the LORD God of Israel."

Before diving into the specifics of the Feast of Weeks, understand that these three specific Feasts in the verses above are considered the High Holy Days. This simply means that the First Day of the Unleavened Bread, the Day of Pentecost, and the First Day of Sukkot (Tabernacles) are the three times annually that every man who is either a natural born citizen or grafted in to God's chosen people is to appear in Jerusalem to present himself with his offering (Deu. 16:16). We will need to understand these things much more deeply later; but for now just know that these Feasts are rich with meaning, extremely important, and absolutely commanded for anyone following the God of the Bible to observe, even though the annual Jerusalem pilgrimage itself is now a dormant commandment.

One of the main reasons that modern pastors and churchgoers are completely unable to understand the Feast of Shabua and its connection to Daniel 9:24 is because *they do not actually observe it every year.* They believe it is not for them but for Jews only. Most people believe that the "law is done away with" or some variation of this false teaching. And because they have never observed it or practiced it, they are left hopelessly guessing in all matters of end times prophecy because all end times prophecy is 100% related to understanding the Holy Days of Yehovah, especially the Feast of Shabuot.

Don't let this be you.

Turn around and start learning about all of the Holy Days. The last chapter of this book describes how to observe all the Appointed Times in a very tangible way that examines both the letter of the law and the spirit of the law.

THE SHABUA AND GOD'S PROPHETIC TIME CLOCK

The timeline in Figure 2.3 provides an overview of what are commonly referred to as the Spring Feasts, and it is based on the whole of the Torah and the Holy Days of Leviticus 23.

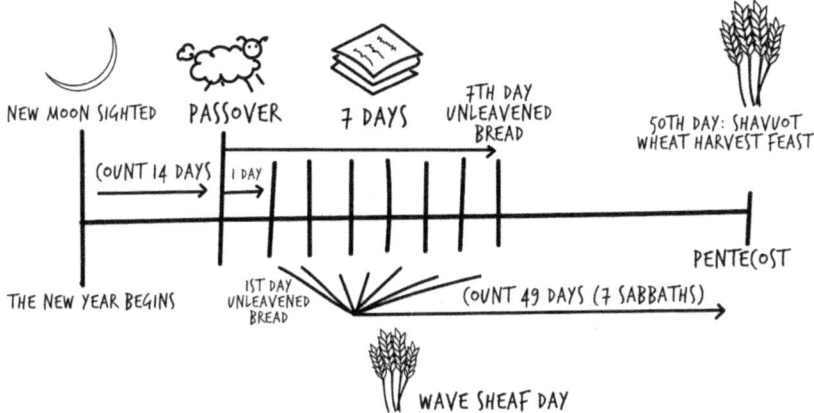

Figure 2.3: The Feast of Weeks Timeline. A renewed moon ("rosh chodesh" in Hebrew) determines the beginning of the Hebrew months since we are specifically told that God set the moon's light in the firmament for the purpose of timekeeping (see Gen. 1:14, Psalm 104:19, Isaiah 66:23). During the season of the first ripe barley from late February to early April, if at least one "omer" (about two liters) of barley will be ready to harvest in the land of Israel on time for wave sheaf day, then the New Year begins with the sighting of a new moon to declare the first month of Abib. A renewed moon is the first crescent sliver visible to the naked eye as the moon renews its light each 29.5-day cycle. Wave sheaf day is the Sunday after the weekly Sabbath and can land on any one of the days 1-7 of Unleavened Bread depending on when the moon was sighted to begin the month. You begin counting seven Sabbaths from this day onward for the celebration of the Feast of Weeks, or Pentecost. Because we count seven sabbaths (49 days) starting from wave sheaf day, Pentecost day will always fall on a Sunday.

This is a simple diagram to understand, but the truths within it are profound. The first thing to know is that if wild, heirloom barley in Israel will be ready for the presentation of one omer for the required Wave Sheaf Day offering to God, then this is the first month called "Abib," and the New Year can begin. Each month, including the first month, begins with the sighting of a new sliver, or crescent moon, in the evening sky. This sighting is what is called the "rosh chodesh" or "new moon" in the Bible. The idea is that the moon is renewing its visible light because this was the purpose why God created the lights in the firmament in order to provide the timing of His seasons. Therefore a dark moon, or conjunction moon, does not fit the Hebrew understanding of a renewed light. It must be the first sliver of the crescent moon that is seen without the aid of binoculars or other technology. You then count 14 days from the New Moon to Passover, keep seven days of eating Unleavened Bread, keep Wave Sheaf Day on the Sunday after the weekly Sabbath during this timeframe, and then you count seven sabbaths to Shavuot.

Let me slow down and explain that a little better.

First, the Bible itself shows us that the Hebrew year occurs from Abib to Abib. This is what Yehovah tells us when Passover is instituted in Egypt during the time of the ten plagues: "This month *shall be* your beginning of months; it *shall be* the first month of the year to you" (Exodus 12:2). It was also during this first month of the year that the children of Israel entered into the promised land under the leadership of Joshua (see Jos. 5:10). I will explore the deep significance of this exact event later in this book when we dive deeper into the chronology of the Bible and we make the connection from biblical creation years to Gregorian years. The main point I need to stress for now is that the Hebrew year does not begin in the fall timeframe around the Jewish *Rosh HaShana*. The modern practices of rabbinical Judaism have dismissed what the Bible says about Abib beginning the year around March timeframe (the first new moon to begin the year can fluctuate from February to early April), and they instead declare the New Year in September or October. *Abib* is a Hebrew word that literally means green, tender, and young ears of barley, and this barley is absolutely not found in September or October in the land of Israel.

"So, why do we need barley to begin the year?"

This is a question I get asked all the time. The answer is found inside of chapter 23 of the book of Leviticus where the instructions for all of the Appointed Times of God are clearly presented. I encourage you to stop, read, and study the entire chapter so you can cross examine what I am showing you with what the Scriptures proclaim.

10 "Speak to Bnei-Yisrael and tell them: When you have come into the land which I give to you, and reap its harvest, then you are to bring the omer of the firstfruits of your harvest to the kohen.
11 "He is to wave the omer before Adonai, to be accepted for you. On the morrow after the Shabbat, the kohen is to wave it."
(Lev. 23:10,11 TLV)

The reason I quoted the Tree of Life Version is because many translations do not use the word "omer" and may use another word like "sheaf" that loses the exact Hebrew meaning. An omer is simply a unit of measure that is about two liters. This omer is the firstfruits offering that the priest (kohen) would wave on behalf of the people. As soon as this omer was finished being waved, then (and only then) could the rest of the harvest could be gathered and enjoyed freely by all of the people.

There is profound significance within all aspects of Elohim's Holy Days. When Yeshua rose again from the dead, he did so on the very same day that the firstfruits omer of barley was waved on Sunday. He was the firstfruits of those who had fallen asleep (1Co 15:20). Also remember that the graves of many resurrected saints were opened (Mat 27:52) at the time of the crucifixion, indicating that redemption is connected to the firstfruits harvests of the Bible. Prophetic events yet to be fulfilled in the future will also coincide directly with specific Feast days, so it is essential to practice these instructions if one hopes to obtain any serious comprehension of Bible prophecy.

We are told in Leviticus 23 that the firstfruits of the barley crop are to be collected on the Sunday after the weekly Sabbath during this specific time frame in the first month of the year. This Sunday is called Wave Sheaf Day and can land on any one of the seven days of Unleavened Bread depending on when exactly the New Moon was seen in order to begin the year. Wave Sheaf Day can therefore change every year, and its timing depends on when the sighted moon was seen to begin the month. I'll be the first to admit that understanding the nuances of these things is a whole lot easier if you practice doing them every year as prescribed by the Text. You then begin counting from Wave Sheaf Day onward to determine the exact day of Pentecost, which is exactly what we are told in Deuteronomy:

9 "You shall count seven weeks for yourself; begin to count the seven weeks from *the time* you begin *to put* the sickle to the grain.
10 "Then you shall keep the Feast of Weeks to the LORD your God with the tribute of a freewill offering from your hand, which you shall give as the LORD your God blesses you.
(Deut. 16:9,10 NKJV)

Wave Sheaf Day is the time that the sickle is used to harvest the standing grain of barley. Because this day always happens on a Sunday, the 50th Day Pentecost Wheat Harvest Feast always occurs on a Sunday every year also.

Hopefully you haven't gotten lost in these details!

With everything I just showed you in the diagram and also explained, we now have enough information to ask the critically important question that brings us back to fully investigating Daniel's 70 weeks: Where does the "Feast of Weeks" fit into this whole picture, exactly?

The word *weeks* in the Feast of Weeks refers to the period of time where you are counting. Though this phrase does not appear in the Bible, people commonly refer to this time period as "counting the omer." The Bible does tell us that we are to count seven sabbaths, which is the same idea as counting the 49 days in anticipation for the wheat harvest of Pentecost, which is a High Holy day. The importance of this time period is huge. Recall that I mentioned it is referred to as the Feast of Oaths. The process each person goes through every single year is the process of re-affirming your oath and covenant loyalty to God. You are "sevening" yourself, which is another way of saying that you are repeating yourself seven times in a manner whereby you are swearing allegiance to following the Creator for seven weeks. This concept appears in a multitude of Scriptures whereby the priests would take blood and sprinkle it seven times to purify, dedicate, or confirm something (Lev. 4:6; 14:7, Num. 19:4). This act of *sevening* before Pentecost is a form of worship that Yeshua ordained for us to follow.

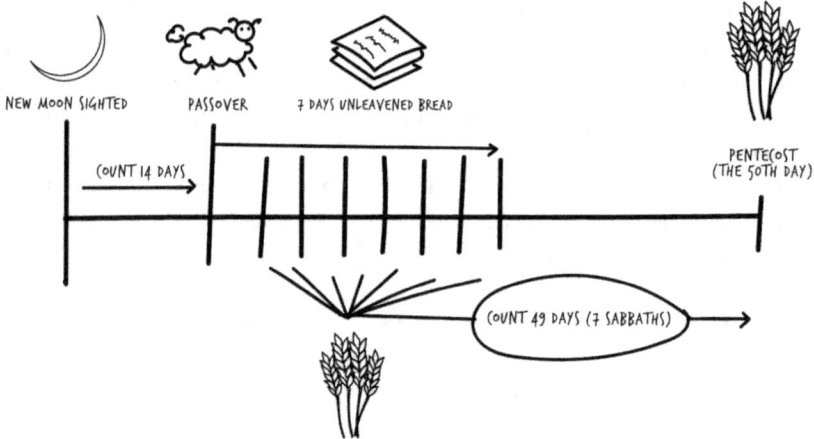

Figure 2.4: The Feast of Weeks Mystery - *"And you shall count for yourselves from the day after the Sabbath, from the day that you brought the sheaf of the wave offering: seven Sabbaths shall be completed"* (Lev. 23:15).

So, do you see the secret of the word *shabua* and the Feast of Shabua yet? The secret is:

7 days per week x 7 weeks = 49 days

As you can see, this is a fundamentally different conclusion than all of modern Christianity or the vast majority of Bible teachers in general ever arrive to. To my knowledge, the only other work to arrive at this same conclusion is *2300 Days of Hell* by the Canadian author Joseph Dumond. I believe he was the first to widely proclaim this understanding when he released his book in 2014.[3]

This concept of counting by 49 is the key to unlocking the entire world of Bible prophecy, which is why you will see the Hebrew word "shabua" (שָׁבוּעַ) inscribed on the golden key found on the cover of this book. Lest you think this is an isolated, cherry-picked concept, I will show you later how this commandment to count by 49 perfectly connects to key passages of Genesis and Leviticus in determining the sum of mankind's history.

Let's now go back and revisit what Daniel was actually telling us. Hopefully you can see the different yet obvious conclusion. Daniel is telling us that "Seventy *shabuim* are determined" which really means the following:

7 days per week x 7 weeks x 70 total weeks = 3,430

I will now show you with 100% certainty that this is not 3,430 days or months, but *years*. This statement should send a chill down your spine because the timeline I am about to reveal to you brings us right to the present day in which we are living and unpacks all of the mysteries of Daniel's prophecy you have probably ever wondered about, including Covid-19, the United Nations, the Great Reset agenda, and more. Before we get into more of the math, we need to finish dissecting the rest of Daniel 9:24.

$$\text{עַל־עַמְּךָ וְעַל־עִיר קָדְשֶׁךָ}$$

Figure 2.5: "For your people and your holy city". The literal reading of this phrase is "upon your people and upon city, your holy" or transliterated as "al ammekah veh-al ir kadshekah".

WHO ARE DANIEL'S PEOPLE AND THE HOLY CITY?

The holy city is pretty easy to figure out. The two Hebrew root words used are "kodesh" and "ir." We will run into the word "kodesh" quite a bit, but for now just understand that it means "set apart" or "holy." Jerusalem is specifically mentioned in the very next verse (Dan. 9:25) regarding the command "to restore and build Jerusalem" where Strongs H3389 or "Yerushalaim" is used by Daniel. *It is quite clear that the set apart city is Jerusalem.* What is not so clear is the identity of Daniel's people because they are a people of 12 tribes just as my map depicts.[4]

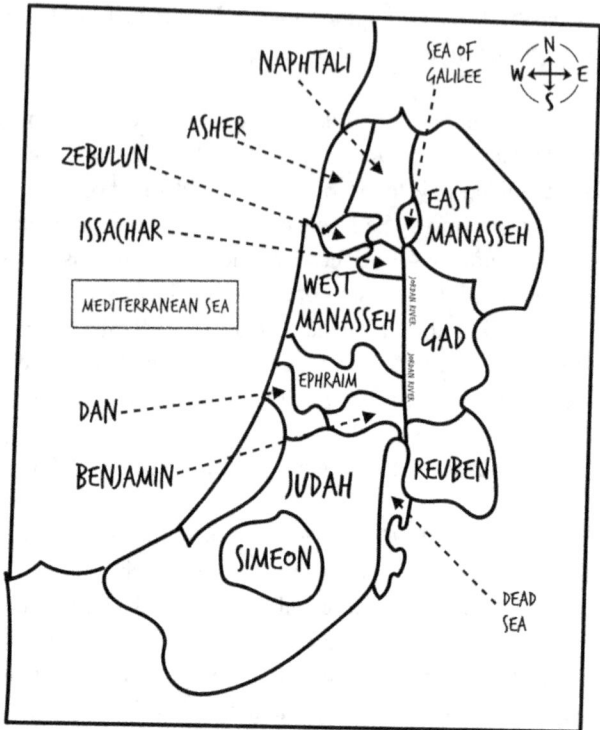

Figure 2.6: The 12 Tribes of Israel Approximately 1200 BC. This is where the Israelites settled after the conquest of Joshua. The tribes of Levi (and Simeon) were dispersed throughout the land as described in Jacob's prophetic blessing and later confirmed by Moses (Gen. 49:7, Deu. 10:9).

Whenever I bring this topic up to the average Christian, Seventh Day Adventist, Evangelical—you name it—I usually get the same few responses. It's humorous to me that people will say with conviction that "Daniel's people are Christians!" when, in fact, there were no such thing as *Christians* on the world stage when this prophecy was written. People will also tell me that Daniel's people are Jews, but this answer also falls flat on its face when you realize that the term *Jew* was also not something that Daniel himself would have been familiar with.

Before going forward, *we must be 110% certain* that we know the identity of Daniel's people at this point because this is the subject matter of the entire prophecy. Failure to understand the subject matter will result in failure to understand the entire prophecy.

My style of studying the Bible is to allow the Bible to explain itself. We should always read the Bible in as self-explanatory a way as possible without adding our own twist. In fact, this approach falls within our Law of Context as explained in the last chapter. That's precisely why I now direct your attention back to Daniel's prayer. Who is he praying for right before he receives the 70 weeks prophecy? Let's take a look:

"O Lord, righteousness *belongs* to You, but to us shame of face, as *it is* this day—to the men of Judah, to the inhabitants of Jerusalem and all Israel, those near and those far off in all the countries to which You have driven them, because of the unfaithfulness which they have committed against You."
(Daniel 9:7)

He was specifically praying for all 12 Tribes—*both* Israel *and* Judah—including all of the exiles that are commonly referred to as the "lost tribes". It is foolish to say that Daniel's people are "Jews only". Someone who was a *Jew* in the New Testament Scriptures refers to someone that belonged to the Southern Kingdom of Israel whose ancestors returned from Babylonian captivity with Ezra and Nehemiah. In today's lingo, someone who is a *Jew* could also refer to someone practicing Judaism, which is also a completely different idea than what we are talking about here. Judaism is a blatant counterfeit of true faith in God due to its utter rejection of Yeshua, for as Paul said, "For we are the circumcision, who worship God in the Spirit, rejoice in Christ Jesus, and have no confidence in the flesh" (Phl. 3:3). Regarding the precise identity of Daniel's people, we should mostly be looking for those people who are attempting to worship the God of the Bible and who have adopted the teachings of Jesus.

The key idea within Daniel's prayer is that there are two houses, or kingdoms, of Israel, and they were scattered around the world because of their unfaithfulness. This is exactly what Moses warned about:

"And the LORD shall scatter thee among all people, from the one end of the earth even unto the other; and there thou shalt serve other gods, which neither thou nor thy fathers have known, even wood and stone."
(Deut. 28:64 KJV)

"And the LORD uprooted them from their land in anger, in wrath, and in great indignation, and cast them into another as it is this day."
(Deut. 29:28 KJV)

The curse and the oath of Moses fell upon them because they broke their marriage covenant with God by being unfaithful and sinning against His commandments.

In order to understand Daniel's people, you must know about the major civil war that *almost* took place in ancient times, and you must also understand that the Nation of Israel was united only under three kings before it was eventually divided in two by God Himself (1Kings 12:24). The first king of united Israel was Saul. He sinned and acted wickedly, so David succeeded him as king. Then David's son, Solomon, reigned in his place. However, Solomon also did wickedly in the eyes of God, so the kingdom was divided because of him. This division occurred after his death when his son Rehoboam began to reign. Jeroboam took over the Northern Kingdom which consisted of 10 tribes (1Kings 11:31), and it is specifically referred to as "Israel" throughout the Scriptures. Rehoboam ruled over the Southern Kingdom of Israel, which consisted of Benjamin and Judah, and that's why it's called "Judah" throughout the Bible. Be aware that the tribes of Levi and Simeon were both scattered throughout the land because of Jacob's prophecy (Gen. 49:5-7).

Figure 2.7: The Two Houses of Israel. These two kingdoms existed as neighbors for approximately 241 years until the North was conquered by Assyria in 722 BC. At times, the two cooperated, but generally there was hostility between the North and South. The North immediately established a different form of religion under its first king, and these 10 tribes of Israel established strong ties with their northern neighbors, the Sidonians. They intermarried and adopted forbidden Canaanite customs (1Ki. 16:31).

Due to time constraints, I'm not going to go over every detail of how, when, and where both of the Kingdoms of Israel migrated to after they fell because this is a very dense topic of historical research. I could dedicate many pages on this topic and barely scratch the surface. There is so much evidence of Hebrew ancestry in the UK, Europe, the US, and other Western nations that if you haven't been exposed to this information before, it will be quite eye opening.

I'll provide a brief overview.

The Northern Kingdom of Israel was more wicked than Judah, and they were the first to be conquered by Assyria under the rule of Tiglath-Pilesar III in 722 BC. Judah was later conquered by Babylon under the reign of Nebuchadnezzar II in 586 BC.

The first critical piece of history to know is that many southerners were also scattered among the nations during the Babylonian conquest. Only a remnant of the Southern Kingdom of Judah returned after the 70 years of captivity in Babylon were completed according to the prophet Jeremiah (Jer. 25:11, 29:10, Dan. 9:2). The scattering of Judah took place once again after the destruction of the temple in AD 70 at the hands of the Romans. The second historical development of critical importance is that the Northern Israelites never returned back to the promised land because there was no such prophecy or word from Yehovah that guaranteed their return. Instead, we are specifically told that they would become wanderers among the gentiles, or nations, of the world (Hos. 9:16); and they would lose their identity because they would become mixed into various nations (Hos. 7:8). The Northern Israelites were given the curse of wandering. This is why we read the following declaration in Isaiah 1:3: "The ox knows its owner And the donkey its master's crib; But Israel does not know, My people do not consider." These words would not have made sense during the time of Isaiah who was a prophet during the days of Uzziah king of Judah (767–740 BC). Yehovah is saying that Israel does not know who their Master is, but they certainly had this knowledge when Isaiah wrote this prophecy and before they were conquered by Assyria. They still knew they were Israelites during the 8th century BC. Of course, this prophecy makes perfect sense these thousands of years later now that all twelve tribes of scattered Judah and especially Israel have no idea who they really are.

Before going forward, the controversial topic of skin color and race must be addressed. First, any serious arguments concerning "race" or "racial" identities are inherently flawed because there is only one race—the human race— as clearly explained in Genesis and skillfully repeated by Paul in Acts 17:26, where he speaks of all nations being "one blood" during a public sermon. Undoubtedly, the question will cross your mind as to what the ancient Israelites looked like and what their features and skin color were like. It is always important to remember that the Israelites who left Egypt in the Exodus were always a mixed multitude. Pay attention to these words of Exodus 12:37,38 (NKJV):

"Then the children of Israel journeyed from Rameses to Succoth, about six hundred thousand men on foot, besides children. A mixed multitude went up with them also, and flocks and herds—a great deal of livestock."

The key takeaway here is that primarily Egyptians but certainly other people groups joined the Israelites after the nation of Egypt had been left in total ruins from God's judgment. Not everyone had Pharaoh's hard heart. There were those that feared Yehovah (see Exodus 9:20) and realized that their country was in a state of hopelessness. These wise people decided to join themselves to the Hebrews and become Israelites. That is why we read of a mixed multitude traveling in the desert. We are also told that Moses himself married an Ethiopian woman (Num. 12:1), which indicates that North Africa all the way down to Ethiopia had received an opportunity to join themselves to the Holy Nation. Even well before the Exodus, Joseph had married the Egyptian woman Asenath, making Ephraim and Manasseh half Egyptian. Taking hard doctrinal stances based on features such as skin color is not only childish (and even cultish in most cases), but it also diminishes the simplicity of the narrative that is presented in God's Word. There were whites, browns, and blacks amongst the Israelites. As you will soon be discovering, however, the primary physical identity of the twelve tribes of Israel can certainly be found within the white-skinned peoples of the world due to the overwhelming evidence of Israel's historical whereabouts. Though there are certainly migration patterns all over the world including India and Africa, the Israelites established the nations and empires connected to their specific birthright blessings from among the European peoples.

THE NORTHERN KINGDOM OF ISRAEL

In the Bible, these people were known as Ephraim, Joseph, House of Israel, Israelite Gentiles, Diaspora, House of Isaac, and Lost Sheep. They were cut off and "divorced" by God because of their excessive spiritual adultery (see Jer. 3:8 and Hos. 1:6), and this fulfillment of prophecy took place around 722 BC when the Assyrians had conquered these ten tribes.

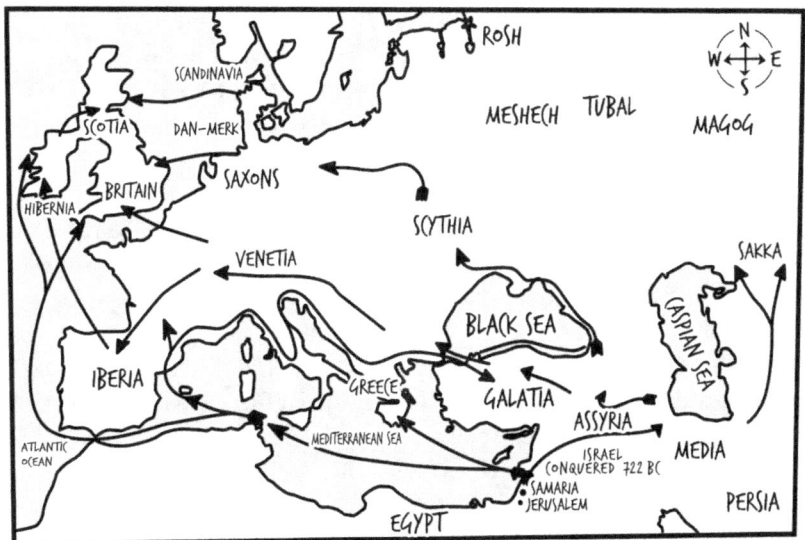

Figure 2.8: The Scattering of Conquered Israel. The black arrows indicate
the various migration routes of the ten northern tribes. As they traveled,
their names changed. They were known as Sakka in Western Asia but
Scythians in Asia Minor and Eastern Europe. The Assyrians also called
them Iskuza, Cimmerians, and Gimiri.[5] These scattered sheep made their
way into the British Isles where they were known as Druids, Celt, and
Culdee. The Iberian Peninsula is named after Eber, the father of the
Hebrews, and its etymology suggests that the name's inherent meaning is
the Hebrew's Land. Their journey through the Caucasus Mountains is
where the term "Caucasian" originates—a term used to describe white-
skinned people and Europeans. Of course, this map has profound
consequences for both North and South America where the descendants
of the Kingdom of Israel have firmly established themselves in the present
day.

This geographical dispersion throughout the world was precisely why
Yeshua said, "I was not sent except to the lost sheep of the House of Israel"
(Matt. 15:24). Part of the good news message (gospel) was that Israel could be
saved by the Messiah's redemptive power in the renewed covenant in His
blood. They were allowed to be in a renewed marriage covenant with the Most
High God, even though they were adulterers that had broken the original
covenant. They were no longer divorced and cut off. Yeshua was raised from
the dead as an eligible bachelor to enter back into marriage with the House of
Israel (Rom. 7:4). This became the primary mission of the early apostles and
believers of the 1st century. They were sent out to the world to share this
message with the Lost Sheep, which was precisely the commission that Jesus
gave as recorded in the first chapter of Acts:

"But ye shall receive power, after that the Holy Ghost is come upon you: and ye shall be witnesses unto me both in Jerusalem, and in all Judaea, and in Samaria, and unto the uttermost part of the earth." (Acts 1:8 KJV)

Pay attention to where the apostles were traveling in Acts because they were indeed obedient in fulfilling this calling. It was all over Asia Minor, Greece, Rome, Spain, and many other places. They were actively trying to reach the diaspora of Israel to tell them the good news about the Messiah's renewed covenant with them. There are many references to the exiles (the diaspora) of Israel in the New Testament, but I especially like Matthew 10:5, James 1:1, and 1Peter 1:1. The apostles were going after the Lost Tribes, or the Israeli Gentiles, which were the Lost Sheep of the House of Israel that had been (and still are) scattered around the known world. That is why Paul preached inside of a Hebrew synagogue for three sabbaths while in the Grecian city of Thessalonica (see Acts 17:2). Paul was actively seeking out those Hebrews that still had a heart to seek the God of the Bible but that also lacked the knowledge regarding the prophetic fulfillment of the Messiah's arrival. It was well known in the first century that the Lost Tribes of Israel were heavily located among the Greeks, and this fact is made plainly evident when the Pharisees raised the question, "Does [Jesus] intend to go to the Dispersion among the Greeks and teach the Greeks?" (John 7:35 NKJV).

With regard to the specific words of Acts 1:8, there is a tragically overlooked message hidden within the phrase "uttermost part of the earth" that Christ stated after His rise from the dead. Just as Jerusalem, Judea, and Samaria are all singular places, it logically follows that the "uttermost part" is also a single location, rather than many locations as most people have presumed. In fact, this is exactly what the Greek language of the Textus Receptus records for us by using the word ἐσχάτου, or eschatou, a "genitive singular masculine adjective"[6] describing a specific location on earth. Clues as to what the commission of Yeshua truly meant to his apostles can be found in a number of sources including Roman writings; and perhaps the most impressive evidence can be found within early Scotland and the Declaration of Arbroath. This document was originally sent as a letter written in Latin from King Edward I of Scotland to Pope John XXII.[7] Archeologist and lost tribes researcher, E. Raymond Capt, notes in his findings:

> "Further evidence that 'the uppermost part of the earth' is intended to refer to Britain is found in the Scottish Declaration of Independence, which was drawn up in 1320 in protest against the attempt by Edward I to conquer Scotland with the help of the Pope. The document is deposited in the National Registry at

Edinburgh, and states: 'The nation of the Scots ... passing from the greater Scythis through the Mediterranean Sea and the Pillars of Hercules, and sojourning in Spain among the most savage tribes through a long course of time, could nowhere be subjugated by any people, however barbarous; and coming thence one-thousand-two-hundred years after the outgoing of **the people of Israel** ... acquired for themselves the possessions of the West. In this kingdom, one hundred and thirteen kings or their own royal stock, no strangers intervening, have reigned, whose nobility and merits ... shine out plainly enough from this, that the King of kings, even our Lord Jesus Christ, after His passion and resurrection, called them; though **situated at the uttermost part of the earth,** almost the first, to His most holy faith."[8] [emphasis added]

This English translation of the Declaration reveals that the ancient Scots clearly identified as Hebrews while also concluding with the same thought of Acts 1:8 so as to provide evidence that they wholeheartedly accepted the message of Christianity when it first arrived to their shores.

The question is, how did this strong acceptance of Yeshua's message come about amongst the British Isles? And, was the Christian religion established in the first century or at a much later time? To answer these questions, it must be first noted that out of all the books of the New Testament, only two—James and the Book of Acts—do not conclude their message with the word *Amen*, which has caused some scholars to believe that these two books might be incomplete as currently presented within our Bibles. While I hold strongly to the fact that the Word of God has been compiled and preserved supernaturally until heaven and earth pass away (Mat. 5:18), it can also be helpful to consider extra-biblical texts to see if they hold any merit when compared to the whole of Scripture. Though considered pseudepigrapha (falsely inscribed), it is well worth mentioning that the twenty-ninth and final chapter of the Book of Acts may have been located inside what is called the *Sonnini Manuscript.* This alleged lost chapter of Acts originates from a Greek manuscript discovered in the archives at Constantinople and presented to the translator, French naturalist Sonnini de Manoncourt, by the Sultan Abdoul Achmet of Turkey. This work was first written in French by Sonnini in the late 18th century and was found within an English copy of his book *Voyage en Grèce et en Turquie* (Travels in Greece and Turkey). This English translation belonged to the library of Irishmen Sir John Newport (1756–1843), being discovered after his death in London in 1871.[9]

This compelling "final" chapter of Acts explains Paul's journey into Spain and Britain before his eventual martyrdom in Rome during Nero's reign.[10] Of the 26 verses of this manuscript, here are the ones of most importance to this discussion (verses 1-4, 7-8, and 13):

> 1 And Paul, full of the blessings of Christ, and abounding in the spirit, departed out of Rome, determining to go into Spain, for he had a long time proposed to journey thitherward, and was minded also to go from thence to Britain.
>
> 2 For he had heard in Phoenicia that certain of the children of Israel, about the time of the Assyrian captivity, had escaped by sea to "The Isles afar off" as spoken by the prophet, and called by the Romans – Britain.
>
> 3 And the Lord commanded the gospel to be preached far hence to the Gentiles, and to the lost sheep of the House of Israel
>
> 4 And no man hindered Paul; for he testified boldly of Jesus before the tribunes and among the people; and he took with him certain of the brethren which abode with him at Rome, and they took shipping at Ostrium and having the winds fair, were brought safely into a haven of Spain.
>
> 7 And they departed out of Spain, and Paul and his company finding a ship in Armorica sailing unto Britain, they were therein, and passing along the South Coast, they reached a port called Raphinus.
>
> 8 Now when it was voiced abroad that the Apostle had landed on their coast, great multitudes of the inhabitants met him, and they treated Paul courteously and he entered in at the east gate of their city, and lodged in the house of an Hebrew and one of his own nation.
>
> 9 And on the morrow he came and stood upon Mount Lud, and the people thronged at the gate, and assembled in the Broadway, and he preached Christ unto them, and they believed the Word and testimony of Jesus.
>
> 13 And it came to pass that certain of the Druids came unto Paul privately, and showed by their rites and ceremonies they descended from the Jews [Judahites] which escaped from bondage in the land of Egypt, and the Apostle believed these things, and gave them the kiss of peace.[11]

There is substantial confirmation to believe this account to be a truthful explanation of Britain's hidden history. Within this manuscript, we see information that during the days of the cruel bondage under the Egyptians, certain Israelites had fled North Africa and arrived in Britain. Many classical writers confirm that the Israelites were already fleeing Egypt before the Exodus took place due to the harsh treatment by the Egyptians. Speaking of the Israelite slaves in Egypt, one 6th century author, Hecataeus of Abdere, tells us that the Egyptians sought to rid these Hebrews from their country, and "the most distinguished of the expelled foreigners followed Danaus and Cadmus into

Greece: but the greater number were led by Moses into Judea."[12] From Greece, it is not outlandish to conclude that the exiled Hebrews eventually migrated further northward, eventually reaching the shores of Britain. There is also tremendous evidence that wise Hebrews fled the Assyrian conquest of Israel in order to find refuge in the British Isles where they eventually became the Druids, Celts, and Culdee. The Druidic system of Britain was both a religious and a pragmatic legal framework from which the nation operated, and its parallels to the Semitic way of life presented in the Torah is apparent. Author Isabel Hill Elder has outlined compelling evidence that the first Christian church outside of Jerusalem was indeed found in the British Isles, noting:

> "Druidism with its self-evident Old Covenant origin, which latter was, indeed, the great 'oral secret' transmitted by Druid sages from generation to generation, its doctrine of the Trinity, worship entirely free from idolatry, furtherance of peace and contribution to the settling of disputes among the laity, high moral tone, and insistence on the liberty and rights of the subject, was a perfect preparation for the reception of Christianity. Upon the introduction of Christianity the Druids were called upon, not so much as to reverse their ancient faith, as to 'lay it down for a fuller and more perfect revelation'. No country can show a more rapid natural merging of a native religion into Christianity than that which was witnessed in Britain in the first century A.D. The readiness with which the Druids accepted Christianity, the facilities with which their places of worship and colleges were turned into Christian uses ... are facts which the modern historian has either overlooked or ignored."[13]

Elder goes on to explain that even the ancient British language did not succumb to Greco-Roman influence in their reference to God, for they always referred to Jesus as *Yesu,*[14] which is an extremely accurate rendering of the original Hebrew name, Yehoshua, given to Jesus along with this name's shorthand equivalent, Yeshua. There is no doubt that first century Britain widely accepted a non-Romanized and pure Christianity over five hundred years before the Roman Catholic St. Augustine had ever arrived with his false claim of being "the Apostle to the English." There is also overwhelming evidence from artifacts, buildings, documents, and deeply rooted traditions that Joseph of Arimathea along with other apostles of Yeshua with him had firmly established Christianity in Britain, and particularly in Glastonbury of Avalon,[15] in the aftermath of the great persecution within Jerusalem (see Acts 8:1).

Critics of the Sonnini Manuscript and the overall narrative regarding Britain's early and widespread acceptance of Christianity rely heavily on the Roman narrative of the Druids being a mostly savage and barbaric people that were only increasingly more civilized with the arrival of Romanized Christianity in the 6th century. The fact that the Druids lacked thoroughly documented works explaining their customs coupled with Roman imperial interests in exploiting the gold, tin, pearls, and wealth of the Isles fully enabled Roman historians to control the narrative. They claimed that the Druidic way of life was filled with "abominable practices" while simultaneously hiding Rome's inhumane methods of subjugation, which included burning down homes and slaughtering large numbers of Druid priests under Suetonius Paulinus, the Roman legate of Britain in AD 61.[16] This tragic carnage of Rome continued well beyond the first century due to Rome's imperialism and love of gain. The stark reality is that history has been purposely obscured by secularists and malevolent elites that have sought to conceal God's Hand throughout world history. The Romanized narratives of history that we have received in all levels of establishment education have been carefully crafted to guarantee confusion over the veracity of God's Word while hiding the proper understanding of who the lost sheep of Israel truly are.

As you will discover throughout this book, the primary areas where both Judah and the Ten Lost Tribes are currently located today are the United States along with the nations of the UK, Australia, Spain, Latin America, and Europe. In fact, it was clearly prophesied by Isaiah in particular that scattered Israel was destined to be located at the coastal extremities of the earth such as North America, the British Isles, Scandinavia, New Zealand, and Australia (Isa. 11:12; 41:8,9; 42:10,12; 49:1,6). Generally speaking, all Western nations have significant amounts of descendants of Abraham, Isaac, and Jacob from both kingdoms of Israel. Sadly, most people think of 1948 UN-created Israel as being the only place of relevance in terms of end-time Bible prophecy. This secular nation state certainly has its place in prophecy, but it is the headquarters of Mystery Babylon Jerusalem, as explained earlier. Israel is roughly the same geographical size as the US state of New Jersey, making it of far lesser importance in terms of understanding the nations of the Lost Tribes of Israel; for indeed, they are nations. This geopolitical reality we now find ourselves in was established long ago in the Scriptures. Besides Abraham himself being directly told that he would be a "father of many nations" (Gen. 17:4), there are numerous other places where this promise is repeated and solidified. Speaking to Abraham regarding his wife, Sarah, it is written:

"As for Sarai your wife, you shall not call her name Sarai, but Sarah shall be her name. And I will bless her and also give you a son by her; then I will bless her, and she shall be a mother of nations; kings of peoples shall be from her." (Gen. 17:15,16)

Speaking to Jacob, Elohim said:

"I am God Almighty. Be fruitful and multiply; a nation and a company of nations shall proceed from you, and kings shall come from your body." (Gen. 35:11)

As you saw in Figure 2.8, Israel was taken captive to Assyria but then migrated extensively throughout Asia minor, Europe, the Caucasus Mountains, and the UK. We can confirm these migratory routes through a variety of archeological and historical witnesses, one of the most important of which can be found in the writings of the Assyrians themselves. Within over 23,000 cuneiform clay tablets of the ancient Assyrians that were later shipped to the British museum, the records of Israel's fall, the various different names they were known by, and their wanderings can be found as documented in E. Raymond Capt's work *Missing Links Discovered In Assyrian Tablets*.[17] Once the veil of false history is lifted from your eyes, you will be able to see that Israel's ancestry and heritage are hiding in plain sight.

Generally speaking, we can designate the "Christian" peoples of the world and those nations with Christian origins such as the United States as being the primary locations of the Lost Tribes of Israel. But, what is a Christian? What does this word really mean? There are many traditions and ideas surrounding the meaning of this label, but Acts 11:26 plainly tells us that the followers of Yeshua and The Way that He promoted were first called "Christians" in Antioch:

"…So it was that for a whole year they assembled with the church and taught a great many people. And the disciples were first called Christians in Antioch." (Acts 11:26b)

The Greek word recorded here for "Christians" is Χριστιανούς (Strong's G5546) and can be transliterated as *Christianos*. This word makes tremendous sense, since we can also look at it as being a mixture of both Greek and Hebrew concepts. The word "christos" in Greek (Strong's G5547) means "consecrated or anointed" and the word for "people" in Hebrew (Strong's H5971) is spelled with the Hebrew letters "ayin" and "mem" to produce "am." As you can see, the believers identified themselves with a label that mixed Hebrew and Greek into the name Christiam, or Christian—a consecrated people to the Lord God Almighty. This became the primary religion of the lost tribes and their nations after the apostles fulfilled their commission to evangelize these lost sheep.

THE SOUTHERN KINGDOM OF ISRAEL

The Southern Kingdom of Judah consisting of Judah, Benjamin, and some of the tribe of Levi also fell into idolatry and lawlessness just like the North. In fact, Jeremiah tells us that the South's sin became even worse than the North, and he declares Israel to be "more righteous" than her sister, "treacherous Judah" (Jer. 3:11). In 586 BC, the Babylonian army came and conquered the House of Judah, just as was foretold by numerous prophets. The key difference between the fall of the South compared with the North is that Judah received a direct promise from God that they would return from captivity once their punishment was complete. The North never had such a promise given to them. More specifically, the punishment of the South was to be a period of seventy years because Judah had been disobedient to observe the commandment to keep the land sabbath, or shemitah, years every seven years that they dwelt in the land. That is why the writer of Chronicles states the following:

"And those who escaped from the sword he carried away to Babylon, where they became servants to him and his sons until the rule of the kingdom of Persia,
to fulfill the word of the LORD by the mouth of Jeremiah, until the land had enjoyed her Sabbaths. As long as she lay desolate she kept Sabbath, to fulfill seventy years."
(2Ch 36:21)

You will discover just how immensely important this idea of keeping the sabbatical years is for understanding end times prophecy. In fact, this is a central and foundational concept that is necessary for decoding the entire 70 weeks timeline. For now, it is important to be reminded of Judah's promise whereby they would return back to the land. Jeremiah states, "For thus says the LORD: After seventy years are completed at Babylon, I will visit you and perform My good word toward you, and cause you to return to this place" (Jer. 29:10). This promise allowed the messianic prophecies concerning Yeshua's birth to take place along with His subsequent ministry, death, burial, and resurrection.

Without the promise of Jeremiah 29:10, the House of Judah would have also been wanderers among the nations in the first century with no homeland of their own. However, history is full of records to confirm that large numbers of the descendants of Judah were also scattered during the Babylonian conquest.

Only a small remnant of Judah returned to the land of Canaan after the captivity was over. Even though this remnant was blessed to return after 70 years of enslavement, they were never fully devoted to following Yehovah. Erroneous and idolatrous practices infiltrated the culture of Judah, and these man-made traditions eventually caused great conflict between Yeshua and His followers during the first century. Arguably, the rise of Judaism as a form of religion can be understood to have begun during the 5th century BC during the days of the Babylonian captivity and onward.

Unlike the Lost Tribes of Israel that have identified heavily with Christianity throughout history, the descendants of Judah can be associated with both Christianity and Judaism. In order to avoid losing their identity around the time of the captivity and to preserve traditions that were esteemed as essential, the Judahites, or Jews, compiled a rigorous set of oral traditions that were partially penned within the writings of the Talmud. These man-made traditions were based on the commentaries and directions of various teachers and rabbis, and the list of new rules continued increasing after the return of the captives. Over time, both written and oral traditions ended up becoming elevated above the Word of God itself, which is why Jesus spent so much time battling the Scribes, Pharisees, and Sannhedrin during His ministry. They were constantly judging Jesus under their false traditions concerning hand washings, extra-biblical regulations for the Sabbath day, and more. Even though the foundations of modern Judaism and its mystical counterpart of Kabbalism can be traced farther back to the fallen days of King Solomon, both the Jerusalem Talmud (4th century) and Babylonian Talmud (5th century) formed the basis of what is commonly understood today as Judaism. To date, practitioners of this religion esteem the writings of the Babylonian Talmud, the Mishna (a rabbinic commentary on the Scriptures), Targums (Aramaic interpretations of the Scriptures), various Midrash commentaries of the rabbis, the Zohar, and also the Kabbalah (teachings of Jewish mysticism). Of all these works, the Talmud, Zohar, and Kabbalah in particular contain open blasphemies that directly contradict the Bible itself. As mentioned before, rabbinical Judaism became the driving force behind the intense persecution of the first century believers after Yeshua's rise from the dead. To this day, Judaism has played a dominant role in the end times, and there is a strict reason why Jesus makes mention of the "synagogue of satan" twice in the book of Revelation, as we will explore later. In light of all this history, we can still generally understand the "Jewish" identity to be directly correlated with the South, and it can therefore be used for locating where Judah might be found today.

What I will provide next is going to help us estimate where the highest concentration of modern day Judahites are located throughout the world. Keep in mind, this data is just a rough estimate because many people (like myself) don't identify as "Jewish", though I personally have evidence of both Jewish and Israeli origins. With that said, three of the tribes (Judah, Benjamin, and some of Levi) can be somewhat located using statistical data provided in censuses. Keep in mind that censuses in many countries do not record religious or ethnic background, leading to a lack of certainty on the exact numbers of Jewish population. Again, this is just a very rough estimate. However, when you look at the highest concentrations of Jews around the world based on the metropolitan areas where they are located, you will find something very interesting. Based on an encyclopedia entry entitled "Jewish population by Metropolitan Area," the majority of modern day self-proclaiming Jews are located in the United States, with New York City and Los Angeles being among the top three locations in the world.[18] NYC has over 1.6 million Jews and LA has over 500,000. Jerusalem is number two on the list of metropolitan areas with the highest numbers of Jews, and it contains over half a million Jews, nearly tying LA. This list goes on to reveal that France, Argentina, Canada, Russia, the UK, Brazil, Australia, South Africa and many other countries have significant numbers of Jews within major cities like Paris, Buenos Aires, and more. Yet, for some strange reason, people still choose to falsely believe that 1948 Israel in the Middle East is the only location of any consequence to end times prophecy. The large numbers of self-proclaiming Jews worldwide simply do not lie.

The Southern Kingdom of Judah is also found in large numbers in Mexico, Central and South America. Regarding Mexico, for instance, Mexican historian Gutierre Tibón notes the following in his *Historia del nombre y de la fundación de México* (History of the Name and Foundation of Mexico):

> "It is not surprising, then, that the Dominican friar Gregorio Garcia (1554-1627) sees Mexico as a Hebrew name, due to the obvious fact that Mexicans descend from the lost tribe of Israel. Mexi or Mesi is the Messiah, and Mexico, the city of the Messiah, the city of Jesus Christ, and not of Huitzilopochtli."[19]
> [translation mine]

This hidden history is not unique to Mexico. Similar evidence, historical documentation, and even legends can be found throughout all of Latin America including the Dominican Republic, Argentina, and Brazil, to name a few. Regarding Hebrew symbolism and coats of arms, the family crest of the lion of Judah is often found in the history of a wide variety of last names and heraldry in Latin America. The lion of Judah is found in my own family crest name through my mother's side of the family. As another example, the name Jimenez reveals the family crest of a wolf, which represents the tribe of Benjamin. Examples of Hebrew culture and symbolism in Latin American history are overwhelming just like they are in Anglo-Saxon culture.

THE SYMBOLS OF THE TRIBES OF ISRAEL

As already alluded to, another simple way to trace the migration and ancestry of all 12 tribes around the world is to study Jacob's blessing upon all his sons in Genesis 48 to 49. It is within these chapters that we can identify all of the symbolism associated with each tribe. When you do this, you will find that the heraldry, banners, and insignia of all Israel are glaringly obvious throughout the flags, seals, and coats of arms of families and nations worldwide. Arguably the easiest symbol to recognize is the lion of Judah, which can be found in the Royal Arms of England, the Scottish red lion, and the Coat of Arms of the King of Spain, to name just a few. Let's first look at an overview of these symbols and then examine them one by one.

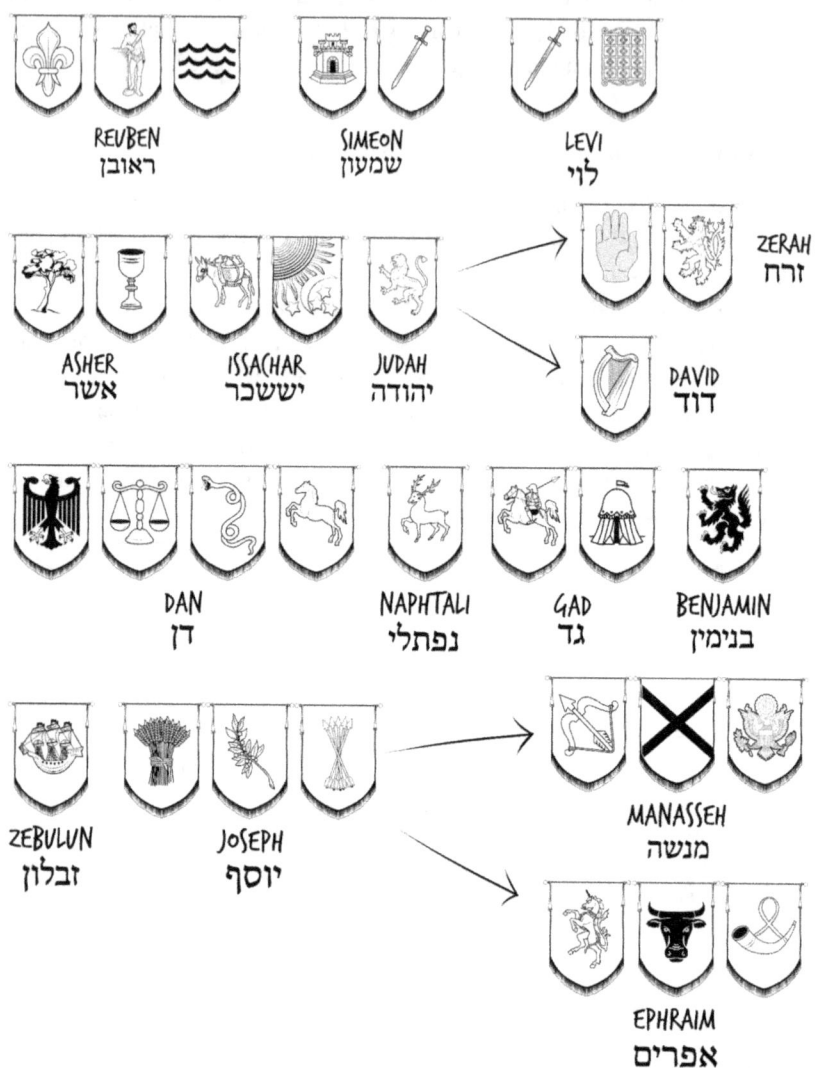

Figure 2.9: The Symbols and Heraldry of the Tribes. Though most of these symbols are given in Genesis right before Jacob is about to die from sickness and he blesses all of his sons (including Joseph's two sons), some symbols are derived from other scriptures, especially the blessing of Moses in Deuteronomy 33. The prophecies of Genesis have now been fulfilled, and these symbols are found in the official insignia of Israelite nations worldwide.

First, it is essential to understand that Jacob first blessed his son Joseph along with his two sons before anyone else received their blessing. This fact may seem trivial, but the writer of Chronicles explains why this was the case.

"Now the sons of Reuben the firstborn of Israel—he was indeed the firstborn, but because he defiled his father's bed, his birthright was given to the sons of Joseph, the son of Israel, so that the genealogy is not listed according to the birthright" (1Ch 5:1)

We read throughout the Torah that the firstborn son of a given family is the recipient of the birthright, or blessing, of his father. This usually included both physical and spiritual blessings. In cases where the firstborn son is the only heir to his father, he would be the immediate legal recipient of his father's inheritance and possessions in the event of his father's death. What 1Chronicles 5:1 reminds us is that Reuben forfeited his God-given birthright even though he was Jacob's true firstborn son that Leah bore him. He forfeited his chance to receive the primary and most significant blessing from among all of Jacob's sons because he slept with his father's concubine, Bilhah, in a very sinful and incestual act. Therefore, since the firstborn son of Leah had forfeited his blessing, the birthright fell onto the firstborn son of Rachel, which was Joseph.

Regarding the specific blessings given to each tribe, it is of utmost importance to realize that Jacob declared that these were to be understood as end times prophecies.

And Jacob called his sons and said, "Gather together, that I may tell you what shall befall you in the last days" (Gen. 49:1)

This book would certainly be incomplete without outlining these prophecies that correspond to both Judah and the lost tribes of Israel in order to properly identify the greatest events of these last days. Heraldry is a sure way to identify Daniel's people of the 70 weeks prophecy. Even though any *single* symbol can be found on a coat of arms or flag pertaining to a nation in our modern-day context, it is more common to find a mixture of Hebrew symbols.

In order to readily identify all of them, it must first be understood that the children of Israel would encamp around the Tabernacle in the wilderness according to a specific East-South-West-North formation. Numbers chapter 2 is the first place we clearly understand that each tribe has its own standard, or symbol, used to identify it. To the east was Judah, to the south was Reuben, to the west was Ephraim, and the north was Dan. Though Numbers 2 does not give us exactly what these standards were, it is within Ezekiel's description of the four living creatures that the connection can be made. Regarding this vision, he wrote, "As for the likeness of their faces, each had the face of a man; each of the four had the face of a lion on the right side, each of the four had the face of an ox on the left side, and each of the four had the face of an eagle" (Eze. 1:10). Ezekiel's vision of the living creatures and their four faces perfectly matches the formation of Israel in the desert. In other words, Reuben was the face of the man in the south, Judah was the face of a lion in the east, Ephraim was the face of an ox in the west, and Dan was the eagle's face in the north. These symbols will become more clear as these four tribes are carefully examined together with all the other tribes and their respective symbols.

REUBEN
ראובן

Figure 2.10: The Symbols of Reuben: Fleur De Lis, Man, and Water

We begin this investigation with Rueben because Jacob declared him to be the beginning of his strength in the last days. In other words, end-times prophecy revolves around the appearance of the Reubenites as a mighty nation. This is what Jacob said:

3 "Reuben, you are my firstborn, My might and the beginning of my strength, The excellency of dignity and the excellency of power.
4 "Unstable as water, you shall not excel, Because you went up to your father's bed; Then you defiled it— He went up to my couch."
(Gen. 49:3,4)

We get the strong impression of Reuben as a man, no doubt handsome, who is driven by a sensuality that overrides his moral character to the point that he is not successful in life. This behavior is manifested when Reuben does the right thing to deliver Joseph out of the hand of his brothers who wanted to kill him, but he did not take full responsibility upon himself as the eldest to do what was right. For as Moses wrote, "And Reuben said to them, 'Shed no blood, but cast him into this pit which is in the wilderness, and do not lay a hand on him'" (Gen. 37:22). Even though his heart's intention was to deliver Joseph out of the hand of his brothers, Reuben had Joseph thrown into a pit rather than do whatever was necessary to protect him and physically defend him if necessary. He could have approached this situation much differently, but he conformed to the mob mentality of his brothers who quickly sold Joseph into slavery from Reuben's pit. Reuben casually slipped away from the scene of the crime because he was not mentioned again until after Judah and the brothers successfully conspired to sell Joseph. Rather than taking full responsibility, he avoided confrontation and eventually joined the brothers in the conspiracy as they all lied to their father together. He would rather live a lie than firmly stand up for what he believed in. Going forward to the time of the famine, Genesis 42:22 reveals that Reuben expressed great anxiety to the brothers while also shifting the blame away from himself as Joseph began putting them to the test. Apparently, he had not changed much from his earlier days.

Reuben is first identified as the gatherer of mandrakes in a scenario where he was "hired" to settle a dispute between Rachel and Leah as recorded in Genesis 30:14. The mandrakes themselves as found in Israel to this day are the Mandragora autumnalis *Bertol.*, which are commonly called the Autumn Mandrake, Devil's Apple, Dudaim, or Love Apple.[20] It is around the time of the firstfruits of the wheat harvest of Pentecost each year that the fruit of the mandrakes appear in the land, though the actual flowers bloom before Abib.[21] Rather than the flowers, it was the fruits themselves that were coveted by the barren Rachel because they were believed to be a natural fertility enhancer. In fact, this account gives us a little insight as to why Rachel was unable to conceive for so long. She was an idolatrous woman as Genesis 31:34 records, and she also put her hope and trust into the mandrakes to help her conceive her first child rather than God Himself. It wasn't until years later after the mandrakes incident that Rachel ever conceived, further humbling her. However, Rachel wishfully "purchased" the mandrakes from Reuben's hand in exchange for his mother Leah having the opportunity to be intimate with Jacob for the night. For this reason, the purple-colored mandrake flowers became a primary symbol of the tribe of Reuben, and it has manifested itself on the world stage as none other than the Fleur De Lis commonly seen among the French people and their territories from antiquity.

In addition to these things, Reuben is remembered for history's most infamous act of adultery, perhaps second only to David and Bathsheeba. By having sexual relations with Bilhah, Jacob's concubine, Reuben not only undermined and disgraced his father's honor, but this incestual act with the mother of Dan and Naphtali also brought great shame to his half brothers. This act forfeited the birthright blessing that belonged to Reuben, and it was passed onto Joseph instead. It is in this context that the symbol of the water is ascribed to this tribe.

Instability, great sensuality, and inconsistent moral character are therefore the prophecies that the tribe of Reuben and his offspring have inherited in the last days. As mentioned, the most perfect description of this prophecy can be found within the nation of France. Not only is Paris well known as one of the most romantic cities in the world, but various other locations like Quebec City, Canada, Aix-en-Provence in Southern France, and New Orleans, USA are all French places known for their romance and sensuality. Words like lingerie, French kiss, boudoir (a woman's private bedroom), and many other words and phrases have been carried over directly into the English language as well as the languages of other Western nations. French culture is also heavily centered around exquisite dining experiences and delicacies that appeal to the senses. Things like creme brulee, crepes, and the Bordeaux wines such as Cabernet Sauvignon, Cabernet Franc, and Merlot have defined the essence of France's culture from antiquity.

Regarding France's instability more specifically, the nation boasts the unsavory fact of having adopted 12 different constitutions and 3 charters from the time of the French Revolution in 1789 to its present-day Fifth Republic with the Constitution of October 4, 1958. Each constitution or charter reorganized the government of France, sometimes significantly, during this 169-year period. By comparison, the United States has only had one constitution from 1776 to the present. Such instability is unique on the world stage and a clear indication that the French people are indeed Reubenites. During the time of Napoleon Bonaparte and his rule over France from 1799 to 1815, the French Empire reached its peak of territorial expansion in 1812, having reached as far as Russia and having direct influence in the Americas. This worldwide presence of the French people satisfied the prophecy of Moses when he said, "Let Reuben live, and not die, Nor let his men be few" (Deu. 33:6). However, the Empire came to a quick end as Britain began revolting against French rule in the north while Russia headed an insurrection of multiple European states against Napoleon in the east. Unable to cope with internal division and numerous war fronts, Napoleon's France readily diminished. Just as Jacob had declared, France would be the first of Israel's strength and power in the last days, but it did not excel. The birthright blessing was instead passed onward to Joseph and his two sons, Ephraim and Manasseh.

JOSEPH

יוסף

Figure 2.11: The Symbols of Joseph: Wheat, Olive Branch, Arrows

22 Joseph is a fruitful bough, A fruitful bough by a well; His branches run over the wall.
23 The archers have bitterly grieved him, Shot at him and hated him.
24 But his bow remained in strength, And the arms of his hands were made strong By the hands of the Mighty God of Jacob (From there is the Shepherd, the Stone of Israel)
(Gen. 49:22-24)

The bundle of wheat, the olive branch bearing fruit, and the bundle of arrows are the primary symbols of Joseph. The wheat should be obvious in its connection to the famine in Egypt and Joseph's wisdom. This tribe received the most significant blessing, and Jacob stated that he had given to Joseph "one portion above your brothers" (Gen 48:22). He was blessed with every possible blessing from heaven above to the great deep beneath the earth. Joseph's two sons, Ephraim and Manasseh, were also to be named among Jacob's sons (Gen. 48:5). Technically speaking, there are therefore thirteen tribes of Israel and not just twelve; however, many people often use both numbers interchangeably. Rather than Joseph taking on an identity of his own on the world stage, the blessing was manifested in the nations of his two sons. That is why you will find these primary symbols of Joseph among the families, cities, and nations of Ephraim and Manasseh.

EPHRAIM
אפרים

Figure 2.12: The Symbols of Ephraim: Unicorn, Bull, and Horn

14 Then **Israel** stretched out his right hand and laid it on Ephraim's head, who was the younger, and his left hand on Manasseh's head, guiding his hands knowingly, for Manasseh was the firstborn.
16 "The Angel who has redeemed me from all evil, Bless the lads; **Let my name be named upon them,** And the name of my fathers Abraham and **Isaac**; And let them grow into a multitude in the midst of the earth."
18 And Joseph said to his father, "Not so, my father, for this one is the first-born; put your right hand on his head."
19 But his father refused and said, "I know, my son, I know. He also shall become **a people,** and he also shall be great; but truly his younger brother shall be greater than he, and his descendants shall become **a multitude of nations."**
(Gen 48:14,16,18,19) [emphasis added]

The first and most important thing to notice is that "Israel" said that Ephraim and Manasseh would have his name upon them along with Isaac's name. That is why throughout the Bible and especially prophetic scriptures, the names *Israel* and *Issac* are used to refer to the ten tribes of the North and are even used interchangeably with Ephraim, who was the chief blessing recipient of Israel. Notice that though Ephraim was not the true firstborn of Joseph, Jacob made a deliberate choice to cross his hands to ensure that his right hand was upon Ephraim's head so that he would receive the greater blessing while his left hand was upon Manasseh's head. The prophecy was that the younger brother, Ephraim, would become a multitude of nations while Manasseh would only be a singular people, or singular nation. Before Moses passes away, he also blesses each of the tribes with somewhat of a repetition of Jacob's original blessing but with added details. In the case of Ephraim and Manasseh, this is what Moses spoke:

"[Joseph's] glory is like the firstling of his bullock, and his horns are like the horns of unicorns: with them he shall push the people together to the ends of the earth: and they are the ten thousands of Ephraim, and they are the thousands of Manasseh." (Deut. 33:17 KJV)

It is within the blessing of Moses that we see the primary symbols of Ephraim being the unicorn, young bull, and the horn. The King James Bible's use of the word *unicorn* is rather widespread, and the underlying Hebrew word (Strong's H7214) used in Deu. 33:17 is said to describe an animal that is now extinct though certainly containing a horn. This unicorn symbol is found in the Royal Coat of Arms of the United Kingdom with a few variations also found throughout Britain. The assignment of the bull to Ephraim is not unique to Moses' departing blessing but is a repetition of the standard presented in Numbers 2 and Ezekiel 1. Like Uncle Sam of the US, the John Bull figure was used in military recruiting posters especially during World War I, further pinpointing Ephraim's identity within the UK. The most important piece of the end-times puzzle, however, is that Ephraim would be ten thousands while Manasseh would only be thousands. This tenfold difference in magnitude between these two brother nations has already played out historically in the most remarkable way.

Immediately after the decline of the French Empire, Britain took over the world stage and expanded greatly. This commonwealth of nations took over the birthright blessing and became the new superpower of history. The nations of the British Commonwealth today are Great Britain, Canada, Australia, and New Zealand together with a combined total of 56 member states that were carried over from the peak of the British Empire. The Empire itself began in 1707 with the Acts of Union and reached its peak of power in the early 1900s. By 1920, Britain controlled almost a quarter of the world's total land area, giving it the nickname as "the empire on which the sun never sets."[22] This was, without a question, the largest empire in all of recorded history.

The inevitable decline of the British occurred in 1946 in the aftermath of World War II. A harsh debt load had accumulated by the time the war was over, and it caused the empire to become nearly bankrupt. With a financial crisis looming, Britain decided to take a 3.75 billion USD loan from the United States.[23] As Proverbs 22:7 states, the borrower is a servant to the lender; and the United States quickly emerged as the superior power over Britain on the world stage. It is not a coincidence that Ephraim, a multitude of nations, came first and then Manasseh appeared as the last Israelite superpower on the world stage.

MANASSEH

מנשה

Figure 2.13: The Symbols of Manasseh: The Bow, Cross, and Great Seal of America

We first see this name mentioned in Genesis 41, where we learn the exact reason why this name was important to Joseph.

Joseph called the name of the firstborn Manasseh: "For God has made me forget all my toil and all my father's house."
(Gen. 41:51 NKJV)

This name literally means *one who forgets*, or *causing to forget*. The nuances here are extremely important for understanding this tribe's place in the last days. Manasseh's land is one in which its people are brought back into balance and inner peace while being disconnected from a past life of hardship or far less desirable circumstances. What else besides the United States of America, the land of opportunity and the melting pot of the world's immigrants, fits the manifestation of this identity so perfectly? Just as the name Manasseh so prophetically describes, most Americans have forgotten their true ancestry and their origins. They simply refer to themselves as "Americans" and give little thought as to how their families ever arrived within the massive country's borders to begin with. If you take a look back at Figure 2.6, pay attention to where Manasseh is on the map. Even though this tribe had an average-sized population of 52,700 during the second census of Israel in Numbers 26, they ended up claiming two large tracts of land labeled East and West Manasseh by the time of the conquest under Joshua. This history is reminiscent of the United States where its population prefers to be spread out across the land rather than highly concentrated in one area as is the case in a country like Indonesia or Japan, for example. Not only that but just like East and West Manasseh were divided by the Jordan River, today's Manasseh is divided into East and West by the Mississippi River. The likelihood of such a significant thing being merely coincidence is impossible. We are also told in Numbers

60

that Machir was one of the ancestral heads of Manasseh. Numbers 26:29 literally refers to the descendents of this patriarch as *ha-mah-kee-ree* in the Hebrew, or Machirites in the English translations. If you say the Hebrew word out loud you can hear the phonetic resemblance to the word *America*. This connection is precisely what Australian lost tribes researcher, Yair Davidiy, lays out in his book *Hebrew Tribes* where he explains that *ha-mah-kee-ree* was Latnised over time to be pronounced as America.[24]

One of the clearest indications that Manasseh's prophetic identity is indeed America can be found within the symbolism of the tribe. Though not unique to the USA alone, the symbols of Figure 2.13 can all be found in the heraldry and official seals of America and its citizens. The "X" shape is derived from the crossing of Jacob's hands to bless Ephraim with his right hand instead of the true firstborn, Manasseh, and it is found in various countries and flags pertaining to Manasseh such as Scotland. The primary colors of America—red, white, and blue—are all colors of the tabernacle and its curtains during the journey through the wilderness. That is why other English Lost Tribe countries like the UK and Australia also have these colors as part of their flags. When examining the Great Seal of the United States, all of the connections to Jacob's blessing over Joseph are plainly evident for all to see. The 13 stars and stripes of the original 13 colonies give us the first clue. Then take a close look at the bald eagle's claws. In one, the eagle is pictured with a fruitful bough of an olive tree bearing 13 olives and having 13 leaves. In the other claw, there are 13 arrows resembling the shots that Joseph endured from his brothers. All of these things point to Manasseh's true identity as being the thirteenth and final tribe of Israel to appear on the world stage and the last of Joseph's two sons to receive his birthright blessing before the end of the age finally comes.

Though America has not yet fallen from its position of prominence as of the time of writing, this event will certainly come to pass soon. God has now sent the dire omen of the triple solar eclipses of 2017, 2023, and 2024 over the nation. This omen is none other than the sign of Jonah referred to by Jesus multiple times in the Gospels. This is the sign that *any* crooked and perverse generation receives before judgment, and it has indeed now appeared to America just like it did to ancient Nineveh in the mid-700s BC. For a deeper look at all aspects of the sign of Jonah, read *Bible Prophecy Secrets II,* the second book in this series. This topic will also be addressed in Chapter 13.

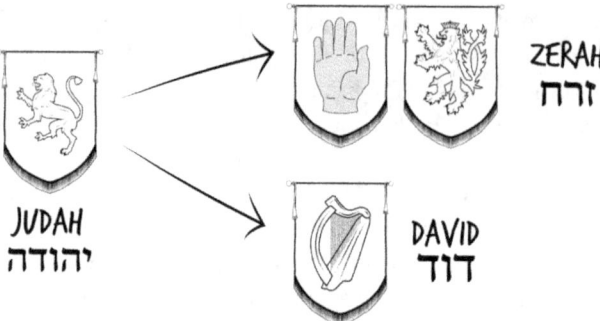

**Figure 2.14: The Symbols of Judah: The Lion, Red Hand of
Zerah, and Harp of David**

Judah is the only tribe containing all four letters of God's name, or Yehovah. This is not a coincidence. Leah declared, "Now I will praise Yehovah" when she bore Judah (Gen. 29:35), and that is why he was called Judah, which literally means *praised*. Jacob then declared in his blessing that Jesus the Messiah (Shiloh) would be born through this tribe (Gen. 49:10), further fulfilling the message contained within Judah's name. Much is said about Judah throughout the Bible. Appearing over 800 times, this name is transferred from the patriarch himself and to the entire Kingdom of Judah in the South also consisting of Benjamin and Levi after the division of United Israel had occurred. As an individual tribe, Judah always maintained a leadership role. Numbers 2:9 reveals that every time the children of Israel journeyed into the wilderness, Judah was always the first tribe to lead them all. Regarding his last-days blessing in particular, this is what Jacob declared:

8 Judah, you are he whom your brothers shall praise; Your hand shall be on the neck of your enemies; Your father's children shall bow down before you.
9 Judah is a lion's whelp; From the prey, my son, you have gone up. He bows down, he lies down as a lion; And as a lion, who shall rouse him?
10 The scepter shall not depart from Judah, Nor a lawgiver from between his feet, Until Shiloh comes; And to Him shall be the obedience of the people.
11 Binding his donkey to the vine, And his donkey's colt to the choice vine, He washed his garments in wine, And his clothes in the blood of grapes.
12 His eyes are darker than wine, And his teeth whiter than milk.
(Gen. 49:8-12)

Notice that these words are only blessings with none of the negative attributes of Judah mentioned by Jacob. We know that Judah was the one that came up with the idea to sell Joseph into slavery. An entire chapter of Genesis is also dedicated to explaining the immorality of Judah's sons that were conceived through the Canaanite woman that he married. In chapter 38, it is recounted how Judah's firstborn Er was evil along with the second born son Onan, so both of them were killed by Yehovah. The young woman Tamar was first married to Er but was then married to Onan after Er's death. Her marriage to Onan was done to fulfill the brother-in-law instruction as found in Deuteronomy 25:5. After the death of the wicked Onan, Tamar was left childless, without a husband, and consequently remained a widow. In ancient times, this was a grave situation for a young woman to find herself in. Having the leadership of a husband and the comfort of children were necessary for survival in a more hostile world where bands of raiders existed and life was more nomadic with far less governmental oversight in place compared to today. The family unit was necessary for dividing agricultural labor and living off of the land. Back in those days, it was shameful to be childless, and it was an honor to have a large family. After Judah permanently delayed Tamar's marriage to his son Shelah, she took it upon herself to deceive Judah by dressing up as a prostitute while successfully luring him into her trap. Just three months later, she was visibly pregnant. Tamar was able to escape the death penalty described in Deuteronomy 22 because although she was technically betrothed to Judah's son Shelah, she was able to prove her innocence by presenting Judah's cord, signet ring, and staff—the very things that she held as a security deposit the day that Judah slept with her. Though Judah never knew Tamar intimately ever again, she gave birth to the twins Zerah (the firstborn with the scarlet thread) and Perez (the one who broke through). Both of these brothers would go on to become major identities of the tribe of Judah throughout history. However, all of these embarrassing details were not overly important to Jacob. Interestingly enough, Judah's conspiracy against Joseph, the corrupt moral character of his first two sons, and his lust for a prostitute are not mentioned in Jacob's departing words of Genesis 49.

Of the symbols of Judah, the lion is by far the most prevalent and easily recognizable. After the dispersion of Judah first by the Babylonians and later by the Romans, this tribe spread across Europe, the British Isles, all over the Mediterranean, and also within the Iberian Peninsula. That is why the lion is found in the emblems and coats of arms of countless families, cities, provinces, royal arms, and national arms of these regions and also throughout the Americas. For example, the lion is a national emblem found in the coat of arms of Sweden, Belgium, Luxembourg, Denmark, Ireland, Canada, Norway, and the Netherlands. As mentioned before, the Royal Coat of Arms of the UK contains the unicorn of Ephraim to the right but also the lion of Judah to the left, indicating its historical origins in both houses of Israel. It is also common to find this symbol expressed as the three lions of Judah. This representation is seen in the national emblem of England and appears in the Royal Standard and the shield of the Royal Arms of Britain.

Based on Jacob's blessing alone, it may seem that the lion is the only symbol of Judah, but as I have recounted, there is more to the story. There is also the blood red hand of Zerah, which is also depicted as a blood red lion. This was the firstborn of Tamar whose red hand came out first. Perez, the second born, brought about the lineage of King David that also eventually gave rise to Jesus the Messiah as recorded in Matthew 1. That is why the harp symbol is associated with Perez. While David's harp is found mostly in Ireland such as County Armagh, it is also found elsewhere as is the case in the British monarchy, which uses both the harp and red lion as symbols. The blood red lion of Zerah is also found in the shield of the Royal Arms of Canada, the Arms of the Dutch Republic, the Seal of the Batavian Common-wealth (Netherlands), the Coat of Arms of Australia, and the Coat of Arms of Scotland, to name a few. The red hand of Zerah is harder to find and appears to be mostly limited to Ireland. The Northern Ireland counties of Antrim, Tyrone, Londonderry, and Fermanagh all have the red hand in each of their coats of arms.

DAN

דן

Figure 2.15: The Symbols of Dan: The Eagle, Scales, Serpent, and Horse

Jacob's blessing upon Dan reveals three of his primary symbols. The fourth, as discussed, is the eagle symbol of Ezekiel's vision and Dan's leadership role as the northern standard of the encampment around the Tabernacle. This is what Jacob said regarding Dan:

16 Dan shall judge his people As one of the tribes of Israel.
17 Dan shall be a serpent by the way, A viper by the path, That bites the horse's heels So that its rider shall fall backward.
(Gen. 49:16,17)

The first verse is where the scales of justice are derived from. One fulfillment of this symbol can be found in the life of Samson the Danite who judged Israel for 20 years during the times of the judges. Both the serpent and the horse alone or with a rider on it can be assigned to Dan. The main idea with regard to the serpent symbol is that it travels and moves in a wave-like fashion, which is exactly how Dan migrated throughout the world in his conquests. More specifically, the hidden identity of the tribe of Dan throughout history can be found within these words from the book of Judges: "Gilead stayed beyond the Jordan, And why did Dan remain on ships? Asher continued at the seashore, And stayed by his inlets" (Jdg 5:17). We are being told that Dan mostly lived a maritime lifestyle and had been doing so from after the time Joshua entered the promised land (1338 BC) until the times of the Judges (about 1200 BC).

History confirms that it was specifically during the time of the Judges that a mysterious people group known as the Sea Peoples emerged on the world stage, which was none other than the tribe of Dan. Lost tribes researcher and author Steven M. Collins presents the following findings regarding the Danites:

> "The Encyclopaedia Britannica records that the Greeks listed the 'Danaans' or 'Danauna' as a distinct, seafaring people who were present in the eastern Mediterranean as early as 1230–1190 B.C. This is exactly the same time frame in which Judges 5:17 ascribes a nautical way of life to the Israelite tribe of Dan. ... These 'Danaans' were part of the seafaring alliance of tribes known as the Sea Peoples who raided and settled Mediterranean coastlands."[25]

As a result of this maritime culture, historical traces of Dan can be found from north of Canaan to Syria, into Asia Minor, and westward to all the way to North Africa. Of course, Dan made his way well within Europe and particularly Greece. Greecian culture and lore was heavily influenced by Dan's activities, and as mentioned, they knew them as the Danaans and Danauna. Regarding their physical appearance, a professor of Assyriology at Oxford University noted that the Danites with their "white skins, blue eyes, and reddish hair" formed a "link between the white-skinned tribes of the Greek Seas and the fair-complexioned Libyans of North Africa."[26] Many scholars have noted that white and fair skin was indeed a major characteristic of the lost tribes of Israel, and Dan was no exception.

Figure 2.16: The Migrations of the Tribe of Dan

Wherever the Danites, or Danes, went they would create a viper's trail and name the locations of their whereabouts after their patriarchal father, Dan. Places, rivers, and cities such as the Dardanelles (strait in northwestern Turkey), Dan's Mark (Denmark), the Danube River, the Tuatha Dé Danann of Ireland, the Bay of Donegal (Ireland's largest bay), and Danelaw in England are all locations that Dan directly influenced and even controlled. Of all these areas, Denmark might have the highest concentration of modern-day Danites, as these Danish people have held strongly to their language, culture, and name for many hundreds of years now.

Dan also left behind his ancient symbols in these numerous locations. The eagle of Dan can be found nearly everywhere in Europe and throughout the Americas. Going back to the Great Seal of the United States, the eagle of Dan is a primary symbol together with the other symbols of Joseph as already described. Germany, Mexico, Poland, and Austria all feature this same eagle. Some say that Russia should be included in this list, however, the Russian eagle is specifically a double-headed eagle and not a single-headed one. This mythological creature can be traced back to the Hittites and other non-Hebrew cultures from antiquity.[27] Sometimes the eagle and snake symbols of Dan were combined into one symbol called a *wyvern*, as currently seen on the flag of Wales or in the heraldry of the old Anglo-Saxon Kingdom of Wessex in England. The horse on its hind legs is usually white and occasionally depicted with a rider. This was a primary symbol of the Saxons before their invasion of Britain and was also heavily seen in the people of Denmark and the Netherlands.[28] The scales of justice can be found scattered throughout various families, cities, and places of the West.

Figure 2.17: The Symbols of Simeon and Levi: Castle, Sword, and Priestly Breastplate

The blessing upon Simeon and Levi was given to them simultaneously, which is why both will be examined together. It was actually more of a prophetic curse than it was a true blessing, but Jacob's words do contain a hidden message that these two tribes would become valiant sword wielding warriors. This is what he said:

5 Simeon and Levi are brothers; Instruments of cruelty are in their dwelling place.
6 Let not my soul enter their council; Let not my honor be united to their assembly; For in their anger they slew a man, And in their self-will they hamstrung an ox.
7 Cursed be their anger, for it is fierce; And their wrath, for it is cruel! I will divide them in Jacob And scatter them in Israel.
(Gen. 49:5-7)

These words were based entirely on the Dinah incident recorded in Genesis 34. After Jacob had fled from Laban and also avoided a hostile confrontation with his brother Esau, he entered Canaan and purchased his first plot of land in a place called the city of Shechem. As Jacob finally started to relax after a life of hardship, another major turn of events took place involving his daughter Dinah. She apparently went out by herself into Shechem without any companion or protection. That was when a prince of the land named Shechem took her "and lay with her, and violated her" (Gen. 34:2). The Hebrew word translated as "violated" is *anah* (Strong's H6031) and is seen for the first time in Genesis 15:13 where God tells Abraham that his descendants will be "afflicted" in a land not their own for 400 years. Therefore, the use of force, oppression, being humbled, or humiliated are all ascribed to this same word throughout the Bible. What we can conclude is that Dinah was pressured into doing something she did not want to do at the very least, and in the worst case scenario she was raped without any consent. Either way, Shechem and his father Hamor agreed to do whatever Jacob wanted in order to make the situation right and give Dinah into a proper marriage with Shechem, who ended up loving Dinah afterwards. Interestingly, it was not Jacob who directly laid out the terms and conditions of an agreement but it was his sons. Dinah's brothers Simeon and Levi certainly played a major part. They spoke deceitfully and demanded that all the men of the city become circumcised, to which Hamor and Shechem agreed.

It is at this point that we understand the "instruments of cruelty" that Simeon and Levi used. They each took their sword and proceeded to kill all the males of the city and plunder everything, including women, children, sheep, oxen, and donkeys. They took all the wealth and possessions of Shechem for themselves. Forced to flee to Bethel, Jacob was once again in a position where he felt vulnerable, threatened, and afraid for his life. Such desperation was never forgotten by him and was highlighted within the language of the prophetic blessing over Simeon and Levi. Jacob's words reveal that not only did they murder many men in cold blood, but they also killed oxen for fun, or for sport. They went on a bloody rampage that Jacob could only describe as an intense and cursed anger. Some say that because these tribes were both scattered in Israel, they did not have clear identifying symbols, especially Levi. This idea is simply not true. Both of these tribes used the sword as an instrument of cruelty, and therefore both have this symbol as an inherent part of their identity. Moses describes Levi as a lawgiver in his blessing of Deuteronomy 33, which is where the linen ephod and particularly the breastplate of the high priest became an identifying symbol of the tribe. Not surprisingly, Moses does not give Simeon a blessing in this same chapter because this tribe revolted under his leadership, having had 59,300 males during the first census of Numbers 1:23 and only 22,200 males 40 years later during the second census of Numbers 26:14. It is clear that Simeon's revolt was at least partly connected to Phinehas' killing of a

Simeonite prince in Numbers 25 during the Baal Peor incident. Unwilling to await the inheritance of the promised land and being led astray into idolatry, the Simeonites took up their swords in search of a better opportunity else-where. Historian Steven M. Collins concludes that the Milesians of Ireland who traveled directly from Egypt to Spain maintained their Scythian (Israelite) origins and memorized legends such as that of the poisonous biting snakes that perfectly match the account of Numbers 21.[29] That is why Simeon can be traced throughout the Iberian Peninsula, Europe, and Britain. The Spar-tans of ancient Greece can also be traced back to Simeon.[30] By comparison, Levi maintained a strong presence in Israel until the Kingdom of Judah was first carried away by Babylon and then later by the Romans who completed the dispersion of the South. The sword emblem itself can therefore be found throughout all countries of the West, and it is fairly ubiquitous.

Genesis 34:24 reveals that the city of Shechem had a gate, meaning that it also had walls and most likely a castle that belonged to Hamor the king and Shechem the prince. Simeon and Levi's conquest of the walled city therefore became an identity for which they have been remembered in heraldry. Based on the Genesis narrative alone, Shechem's castle should be assigned to both Simeon and Levi since the narrative makes no distinction. This emblem also sometimes appears in heraldry as a single tower or a gate. In his extensive 30-year work, Hebrew heraldry researcher W.H. Bennett notes that the fortified castle with a gate is indeed an emblem of both Simeon and Levi, though he claims that it is mostly attributed to Simeon later in history.[31] The castle is found nearly everywhere in the British Isles and also has a strong presence in Spain, especially in the 11-12th century Spanish Kingdom of Castile, or *el Reino de Castilla*. In Spanish, this kingdom's name literally means *the reign of the castle.* For this reason, the castle has a prominent place in all of Spanish and Latin American heraldry, where numerous descendants of the lost tribes and particularly Simeon and Levi were scattered.

Regarding Levi more specifically, this tribe is one of the difficult ones to directly pinpoint. Since the word for priest in Hebrew is *kohen,* it is commonly believed that Levi can be located amongst those bearing the Cohen surname along with its variations. The breastplate of the high priest is also ascribed to Levi alone, and it appears in heraldry in unique ways. For exam-ple, the Coat of arms of the Westminster City Council (within London) features a gate with exactly twelve squares in what appears to be a normal iron grid pattern. Such a gate fits the description of the city of Shechem, and this unique pattern containing the same number of gemstones as the breastplate is not a coincidence. This same gate also appeared as the official emblem of the British Customs and Excise Service along with the Canadian Customs cap badge.[32] This emblem can also be found in the heraldry of specific families such as the Ramos coat of arms from Spain.[33]

ZEBULUN

זבלון

Figure 2.18: The Symbol of Zebulun: The Ship

Zebulun shall dwell by the haven of the sea; He shall become a haven for ships, And his border shall adjoin Sidon.
(Gen. 49:13)

If you look back at Figure 2.6, you will notice that Zebulun was a tribe with no access to water, making it clear that Jacbo's blessing was to occur much later in the tribe's history and after the dispersion. In order to identify this tribe in the last days, we must be looking for a people group that were seafarers with plenty of ports and harbors for their ships. Because the boat itself is common in heraldry everywhere around the world, Zebulun must be identified by also taking notice of other Hebrew symbols that may be found on the same coat of arms. One perfect example is New Zealand, which features three boats of Zebulun in the middle together with the wheat of Joseph on its official coat of arms. Another example is the flag of the city of Nieuwpoort, Belgium, which features the lion of Judah riding a boat of Zebulun. However, if there is one single nation that perfectly embodies the end-times identity of Zebulun it is none other than the Netherlands. The boat is the ancient emblem of Holland, and the old crest of the Dutch Republic features a ship with seven shields representing each of the seven provinces.[34] During this time period, William of Orange initiated the Dutch Revolt against Spain, and an old statue at Het Plein in The Hague is still preserved to this day bearing a quote from this key figure together with the ship emblem. Before considering Holland's connection any further, let's first look at the blessing of Moses over Zebulun:

"They shall call the people unto the mountain; there they shall offer sacrifices

of righteousness: for they shall suck of the abundance of the seas, and of treasures hid in the sand."
(Deu. 33:19 KJV)

Because of the low elevation of the Netherlands, about two thirds of the
country is vulnerable to flooding, but due to the great ingenuity of the Dutch,
a system of dikes, dams, canals, and floodgates were constructed to keep
various areas of Holland dry for habitation and agriculture. Without these
flood control measures in place, many cities would be underwater including
Amsterdam. As the King James Version so cleverly states, it appears that the
Netherlands has "sucked" the water out of their country so that their land
could be usable and cultivated, thereby yielding treasures and prosperity that
would have been hidden otherwise.

ISSACHAR
יששכר

**Figure 2.19: The Symbols of Issachar: The Donkey and Sun,
Moon, & Stars**

14 Issachar is a strong donkey, Lying down between two burdens;
15 He saw that rest was good, And that the land was pleasant; He bowed his
shoulder to bear a burden, And became a band of slaves.
(Gen. 49:14,15 NKJV)

Most commentators say that Issachar only had one symbol, the donkey. While
this is certainly the primary symbol within Jacob's blessing, we are also told
that men of Issachar had "understanding of the times" in 1 Chronicles 12:32,
which connects back to Genesis 1:14 and the time keeping of the celestial
bodies. Since we are given little details about Issachar throughout the Bible
besides this description, the secondary symbol of the sun, moon, and stars can
also be assigned to this tribe. However, these secondary symbols should be
found alongside other Hebrew symbols for clear confirmation since they
appear often throughout the world.

Abraham Ojeda

When seeking for the donkey in particular, it appears to be found mostly in Germany. The Borough of Maulbronn in Germany has a coat of arms picturing a golden colored donkey carrying a load on his back while approaching a trough of water. The Borough of Tussenhausen features a black donkey on its coat of arms with a crown on its head and what appears to be a cloud covering half of its upright body. The town of Haldenwang again pictures a black donkey on its coat of arms while the town of Oberohrn contains a white one. The municipality of Rettenbach in Bavaria, Germany again pictures a black donkey. Of course, the donkey again appears in a variety of family last names of Germanic origin. The prophetic assignment of Issachar to Germany makes sense. He lies down between two "burdens," and the underlying Hebrew word, *mishpath*, is also used in the Bible to refer to a sheepfold. For more clarity, simply compare this concept to verses like Micah 2:13 where God presents the metaphor of His people being like sheep behind a gate that He opens. The prophecy of Issachar is speaking of a nation that is caught in between two people groups, or separate sheepfolds, that both undermine the free will and sovereignty of this nation for their own benefit. This paradigm certainly fits Germany, a nation upon which all of the monetary blame of World War 1 was placed during the Treaty of Versailles. Such mistreatment of Germany, its subsequent monetary hyperinflation, and internal strife led to the rise of Adolf Hitler's Germany. The swastika is actually an ancient symbol of the sun and therefore correlates with the sun, moon, and stars insignia of Issachar. Again, Germany was caught between the powers of the West (Europe) and East (Russia) who both brought the nation once again under their will at the conclusion of World War 2. In fact, the Iron Curtain and its physical manifestation within Germany as the Berlin Wall greatly exemplifies the wording of Jacob's blessing. West Germany stabilized itself through cooperation with other countries of the West while East Germany languished under Soviet Communism. Germany has been unique in history in that it has been under the burden of pressure from its neighbors to the East and to the West. Though other identities may be possible for end-times Issachar, Germany seems to be the most fitting.

GAD
גָד

Figure 2.20: The Symbols of Gad: The Soldier and the Encampment of Troops

"Gad, a troop shall tramp upon him, But he shall triumph at last." (Gen. 49:19)

The two symbols of Gad are the armed rider, or troop, and a military-styled encampment, or a tent. Moses refers to Gad as a lion in Deuteronomy 33 just like he did with Dan, but because the lion was the primary symbol of Judah, this emblem was never a primary symbol of Gad or Dan. It is possible that the lion may have not even been used at all to avoid misidentification with the Judahites. The armed horseman can be seen in prominent emblems throughout Europe. The country of Lithuania features this emblem on its coat of arms as does the country of Russia. Though the primary emblem of Russia is the two-headed eagle, its capital city of Moscow does feature the horse and rider on both the flag and the coat of arms. The armed rider is also found in the town of Brušperk in the Czech Republic as well as various locations in Scotland, Denmark, and France. The tent symbol itself does indeed exist in small communes of France such as La Châtre, but it is a rare symbol. At this moment in history, it is not yet clear which nation has fulfilled or will fulfill the "triumph" prophecy of Gad, but we should be watching for some nation to overcome adversity and administer true justice as described in Deuteronomy 33:21.

ASHER
אשר

Figure 2.21: The Symbols of Asher: The Olive Tree and the Cup

"Bread from Asher shall be rich, And he shall yield royal dainties." (Gen. 49:20)

Jacob's blessing reveals the primary symbol of Asher as the royal cup. This cup can be found in various coats of arms in Sweden, Germany, England, and Denmark. It is then Moses who gives Asher its other main symbol of the olive tree when he said, "Asher is most blessed of sons; let him be favored by his brothers, and let him dip his foot in oil" (Deut. 33:24). The oil is directly connected to olives, which were abundant along the coastal areas of Lebanon where Asher's ancient territory was located. Moses also went on to say, "Your sandals shall be iron and bronze; as your days, so shall your strength be" (Deut. 33:25). By this, Moses gave us a clue as to where Asher might be found in the last days. He will have access to iron and bronze and therefore be a miner of the soil. Because Asher's territory contained the cities of Tyre and Sidon, they developed a very close relationship with the Phoenicians—the seafaring Canaanites who mingled with the Israelites and together dominated trade in the entire Mediterranean. The Phoenicians, together with the Asherites and other Israelites, went as far as the British Isles where tin, iron, and copper mining were abundant. They also colonized all of Europe together, which is why the symbols of Asher are found throughout all countries of the West.

NAPHTALI
נפתלי

Figure 2.22: The Symbol of Naphtali: The Deer

"Naphtali is a deer let loose; He uses beautiful words."
(Gen. 49:21)

The word used in Hebrew to describe Naphtali can be transliterated as *ayala,* which is a feminine noun referring to a doe or hind (female deer), rather than a stag. Using a feminine noun to describe a patriarch of Israel was certainly an intentional choice by Jacob. The female deer is mentioned throughout the Scriptures as being swift on its feet; and Job, David, and Solomon speak directly of the deer's sexual reproduction with an emphasis on giving birth to offspring. Wherever Naphtali is located today, we should be looking for a people group whose identity is somehow connected to women being let loose to embrace their maternal nature. The other major clue should not be ignored. Naphtalites are also marked by beautiful words, speeches, or sayings. When combining these concepts together there is certainly a nation and an entire region that fits this identity. Though the deer itself is found in a wide variety of surnames and municipalities throughout England, Germany, Poland, and Holland, it is actually the nation of Sweden that appears to fulfill a primary role in Jacob's prophecy. Regarding the "beautiful words" portion of the blessing, Sweden is the nation that has been issuing the annual Nobel Prizes since 1901 to commemorate special achievements worldwide. These gold-plated medals are considered the most prestigious awards in the world for each of six distinct categories, and the ceremonies involved with their presentation and acceptance are surrounded by flowery speeches and words. It is no surprise then that the deer is found throughout a variety of surnames in Sweden and all of Scandinavia. Regarding motherhood and the raising of children, a recent UNICEF report found that the Nordic countries of Sweden, Norway, Iceland, and Estonia all ranked the highest for family-friendly policies in OECD and EU countries.[35] In Sweden, for example, the 1974 Parental Leave Act introduced 180 days of state-funded parental leave from work responsibilities, which could be shared between the farther and mother as they see fit. However, this law has since been updated, and up to 18 months of leave are allowed,[36] with parents receiving 80% of their salary during their parental leave.[37] This national policy allows enough time for a child to be weaned, if the parents so choose. Such a paradigm also reduces the tremendous pressure that women from other countries often have to face in balancing motherhood with a career. Rather than the "deer let loose" being a reference to sexual promiscuity, as the majority of lost tribes commentators often argue, a far more reasonable interpretation involves maternity and the unique protections granted by law for the Nordic countries where Naphtali's identity is found today.

BENJAMIN
בנימין

Figure 2.23: The Symbol of Benjamin: The Wolf

"Benjamin is a ravenous wolf; In the morning he shall devour the prey, And at night he shall divide the spoil."
(Gen 49:27)

Benjamin only had one symbol assigned to him—the wolf. Besides the castle and the lion of Judah, this is one of the most common symbols in all Spanish and Latin American heraldry, being seen in the family crests of Lopez, Jimenez, Ayala, Romero, Navarro, Estrada, and others. Besides numerous surnames, the wolf is found throughout Europe in the coats of arms of various towns and municipalities such as Northern Ireland's capital city Belfast where a chained wolf is depicted. The town of Lobez, Poland has a wolf in its coat of arms as well as the German towns of Passau and Remagen together with the District of Prignitz in Germany. Switzerland also features the wolf emblem in its Borough of Vauffelin.

Going back to ancient times, Benjamin was directly responsible for a civil war that broke out between them and the rest of the tribes as recorded in Judges 19-21. Because God's hand was against Benjamin's wickedness, the number of Benjamites was reduced from 26,700 down to only 600 men. That is why Benjamin became the least of the tribes throughout history after he fought foolishly against all Israel. Out of this tribe came one of the most prominent men of faith in history—Saul of Tarsus, who eventually became the Apostle Paul. His birthplace, Tarsus, is a town located just off the coast of the Mediterranean in modern-day Turkey. The maritime presence of Benjamin in Asia Minor indicates that they had already been scattered throughout the Mediterranean during the time of Christ. However, Jacob's blessing makes it clear that he would find an end-times home elsewhere.

Since the wolf is a creature of cold climates, it would make sense to be looking for Benjamin in the northern regions of the world such as North America and the Nordic countries. Collins concludes that the wolf of Benjamin is directly tied to the ancient Viking culture of Scandinavia, and he specifically points to Norway and its wolf-like wars against all other nations of Europe as being the fulfillment of Jacob's prophecy.[38] This idea makes sense, since Scandinavia was one of the last places in Europe to adopt Christianity, and some still hold strong to the pagan gods of norse mythology to this day.

WHAT ABOUT THE "STAR OF DAVID"?

I challenge you to search for the phrase "star of David" in the entire Bible. You won't find it anywhere. This symbol is not biblically associated within any patriarchal blessing, neither Jacob or Moses. It was never a banner of Judah or any of the other tribes when they encamped in the wilderness. Yet, for some odd reason this six-pointed star has become synonymous with "Israel" in people's minds. Whenever the common person considers the Hebrew or Jewish identity today they automatically think of the hexagram symbol which is sometimes referred to as the seal of Solomon. It is nicknamed such because this final king over United Israel fully immersed himself in the occultic arts after being led astray by his many foreign wives, and somewhere down his descent into paganism this symbol emerged as a "good" thing. However, the Bible has a different name for this particular star.

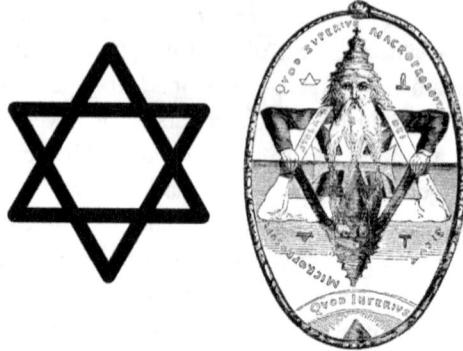

Figure 2.24: The hexagram (left) and one popular rendition of the Seal of Solomon (right). The ouroboros—Leviathan eating its own tail—is pictured around the entire seal along with the Great Pyramid of Giza at the bottom. Some say that Solomon wore a similar hexagram ring as a good luck charm to keep demons away, and people make it akin to the use of white magic (good magic). However, there is no escaping the various pagan and occult practices that are clearly associated with the hexagram and the other evil symbols of Solomon's seal.

The truth is that, yes, while this symbol can indeed be found in the pages of Scripture, it's something that Yehovah Himself describes as blatantly evil and idolatrous. In fact, this pagan symbol actually predates the arrival of King Solomon's reign, and it was surely not something that would be found in David's possession since he was a man after God's heart. The prophet Amos provides us with this needed insight:

25 "Have ye offered unto me sacrifices and offerings in the wilderness forty years, O house of Israel?
26 But ye have borne the tabernacle of your Moloch and Chiun your images, the star of your god, which ye made to yourselves.
27 Therefore will I cause you to go into captivity beyond Damascus," saith the LORD, whose name is The God of hosts.
(Amos 5:25-27 KJV)

We are being told here that during the forty years of wandering in the wilderness and before the righteous Joshua generation rose up, the newly freed Egypt generation of Israel was seduced by the paganism of several idols. The prophet Amos tells us about God's disdain for the idols of Moloch and Chiun along with the star associated with either of these false deities. Most likely, these pagan entities somehow made their way into the hearts and minds of

Israel due to the influence of the polytheistic nation of Egypt. I will further contend that these false gods can be traced back to the time of Nimrod, since this was a man that brought the emergence of dark arts and occultism in a major way during the early post-flood world. Regarding the star of Moloch, we receive more confirmation that this is actually the correct name of the supposed "star of David" from the last words of Stephen the martyr in the book of Acts. Quoting Amos, Stephen provides a little more clarity as to what took place during the days following the exodus:

41 "And they made a calf in those days, offered sacrifices to the idol, and rejoiced in the works of their own hands.
42 "Then God turned and gave them up to worship the host of heaven, as it is written in the book of the Prophets: 'Did you offer Me slaughtered animals and sacrifices during forty years in the wilderness, O house of Israel?
43 You also took up the tabernacle of Moloch, And the star of your god Remphan, Images which you made to worship; And I will carry you away beyond Babylon.'"
(Acts 7:41-43 NKJV)

Before he is killed by the council of Pharisees, Stephen tells us that God had handed over Israel to have a debased mind and to worship the host of heaven, particularly by using the "star of Remphan" which can be understood to be the star of saturn, or rephaim. Stephen confirms that the religious establishment of Judah in the first century had a reprobate mind full of idolatry. In his letter to the Romans, Paul states that when people choose not to retain God in their hearts and minds, they are given over "to a debased mind, to do those things which are not fitting" (Rom. 1:28b). In other words, this particular star symbol has always been something extra-biblical and of ancient origin, and when Stephen exposed its wickedness, it cost him his life.

Many fail to realize that the hexagram's use has been widespread in all manner of different religions from Jainism, Taoism, Buddhism, Hinduism and a wide variety of secret societies and cults including the Freemasons. It was also featured prominently in the occultic books and works of Aliester Crowley (1875–1947), the father of modern satanism. Because of the hexagram's absence within the correct context of patriarchal blessings or other God-breathed descriptions of Israel, there is only one conclusion that ever needs to be made regarding this star of occultism and witchcraft—it is an abomination to the Most High God. That is why 1948-Israel flies the flag of this star of Remphan, so that God's people can identify what Mystery Babylon really is, as we will discuss in further detail later. Though it is a pagan and godless symbol, the star of Remphan is still associated with Judaism and therefore may be used in helping to identify where Judahites are located today. However, the primary and biblical symbols of the tribes should take precedence over false symbols such as this star.

DISCOVERING YOUR IDENTITY IN THE TRIBES TODAY

With a clear understanding of the symbolism of the tribes of Israel, you can now research your own last names from both your mother's and father's side of the family to see what kind of heraldry corresponds with your lineage. There are a few ways to do this. One company named Swyrich Corporation is currently an industry leader in last name histories, coats of arms, and heraldic clipart, and this company began researching and writing family name history documents in 1968. They now boast the ability to provide millions of histories worldwide. Even though not every single name under the sun is catalogued by them, it will be well worth your time to visit their partner website at House of Names[39] where they offer detailed family histories including surname histories. They also provide the meaning behind each symbol found in a coat of arms along with downloadable artwork for just a few dollars. A handful of other websites are also available to help with your research, but House of Names will be a great starting point. Simply type in your last name and search for available information on their website.

For a deeper dive into this topic, I have also provided a *Recommended Reading* list in the back of this book. The sequel to this book, Bible Prophecy Secrets II, will further illuminate the hidden history of both Britain and especially the United States of America in a way that connects archeology, history, and the recent solar eclipse omens that took place over the US from 2017 to 2024. In addition, authors like Steven Spykerman and Steven M. Collins have gone to great lengths to demonstrate the identity of Israel's tribes in these last days. Rather than risk losing track of the main purpose of this book, I will simply point you in the right direction if you wish to put even more puzzle pieces together.

With all these things considered, are you now seeing what I'm seeing?

The Judahites and also the Lost Northern Tribes have been scattered throughout the entire world, but the highest concentrations are within the United States, the UK, Europe, Australia, New Zealand, and various Latin American countries. Doesn't it make sense now? Do you understand why the USA has been so prosperous? Do you see why Europe and the UK have been so blessed? Remember God's blessing upon Isaac:

"And I will make your descendants multiply as the stars of heaven; I will give to your descendants all these lands; and in your seed all the nations of the earth shall be blessed"
(Genesis 26:4)

This promise to Abraham's seed was unconditional, meaning that it was not dependent on the performance, geographical location, or the righteousness of the people. This blessing is God's decree and therefore permanent and unable to be altered. Like I said, this topic is quite huge, and many books have been solely dedicated to this topic.

Now that we have established the identity of Daniel's people, let's go back to the prophecy of the 70 weeks.

THE COMPLETION OF THE THREE EVILS

What would you say is the definition of *sin* in the Bible?

When I ask people this question, the vast majority fail to realize that there are at least three words in the Hebrew language that are used to describe sin. People will usually say that "sin is missing the mark of perfection." Others will say that being a sinner means that someone is not living a perfect life.

These modern definitions that have to do with the idea of being perfect aren't found in the Hebrew language. Remember when we looked at the word *anomia* which is the word for *sin* throughout the Greek New Testament? It doesn't have anything to do with perfection, either, as we found out in Chapter 1 of this book; but it simply means lawlessness or in a state of breaking God's Law.

One of the best places in the entire Bible to study all three Hebrew definitions of *sin* is right here in Daniel 9:24. Let's take a look.

לְכַלֵּא הַפֶּשַׁע ולחתם חטאות וּלְכַפֵּר עָוֹן

Figure 2.25: "...To finish the transgression, To make an end of sins, To make reconciliation for iniquity...". The transliteration of this phrase is "lekalle hapesha vlhitim kht'vt ulkaper aon".

The first word we need to look at is "finish." What does it mean to *finish?* This root word is Strong's H3607 (kaw-law'); and according to BLB it is "a primitive root; to restrict, by act (hold back or in) or word (prohibit):—finish, forbid, keep (back), refrain, restrain, retain, shut up, be stayed, withhold."[40] We can conclude that there will be an end or prohibition of transgressions once the seventy shabua are completed. There will be a forbidding, a finishing of transgression.

When you look up the word *transgression* you will find that it is the Hebrew word *pesha* (Strong's H6588; peh'-shah). It is a revolt on a national or individual level.[41] It is a rebellion that is religious and moral in nature, and this concept is similar to the word *trespass*. In other words, transgression is a clenched fist of rebellion directly against God Himself. This is intentional sin against God, and we are being told that it will be finished at the end of the 70 weeks prophecy.

Now let's look at what it means to *make an end of sins*. There are only two words used in the Hebrew text to express this thought. The first word is Strong's H2856 which is pronounced khaw-tham', and it means "to make an end, mark, seal (up), or stop."[42]

When you look up the word *sin,* it is Strong's H2403, which is pronounced khat-taw-aw't. This word has a wide range of uses including guilt associated with sin, the punishment for sin, the offering for sin, and even purification for sin.[43] When looking closely at the various places throughout Scripture where this word is used, the best definition I can give this word is that it is an offense against God through disobedience of a direct or written command, and this offense can be unintentional due to a lack of awareness or knowledge of God's instructions.

As you can see, there is a huge difference between transgression and sin. The former is open rebellion whereas the latter can be unintentional.

Finally, let's look at what it means to *make reconciliation for iniquity.* Again, two Hebrew words are used here. The first is Strong's H3722 which is pronounced kaw-far' and is used to describe the abstract concept of covering or making atonement for sins.[44] It is the idea of making reconciliation between God and man through a legal process.

The true understanding of this reconciliation spoken of here by Daniel is made clear after looking up the word *iniquity.* This is Strong's H5771 or 'âvôwn. This word means perversity including moral evil. Other definitions include fault, iniquity, mischief, and punishment (of iniquity).[45] This word is different from transgression and sin because it describes the corruption that exists within mankind in his fallen state and is reminiscent of the word *depravity* or *immorality.*

So, we can conclude once all of the 70 shabua are completed, there will be an end of transgression, which is rebellion (willful, on-purpose disobedience to God Himself); there will be an end of sin, which is an offense against God; and lastly, there will be reconciliation of immorality and depravity (iniquity).

We are being told that there will be a state of purity and righteousness in the world after this prophecy is finished. How exciting is that!

As I will demonstrate in Chapter 13, I am convinced that the *reconciliation for iniquity* spoken of here is referring to the prophecy of the New Covenant that Yeshua initiated at the Lord's Supper the evening before He was crucified. It was *initiated,* but it was not 100% fulfilled. The majority of modern day seminaries, pastors, and Bible teachers like to falsely claim that the New Covenant was already completely fulfilled, but was it really? Let's take a quick look at it.

31 "Behold, the days are coming, says the LORD, when I will make a new covenant with the house of Israel and with the house of Judah—
32 "not according to the covenant that I made with their fathers in the day *that* I took them by the hand to lead them out of the land of Egypt, My covenant which they broke, though I was a husband to them, says the LORD.
33 "But this *is* the covenant that I will make with the house of Israel after those days, says the LORD: I will put My law in their minds, and write it on their hearts; and I will be their God, and they shall be My people.
34 "No more shall every man teach his neighbor, and every man his brother, saying, 'Know the LORD,' for they all shall know Me, from the least of them to the greatest of them, says the LORD. For I will forgive their iniquity, and their sin I will remember no more."
(Jeremiah 31:31-34)

Many people claim that this prophecy was already fulfilled by Jesus at the cross; but that's simply not true. For roughly 2000 years now since Yeshua was on earth, we have still needed teachers to teach the Bible. People are still saying "Know the Lord" and teaching their neighbor. This prophecy of the New Covenant explicitly states that no one will be teaching anyone anymore because everyone will have such intimate knowledge of God with His instructions written on their hearts!

There will be a future time when the regathered 13 tribes of Israel will be brought back to the land of Israel, and God will actually write his Torah on their hearts. The "reconciliation for iniquity" spoken of by Daniel the prophet will finally take place when these elect are gathered from the four corners of the world and forgiven of all their iniquity. I will discuss this amazing prophecy of the regathering, or Greater Exodus, in more detail in Chapter 13.

וּלְהָבִיא צֶדֶק עֹלָמִים

Figure 2.26: "To bring in everlasting righteousness". The transliteration of this phrase is "ulhabi tsedek olamim" and is read literally as "and to bring in righteousness everlasting".

THE COMING EVERLASTING RIGHTEOUSNESS

Okay, so what are the words used in Hebrew for "everlasting righteousness"?

The first root word we should look at is pronounced oh-law-meem. This word is derived from Strong's H5956, and the BLB entry states: "concealed, i.e. the vanishing point; generally, time out of mind (past or future), i.e. (practically) eternity; frequentatively, adverbial (especially with prepositional prefix) always:—alway(-s), ancient (time), any more, continuance, eternal... perpetual...without end)."[46] This word simply means a state of perpetuity. Forever.

The next word is pronounced "tseh'-dek" and means "the right (natural, moral or legal); also (abstractly) equity or (figuratively) prosperity: even, (that which is altogether) just(-ice)."[47]

So, we are being told that there will be perpetual legal justice and prosperity at the completion of the 70 Shabua. I think it's almost time for us to revisit those camps that believe that all 70 weeks have already been completed at some point in the past. But before we do, let's take a look at what Daniel wrote next regarding vision and prophecy.

וְלַחְתֹּם חָזוֹן וְנָבִיא

Figure 2.27: "To seal up the vision and prophecy". The transliteration of this phrase is "vehlakhtom hazon vehnabi".

TO SEAL UP VISION AND PROPHECY

Let's look at these three root words used here to understand what is meant by *to seal up vision and prophecy:*

1. "khaw-tham'; a primitive root; to close up; especially to seal:—make an end, mark, seal (up), stop;[48]
2. khaw-zone'; from H2372; a sight (mentally), i.e. a dream, revelation, or oracle:—vision;[49] and

3. naw-bee'; from H5012; a prophet or (generally) inspired man:—
prophecy, that prophesy, prophet."[50]

Are you seeing what I'm seeing here?

It is very straightforward what we are being told here. There will be an
end of visions, dreams, revelations, and prophetic messages that would
normally be proclaimed by those with inspiration from Elohim. This verse is
talking about people inspired by the Holy Spirit to share a word or vision
concerning a future outcome, but it is also referring to all of the prophets of
the Bible that had proclaimed their messages of future events. Either way, this
reality of inspired prophecy is supposed to stop at the end of the 70 shabua.

וְלִמְשֹׁחַ קֹדֶשׁ קָדָשִׁים:

**Figure 2.28: "And to anoint the most holy". The transliteration
of this phrase is "vehlimshoakh qodesh qadashim" and is
read literally as "and to anoint the holy holies."**

TO ANOINT THE MOST HOLY

Now, let's look at the very last line to finish dissecting Dan. 9:24. This line is
interesting and can ignite a lot of speculation. What does it mean to "anoint
the most holy"? Here is what BLB says about the Hebrew root word *anoint:*
"maw-shach'; a primitive root; to rub with oil, i.e. to anoint; by implication, to
consecrate; also to paint:—anoint, paint."[51]

I encourage you to do a word study and find every single place the word
anoint is used in Scripture. It is fascinating; and it almost always is accompanied by the use of oil, most likely olive oil since olives were famously grown
in the land of Israel from antiquity. Anointing is the simple act of rubbing oil
onto something. Kings were anointed; so were pillars, stones, and temple
items. In Exodus 29:2, we even see unleavened bread wafers anointed with
oil. The bottom line is this: many things can be anointed with oil.

Where we get clarity on this verse is from the use of the phrase "qodesh
qadashim." The Hebrew word for *holy* is used twice, but the second time it's
plural as noted by the "-im" ending of the word, which indicates more than
one. For example, Elohim is a masculine plural noun, meaning that God is one
person but with three distinct parts. Here's what a deeper look at *qodesh*
reveals: "ko'-desh; from H6942; a sacred place or thing; rarely abstract, sanc-
tity:—consecrated (thing), dedicated (thing), hallowed (thing), holiness,
(most) holy (day, portion, thing), saint, sanctuary."[52]

When you see the words "qodesh qadashim" used twice like this, it can refer to a few things. We see this double holy mentioned in Exodus 26:33 speaking of the Holy of Holies in the Tabernacle (see also 1Kings 8:6). This was the place where the Ark of the Covenant was placed, and the High Priest was only allowed to enter inside once a year to make atonement. This "kodesh kadashim" can also refer to a thing that is considered most holy, which is the case in Lev. 2:3 where it is referring to part of a grain offering for Aaron and his son's. In Ezekiel 48:12, "kodesh kadashim" refers to a portion of land in the New Jerusalem.

With this understanding, you now know that "kodesh kadashim" could refer to a wide variety of things such as the Holy of Holies, a grain offering, sin offering, portion of land, and more. It is up to you to use discernment to figure out what is being spoken of here. I don't believe the answer is all that straightforward, but the vast majority of people tend to say that this anointing of the "kodesh kadashim" simply refers to the sprinkling of Yeshua's blood on the heavenly altar spoken of in Hebrews 9:12. But is it? I will make the argument that this popular idea of mainstream Christianity is probably not what Daniel was referring to because the 70 shabua prophecy does not have anything at all to do with the first coming of the Messiah. I'll prove it to you later when we start calculating all of the years. Honestly, the anointing of the "holy holies" is a true mystery.

What I do know is that there are still anointings yet to take place that we are specifically told about in the book of Revelation and other prophets. Since we are talking about end times events, I think these are the appropriate places to be looking for clues.

Remember that *kodesh* can refer to a saint, which is a person who is considered set apart in the eyes of God. Therefore, kodesh kadashim could refer to holy saints, or holy set apart people. Therefore, this mystery in Daniel could easily be referring to the sealing of the 144,000 Israelites in Revelation chapters 7 and 14. Lost tribes researcher Dumond also points out this possibility in *2300 Days of Hell.*[53] These people are going to be sealed on their foreheads, which is how anointing with oil usually took place throughout the Scriptures. I will be spending time unpacking the secrets of the 144,000 in a later chapter, and if you haven't done a deep study on this topic, I know this is going to be a major eye opener for you.

DEBUNKING CAMP #2:

At this point we are able to easily prove that any interpretation proclaiming that the 70 weeks were already finished at some point in the past is completely wrong. Just take a look back at Figure 1.4 and the Seventh Day Adventist chart one more time.

According to the SDA chart, the 70 weeks of Daniel 9:24 were all completed by the year AD 34. But let me ask some pretty obvious questions now that we have looked up the Hebrew words of this verse and applied our three laws of interpretation. Has there been an end of sins since the year AD 34? Have transgressions and human depravity been finished? If you take a look at what's going on in the nightly news, the answer should clearly be *no.* Are there no more visions and prophecies taking place today? In other words, has there been a complete end of prophecy since the year AD 34?

I encourage you to be brutally honest with yourself if you find yourself having an emotional response while I am challenging the end times doctrine of Camp #2. Did you know that John received the book of Revelation on the Island of Patmos sometime between 68 and 96 AD? There is conflicting information out there, but it is undisputed that the book of Revelation was recorded well after the year AD 34. Based on this early church history alone, the SDA position falls flat on its face. Similarly, the Jehovah's Witnesses teach that AD 36 was the year that all 70 weeks were completed. These teachings are completely and utterly false. Unless of course, the book of Revelation is not a legitimate vision from God that was written down by inspiration of the Holy Spirit and preserved for God's people to study?

Anyone who teaches that the 70 weeks were fulfilled sometime in the past are (without realizing it) also declaring Revelation to be an illegitimate prophecy because no more visions or prophecies should ever take place after the 70 weeks are finished. The situation becomes even more problematic for the SDA since both the Millerites and Ellen White's works were founded upon visions, dreams, and special revelations that were recorded in various writings. Without getting lost in the details here, the bottom line is that both the SDA and JW organizations consider Revelation to be Scripture and therefore are hypocrites by teaching that all 70 weeks were completed sometime in the 30s AD because vision and prophecy have absolutely *not* been stopped since then.

Also, notice something else that's really important here that I have already been alluding to.

Daniel's prophecy should also be interpreted to say that 100% of visions and prophecies in the entire Bible will be *completed* at the end of the 70 weeks. Anyone who is being intellectually honest with themselves cannot seriously hold to a doctrinal position where all 70 weeks have been completed at some point in the past. Too many prophecies have not happened yet! It's really hard to fathom, but a lot of religious camps have been teaching this boldfaced lie of a completely historical 70 weeks fulfillment for quite some time now and getting away with it. It's shocking to see the Bible completely butchered and misrepresented like this, but we're just at the tip of the iceberg of truth.

The best is yet to come.

Chapter 3
The First 7 Shabua and Moses'
120 Cycles Prophecy

Now that you have seen how I study the Bible in a word-for-word method, I am going to move just a little faster through the rest of the prophecy. I trust that you will be looking up the words yourself on blueletterbible.org or a similar resource with a Strong's concordance and an interlinear text. Let's now take a look at the next verse throughout this chapter:

"Know therefore and understand,
That from the going forth of the command
To restore and build Jerusalem
Until Messiah the Prince,
There shall be seven weeks and sixty-two weeks;
The street shall be built again, and the wall,
Even in troublesome times."
(Dan. 9:25)

First, let's consider Proverbs 25:2 together; here's what it says: "*It is* the glory of God to conceal a matter, But the glory of kings *is* to search out a matter." The reason I am focusing on this verse like a laser beam before going forward is because the information you are about to learn is going to be very specific. It is not guessing games.

A lot of people have accused me of being a false prophet and insane date setter like I'm part of some sort of kool-aid drinking cult or something. All I am doing is presenting what the Hebrew Scriptures already reveal to us about the 70 Shabua of Daniel on an accurate and well-researched timeline of events. It is the glory of kings to understand the secrets that I am about to present to you.

Now, let's go ahead and break this verse down line by line.

Figure 3.1: "Know therefore and understand". The transliteration of this phrase is "vetedah vetaskel".

KNOW THEREFORE AND UNDERSTAND

The next secret of this prophecy is that we are explicitly commanded to know and understand. This is the meaning of the two Hebrew root words, *yada* and *sakal*, that are used here. In other words, this is not a suggestion. It is a command.

Know with your head first, and then understand with your heart through proper application of the head knowledge.

Too many people make up excuses in order to make themselves comfortable with a mediocre understanding of prophecy and then often misquote the *"no man knows the day or hour"* one-liner from Jesus in the New Testament.

Don't be like that.

The Scripture here is telling you to understand. Yeshua never contradicted any of the Scriptures, and He was actually talking about something else when He said those words, which is a different topic I will address in Chapter 14 where I explain the Feast of Trumpets.

מִן־מֹצָא דָבָר

Figure 3.2: "From the going forth of the commandment". The transliteration of this phrase is "min motsa dabar".

FROM THE GOING FORTH OF THE COMMAND

When you take a look at the Hebrew for this line, you will notice that there are only three words used—*min motsa dabar*—whereas in English there are seven. We are being told to begin counting the entire 70 shabua beginning with a command that was spoken. It was a command given by speech, which is what *dabar* tells us when looking at the Strong's concordance entry.

This is a big clue.

We will revisit this line of Daniel 9:25 later after we establish more clarity on the bigger picture. Without understanding the overall context, you will be left helplessly guessing as to which spoken command in all of history this might be referring to. The information in this chapter is about to shave off hundreds of hours of study from your journey.

לְהָשִׁיב וְלִבְנוֹת יְרוּשָׁלַם

Figure 3.3: "To restore and build Jerusalem". The transliteration of this phrase is "lehashib velibnot yerushalam".

90

TO RESTORE AND BUILD JERUSALEM

Lets keep looking at more Hebrew to unlock the mystery by understanding the root words used here.

Shoob Bana Yerushalam.

The root word *shoob* is the same word used to describe repentance, or turning back to God. Since there are so many Strong's usages for this word, it would be best to look at the "law of first mention" verse to understand it, which is Genesis 3:19. Man "returns" to dust. So, the idea is to go back to the starting point. Restore. Return again.

Bana (build or rebuild) and *Yerushalam* (Jerusalem, the capital city of ancient Israel) are both straightforward to understand.

Figure 3.4: "Until Messiah the Prince". The transliteration of this phrase is "ad mashiach nagid".

UNTIL MESSIAH THE PRINCE

This is where things get interesting and radically different from the mainstream points of view. Most people take "Messiah" to mean it is talking about Jesus; but the Hebrew word "mashiyach" that is used here is found throughout the Scriptures to refer to a wide variety of people. This root word (Strong's H4899) is extremely similar to the word we saw in Dan. 9:24 (Strong's H4886) speaking of "to anoint" the qodesh qadashim. It simply means *anointed.*

Just look at the Strong's entry for H4899 and see how "mashiyach" is used. Is this word ever used in any of the Hebrew Scriptures to refer to *the* Messiah Yeshua? I challenge you to find a place where the Old Testament speaks of the coming Messiah using this word *mashiyach.* You'll find out that this is a bigger challenge than you might expect.

Now, just for fun, let's take the logic of modern day, Western religions while looking at a random verse that uses the word *mashiyach* to describe a particular person:

"Look, this day your eyes have seen that the LORD delivered you today into my hand in the cave, and *someone* urged *me* to kill you. But *my eye* spared you, and I said, 'I will not stretch out my hand against my lord, for **he** *is* **the LORD's anointed.**'" [emphasis added]
(1Samuel 24:10)

This verse is talking about how King Saul was delivered into David's hand inside of a cave where Saul was having a bathroom break. David was tempted but did not rise up and kill Saul, even though he had the opportunity to do so. Now, if I wanted to, I could actually translate this verse using the word "Messiah" with a capital "M", and it would still be a technically correct and literal translation of the Hebrew language into English:

"Look, this day your eyes have seen that the LORD delivered you today into my hand in the cave, and *someone* urged *me* to kill you. But *my eye* spared you, and I said, 'I will not stretch out my hand against my lord, for **he** *is* **the LORD's Messiah.**'" [emphasis added]
- 1Samuel 24:10

Is this verse talking about Yeshua the Messiah? Of course not. The bottom line is that the word messiah, or mashiyach, is used in a ton of places throughout the Hebrew Scriptures. It is not blasphemy or somehow irreverent to God to use the word *messiah* to describe various people that were simply *anointed.*

It's just how the Hebrew language works.

But to automatically assume that Daniel 9:25 can only be talking about the one true prophesied Messiah Yeshua shows a huge disconnect of our modern culture from the understanding of extremely simple Hebrew words.

Just because the translators (in nearly every Bible) of Daniel 9:25 decided to capitalize the first letter of the word *Messiah* doesn't mean that the *anointed* being spoken of here is absolutely and indisputably Jesus of the New Testament. In fact, the numbers simply do not work. In just a moment, I will show you using mathematical proof exactly who this really is talking about. I will show you the correct interpretation of the *anointed prince.*

Now, let's take a look at the word *prince,* or *nagid,* in the Hebrew.

If this is talking about Yeshua, was He ever referred to as "Nagid" in the Scriptures? We have heard of Him being referred to as the "Prince" of Peace, right?

Well, sort of.

It turns out that the only time that Yeshua is referred to as the Prince (of

Peace) in the Hebrew, the word "sar" (Strong's H8269) is used by Isaiah the prophet, but not "nagid" (Strong's H5057). Though these words seem similar, they are very different. Here is what Isaiah wrote:

"For unto us a Child is born,
Unto us a Son is given;
And the government will be upon His shoulder.
And His name will be called
Wonderful, Counselor, Mighty God,
Everlasting Father, **Prince of Peace.**"
(Isaiah 9:6) [emphasis added]

Daniel chose to use the word *nagid* instead of *sar* because He wasn't referring to Jesus or attempting to quote Isaiah 9:6 where Yeshua is called the *sar shalom.*

When you look into the word *nagid,* you will find that the word refers to a governmental leader, ruler, or commander. This word does not fit the description of the first coming of Christ, which is why the Holy Spirit did not inspire Daniel to write it down that way. The law-of-first-mention verse is 1Samuel 9:16, which refers to Saul as the military commander and first king of Israel:

"Tomorrow about this time I will send you a man from the land of Benjamin, and you shall **anoint him commander [nagid]** over My people Israel, that he may save My people from the hand of the Philistines; for I have looked upon My people, because their cry has come to Me." [emphasis added]

By the way, Saul was "messiah-ed" or "anointed" by Samuel the prophet when he poured his horn full of oil on Saul's head (1Sa 10:1).

SAUL   SAMUEL

Figure 3.5: The First Anointed Prince of the Bible. King Saul
fits every description of the word *nagid,* being the military
commander, prince, and governmental leader of United
Israel.

In other words, King Saul was the very first *mashiyach nagid,* or anointed prince, in the entire Bible. However, when you look at all the places "nagid" is used, there is one unique person that God Himself refers to over and over as a *prince*, both in history as well as prophetical wording. It also happens to be precisely who Daniel 9:25 is referring to.

And that person is…

…

I'll show you who this is later. For now, I'll give you a hint: God made an eternal covenant with this person and his lineage that was unlike anyone else in the entire Bible.

שָׁבְעִים שִׁבְעָה וְשָׁבְעִים שִׁשִּׁים וּשְׁנָיִם

Figure 3.6: "Seven weeks and sixty two weeks". The transliteration of this phrase is "shabuim shiba vehshabuim shishim ushnayim", and the literal reading is "weeks seven and weeks threescore and two." Regarding the English translation, whenever you see words italicized throughout the Scriptures, in this case *"there shall be,"* the translators have added these words for clarity. They are not found in the original Hebrew text.

SEVEN WEEKS AND SIXTY TWO WEEKS

This next line is straightforward. We are simply being told:

"Seven Shabuim"

And

"Sixty Two Shabuim"

We can assume that Dan. 9:25 is talking exclusively about the first seven shabua, and I will prove it to you in just a moment. The math for this time period works out to be the following:

$$7 \times 49 = 343 \text{ years}$$

We will talk more about the other **62 x 49 = 3,038 years** very soon.

תָּשׁוּב וְנִבְנְתָה רְחוֹב וְחָרוּץ וּבְצוֹק הָעִתִּים

Figure 3.7: "The street shall be built again, and the wall, Even in troublesome times." The transliteration of this phrase is "tashoob venibnetah rekhob vekharuts ubtsoq ha-itim".

THE STREET AND WALL

When you look up all the words of the final line of this verse, you will notice that we are again being told details about Jerusalem here. In other words, the central subject of the prophecy is being repeated. The words to pay close attention to here are "rekhob" (street) and "kharuts" (wall). These things will be built; but what are they? And if you look up the word "tsoq" it means pressure or distress; troubling times. When did this take place, exactly?

We will revisit this line later, but let's recap some ideas first. In order to figure out the first seven weeks of the prophecy, we have to understand:

1. There is a spoken command to build Jerusalem, the literal capital city of Israel, along with the "rehob" and "harus" during times of distress.
2. The first seven weeks, or 343 years, lasts from the time a specific spoken command is given until a specific anointed prince.

I'll now unlock the secret of how all this information fits together.

THE ANCIENT MYSTERY OF MOSES REVEALED

I am now about to present a specific prophecy of Moses that connects all of the dots of the 70 shabua prophecy. For some reason, this is one of the most overlooked, misunderstood, and outright ignored scriptures of the entire Bible. Pay careful attention to this prophetic declaration given by Yehovah right before He is about to judge the earth with a worldwide flood and just before He calls Noah to build the ark: "And the LORD said, 'My Spirit shall not strive with man forever, for he *is* indeed flesh; yet his days shall be one hundred and twenty years'" (Gen. 6:3).

There are only two ways that establishment religious leaders and pulpits out there have ever interpreted this verse. First, it is asserted that Noah was 480 years old when God told him to build the ark, and he completed it when he was 600 years old, which was the same year that the flood waters came. Therefore, the 120 years spoken of in Genesis 6:3 simply refers to the short time period before the flood destroyed the earth. Of course, this statement is completely false because Noah received the commandment to build the ark when he was 500 years old as explicitly stated in Genesis 5:32 (compare with Gen. 6:10). The 120 "years" therefore cannot be referring to this time period. The second and most popular way that the religious establishment explains this verse is by stating that it merely refers to the average age, or lifespan, that people would live after the flood. Some say that the earth's climatic and environmental conditions were altered, causing lifespans to be greatly reduced from that of the pre-flood world. While the Bible does clearly show through the genealogical records of Genesis that the lifespan of mankind was significantly decreased after the flood, the actual numbers provided in the Bible are completely incompatible with this teaching. For example, Abraham lived to be 175 years old (Gen. 25:7), his son Isaac lived to be 180 (Gen. 35:28), and much later on in history, Aaron was 123 when he died (Num. 33:39). Then suddenly, as becomes commonplace later in history, we see that David only lived to be 70 years old (2Sa. 5:4). All of these examples are inconsistent with the false teaching that people born after the flood were only allotted to live exactly 120 years. If the prevailing 120-year lifespan theory were true, at what exact point in time did God's declaration become the law of the earth? The clear-cut answer to this theory is hopeless to discern from the Bible alone. Thankfully, there is a far more simple, yet hidden, explanation for Genesis 6:3.

But first, let's just see if modern science can tell us whether or not the prevailing 120-year lifespan theory is true.

When I first investigated the topic of longevity, I was really big into fitness, dietary supplements, and nutrition. I even worked as an analytical chemist professionally testing and studying specific supplement formulations that focused on living longer like Niagen and BioPQQ. In my journey to better understand human nutrition, I came across the Blue Zone diet and information related to the whole idea of Blue Zones. Here's what an article from Interesting Engineering has to say:

> "Blue Zones are areas of the Earth where people live the longest, often reaching well beyond 100 years of age. Compare that to 73.4 years, which was the worldwide average life expectancy in 2019, according to the WHO."[1]

In other words, these blue zone people are the gold standard of health and wellness worldwide. They are beating the statistics for longevity. They are outliers of healthy human aging; and if you go to www.bluezones.com, you will find even more information about what makes these places unique and why blue zone residents live so long.[2]

But...

Even these people don't live to be 120 years old on average. They only live to be a little over 100. In my pursuit of getting to the bottom of this rabbit hole, I really wanted to know whether or not Genesis 6:3 is literally referring to a person's lifespan, so I researched the oldest people in the world that have been recorded in recent history. With medical advancements, life extension technologies, and advancements in supplementation, surely people have been hitting the 120-year mark, right?

According to the Gerontology Research Group (GRG), an organization that verifies and catalogs the oldest people in the modern world, the oldest living person at the time of the writing of this book is Maria Branyas Morera from the US at 115 years old.[3] The vast majority of the people documented on this sight range from 110-115 years old. Only a few outliers have lived beyond this range; and at the time of writing, only eight people are confirmed to be alive that classify as *supercentenarians*—the oldest people in the world—with an average age of 115.[4]

Let's not lose sight of the bigger picture.

Every single one of these people on the GRG website are extreme outliers in a world of eight billion people. If Gen. 6:3 were *really* speaking of someone's lifespan, then people living to 120 would not be the wildly rare exception but the norm. The ratio would not be one billion to one!

I had been aware of this reality for the longest time, yet I never properly questioned Genesis 6:3. It always remained a complete mystery to me. What was it possibly talking about? Let's take a closer look at this verse, but pay close attention to the words in bold:

"And the LORD said, 'My Spirit shall not strive with man forever, for he *is* indeed flesh; yet **his days shall be one hundred and twenty years**.'" Gen. 6:3

I'm about to present a real challenge to you. Let me start by raising this question: does the Bible contradict itself? Well, do you remember one of our golden rules from Chapter 1? The Bible is Absolute Truth, and there are no errors, just as the prophet Samuel expressed when he said, "Moreover, the Eternal Glory of Israel does not lie or change His mind. For He is not human that He should change His mind" (1Samuel 15:29 TLV).

Okay, so then how is this following verse I'll show you *also* true—is there a contradiction? (Of course not, as I'll show you):

"The span of our years is seventy—or with strength, eighty—yet at best they are trouble and sorrow." (Psalm 90:10 TLV)

For the untrained and unskilled with the Word of God (which sadly, is the vast majority of people), there's no logical explanation when comparing Genesis 6:3 with Psalms 90:10 except that the Bible contradicts itself. In one passage it is translated to say that the lifespan of man is 120 years, but in another place it says that 80 years is as good as it gets for those who have a strong will to live.

Whenever there is an apparent contradiction in the Scriptures, it is never the Scriptures that are false, but it is our lack of understanding that leads us to believe false things about the Scriptures. Like I have said before, every cult and Mystery Babylon religion is guilty of committing the grave error of misinterpreting the Bible at least once.

Let's not fool ourselves any longer. Nobody lives to be 120 years old. It is extremely rare, and only certain people that live in the unique blue zone areas of the world live to be just a little over 100—but these are not typical cases.

Now let's go back to the Interesting Engineering article that I cited earlier. The author mentions that even the World Health Organization 2019 statistics show that 73.4 years used to be the average lifespan.[5,6] I say *used to be* (in the past tense) because this was before the COVID pandemic, vaccine agenda, and all of the artificial problems of today. Pre-2020 was the peak of modern civilization in terms of convenience, abundance, and quality of life. I'll show you exactly why life will never be the same beginning from March 2020 onward as we continue unpacking the secrets of biblical prophecy together.

I must pause for a quick moment and give credit to whom credit is due. If it weren't for the innovative work of Canadian author Joseph Dumond and his blog at sightedmoon.com, it probably would have taken me many years to finally connect the dots here and understand what Yehovah was proclaiming in Genesis 6:3. Let's take a look at it one more time:

$$\text{וְהָיוּ יָמָיו מֵאָה וְעֶשְׂרִים שָׁנָה}$$

Figure 3.8: "...yet his days shall be one hundred and twenty years." The transliteration of this phrase is "vehayu yamayv mehah veh-esrim shah-nah". The secret is in the final word "years" or "shanah".

"And the LORD said, 'My Spirit shall not strive with man forever, for he *is* indeed flesh; yet his days shall be one hundred and twenty **years**.'" Gen. 6:3 (NKJV)

It turns out that this Hebrew word "shanah" (Strong's H8141) has been mistranslated into English as *years*. It should *not* say "years"; it should say "divisions of time" or "revolutions of time" just as the Strong's concordance has laid out so clearly.[7] In other words, we must consider this prophecy to be 120 cycles in duration. Here's how I would translate Genesis 6:3:

"And the Yehovah said, 'My Spirit shall not strive with man forever, for he is indeed flesh; yet his days shall be one hundred and twenty **periods of time**.'"

The next logical questions you should have are, "What are these periods of time? How long are they?". When I first started digging into this massive gold mine, I had to start by asking, "*What if..?*"

What if these periods of time are also specifically *shabua* just like in the 70 *shabua* of Daniel 9 prophecy? What if we are actually being told here that the days of man "shall be 120 Shabua?" What if these are the periods of time being spoken of here? Well, we can easily put that theory to the test and find out if it's true or not.

Let's do the math:

120 x 49 = 5880 years

Yes, what I am now proposing is that the entire history of man as we know it will only last for 5880 years. Based on this information alone, you can now create an Excel, Numbers, or OpenOffice spreadsheet and begin the process of data entry, as follows:

Shanah Cycle #1: 1 - 49
Shanah Cycle #2: 50 - 98
Shanah Cycle #3: 99 - 147

...

Shanah Cycle #120: 5832 - 5880

All of this work has already been done for you in the back of this book (see Appendix A). What I will now show to you is how we can properly connect these ambiguous creation years to our everyday Gregorian years of BC and AD.

To unlock Daniel's prophecy and to also see exactly where we are in our modern day context, the first thing we need to do is simply look at the genealogical records of the Bible and start adding up the years to see how everything fits. Again, the only reason we are adding up all these numbers is because this is how we establish a connection to Gregorian years so we can understand exactly where we are in the entire 120 Shanah of mankind.

ADDING UP THE CHRONOLOGY

This next exercise is really easy. Just grab your Bible because all of the information you need to figure out the math is right there.

Note: I am going to be using the KJV because of its accuracy in following the Masoretic text as I go through the following biblical chronology. If you need help counting it all, I recommend using the chart in an article from Wikipedia entitled "Genealogies of Genesis."[8] This encyclopedia entry provides a nice overview of the chronological records of Genesis, but use the Hebrew Masoretic and Latin Vulgate texts for determining the years because the other sources are inaccurate.

All you do is add up the ages of the fathers when they have their first born sons in order to figure out the total number of years.

Figure 3.9: Adding up the years from Adam to Abraham.

Adam begat Seth at 130 years old.
Seth begat Enosh at 105
Enosh begat Cainan at 90.
Cainan begat Mehalalel at 70.
Mehalalel begat Jared at 65.
Jared begat Enoch at 162.
Enoch begat Methuselah at 65.
Methuselah begat Lamech at 187.
Lamech begat Noah at 182.
Noah begat Shem at 502.
Shem begat Arphaxad at 100.
Arphaxad begat Salah at 35.
Salah begat Eber at 30.
Eber begat Peleg at 34.
Peleg begat Reu at 30.
Reu begat Serug 32.
Serug begat Nahor at 30.
Nahor begat Terah at 29.
Terah begat Abraham at 70.

Genesis chapter 5 gives us all the years from Adam to Noah while Genesis chapter 11 then brings us from Noah's son Shem to the birth of Abraham. The apocryphal book of Jasher notes that Noah was 502 years old when he begat Shem, but you can simply calculate Noah's age based on Shem's age being 100 when his son Arphaxad is born to him, which was two years after the flood (Gen. 11:10). Because we know that Shem was 100 years old two years after the flood and because we are told that Noah was 600 when the flood waters came (Gen. 7:6), then that means Noah was 502 when Shem was born. Finally, add all of these numbers together.

You will get 1948 years of human history from Adam to Abraham, and this is an undisputed fact. The problems and disagreements start to happen amongst scholars, teachers, and Bible students after this point in history.

The major problem is that we simply cannot keep going forward in time by continuing to add up the ages of the fathers when they have their first born sons. Just try it, and you'll see the problems. Yes, we can add up Isaac, Jacob, and Joseph. After Joseph, there is a gap in the chronology until the Exodus. Though there are ways to estimate this timeframe, you will eventually arrive at the books of the Judges, Samuel, and the Kings and will be unable to continue because we are not given every single firstborn son of a particular lineage in order to determine a chronology. The times of the Judges in particular are inconclusive for establishing exact numbers for our timeline. Getting to the times of the New Testament and the modern time period we are now living in becomes problematic at this point. It even seems impossible; and although Matthew 1:17 provides for us the generations of Yeshua's lineage, it doesn't actually give us exact years that we can decisively use for our chronology.

Thankfully, there's a secret time clock hiding in plain sight for all those with spiritual eyes to see it. Right there in the pages of the Torah—specifically within Leviticus—Elohim has made His secret counsel known to us.

TO WHOM MUCH IS GIVEN, MUCH IS REQUIRED

This information is not supposed to be just for a select group of privileged people. I don't consider myself special or better than anyone else. When I stop and think about all of the people out there that have been studying the Bible for decades...

When I think about all the people that came before me...

When I think about all the DVDs, presentations, and books that have been written about Bible prophecy...

When I think about all of these things and realize that the vast majority of people don't understand what I am about to show you, I experience a feeling that is hard to describe. You, too, will have the generational blind-fold taken off of your eyes. It is absolutely mind blowing and utterly humbling. The only verses that come to mind to explain this phenomenon are these:

99 "I have more understanding than all my teachers,
For Your testimonies *are* my meditation.
100 "I understand more than the ancients,
Because I keep Your precepts.
101 "I have restrained my feet from every evil way,
That I may keep Your word.
102 "I have not departed from Your judgments,
For You Yourself have taught me."
(Psalm 119:99-102)

It is only through meditating on the Word with the sole intention of practicing it and obeying it that the writer can then say that he has been taught directly by Yehovah Himself. The number one problem that Christianity and Western religions have today is that most of them teach that God's laws, precepts, statutes, and judgments are "for Jewish people," they are "done away with," and "nailed to the cross" based on twisted interpretations of Paul's letters; or even worse, they say that God's instructions in the Torah "are a yoke of bondage."

Yeshua did not destroy His own Law.

The sin of misunderstanding, misapplying, and misrepresenting the Word of God is why nobody had been able to truly understand the secrets of Bible prophecy all this time. Yes, of course it was made clear to Daniel that the words were to be sealed until the time of the end. But you are about to discover just how close to the end we actually are! These secrets should have and could have been discovered and proclaimed widely much sooner than now!

Being a practitioner of the Bible is how we are able to learn the Word on a much deeper level of actual experience rather than head knowledge alone. Head knowledge alone is insufficient to arrive at the understanding I am about to reveal to you, which is why the most famous churches and ministries are unable to teach these things. If you don't take anything else away from this book, please simply remember that humbly observing the Torah of Yehovah is the secret to experiencing a fulfilling, profound, and blessed life. Toward the end of his life, Solomon made it very clear that keeping God's instructions is the true purpose of mankind (Ecc. 12:13).

KEEPING TRACK OF TIME, ELOHIM'S WAY

It's now time for us to look at Leviticus 25 from the TLV. Pay attention to the words in bold.

1 Then *Adonai* said to Moses on Mount Sinai,
2 "Speak to *Bnei-Yisrael* and tell them: **When you come into the land which I give you, then the land is to keep a *Shabbat* to *Adonai*.**
3 For six years you may sow your field and for six years you may prune your vineyard and gather in its fruits.
4 But in the seventh year there is to be a *Shabbat* rest for the land—a *Shabbat* to *Adonai*. You are not to sow your field or prune your vineyard.
5 You are not to reap what grows by itself during your harvest nor gather the grapes of your untended vine. It is to be a year of *Shabbat* rest for the land.
6 Whatever the *Shabbat* of the land produces will be food for yourself, for your servant, for your maidservant, for your hired worker and for the outsider dwelling among you.
7 Even for your livestock and for the animals that are in your land—all its increase will be enough food.
8 **"You are to count off seven *Shabbatot* of years—seven times seven years**, so that the time is **seven *Shabbatot* of years—49 years.**
9 Then on the tenth day of the seventh month, on *Yom Kippur*, you are to sound a *shofar* blast—you are to sound the *shofar* all throughout your land.
10 **You are to make the fiftieth year holy,** and proclaim liberty throughout the land to all its inhabitants. It is to be a **Jubilee** to you, when each of you is to return to his own property and each of you is to return to his family.
11 **That fiftieth year will be your Jubilee. You are not to sow,** or reap that which grows by itself, or gather from the untended vines.
12 **Since it is a Jubilee, it is to be holy to you. You will eat from its increase out of the field.**
20 And if you say, "What shall we eat in the **seventh year**, since we shall not sow nor gather in our produce?"
21 'Then I will command My blessing on you in the **sixth year**, and it will bring forth produce **enough for three years.**
22 **And you shall sow in the eighth year**, and eat old produce until the **ninth year**; until its produce comes in, you shall eat of the old harvest. (Leviticus 25:1-12; 20-22 TLV)

Do you see it? **7 x 7 = 49**

This passage reveals how we are supposed to count the years of history from a solely biblical standpoint in cycles of sevens and forty nines. What is spoken here is radically different from any modern method of historical time-keeping, including the Gregorian calendar that we are accustomed to. Every seventh year in a cycle is to be a Sabbatical, or Sabbath, Year. This year is also called a Shemitah year due to the Hebrew word (Strong's H8059) used in Deuteronomy 15:1 to describe the year of "release" of debts and financial burdens.

In Lev. 25:8 we see the exact same concept of a *shabua* that Daniel simply repeated for us later in the 70 shabua prophecy. Leviticus brings even more clarity. Understanding this major concept of seven Sabbatical Years in a 49-year cycle is critical to keeping track of time, God's way.

The key words here are that "you are to count...so that the time is seven Shabbatot of years—49 years" in Lev. 25:8. We are commanded to count by 49-year periods. Notice something extremely important. We *are not* commanded to count by 50-year cycles. We are told to acknowledge the 50th year as the Year of Jubilee, but we are not actually told to count by 50-year cycles. We are commanded to count only by 49-year cycles.

Let me paint this picture using a simple diagram because I find that these sorts of illustrations help immensely.

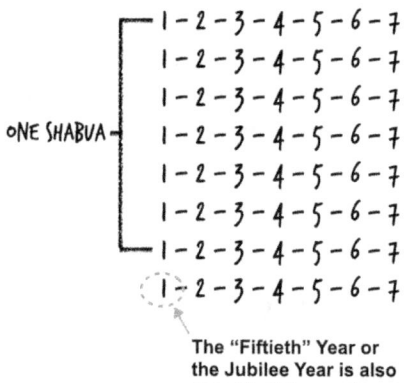

The "Fiftieth" Year or
the Jubilee Year is also
Year #1 of the next cycle

Figure 3.10: Counting the Pattern of Sevens. One shabua is a
49-year period as described in Leviticus 25, hidden within
Genesis 6:3, and also hidden within the Feast of "Weeks"
concept that Daniel cleverly used to "seal up" the words of
his prophecy.

This pattern of counting by sevens is present from the creation week in Genesis chapter one. We all count seven days in a week and not eight, and this same concept is true when we are talking about the 49-year cycles of history.

The 50th year of Jubilee is the same thing as year number one in the very next 49-year cycle just like the eighth day would actually be the first day of the next week. Just like there is no such thing as an eight-day week there is also no such thing as a 50-year shabua cycle.

Just with the information that I have already shown you inside of Daniel's prophecy, you should already know that 49-year cycles are the correct interpretation, otherwise Daniel would have used the Hebrew word *yobel* (Strongs H3104 which means "Jubilee") instead of *shabua*. I don't mean to belabor the point here, but the false interpretation of counting by 50-year cycles has been pushed by a growing number of voices and ministries out there, and as a result, many people are being led astray into completely fraudulent interpretations of Scripture and very misguided understandings of end times events. The pattern of Scripture reveals that mankind's days will be 5,880 years (49x120) and *not* 6,000 years (50x120).

ADDING THE YEARS FROM ABRAHAM TO THE EXODUS

In order to continue interpreting the Genesis 6:3 prophecy, we must look at key numbers associated with the Exodus out of Egypt. I first learned about this next logical progression in the chronology from an old video presentation Joseph Dumond gave for Stan Johnson's Prophecy Club. This information was later repackaged inside of his *Remembering the Sabbatical Years* book,[9] but I struggled getting through the nonessential details and dense presentation. I will do my best to keep this section concise and simple to understand using diagrams.

Genesis 12:4 tells us that Abraham was 75 years old when he left his homeland of Haran in order to follow Yehovah and be obedient to His voice. Three chapters later in Genesis 15:18 we see the exact moment in history where Yehovah cuts a covenant with Abraham. This particular day is profound from both a chronological and prophetic standpoint. A deep sleep fell upon Abraham after he had slain the sacrifices of the covenant, and the flaming torch passed between the sacrificial pieces in order to confirm the oath between the Most High and Abraham (along with his descendants). At this point, we need to pause and look at what Paul said through inspiration of the Holy Spirit.

"Now to Abraham and his Seed were the promises made…And this I say, that the law, which was four hundred and thirty years later, cannot annul the covenant that was confirmed…"
(Gal. 3:16,17 NKJV)

What Paul is telling us is that the law as given from Mount Sinai came 430 years after this particular moment in history when Abraham fell into a deep sleep and the covenant promise was given to him. Keep that in mind as we move forward because it will serve as one witness of the chronology that I am going to unpack for you. Let's now take a look back at these words of Genesis 15:13:

"Then He said to Abram: 'Know certainly that your descendants will be strangers in a land that is not theirs, and will serve them, and they will afflict them four hundred years.'"

We are given yet another number. Yehovah says that Abraham's descendants are to be mistreated in a land not their own for 400 years. We are also going to use this number alongside the 430 years that Paul told us about to prove the correct chronology.

Now remember, we left off with 1948 years from Adam to Abraham. We are told in Genesis 21:5 that Isaac is born when Abraham is 100 years old. Simply add this number to 1948 to arrive at 2048 years after creation (remember, these are *not* Gregorian years).

So, now what? How do we connect this information to the 400 or 430 years prophecies? How do we continue moving forward in time?

We have to answer two questions:

1. What was the moment in time when Abraham received the covenant promise? What was the creation year? How old was Abraham?
2. When exactly was the start date when Abraham's descendants were mistreated in a land not their own? Did this begin in Egypt under the harsh treatment of the Pharaohs, or was it sooner?

Let's begin with the first question.

We can figure out Abraham's age by understanding the timeline from Ishmael being born through Hagar, Sarah's Egyptian handmaid. Remember, the covenant promise was given in chapter 15. In the *very next* chapter, we are told in Genesis 16:3 that after Abraham had been dwelling ten years in the land of Canaan, he decided to go ahead and listen to Sarah and have intimate relations with Hagar in order to bear children. Because we were already told that Abraham was 75 when he left his homeland of Haran, he was 85 when he took Hagar as a wife. Hagar conceived and gave birth to Ishmael in Gen. 16:16, and we are told explicitly in the Text that Abraham is 86 years old.

Therefore, Abraham was between 75 and 85 years old when the covenant promise was given to him in Genesis 15:18.

If the details seem a little overwhelming at this point, don't worry. I'll show you a chart in a moment.

Let's now address the second question.

The prophecy of Abraham's descendants being mistreated actually begins with Isaac, as I will show you in a moment. It is Genesis 21 that gives us the account of Isaac growing up and becoming weaned, and it is the day that Isaac is weaned that Abraham throws a great feast. In my original *70 Shabua Decoded* presentation that was available for free on my website for about a year, I overlooked some of the Hebrew language here and slightly miscommunicated the events surrounding this topic. Isaac was in fact weaned, Abraham threw a great feast that day, and then at some point later in the future, we see this take place:

"And Sarah saw the son of Hagar the Egyptian, whom she had borne to Abraham, scoffing."
(Gen. 21:9)

The word here for *scoffing* is Strong's H6711 and can mean to mock, make sport, or make a toy of. When the Philistines gouged Samson's eyes out, threw him in prison, and then later summoned him for personal entertainment, Judges 16:25 uses this same Hebrew word where it says, "…Call for Samson, that he may *perform* for us…". Another time this word is used is in the account of Gen. 39:14-17 where Potiphar's wife tries to frame Joseph as if Joseph is trying to have sex with her. Pay attention to the word *mock* when she says, "See, he has brought in to us a Hebrew to *mock* us. He came in to me to lie with me, and I cried out with a loud voice" (Gen. 39:14). Even though this Hebrew word could also mean to simply *laugh*, something bigger and more problematic than laughing is going on here in Gen. 21:9 because Abraham was greatly displeased with what happened, and God Himself even tells him that it's okay to send Hagar and Ishmael away from Isaac.

When I think of this account and what happened, my mind goes to Proverbs 17:17 which states, "A friend loves at all times, And a brother is born for adversity."

Gen. 21:9 could be talking about physical violence, an act of sexual perversion, or even harsh words. The bottom line is that this event of Ishmael mocking Isaac actually begins the counting of the 400 years of mistreatment in a foreign land, and the 430-year count from the time of the covenant begins when Abraham is between 75 and 85 years old. Here's how this information all fits together on a chart, and I will prove to you that this is the correct interpretation as we move forward to the time of Joshua.

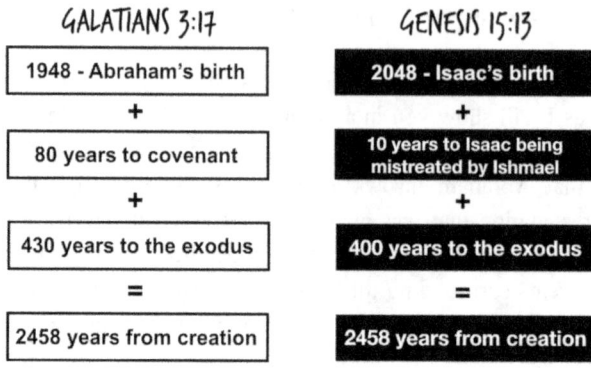

Figure 3.11: The Hidden Prophecies of Paul and Moses. These two numbers given to us from both the Old and New Testaments regarding the Exodus must be used to establish the overall chronology of events.

What I am going to show you is that Abraham was 80 years old when the covenant was made. If we use the number that Paul gave us from the covenant to the law at Sinai, then the math works out to be exactly 2458 for the year of the exodus from Egypt. I am also going to prove to you that Isaac was actually 10 years old when he was mistreated by Ishmael, and when we add 400 years to this starting point of mistreatment, we will also arrive at the year 2458 for the exodus when this period of time is over.

NUMBERING THE YEARS FROM THE EXODUS TO JOSHUA

Our current assumption is that the year for the Exodus is 2458. The next step is to simply figure out the order of events from the books of Exodus through Deuteronomy and finally, when the nation of Israel enters the promised land in Joshua chapter 5.

What many academic works and various chronologists fail to realize is the fact that the nation of Israel began traveling to the promised land in the second year after the exodus, meaning that they were at Sinai for about two years. We are explicitly told this fact in Numbers 10:11: "Now it came to pass on the twentieth day of the second month, in the second year, that the cloud was taken up from above the tabernacle of the Testimony."

Of course, we know the sad ending to the story after Numbers chapter 10. The people complained for meat. Miriam gets leprosy for questioning Moses' leadership. We then arrive at the scene of the 12 spies being sent out in Numbers 13 at the command of Yehovah. Of the twelve spies that are sent out, only two bring a good report, but the other ten bring a report that causes extreme anxiety among the people. We read that the people wept all night and determined in their hearts to select a leader to return back to Egypt (Num. 14:1-4). It is this staunch rebellion that causes Yehovah to swear this oath in Numbers 14:34: "According to the number of the days in which you spied out the land, forty days, for each day you shall bear your guilt one year, namely forty years, and you shall know My rejection."

The decree from the Throne was that Israel would wander for 40 years. Once this time period was over, the following event happens which is extremely important for decoding Genesis 6:3 and the 120 periods of time:

10 "Now the children of Israel camped in Gilgal, and kept the Passover on the fourteenth day of the month at twilight on the plains of Jericho.
11 And they ate of the produce of the land on the day after the Passover, unleavened bread and parched grain, on the very same day.
12 Then the manna ceased on the day after they had eaten the produce of the land; and the children of Israel no longer had manna, but they ate the food of the land of Canaan that year."
(Joshua 5:10-12)

We are told that the manna ceases, the children of Israel enter the promised land, and they eat the food of this land starting on the 16th day of the first month (Abib) of the Hebrew calendar. The words of immense importance are that *they ate the food of the land*. By implication, they did not plant or sow this food. Of course, they couldn't have possibly farmed the land because they had *just* entered the land. The crops that they were eating were planted and tended to by the Canaanites. This fact may seem trivial, except that we were given this specific prophetic declaration in Leviticus 25:2 before this event took place:

"Speak to the children of Israel, and say to them: 'When you come into the land which I give you, then the land shall keep a sabbath to the LORD.'"

We already looked at this verse earlier in this chapter, but now it's time to dig a little deeper. The question we need to be asking ourselves is *what kind of land sabbath is Lev. 25:2 talking about?* Recall that God keeps time in cycles of 49 years. After every six years, there is a land sabbath on the seventh year. After the 48th year in a 49-year cycle, there is a 49th-year sabbath, of course, but it is immediately followed by the 50th year of Jubilee, which is also a land sabbath.

So, which is it? Are we talking about one out of the six 7th years in a cycle, the 49th year, or the 50th year in Joshua 5:10?

What I am about to mathematically prove to you is that the children of Israel entered the promised land exactly on a Jubilee year. It wasn't simply one of the 7th years in a cycle, or even the 49th year, but it was in fact the 50th year of Jubilee in a cycle. The Jubilee is special. It is a proclamation of liberty in which everyone is supposed to return to the land of their possession (Lev. 25:10). Just like other sabbath years, sowing the land and the act of harvesting food for the purpose of storing up for long periods of time (as opposed to daily harvesting only) is prohibited (Lev. 25:11). Land (with the exception of parcels within walled cities) was to be restored back to its original owner in a Jubilee year (Lev. 25:28). Hired servants were also released (Lev. 25:54), and therefore, people were set free. It was a time of rejoicing and financial reset.

The fact that Yehovah brought the people into the promised land on a Jubilee year was highly significant. He, in His divine foreknowledge, already knew that the children of Israel would be faithless and wander for 40 years. He knew that the appointed time for the righteous Joshua generation to rise up and enter the land would be on the Jubilee when the captives return home and are set free. It is amazing when you step back and look at the bigger poetic picture and its significance.

Here's how we know mathematically that this year was a Jubilee year. We take the year of the Exodus which is 2458 after creation, we add two years for when Israel leaves Mount Sinai, and we add the 40 years of punishment.

We get 2500 years exactly.

If the year 2500 after the creation of Adam is the 50th year of Jubilee, then that means that the year 2499 is the 49th year of the shanah cycle. Now, let me remind you of the questions that I presented near the beginning of this chapter.

What if the periods of time of Genesis 6:3 are also *shabua* just like in the 70 *shabua* of Daniel 9 prophecy? What if we are actually being told here that the days of man "shall be 120 *shabua*?"

All we must do now is simply divide 2499 by 49 and we should get an exact, whole number with no decimals whatsoever; then we will know for sure that we have interpreted the events of Joshua 5:10 perfectly.

And, in fact, when you do the math, here's what you get:

2499 ÷ 49 = 51

Joshua 5:10 reveals to us that there had been exactly 51 shanah (or shabua) cycles in the entire history of the 120 shanah of mankind that were completed at this exact point in history. Now we just need to figure out how to calculate the other 69 shanah cycles. We also need to figure out how these cycles correctly link together with the 70 shabua of Daniel. The way we solve the mystery and get to the present day is by figuring out where all the remainder of the Sabbatical (7th or 49th) and Jubilee (50th) years are throughout history.

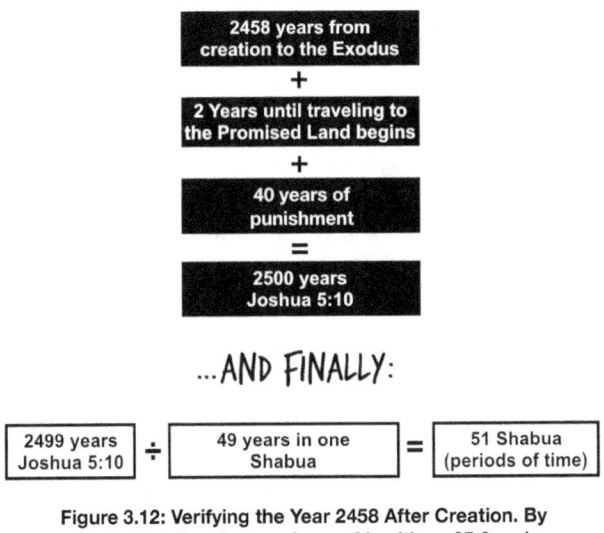

... AND FINALLY:

Figure 3.12: Verifying the Year 2458 After Creation. By understanding the prophecy of Leviticus 25:2 and Joshua's entrance into the promised land, we can mathematically verify the correct interpretation of the 430- and 400-year prophecies of Paul and Moses, respectively.

CONNECTING CREATION YEARS TO GREGORIAN YEARS

Here's the secret: we actually only need *one* accurate, verifiable event in history that occurred on a 7th, 49th, or 50th year in order to properly connect all of the creation years that we have calculated so far to the contemporary dating of Gregorian years. I will reveal several such verifiable dates, but we really only need *one*. In other words, if we know that "X" event was a biblical year of land rest that occurred in the year "# BC" or "AD #", then we can assign Gregorian years alongside creation years in a chart or table and organize all of this information perfectly. A chart like this can be easily created inside of Excel, OpenOffice, or any spreadsheet software, and if you have the time and ability to do so, give it a shot.

Let's pause for just a moment, though. Do you realize the importance of what I am saying?

Once we know the Gregorian years for the creation year chronology we have developed so far using only the Bible, we can understand what the creation year 5880 is in Gregorian years. We can therefore understand exactly when the 120 shanah cycles of mankind will end as recorded in Gen. 6:3. We will know the end of history. We will know the *time of the end* that was prophesied by Daniel, including the final, 70th shabua of history.

As we begin to look at outside sources throughout history to understand the Gregorian dating of the biblical years of land rest, always remember that a Textbook Hebrew year occurs from Abib to Abib (as discussed in the last chapter) kind of like how a Gregorian year occurs from January to January.

With that said, I will now provide you with twelve dates for Sabbatical years as documented and clearly presented within the book *The Sabbath and Jubilee Cycle Volume One* by Qadesh La Yahweh Press.[10] These are listed in the next chart.

Sabbatical Year	Historical Accounts
701 BC	Destruction of Sennacherib's Army Outside Jerusalem
456 BC	Reading of the Entire Torah (Nehemiah 7:73-8:18)
162 BC	Siege of Jerusalem by Antiochus Eupator
134 BC	Murder of High Priest Simon and Rise of John Hyrcanus
43 BC	Decree by Gaius Julius Caesar
36 BC	Herod's Conquest of Jerusalem
22 BC	The 16th Year of Herod's Reign
AD 42	Jewish Protest Against Gaius Caligula Caesar
AD 56	A Note of Indebtedness In Nero's Time
AD 70	Conquest of Jerusalem by the Romans
AD 133	Rental Contracts During Bar Kochba Revolt
AD 140	Sabbath Year (Murabba'at Land Deed Document)

Figure 3.13: The 7th and 49th Years of History.

This work is available to download for free, and I have included a link for you in the notes section of this book. These dates are backed by significant research of historical records such as *Antiquities of the Jews* by the early historian Josephus, Apocryphal works (Maccabees, Esdras, etc.), and many other ancient sources.[11,12] The eye-opening discussions around the various errors that chronologists make when trying to figure out the correct numbering of Sabbatical years also makes *The Sabbath and Jubilee Cycle* well worth the read. Now remember, we only need one bulletproof Gregorian date in order to connect to the creation years chronology. I will address which one of these dates is the most undisputed and accurate in a moment.

In addition to these dates, Joseph Dumond has also conducted independent research over the course of many years now in putting together a list of sources that shed light on the Gregorian datings of Sabbatical years. His website details the discovery of the Tombstones of Zoar. What we find in Zoar is fascinating, to say the least. This is a place outside of the land of Israel south of the Dead Sea in what would be considered the ancient territory of Moab, and it is here in Zoar that we find a community of Hebrews living after the time of the destruction of the Temple in AD 70.

Figure 3.14: The Tombstones of Zoar. Because these grave inscriptions refer back to the destruction of the temple in AD 70 which was a sabbath year, they can be used to verify more sabbatical years throughout history.

Their tombstones are unique in that they have intact Hebrew inscriptions on them with a glance at how these ancient Hebrews kept track of time. Dumond has even paid for the translation of some of these artifacts himself, and here is what his article "45 Sabbatical Year Proofs With Documentation" says about one specific tombstone:

"Tombstone #7 - 427 CE Naveh's # 5. Published (by Naveh) in 1987; painted red. It is missing the three first lines. The height preserved is 35cm and is 10cm thick. '[this tombstone of X] [son/daughter of Y who died] [on day Z (of the Sabbatical)] 26 days in the month of Nissan (1st month) in the year of the Shemitah, year 3 hundred 57 years to the destruction of the temple Shalom Shalom' [357 + 70 = AD 427]".[13]

These artifacts reveal many important truths. First, because these Hebrews are referring back to the destruction of the Temple (which we know to be the sabbatical year of AD 70), we can assign a Gregorian date to what the tombstones say. In this example, we see that this person died in AD 427. They also inscribed on the stone that AD 427 was a Shemitah, which is the same thing as a Sabbatical year. Do the math, and this year fits perfectly with all of the other dates from the chart I showed you, which is remarkable.

What we are also seeing in these tombstones is that God's people have always been keeping track of time using Sabbatical cycles, or periods of 49 years; and they have also been diligent to keep track of when the 7th years of rest occurred throughout history in order to observe them. Now do you see why Daniel's prophecy was sealed until the time of the end? This knowledge of keeping track of time God's way with a heart of obedience has mostly been lost from the consciousness of His people, and one of the purposes of this book is to help restore that consciousness.

Because of this discovery, there are more dates that we can add to our list of known Sabbatical years throughout history. I won't take the time to list them here, but leaning upon Dumond's investigative work, we can conclude that there are at least 23 more dates from the tombstones of Zoar[14] that match the chronology of the Sabbatical and Jubilee years that I have already shown you in this book.

THE ONE BULLETPROOF GREGORIAN DATE

Recall that we only need one verifiable date that connects the Creation Years timeline to a fully documented Gregorian date of history in order to finish interpreting Gen. 6:3. This one easy date that is the most verifiable and undisputed in history is 701 BC, which we can confirm with both Scripture and historical sources. Here is what 2 Kings 19:29 says about this date:

"This *shall be* a sign to you: You shall eat this year such as grows of itself,
And in the second year what springs from the same; Also in the third year sow and reap, Plant vineyards and eat the fruit of them."

Sounds familiar, doesn't it?

That's because it is a repetition of the same concept from Leviticus 25, specifically verses 21 and 22. Before we can discuss this Sabbatical year, the context is paramount.

The prophet Isaiah was sent by Elohim to deliver this specific word to King Hezekiah of the southern kingdom of Judah. During this time period, King Sennacherib of Assyria was waging war against many nations and was the elite military power in the world right before Babylon rose to world domination. In fact, the Assyrians had already conquered the northern kingdom of Israel roughly 20 years prior to the events of 2 Kings 19. Hezekiah found himself stressed out. He was afraid; but he cried out to Yehovah and asked to be delivered from the hand of Assyria. His prayer was answered.

Yehovah told him that he was going to be safe from Assyria, and that He was going to give Hezekiah a particular sign. Scripture tells us that eventually 185,000 Assyrian soldiers were killed in one night by the Angel of Yehovah (2 Ki. 19:35), just as Isaiah had prophesied (Isa. 37).

Let's take a look at 2 Kings 19:29 again. We are told it is a sign. This is the same Hebrew word (Strong's H226, or "oth") that is used in many places such as Exodus 31:13 in which the sabbaths are to be a *sign* between God and His people. In other words, Yehovah told Hezekiah that He gave him the sign of the sabbath to confirm His word that Judah would not be conquered by Assyria. Now here's the verse again in light of this truth and also Leviticus 25:

"This *shall be* a sign to you: You shall eat this year [the 49th year] such as grows of itself, And in the second year [the 50th year] what springs from the same; Also in the third year [the 51st year] sow and reap, Plant vineyards and eat the fruit of them." (2 Kings 19:29)

Recall from Leviticus 25 that it is only during the 49th and 50th years that we are commanded to observe back-to-back sabbath years. Again, this is the only time in a cycle that the double sabbath year takes place. That is what makes this sign to Hezekiah so clearly identifiable from the Scriptures alone. Based on various historical records, we can also prove that 701 BC is this Sabbatical Year (49th), and 700 BC is this Jubilee Year (50th) spoken of in 2 Kings.

In fact, it is universally accepted by scholars that 701 BC was the date of Sennacherib's failed invasion attempt of Judah. Edwin R. Thiele in his book, *The Mysterious Numbers of the Hebrew Kings*, says,

"The date of 701 for the attack of Sennacherib in the fourteenth year of Hezekiah is a key point in my chronological pattern for Hebrew rulers. ...Full confidence can be placed in 701 as the fourteenth year of Hezekiah, and complete confidence can be placed in any other dates for either Israel or Judah reckoned from that date in accord with the requirements of the numbers in Kings."[15]

The reason that Thiele and many others assert that 701 BC is a verifiable and bulletproof date in history is because of the overlap of historical records that can prove this date with a high degree of accuracy. For example, the combination of Sennacherib's Annals, the Assyrian limmu, the Assyrian eponym, and Ptolemy's Cannon can all be used to pinpoint 701 BC as the year in which Sennacherib tries to attack Judah. These are records, cuneiform artifacts, and lists that provide detailed accounting of kings and events for that specific time period. For a deeper dive into 701 BC and its authenticity in the Sabbatical years, make sure to read *The Sabbath and Jubilee Cycle* in which the authors address Assyrian propaganda, common misconceptions, and other details surrounding this particular year.[16]

FROM JOSHUA TO HEZEKIAH'S 14TH YEAR

Now what do we do? We have the creation year 2499 which was the 49th year of the shabua cycle immediately before Joshua enters the promised land. We also have the Gregorian year 701 BC which was the 49th year of a certain shabua cycle and the 14th year of Hezekiah's 29-year reign. How do we connect them?

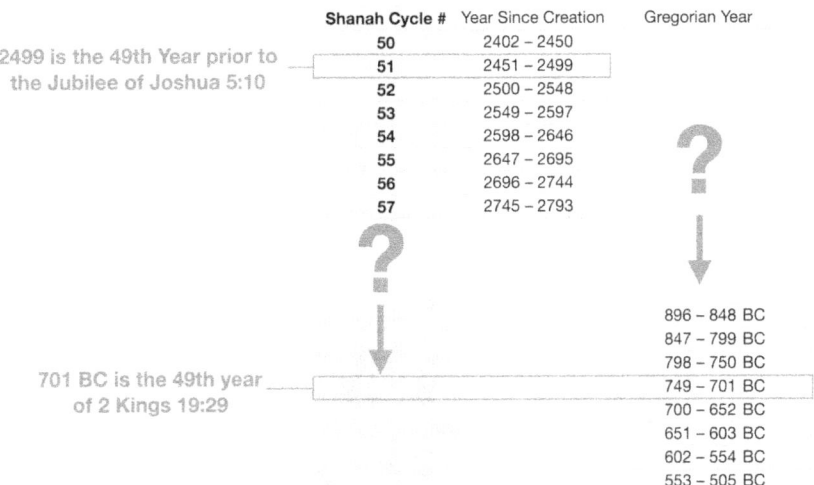

	Shanah Cycle #	Year Since Creation	Gregorian Year
	50	2402 – 2450	
2499 is the 49th Year prior to the Jubilee of Joshua 5:10	51	2451 – 2499	
	52	2500 – 2548	
	53	2549 – 2597	
	54	2598 – 2646	
	55	2647 – 2695	
	56	2696 – 2744	
	57	2745 – 2793	

	Gregorian Year
	896 – 848 BC
	847 – 799 BC
	798 – 750 BC
701 BC is the 49th year of 2 Kings 19:29	749 – 701 BC
	700 – 652 BC
	651 – 603 BC
	602 – 554 BC
	553 – 505 BC

Figure 3.15: Constructing Our Spreadsheet. We still must connect Creation Years to our contemporary Gregorian (BC to AD) years.

What I am going to show you next is not absolutely necessary because the dates between the shabua of the burning bush (and the Exodus) to the shabua when the anointed prince (that I will explain in a moment) arrives can't fit any other way. But for the sake of offering a different mathematical perspective, here is how we can pin the year 701 BC to a specific 49th year in our creation timeline. All we have to do is *generally* understand the timeline from Joshua, the Judges, Samuel, Saul, David, Solomon, and the Kings of Israel until we get to Hezekiah's 14th year as king of Judah. Again, we must estimate because we don't know all of the years after Joshua enters the land.

My next chart was put together based on my own research along with the chronological research presented in *Mysterious Numbers of the Hebrew Kings* and also in *A Biblical History of Israel.*[17,18] As I will explain in a moment, we can know the year of Solomon's death to be 931 BC, and since we know the timing and significance 701 BC, we can understand that there are actually 230 years between these dates.

Time Period	# Of Years
Joshua's Conquest of Canaan	7
Elders That Outlived Joshua	?
Judges Period and Eli's Judeship	Approx. 350
Samuel's Judgeship (Between Eli and Saul)	12
Saul's Reign	20
David's Reign	40
Solomon's Reign	40
Rehoboam (931 BC) to Hezekiah's 14th (701 BC)	230
Total Years	**699**

Figure 3.16: From Joshua to Hezekiah's 14th Year – An Estimate

Keep in mind that the years of the Judges most likely overlap in different places and are ambiguous in and of themselves for establishing a timeline. Likewise, we don't know the exact years of the events of the book of Joshua, and therefore, my chart presents rough estimates. Remember, we are told in 2Kings 18:13 that it was the 14th year of King Hezekiah when Sennacherib foolishly attempted to attack Jerusalem in 701 BC. All we do is add up the number of years, and you will get 699. We then pick up where we left off:

$$2499 + 699 = 3198 \text{ creation years}$$

This year, 3198 (which is just a very rough estimate), tells us that we need to be looking somewhere around the 64th, 65th, and even 66th Shanah of mankind in order to connect 701 BC into our timeline.

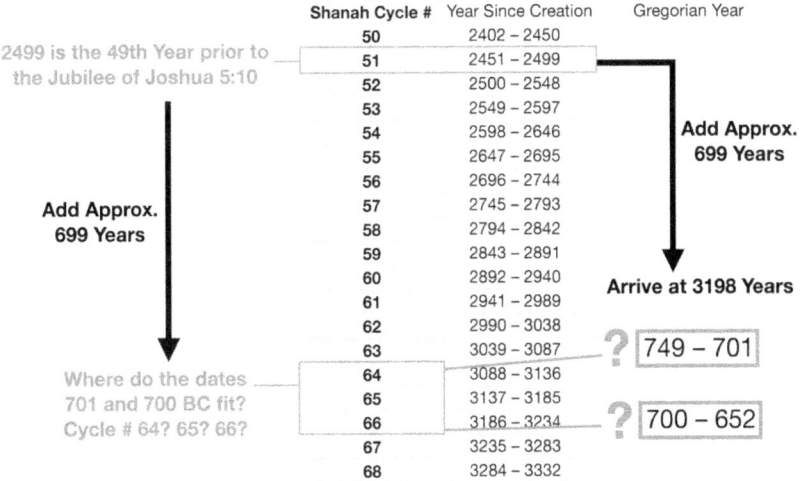

Figure 3.17: A Different Mathematical Perspective. Using the ambiguous years given in the books of Joshua and the Judges, we can estimate that we must be looking to connect 701 BC into the timeline somewhere within the 64th, 65th, or 66th Shanah Cycle.

So, what did I just prove?

My chart proves that, though we don't know all the dates from Joshua to the Judges, we can reasonably estimate. We get actually really close, and what I will more clearly demonstrate to you in just a moment is that we can declare 701 BC to be the year 3136 after creation. This is absolutely the only way the math works upon further examination. Again, I will prove this mathematically once we further interpret the remainder of Daniel 9:25.

5880: THE FINAL GREGORIAN YEAR FROM ABIB 2044 TO ABIB 2045

We can now go back in time and have a complete list of dates for the Sabbatical years and the 120 Shabua of mankind as prophesied by Moses. At the end of this book in Appendix A, you will find my spreadsheet that has been constructed based on all of this information. You should review it and verify it for yourself, especially once we are done dissecting Daniel 9:25.

2499 is the 49th Year prior to the Jubilee of Joshua 5:10	50	2402 – 2450	1435 – 1387 BC
	51	2451 – 2499	1386 – 1338 BC
	52	2500 – 2548	1337 – 1289 BC
	53	2549 – 2597	1288 – 1240 BC
	54	2598 – 2646	1239 – 1191 BC
	55	2647 – 2695	1190 – 1142 BC
	56	2696 – 2744	1141 – 1093 BC
	57	2745 – 2793	1092 – 1044 BC
	58	2794 – 2842	1043 – 995 BC
	59	2843 – 2891	994 – 946 BC
	60	2892 – 2940	945 – 897 BC
	61	2941 – 2989	896 – 848 BC
	62	2990 – 3038	847 – 799 BC
701 BC is the 49th year of 2 Kings 19:29	63	3039 – 3087	798 – 750 BC
	64	3088 – 3136	749 – 701 BC
	65	3137 – 3185	700 – 652 BC
	66	3186 – 3234	651 – 603 BC
	67	3235 – 3283	602 – 554 BC
	68	3284 – 3332	553 – 505 BC

Figure 3.18: Filling Out the Chart. Understanding 701 BC to be the year 3136 after creation allows us to visualize the entire 120 Cycles of mankind.

With the understanding that 701 BC is 3136 after creation, we can now see that the year of Joshua 5:10 (2499 after creation) is in fact 1338 BC; and of course, we understand that the Jubilee Year of 2 Kings 19:29 (3137 after creation) is 700 BC.

We can also determine the date of the Exodus, which we will be relying on for additional calculations. This date of the Exodus can be calculated by simply taking the Gregorian date of 2500, which is 1337 BC, and working backwards (remember that when going backwards in BC years the numerical value of the year will increase):

1337 BC – 40 years of wandering – 2 years at Sinai = 1379 BC

We can now see that the year of the Exodus (2458 after creation) is 1379 BC. All of the other Creation Year dates presented so far can also be assigned a Gregorian Year. This breakthrough understanding of history will undoubtedly lead to many new discoveries and significant numerical patterns.

Shanah Cycle #	Year Since Creation	Gregorian Year
113	5489 – 5537	AD 1653 – 1701
114	5538 – 5586	AD 1702 – 1750
115	5587 – 5635	AD 1751 – 1799
116	5636 – 5684	AD 1800 – 1848
117	5685 – 5733	AD 1849 – 1897
118	5734 – 5782	AD 1898 – 1946
119	5783 – 5831	AD 1947 – 1995
120	5832 – 5880	AD 1996 – 2045

Figure 3.19: Finishing the Chart. Man's days will only last until 2045.

Finally, you can now see that the final year Abib 2044 to Abib 2045 will mark the end of the history of mankind (as we currently know it), and this final shabua we are living in began in Abib 1996. As I will continue to prove to you, 1996 to 2045 is the final, 70th shabua of Daniel. This is the time of the end and the "last days" spoken of by all of the prophets in which all prophecy must be fulfilled, including the abomination of desolation, Great Tribulation, and the return of Yeshua on the clouds.

EXAMINING DANIEL 9:25 WITHIN THE 120 SHANAH

Let's go back to where we left off. Here is Daniel 9:25 again just to refresh our brains:

"Know therefore and understand,
That from the going forth of the command
To restore and build Jerusalem
Until Messiah the Prince,
There shall be seven weeks and sixty-two weeks;
The street shall be built again, and the wall,
Even in troublesome times."

Recall that I already mentioned we need to understand the following things in order to fully unlock the 70 weeks of Daniel:

1. There is a spoken command to build Jerusalem, the literal capital city of Israel, along with the "Rekhob" and "Kharus" during times of distress.
2. The first seven weeks, or 343 years, lasts from the time a specific spoken command is given until a specific anointed prince.

3. The other sixty-two weeks, or 3,038 years, is another distinct period of time that happens after the first seven weeks.

The beautiful thing about the foundation we have just laid is that under-standing this prophecy just became a whole lot easier. We have a framework of dates to work with now when we understand that 701 BC is 3136 after creation. We understand the shabua cycles like a true ancient Hebrew would. We are now ready.

THE PARABLE AND DARK SAYINGS OF PSALM 78

When I first began studying these things very deeply and thinking about them constantly, I believe that Elohim showed me something very special inside of Psalm 78 that I now want to pass on to you. This is a very significant Psalm that reads unlike any other Psalm in the Bible. Here are the first three verses:

1 "A Contemplation of Asaph. Give ear, O my people, *to* my law; Incline your ears to the words of my mouth.
2 I will open my mouth in a parable; I will utter dark sayings of old,
3 Which we have heard and known, And our fathers have told us."
(Psalm 78:1-3)

The writer, Asaph, speaks of a "parable" and "dark sayings," but when you look at the entire Psalm from beginning to end, you are left scratching your head. What exactly is so mysterious about it? It's rather straightforward.

Asaph speaks of a future generation to come that would know and under-stand what is being spoken of. He prophesies of a future generation that would not forget the Law of Yehovah. There are even interesting parallels to the book of Hosea and other historical events. But the main thought of this Psalm begins with the Exodus from the land of Egypt in 78:12 and concludes with the anointing of David as the shepherd over God's people in 78:70.

Well, it just so happens that this parable of Psalm 78 matches exactly what Daniel was shown in the 70 shabua prophecy. Asaph was actually verifying the correct understanding of the prophetic mystery of the 70 shabua of Daniel for those of us living in the last days. This is the reason the Holy Spirit breathed the words "parable" and "dark sayings" inside of this Psalm.

MOSES AND THE BURNING BUSH

Of all the spoken commandments in the Bible that could possibly fit into the timeline of Dan. 9:25, none is more significant than that Moses and the burning bush, where Yehovah declares:

"Come now, therefore, and I will send you to Pharaoh that you may bring My people, the children of Israel, out of Egypt."

(Exodus 3:10)

Pay very close attention to the underlying Hebrew words that have been translated as follows in Dan. 9:25:

"...*That* from the going forth of the command..."

We have Strong's H4161, "motsa", which is translated as "from the going forth." We also have Strong's H1697, "dabar", which is translated as "of the command." When you look up the word "motsa", it has quite a broad range of uses. Here's what the entry says inside of the BLB definitions section:

> "מוֹצָא **môwtsâ'**, mo-tsaw'; or מֹצָא môtsâ'xlit môtsâ corrected to môtsâ'; from H3318; a going forth i.e. (the act) an egress, or (the place) **an exit**; hence, a source or product; specifically, **dawn, the rising of the sun (the East)**, exportation, utterance, a gate, a fountain, a mine, a meadow (as producing grass):— **brought out**, bud, that which came out, **east**, going forth, goings out, that which (thing that) is gone out, outgoing, **proceeded out,** spring, vein, (water-) course (springs)."[19] [emphasis added]

Do you see what I see? I put certain words in bold to make it easier to see the common thread in this word's usages. Now let's take a look at the BLB entry for "dabar", and you will find under the Outline of Biblical Usage that it is used to say "speech, word, speaking, thing."[20]

Put these two words together, and "motsa dabar" could easily be interpreted as the "the spoken command to exit towards the east." It could also be literally translated as "brought out eastward by speech." This is exactly what happened when the children of Israel left Egypt in the Exodus. God's people had to travel east out of Egypt and across the Red Sea in order to reach Mount Sinai and eventually the promised land under Joshua. Jerusalem is east of Egypt.

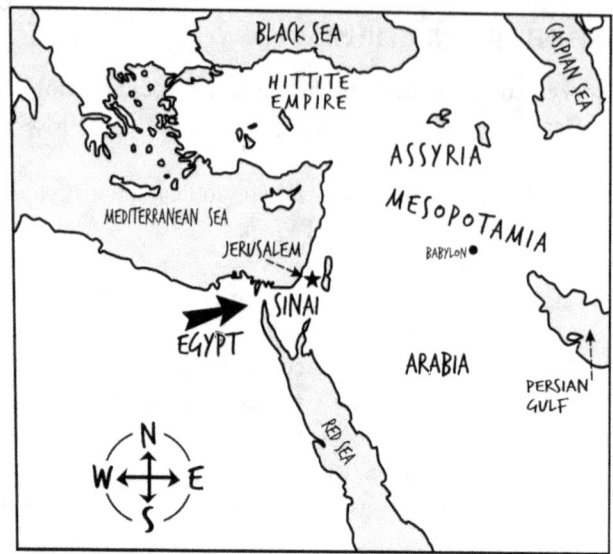

Figure 3.20: The Command to Exit East.

Let's briefly revisit the mainstream interpretations of this prophecy from *every single religion* out there. Everyone without exception teaches that the 70 weeks prophecy has something to do with a declaration of Artaxerxes given to Nehemiah in order to rebuild the Temple in Jerusalem. Everyone teaches that this event begins the counting of the 70 weeks prophecy, and in doing so, they have ignored the fundamental definition of the word "motsa". It is literally, physically impossible to travel east from the land of Babylon where Judah was in exile in order to reach Jerusalem and rebuild the Temple.

The only direction to get to Jerusalem from Babylon is west. There's absolutely no way around this fact. The decree of Artaxerxes was also arguably not even a spoken command or a command given by speech. Regardless of the nuances, the so-called "decree" of Artaxerxes cannot mathematically fit within the biblical 70 shabua framework. It only "fits" (forcibly, at best) inside of a false, Greco-Roman 490-year framework.

UNTIL MESSIAH THE PRINCE

Like we already discussed in the beginning of this chapter, Dan. 9:25 fascinates me because it is translated as "...Until Messiah the Prince..." with the letter *m* in *messiah* capitalized along with the first letter in the word *prince*.

Did you know that the biblical Hebrew language does not have lowercase letters? They are all uppercase. When you see this liberty taken by Bible translators just take special note of it. They are no longer doing their job of being a translator, but they are taking on the role of an interpreter instead. All Bible translations that I know of render the passage in this way so as to automatically make the reader think this passage has maybe something to do with Jesus the Messiah. Sometimes (as is a classic example here) it is extremely difficult to read the Bible without hearing the voices and thoughts of men shouting inside our heads as we try to read the Text for ourselves. By default, we have all read this verse in times past and had our judgment severely clouded by the interpretations of men without realizing it.

There are only two Hebrew words used here. The first is Strong's H4899, "mashiyach", and Strong's H5057, "nagid". We already covered how King Saul, the first king of Israel, was also the first *mashiyach nagid* mentioned in all the Scriptures. Well, you probably easily guessed who this is really talking about by now. When you carefully examine the timeline I have already revealed to you, David is the only *mashiyach nagid* that fits perfectly into the prophecy, which is exactly what the parable and dark mystery of Psalm 78 told us.

Go look up where the word *nagid* is used and you will find interesting prophetical and historical wording throughout the Text referring to King David. God made an eternal covenant with David. There are so many Scriptures to talk about when it comes to David's kingship. Just look what Samuel told Saul after Saul disobeyed the commandment of God and lost his kingship:

"But now your kingdom shall not continue. The LORD has sought for Himself a man after His own heart, and the LORD has commanded him to be commander [nagid] over His people, because you have not kept what the LORD commanded you." (1Sa. 13:14)

The title of nagid is used many times in Scripture to refer to David. Here's what David said while giving a speech in Jerusalem. He is saying he was chosen to be prince (nagid) forever:

"However the LORD God of Israel chose me above all the house of my father to be king over Israel forever, for He has chosen Judah to be the ruler [nagid]. And of the house of Judah, the house of my father, and among the sons of my father, He was pleased with me to make me king over all Israel." (1Ch. 28:4

THE FIRST 343 YEARS: FROM MOSES TO DAVID

We have already established that the date of the exodus from Egypt to be 1379 BC. But when was the spoken command at the burning bush given by the Great I AM? Can we know this date *for sure?* The answer may surprise you.

If you have ever worked with livestock, what I am about to explain is common sense. Sadly, many people are disconnected from living off the land and working in agriculture, so if you find yourself in that position, don't stress. However, the Bible was written through the lens of a culture that was fundamentally agrarian and radically different from the modern day industrialized societies the majority of us find ourselves in. The more you experience living a rural, simple life, the easier it will be to learn biblical truth.

In order to understand the timing of the burning bush, we have to examine the events of the ten plagues of Egypt. We have to understand exactly how long Moses and Aaron were performing their work as the two witnesses of Yehovah. The first clue is given to us in Exodus 9:3-7. After the plagues of blood, frogs, lice, and flies, there is the fifth plague that specifically brings death on every single one of the livestock of Egypt—from horses to sheep and everything in between. The language here in the Scriptures tells us assertively that none of the livestock of Egypt survived (Exo. 9:6).

Here is where things get interesting.

The very next plague causes boils and sores to break out on both "man and beast" (Exo. 9:9). The seventh plague arrives next and brings hail mixed with fire on the Egyptians who did not fear the word of Yehovah. We are told explicitly that both the servants and livestock that were left in the open fields were killed by this plague.

Finally, we are told that during the tenth and final plague, all of the first-born of both man and livestock were killed at midnight (Exo. 12:29). In other words, if 100% of the livestock were killed during the fifth plague, how did the Egyptians have livestock during the sixth, seventh, and even tenth plagues? The answer to this question is the key to understanding the chronology.

For many years, I thought that the ten plagues of Egypt happened in a short period of time, maybe a year at most. When you read the Text, it just seems quick, decisive, and action-packed. In order for these events to happen realistically, though, it took time.

After the fifth plague, the Egyptians must have purchased and acquired livestock from neighboring countries that were not impacted by the plagues. Pharaoh's heart was hardened, and he and his people defiantly acquired more animals while not letting Israel go free. This explanation satisfies the events of the sixth and seventh plagues, but there would need to be at the very least one complete breeding cycle in order for the tenth plague and the death of the firstborn to take place. More realistically, though, two or more breeding cycles would make sense because the livestock would need to multiply to a large enough number to require servants being out in the fields managing the animals during the seventh plague of hail.

What I will prove to you mathematically is that Moses and Aaron worked for 3-1/2 years before the Exodus actually took place. Yehovah likes to work in very predictable patterns and with very specific structure. He doesn't work randomly. This is the same thing that will happen in the future when the two witnesses will be sent by God (before the Greater Exodus of scattered Israelites worldwide takes place) as described in Revelation 11:3:

"And I will give *power* to my two witnesses, and they will prophesy one thousand two hundred and sixty days"

Notice the math here: 360 (days in one year) x 3.5 (years) = 1260 days

This is the 3.5-year period of Revelation that I believe was also the same amount of time that Moses and Aaron performed their work as the original two witnesses of Scripture. Therefore, the spoken command of the burning bush occurred in either 1382 or 1383 BC (3.5 years before 1379 BC).

For the well-studied in the subject of time-keeping, yes, I am saying that there are 360 days in a Hebrew year generally speaking. Remember, the sighting of a new crescent moon is necessary to declare the beginning of each month. Based on modern science and technology, we know that it takes the moon about 29.530 days in its cycle around the earth to arrive at the same phase of a new moon. What this means practically is that a biblical month can only have 29 to 30 days but certainly no more than 30 days. This also means that the moon makes about 12.4 circuits around the earth in a year. That is why a Hebrew 13-month year occurs sometimes with an added month in order to avoid calendrical drift where, for example, Passover would erroneously take place in the winter. This occasional addition of a 13th month is solely dependent on the readiness of the Abib barley to begin the year. I realize this is more of an advanced topic but wanted to address it before moving on. More calendar insights will be provided at the very end of this chapter. It's now time for some more calculations.

343 YEARS: FROM MOSES TO DAVID

The Command is to Moses at
the burning bush in 1383 BC

KEY: We start counting by Shabua
Cycles starting with the 51st Shanah

The count is
EXACTLY
7x49 or
343 years

David is born in 1040 BC

120 Shanah Cycle #	Year Since Creation	Gregorian Year	70 Shabua Cycle Count
50	2402 – 2450	1435 – 1387 BC	
51	2451 – 2499	1386 – 1338 BC	1
52	2500 – 2548	1337 – 1289 BC	2
53	2549 – 2597	1288 – 1240 BC	3
54	2598 – 2646	1239 – 1191 BC	4
55	2647 – 2695	1190 – 1142 BC	5
56	2696 – 2744	1141 – 1093 BC	6
57	2745 – 2793	1092 – 1044 BC	7
58	2794 – 2842	1043 – 995 BC	8
59	2843 – 2891	994 – 946 BC	9

Figure 3.21: The First Seven Shabua of Daniel's Prophecy. This chart proves that our earlier assumption is correct, where 701 BC is the year 3136 After Creation.

Since 1382 or 1383 BC was the date of the burning bush, all we do is add 343 years (the first seven weeks) and we will arrive at the time of 1039 or 1040 BC. I will show you that 1040 BC is the correct date. Since we know this prophecy is talking about David, all we have to do is pinpoint a date that is verifiable and accurate somewhere in the chronology of David. One such date is the death of Solomon, which is widely confirmed to be around 931 BC.[21,22]

The Scriptures tell us that King Solomon succeeds David and reigns 40 years (1Kings 11:42). Since Solomon's death is roughly 931 BC, all we have to do is work our way back in time. Subtract 40 years and you arrive at 971 BC—the year when Solomon begins his reign. It is 2Samuel 5:4 that gives us the details of David's reign:

"David was thirty years old when he began to reign, and he reigned forty years."

We therefore start at 971 BC and subtract another 40 years, which brings us to 1011 as the year that David begins his reign. If you simply go back in time 30 years from 1011, you will arrive at 1041 BC. We can safely declare that this calculated value of 1041 BC falls within the required timeframe, due to:

1. the inherent difference between Gregorian years (365.25 days per year; January to January) and Hebrew years (354 or 383.5 days per year; Abib to Abib) when comparing the biblical narrative to secular dating; and
2. the fact that historians such as Gershon Galil and Kenneth A. Kitchen have determined David's reign to have ended in 970 BC rather than our calculated value of 971 BC.

Remember, we are looking for 343 years from the burning bush in 1383 BC. Therefore, the exact birth year of David the Prince of the Daniel 9:25 prophecy is the Gregorian year 1040 BC. That's right! We have officially mathematically proven when the first seven shabua of Daniel's prophecy have taken place. As a result, we now know when the clock starts for the 70 shabua and when it ends.

Herein lies the proof of our earlier assumption.

Notice that this 343-year period lines up with our assignment of 701 BC as the Creation Year 3136. Based on my chart that estimates the timeline from Joshua to Hezekiah, we could have associated 701 BC with two other possible 49th years in order to establish the connection between Gregorian and Creation years. However, the command at the burning bush in 1383 BC during the 51st Shanah perfectly lines up with the fact that Joshua entered the promised land in the very first year of the next (52nd) Shanah in 2500. Just do the math:

3.5 yrs (Moses & Aaron Ministry)
+ 2 yrs (until travel to Promised Land begins)
+ 40 yrs (wandering)
= 45.5 yrs

Now take 1383 BC and add those 45.5 yrs to get 1338 (and a half) BC, which lines up with 2499 and 2500 where Joshua enters into the promised land during the Jubilee year. Again, make sure to take a look at the charts in the back of this book if this information is going over your head.

Let's summarize everything.

What I have just proven is that the years from Solomon's death in 931 BC to David's birth in 1040 BC can be used as a separate chronology from which to calculate the 49 x 7 years farther back to the exact year of the burning bush command in 1383 BC. Then, when we add the 45.5 years to the time of the burning bush, we see that the Gregorian year 1338 BC lines up perfectly on our biblical timeline with the year 2499 After Creation, which was the year before Joshua entered the promised land. As we should expect to see, this 49th year of 1338 BC occurs 13 complete Shanah cycles before the 49th year of 701 BC, meaning that these two 49th years of history are perfectly harmonized within the timeline.

Therefore:

701 BC = 3136 After Creation

TO RESTORE AND BUILD JERUSALEM

For the more skeptical mind, the idea of *rebuilding* Jerusalem might be the last remaining stumbling block at this point. However, this is easy to explain now that we have established exactly *who* and *what* the first seven shabua are talking about.

Remember, Yehovah is the same yesterday, today, and forever; He does not change.

Of all the places on Earth, there is one place that is special to Yehovah's heart, and this place is the city of Jerusalem. Recall that this city is the primary subject of Daniel's 70 weeks prophecy together with all 12 tribes of Israel.

Before the Israelites entered the promised land under Joshua, Moses reminded them of various laws and instructions that were taught to the older generation that had already perished in the wilderness. Moses told them that when they entered the holy land, there was one place that all men were required to appear three times every single year (Deut. 16:16). We will explore the prophetic significance of this specific idea when we talk about the year 2020. For now, understand that Jerusalem always has and will be the place of Yehovah's name just like we are told in 1Kings 11:36:

"And to his son I will give one tribe, that My servant David may always have a lamp before Me in Jerusalem, the city which I have chosen for Myself, to put My name there."

This city was also the place where Melchizedek—King of "Salem" or Jerusalem—came from when he met Abraham in the account of Genesis 14:18:

"Then Melchizedek king of Salem brought out bread and wine; he *was* the priest of God Most High."

We aren't told much about Melchizedek in the Scriptures except for within this passage in Genesis along with Psalm 110 and Hebrews chapters 5-7; but what we do know is that this person was operating as a priest within Jerusalem long before the Israelites ever entered the land under Joshua. Therefore, we can conclude that Jerusalem has always been set apart as the central location of proper worship towards Yehovah, even though this city falls well short of that identity today.

The implications here are important for understanding Daniel's prophecy. We can conclude that to "restore" and "build" Jerusalem meant that Yehovah wanted to make this city a place of worship for Himself once again, since that was the purpose of this city even before Abraham received the covenant in Genesis 15. There is also a connection to the parable of Psalm 78:68,69 in which Asaph describes God's sanctuary being built in Zion (Jerusalem).

Here's how this information ties directly to King David. One of the first things he did when he obtained power was conquer Jerusalem, which had been controlled by the Jebusites.

6 "And the king and his men went to Jerusalem against the Jebusites, the inhabitants of the land, who spoke to David, saying, 'You shall not come in here; but the blind and the lame will repel you,' thinking, 'David cannot come in here.'
7 "Nevertheless David took the stronghold of Zion (that is, the City of David).
8 Now David said on that day, 'Whoever climbs up by way of the water shaft and defeats the Jebusites (the lame and the blind, who are hated by David's soul), he shall be chief and captain.' Therefore they say, 'The blind and the lame shall not come into the house.'
9 "Then David dwelt in the stronghold, and called it the City of David. And David built all around from the Millo and inward.
10 "So David went on and became great, and the LORD God of hosts was with him."
(2 Samuel 5:6-10)

This restoration of Jerusalem as the place of worship happened during a time of war with multiple countries, including the Philistines. The building of Jerusalem during this timeframe therefore fits the description of the "troublesome times" in Daniel's prophecy.

Abraham Ojeda

THE STREET AND THE WALL

The last things we need to examine from Dan. 9:25 are the "street" (Strong's H7339, or "rekhob") and "wall" (Strong's H2742, or "kharus"), which are actually described in this verse I just showed you from 2Sa. 5:9:

"Then David dwelt in the stronghold, and called it the City of David. And David built all around from the Millo and inward."

If you look up the word "rekhob" it actually means a broad open place or plaza. The "kharus" is a moat, or trench; and this word has therefore been incorrectly translated as "wall" to better suit the false, mainstream interpretation that this prophecy involves Nehemiah's rebuilding of Jerusalem after the Babylonian captivity. Look up the word "Millo" (Strong's H4407) and the next Hebrew word translated as "and inward" (Strong's H1004, "bayith"). We can conclude that David fulfilled Daniel's prophecy because he built the fortifications around Jerusalem and the open place within it as stated in 2Sa. 5:9.

David is the only anointed *nagid* who fits the description of having built the fortifications and inward place of Jerusalem along with the lesser known place called the City of David. This was the ancient core fortification within Jerusalem and the location of Solomon's Temple with the Gihon spring being the source of cleansing water along with the moat described in Daniel's prophecy. In other words, yes, I am boldly stating that the modern "Temple Mount" with the Dome of the Rock is not the true location of the ancient Hebrew temples. This location is actually an old Roman fortress and cannot fit the descriptions provided in the Scriptures. This is a separate topic of deep study in and of itself, so I won't be going into more details here.

Yeshua the Messiah did not do this restoration spoken of in Daniel. It is not recorded in any of the Gospels that He was digging trenches for the purpose of making moats or building fortifications around Jerusalem during His earthly ministry. This prophecy is *not* talking about Yeshua. It is also not recorded in Scripture that Nehemiah dug trenches or a moat. His work consisted of repairing walls, gates and these sorts of projects. No matter which way you look at the Nehemiah and Ezra restoration of Jerusalem after the Babylonian exile, the numbers simply do not fit into the prophecy with the correct understanding of 49-year cycles. The earthly ministry of Jesus also does not fit mathematically.

We have now completely solved the mystery of Daniel 9:25!

...BUT WHAT ABOUT MATTHEW 24:34?

Before moving forward, let's address what Yeshua said in Matthew. I know the information I have presented so far is difficult to digest for the camps that believe in a historical and complete 70 weeks fulfillment such as the SDA, JW, and traditional Catholics. It is verses like this one in Matthew 24:34 that really do make it seem as if all 70 weeks have already happened some time in the past:

"Assuredly, I say to you, this generation will by no means pass away till all these things take place."

Yeshua just finished talking about a lot of end times prophetic events during chapter 24 of Matthew because his disciples explicitly asked him what to expect during the time of the end in Mat. 24:3. He specifically talks about the abomination of desolation in verse 15 along with many other specific topics. In fact, it is *because* of Mat. 24:34 that I have personally heard many evangelicals and Christians teach that the Grecian ruler Antiochus Epiphanes in the book of 1Maccabees already fulfilled the abomination of desolation prophecy almost 200 years before Yeshua was even born. We will talk more about the abomination of desolation later because it is a future event that will be happening *very* soon.

So, why did Yeshua say that the specific generation that He was living in would not pass away until all these things in Matthew 24 already happened?

The answer is simple:

That's not what He actually said!

Look up the Greek word used for "generation," and you will discover the deeper meaning. This word "genea" (Strong's G1074) could be translated as "time, age, or nation,"[23] so here's how I would translate Matthew 24:34:

"Assuredly, I say to you, this *period of time* will by no means pass away till all these things take place."

Now do you see the connection to Genesis 6:3? Lets just take a look at Gen. 6:3 one more time:

"And the LORD said, 'My Spirit shall not strive with man forever, for he *is* indeed flesh; yet his days shall be one hundred and twenty *periods of time*.'"

Yeshua was saying that the very final period of time—the very final shanah of the complete history of the entire 120 shanah of man, which is the same exact thing as the 70th shabua of the Daniel 9 prophecy—would *not* pass away until all things happen exactly as they have been prophesied. In other words, Moses, Daniel, and Yeshua are the three witnesses of Scripture that proclaim the exact same message of the last days of the history of mankind. All of the things Yeshua spoke about including earthquakes, wars, and the Great Tribulation will in fact take place before the final cycle from 1996–2045 is complete.

SHANAH = SHABUA = GENEA

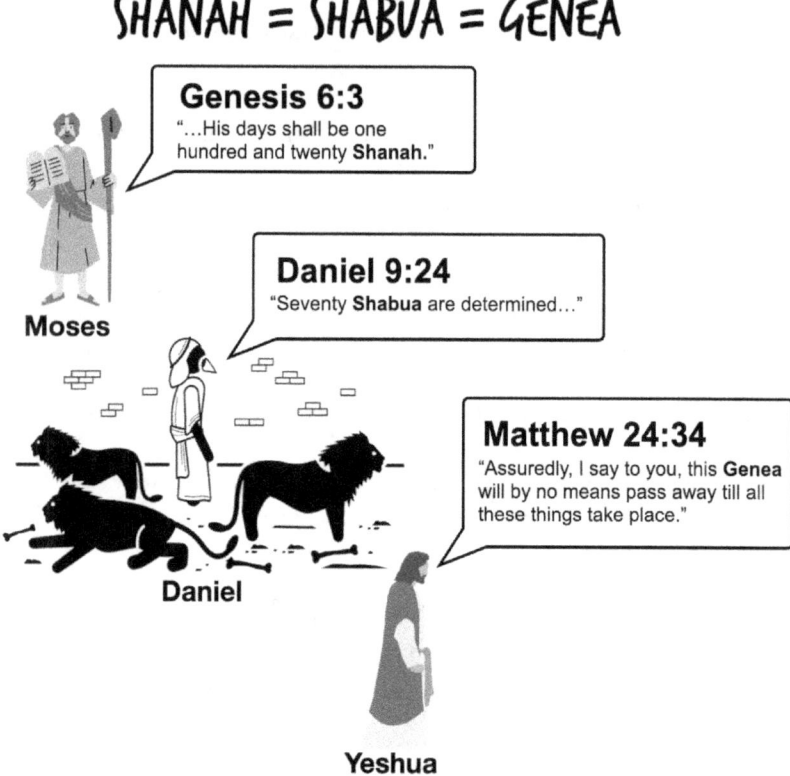

Genesis 6:3
"...His days shall be one hundred and twenty **Shanah**."

Moses

Daniel 9:24
"Seventy **Shabua** are determined..."

Matthew 24:34
"Assuredly, I say to you, this **Genea** will by no means pass away till all these things take place."

Daniel

Yeshua

Figure 3.22: The Three Witnesses of the Final Cycle of Mankind.

WHAT ABOUT THE JEWISH CALENDAR AND ITS TIMELINE?

For every truth in the Bible, the devil has created a counterfeit half truth or blatant lie for his own people to blindly follow. Judaism with its endless web of lies and man-made traditions has corrupted the ability of many to discern important concepts from the Hebrew Scriptures, especially the Torah. The true calendar of Yehovah is among these key concepts.

Back in ancient times, Judah had always kept track of time according to the instructions of the Torah. After their return from Babylonian captivity, Judah continued keeping track of time properly as recorded in the book of Nehemiah, but, as I explained in Chapter 2, they carried the teachings of the Talmud with them—teachings that were diametrically opposed to Yeshua's ministry. From the time of their return until about AD 425, Judah set up and relied on the Sanhedrin, or assembly, of elders that were responsible for declaring the beginnings of months and years. Recall that I mentioned a lunar month being about 29.5 days in duration. Towards the end of a given month, the Sanhedrin would summon and cross examine witnesses who claimed to have seen the new moon, which was always understood to be the very first sliver of a renewed crescent moon. This new moon is visible on the 29th or 30th day of a given month. If the witnesses' accounts were corroborated, then the evening that the crescent moon was sighted would begin the first day of the next month. If no witnesses came forth to confirm a new moon sighting by the 30th day, then the evening would begin the new month by default because a biblical month cannot have more than 30 days. Now, consider also that a lunar year consists of 354 days (29.5x12) while a solar year consists of about 365.25 days. The difference between these two is about 11 days. As already discussed, Passover must always take place in the springtime each year, around March. However, without some sort of regular adjustment to a solely lunar-based calendar system, Passover would occur 11 days earlier each year. It would eventually drift into the winter, then the fall, then summer, and would ultimately drift back into the springtime but only to start this drifting process once again. In fact, since the Muslim calendar is a strictly lunar one, it falls into this exact pattern, which is why the month of Ramadan, for example, shifts drastically over time and into different seasons of the year. Such a system is in disobedience to the Bible because the keeping of Passover is set during the month of Abib (the first month) in the land of Israel—the month of the first barley. That is why the Hebrew calendar is intercalated, which is to say that a 13th month is added in a given year in order to correctly adjust the timing of Abib to take place when the firstfruits of the barley are ready to harvest in the land of Canaan. The only requirement for the declaration of the Abib and the New Year is the presence of *one omer* of firstfruits barley (Lev. 23:10). Sometimes this declaration must be delayed, and a 13th month is therefore needed so that the barley has more time to properly ripen. The Sanhedrin was also put in charge of determining the need for the 13th month (also called Adar II or Adar Bet) declarations. Some contend that this 13th month concept is pagan and comes from the Talmud, but the specific dates given from Ezekiel 1:1 to the time of Ezekiel 8:1 are in perfect agreement with the need for 13th month declarations, since the time keeping presented in these chapters of Ezekiel cannot be calculated any other way.

Though the Sanhedrin kept track of time biblically for centuries, the destruction of the temple in AD 70 along with subsequent Roman oppression inherently shifted the culture of Judah. Persecution together with the scattering of Judah out of the land of Canaan gave the Sanhedrin the idea to establish a fixed Jewish calendar in AD 358 before they, too, were ultimately disbanded. Their reasoning was that because the temple was destroyed and many in the holy land were dispersed by the Romans after the failed Bar Kokhba revolt, a universal method of time keeping was necessary for those that were no longer able to receive new moon reports or understand the state of the Abib barley due to their displacement. This fixed calendar of Judaism that still continues to be used today is the Hillel II Calendar, named after Hillel II the Nasi who was the last leader of the Sanhedrin between AD 320 and 385. The development of this calendar is seen as the last great decision of this religious body. It is a pre-calculated "lunisolar" calendar, which means it consists of two components. First, the months themselves are based on lunar months. Hillel II approximates the period between new moons, and therefore a given month does not always begin on the same day that the actual new moon is sighted. In other words, new months in the Hillel II system sometimes occur on conjunction (dark) moons rather than biblical crescent moons. That is why the Feast of Trumpets, which is strictly based on the sighting of a new moon according to the Bible, is celebrated by Jews for two full days when it really should be one. They are attempting to overcompensate for their calendar's approximations in order to align with the proper observance of this Holy Day. Secondly, the years of the Hillel II calendar are based on solar years. As mentioned, the difference between the duration of a lunar year and a solar year is about 11 days, and the Hillel II calendar therefore adds 13th months periodically in order to synchronize the twelve lunar cycles with the longer solar year. Rather than adding these 13th months as needed according to the readiness of the barley (Abib) offering required by the Bible, the Jews adopted a standardized approach according to a 19-year cycle known as the Metonic cycle. During this cycle, the Jews insert the 13th extra months in 7 of these 19 years, namely the 3rd, 6th, 8th, 11th, 14th, 17th, and 19th years of the Metonic cycle. This disconnect of the Hillel II calendar from the agricultural time clock of the Bible is why more false ideas and traditions of Judaism continue to permeate this subject matter. For example, the Jews now declare the New Year, or Rosh Hashanah, as beginning in the fall timeframe (Sept.-Oct.) rather than the month of Abib around March. This is just the tip of the proverbial iceberg when it comes to the lingering consequences that fourth-century Judaism has had on the minds of believers. The Hillel II calendar invention continues to greatly influence Jews, Messianics, and Christians alike.

In addition to all of these errors of the calendar, Judaism has also fallen into disagreement with the clear chronology of the Scriptures. For example, this book has been written in the Gregorian year 2024, which the Jews say is the year 5784 since creation; however, using the timeline that I have presented in this chapter, the year 2024 is actually 5860. The difference between these two dates is about 76 years, and the mystery of this particular number is found in Matthew 1 and the genealogical record of Yeshua. As I mentioned in this chapter, Matthew 1 is not useful in determining the chronological events of the history of mankind and the 120 shanah cycles. As you will see, four kings were intentionally omitted from the genealogical timeline of Yeshua. It is this omission that actually makes Matthew 1 useful for understanding why Judah, from which the gospel writer Matthew originated, and later Judaism as a whole intentionally deviated from the timeline of the Bible. Pay attention to these words from Matthew 1:7-9:

7 Solomon begot Rehoboam, Rehoboam begot Abijah, and Abijah begot Asa.
8 Asa begot Jehoshaphat, Jehoshaphat begot Joram, and Joram begot Uzziah.
9 Uzziah begot Jotham, Jotham begot Ahaz, and Ahaz begot Hezekiah.

As I mentioned, this sequence of kings beginning with Solomon does not match what the Bible recorded about the kings of Judah. After Joram, his son Ahaziah reigned one year (2Ch. 22:1). Upon dying at the hands of Jehu, his mother Athaliah conjured up a conspiracy to kill all of the royal heirs of the house of Judah so that she could reign for six years (2Ch. 22:10). A priest by the name of Jehoiada then gathered Judah together and overthrew her wicked reign and installed the next rightful heir, Joash, to the throne. He reigned for 40 years. Amaziah reigned after the death of Joash for 29 years. Finally, Amaziah's son, Uzziah, ruled after him, and we can now see that the rulers omitted by Matthew from Joram to Uzziah were wicked rulers that departed from following Yehovah and His instructions during their reigns. This time period (1+6+40+29) is equal to roughly 76 years.

The fact that Matthew purposely removed these 76 years from the chronology of Yeshua means that the culture of Judah had already distanced itself from the history of these rulers for quite some time. Though many theories could be offered as to why this was the case, it is worth considering why the Holy Spirit would inspire Matthew to preserve the good news of Yeshua's arrival in such a way. We find this reason within some of the final words of

Moses' ministry.

18 "Now when someone hears the words of this oath and in his heart
considers himself blessed, thinking, 'Shalom will be mine, even though I walk
in the stubbornness of my heart'—thus sweeping away the moist with
the dry—
19 Adonai will be unwilling to forgive him. For then the anger of Adonai and
His jealousy will smoke against that person. So all the oath that is written in
this scroll will settle on him, **and Adonai will blot out his name from under
the heavens."**
(Deu. 29:18,19 TLV) [emphasis added]

If you look back at the events of Matthew's omitted 76 years you will discover
that none of these rulers of Judah—Ahaziah, Athaliah, Joash, Amaziah—died
peacefully. They all died at the hands of conspirators or soldiers. They died
bloody deaths. In other words, they were all judged. This was the case because
each of these four rulers walked in open rebellion against God. Even Joash
ended up rebelling against God in his old age, and he fell into the curse of
obscurity though he was blessed with a long life of 130 years. Apparently, this
curse had already come to pass by the time of the first century AD when
Matthew wrote his account of Yeshua's life. It must have been a common
practice to remove, or blot out, the names of these four wicked rulers in official documents and records like Matthew's book. Though this curse of the 76
blotted-out years is understandable and biblical, it is still not excusable for the
truth of the Word of God and the 120 cycles of mankind to remain veiled
under the false pretenses of Judaism and its incorrect timeline.

Chapter 4
The Next 62 Shabua and Destruction of the Anointed

We are now ready to tackle Daniel 9:26 of the 70 shabua prophecy.

"And after the sixty-two weeks
Messiah shall be cut off, but not for Himself;
And the people of the prince who is to come
Shall destroy the city and the sanctuary.
The end of it *shall be* with a flood,
And till the end of the war desolations are determined."
(Dan. 9:26)

I must now warn you to consume this information responsibly. What I am about to explain will begin to naturally shift your entire worldview into a place of properly understanding current geopolitical events and the direction our world is heading. When Daniel first saw the vision of the 70 shabua prophecy, he was put into a state of despair for three weeks as recorded in Daniel 10:2.

Once you see this prophecy fully unlocked, you will understand exactly why this happened to Daniel. You will see and understand what it is that he saw that made him unable to drink or eat his regular food or anoint himself. A similar thing will happen to you. This is natural.

Part of the healing process is to share this information with others while informing and warning them of what's coming. It's high time to tell the world they need to fully surrender to the Most High God before it's too late. This is the number one reason I took the great time and effort to write this book. I wanted it to be as easy as possible for people to know and understand the 70 shabua prophecy. Now it's your turn to join me in spreading the word. Be a blessing, walk in obedience to God, and shine like the stars of heaven forever.

I now direct your attention to the 120 cycles charts of Appendix A in the back of this book. We are living in the final shabua from 1996 to 2045, but we left off in the 58th shanah (from 1043 - 995 BC) of the entire 120 shanah with the birth of David in 1040 BC. How *exactly* do we count the 70 shabua? I

explained this concept at the end of the last chapter, but let me break it down
step by step now that we are in Daniel 9:26.

וְאַחֲרֵי הַשָּׁבֻעִים שִׁשִּׁים וּשְׁנַיִם

Figure 4.1: "And after the sixty-two weeks". The
transliteration of this phrase is "veh-ah-khareh ha-
shabuim shishim ushnayim" and can be read literally as
"And after the weeks, threescore and two."

AND AFTER THE 62 WEEKS

The math should be straightforward at this point:

62 x 49 = 3038 years

Your immediate, knee-jerk reaction might be to do the following and take
David's birth year, which marked the end of the first 7 Shabua, and simply
add these years:

1040 BC + 3038 years = AD 1999

You should get 1999 because there is no such thing as a *year zero* in
counting from BC to AD. The math here might go over your head if you are
unfamiliar with calculating numbers in a chronology that crosses over from
BC into AD dates. All you do is subtract the number of the BC date from the
total period of time and add 1. In this particular case: 3038 – 1040 + 1 = AD
1999. Let's now examine this number. If you add the final, 70th shabua of
Daniel, you will get:

1999 + 49 years = 2048

This is a problem! If we add 49 years to 1999, we go *beyond the year
2045* by three years and therefore beyond the cut off date for the 120 shanah
of mankind. Something is off. It doesn't work.

Here's how you figure out how to count the 70 shabua from start to finish.
We already calculated the command to Moses at the burning bush to be the
year 1383 BC which is four years after the beginning of the 51st shanah. The
count is *exactly* 7x49 (or 343) years to 1040 BC when David is born. Here's
the key. We simply start counting the 70 shabua cycles starting with the 51st
shanah, and we will arrive at Abib 1996 to Abib 2045 for the 70th shabua. In
other words, though we use the period from the burning bush commandment
to David's birth as confirmation of the correct interpretation, we use the actual
cycles in which these events took place—chiefly, the burning bush—to begin
the clock of the 70 shabua. Therefore, the clock begins with the Jubilee Year
of 1386 BC (or 2451 After Creation).

Cycle #51 out of 120 Shanah
is Cycle #1 of the 70 Shabua

120 Shanah Cycle #	Year Since Creation	Gregorian Year	70 Shabua Cycle Count
50	2402 – 2450	1435 – 1387 BC	
51	2451 – 2499	1386 – 1338 BC	1
52	2500 – 2548	1337 – 1289 BC	2
53	2549 – 2597	1288 – 1240 BC	3
54	2598 – 2646	1239 – 1191 BC	4
55	2647 – 2695	1190 – 1142 BC	5
56	2696 – 2744	1141 – 1093 BC	6
57	2745 – 2793	1092 – 1044 BC	7
58	2794 – 2842	1043 – 995 BC	8
59	2843 – 2891	994 – 946 BC	9
↓	↓	↓	↓
120	5832 – 5880	AD 1996 – 2045	70

Burning Bush
1383 BC

343
Years

Birth of David
1040 BC

Figure 4.2: Counting the 70 Weeks. You must think about history in terms of cycles because this is the way Elohim keeps track of time. Cycle 51 out of the 120 Shanah is where the first Cycle of the 70 Shabua begins.

This information has already been organized for you in Appendix A with all 70 Shabua counted out alongside the entire 120 Shanah of mankind. Let's now look at the next line of Daniel 9:26.

Figure 4.3: "Messiah shall be cut off". The transliteration of this phrase is "yikaret mashiyach" or "shall be cut off, anointed".

MESSIAH SHALL BE CUT OFF

Now that we understand how to count the 70 shabua, we need to be asking ourselves some serious questions because we are being told in Daniel 9:26 that after the year 1995, something significant is going to take place. What exactly happened after the year 1995 was finished? Is anything significant about 1996, the first year of the 70th shabua? Did *anything* important happen? What are we supposed to be looking for during this final shabua of mankind that we are currently living in?

As we move forward through the prophecy, we are about to see strange words used by the translators because they had no clue what Daniel's 70

Weeks prophecy was talking about at all. Though this problem is understandable, it does mean that we have to proceed carefully.

Now we have another mystery. Who is the *mashiyach* of Dan. 9:26? It can't be David since he already died a while ago! Is it Jesus? Of course not.

It turns out there are two different *mashiyach* in this prophecy.

When the word "mashiyach" was first introduced in Chapter 3, recall that I said it never refers to the Messiah Yeshua in the Old Testament. In fact, the two places where the translators attempt to use the English word "Messiah" to describe Yeshua both happen to be right here in the 70 weeks prophecy. Messiah is incorrectly translated both times, as you will find out. In other words, *mashiyach* is never translated as "Messiah" anywhere else except Daniel. Like we already discussed, this word (Strong's H4899) simply means *anointed* or *saint*, which is a set apart person in the eyes of God. Of all the places where *mashiyach* is used, there is one place that is extremely relevant to this mystery of Daniel 9:26.

"The breath of our nostrils, the anointed of the LORD,
Was caught in their pits,
Of whom we said,
'Under his shadow We shall live among the nations.'"
(Lamentations 4:20)

As you see here, the word *mashiyach* is translated as *anointed* in English. If you are unfamiliar with Lamentations, Jeremiah wrote this book to describe in detail the destruction of Zion (Jerusalem) and the Southern Kingdom of Israel while he was in a state of immense despair and weeping over all of the death and destruction that he saw. The parallels between Lamentations and the book of Daniel are beyond mere coincidence. Just take a look at these words from Lam. 2:3:

"He has cut off in fierce anger
Every horn of Israel;
He has drawn back His right hand
From before the enemy.
He has blazed against Jacob like a flaming fire
Devouring all around."

Just as it was in the days of Jeremiah, so it will be now at the end of the age. The same exact language is consistently used by the Holy Spirit to describe the destruction of rebellious Israel. The Hebrew root word from Dan. 9:26 that is translated as "cut off" is Strong's H3772, or *karat*. Though it is slightly different, the Hebrew word found in Lam. 2:3 (Strong's H1438, or *gada*) is also translated as "cut off"; but it is a verb that is often translated alongside the word "down", such as cut down, chop down, or break down.

We will talk about this more when we explore the abomination of desolation, but the language of Lam. 2:1,2 and specifically the words "cast down from heaven to earth" and "down to the ground", perfectly match the language in Dan. 8:10-12. As I will show you later, we now have a clearer picture of who the "little horn" of the Daniel 8 prophecy is referring to. You will be stunned if this information is new to you.

Notice also this next parallel. Do you believe in coincidence? I don't; especially when it comes to the inspired Word of Elohim. Patterns are extremely important for letting the Text interpret itself properly and avoiding false teachings. Let's continue cross examining Lamentations chapter 2 with Daniel.

"My eyes fail with tears,
My heart is troubled;
My bile is poured on the ground
Because of the destruction of the daughter of my people,
Because the children and the infants
Faint in the streets of the city."
(Lam. 2:11)

Do you remember the verse I mentioned from Daniel 10 at the beginning of this chapter? Let's refresh our minds:

2 "In those days I, Daniel, was mourning three full weeks.
3 I ate no pleasant food, no meat or wine came into my mouth, nor did I anoint myself at all, till three whole weeks were fulfilled."
(Dan. 10:2,3)

Daniel wasn't able to eat. Jeremiah was sick to his stomach. Both of their hearts were deeply troubled. The only difference is that Jeremiah had freshly witnessed a real-life event in front of his eyes. Daniel saw the real-life events of the 70 shabua prophecy, but it was only a vision. It didn't actually happen, yet.

Remember the subject matter of the 70 shabua prophecy. Because Daniel had copies of the Jeremiah Scroll and Lamentations, he specifically chose to use the code-word "messiah" or "mashiyach" to refer to his people during the final shabua after the year 1995. These are his people that have been scattered throughout the entire world. These *anointed* are his people that are highly concentrated in the USA and the West. He is talking about us right now. Something is about to happen that will radically and fundamentally alter the history of what we call the *Western* nations.

וְאֵין לוֹ

Figure 4.4: "But not for himself".

BUT NOT FOR HIMSELF

This is one of those lines in the prophecy that is translated strangely. Now that we understand that *the anointed* refers to the scattered people of the twelve tribes of Israel worldwide during the last days, why would it say "but not for himself"? This phrase is nonsensical.

Two Hebrew words are used here in this phrase. The first is וְאֵין (Strong's H369) and the second word is לוֹ (no Strong's entry). The first word is derived from the root word that can be transliterated as *ahyin*. As it appears in Dan. 9:26, the word is pronounced *vahyen* and occurs this way 239 times in 211 verses in the Masoretic Hebrew (WLC) text.[1] I carefully studied this word and put together a list of nearly all the different ways that it has been translated into English.

I took this same approach for the second word that can be transliterated as *lo*. Interestingly, no Strong's entry is linked to this word, probably because of its ubiquitous usage. It occurs 1,056 times in 1,044 verses in the WLC.[2]

When doing a direct search in the WLC for the exact two Hebrew words *vahyen* and *lo* just as they appear in Dan. 9:26, you will find an exact match in Jeremiah 50:32, and you will also find a close match in Ecclesiastes 4:8.[3] Based on all of this research, I would re-translate the first two lines of Dan. 9:26 as follows:

"And after the sixty-two weeks, the anointed shall be cut off, and they will have nothing."

Therefore, we must expect that sometime between 1996 and 2045, the anointed people of God will be destroyed and taken into some form of captivity whereby they no longer have the ability to buy or sell. They will have nothing. This reality means that we should expect a major world war at the very least in which the Western nations will be out gunned and ultimately overthrown. In fact, Daniel 9:26 is clearly warning us about World War 3. The next words of the Hebrew language provide further clarity.

וְהָעִיר וְהַקֹּדֶשׁ יַשְׁחִית עַם נָגִיד הַבָּא

Figure 4.5: "And the city and the sanctuary, shall destroy the people of the prince that shall come." These next Hebrew words can be transliterated as "vehair vehaqodesh yashit am nagid haba".

AND THE CITY AND THE "HOLY" SHALL BE DESTROYED

As you can see from Figure 4.5, these next words of the Hebrew are written in a different order than what appears in the English translations. This line serves as a reminder of why it is crucial to be looking at every Hebrew word in order to completely understand the "sealed" writings of the 70 shabua prophecy. The main idea here is that a certain *people* are going to be responsible for the destruction. We will discuss this idea more later. First, here's how the entire thought reads extremely literally and in the exact order of the letters of the original Hebrew:

"And the city and the holy will be destroyed by the people of the prince that shall come."

When you dissect this entire thought in a word-for-word manner, you can already see that the subject matter is being repeated once again, namely, Daniel's people and the holy city. It is at this point that you should recognize that we need to be watching out for the destruction of Jerusalem during this final 49-year period. We will touch on this extremely important and time sensitive topic when we explore the abomination(s) of desolation in Chapter 6.

We are being told that the "city" and the "holy" are going to be destroyed. First, let's look at "holy." Yes, I understand that the KJV, NKJV, ESV and other Bibles translate "holy" as "sanctuary"; however, the Hebrew word that Daniel used is "kodesh" (Strong's H6942). He did *not* use the word that is always used for a literal, physical "sanctuary" of a tabernacle or temple throughout the Scriptures, which is "miqdash" (Strong's H4720). Therefore, we must once again understand that the "holy" or "set apart" or "saints" is the same thing as the "anointed" or "mashiyach" which is the same thing as Daniel's people of all 12 tribes during these last days. The subject matter is simply being repeated once again in this line of Daniel 9:26.

I urge you to *not* be like the many Westerners and religious people that think a third temple in Jerusalem with a sanctuary is absolutely necessary in order for this prophecy to ever take place. I will address the rebuilding of a temple in Chapter 9. For now just understand that a physical temple is not necessary for this prophecy to be fulfilled because it indeed already has been happening whether we like it or not.

I will also continue to make the strong case that the *anointed* is referring to people who have confessed Jesus to be Lord of their lives and have received the anointing of the Holy Spirit through surrender and confession for salvation (Rom. 10:10). Here's the harsh reality you need to know about the mystery of the anointed. The curse of destruction in this prophecy applies to all of the bloodline seed of Abraham along with all Christians who, as Paul said, do not obey the truth and therefore will experience indignation and wrath (Rom. 2:8). Like I mentioned in Chapter 1, God never changes His mind. He is not human that He should change His mind. The definition of sin is the same in the Old Testament, New Testament, and beyond.

Sin will always be disobeying the spoken or written instructions (Torah) of God. Since the vast majority of Christians have a desire to follow Jesus but do not obey His commandments while also boldly teaching that "the law is done away with and no longer important," they will be suffering the wrath of this prophecy. The Word Made Flesh made it clear that if we love Him, we must keep His commandments; and He explicitly stated that we are to observe the things Moses commanded (John 14:32; Matt 23:2,3). If you haven't already, it's time to turn around and start observing God's instructions (the weekly sabbaths, feasts, dietary laws, etc.)—not in a spirit of religious pride and self-righteousness, but in a spirit of love for Yeshua and His renewed marriage covenant with us.

This killing off of the saints is also described in detail in Revelation chapters 12 and 13 when the dragon makes war with the offspring of the woman, which is symbolic of the entire nation of Israel. I will boldly make the case that the woman is the scattered seed of Abraham worldwide along with the born-again Christian communities that make up the single largest group in this identity. I believe the "dragon" spoken of in Revelation 12:17 will rise up immediately after the abomination of desolation is deployed against 1948 Israel and Jerusalem. We again see the fulfillment of Daniel's prophecy when it speaks of the saints being persecuted and destroyed under a one world government system in Revelation 13. These ideas will be explored in a lot more detail later.

As I already mentioned, we must understand that Daniel is repeating the subject matter of the "city", Jerusalem, because the word he chose to use can be transliterated as "va-ha-ir", which is a feminine *singular* noun referring to *one* city. In other words, the prophecy is telling us that Jerusalem and then all of scattered Israel worldwide will be decisively defeated, and many will be destroyed. Speaking of this exact outcome, Jeremiah gives us the following warning:

For I am with you,' says the LORD, 'to save you; Though I make a full end of all nations where I have scattered you, Yet I will not make a complete end of you. But I will correct you in justice, And will not let you go altogether unpunished.'
(Jer. 30:11)

The heaviness of Daniel's prophecy can be overwhelming, which is why it is important to always remember that God will save a remnant through these coming events. God says that He will save His people but that He also must punish their nations for their sins. That is why we must expect a complete end to all of the powers of the West including the United States, UK, and EU. Pray sincerely and often that you can be counted worthy to escape the coming war and events, if of course it is God's will for you to do so. For as Jesus said to the church of Smyrna:

"Do not fear any of those things which you are about to suffer. Indeed, the devil is about to throw some of you into prison, **that you may be tested,** and you will have tribulation ten days. Be faithful until death, and I will give you the crown of life." (Rev. 2:10) [emphasis added]

The church of Smyrna was one of the seven churches of Revelation that did not walk in a way that was wholly pleasing to God. That is why He said that He must test them. The only church out of the seven that did please God in all of their ways was the church of Philadelphia. There is a specific reason why, and I will explain it to you in Chapter 12.

Finally, the next word we need to look at carefully here is "destroyed" or "destroy" because this Hebrew word tells us in what sort of manner the evil people will be cutting off God's anointed. In the original and first edition of this book, I maintained the point of view that Klaus Schwab and the World Economic Forum have played a direct role in the fulfillment of Daniel 9:26. I still hold to this viewpoint. However, while many of the ideas that I first brought up were extremely valid, I now believe there are two different ways of looking at the Hebrew word "destroy" in order to help identify who the "people" and "the prince" of this prophecy are referring to. Consequently, I will be offering two possible interpretations.

While the word "shahat" (Strongs H7843), or destroy, inherently carries the idea of destruction and ruin, it can also be understood as corruption—morally, physically, and genetically. As it appears exactly as written in Daniel 9:26, the Hebrew word "yashit" is written as "יַשְׁחִית", and by using the BLB word search tool within the whole Masoretic Text (WLC) for this Hebrew spelling, you will find that this word only appears written this exact same way three times in the entire Bible—Dan. 9:26, Dan. 8:24, and Dan. 8:25.[4] Because of the nature of the prophecy of Daniel 8 that I will fully unpack in Chapter 6, we can safely conclude that Klaus Schwab has played a direct role in the fulfillment of this prophecy. As I stated, however, there is another interpretation.

Before looking at the two different interpretations present in Daniel 9:26, let's take a closer look at the three Hebrew words from Figure 4.5.

$$\text{עַם נָגִיד הַבָּא}$$

Figure 4.6: "The people of the prince that shall come". These next Hebrew words can be transliterated as "am nagid haba".

As you can see, it turns out that there are two different *nagid* in Daniel's 70 weeks prophecy! The first one was King David, of course, but the second one mentioned is not clear at this moment in history. We do have plenty of clues. The main idea is that the people themselves are the responsible agents for the destruction or corruption. By implication, we sort of then get the idea that the prince will arrive later after the destruction is fully complete. The prince (military commander or governmental leader) may or may not have already been revealed at this moment in time, depending on your interpretation of this verse.

INTERPRETATION #1: KLAUS SCHWAB'S WORLD ECONOMIC FORUM

Within this interpretation, it is important to pay close attention to the word "destroy," which was the Hebrew word "yashit" in Figure 4.5 that is derived from the root word "shahat."

Going back to our three laws of interpretation, we will be leaning heavily on the law of first mention this time around to fully understand what is being prophesied here. With this approach, it is quite telling of what the COVID-19 agenda was *really* about. The first time you see the root word *shahat* used in the Scriptures is Genesis 6:11,12, and this is what Moses says:

11 "The earth also was corrupt before God, and the earth was filled with violence.
12 So God looked upon the earth, and indeed it was corrupt; for all flesh had corrupted their way on the earth."

Those two places where you see the word "corrupt" translated into English are based on the same word *shahat* that Daniel used. He was likely referencing Genesis when he was sealing up the words of the prophecy just as he was commanded. Here's why. Genesis 6:1-12 is one of the most important passages of Scripture for understanding a wide variety of topics in the Bible, including why the Israelites conquered the promised land filled with "giants"; the fight between David and Goliath; various end times prophecies; and more. If this information about the giants is new to you, I'll try my best to summarize what has already been proven through the investigative work of Steve Quayle and others that have made documentary films detailing historical writings, eyewitness accounts, artifacts, monolithic structures, and other evidence showing the existence of literal giants.

What those verses in Genesis 6 are describing is the fact that the seed of man was mixed with the seed of the fallen angels who rebelled against Elohim and left their heavenly place (Jude 1:6). Here's what Genesis 6:1-5 tells us:

1 "Now it came to pass, when men began to multiply on the face of the earth, and daughters were born to them,
2 that the sons of God saw the daughters of men, that they *were* beautiful; and they took wives for themselves of all whom they chose.
3 And the LORD said, 'My Spirit shall not strive with man forever, for he *is* indeed flesh; yet his days shall be one hundred and twenty years.'
4 There were giants on the earth in those days, and also afterward, when the sons of God came in to the daughters of men and they bore *children* to them. Those *were* the mighty men who *were* of old, men of renown.
5 Then the LORD saw that the wickedness of man *was* great in the earth, and *that* every intent of the thoughts of his heart *was* only evil continually."

Don't be deceived by the English translation. The "sons of God" is not speaking of mortal men, but it is in fact speaking of angelic beings that rebelled against God. These angels "came in to" women, which is an act of literal, physical intercourse to produce offspring. The key Hebrew word of this passage is found in Gen. 6:4. It is translated as "giants" in English, but the actual word is "nephilim" (Strong's H5303). Before we investigate this word further, you should be aware that this is not the first time that the Scriptures told us about the seed of satan that would be at war with the seed of Adam. This is what Gen. 3:15 says:

"And I will put enmity
Between you and the woman,
And between your seed and her Seed;
He shall bruise your head,
And you shall bruise His heel."

Elohim tells us that satan (the great serpent of old) was indeed going to have his own "seed," or literal physical offspring, but it was going to be the Holy Seed that would come from the woman as Yeshua the Messiah that would crush the serpent's head. This is the first explicit prophecy of a Messiah that would come and conquer satan and give men the power through faith to once again claim the dominion that had been lost because of the sin of Adam. We now have spiritual dominion over the powers of darkness in Yeshua's mighty name. We have the ability to cast out demons and perform the miraculous works of the Kingdom. We are able to live in victory over sin through the power of the Holy Spirit working within us. All things have been made new.

However, don't neglect the plain truth that satan had literal, physical descendants. These are the nephilim. Now you understand why cultures from ancient times until now have always passed on legends of supermans, spider-mans, thors, mythical creatures and monsters just like in the modern day "superhero" movies. The reason why the old world before the flood was completely destroyed is because all flesh had become corrupt. What this really means is that mankind had lost its original state of being created in the image of Elohim. Mankind had become genetically tainted through the seed of the serpent and the reign of the nephilim. The only way to cleanse the earth of the serpent's genetic destruction was through the flood waters. The Word tells us that Noah was "perfect in his generations" during this period of history (Gen. 6:9). The word "perfect" ("tamim", Strong's H8549) actually means to be without spot, without blemish, complete, and whole. Noah and his sons were the only ones on the earth that were not genetically tainted with the seed, or DNA, of the serpent. They were genetically pure and able to continue the human race as created in God's image.

Going forward in history, it was actually descendants of the nephilim that instilled so much fear into the Moses generation of Israelites that they became faithless and unable to conquer the land of Israel. This is what Numbers 13:32,33 says:

32 "And they gave the children of Israel a bad report of the land which they had spied out, saying, 'The land through which we have gone as spies *is* a land that devours its inhabitants, and all the people whom we saw in it *are* men of *great* stature.

33 There we saw the giants (the descendants of Anak came from the giants); and we were like grasshoppers in our own sight, and so we were in their sight.'"

This is the second and only other time we see the word *nephilim* used in the Scriptures. The ten spies gave the bad report, and the sin of cowardice led to the wandering in the wilderness for 40 years. They described themselves as grasshoppers compared to the stature of these Anakim giants. As you study the Scriptures and especially the Torah, you will see the seed of the serpent all over the place. They go by different names, but they are all seed of the serpent.

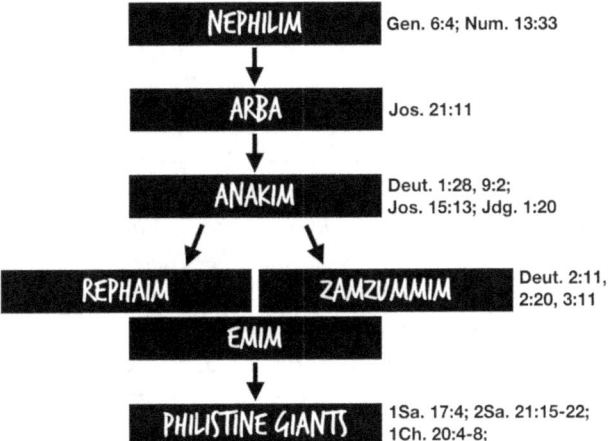

Figure 4.7: The Generations of the Giants.

Let's take a moment to address key questions. You might be wondering, "Wait a minute...I thought the seed of the serpent was supposed to be destroyed during the flood? How did they survive after the flood?"

Honestly, nobody knows for sure. We can only speculate.

One idea is that Nimrod was becoming a mighty hunter in Genesis 10:9, which could be interpreted to mean that he was somehow exercising black magic rituals and using sorcery to open portals or gates in order to somehow resurrect the nephilim or allow the nephilim to return to earth. This theory has merit, and it easily explains why the tower of Babel and the confusion of languages occurred. God wanted to prevent the spread of dark magic practices that satan was teaching Nimrod directly. In fact, God explicitly tells us that it is the sin of magic and sorcery that causes nations to become dispossessed, uprooted, destroyed, and conquered (Deut. 18:12). Such was Babel's fate, as it was overthrown by God Himself.

Another idea is that some of the nephilim were sea monster hybrids of some sort, and they were able to survive the flood waters by living underwater. They then somehow made contact with humans and were able to reveal the magic, science, and rituals necessary to allow the nephilim to return. This idea also has merit within the legends of Mesopotamia that describe half-man and half-fish creatures that made contact with humans. It also explains the lore behind things like the loch ness monster, the dagon fish god, mermaids, the Leviathan (the demon of pride, Job 41:34), and other demonic sea creatures that are scattered throughout both biblical and occultic literature.

Since the nephilim is not the focus of this book, I will now refer you to other works for a deeper look into this topic. Again, I must warn you that the rabbit hole of discovery never ends. It's important to understand these things but not become consumed with them. Knowledge for the sake of knowledge is not the goal of this book but instead, knowledge leading to righteous living in the power of the Holy Spirit. With that said, you can learn more about this topic in *The Genesis 6 Conspiracy* by Gary Wayne, *Archon Invasion - The Rise, Fall and Return of the Nephilim* by Rob Skiba, and *True Legends - Tales of Giants and the Plumed Serpents* by Steve Quayle.

Regarding the Book of Enoch, however, my stance is that I absolutely do not hold this book with the same authority and authenticity as the Bible itself, especially due to its clear association with the mystical Essene cult (see Chapter 11). I highly and strongly encourage you not to view Enoch as being equal to the writings of Moses, Yeshua, or any other book of the inspired Word of God. I've seen too many people become obsessed with Enoch and create all sorts of doctrines from it to their own destruction, but this recently re-discovered book of the Dead Sea Scrolls simply does not have a track record of hundreds or thousands of manuscripts like the Old and New Testaments do. To make matters more troublesome for Enoch, there is no intact Hebrew copy of this text preserved for us, and it has been almost exclusively recorded in the ancient Ethiopian dialect of Ge'ez.[5] This is a really big problem since Yeshua told us that neither one yod or dot would disappear from the inspired Hebrew Words of God until heaven and earth pass away (Mat. 5:18). With that said, Enoch does not pass the test of true Hebrew Scripture, it is anecdotal (at best), and is far too unreliable to spend any serious time on.

Now, let's discuss who the *nagid* of this prophecy might be referring to and how he connects to the corruption of the anointed. Just like in the first edition of this book, the case can be made that Daniel 9:26 is referring to a certain shadow government elitist mostly hiding out of the view of main-stream public media, and yet, is one of the most powerful men on the entire geopolitical stage at this time in history. He yields more power and influence than the Pope. Part of what makes him such a cunning and nearly immeasur-able force is the fact that there is a hidden partnership between hundreds of non-governmental organizations (NGOs), non-profit organizations, charities, and funds that are directly under his control throughout the world.

This man is German-born Klaus Schwab, leader of the World Economic Forum (WEF), formerly known as Davos—an organization that he founded in 1971. His now widely influential WEF think tank has been heavily criticized as an elitist gathering of the super rich and the premier breeding grounds for illicit world government agendas.

Schwab or a successor of his could be the *nagid* spoken of in Daniel 9:26. Let me provide the evidence, and I urge you to continue to maintain an open mind while also testing what I am presenting. The importance of the WEF's role in the last days will become clear as we dissect the events of the "middle of the week" spoken of in Daniel 9:27 which, by the way, was the Gregorian year 2020.

Of all the candidates that could possibly be this *nagid,* Klaus Schwab has really been making a name for himself and also has been instrumental in the fulfillment of Dan. 9:26 and the "cutting off" of the anointed. He literally wrote the book on the COVID-19 pandemic of 2020 and entitled it *COVID-19: The Great Reset.* Even though Schwab has been operating behind the shadows as the executive chairman and founder of the WEF since the early 1970s, it wasn't until 2020 and his planned takeover of the world economy that his full power and fierceness was revealed. Schwab is a man with author-ity, having many powerful people under his direct command.

If you have not investigated the Great Reset agenda, there are many resources available both online and in print to fully understand the role of the WEF in the cutting off of the anointed. One particular video was removed from the official WEF website and social media platforms after massive backlash. Thankfully, there is a place called archive.org where you can still watch it. The video is entitled "8 Predictions for the World in 2030" which was based on a 2016 article by the same name; and it says, "You'll own nothing. And you'll be happy."[6,7] This sounds *exactly* like the prophecy, doesn't it? The video goes on to describe the fall of the United States, the collapse of Western values, an increased cost of living due to energy becoming increasingly taxed by global government, and much more. If you read in between the lines, it's clear that all of these predictions are not simply bleak outlooks or pessimistic thoughts of a lone wolf employee working for the WEF. These are their actual operating procedures for an eventual consolidation of power.

So, what is the Great Reset agenda? It is the controlled destruction of the existing power structure of the West in order to redistribute its wealth and resources into the hands of a small ruling class of elites while the entire world suffers from engineered poverty that is enforced by a global totalitarian (total control) system. The COVID-19 agenda was simply the first step in establishing this economic and spiritual reset.

Anyone who has investigated COVID-19 beyond the superficial lens of the controlled mainstream media has understood the true agenda behind the pandemic. Robert F. Kennedy Jr. sums it up well, stating:

> "Government technocrats, billionaire oligarchs, Big Pharma, Big Data, Big Media, the high-finance robber barons, and the military industrial intelligence apparatus love pandemics for the same reasons they love wars and terrorist attacks. Catastrophic crises create opportunities of convenience to increase both power and wealth."[8]

I will explain who the people are behind these institutions mentioned by Kennedy and how they are relevant to Daniel's prophecy in a moment. Let's first take a closer look at Schwab himself. Even though his book is written in a purposely vague and subliminal style, he clearly states the exact same thing as Kennedy in his *COVID-19: The Great Reset* book. Praising the return of big government, Schwab says:

> "One of the great lessons of the past five centuries in Europe and America is this: acute crises contribute to boosting the power of the state. It's always been the case and there is no reason why it should be different with the COVID-19 pandemic."[9]

The elephant in the room, of course, is that Schwab himself has been and continues to be the direct and greatest recipient of power as a result of the pandemic. How? Like I mentioned earlier, Schwab has enriched himself in power through all of the partnerships under his authority. Dr. Joseph Mercola in his groundbreaking book, *The Truth About COVID-19*, does an excellent job shining a light on the cockroaches of this world government system. He states:

> "Beyond its effects on health and the health care industry, COVID-19 has empowered the global elite more than ever before to manufacture lies and half-truths. Uber-powerful Silicon Valley Big Tech corporations (Facebook, Google, Microsoft, and Amazon), Big Pharma, the World Health Organization (WHO), and philanthropic giant Bill Gates have indentured politicians and scientists from across the political spectrum. The result is fearmongering, political polarization, and social engineering—all wrapped in a disguise of protection."[10]

From Event 201 (a prominent simulation exercise of a global pandemic that happened in 2019) to the actual rollout and consequences of the pandemic, Dr. Mercola tells it all. Just as a reminder, the topic of COVID-19 is not the focus of this book. However, due to its key role in properly understanding the prophecy of Daniel's 70 shabua, if you have not yet properly investigated all of the events and literature surrounding the Wuhan gain-of-function pathogen known as *2019 novel coronavirus*, then I highly encourage you to read Dr. Mercola's book.

I should pause and warn you, too. The rabbit hole of discovery never ends, and much of this information can have the tendency to cause unnecessary fear and worry in your life. Don't let it.

It's good to be aware and awakened to the world around us; but don't be consumed by the negativity, hopelessness, and despair that often becomes a stronghold for people that spend too much time studying the conspiracies of the global elites and world government agendas. Remember, we *want* all of our Father's prophecies to take place. We want the 70 shabua to be fulfilled. We want Yeshua to return on the clouds with power and great glory. The sooner the bad stuff gets over and done with, the sooner we get to see God's light shining even brighter through the many truly amazing prophecies of the Bible that are finally going to take place.

Now, let's get back to Daniel's prophecy.

Remember that the Hebrew words are telling us that it is the *people* of the prince that are going to be the ones destroying (corrupting) the scattered 12 tribes of Israel worldwide. So, who might these people be? Take a look at the *partners* section of the official WEF website, and you'll have the complete list from 0-Z of various entities that work directly with Schwab's organization.[11] From Amazon to Ripple (the XRP cryptocurrency company) and even the Bank of China—it's all there. If you want to understand more of the intricacies of how the WEF operates and implements global agendas, all you need to do is listen to any one of the annual World Economic Forum conferences, and you will have all the answers you have ever been looking for. I personally was only able to listen to maybe two hours of the May 2022 conference in Davos, Switzerland on YouTube because it upset my stomach when I was listening to all of the lies and deceptions that were presented during this meeting.

It's not just businesses, multinational corporations, and these sorts of entities that are the *people* of this prophecy. We also need to carefully examine the Young Global Leaders of the WEF. I exposed this indoctrination program inside of the Overcome Babylon podcast when I broke down this prophecy step by step in Episode #5. The WEF has been grooming and training politicians within this coaching system with the explicit goal of installing these people inside the highest political ranks of society in order to carry out WEF orders.

Yes, you read that right.

Installing.

They manufacture political outcomes in order to get their people right where they want them to be, and this has been taking place for many years now. During a Harvard Kennedy School's Institute of Politics meeting in 2017, Schwab was being interviewed by a man named David Gergen, and he plainly revealed many dark secrets of the WEF on camera. He said that they successfully "penetrate the cabinets" of presidents; and speaking of Prime Minister Trudeau of Canada, Schwab admitted, "...Half of this cabinet or even more than half of this cabinet are our actually young global leaders of the World Economic Forum."[12] In fact, Schwab explicitly says during this same interview that Justin Trudeau, Angela Merkel (Germany), Vladimir Putin (Russia), Emmanuel Macron (France), and Alberto Ángel Fernández (Argentina) are all graduates of the Young Global Leader program.[13] Think about the profound consequences of that statement. Think about all of the hidden power that Schwab has had without most people realizing it.

Think about the great mystery of the WEF system and how it relates to Bible Prophecy in these last days.

If you're still not convinced that Klaus Schwab might be the prince of Daniel 9:26, don't overthink it for now. This is only one interpretation. However, I will later show you exactly how he is described in chapter 8 of the book of Daniel and the "two thousand three hundred" prophecy.

So far I have given you an overview of all the people that work for this prince. Now I am going to show you the most important people to take note of, but before I do, remember that they are supposed to *destroy or corrupt,* according to the underlying Hebrew word *shahat.*

It is with the proper understanding of *shahat* being genetic corruption that you can fully understand exactly how the numerous "scientific advancements" of this final, 70th shabua have been playing a role in destroying the anointed. Of course, the COVID-19 agenda was the latest and greatest abomination that God's people have faced during these last days, but things like pharmaceuticals of all kinds, vaccine technologies, GMO crops, various chemical poisons in the food and water supply have all become increasingly severe and harmful to the point of death during the end times.

This corruption has been happening like never before with the newly designed mRNA vaccine gene therapy technologies that were disguised as COVID-19 "vaccinations." A new study conducted by Phinance Technologies looked at all of the 2022 data related to excess deaths, vaccine injuries, and complications caused by the COVID-19 shots and reported economic damages of nearly $150 billion, with tens of millions injured, disabled, or killed.[14,15] All of these things are building up God's wrath that will finally be unleashed in the book of Revelation. We get this clarity during the seventh trumpet in Rev. 11:18, where an angel proclaims:

"The nations were angry, and Your wrath has come,
And the time of the dead, that they should be judged,
And that You should reward Your servants the prophets and the saints,
And those who fear Your name, small and great,
And should **destroy those who destroy the earth**."
[emphasis added]

The reason why we should eagerly desire the book of Revelation to take place is because God will finally repay His enemies. He is going to destroy the people of the prince that destroyed the earth with all of their genetic abominations of GMOs, vaccine technologies, and other scientific atrocities. He will also judge the current ruling class because of the destruction of the earth that they are about to engineer through the provocation of worldwide nuclear war. I will explain this idea more in Chapter 6 and the abomination(s) of desolation.

As mentioned, the list of the people of this prince is quite large. One of the main ones is Yuval Noah Harari, a department head at the Hebrew University of Jerusalem.[16] During a WEF annual meeting in 2018, he said this extremely disturbing and downright blasphemous statement describing the mixing of man's genetics with technology:

"Science is replacing evolution by natural selection with evolution by intelligent design. Not the intelligent design of some God above the clouds, but our intelligent design and the intelligent design of our clouds—the IBM clouds, the Microsoft clouds—these are the new driving forces of evolution."[17]

Harari wants to be like God, having the power to evolve men into his own image. He has gone on to describe humans as hackable animals that with proper implantable devices could be controlled, tracked, and easily manipulated by a dictatorship. These words echo the exact thought of Daniel's chosen word *shahat*. Daniel appears to be warning us to expect a Genesis 6 kind of event in the last days. He was likely warning us of technological abomination.

Next we have Bill Gates. Many tend to elevate Gates beyond his true role as a subordinate of the WEF because they don't understand this hidden power structure from a biblical standpoint. Gates is only a cog in the WEF machine. There are so many obvious lies and evil agendas tied to Gates that a whole book could be written about his works alone. Simply pay attention to his activity around the time of the pandemic. There was a very interesting video released from his official YouTube channel entitled "Does saving more lives lead to overpopulation?" that puts a strong emphasis on control and management of the world's population in a vague and subliminally evil way. Speaking of the future, he states:

"…The population is going to get so big, that feeding everybody and maintaining the environment is going to be impossible…The population goes down as we improve health."[18]

In other words, Gates is saying that the environment is more important than people are, and the earth has too many people on it. Of course, it's completely vague and unclear exactly what standard is being used to quantify that there are too many people, but that's what Gates asserts.

Earth worship is the religion being promoted here. The idea is that the earth must be protected at all costs, and the population should go down as more scientific schemes disguised as beneficial things like healthcare and technology are used to successfully reduce the human population. The real goal is to kill people using social engineering and eugenics. Consider these ideas to be a warm up exercise before the deeper dive in the next chapter where I fully explain the *covenant made with many* of Daniel 9:27.

Unfortunately, you must understand the pseudo-religion of the ruling class in order to comprehend prophecy. I say *unfortunately* because it's not the most thrilling and edifying stuff to read. But we were born for such a time as this.

Paul said it best that the job of believers should be to completely avoid the works of darkness and work instead to expose them (Eph. 5:11).

We can be extremely confident in our accusations of Bill Gates as a genocidal mass murder of God's people. All you need to do is simply recognize the strange and contradictory nature of his idea that *population goes down as health improves.* This is the complete opposite of the truth. It is an inversion of reality. Good health should increase the quality of life and naturally lead to a bigger, better, happier population. Gates's words after the COVID-19 pandemic are even more telling of his true nature. Almost a month after the pandemic was declared he stated, "I am optimistic that one of the vaccine efforts will give us a vaccine in the next 18 months...That's how we are going to end this pandemic."[19]

Healthy eating, living an active lifestyle, and spending time in nature weren't the answer to the pandemic. No. According to Gates, vaccines were the only acceptable solution. A little digging into Gates activities with the WEF reveals that he had already been gathering and enriching his foundations with vaccine development money in the billions of US dollars, and it was actually his vaccine initiative called the Gavi Alliance that was instrumental in the rollout of COVID vaccines, even though he fully knew they did not actually work to prevent disease.

During the May 2022 WEF annual meeting, Gates actually openly admitted that "[The vaccines of today] don't have much in the way of duration and they are not good at infection blocking."[20] Immediately after Gates said this statement on stage with all cameras and eyes on him, you could see his eyes look to the left and right with an obviously guilty and regretful look on his face, clearly thinking to himself, "Oh...did I *really* just say that out loud? I really hope no one noticed...". I'll never forget that embarrassed look on Gates' face after he openly said that the vaccines of today including all of his personal work in the COVID vaccines are *not good* at stopping infection. So, if they are not good at preventing disease, then what was the whole purpose? Let's take a look at Dr. Mercola's perspective once again:

> "The idea behind these mRNA vaccines is that by creating the SARS-CoV-2 spike protein, your immune system will produce antibodies in response. What has not been factored into this treatment is how to shut off the production of these proteins once they aren't needed. What happens when you turn your body into a viral protein factory, thus keeping antibody production activated on a continual basis with no ability to shut down?"[21]
>
> Of course, not all of the vaccines for COVID were of the mRNA kind, but Dr. Mercola's point is that genetically engineering people's bodies to produce

spike proteins forever is very unnatural and has led to extreme side effects of all kinds and ultimately, death. Dr. Mercola goes on to state the following:

"Some of these effects, such as systemic inflammation and blood clots, resemble severe symptoms of COVID-19 itself…Within weeks of the vaccines becoming available (primarily to front-line health care workers and nursing home residents), reports of serious side effects started emerging in popular media and on social media networks. Among them:

• Persistent malaise and extreme exhaustion.

• Anaphylactic reactions.

• Multisystem inflammatory syndrome.

• Chronic seizures and convulsions.

• Paralysis, including cases of Bell's palsy.

• At least 75 cases of sudden death (55 in the US and 20 in Norway), many occurring within hours or days."[22]

The whole point of the vaccine agenda was not to help people and prevent disease. It was to use pseudo-science as the manipulation tool in order to inject people with a mysterious vaccine technology that leads to disease, genetic corruption, and a slow enough death so as to not be too noticeable in the eyes of the unsuspecting victims. Daniel already told us this would happen. This was spiritual warfare from the enemy of our souls that was physically manifested in the form of lies, syringes, and needles in order to successfully inject a spirit of fear, disease, and death into people on a mass scale.

Before moving forward, if you have fallen victim to this vaccine agenda and have taken any of the vaccines of the enemy, then it's time to rise up and claim victory right here and right now. Meditate upon these words of Yeshua's from Mark 16:17,18:

17 "And these signs will follow those who believe: In My name they will cast out demons; they will speak with new tongues;
18 they will take up serpents; and if they drink anything deadly, it will by no means hurt them; they will lay hands on the sick, and they will recover."

Do you believe Jesus' words? Our Master makes it very clear. He is telling us that even if you drank something deadly, it will by no means hurt you. Now it's time to claim this blessing in your life. It doesn't matter where you are reading this. Who cares who is around you. Who cares what anyone thinks or has to say about it. You are going to take back what the enemy has stolen right now in Jesus' mighty name. You are going to pray a prayer with me that will restore and heal you from this spiritual darkness that was forced upon you by many evil and powerful people. The word says by Jesus' beatings, bruisings, whippings, and lashes we are healed; it is by His stripes we are healed (Isa. 53:5). Is there anything too hard for Him to heal? Is His arm too short that He is unable to reach you and save you? He can and *will* even restore you from these injections. I don't care what anyone has to say about it. I know what the Word of God says, and now you do, too. Pray this prayer with me right now with just a mustard seed of faith, and watch what happens.

You have nothing to lose.

"Lord Jesus, I acknowledge You right here right now. You are the Lord and God of my life. I also acknowledge and receive the presence of the Holy Spirit that raised Christ from the dead. Please, rest upon me Holy Spirit of power and fire. I recognize the power that is within me. I don't want to suppress Your power through unbelief anymore. I don't want to doubt You anymore. Forgive me of all my sins against You. I want to see Your healing power at work right now. Please, forgive me for giving in to the spirit of fear that was pushed on me through the TV, my doctor, the media, my job, and even those close to me. I forgive all those people that deceived me. You deal with them, Father. I choose not to be angry any longer! I'm sorry for not trusting You to protect me from all diseases. I'm sorry for lacking trust in Your finished work on the cross. I accept your forgiveness right now. I am a child of the King. This vessel is reserved for the King of Kings only. Any unclean spirit, demon, or evil spirit attached to me through a spirit of fear, I cast you out of my body right now in the mighty name of Jesus! Any spirit of death, any spirit of disease, infirmity, or illness that has attached itself to me as a result of taking a COVID vaccine, I cast you out right now with all power and authority of Jesus' name. You have no choice but to submit to my Master, Jesus. Get out right now—all the way! Holy Spirit, come and burn these evil spirits out of my body, and fill me with your healing power and comfort, Mighty Comforter. In the powerful name of Jesus, Amen!"

The reason I had you pray that prayer is because it's true. These injections are just a reflection of the spiritual dimension. It is the spirits of fear, death, and infirmity that all people who took the vaccine must rebuke and cast out in the name of the King of kings, Jesus Christ. Yes, there are chemicals, compounds and things of this nature in the injections. However, all disease is fundamentally spiritual in nature, and His stripes *will* heal you, if you let Him!

If you prayed that and have felt the fire and power of God in your life, hallelujah! Take a moment to breathe. Rest.

Now, let's go back and talk about the people of Schwab and his organization. The head of Pfizer, Albert Bourla, is someone that played a huge role in the destruction of the anointed with his mRNA vaccine that received billions of dollars in funding and distribution along with emergency use authorization during the pandemic. To this day, new and updated Pfizer Covid vaccines and boosters continue to get immediate approval from Western countries. Of course, Bourla is only one of many key partners of the WEF. The list feels never ending. During the 2022 WEF conference, Bourla and Schwab were speaking to one another on stage, and Schwab then proceeded to state the obvious fact that the WEF has "many children" under its command, including but not limited to the Bill and Melinda Gates Foundation, The World Health Organization, and the Gavi Vaccine Alliance.[23]

Now that you understand all of the nuances of the Hebrew word *shahat,* we can now have a more educated conversation about other events of the 70th shabua of Daniel. The current focus of the people of the WEF has been to condition the world to accept global government and also to genetically corrupt and alter humans into genetically modified organisms. This seems to be the primary agenda. Regarding the WEF's role in the "corruption" of Jerusalem, it has been reported that Israel was one of, if not *the* most highly vaccinated nations in the world, with 85% of its population inoculated with at least one Covid vaccine,[24] 63% injected twice, and 46% injected three times.[25] There is no doubt that if the WEF continues in its current trajectory they will usher in more pandemics and more vaccine technologies with sophisticated delivery mechanisms that many speculate will be directly tied to an internet-based "mark of the beast" digital currency system. In this scenario, most likely a successor to Schwab will assume power and implement these plans in the event that the WEF continues its consolidation of power throughout the world.

However, the literal, physical destruction of the earth and the ruin of Jerusalem itself will also come very soon as I will reveal to you. Will WEF and its people also be responsible for this coming *physical* destruction? Well, this is where we must certainly consider an alternate interpretation regarding the people of a prince who is to come. In fact, this second interpretation that I will now present agrees with numerous prophecies throughout the Bible and seems more plausible overall.

INTERPRETATION #2: A COMING ISLAMIC WORLD LEADER

When taking a different approach to the word "shahat," there is room to inter-pret Daniel's prophecy as pertaining to a rising power from the Middle East that will make war against Jerusalem and the West in a decisive fashion. This more literal understanding of the word *destruction* makes it quite clear that it is through warfare that these events will unfold, and the whole context of Daniel 9:26 seems to provide a lot of weight to this outcome. As I will show you throughout this book, Bible prophecy in general is quite clear that the West will be defeated militarily and at the hands of a Muslim-Russian-Chinese alliance of nations. Of all the powers in the world that have a bitter hatred and resentment toward the West and particularly 1948 Israel, it is the people of Iran and their current leader, Seyyed Ali Hosseini Khamenei—the Supreme Leader of Iran since 1989. He has often referred to the United States as the *great satan* while expressing deep-rooted animosity for Zionism and Israel. Children and youth under this regime are even made to recite the words "death to Israel, death to America, and death to the UK" when attending public schools each day. Because of Iran's adoption of Islam as the official religion since the time of the 1979 Revolution, it provides an excellent case study as to what a coming Islamic new world order would look like in practice. While it is technically not illegal to be a Christian in Iran, the law is inherently against all followers of Jesus. Not only is converting from Islam to Christianity considered illegal, but evangelizing anyone to the Christian faith is also considered the crime of apostasy that is punishable by death. Due to the subjective interpretation of *evangelism*, every authority in Iran such as Revolutionary Guards, policemen, and judges are able to interpret the law for themselves without any level of accountability, due process, or other routine protections common to Western countries.[26] Such a system has led to the imprisonment, torture, and brutal execution of countless political prisoners, non-Muslims, and Christians in Iran for over four decades.

Now, am I suggesting that the current Ayatollah Khamenei himself is the prophesied prince of Daniel 9:26? Well, let's first pay attention to the words of Jesus when He said, "Therefore if they say to you, 'Look, He is in the desert!' do not go out; or 'Look, He is in the inner rooms!' do not believe it" (Matthew 24:26). Speaking of the coming false messiah, Jesus is very clear that one such imposter and miracle worker will be seen in the "desert." What better description of a coming Muslim world leader can we find in the Scriptures? Clearly, the Middle East is one location that cannot be overlooked when considering the coming of the man of lawlessness commonly referred to as the antichrist. This will be a key topic of Chapter 13.

However, there is currently not a man that perfectly fits the description of the prophesied antichrist. Though Revelation 13 speaks of different beasts, it is important to emphasize that the coming antichrist figure will perform signs and miracles, even making "fire come down from heaven" (Rev. 13:13). Therefore, neither Schwab or Khameini currently fit the description as being the false messiah that will deceive the whole world. However, both of these governmental leaders are playing their own major roles in the end times. The people of Khameini, including Hezbollah, Hamas, and numerous Arab militias, will surely be responsible for the coming destruction of Jerusalem. There is also little doubt in my mind that a religious and political Muslim world leader will emerge in the aftermath of the abomination of desolation that will be taking place very soon.

With regard to the role of Islam in the end times, the Muslim world believes that a descendant of Muhammad will arrive to destroy evil and injustice from the earth during a brief "golden age" lasting between seven to nine years and right before the end of the world.[27] This coming messiah, or nagid, figure is called the Mahdi. The Bible itself seems to strongly confirm this idea in general. Just pay attention to these words of Isaiah 14:12: "How you are fallen from heaven, O Lucifer, son of the morning! How you are cut down to the ground, You who weakened the nations!" This verse echoes what we see in Revelation 12, specifically verses 9 and 12:

9 So the great dragon was cast out, that serpent of old, called the Devil and Satan, who deceives the whole world; he was cast to the earth, and his angels were cast out with him.
12 "Therefore rejoice, O heavens, and you who dwell in them! Woe to the inhabitants of the earth and the sea! For the devil has come down to you, having great wrath, because he knows that he has a short time."

We see multiple confirmations of the Mahdi prophecy of Islam within these verses. First, we see that Rev. 12:12 speaks of the devil having a "short time" to perform his work of deception, which seems to match the idea of the short *golden age* expected by Muslims. But perhaps the most eye-opening connection to the coming of the Islamic antichrist can be found in the exact Hebrew words of Isaiah the prophet where he writes, "How you are fallen from heaven, O Lucifer" (Isa. 14:12). The English word "Lucifer" is incorrectly translated and was lazily carried over from the Latin Vulgate. The actual Hebrew word used here is "הֵילֵל" which can be transliterated as *"heylel"* (Strong's H1966). Because of flexibility in the Masoretic assignment of vowel sounds, this word could also technically be pronounced "haylal." This is the exact same word as the Arabic "حلال" which is anglicized as *halal* and means to be permissible according to Islamic dietary laws. This word is kind of like the Jewish word kosher, which means to be allowable according to the dietary traditions of Judaism. The perfect match of the Hebrew word *haylal* (poorly translated as Lucifer) to the Arabic word *halal* indicates a correlation well beyond coincidence. Assuming that Jesus was warning us of a coming Islamic Mahdi in the last days, we can now see a clearer message at the end of Revelation 13:

16 He causes all, both small and great, rich and poor, free and slave, to receive a mark on their right hand or on their foreheads,
17 and that no one may buy or sell except one who has the mark or the name of the beast, or the number of his name.
18 Here is wisdom. Let him who has understanding calculate the number of the beast, for it is the number of a man: His number is 666.
(Rev. 13:16-18)

What we are likely being shown in these verses of Revelation is that the coming rule of satan will be disguised under the system of a worldwide Islamic Caliphate. This system of government is by definition a monarchical government based on a claim of succession to the Islamic State of Muhammad. Under such a system, only those who accept the "mark of the beast" will be able to buy and sell the things that are labeled as *halal* and permissible under the rule of this coming kingdom. Even today, the label of *halal,* which can also be ascribed to Lucifer, is presented as an official seal on the foods and consumable products of the Muslim world. This is one of the names of the coming beast and his system.

In addition to the word *halal,* there is more information underneath the surface of the number "666" when examining the original Greek language. When John wrote down the book of Revelation, he was commanded to send it as seven separate letters to different churches in Asia Minor. These were Greek-speaking territories in those days, and therefore, it would be foolish to attempt to understand the mark of the beast without examining the original text. Many of the most popular commentators and Bible teachers out there have erroneously investigated the English translation of "666," and many have heavily relied on the use of Gematria to arrive at various false conclusions while not realizing Gematria's origin in the satanic teachings of the Kabbalah and the Talmud. That is why Jewish Gematria is not listed under any of the three laws of interpretation in this book. In the wake of the recent vaccine agenda, many were also quick to adamantly proclaim the "mark" to be any one of the mRNA vaccines that were released in the aftermath of 2020. Again, these ideas fall well short of understanding the nuances of the Bible. In this case, all that is needed is a deeper look at the Greek text.

Figure 4.8: The Three Greek Letters of "666". These letters are pronounced "Chi Xi Stigma" and represent the numerical value of 666 (600, 60, and 6, respectively).

Pictured in Figure 4.7 are the three Greek letters representing the numerical value that is often translated as *666* into the English language. This image is often what you will find in online, digitized manuscripts of the Textus Receptus. However, this is one of the few cases where it is necessary to go back to a copy of the original handwritten manuscript to see if there is additional information. There is one such manuscript that has now been made available online by the Vatican Library called the Codex Vaticanus. This is a manuscript that dates to the fourth century and contains nearly all of the Christian canon in Greek. Within the online digital version, simply navigate to page 1530 of "Apocalypsis," and you will find Revelation 13:18 near the upper right hand side of this page with the Greek letters "666" appearing exactly as it had been preserved in the manuscript.[28] Because the images online are so blurry and low quality, I created Figure 4.8 as a near replica to reveal precisely what the Greek looks like.

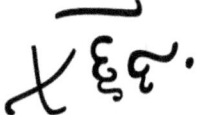

Figure 4.9: "666" In The Original Greek Manuscript of the Codex Vaticanus.

As you can see, the letters look very different from digitized manuscripts or interlinear study tools. The imperfections in the handwriting are evident, but even more importantly, the intentional markings seen by John have been preserved—markings that are not visible in either Greek print reproductions or in English translations. With this exact visual representation of the "666" mark that John saw, it is now possible to make the necessary connections to Islam, for it is within the Arabic language that this particular representation of the Chi Xi Stigma can be found. More specifically, it is the Arabic phrase *bismillah,* or "in the name of Allah", that correlates to the letters of John's vision.

The bismillah is one of the most important phrases in all of Arab culture, having its place in both religious and political environments. In fact, this phrase regularly appears in the constitutions of countries where Islam is either the official religion or where an Islamic majority exists, such as Iran, Iraq, Afghanistan, Egypt, Bahrain, Bangladesh, Brunei, Kuwait, Libya, Maldives, Pakistan, Saudi Arabia, Tunisia and the United Arab Emirates. The standardized print version of this phrase *bismillah* looks like the following:

" بِسْمِ ٱللَّهِ " or " بسم الله "

or in calligraphy, "  "

Already, you can see the resemblance to Rev. 13:18. However, in the Arabic world there is the widespread use of artistic calligraphy with varying stylized representations of the bismillah depending on the artist's interpretation. That is why a simple online search for this phrase will yield a multitude of different images. One such representation depicts the widely used crossed swords of Islam right next to the phrase "in the name of Allah", and when put together in this fashion perfectly matches John's vision.

Figure 4.10: The Swords of Islam and Bismillah. The crossed swords are very common in the Islamic world such as the Emblem of Saudi Arabia or the Victory Arch of Baghdad. In Shia Islam, one key symbol is the Zulfiqar (the Sword of Imam Ali) often depicted with a deep notch to almost appear as two swords or also as two crossed swords with both having the notch at the end of the blade. The crossed swords are also common insignia among Islamic soldiers, militia groups, and organizations such as the Muslim Brotherhood.

To the best of my knowledge, it was Walid Shoebat, a self-proclaimed former Muslim terrorist turned Christian, who first widely proclaimed this understanding of the crossed swords and bismillah together since the late 1990s.[29] Since then, many people have begun seeing how this view of the bismillah gives the book of Revelation tremendous new relevance in light of the events now unfolding in the Middle East, especially since armed Islamic militants are often seen wearing a head covering or right-handed armband with the bismillah marked into the cloth. In fact, that is exactly what the Greek word translated as "mark" in Rev. 13:16 means—to stamp or to imprint, as onto cloth (see Strong's G5480). Putting all of these pieces of this prophetic puzzle together now allows us to examine the bismillah alongside the original inscription from the Codex Vaticanus. When modified only slightly, there is no escaping the obvious connection.

Figure 4.11: The Mark of Revelation 13:18. By rotating the letter Xi and moving the long pen stroke that looks like an English "L" into the correct location, you can see that the two symbols are nearly identical.

This radically different understanding can now be applied to the book of Daniel and particularly Dan. 9:26. The first part of this verse can now be translated as saying, "And the Islamic people of a coming Mahdi will destroy Jerusalem along with the Jewish and Christian people." This interpretation echoes what Jesus said concerning a coming persecution where, "They will put you out of the synagogues; yes, the time is coming that whoever kills you will think that he offers God service" (John 16:2). There will be a coming persecution in the name of Allah where a unified Islamic world will believe they are doing a good service by imprisoning, torturing, and beheading their opposition.

After Jacob wittingly stole his brother Esau's birthright, Isaac blesses his firstborn son Esau by stating the following:

39 Then Isaac his father answered and said to him:
"Behold, your dwelling shall be of the fatness of the earth,
And of the dew of heaven from above.
40 By your sword you shall live,
And you shall serve your brother;
And it shall come to pass, when you become restless,
That you shall break his yoke from your neck."
(Gen. 27:39,40)

Again we see a reference to the sword of Islam. The Hebrew word used to describe the "fatness" of the earth is pronounced *mishmanneh* (from Strong's H4924) and can refer to oil generally speaking and also olive oil. This word is the key giveaway that Esau's descendents currently dwell in the petroleum-rich countries of the Middle East where there also happens to be olive oil in great abundance. This dual meaning of "fatness" cannot be overlooked. There is also evidence that this breaking of Jacob's yoke has never occurred in any significant way throughout history. Though many scholars say that Esau's geographical location is limited only to modern-day Jordan due to the location of Mount Seir, the prophecy of Isaac should be understood as having wide-spread consequences for the whole Middle East. Especially in the last several hundred years, the British Empire and the United States after it have success-fully imperialized the Middle East where the bloodline descendents of Esau are dispersed today. Whether it has been British Petroleum in Iraq or the American Conoco oil fields in Syria, the descendants of Jacob have been relentless in their exploitation of the resources of various Arab nations. In fact, pay close attention to Obadiah's prophecy. We can see that the words of this minor prophet have not yet been fulfilled because his book concludes with the fact that Yeshua will reign in Zion with the whole kingdom of United Israel restored under Him. The majority of this prophecy has to do with Edom (Esau) and his mistreatment of his brother Jacob. Right there in the Oba. 1:10 we read, "For violence against your brother Jacob, Shame shall cover you, And you shall be cut off forever." This is no doubt a reference to Esau, and the Middle East generally speaking, breaking off Jacob's yoke of imperialism that has not yet taken place. Once again we see a last days patriarchal prophecy within Genesis that correlates with both the prophetic Scriptures and also the Gospels. The restlessness of Esau is approaching quickly, indeed.

Now that we have examined the two primary and different interpretations available within the first part of Daniel 9:26, it is time to understand the second half of this verse.

Figure 4.12: "And the end thereof, with a flood". This phrase
can be transliterated as "vehqitso bashetef".

THE END OF IT SHALL BE WITH A FLOOD

The next lines are straightforward to understand. The first word we will look at is "end" (Strong's H7093), and it can be understood to mean "at the end of time" according to the BLB description.[30] As I will show you, there is a specifically appointed period of time in which this destruction is taking place. It has a definite ending point, and that's what Daniel is telling us here.

The next word "flood" ("shetef", Strong's H7858) is interesting because it is different from the Hebrew word "mabul" (Strong's H3999) used to describe Noah's flood. This is an uncommon word. It can be used figuratively, or it can be used to speak of literal flood waters. This word "shetef" can also be used to describe the anger of God or His judgment (see Psalm 32:6 and Nahum 1:8), and I believe that this idea is part of what Daniel was portraying. It's not completely clear what is being spoken of here, but I believe that after the specifically appointed period of time, the ruling prince and world governmental power is going to be overthrown by God Himself in His wrath. The anointed people will be declared justified (as I will show you in the next chapter), and the wrath will be accomplished. In other words, I do not believe that this flood of destruction is going to happen to the saints that are still alive at the end of this judgment period, but it likely applies to the oppressors themselves.

וְעַד קֵץ מִלְחָמָה נֶחֱרֶצֶת שֹׁמֵמוֹת

Figure 4.13: "And unto the end of the war are determined desolations". This phrase can be transliterated as "veh-ad qets milkhama nekheretset shomemot".

AND TILL THE END OF THE WAR DESOLATIONS ARE DETERMINED

Based on what is being described here, the countries containing Daniel's people will be entering a WWIII scenario where there will be intense fighting. They will fight, but will they win? I think you understand the answer by now. We will find out even more details when we look closely at Daniel 9:27. This war already began with Vladmir Putin's special military operation in Ukraine on February 24, 2022—a war that was originally stirred up by hidden factions of the United States government all the way back in 2014 and only put on a brief hold during the Donald Trump presidency from 2016-2020. The global elites have always wanted the war we are seeing now. They have always wanted to create chaos between a Muslim-Russian-Chinese alliance versus the West in order to usher in a one world government system in the aftermath of a short-lived nuclear war.

The next key word to focus on is "desolations" ("shomem-oht", Strong's H8074), which is the same word used in the next verse speaking of the abomination of *desolation*. This word has quite a range of uses and nuances in the Bible. Remember what Daniel was praying right before he received the 70 shabua prophecy? This is what he said in Dan. 9:11:

"Yes, all Israel has transgressed Your law, and has departed so as not to obey Your voice; therefore the curse and the oath written in the Law of Moses the servant of God have been poured out on us, because we have sinned against Him."

The curse and oath are found in very specific places of the Torah. Based on everything we have uncovered so far, I can tell you with firm conviction that Daniel was quoting Leviticus 26 where this word *desolation* is used six times to describe Elohim's curses for disobeying His instructions. Here they are:

22 "I will also send wild beasts among you, which shall rob you of your children, destroy your livestock, and make you few in number; and your highways shall be **desolate**."
31 "I will lay your cities waste and bring your sanctuaries to **desolation**, and I will not smell the fragrance of your sweet aromas."
32 "I will bring the land to **desolation**, and your enemies who dwell in it shall be astonished at it.
34 "Then the land shall enjoy its sabbaths as long as it lies **desolate** and you *are* in your enemies' land; then the land shall rest and enjoy its sabbaths.
35 "As long as *it* lies **desolate** it shall rest—for the time it did not rest on your sabbaths when you dwelt in it.
43 "The land also shall be left empty by them, and will enjoy its sabbaths while it lies **desolate** without them; they will accept their guilt, because they despised My judgments and because their soul abhorred My statutes."
(Lev. 26:22,31,32,34,35,43) [emphasis added]

I know I have already made this clear, but the blessing and the curse of the oath written in the Law of Yehovah still apply to us to this very day. All of the descendants of Abraham are bound to this covenant because their ancestors swore an oath of allegiance to the God of the Bible. Those that have said "yes" to Jesus as Lord of their lives have also entered into the renewed covenant in His blood. These curses still apply to this very day thousands of years later because God does not change His mind.

The covenant cannot be dismissed until heaven and earth pass away (Matt. 5:18). We can't even talk about the blessings because no majority of people on a national scale have bothered to follow God's instructions now for many hundreds of years. No nation has ever committed in any large-scale way to do God's instructions (Torah) that Moses wrote down for us. There are many places throughout Scripture that speak of the consequences of breaking the Torah, but Hosea paints an extremely relevant picture for us when he says:

"My people are destroyed for lack of knowledge.

Because you have rejected knowledge,
I also will reject you from being priest for Me;
Because you have forgotten the law of your God,
I also will forget your children."
(Hos. 4:6 NKJV)

That's why the curses are now coming down on us. The vast majority of God's people have forgotten the instructions of their God. They have rejected the Torah and considered it a strange thing.

The next word we need to look at is "determined" ("kharats", Strong's H2782). This word is straightforward. It means "decisive decree", and it can also mean "cut" or "mutilate."[31] The idea is that there is nothing that can stop all of these things from taking place. They are absolutely determined within the very heart of Elohim Himself.

You now understand what happens after the first 69 weeks of the prophecy. You now understand why there has been out of control inflation. You now know why there have been supply chain problems and shortages of food and all kinds of goods and supplies. You see why the experimental vaccines were rolled out to purposely harm people and why horrifying treatments like remdesivir with an extremely high mortality rate were used in hospitals as the only approved treatment for Covid-19 before the vaccines showed up. I could go into a lot more detail with the 5G control grid in place and much more evil being rolled out on a weekly basis. It's really not fruitful. The bottom line is this: the USA and the nations of the West are being cut off.

That doesn't mean we live in hopelessness and fear. Quite the opposite. Come back into covenant through the finished work of the cross. Do not rely on your performance or self-righteousness. Trust in Yeshua. Then let him break the curses of the law that still remain over those who do not confess and repent of their sin. Let Him break the curse of the law in your life just as described in Gal. 3:13. He has already redeemed you. Just accept it, and walk in newness of life. Then you can rightfully claim this blessing of Ezekiel 11:16:

Therefore say, "Thus says the Lord God: 'Although I have cast them far off among the Gentiles, and although I have scattered them among the countries, yet I shall be a little sanctuary for them in the countries where they have gone.'"

Let Him be your sanctuary of rest and peace that surpasses all understanding through all of the hardship and tribulation that the world will be facing.

Chapter 5
Daniel's 70th Shabua and the Year 2020

We will now take a closer look at the 70th shabua of Daniel, the covenant made with many, and more. Due to the amount of information contained in Daniel 9:27, I will be dividing the analysis of this verse into two parts, Part A and Part B; and the second half will be continued in Chapter 6. Here are the primary words from Dan. 9:27a as we continue to let the Word of God accomplish its work in us:

"Then he shall confirm a covenant with many for one week;
But in the middle of the week
He shall bring an end to sacrifice and offering.
And on the wing of abominations shall be one who makes desolate,
Even until the consummation, which is determined,
Is poured out on the desolate."
[emphasis added]

Now that we are finally here, let's first take a look at what 70th shabua looks like in a chart format according to Gregorian years with all the years of rest listed in this cycle. To see the Hebrew (Creation) years, visit Appendix B in the back of this book.

	First Seven	Second Seven	Third Seven	Fourth Seven	Fifth Seven	Sixth Seven	Seventh Seven
	1996	2003	2010	2017	2024	2031	2038
	1997	2004	2011	2018	2025	2032	2039
	1998	2005	2012	2019	2026	2033	2040
	1999	2006	2013	**2020**	2027	2034	2041
	2000	2007	2014	2021	2028	2035	2042
	2001	2008	2015	2022	2029	2036	2043
7th Year Rest	2002	2009	2016	2023	2030	2037	2044, Aviv 2045

Figure 5.1: The 70th Week of Daniel. The year 2020 has a major place in Bible prophecy.

Amazing, isn't it? This is the mystery of the 70 shabua of Daniel that was sealed until the last days. We are here now. We are living through it. Mathematically and biblically, this is the one and only true meaning of the prophecy. Everything else that we were ever taught was a distracting lie meant to keep us from being diligent students of the Word. Praise God that He is still speaking to His people and revealing His wise counsel to all those who simply ask and seek with all their heart. As you can see in this chart, we are now past the year 2020, which was the exact middle of the 70th week of Daniel. Let us now take a look backwards and find out exactly what the Word already warned us about. Like people say, hindsight is 20/20 vision.

$$\text{וְהִגְבִּיר בְּרִית לָרַבִּים שָׁבוּעַ אֶחָד}$$

Figure 5.2: "And he shall confirm the covenant with many for week, one". This line can be transliterated as "vehigbir berit larabim shabua echad".

THEN HE SHALL CONFIRM A COVENANT WITH MANY FOR ONE WEEK

So, what is this 49-year covenant that we need to be looking for? Has it already been fulfilled, or are we currently living through it? First, I will point out that the English use of the word "he" in referring to a single person that is responsible for this covenant does not make sense in light of the evidence I will present. If you look closely at the Hebrew language, the use of the pronoun "he" is based on an assumption of the translators that the same "coming prince" from the previous verse is also responsible for this covenant with many. Again, this is an assumption only. As I will demonstrate, the use of the word "he" is only a filler word because the translators did not understand this prophecy like you are about to.

In order to completely discern what this covenant is all about, the Hebrew words need to be carefully examined. The word "confirm" ("gabar", Strong's H1396) means to strengthen or make strong; the word "covenant" ("berit", Strong's H1285) means treaty, alliance, league, or constitution; and finally, the word "many" (rab", Strong's H7227) means numerous, mighty, or multitude. Now we just need to look for a strengthened constitution of some sort that has been made with vast multitudes of people for exactly 49 years.

The first covenant I researched when I started investigating this topic was the League of Nations that was established in the aftermath of WWI. It was created as Part I of the Treaty of Versailles (the same treaty that put all of the blame and monetary damage of WWI on Germany, which led to the rise of

Hitler). This covenant was a peace treaty that was formed in order to prevent war through diplomacy, disarmament, and arbitration. This league fits the definition of "berit." At its peak, 58 different countries signed on to this covenant, so this fits the definition of the root word "rab"; however, the League of Nations only lasted from 1920-1946, and fell apart after it failed to prevent WWII.[1]

Next on the list of suspects is the Geneva Conventions. Established in the aftermath of WWII, this document clearly defines the international legal standards for humanitarian treatment in war, including the basic human rights for wartime prisoners; the wounded and the sick; and also civilians during war. It is actually a series of four treaties and therefore fits the definition of "berit." Though it was ratified by all 196 countries in the world (absolutely fitting the description of "many"), this covenant has been in effect since the year 1949 to the present day, which currently makes it 73 years old and does not fit the definition of being one shabua.[2]

There are numerous treaties, alliances, and leagues to be looking for, but how does something like the Nuremberg Code fit into this picture? This document was next on my investigative hunt. This was considered the most important document in the history of medical and clinical research ethics because of its enormous influence on human rights worldwide. It was first developed by the United States, Great Britain and the Soviet Union in the aftermath of WWII and the defeat of the Hitler's National Socialist regime. If you recall, these are the standards that were used to hold legal trials and hold Nazi war criminals accountable for human experimentation. Too bad this document wasn't enforced in light of the COVID vaccine rollout, right? That's the problem with the Nuremberg Code. It was never officially ratified (accepted as law) by any nation.[3] Nonetheless, it has strongly influenced a variety of governing bodies and different legislation worldwide. The other problem is that this code has been in existence from 1947 to the present (over 75 years old), which again is not one shabua.

The next logical place we need to focus on like a laser beam is the United Nations. Headquartered in New York City, this organization was created as the successor of the failed League of Nations covenant. It was created in 1945 shortly after WWII with the goal of preventing more wars and establishing world peace. It had 51 member countries the year it was founded and has since grown to be the largest and most all-encompassing world governing body with numerous sub-entities (WHO, UNEP, UNESCO, etc.).[4] The UN even has its own standing army of thousands of soldiers known as peace-keeping troops. Though this covenant contains 193 countries in the world (fitting the description of "rab"), this covenant itself does not fit into the parameters of being 49 years old. However, many groups exist within the UN, and when you look very closely at all of them, there is one that fits the exact description of Daniel 9:27.

The UN has 15 agencies that do its work. The UN Security Council describes itself as upholding international peace and security. The World Bank boasts supporting the developing countries through technical assistance. UNSECO claims to use education, science and culture to inspire people. By the way, the word *inspiration* is a spiritual and religious term. Pay attention to that wording moving forward.

Of all of the different entities, institutions, and tentacles within and around the UN monster, there is one that perfectly fits the parameters of the covenant made with many described by Daniel. It is the United Nations Environmental Program (UNEP). A look at the official logo shows mother earth, or gaia, worship with a woman extending her arms outward left and right with the laurel wreath of the false Greek god, apollo, under her feet.[5] From a biblical standpoint, apollyon which is synonymous with apollo, is the great serpent and satan himself that will be released from the bottomless pit in the very near future as described in Rev. 9:11. As you will soon find out, UNEP is the religious arm of the UN organization that Daniel saw in his vision.

UNEP - THE COVENANT WITH MANY

Out of a possible 196 countries, 113 joined the UNEP religious covenant when it was first introduced in 1972. This covenant was already under development before 1972, and the groundwork was laid in several conferences, writings, and meetings amongst the global elites. However, this covenant was officially presented in Stockholm, Sweden from June 5-16, 1972, and it was entitled *Report of the United Nations Conference on the Human Environment.*[6] Before we dive into the details of this covenant, the next figure provides an overview of its development and the different people and works involved.

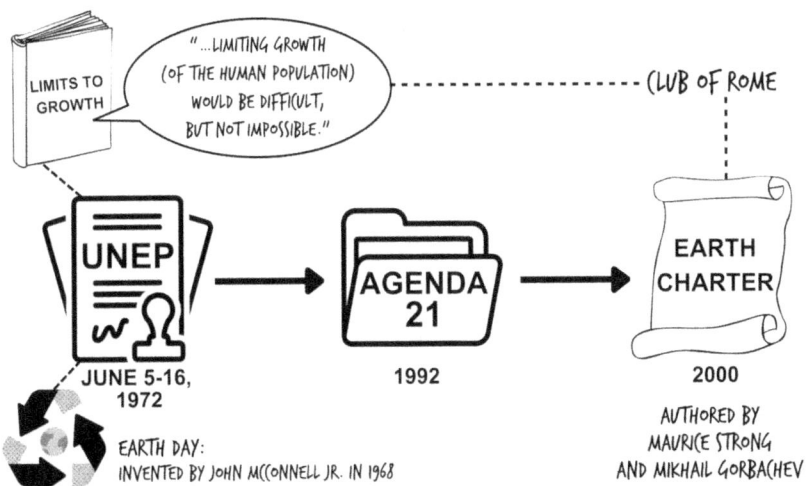

Figure 5.3: The United Nations Environmental Program.

As you can see, there were other major influences behind the invention of the UNEP covenant. In a now deleted interview, Klaus Schwab stated that he directly helped the Club of Rome in its early days to establish itself as a climate change and world government think tank. Similar to the WEF, the Club of Rome is an organization that is only slightly older but that shares the same ideals. Depopulation, earth worship disguised as environmentalism, and pseudo-science are their doctrines. One of the works of the club that really influenced UNEP was a book entitled *Limits to Growth*. The authors plainly state, "Deliberately limiting growth [of the human population] would be difficult, but not impossible."[7] The authors are stating extremely plainly that they intend to murder people on a large scale. Genocide is the goal. This book isn't an accident because it was the very first report of the club in 1972, and its publication suspiciously coincided with the UNEP meeting that same year. Of course, members of the club were also present at the UNEP meeting. Without getting too lost in the details, just understand that UNEP is more of a formal and vague constitution of dry, legal language; but if you want to know the true intentions of UNEP, *Limits to Growth* gives all the answers. There are also many other influences like the Pentecostal Christian John McConnell, Jr. who coined the term *earth day* in 1968, decided on the spring equinox observance of this new "holiday" in 1969, and then sparked global governmental adoption originating in San Fransisco.[8]

If there is any doubt in your mind as to the true intentions of the people behind UNEP, we are about to look at their own words and dissect the true meaning of what they proclaimed. Right from the very first page and the very first statement, this is what they write:

> "*The United Nations Conference on the Human Environment,*
>   Having met at Stockholm from 5 to 16 June 1972,
>   Having considered the need for a common outlook and for common princi-
> ples to inspire and guide the peoples of the world in the preservation and
> enhancement of the human environment...".[9]

We talk a lot about "inspiration" and "being led" or "guided" by God or the Holy Spirit quite a lot in Christianity and biblically based religions. The words being used here are extremely religious in nature, make no mistake about it. They are stating that their express purpose is to make people think correctly about the environment. In reality, that is the job of the Bible. The Bible is the instruction manual for all things. What they are actually doing is elevating themselves as authorities above the Scriptures. Let's read on and see what they say under *Principle 1* on page 4:

> "Man has the fundamental right to freedom, equality and adequate conditions
> of life, in an environment of a quality that permits a life of dignity and well-
> being, and he bears a solemn responsibility to protect and improve the envi-
> ronment for present and future generations.

In this respect, policies promoting or perpetuating *apartheid,* racial segrega- tion, discrimination, colonial and other forms of oppression and foreign domi- nation stand condemned and must be eliminated."[10]

The first part of this statement sounds nice and flowery. Of course people should be good stewards of the earth. We should do unto others as we would want done unto us. But do you see the glaring problem with the second part of what they are stating? "Promoting" or "perpetuating" are very subjective terms, along with "other forms of oppression." This wording leaves the door wide open for the interpretation to be extremely subjective regarding ideas of racism and discrimination. What if one day the UN decides that Christianity and any Bible-based religion is to be considered "oppressive"? Then what?

That's the problem.

Their goal is to try to get as many people completely invested and sucked into the religion of earth worship to the point that their followers will violently oppose even a perceived threat to the cult. The UN will say, "jump" and people will be asking, "how high?". Here's how I would translate *Principle 1* from UNEP: "If we don't like you, we'll eliminate you, for the greater good of the environment." Now let's take a look at *Recommendation 12* and see the direct influence that *Limits to Growth* had in the creation of UNEP:

"1. *It is recommended* that the World Health Organization and other United Nation agencies should provide increased assistance to Governments which so request in the field of family planning programs without delay.

2. *It is further recommended* that the World Health Organization should promote and intensify research endeavour in the field of human reproduction, so that the serious consequences of population explosion on human environment can be prevented."[11]

I think you are starting to see the thought pattern of UNEP. Everywhere you look there is a thought about killing people; reducing population; eliminating. If you are from the US then you are very familiar with Planned Parenthood and their "family planning" programs, which are the physical manifestation of this UNEP religious covenant. This organization alone has been responsible for the murder of millions upon millions of babies along with the prevention of pregnancy through the taxpayer funded distribution of contraceptives. It is not by accident. Hollywood, the media, universities, and celebrities of all kinds have been instrumental in furthering this covenant's agenda.

Under the second point, UNEP is calling upon the WHO to prevent people from reproducing naturally because of the lie of overpopulation. Elohim told us to be fruitful and multiply, and He never made any statement regarding overpopulation. He did tell us that man's days would only be 120 periods of time, and now that you understand this profound biblical truth, this idea of overpopulation should completely vanish from your mind. We are almost at the end of time, and of course humankind as we know it will not exponentially increase forever to the point where there are 500 billion people or more on the planet. Elohim will not allow this to happen under the current paradigm of sin and lawlessness abounding because it is not His will.

THE AGENDA 21 INITIATIVE

Out of the environmental covenant of UNEP sprang up many other works, initiatives, and entities. Of particular importance is the *Earth Summit Agenda 21* that was released in 1992. This agenda is the fundamental reason why restrictive building codes have been enforced in nearly every county of the United States and the local jurisdictions of other Western countries. It is the driving force behind restrictive land use regulations that prevent people from living on their own purchased land and homesteading. This agenda is the one that has stripped people of their freedoms, made the cost of living rural more prohibitive, and has encouraged the herding of people into urban areas like cattle where they can be more easily manipulated and controlled. In her eye-opening book, *Behind the Green Mask: U.N. Agenda 21,* Rosa Koire states:

> "In a nutshell, the plan calls for governments to take control of all land use and not leave any of the decision making in the hands of private property owners. It is assumed that people are not good stewards of their land and the government will do a better job if it is in control. Individual rights in general are to give way to the needs of communities as determined by a globalist governing body. Moreover, people should be rounded up off of the land and packed into human settlements or islands of human habitation, as they are called in the UN Agenda 21 documents, close to employment centers and transportation."[12]

Behind the illusion of local political structures and elected governments lies world government agendas that are ruthlessly established through extremely crafty and illegal means. One of the curses of Leviticus states, "Those who hate you shall reign over you, and you shall flee when no one pursues you" (Lev. 26:17b). Ultimately, it is God that raises up leaders and hands people over to curses. This is merely a cause-and-effect consequence of disobeying God's righteous instructions. The UN is only fulfilling its role within the biblical parameters of end times prophecy.

THE EARTH CHARTER BLASPHEMY

In 2000, the Earth Charter covenant furthered the agenda of UNEP and created a blatant mockery of the Bible. Authored by Club of Rome members Maurice Strong and Mikhail Gorbachev, this charter further revealed the true religious nature of the UNEP covenant with many. Before discussing what the Earth Charter is all about, I first encourage you to watch a documentary that was put together by Brian Moonan called *Agenda 21: The Earth Charter, the Ark of Hope, and the New World Order.* YouTube has censored this video, so go to his Vimeo to check it if it's still there (I provide a link in the notes section for this chapter).[13] The main idea is that this document has been placed inside of a blasphemous replica of the ark of the covenant of the Bible, and this fake ark was celebrated in a long pagan ritual in which religious symbols of pagan worship were placed in and around it. If you can stomach it, go see for yourself on Linder's ark of hope website.[14] With that said, here are some of the things that the Earth Charter itself says:

"7. Adopt patterns of production, consumption, and reproduction that safe-guard Earth's regenerative capacities, human rights, and community well-being.

d. Internalize the full environmental and social costs of goods and services in the selling price, and enable consumers to identify products that meet the highest social and environmental standards.

e. Ensure universal access to health care that fosters reproductive health and responsible reproduction.

f. Adopt lifestyles that emphasize the quality of life and material suffi-ciency in a finite world."[15]

We once again see this extremely strong emphasis on human reproduction and making sure that it is "responsible." Of course, by now you understand what they *really* mean by these statements. We also see a more detailed explanation of what UNEP told us under *Principle III. Social and Economic Justice:*

"a. Eliminate discrimination in all its forms, such as that based on race, color, sex, sexual orientation, religion, language, and national, ethnic or social origin."[16]

We again see this language that we are to *eliminate* unwanted behaviors. Not only do these things have absolutely nothing to do with the environment, but they are 100% anti-Bible. The LGBT stance within the Earth Charter is what makes it inherently hostile to all followers of the Bible. There are more things that could be discussed concerning the Earth Charter and the blasphemous ark of hope in which it has been placed. The main idea is that the elites are worshiping this Earth Charter using magic and rituals. They are mocking the Ten Commandments. They are mocking the Ark of the Covenant of the Most High Elohim. All of these things are what Daniel saw in his vision that amazed him. What I will demonstrate mathematically in just a moment is that the start of UNEP in 1972 is in fact *the covenant made with many* that lasted from 1972 to 2020. This was a 49-year period exactly as described by Daniel; but first, we need to fully understand the year 2020.

$$\text{וַחֲצִי הַשָּׁבוּעַ יַשְׁבִּית זֶבַח וּמִנְחָה}$$

Figure 5.4: "And in the midst of the week, he shall cause to cease the sacrifice and the oblation." This phrase can be transliterated as "vakhatsi ha-shabua yashbit zebakh uminkha".

BUT IN THE MIDDLE OF THE WEEK, AN END TO SACRIFICE AND OFFERING

Let's examine the Hebrew words once again with special attention to the BLB entries. The word "middle" ("chaytsi", Strong's H2677) means half, middle, midnight, or in the midst of. The root word for "cease" ("shabbat", Strong's H7673) means to rest, still, take away, suffer to be lacking, put away, exterminate, cause to destroy, cause to fail, and it also means "sabbath" day.[17] The word "sacrifice" ("zebakh", Strong's H2077) has a wide range of uses including sacrifices of righteousness, sacrifices of strife, sacrifices to dead things, the covenant sacrifice, the passover, annual sacrifice, or thank offering.[18] The word "offering" ("minkhah", Strong's H4503) could be used to mean gift, tribute, present, oblation, sacrifice, grain offering, or meat offering.[19]

People use these two words—sacrifice and offering—to make the strong case that a physical temple must be built in Jerusalem in order for the 70th week of this prophecy to ever take place. This common misconception happens because people think that the pre-tribulation rapture of the church must take place before the 70th week ever begins, or they think that the antichrist figure is supposed to show up first and sacrifice a pig on the altar of a rebuilt Jewish temple. You should know better than that by now. We have to consider all possibilities. We have to consider every aspect of what these words are truly talking about because it has already taken place in the Gregorian year 2020, which is the exact middle of this final 49-year period of history as depicted in Figure 5.1.

Sadly, people can make the Bible say whatever they want. To be thoroughly transparent, this secret of Daniel's prophecy was incredibly hard for me to understand. Since we already know the timeline and know that the entire 120 shanah and 70 shabua of Daniel fit so perfectly into this picture, we only need to figure out the meaning of what Daniel wrote here. Just take a look at all of the different sacrifices and offerings spoken about in the Bible, and you will begin to realize just how intentional Daniel's word choices are in these lines of the prophecy.

Name of Offering	(Strong's Number) Definition
freewill offering	(H5071) voluntary, of one's own free-will
sin offering	(H2403) offering for purification from sins
trespass offering	(H817) guilt, trespass, at-fault offering
burnt offering	(H5930) a thoroughly whole burnt offering
drink offering	(H5262) something poured out as an offering
wave offering	(H8573) literally swinging, waving in the air
heave offering	(H8641) contribution of grain, money, etc.
meat offering	(H4503) gift, tribute, present, oblation, grain or meat
peace offering	(H8002) (H2077) sacrifice for alliance / friendship
sacrifice of thanksgiving	(H2077) (H8426) confession, praise, thanks, songs
fire offering	(H801) offering made by fire, fire offering

Figure 5.5: Types of Offerings in the Bible

Remember one of our fundamental rules for understanding this prophecy: knowing the subject. Who is the subject of this prophecy? It is Daniel's people and his holy city, Jerusalem, of course. That being said, here is the key verse that must be heavily considered:

"And to his son I will give one tribe, that My servant David may always have a lamp before Me in Jerusalem, the city which I have chosen for Myself, to put My name there."
(1Kings 11:36)

We know for a fact that Elohim chose Jerusalem as the place to put His name. With that piece of information, we can now fully understand what the Torah already told us in Exodus 34:18,22,23:

18 "The Feast of Unleavened Bread you shall keep. Seven days you shall eat unleavened bread, as I commanded you, in the appointed time of the month of Abib; for in the month of Abib you came out from Egypt.
22 "And you shall observe the Feast of Weeks, of the firstfruits of wheat harvest, and the Feast of Ingathering at the year's end.
23 "Three times in the year all your men shall appear before the Lord, the LORD God of Israel."

The three times every single year when all men were supposed to appear in Jerusalem are Unleavened Bread, the Feast of Weeks (Pentecost), and the Feast of Ingathering during the First Day of Sukkot. This command is again repeated in Deuteronomy 16:16,17:

16 "Three times a year all your males shall appear before the LORD your God in the place which He chooses: at the Feast of Unleavened Bread, at the Feast of Weeks, and at the Feast of Tabernacles; and they shall not appear before the LORD empty-handed.
17 "Every man *shall give* as he is able, according to the blessing of the LORD your God which He has given you."

Do you see the connection yet? Three times a year, all males are supposed to make a pilgrimage to Jerusalem to observe these three holy days. Three times a year, all males are required to present a *gift offering,* according to their ability to do so. Think about it carefully. Think about *why* Daniel chose the Hebrew words that he did to describe COVID-19 and a worldwide pandemic. Although the "Three Pilgrimage Festivals" (as they are commonly referred to) are no longer regarded as obligated by the majority of Jews, Messianics, and followers of the God of the Bible worldwide, this gross negligence does not mean that the commandment has ceased to exist, and I will make the case that this is one of those commandments that is partially dormant until the return of Yeshua to establish His kingdom. When He returns, it will still be absolutely commanded for God's people to appear in Jerusalem three times a year. Going back to the first century, this is exactly what we read about in Acts 2:5,9-11 during the Feast of Pentecost and the tongues of fire:

5 "And there were dwelling in Jerusalem Jews, devout men, from every nation under heaven."
9 "Parthians and Medes and Elamites, those dwelling in Mesopotamia, Judea and Cappadocia, Pontus and Asia,
10 "Phrygia and Pamphylia, Egypt and the parts of Libya adjoining Cyrene, visitors from Rome, both Jews and proselytes,
11 "Cretans and Arabs—we hear them speaking in our own tongues the wonderful works of God."

Think about the profound truth of the Scriptures. Why are they described as *devout men?* What exactly makes them so dedicated and determined to be physically present in Jerusalem?
That's the secret.

Even after the Yeshua the Messiah rose from the dead, all of these people still understood, obeyed, and kept the commandment from the Torah that required them to meet in Jerusalem *three times a year.* These men didn't care how much travel they had to do by camel and donkey to get there. They weren't bothered by jobs or responsibilities that would hinder them from extended travel. They set aside enough money each year in order to make the trip. They were absolutely determined. In this case, it was the feast of Shavuot (Pentecost), but we can assume these devout people regularly observed the other two annual feasts as well.

Many teach that Yeshua abolished, did away with, nullified, destroyed, or changed His mind about His own Torah. This is a completely false, fake teaching. *It's simply not true.* Sadly, this false teaching and mindset is exactly why so many Bible teachers and pastors are hopelessly lost and confused when trying to explain end times events. Only the *devout* men that took the Word of God seriously were the first recipients of the Holy Spirit in the form of tongues of fire. Still today, only the devout men and women that respect God's Torah and do their best to honor His commandments are the recipients of the profound blessings of *true freedom and fullness* that are only obtained from a complete understanding of Scripture. Only the devout people of today can understand how Daniel chose to seal up the words of this prophecy so that only God's intended recipients would receive the message.

Indeed, the secret of this prophecy and the year 2020 has now been revealed to you!

Daniel used the word "zebakh" because it can be used to specifically refer to all the *annual sacrifices* mentioned in Exo. 34 and Deut. 16 where every male is required to appear in Jerusalem every year. Daniel used the word "minkhah" because it describes the *gift offering* that is required to be presented in Jerusalem three times a year.

Do you understand what Daniel 9:27a truly means now?

Everyone in the entire world knew that Covid-19 was a significant event. Everyone knew that something fundamentally changed in the world. But did you realize *why* it was so significant from a biblical perspective? The bottom line is this: The ability to freely travel to Jerusalem for the Three Feasts was "caused to fail" which is what the word "shabbat" means within the exact context of Daniel's Hebrew word choices. The "nagid" (prince/commander) of the WEF and his people shut down economies, businesses, airlines, governmental activities, and life as usual. During 2020-21, I personally knew people living in Israel that could not travel a certain distance from the front door of their homes except for buying groceries and for so-called "essential" travel.

Now, here's where the truth of the Scriptures comes to life even more and becomes even more powerful. Do you remember exactly *when* the World Health Organization declared COVID-19 to be a global pandemic? Well first, what is a pandemic, anyways? Unlike an outbreak or an epidemic of contagious disease, a pandemic is the most severe spreading of illness and disease beyond a local area that spreads across entire countries and continents.[20] The WHO made their declaration of a global pandemic exactly on March 11, 2020. The Director-General, Dr. Tedros Adhanom Ghebreyesus, said this in his official statement:

> "There are now more than 118,000 cases in 114 countries, and 4,291 people have lost their lives. ...WHO has been assessing this outbreak around the clock and we are deeply concerned both by the alarming levels of spread and severity, and by the alarming levels of inaction. We have therefore made the assessment that COVID-19 can be characterized as a pandemic. ...WHO's mandate is public health. But we're working with many partners across all sectors to mitigate the social and economic consequences of this pandemic."[21]

The word *mandate* is just a watered-down synonym for *edict, command, decree, or law.* Did you notice the key phrase? They are working with many *partners* to make sure that everything was coordinated exactly as battle planned. As I have already discussed, Schwab and the WEF were behind the whole pandemic; but it was God's hand that directed this history-changing event. Not only did the WHO make the public declaration of a pandemic on Wednesday March 11, 2020, but this was also *the exact day* that that Passover was observed that year based on the new moon for that cycle and also accurate reports from Rivkah Biderman and Joseph Dumond of the barley being indeed *abib* and ready for the presentation of the one omer for wave sheaf day on Sunday March 15th. My next figure shows you the breakdown for all of the Spring Holy Days for the year 2020. Because no new moon was sighted in the land of Israel on February 24, the next day became the first day of the month by default, as Devorah Gordon explained in her new moon observation report.[22] Remember, a Hebrew month cannot have more than 30 days. Also keep in mind that a Hebrew day is always from evening to evening, and each vertical line on my timeline represents the evening. In the case of the seven days of unleavened bread, the gaps in between the lines represent the daytime. For example, where you see the counting of the Feast of Weeks, the line is pointing to Saturday evening to begin the next Hebrew day and the counting of the seven sabbaths to Pentecost.

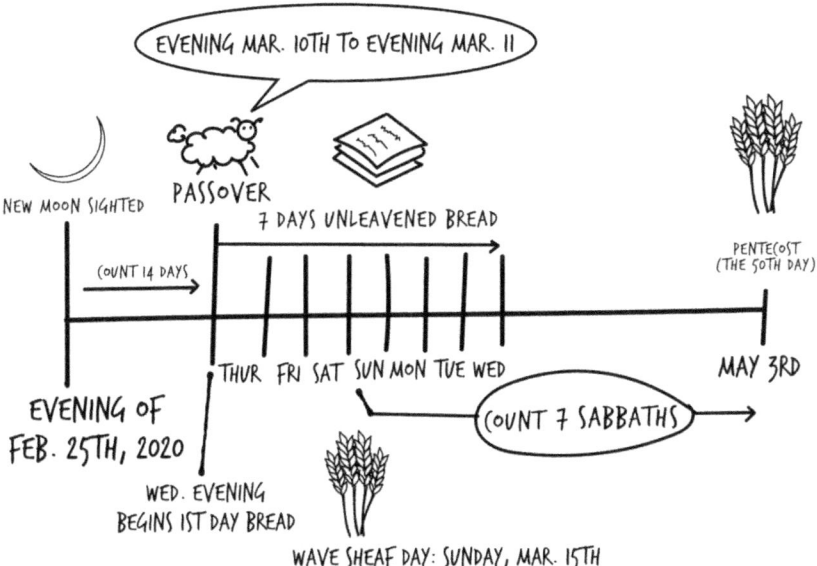

Figure 5.6: Covid-19 and the Middle of the Week.

The Most High has not done away with His Holy Days. They are not "Jewish" as people commonly refer to them. They are not for specific people groups only. Anyone who follows the God of the Bible must uphold His marriage covenant with His people. The biggest and most important events in human history always have and always will continue to occur during His appointed times. These Holy Days are the Law of Earth.

Because of this one declaration by the WHO that Elohim Himself orchestrated, the entire world's borders were shut down, some for much longer periods than others. Canada, for example, had refused to let their people go in and out of the country freely without the experimental vaccines for quite some time even after the pandemic was waning. Travel became severely limited beginning with 2020 and continuing well afterwards. The most important thing you must be aware of is that traveling to Jerusalem to observe the Feast of Unleavened Bread and the other two Feasts of the holy calendar of God was caused to fail after this declaration, and Daniel obediently sealed up the prophecy using this description. We will discuss more nuances of correctly determining the Holy Days in later chapters.

REVISITING THE COVENANT WITH MANY

Now that we fully understand the role of Covid-19 in prophecy, we can also understand exactly when the *covenant made with many* came to an end. The UNEP religious covenant began in the week of June 5th, 1972. Generally speaking, a Hebrew year has 360 days in it rather than the 365 days of the Gregorian solar calendar (or 366 in a leap year). We briefly discussed this math concept when we talked about the first 343 years of Daniel's prophecy from Moses at the burning bush to the birth of David. Moreover, during the days of the flood and the months of rain, Noah could not literally see the crescent new moon to perfectly keep track of time during his days on the ark. If you examine Genesis 7, you will find that he kept track of time by counting the days and assuming 30-day months. Similarly, we do not have accurate records of all the Holy Days and all 12-month years alongside the occasionally intercalated 13-month years to perfectly examine the 49-year period of the UNEP covenant. Let's estimate using 30-day months and see what we find. With this understanding, we can do the following:

49 years x 360 days/per year = 17,640 days

If we assume that UNEP began exactly on June 5th, 1972, we simply add these 17,640 days using some sort of online date calculator tool. You will arrive at the date of September 21, 2020.

We know exactly what we are looking for, and we know who the key players are, which makes this 49-year period really straightforward to understand. In the original analysis presented in the first edition of this book, I stated that it was necessary to follow the WHO official timeline for the pandemic, since this arm of the UN was used heavily during the year 2020. Though this information is technically correct, there is a more refined way of looking at what happened on September 21, 2020 that I will explain once I first recap my findings from the original analysis.

It was on this date of September 21 that the interactive timeline on the WHO website cited a press release entitled "Boost for global response to COVID-19 as economies worldwide formally sign up to COVAX facility."[23,24] Therefore, I concluded that a new covenant with many began that superseded and nullified the original UNEP covenant with many. I called it the COVAX covenant wherein exactly on September 21, there were 156 countries (economies) representing two thirds of the world's population that signed formal agreements with COVAX for vaccine development.[25] The press release by Bill Gates and Gavi-backed COVAX admits that the entire success of the vaccine rollout hinged on their ability to get funding and cooperation from many countries. Because of this COVAX covenant, they could now reach their goal of 2 billion doses by the end of 2021. Just about a month later on October 19, 2020, 184 countries had joined COVAX with even more eventually participating.[26] Since the Hebrew word for *covenant* could also be translated as an *alliance,* it is fitting that this is how Gavi refers to itself. These COVAX vaccines were completely experimental in nature and did not go through the proper multi-year clinical trials and scientific scrutiny that vaccines normally go through before they are released to the public. This new vaccine-related covenant in 2020 therefore broke the original covenant that was made in 1972 and the Earth Charter. Under the heading *"Principle IV. Democracy, Nonviolence, and Peace"* the document states the following:

> "13. Strengthen democratic institutions at all levels, and provide transparency and accountability in governance, inclusive participation in decision making, and access to justice.
>
> a. Uphold the right of everyone to receive clear and timely information on environmental matters and all development plans and activities which are likely to affect them or in which they have an interest.
>
> b. Support local, regional and global civil society, and promote the meaningful participation of all interested individuals and organizations in decision making.
>
> c. Protect the rights to freedom of opinion, expression, peaceful assembly, association, and dissent."[27]

Paying close attention to letter "c." because no one ever voted for their government to spend billions and billions of dollars on vaccine manufacturing. There was no "transparency" or "accountability" like the original covenant stated above. The new COVAX alliance superseded and became more important than the original UNEP covenant and all of its bylaws and ordinances as found in the Earth Charter.

Now let's look at another place in the Earth Charter that gives us more clarity on exactly why the original UNEP covenant was diminished on Sept. 21, 2020. Under the heading *"Principle I. Respect and Care for the Community of Life,"* the document says:

> "3. Build democratic societies that are just, participatory, sustainable, and peaceful.
>
> a. Ensure that communities at all levels guarantee human rights and fundamental freedoms and provide everyone an opportunity to realize his or her full potential.

b. Promote social and economic justice, enabling all to achieve a secure and meaningful livelihood that is ecologically responsible."[28]

Once the vaccines were made available, many lost their jobs because they did not have the ability to choose to say *no*. The right of participatory dissent and the basic human right of making personal medical decisions was lost because of the so-called pandemic. This was absolutely unprecedented in history. Even under the old covenant made with many, UNEP, people still had the ability to make personal health choices. Under this new paradigm shift, those with opinions that challenged, questioned, or even made simple evidence-based conclusions that differed from the mainstream media and governmental narratives were silenced and oppressed. Many were monetarily punished. All of these actions nullified and destroyed the 1972 covenant that was supposed to guarantee (at least, in writing) freedom of opinion and many other rights and freedoms.

Now, as I said, there is a more refined way of examining the date of September 21, 2020 because it was on this date that the UN itself declared the beginning of a new covenant of which the COVAX covenant was only a contributing part of. This aforementioned date marked the 75th anniversary of the United Nations. As stated in Resolution 75/1, the UN announced that they were strengthening the UN system specifically with the implementation of a prior Resolution 70/1 from September 25, 2015.[29] This older Resolution is none other than *The 2030 Agenda for Sustainable Development*, which they then declared exactly on September 21, 2020 to be "our road map and its implementation a necessity for our survival."[30] Though this agenda was already adopted back in 2015, it suddenly became the primary and most important agenda of the UN. They went on to say that the next ten years from 2020 to 2030 would be the most critical years for humanity in which the world would need to "build back better" in the aftermath of the Covid-19 pandemic. Of course, this was the exact same statement that was echoed by Klaus Schwab and nearly every Western politician after 2020, including Justin Trudeau and Joe Biden. The UN further stated that they are determined to implement the 2030 Agenda in full and on time. This strengthening of the UN system under Agenda 2030 superseded the old covenant of UNEP that had begun in 1972.

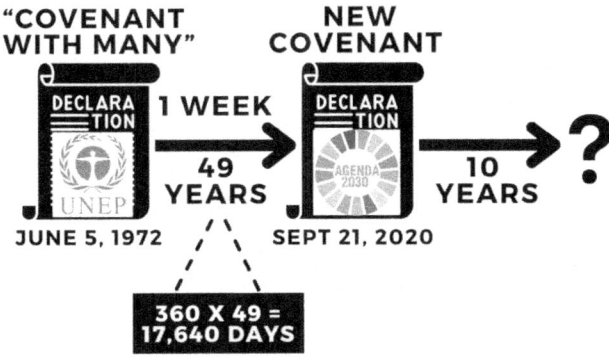

Figure 5.7: September 21, 2020 and the New Covenant: Agenda 2030.

Recall that the very first Hebrew word of Dan. 9:27 is "gabar" which means to strengthen (Strong's H1396). We are able to firmly conclude that the adoption of Agenda 2030 put an end to the original covenant with many due to the strengthening and confirming declaration associated with September 21, 2020. In other words, just as the original covenant of 1972 began with a "gabar," the new covenant of 2020 began with a "gabar," or confirmation.

This series of events begs the question: What exactly *is* Agenda 2030? As is the case with most UN documents, the Agenda 2030 whitepaper uses vague and dry legal language that the average person would not be able to properly interpret beyond the superficial mask of benevolence. The ideas surrounding the 17 Sustainable Development Goals (SDGs) are presented in various works explaining this agenda, often with an accompanying rainbow wheel symbol, claiming that these SDGs are necessary for the planet's freedom, peace, and prosperity. The investigative journalists at Muckraker have done an excellent job covering all of the real-world developments that this new agenda is directly responsible for. In a Muckraker article entitled "The 2030 Mass Migration Agenda", Thomas Hicks outlines the following:

> "Agenda 2030 outlines a blueprint for world socialism, stating that we are embarking on a 'collective journey.' What is largely undiscussed is the agenda's plan for mass migration. The Agenda 2030 white paper only mentions migration in regard to ensuring 'safe, orderly, and regular migration involving full respect for human rights and the humane treatment of migrants.' However, in a report by the IOM (International Organization of Migration) titled 'Migration and the 2030 Agenda', an intentional mass migration plan is presented. The 156-page paper almost immediately states 'The 2030 Agenda recognizes migration as a core development consideration, which marks the first time

migration is integrated explicitly into the global development agenda' … The collapse of the US southern border is part of a deliberate and carefully executed plan to usher in Agenda 2030. The United States is the largest financial contributor to the United Nations. Despite this, it is clear that the UN has become a creature that not even its master can control, with an agenda to change the United States of America as we know it."[31]

Of course, the unprecedented devastation of mass illegal migration is not limited to the US alone. The UK and Europe have also experienced massive inflows of migrants. In 2022, just seven years after Agenda 2030 was first adopted and two years after its strengthening, "official" numbers revealed that 23.8 million non-citizens were living in the EU, with the highest concentrations in Italy, France, Sweden, Germany and the UK.[32] Due to the improper vetting of these migrants, the US along with these aforementioned countries have seen more organized crime,[33] property theft, gang violence, and incidents of rape[34] making the news headlines regularly. In North America, a recent investigative report revealed that the Chinese Communist Party has been working with Canadian banks in Toronto together with the Mexican cartels to facilitate global money laundering and drug trafficking operations that are being used against Western nations where, for example, fentanyl has been claiming the lives of tens of thousands annually.[35] The mainstream media has been systematically downplaying and hiding these facts from the general public, which is also a major part of how the UN has operated historically. In order for this system of socialist world government to succeed, it must redistribute the resources of the wealthy Western nations into the hands of foreigners and invaders. Again, we see that the anointed are slowly being cut off, and they will ultimately have nothing at some point during the 70th week of Daniel. These events associated with *the covenant with many* provide further evidence that the West is where the lost tribes of Israel—the anointed descendants of the Mount Sinai covenant—are located today. Agenda 2030 also ties directly into the playing out of the "locusts" prophecy of Revelation 9. This is a prophecy we will need to explore later.

THE MYSTERY DANIEL 9:27A REVEALED

We have now successfully divided the Word of God and understood the secrets of Daniel's prophecy inside the first half of this verse. Let's just take a moment to recap some ideas.

First, UNEP was the mysterious covenant with many for 49 years. Of course, the environmental religion of UNEP is still alive and well. Going "green" and many other narratives are still very much a part of western society because they are still being pushed on the people through big tech, big government, and multinational corporations currently under WEF leadership. However, when Sept. 21, 2020 came around—and indeed, the pandemic declaration of March 11, 2020 before that—there was a paradigm shift. Not only was the covenant of UNEP shoved aside in the false name of health, public safety, and disease prevention, but the 17 Sustainable Development Goals became the primary agenda on this 75th anniversary meeting of the UN. The odds of our 49-year count of one shabua from 1972 to 2020 also coinciding with such a pivotal event are mathematically impossible to be mere coincidence. Agenda 2030 and its underlying initiatives such as the COVAX vaccine rollout became the new covenant with many, and through its successful conditioning of the general population, it will ultimately lead to widespread acceptance of the final covenant with death and the mark of the beast on the right hand or forehead. The only outcome that remains unclear is whether or not the WEF will remain the major power on the world stage or if they will be superseded by a Mahdi from the Middle East. Perhaps these two will somehow merge, borrowing the technological sophistication of the WEF while relying on Islam's sword to enforce said technologies using a religious motive. The answer will be revealed soon. For now, we can see that Daniel's 70 weeks prophecy has had multiple major players in it. It is not simply talking about one prince or one antichrist only from start to finish. There are contributing groups and elitist forces that have made the fulfillment of this ancient prophecy possible. That is why I stated at the beginning of this chapter that the translators' use of the word "he" in establishing a single person, or antichrist, as being solely responsible for the *covenant with many* is nonsense.

The majority of mainstream Christian doctrines have been continuously littered with the idea that an antichrist figure will walk into a newly-built Jewish temple, declare himself to be God, and then initiate a 7-year peace covenant with many. They go on to say that this 7-year covenant is the same thing as the 70th week of Daniel, and the abomination of desolation is surely going to be an event where this same antichrist will be sacrificing perhaps a pig on the altar of the Jewish temple at exactly three and a half years into this 7-year covenant. Most Christians assert that this event will then begin the Great Tribulation that will last another three and a half years to then finish the 70th week of Daniel.

I realize you probably had a hard time keeping yourself from cracking a big smile as I recounted these foolish ideas, provided of course that you have acknowledged all the conclusive evidence I have presented so far. By now, you understand all of those cherished Christian doctrines to be completely and utterly false. Concerning the abomination of desolation, there is tremendous clarity available right inside the pages of Scripture that will leave you awestruck. You will be utterly amazed at why people fail to readily accept these facts to begin with. The problem is that the mass-indoctrination spell any given person has been put under must be first recognized and only then overcome. If you have made it this far in the book, you are well on your way to completely breaking loose of the death grip of cold and outdated end-times teachings.

Moving on to Daniel 9:27b, we will uncover the most important and time-sensitive message out of everything that I have shown you so far because it tells us to expect something huge to take place in the Middle East very soon after the year 2023.

Brace yourself.

Chapter 6
September 22, 2023 - The Nuclear Abominations of Desolation

It's now time to completely understand the abomination of desolation spoken of by Daniel the prophet and further explained by Yeshua in the Gospels. Before moving forward, I want to thank you and congratulate you for making it this far! You have undoubtedly felt the leading of the Holy Spirit. Elohim has given you a genuine desire to know and understand the secrets of the Bible. You were hungry and thirsty for righteousness, and you have been filled, just as Yeshua promised (Mat. 5:6). Only one large secret remains to be understood in Daniel. This is what he wrote for us in Daniel 9:27b:

"…And on the wing of abominations shall be one who makes desolate,
Even until the consummation, which is determined,
Is poured out on the desolate."

It is with great responsibility on my shoulders and a great sense of urgency that I now unpack these words with you. The understanding you are about to gain may affect your decision making going into the future, and it should. Let the Holy Spirit lead you into all truth, and let Him direct your steps. Here is what Proverbs 27:12 has to say:

"A prudent *man* foresees evil *and* hides himself;
The simple pass on *and* are punished."

We see this pattern throughout the Scriptures from Genesis to Revelation. Lot was told to physically leave Sodom and Gomorrah before it was destroyed. Likewise, an angel has proclaimed to those of us living in the last days to come out of Babylon, "…Lest you share in her sins, and lest you receive of her plagues" (Rev. 18:4). Be wise. Be prudent. Time is truly of the essence, and the sooner you understand the words of Yeshua concerning the abomination of desolation, the sooner you can become fully spiritually prepared for what the world will be facing.

DIVISIONS OF THE BOOK OF DANIEL

I'm not going to be like the majority of Bible teachers that will spend lots of time on history lessons about the statue in Daniel chapter 2 or various nuances inside the book of Daniel. We are short on time. There are only a few truths that are truly pressing at this point in history, and we are going to focus on them without getting distracted. The first thing we will do is pause and look at an overview of the Book of Daniel. This is necessary for a few reasons. The first thing we need to do is understand the context of the entire book so that we can recognize where future events fit into the puzzle.

Division	Theme	Language
Chapters 1-6	Life of Daniel (Prophetic Statue Dream Ch. 2)	Mixed
Chapter 7	Four Huge Beasts from the Sea	Aramaic
Chapter 8	The Ram, The Male Goat, and The Horn	Hebrew
Chapter 9	The 70 Shabua	Hebrew
Chapter 10	Man Dressed in Linen with a Belt of Fine Gold	Hebrew
Chapter 11	Kings of the North and South	Hebrew
Chapter 12	Sealed Until The Time of the End	Hebrew

Figure 6.1: The Major Themes of Daniel.

Some of the book of Daniel is written in Aramaic, which was the most widely spoken language of the world during the days of Daniel. For example, chapter 4 of Daniel is written in Aramaic and includes King Nebuchadnez-zar's direct words and his first-person account of his God-given madness and subsequent restoration to kingship. The chapters that we will be dissecting in order to understand Dan. 9:27b were all originally written in Hebrew.

With regards to Daniel chapter 8, I am going to spend a little more time explaining how Klaus Schwab and the year 2020 once again fit into the puzzle. Because we now know what Dan. 9:24-27a is saying, we can truly understand other sections of Daniel like this one that were also sealed until the time of the end.

When I first published this information inside the Overcome Babylon podcast, I made the mistake of labeling Schwab as the little horn speaking pompous words in Daniel chapter 7. However, I now understand this to be a different person than Schwab since this particular chapter makes no mention of the abomination of desolation *and* it was also written in the different language of Aramaic rather than Hebrew. I believe this distinction was made on purpose through inspiration of the Holy Spirit to let us know that Schwab is different from the very last one-world leader that assumes power immediately after him. As mentioned in Chapter 4, this very final leader will work with all the power of satan and with false miracles and wonders to deceive the nations. I do not believe Schwab will be this person.

THE ABOMINATION OF DESOLATION IN HEBREW AND GREEK

The first time I deeply studied through this prophecy I was blown away by how many times the abomination of desolation is mentioned in both the Old and New Testaments. When the Holy Spirit says something once, we better listen. When He repeats something six complete times, then obviously it's to be taken extremely seriously. The next figure shows an overview of all the places this prophecy is mentioned.

In The Old Testament	In The New Testament
"And on the wing of abominations shall be one who makes desolate…" - Dan. 9:27	"Therefore when you see the *'abomination of desolation,'* spoken of by Daniel the prophet, standing in the holy place…" Mat. 24:15
"And forces shall be mustered by him, and they shall defile the sanctuary fortress; then they shall take away the daily *sacrifices,* and place *there* the abomination of desolation." - Dan. 11:31	"So when you see the *'abomination of desolation,'* spoken of by Daniel the prophet, standing where it ought not…" - Mark 13:14
"And from the time *that* the daily *sacrifice* is taken away, and the abomination of desolation is set up, *there shall be* one thousand two hundred and ninety days. - Dan. 12:11	"But when you see Jerusalem surrounded by armies, then know that its desolation is near." - Luke 21:20

Figure 6.2: The Abomination of Desolation Prophecy.

When it comes to last days prophecies, the abomination of desolation is mentioned by name more than any other single event, and in my opinion it is second only to the Greater Exodus of all 13 Tribes of Israel and also the Day of the LORD. It is discussed in Dan. 9:27, 11:31, and 12:11 along with Mat. 24:15, Mark 13:14, and Luke 21:20. Let me emphasize something before moving forward. Chapters 9, 11 & 12 of Daniel all have future prophetic events that have not yet taken place, and Yeshua was quoting these chapters when He spoke to us in the Gospels. Please let these Hebrew Scriptures define your understanding of this topic and not the New Testament Greek. Stick to the law of first mention, and all things will become crystal clear, just as Yeshua intended them to be. Also keep in mind that these prophecies, just like the 70 shabua prophecy, were sealed until the last days. The translators of English Bibles have inserted a lot of filler words that have no underlying Hebrew letters connected to them. These filler words like "some" and "sacrifices" can usually be easily identified in your Bible because they are italicized to distinguish them as filler words with the intention of making the text easier to read. However, when we are dissecting lines of Hebrew prophecy that were deliberately written in code, we have to throw out these English words and make a strong effort to ignore the bias of the translators.

In the original edition of this book first published on May 8, 2023, I had erroneously included Daniel 8:13 in the chart above, which states: "How long *will* the vision be *concerning* the daily *sacrifices* and the transgression of desolation...". Because of an event that occurred on May 5, 2023 just three days before the release of the first edition of this book, we now know what Daniel 8 and the vision of the evenings and mornings is truly speaking about. I had missed this event's significance. The English language used here speaking of the "transgression of desolation" had tricked my mind into associating this passage as speaking of the "abomination of desolation." My original analysis was mostly accurate, as you will see, but we now have a much more refined understanding of not only Daniel 8:13 but chapter eight as a whole, which was one of the main reasons why it became necessary for me to produce this updated edition. Before digging into the first mention of the abomination of desolation in Daniel 9:27b, let's first discuss what the "transgression of desolation" prophecy *really* is and why it is different from the abomination of desolation.

DANIEL CHAPTER 8

The fundamental idea for understanding this entire chapter is found in this verse:

"And the vision of the evenings and mornings
Which was told is true;
Therefore seal up the vision,
For it refers to many days *in the future.*"
(Dan. 8:26)

We are once again told that Daniel was commanded to seal up the words of this prophecy by purposely writing them down in a coded way. He wrote these words so that they would not be easily understood. Just like the 70 weeks vision, this prophecy is not meant to be merely read but studied.

The little horn is the central focus of Daniel chapter 8, and it was prophesied that this power would be responsible for the destruction of many people. But what is the true identity of this little horn?

Let me bring you up to speed. The first verses of Daniel 8 record a vision that Daniel had about two different geopolitical powers—a Persian Ram from the East and a Greek Goat from the West—that were attacking one another, with the Goat prevailing. An angelic messenger by the name of Gabriel speaks these words to Daniel after he had the vision, and he explains the meaning:

"19...'Behold, I am going to inform you about what will happen later in the time of wrath, for the vision pertains to the appointed time of the end.
20 The ram that you saw with the two horns stands for the kings of Media and Persia.
21 The buck, the male goat, is the king of Greece; and the large horn between his eyes is the first king.
22 The four horns that replaced the one that was broken represent four kingdoms that will arise from this nation, though not with its power.
23 Now toward the end of their reign, when the measure of transgression is completed, a stern-faced king, a master of intrigue, will arise."
(Dan. 8:19-23 TLV)

We know that we are in the appointed time of the end, so it is high time to understand the words of this prophecy. The Ram with two horns is the kingdom of the Medes and the Persians, which is the same silver empire of Daniel's statue (Dan. 2). The one-horned Male Goat is Alexander the Great that conquered the Medes and the Persians from the West. He was the first ruler of Greece after he finished conquering the world (1Maccabees 1:1), and he is represented as the bronze empire of Daniel's statue (Dan. 2). After becoming ill, Alexander the Great died after reigning only 12 years, and his kingdom was divided amongst his four generals, which are represented as the four horns of the Male Goat. Feel free to research these things as needed while paying close attention to Gabriel's interpretation. The main idea is that there is a power (goat) from the West that is the central focus of this Daniel 8 prophecy and of specific events during the 70th week of Daniel. As I will show you, the little horn described in Dan. 8:23 has already appeared on the scene during these very last days we are living through, and he is from the West as opposed to being from the East (Persia or Iran).

Our focus begins with the "little horn" because it is responsible for the prophecy of the evenings and mornings described in this same chapter. Here is what Daniel recorded for us:

"And out of one of them came a little horn which grew exceedingly great toward the south, toward the east, and toward the Glorious *Land.*"
(Dan. 8:9 NKJV)

We are now at the exact moment in history when the little horn of the Male Goat has risen up and fulfilled the "transgression of desolation" (Dan. 8:13). Keep in mind that it is specifically because of transgression—open rebellion against the God of the Bible and His Torah—that all these things have taken place. Look at what Dan. 8:23 says about this mysterious little horn (compare this NKJV translation to the TLV quoted earlier):

"And in the latter time of their kingdom,
When the transgressors have reached their fullness,
A king shall arise,
Having fierce features,
Who understands sinister schemes."

This little horn is the World Economic Forum, and more specifically, Klaus Schwab. The little horn of the male goat began its authority as being little and insignificant, but it then grew to become exceedingly great throughout the world. Make no mistake about it. Daniel was describing Schwab, who was insignificant until 2020; and after the pandemic, he truly became great. Notice that these events are during the "latter time" of the kingdom of the West. This language further adds validity to the analysis presented in Chapter 4, where Islam and the East will rise up and prevail as the head of the next world order. This outcome will become more apparent after we discuss the abomination of desolation later in this chapter.

I have already described the sinister schemes of the WEF, but I now want to point your attention to the symbolism that Klaus Schwab uses to identify himself and his people. The World Economic Forum 2022 annual meeting opened the eyes of many people to the possibility of Schwab playing a biblical end times role and further confirmed what I have already been showing you from Daniel.

Based on charges of simply appearing suspicious, journalist Jack Posobiec was detained by police for covering the secret world government meeting in May 2022 in Davos, Switzerland. Someone with a smartphone recorded this encounter with police, and the video clip and interaction went viral on social media. The problem is that it wasn't just ordinary police that harassed Posobiec. It was World Economic Forum police wielding sub-machine guns and wearing identification patches on their arms that actually depicted a one-horned male goat. Here's what journalist Adam Eliyahu Berkowitz had to say about the symbolism seen during Posobiec's arrest:

> "The World Economic Forum Police patch on the officer's uniform features what appears to be a side view of two goats, apparently in reference to the goat on the flag of the local Grisons, or Graubünden, Canton (governmental region) of Switzerland in which Davos is located, and a stylized rough crystal formation at the bottom. According to *Reuters,* the WEF security patch was patterned after the region's emblem, which is also featured on the patches of the local police force. However, all the local police patches have historically featured a ram with two horns. Throughout the years, the ram on the WEF patch is depicted in silhouette, showing a ram with only one horn."[1]

In other words, contrary to the disinformation of the mainstream media outlets like Reuters who were "fact-checking" and controlling the narrative on social media, the WEF patch is *not* the same thing as what is seen on local police patches. The one-horned goat is unique to the WEF's identity and absolutely connects to the prophecy of Daniel.

Figure 6.3: The Official Badge of World Economic Forum Police. This was the same badge seen by journalists in 2022, and it has consistently been the official police logo for decades.

Now look at what Dan. 8:24 says concerning Schwab:

"His power shall be mighty, but not by his own power;
He shall destroy fearfully,
And shall prosper and thrive;
He shall destroy the mighty, and *also* the holy people."

As I have already shown you, the WEF does not have its own standing army, physical borders, or any of the visible power structure that people normally think of when they imagine empires, kingdoms, and nations. Its power is not its own. Schwab's power comes from non-governmental partnerships, infiltrations into political systems, the military strength of other nations, and even the UN itself to carry out its orders including the Great Reset. Just look at how the little horn is further described in Dan. 8:25, and the connection to Schwab becomes obvious:

"Through his cunning
He shall cause deceit to prosper under his rule;
And he shall exalt *himself* in his heart.
He shall destroy many in *their* prosperity.
He shall even rise against the Prince of princes;
But he shall be broken without *human* means."

Deceit, lies, and propaganda have been the number one tools of Schwab. From carbon-neutrality (which is just another fancy word for *global taxation* to make the elite richer) to depopulation disguised as healthcare, everything that the little horn and his people promote is a never-ending web of evil agendas. The good news is that the WEF will come to an end, and I will show you a timeline later in this book that will shed light on when this might be taking place. It will happen very soon.

DANIEL 8:10 - STARS TO THE GROUND

We will unpack this prophecy in much the same way that we were able to understand all of Daniel chapter 9. First, let's dissect Dan. 8:10 which gives the following description of the little horn:

"And it grew up to the host of heaven; and it cast down *some* of the host and *some* of the stars to the ground, and trampled them."

וַתִּגְדַּל עַד־צְבָא הַשָּׁמָיִם וַתַּפֵּל אַרְצָה מִן־הַצָּבָא וּמִן־הַכּוֹכָבִים וַתִּרְמְסֵם

Figure 6.4: Daniel 8:10 in Hebrew

As I will prove to you, when Daniel writes "stars," he is actually referring to the scattered descendants of Abraham from all 12 Tribes of Israel in the last days. I'll give you my complete translation of Dan. 8:10 after breaking down this verse step by step.

Revisiting Daniel 8:25 for a moment, we are reminded that the little horn will come to an end according to the will of Elohim. Knowing this, when you look at Dan. 8:10 and see the word "host" (Strong's H6635) mentioned for the first time, it could also be translated as the *appointed time (of heaven),* which is a proper decoding of Daniel's words.

The next word translated as "and it cast down" (Strong's H5307) could also mean to fall down violently to death, to cause to fall, to overthrow, and these sorts of ideas. That's why I will choose the word *destroyed* in my translation because it summarizes this idea better.

Next we have "of the host" which is translated from two Hebrew words that can be transliterated as "min ha-tsaba" (Strong's H4480 and H6635). This exact phrase with the same vowel marks appears one other time in the Bible in 2Ch. 28:12 and is translated as "from the war" which is why I also will choose this phrase rather than "of the host."[2] These words *(from the war)* also match exactly what we see in the very last line of Dan. 9:26. Notice that both times the word "some" is translated there is no underlying Hebrew word. These are filler words that the translators threw into the English text simply because they wanted to.

This next phrase "of the stars" is where we get the true meaning of what Daniel was prophesying, and this phrase also happens to perfectly match what I have already shown you from the 70 shabua prophecy. Again we have two Hebrew words appearing together that can be transliterated as "oo-min ha-kokab-eem" (Strong's H4480 and H3556). We must rely heavily on the law of first mention in order to determine what Daniel was *really* saying, and when you apply this principle, you will find the word *stars* is used for the very first time in the creation week (Gen. 1:16); and interestingly enough, the second time it appears in the Bible it is used figuratively to describe the innumerable descendants of Abraham throughout the world (Gen. 15:5). This is why I will translate Daniel's words to say *the descendants of Abraham.*

Finally, here is how I would translate Dan. 8:10 in a more literal, word-for-word and decoded understanding that accurately ties into the 70 shabua prophecy:

"And it became great until the appointed time of Heaven; and it destroyed from the war the descendants of Abraham in the earth, and oppressed them."

The Holy Spirit breathed these words to us and is testifying that indeed the destruction of the seed of Abraham in the last days must take place because of the specific sin of rebellion against Yehovah and His Torah. The "war" spoken of here is perhaps not a reference to World War 3 as I had originally presumed but instead a war on the truth of the word of God, which is exactly what the Covid-19 agenda was.

DANIEL 8:11 - BY HIM THE DAILY WERE TAKEN AWAY

This verse helps us further understand all of the biblical events concerning the year 2020 and the middle of the 70th shabua. Dan. 8:11 says the following:

"He even exalted *himself* as high as the Prince of the host; and by him the daily *sacrifices* were taken away, and the place of His sanctuary was cast down."

וְעַד שַׂר־הַצָּבָא הִגְדִּיל וּמִמֶּנּוּ הרים הַתָּמִיד וְהֻשְׁלַךְ מְכוֹן מִקְדָּשׁוֹ

Figure 6.5: Daniel 8:11 in Hebrew

The first question we will seek to answer is, who are the *prince* and the *host* that the little horn has greatly exalted himself above? Let's begin by looking at the word "exalted" (Strong's H1431). When doing a word search for this Hebrew word with the exact vowel sounds, you will find that it is used a number of times in the context of betrayal like that of Judas Iscariot in Psalm 41:9. Other passages like 1Sa 20:41 speak of being comparatively greater while passages like Psalm 126:2,3 speak simply of Yehovah's great-ness. These usages of the word lead me to believe that this exaltation has to do with a subverting behavior or a great takeover of existing power.

Though the word *Prince* is capitalized, you know better by now that the Hebrew language only has uppercase letters. This word is Strong's H8269 and can be transliterated as "sar". It is used throughout the Bible to refer to a prince, general, ruler, leader, official, and other words associated with supreme leadership. This is not talking about Jesus. It turns out that there is yet another prince being spoken of within the context of the 70th shabua. We have already discussed Director-General of the WHO, Dr. Tedros Adhanom Ghebreyesus, who caused the pandemic of 2020 to be declared, but I believe this verse is talking about the highest ranking official in the entire United Nations organization—the Secretary-General António Guterres. It will be clear in a moment why I am arriving at this conclusion.

The word *host* (Strong's H6635) that we already explored in the very last verse as *appointed time* or *war* is being translated correctly as "host" or "armies". I believe this word is speaking of the United Nations and all of the host under its authority. I believe Daniel saw the UN gathered together in its headquarters during his vision. I believe he saw the Secretary-General being subverted and tricked into following the leadership of Schwab and the WEF. In other words, this prophecy is most likely speaking of Schwab exalting himself even as high as the Secretary-General of the UN.

The next word we are going to focus on heavily is "daily" which is the Hebrew word "tamid" (pronounced tah-meed'; Strong's H8548). The law of first mention verse is Exo. 25:30 where it speaks of the showbread being *tamid* in the tabernacle. Exo. 27:20 tells us that the lamps are to have enough oil to give light in a *tamid* manner. Exo. 30:8 tells us of incense being *tamid*. The more you look into this word the more you will find that it has to do with ceremonial tabernacle or temple worship. Of all the places where we receive clarity on what exactly the mystery of the *tamid* could be talking about, Revelation 5:8 provides the most clarity:

"Now when He had taken the scroll, the four living creatures and the twenty-four elders fell down before the Lamb, each having a harp, and golden bowls full of incense, which are the prayers of the saints."

By understanding Daniel's use of the word "tamid" and connecting it to Revelation, we can establish the perspective that the "prayers of the saints" are considered the "tamid" that is always present before Yehovah throughout all generations, and this concept is further repeated in Rev. 8:3,4. This is yet another clue in understanding Daniel 8:11:

3 Then another angel, having a golden censer, came and stood at the altar. He was given much incense, that he should offer it with the prayers of all the saints upon the golden altar which was before the throne.
4 And the smoke of the incense, with the prayers of the saints, ascended before God from the angel's hand.
(Rev. 8:3,4)

Just as literal incense was *tamid* in the times of the tabernacle and later the temples, the figurative incense before God's throne is now the prayers of the saints, and these are also *tamid,* or perpetual.

We now need to look at two more words and then Dan. 8:11 will become clear. The first word is "place" (mah-kone; Strong's H3559) and the second word is "sanctuary" (miqdash; Strong's H4720). A closer look at all possible meanings here reveals to us details surrounding the year 2020. *Place* has the meaning of dwelling, abode, or habitation. *Sanctuary* can refer to places of worship of all kinds such as pagan, Jewish, Islamic, or even legitimate places to worship Yehovah. Here is one example from Isaiah 16:12 speaking of Moab having a pagan "sanctuary" to pray within:

"And it shall come to pass,
When it is seen that Moab is weary on the high place,
That he will come to his sanctuary to pray;
But he will not prevail."

Once you realize that this *place of worship* goes beyond the traditionally accepted view that a physical temple must be built in Jerusalem in order for these events to take place, your mind can go to the correct place of understanding. With that said, here is how I would translate Dan. 8:11:

"He even exalted himself as high as the Secretary-General of the United Nations; and by him the prayers of the saints were cast down, and their places of worship were cast down."

As we have already discussed, the plan-demic of 2020 caused to fail (shabbat) the prayers, places of worship, and the annual pilgrimage sacrifices of God's people worldwide. Beginning on March 11, 2020, church doors were closed worldwide through "health mandates" that Schwab and his people forcibly established using the UN, the WHO, and various global agencies all the way down to the local government level.

Figure 6.6: The Sanctuary of Abraham's People Was Cast Down

The prayers of the descendants of Abraham were taken away, and they were not allowed to assemble freely and exercise freedom of religion. What had been *tamid,* or perpetual, had been completely disrupted by the events of 2020 and the pandemic declaration of the WHO.

DANIEL 8:12 - BECAUSE OF TRANSGRESSION

As I have already mentioned, these dreadful end times events have taken place because of national, moral rebellion against God and His instructions, which is different from unintentional sin. This is what Dan. 8:12 says:

"Because of transgression, an army was given over *to the horn* to oppose the daily *sacrifices;* and he cast truth down to the ground. He did *all this* and prospered."

וְצָבָא תִּנָּתֵן עַל־הַתָּמִיד בְּפָשַׁע וְתַשְׁלֵךְ אֱמֶת אַרְצָה וְעָשְׂתָה וְהִצְלִיחָה

Figure 6.7: Daniel 8:12 in Hebrew

Let's break this Scripture down. Just like in the previous verse, there are filler words added in italics such as "sacrifices" and "to the horn." The word "army" is actually the same word "host" that we have already looked at in the previous verses. Based on this understanding, we know that Daniel was describing the host of the UN power structure that was given to Schwab in order to carry out the Covid-19 agenda.

When this verse speaks of the truth being cast to the ground, you should automatically ask the question, "What is truth?". Of course, we understand the Bible to be absolute truth from cover to cover. But more specifically, Daniel was speaking of the foundational truth of the Torah being trampled on. Just look at what Exodus 15:26 says:

"…If you diligently heed the voice of the LORD your God and do what is right in His sight, give ear to His commandments and keep all His statutes, I will put none of the diseases on you which I have brought on the Egyptians. For I *am* the LORD who heals you."

This same thought of Yehovah healing His people is repeated in the prophecy speaking of Jesus' work of salvation on the cross in Isaiah 53:5. In the New Testament, it is further reinforced that healing miracles will always follow as visible signs amongst all true disciples of Jesus (Mar. 16:17). Because of the WHO and the plan-demic, the truth of God's promises were cast down to the ground. The principalities and powers of darkness successfully cast extreme doubt into people's minds as to whether the healing power of Almighty God is real or not. People were completely tricked into thinking that they needed a vaccine in order to be protected from disease. They were deceived into thinking that losing their jobs, forfeiting the ability to travel, and possibly hurting loved ones around them was of more importance than the truth of the Word of God. People believed that the lies of social distancing, wearing masks, and vaccinations were all righteousness and good works. Regarding disease prevention and quarantines, the Bible is not silent, but it is in fact lepers and diseased people that are to be sent away and isolated from the general population (Num. 5:2). Elohim's instructions tell us to quarantine the sick and *not* the healthy.

2300 DAYS: THE BIG PICTURE OF DANIEL 8

What I love about Daniel is that we are given so many numbers to work with. Unlike Revelation, this book is much simpler to understand and provides clear timelines for those of us living in the last days to use as navigation tools in the world's ocean of deception. These truths of Dan. 8:13,14 are going to provide much needed clarity:

13 "Then I heard a holy one speaking; and *another* holy one said to that certain *one* who was speaking, 'How long *will* the vision *be, concerning* the

daily *sacrifices* and the transgression of desolation, the giving of both the sanctuary and the host to be trampled underfoot?'

14 "And he said to me, 'For two thousand three hundred days; then the sanctuary shall be cleansed.'"

As you can see, there is a conversation happening between two different angelic messengers and Daniel. It is within this conversation that we understand that the "transgression of desolation" is a key idea. Because of Daniel's use of the same root word *shamem* (desolation) just like in Dan. 9:26 and 9:27b of the 70 shabua prophecy, I had been tricked into thinking that this was a reference to the abomination of desolation. English translations such as the KJV, NKJV, ESV, and more are also similarly misleading. It is in fact the TLV that provides the most accurate translation of Daniel 8:13 in particular, and I will explain why these following words are a perfect reflection of the Hebrew language:

Then I heard a holy one speaking, and another holy one said to him, "How long will it take for the vision to be fulfilled—the vision concerning the daily sacrifice, **the rebellion that causes desolation,** the surrender of the sanctuary and **the trampling underfoot of the Lord's people?"**
(Dan. 8:13 TLV) [emphasis added]

As you can see more clearly in this translation, it is in fact the rebellion against God that is the source of a specific desolation. This desolation is directly connected to the vision of evenings and mornings—a prophecy that I will unpack in a moment.

8:13 וָאֶשְׁמְעָה אֶחָד־קָדוֹשׁ מְדַבֵּר וַיֹּאמֶר אֶחָד
קָדוֹשׁ לַפַּלְמוֹנִי הַמְדַבֵּר עַד־מָתַי הֶחָזוֹן הַתָּמִיד וְהַפֶּשַׁע
שֹׁמֵם תֵּת וְקֹדֶשׁ וְצָבָא מִרְמָס׃

Figure 6.8: Daniel 8:13 in Hebrew

There are a few words here in Daniel 8:13 that need a little explaining before we understand the full mystery. We again see the mistake of the English translators in using the word "sanctuary" when the underlying Hebrew word *qodesh* simply means *holy* just like we already saw in Dan. 9:26. The translators were biased and projecting their imagination of a physical temple to be rebuilt in Jerusalem. They should have simply used the word *holy* in both Dan. 9:26 and Dan. 8:13. Of course, we now clearly know this word to be describing both the physical and spiritual (grafted-in) seed of Abraham throughout the world. It is all twelve tribes of Israel scattered throughout the world that have refused to obey the voice of God and walk in His Torah. What Dan. 8:13 is telling us is that the host (saba) of the seed of Abraham (the qodesh) were trampled like slaves and subdued. They were trampled by the enemy—the male goat with the little horn that became great.

Now let's take another look at Dan. 8:14. It is of critical importance to pay attention to the Hebrew language here. We are being presented with specific numbers, and if we are to be obedient to know and understand the prophecy, as we are commanded, then calculations are needed. This is the first place in this book where future dates will be presented. Multitudes of religious people toss around the label of "date-setting" like a curse word against those, like myself, who have done the due diligence to present new findings. Most of the time, the term "date-setter" is used by insecure people in order to readily dismiss new information that overwhelms them or that puts a perceived pressure on them to have to search it out. The source of this behavior is rooted in pride because it takes humility to be able to admit a current lack of knowledge while simultaneously having deep-rooted beliefs and traditions proven to be wrong.

וַיֹּאמֶר אֵלַי עַד עֶרֶב בֹּקֶר אַלְפַּיִם וּשְׁלֹשׁ מֵאוֹת וְנִצְדַּק קֹדֶשׁ

Figure 6.9: Daniel 8:14 in Hebrew. A literal, word-for-word reading of this verse is as follows: "He said to me, 'For evening morning two thousand three hundred then will be properly restored the holy." The Hebrew can be transliterated as "vayomer elay ad ereb boqer alpayim ushlosh meh-ot venitsdaq qodesh."

Again, we already know, based on our understanding of the 70 shabua, that Dan. 8:14 is speaking of the set-apart people of the twelve tribes when it uses the word "holy" (qodesh, Strong's H6944) at the end of the verse. Before doing some math, we must look at the word "cleansed" (Strong's H6663) which means to have a just cause, to be in the right, or to be put and made right. What I will now reveal to you are the two interpretations of the 2300 evening-morning vision. The first interpretation is the same one I had presented in the first edition of this book, namely:

March 11, 2020 + 2300 Days = Sunday, June 28, 2026

My reasoning behind this interpretation was that, considering all of the evidence already presented, Covid-19 and the pandemic declaration on

Passover 2020 began the prophetic time clock of the 2300 evenings-mornings. In other words, I interpreted "evening morning" to be one day, and therefore, judgment is to be expected from March 11, 2020 until June 28, 2026. Abraham was told in Genesis that his descendants were going to be mistreated for 400 years in a land not their own. The captivity of Judah in Babylon was 70 years long, just as God told Jeremiah. Yet, according to this first interpretation, this short period of harsh judgment upon Abraham's rebellious descendants and nations should only last from 2020 through 2026, after which they will be declared justified. However, now that I have understood a major event that took place on May 5, 2023, I will admit that my first interpretation clearly falls short in light of this second interpretation that I will now explain.

It is now quite obvious with new supporting evidence why Daniel deliberately chose not to use the Hebrew word for day, or *yom,* when writing down his vision of the "2,300 evening-morning." Since this prophecy was written in code, the absence of such an obvious word choice really means that Daniel was not speaking literally of *2,300 days.* He simply wrote down the two parts of a day—evening and morning—and in the Hebrew Scriptures we know that one *yom* is from evening until the next evening that begins a new day.

As we know, the Covid-19 pandemic was declared on March 11, 2020. At first, life was restless. The media generated enough hype to shut down daily life while erasing trillions from the world economy and forcing millions of people into poverty. Restrictions of all kinds abounded, and the world felt like an open-air prison. We all know the story. Over time, however, things started loosening up. Towards the end of 2021 when the first vaccines were being rolled out, many places in the US started lifting mask mandates and other restrictions. By the time 2022 came around, life was slowly but surely coming back to normal. When 2023 arrived, many people looked back on Covid-19 and laughed as if it had been a distant memory. That is why on May 5, 2023 when the Director-General of the WHO, Tedros Adhanom Ghebreyesus, briefed the media in Geneva and declared an end to the Covid-19 public health emergency,[3] many people failed to notice. In fact, his X (formerly Twitter) post briefly describing this declaration was met with mockery and scorn in the comments section below it.[4] People had already moved on from Covid and the coordinated fearmongering and hysteria promoted by the media industrial complex. Nevertheless, when it comes to Bible prophecy, you should understand by now just how important declarations and spoken words are when made by high-ranking officials.

The officially declared duration of the Covid-19 pandemic was from March 11, 2020 to May 5, 2023. The exact number of days between these two dates is 1150. When multiplying this number by two you will get 2300. Therefore, Daniel was stating that trampling underfoot of scattered Israel by the one-horned male goat and the governing bodies that he hijacked would only last for 1150 days, which combined is a grand total of 1150 evenings and 1150 mornings for a total of 2300 "evening-morning", as recorded in Hebrew. After May 5, 2023, life was fully restored back to normal. The scattered seed of Israel was restored and put back into their place of freely assembling and doing business. Though there still remains a heightened awareness of world government coupled with fears of new pandemic agendas that could emerge any time, the holy people of Jacob are now back to normal, which is what we were told would happen once the 2300 evening-morning judgment period was over.

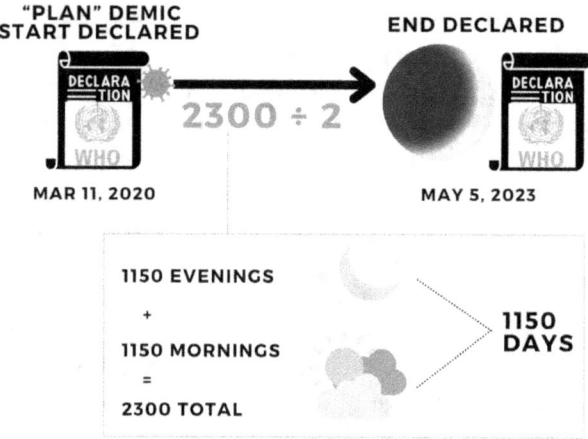

Figure 6.10: The 2300 Evening-Morning Prophecy of the Last Days. The pandemic began with Wuhan and ended with Wuhan, since this same Chinese city saw a lunar eclipse the exact day that the pandemic was declared to be over.

It is also important to be reminded of what God said in Genesis. Speaking of the sun, moon, and stars, the Word states:

Then God said, "Let there be lights in the firmament of the heavens to divide the day from the night; and let them be for signs and seasons, and for days and years"
(Gen. 1:14)

It is highly relevant for God's people to be paying attention to His signs as revealed in the heavens when attempting to understand Bible prophecy. They are to provide insight on various aspects of world events and oftentimes provide deeper insights into the something written in the Word of God. In the case of the Covid-19 pandemic and its 1150-day duration, there was a celestial event that occurred on May 5, 2023 that coincided with the end of this time period. Though the origins of the virus are still disputed to this day, the official narrative is that the novel coronavirus was first discovered in December 2019 within the central Chinese city of Wuhan where the Wuhan Institute of Virology (WIV) had been studying coronaviruses in bats for over a decade[5] and likely conducting gain-of-function bioweapons research. When Ghebreyesus held his emergency meeting to declare an official end to the pandemic, there also happened to be a penumbral lunar eclipse that maintained the highest visibility over the center of China and in very close alignment to the city of Wuhan.[6] That is why you see a partial lunar eclipse depicted in Figure 6.10 because this celestial event was a visible confirmation from the heavens that the prophecy of the 2300 evening-mornings was complete. Does this mean that we should discard the date of Sunday June 28, 2026 that was presented in the original interpretation? Perhaps. However, due to the layers of outcomes that tend to exist within prophetic Scriptures, I would make a note of it and wait to see if anything significant might unfold on that date. For now, it is clear that the primary interpretation of Daniel 8 has now come to pass.

However, a few questions still remain. What exactly was the purpose of the 2300 evening-morning judgment, and what comes next now that it is over? I can answer this question with utmost conviction because my life was radically changed forever by the pandemic and lockdowns. Even though I was already homesteading and living off grid as early as 2018, my heart was only partially devoted to following God. My focus for many years was swallowed up by the cares of this world especially regarding business, real estate, and online marketing. I would occasionally dabble with marijuana and participate liberally in hangouts with people that had diametrically opposed lifestyles to mine. Even though I had a heart to follow Yeshua and observe His Torah after my great awakening in 2016, I always struggled with various pet sins like pornography. As a result of this mountain of compromise and lack of leadership, my marriage struggled greatly. My inward suffering finally stopped in late 2019 when I cried out to Yeshua with my whole heart. That November was the moment when I finally had a true encounter with the Living God—an encounter so profound that I literally felt demons vibrating out of my skull during an early-morning prayer session. Before that day, I didn't really understand what demon possession was or if it could affect me. Yeshua taught me directly what it means to cast out unclean spirits, and I was never the same person again. When the pandemic came around just a few months later, I understood why my radical encounter with God had taken place at that specific moment in my life. God used the pandemic to intensely refine those who were already His. Some, like me, had been spiritually prepared immediately before the pandemic, and the dystopian lockdowns allowed us to maintain our focus on Yeshua's narrow road while recognizing that all sides of the political spectrum were actively colluding against us. Many others became intimately acquainted with the evils of world government only after the pandemic, and the terrifying prospect of this reality stirred up their hearts to truly investigate good and evil. For many, the pandemic was the first time where life's circumstances forced them to ask the hard questions about life. Without a job or even a church to go to, people were drawn into a true relationship with God for the first time ever. Christian culture felt disenfranchised by their church doors closing. Even unbelievers were shocked at how pastors were complying with illegal mandates while so readily forfeiting their birthright of freedom of speech and assembly. All of these events forced people to realize that finding God was something that would only take place outside of a church building. Astonishing events such as the February 2023 Asbury University Revival in Kentucky took place during the 1150-day timeframe, where countless young men and women re-dedicated their lives to Christ while many confessed Jesus as Lord for the first time ever.[7] This movement spread to other universities in the US and even traveled worldwide.

Though the prevailing culture of the West today continues to be one of debauchery and lawlessness, the pandemic was a horrifying enough event to usher in a small revival of true and authentic pursuit of Elohim. These circumstances also contributed to my decision to begin the Overcome Babylon podcast in 2022, and since doing so, I have received multitudes of emails, phone calls, and messages telling of revolutionary encounters with Yeshua similar to what I experienced in 2019. There was a sweeping movement of the Holy Spirit that was a direct byproduct of the pandemic. The eyes of many were finally opened enough to see the deception and evil of the media industrial complex like never before. However, because of the prevailing and currently ongoing rebellion against God and His Law, there is still more judgment coming to the West. The very next event on the prophetic map is the abomination of desolation.

DANIEL 9:27b - ON THE WING OF ABOMINATIONS

Now that we understand Daniel 8 we have a solid foundation for interpreting the remainder of Daniel's 70 weeks prophecy. Once again, this is what Dan. 9:27b says:

"...And on the wing of abominations shall be one who makes desolate,
Even until the consummation, which is determined,
Is poured out on the desolate."

וְעַל כְּנַף שִׁקּוּצִים מְשֹׁמֵם
וְעַד־כָּלָה וְנֶחֱרָצָה תִּתַּךְ עַל־שֹׁמֵם׃

Figure 6.11: Daniel 9:27b in Hebrew. This phrase can be transliterated as "veh-al kanaph shiqutsim meshomem veh-ad kala veh-neh-eratsa titak al shomem".

The two most important words here are "wing" (kanaf, Strong's H3671) and "abominations" (shih-koots-eem, Strong's H8251). *Kanaf* is first mentioned in Gen. 1:21 speaking of the creation of every "winged" bird after its kind. This word has been used throughout the Bible to speak of wings, extremities, edges, and something winged. The word *shihkootseem* is the plural form of a noun that is used to describe spiritually disgusting things, idols, and especially things that are idolatrous. That's why the word *abominations* in the title of this chapter is plural. We should expect to see more than one abomination. The first time we see this word used is the following verse in Deut. 29:17:

"and you saw their **abominations** and their idols which *were* among them—wood and stone and silver and gold" [emphasis added]

Shortly before his death, Moses spoke these words to the Joshua generation regarding the idols of the inhabitants of the land that they were never to mix themselves with, lest they develop a spiritual root of bitterness producing evil fruit. Another excellent verse is from 2Ki. 23:24:

"Moreover Josiah put away those who consulted mediums and spiritists, the household gods and idols, all the **abominations** that were seen in the land of Judah and in Jerusalem, that he might perform the words of the law which were written in the book that Hilkiah the priest found in the house of the LORD." [emphasis added]

As you study this word *abominations,* you will tend to find it right alongside idolatry just like in these two verses. In other words, the word "shihkoots" is usually used in the same way that "idol" is used. It is used to describe a wide variety of things that God considers disgusting filth. When I was first attempting to understand exactly what Dan. 9:27b is describing, I came across these verses here from Ezekiel 24:4-6:

4 "...Everyone of the house of Israel who sets up his idols in his heart, and puts before him what causes him to stumble into iniquity, and then comes to the prophet, I the LORD will answer him who comes, according to the multitude of his idols,
5 "that I may seize the house of Israel by their heart, because they are all estranged from Me by their idols.
6 "Therefore say to the house of Israel, 'Thus says the Lord GOD: 'Repent, turn away from your idols, and turn your faces away from all your abominations.'"

Idols and abominations cause people's hearts to become estranged from a relationship with God. With that said, let me present an obvious question. We have been dealing with the topic of national, moral rebellion against God. I have been showing you that because of transgression, destruction must take place according to the words of Daniel. So, when was the last time that the United States, the UK, or any other Western nation put its faith 100% into the God of the Bible to defend them militarily? When was the last time that *any* nation placed their faith and trust in God to defend them from their enemies?

From the ancient days of the Torah until now, war was always meant to be an act of faith. Victory was always guaranteed by the supernatural power of God to any nation that did not set up any idols, abominations, or anything else in their hearts other than the one true God, Yehovah. Trusting in God for salvation is not a New Testament concept only. It was a way of life for the Israelites. Just look at what Deut. 20:1 says:

"When you go out to battle against your enemies, and see horses and chariots *and* people more numerous than you, do not be afraid of them; for the LORD your God *is* with you, who brought you up from the land of Egypt."

Also take a look at what Num. 10:9 says:

"When you go to war in your land against the enemy who oppresses you, then you shall sound an alarm with the trumpets, and you will be remembered before the LORD your God, and you will be saved from your enemies."

If you read these verses carefully, it is overwhelmingly clear that military strength and protection is a spiritual reality rather than a physical one. Regarding the last days and the judgment of all 12 tribes of Israel, Moses says this:

15 "But Jeshurun grew fat and kicked;
You grew fat, you grew thick,
You are obese!
Then he forsook God *who* made him,
And scornfully esteemed the Rock of his salvation.
28 "For they *are* a nation void of counsel,
Nor *is there any* understanding in them.
29 "Oh, that they were wise, *that* they understood this.
That they would **consider their latter end!**
30 "How could one chase a thousand,
And two put ten thousand to flight,
Unless their Rock had sold them,
And the LORD had surrendered them?"
(Deut. 32:15;28-30) [emphasis added]

The name *Jeshurun* simply means *upright one* and refers to all Israel. Indeed, the descendants of Abraham have grown fat, prosperous, and have forsaken God and His holy covenant. If only the people of Abraham had understood the nature of both physical and spiritual warfare, then they would have trusted in God Himself as their protection and not their abominations. This "latter end" prophecy of Moses is the secret of Daniel 9:27.

If the nations of the United States, UK, and all the West did not forsake God…

If they did not put their trust in their own military intelligence, 21st century technologies, weapons of mass destruction, missile defense systems, rockets, planes, fighter jets, and naval ships…

If they did not put their trust in the idols of the military industrial complex, then they would have been delivered from what is about to happen.

Based on this end times connection from Moses and the proper understanding of *abominations,* this is how I would translate Dan. 9:27b:

"And on the wing of military technologies will be one who causes desolation,

Even until the end, which is decreed, is poured out on the ones who make desolation"

We can see that there will be desolation, but at the end of it all, the ones responsible for this destruction will have the same measure of judgment poured out on them. This idea is mirrored in the Day of the LORD (Yehovah) prophecy of Obadiah:

"For **the day of the LORD** upon all the nations is near; As you have done, it shall be done to you; Your reprisal shall return upon your own head.
(Oba. 1:15) [emphasis added]

People and nations reap what they sow, and we know how this story is going to end. Zechariah 14 gives us the details of how the Day of the LORD is to unfold both when Jerusalem is first judged and finally, when it is redeemed. Pay close attention to verse 12 where it speaks of God repaying His enemies once the current judgment period is finally over:

1 Behold, **the day of the LORD** is coming, And your spoil will be divided in your midst.
12 And this shall be the plague with which the LORD will strike all the people who fought against Jerusalem: **Their flesh shall dissolve** while they stand on their feet, **Their eyes shall dissolve** in their sockets, And **their tongues shall dissolve** in their mouths.
(Zec. 14:1,12) [emphasis added]

Why would Yehovah strike the nations with a plague in which their eyes and tongues dissolve immediately, as if by the inferno of an unquenchable fire? As Obadiah stated, they will reap what they have sown. These verses together with what I will explain next provide clear context and evidence as to why nuclear desolation and weapons of mass destruction should be expected on a large scale, beginning in Jerusalem, as you will see.

Because Daniel was sick for three weeks after seeing this prophecy in a vision, I believe that these words are speaking of nuclear warfare. If you have never watched documentaries about the atomic bombings of Hiroshima and Nagasaki during WWII, I highly recommend looking into it. When you hear first-hand accounts of the devastation, the immediate effects of radiation, and the long-term consequences of this unique kind of warfare, your stomach will feel uneasy. I recently rewatched a documentary and thought to myself, "How could humans do this to one another?" It is utterly atrocious to see what nuclear war did to buildings, homes, and the society of Japan back in those days.

The issue is that the nuclear weapons that are armed and on standby today are exponentially more catastrophic than the two atomic bombs of WWII. I specifically believe that Daniel saw a vision of multiple military aircraft deploying nuclear weapons. Even though nuclear weapons can be deployed in different ways, I think Daniel attempted to describe some sort of fighter jet or aircraft causing the desolation. I'm not saying that's the *only* source of the desolation. I'm simply stating that Daniel wrote down aircraft as the key component of a larger-scale nuclear war when he spoke of the *wing of abomination.*

שִׁקּוּצִים מְשֹׁמֵם

"MEH-SHOH-MEM"   "SHIH-KOOTS-EEM"

...SHALL MAKE
DESOLATION   ABOMINATIONS...

Figure 6.12: On The Wing of Military Technology. Remember to read the Hebrew from right to left in my illustration (therefore, it is plural "abominations" that "shall make desolation").

The reason I am focusing on jets with nuclear capabilities is because Daniel said he saw a "wing." My mind easily jumps to aircraft, and military personnel are known to commonly refer to their jets and cargo planes as "birds." To be fair, he could also be referring to any part of the "nuclear triad" as it is called here in the US, which includes (1) Land-based ICBMs, (2) Air-Launched Missiles, and (3) Submarine-Launched Missiles. All of these things are idols that the nations worship as their source of strength and security, rather than the one true God.

Let's now investigate the military technology currently on the table. Back in mid-2020, the *Defense News* released an article stating that the US fighter jet F-15E had become the first aircraft compatible to carry and deploy the latest nuclear bomb design.[8] This information confirms our suspicion of what

Daniel could have seen. Then in October 2021, the *Air Force Times* released an article speaking of the US F-35 fighter undergoing a makeover to be able to carry and deploy nuclear bombs.[9] Less than a year later, the modifications to the F-35 were completed, and the US was even making them available for sale, with Germany adding them to their defense arsenal.[10] The evidence is overwhelming. This technology exists, it's available, and I believe Daniel saw fighter jets deploying these abominations that cause extreme desolation, or weapons of mass destruction, in his vision.

The next logical question is, *who* is going to be responsible for dropping the bombs? This will be the major subject of Secret II of this book. For now, I direct your attention to the work of Joel Skousen, the founder of the news website World Affairs Brief and creator of the groundbreaking nuclear survival publication, *Strategic Relocation: North American Guide to Safe Places.* Based on his career work as a consultant for prominent people looking to build high security shelters, bunkers, and off-grid doomsday structures, Skousen has been predicting a nuclear WWIII scenario for decades. In an interview with Alex Jones, he makes mention of high profile US government officials across the board that have been coming to him specifically for nuclear war preparation.[11] In other words, the higher level intelligence community and high ranking officials know that nuclear war has been programmed into the New World Order's desire for order out of chaos. Out of the chaos of WWIII, they hope to finally achieve that totalitarian, one-world government spoken of in the Bible. Skousen has been making the case for many years now that the geopolitical stage has been set for the US to go to war with a Russian and Chinese alliance of nations and ultimately lose due to corruption and betrayal from within. Of course, we don't need Skousen to tell us about this reality. We know what the Bible says now, and I will show you even more biblical evidence later.

Without getting lost in the details of the Ukrainian conflict that began WWIII, just be aware that all of this warfare started because the US was ready once again to provoke Russia into an all-out nuclear war. The mainstream media narrative that Russia was the greatest threat and enemy of the US isn't something new. It first took hold in the days of the Cold War. It was then restarted under Barack Obama and Hillary Clinton. In fact, Clinton made it clear that if she were elected president (instead of Donald Trump), she would make sure that Russia would remain an primary enemy of the US and be treated with great hostility. However, Clinton was not aware of the prophetic time clock of the Most High. Trump took the stage of the presidency, and open warfare was put on hold. However, it should also be noted that during the Trump years, the military industrial complex continued its active training and exercises for NATO's future clash with Russia. Official NATO documents reveal that US funding steadily increased from about $642 Billion in 2017 to $770 Billion at year's end in 2020,[12] despite Trump's public theatrics threatening to defund and withdraw from NATO.[13] Trump's rhetoric was only meant to distract the gullible public from the true agenda of the Western elites, which was to print mountains of debt during the pandemic that would later be used finance new lucrative wars during the Joe Biden years, all with the hopes of eventually ushering in a new world order after the fact.

At this point in history, God's judgment is ripe for the harvest, and transgression has reached its climax. Because of the recent Ukrainian conflict, Russia has made it clear that it is now ready to retaliate against the US with its Satan II missile—a nuclear weapon designed with 15 warheads that is capable of destroying an area the size of the United Kingdom with one strike.[14] When Vladmir Putin invaded Ukraine on February 24, 2022, that was the day when I knew without a shadow of a doubt what the 70 Shabua of Daniel and the abomination of desolation prophecies were talking about. I understood the true meaning of the Gog and Magog prophecy. Everything dawned on me, weighed heavy upon my shoulders, and that's the exact moment that the Holy Spirit gave me the conviction to immediately launch my Overcome Babylon podcast with the hopes of reaching as many people as possible with the truth of the Word of God before life as we knew it completely and utterly changed. Then, with the new theater of war opening up in the Middle East after the events of October 7, 2023, it became even more obvious that the world was headed in an irreversible direction. I will discuss Iran, its proxies, and October 7 heavily in this chapter along with Chapter 7.

DANIEL 11:31 - THE SANCTUARY FORTRESS

As long as you never lose sight of the main subject of Daniel's 70 shabua prophecy, you will never be confused when reading the other things he wrote about the abomination of desolation. Regarding the Kings of the North and South; the ships from Cyprus (literally, *Kittim* or Western lands); and various nuances within Daniel 11, I will boldly admit that I don't know exactly what all these things mean at this point in time. However, I will certainly offer an intriguing interpretation in Chapter 11 because the ongoing war between the Jewish President Voldomyr Zelenskyy of Ukraine and President Vladmir Putin of Russia seems to be perfectly connected. While it is important to fully decode Daniel 11 at some point, it is not absolutely necessary for understanding the abomination of desolation that will be happening *soon*. This is what Dan. 11:31 says:

"And forces shall be mustered by him, and they shall defile the sanctuary fortress; then they shall take away the daily *sacrifices,* and place *there* the abomination of desolation."

וּזְרֹעִים מִמֶּנּוּ יַעֲמֹדוּ וְחִלְּלוּ הַמִּקְדָּשׁ הַמָּעוֹז
וְהֵסִירוּ הַתָּמִיד וְנָתְנוּ הַשִּׁקּוּץ מְשׁוֹמֵם:

Figure 6.13: Daniel 11:31 in Hebrew. A literal reading and correct order of this verse can be rendered as follows: "And arms on his part shall stand, and they shall pollute the sanctuary of strength; and shall take away the daily; and they shall place the abomination that makes desolate."

Several major concepts from prior analyses are being repeated in this verse. At this point, I know I am getting very repetitive when I tell you that "sacrifices" is a filler word. Sorry. The main thing I want you to see here is that the "sanctuary fortress" is speaking of the city of Jerusalem, and there is a connection to the New Testament that we need to make in order to fully understand this event. We have already talked about the first word Daniel used for "sanctuary" which is "miqdash" (Strong's H4720); and this word is trans-lated correctly into the English. The other word "fortress" ("mah-oz", Strong's H4581) has been used in the Bible to mean refuge, stronghold, or military fortress. We already covered this topic in Chapter 3, but Jerusalem is explic-itly regarded as a stronghold in the Old Testament, specifically in 2 Samuel 5:6,7. We already talked about how David fortified Jerusalem with various military defenses. The book of Nehemiah had not yet been written when Daniel was alive, so when he was writing these words in secret code, he was drawing upon the inspiration of the Torah and Prophets that speak many times of Jerusalem being a fortified sanctuary for God's people.

I will now attempt to translate Dan. 11:31 with our firm understanding of the 70 shabua, but before I do, here's the verse from Luke 21:20 where Yeshua confirms the presence of military forces and armaments surrounding Jerusalem during this same event:

"But when you see Jerusalem surrounded by armies, then know that its deso-lation is near."

Of course, this verse has never felt more real after the events of October 7, 2023 and the rise of Hamas, Hezbollah, the Houthis, and various Arab militias that are allied with Iran, who in turn are allied with Russia and China. Add the nuclear-armed nation of North Korea into the mix along with other members of the current BRICS-10 alliance of nations, and there should be absolutely no doubt in your mind that we are finally here at this moment in the prophetic timeline. I will fully explain the importance of BRICS later in Chapter 11. After taking all of these things under consideration and carefully dissecting each Hebrew word, here is how I would translate Dan. 11:31:

"Military arms will be set up by the King of the North and shall defile the set apart stronghold of Jerusalem; the prayers of the saints shall be taken away; the nuclear abomination appointed."

With the exception of the King of the North, I removed the pronouns often present in English translations because it is not any particular "they" or a singular "him" that is responsible for all these events because, as I have shown you, there have been multiple players in the fulfillment of Covid-19 and also with the coming nuclear abomination. The role of the King of the North will be explored in more detail in Chapters 7 and 11. Now, before offering more of my personal commentary, the angelic man clothed in linen who described the whole sequence of events in Daniel 11 also offers Daniel a clear explanation of Dan. 11:31 after he was asked for additional clarity. Here is the messenger's response:

"And from the time *that* the daily *sacrifice* is taken away, and the abomination of desolation is set up, *there shall be* one thousand two hundred and ninety days.
(Dan. 12:11)

We already know when the daily ("tamid") was taken away in the middle of the 70th shabua—March 11, 2020. We understand this event to be the closing of church doors worldwide due to the pandemic. We also know that this is the same event when "sacrifice and offering" were caused to fail (shabbat), which was the ability to travel to Jerusalem to observe the three annual pilgrimage festivals and present the gift offerings ("zebakh" and "minkhah") as required by the Torah. With these things in mind, here is what Daniel 12:11 is showing us:

March 11, 2020 + 1290 Days = Friday, September 22, 2023

Now, I know what you're thinking. *"Nothing happened. This date of September came and went, and it was of no consequence whatsoever. Where*

were the bombs? You are wrong about everything!" This all-too-common attitude toward this prophecy plagued the comments sections of various videos I
uploaded and incessantly dripped through my email inbox like a hopelessly
leaky faucet. That is, of course, because I also misunderstood this prophecy
and presented my flawed interpretation in the first edition of this book. The
complete understanding of the abomination of desolation hinges around the
meaning of one Hebrew word—a word that I had failed to properly weigh and
consider in all of my research of prophecy, which is why I had been strongly
warning of a likely nuclear war scenario beginning on the exact date of
September 22, 2023. The next figure reveals this one critically important
word.

וְלָתֵת

**Figure 6.14: The word "set up" in the Hebrew language. As it appears in
Daniel 12:11, this word can be transliterated as "veh-lah-tet".**

The two English words "set up" are translated from the Hebrew word
velatet. The root word is Strong's H5414 and is pronounced *natan*. The root
word itself is ubiquitous, appearing over 2,000 times in the Masoretic Text, so
the better approach to analyzing the exact meaning in Daniel 12:11 is to
perform a direct word search for "וְלָתֵת" in the WLC text. You will find that
this exact spelling with the same vowel signs is only found in five other verses
of the Bible. Including Daniel, here are the six different ways that *velatet* is
translated in the King James Bible in the order that they appear:

1. Gen. 42:25 - and give
2. Exo. 32:29 - and to give up
3. Deu. 23:14 - that He may bestow
4. Jer. 17:10 - even to give
5. Jer. 19:12 - and make
6. Dan. 12:11 - and set up

I particularly like Jeremiah 19:12 because as I will explain here and further
prove to you in the next chapter, the abomination of desolation was indeed
made and *set up* on September 22, 2023. The true nature of this prophecy only
became abundantly clear exactly two weeks later on October 7, 2023 when
there was a "surprise" military attack against Israel.

This attack took place exactly 50 years after the Yom Kippur War of 1973
and similarly took place on a festival of Judaism called "Shemini Atzeret", or

the 8th Day after Sukkot (according to the time keeping of the erroneous Hillel II calendar). The official narrative is that Hamas along with other Palestinian militias were able to initially launch at least 3,000 rockets against Israel in a rapid barrage while then successfully using paragliders, boats, and vehicles to infiltrate the most heavily surveilled and guarded border in the entire world—the Israel-Gaza border—that is littered with Israeli military bases and fortifications.[15] In what has since been termed the "9-11 event" of the Jews, the Gaza-Israel border was successfully overrun by Palestinian militants, which allowed them to infiltrate the Zikim military training base[16] and overrun two other bases in the region,[17] giving weight to the argument that this operation was not for the purposes of brute psychological terrorism but of intelligence gathering. Given the actions of Palestinian forces, it appears that their primary objective was to infiltrate Israeli military installations with the hopes of breaching computer servers and gathering intelligence on Israel's mysterious nuclear weapons program, among other data. However, the mainstream media was very quick to label all of the actions of Hamas as only "9-11" styled terrorism and nothing more. Actually, this description couldn't be more accurate. October 7th was a 100% synthetic, orchestrated, and "allowed" attack on Israel exactly like 9-11 was on the United States.

It has been reported by the *New York Times* and other media outlets that Israel already had the detailed battleplans of Hamas's October 7th operation over a year in advance.[18] Just three to four months before the attacks, Israeli surveillance soldiers serving on a base in Nahal Oz reported information to their senior leadership concerning suspicious training activity of Hamas operatives but were ignored.[19] Two soldiers, Yael Rotenberg and Maya Desiatni, stated in a Kan News interview that their warnings to leadership were dismissed, with Rotenberg stating she saw "Palestinians dressed in civilian clothing approach the border fence with maps, examining the ground around it and digging holes" but was told they were only farmers, and there was nothing to worry about.[20]

The attacks conveniently came at a time when Israel's internal political division had reached hostile territory. Amid ongoing peace negotiations with Saudi Arabia, National Security Minister Itamar Ben Gvir threatened to implode the Israeli government over any concessions to the Palestinians in a press release dated Sept. 23, 2023.[21] The National Security official's words proved to be more than empty rhetoric just thirteen days later when an apparent stand down order from the top down was given to the IDF. This new war was then used by Netanyahu to rally as much support as possible to fight the straw man of Hamas while insisting that internal political strife must be put on hold for the greater good of the country. War became the scapegoat upon which to deflect attention away from all of the division present within Israel's leadership.

Many people dismiss both political and geopolitical news developments because they deem them to be of no consequence to their daily lives. The past decade of Israel's history provides a worthy case study of why this attitude is not based in reality. Having held office for over 16 years, including a political stint in the 1990s, Benjamin Netanyahu has now stood as Israel's longest serving Prime Minister in the history of the nation. This tenure has been heavily contested, however. Netanyahu's ultranationalist and ultra-Orthodox positions have been widely unpopular as evidenced by hotly battled election cycles. Going back to the very last election of 2022, Israel remained divided over Netanyahu, who has been on trial for "charges of fraud, breach of trust and accepting bribes in three corruption cases."[22] The Times of Israel reported that Netanyahu and his Likud Party's narrow 30,000 vote "victory" was possible due to the nature of how the voting blocs are structured.[23] A pragmatic look into the official numbers reveals that the Likud Party was able to maintain power with only a disproportionate 23.4% share of the entire country's vote.[24] To say that Netanyahu is wildly unpopular with the Israeli people as a whole would be an understatement. That is why anti-war riots and demonstrations have ensued regularly within Israel's borders amid the ongoing actions of Netanyahu's "pure" right-wing government. Beyond Zionist borders, the international community has also been vocal in expressing condemnation over the atrocities of the Israel-Palestine conflict. While official numbers say that a little over 1,000 Israelis were killed as a direct result of the Oct. 7 attacks, there is strong evidence that a good number of these casualties were the direct result of Israel's Hannibal Directive[25] (or approved friendly fire) rather than directly from Palestinian militants themselves. In contrast, a July 2024 scientific study published by The Lancet reveals that the current death toll of 38,000 Palestinians in the ongoing Israeli bombardment campaigns is a gross misunderstanding because this figure does not take under consideration the numbers of bodies buried under rubble; the lasting effects of disease and starvation; and the collapse of basic infrastructure. Their scientific analysis concludes that the real number of casualties could exceed 186,000 Palestinians, most of them women and children, at this point in the war.[26,27] In light of all this evidence, the International Criminal Court (ICC) issued warrants in May 2024 for the arrests of Hamas leaders but also Benjamin Netanyahu and Yoav Gallant (the Minister of Defense of Israel), alleging the following:

- "Starvation of civilians as a method of warfare as a war crime contrary to article 8(2)(b)(xxv) of the Statute;
- Wilfully causing great suffering, or serious injury to body or health contrary to article 8(2)(a)(iii), or cruel treatment as a war crime contrary to article 8(2)(c)(i);
- Wilful killing contrary to article 8(2)(a)(i), or Murder as a war crime contrary to article 8(2)(c)(i);
- Intentionally directing attacks against a civilian population as a war crime contrary to articles 8(2)(b)(i), or 8(2)(e)(i);
- Extermination and/or murder contrary to articles 7(1)(b) and 7(1)(a), including in the context of deaths caused by starvation, as a crime against humanity;
- Persecution as a crime against humanity contrary to article 7(1)(h);
- Other inhumane acts as crimes against humanity contrary to article 7(1)(k)."[28]

The international pressure and condemnation of the Zionist establishment and its unwavering supporters like the US has now reached the point of no return. We now see that Jerusalem and 1948 Israel as a whole are currently getting surrounded by the Axis of Resistance headed by Iran, and the ongoing hostilities are soon going to have massive and far reaching consequences for ordinary citizens of the West. At some point, we are warned that we are to expect the abomination of desolation to be visible, according Yeshua's words, at which time those still alive in Judea (modern Israel) must flee to the hills.

Before getting to the New Testament's description of the coming abomination of desolation, the "set up" must still be properly examined. We have investigated the internal political division present within Israel before Oct. 7, the Security Minister's threats to implode the government, and finally, the intentional stand-down order given to the military that coincided with a major national holiday and therefore decreased security. It must now be understood *why* Hamas and all of the various militia groups including Hezobollah were ready to cross this red line and pursue war with Israel. They knew that they would be placing tremendous risk upon the whole civilian population of Palestine after this decision was made. They knew that Israel's response would be disproportionate and catastrophic. Certainly, there must be more to the story from the standpoint of the Axis of Resistance that we must consider properly if we ever hope to understand this prophecy. One major clue was given to us in the aftermath of the Oct. 7 event. Less than one month after the attacks, Congress met to enact House Resolution 559 into law on November 1, 2023. This declaration is entitled "Declaring it is the policy of the United

States that a nuclear Islamic Republic of Iran is not acceptable," and here is an excerpt of this declaration:

> "...Whereas IAEA investigators found uranium particles enriched to 83.7 percent at Iran's Fordow nuclear facility in January 2023;
>
> Whereas uranium enriched to 90 percent is weapons-grade material;
>
> ...[The] House of Representatives declares it is the policy of the United States—
>
> (1) that a nuclear Islamic Republic of Iran is not acceptable;
>
> (2) that Iran must not be able to obtain a nuclear weapon under any circumstances or conditions;
>
> (3) to use all means necessary to prevent Iran from obtaining a nuclear weapon; and
>
> (4) to recognize and support the freedom of action of partners and allies, including Israel, to prevent Iran from obtaining a nuclear weapon."[29]

While most people became immediately distracted with Hamas and Hezbollah after the events of October 7, the real agenda of the Western establishment began to finalize itself with this particular resolution. Its language provides several details not only concerning the geopolitical environment before the attacks but also key details about Daniel's prophecy that have now become crystal clear. The House makes reference to a report from the International Atomic Energy Agency (IAEA), which was further confirmed by other reports detailing that Iran's enrichment of uranium increased to 84% by February 2023.[30] The language here softens the reality that Iran's nuclear weapons program is fully operational at this time. Just think about it carefully. If Iran already had uranium enriched at 83.7% in January 2023, what is the likelihood that they already had 90% (weapons-grade) enrichment eight months later? Not only does HR 559 essentially prove that Iran was well in possession of nuclear weapons by the time of the aforementioned prophetic date of September 22, 2023, but it explains why Iran was finally ready to activate its proxy armies and militia partners just two weeks later. It further explains why Iran directly attacked Israel on April 13, 2024 with a barrage of over 300 drones and missiles.[31]

Iran is now ready to wage an all-out war against Israel and the West. They are ready to engage in a war that they believe they can win, and that only means one major thing. Iran possesses the nuclear weapons—the abominations of desolation—that will be deployed using their wing of military technology. Iranian lawmaker and member of parliament Ahmad Bakhshayesh

Ardestani shared this precise sentiment to the Rouydad 24 website shortly after the April 13 attack.

The *Iran International Newsroom* publication translates Ardestani's insider point of view for us, relaying the following:

> "'In my opinion, we have achieved nuclear weapons, but we do not announce it. It means our policy is to possess nuclear bombs, but our declared policy is currently within the framework of the JCPOA. The reason is that when countries want to confront others, their capabilities must be compatible, and Iran's compatibility with America and Israel means that Iran must have nuclear weapons,' Ardestani was quoted as saying."[32]

The JCPOA referenced is an acronym for the Joint Comprehensive Plan of Action, also known as the Iran Nuclear Deal, that former President Trump abandoned in 2018. Trump further exacerbated tensions two years later by killing Iran's major general, Qasem Soleimani, in 2020. These conditions coupled together with Israel's constant bombardments of Iranian interests have brought these soured relations to the end game that we are now witnessing. Going back to the words of Ardestani, this news story also made major headlines in the US, with Fox News covering the development while simultaneously downplaying the severity of the situation, selling the idea that Iran is "still a ways away" from having a "deliverable device."[33] Without a proper understanding of Bible prophecy, most people will be led astray and caught completely unaware by what Iran is about to do. Though impossible to prove at this moment in time for obvious reasons, it is my firm conclusion that Iran set up one or more nuclear weapons on September 22, 2023 that will be used against Israel to initiate the Great Tribulation. Regarding this event and this time period, we are told by the angelic messenger of Daniel 12 that "there shall be a time of trouble, such as never was since there was a nation, even to that time" (Dan. 12:1). Make no mistake about it, the abomination of desolation will usher in something unprecedented on the world stage, and this book is the advanced notice that the media and religious industrial complexes are hiding from you.

Now that we have explored the Hebrew foundation that Yeshua Himself was quoting in the New Testament, let's go ahead and see what the Master had to say about the coming abomination of desolation.

MATTHEW 24: WHOEVER READS, LET HIM UNDERSTAND

The entire context of Matthew 24 begins with Yeshua's disciples asking Him how they will be able to discern the last days of mankind. Yeshua begins with a warning not to be deceived and proceeds to speak of many troubles. Shortly after speaking of conflict and wars, he then proceeds to reveal to us this mystery regarding the abomination in Mat. 24:15:

"'Therefore when you see the *"abomination of desolation,"* spoken of by Daniel the prophet, standing in the holy place' (whoever reads, let him understand),"

It should be obvious that the "holy place" is simply referring to the city of Jerusalem based on everything I have already shown you and also the verses that follow this one in Matthew. Let me go ahead and address this word "standing" (Strong's G2476), which I have seen many people use to falsely interpret this verse as speaking of a sacrificial animal, statue, or some sort of physical object or idol somewhere in or around Jerusalem, and oftentimes a temple in the city. We never saw any such language literally referring to something "standing" or "being upright" in the Hebrew Scriptures.

Not once.

It turns out that this Greek word carries the meaning of making firm, establishing, or sustaining the authority or force of anything. In other words, Yeshua perfectly agrees with Daniel by telling us that the abominations will be firmly established in and around Jerusalem. Now let's look at the next verse where Jesus says, "then let those who are in Judea flee to the mountains" (Mat. 24:16). Yeshua is warning us that we are to get away from the cities, towns, and areas within Judea. As I have shown you, He is most likely talking about nuclear fallout and radiation.

Because this event is set to take place specifically in Jerusalem, the bystanders living in the land of Israel must immediately flee to higher ground before the winds and weather patterns distribute the radiation further throughout the country. However, at the same time, I don't know if this is going to be a catastrophic event that will devastate infrastructure and completely demolish Jerusalem off of the face of the earth because it is likely going to be used as the headquarters of the new world order as implied by Revelation 11:2. I believe it is more probable that neutron bombs are going to be used. This specific kind of technology only releases mostly deadly gamma rays within a small radius (only a few miles) of the actual blast site.[34] Gamma rays are simply light rays. The sun releases gamma rays, for example. These light rays become weaponized through the nuclear device itself and when released in a blast, these light rays kill biological life without actually destroying buildings and infrastructure. It is my speculation that these specific kinds of nuclear weapons could be used in Jerusalem and Judea in order to kill military personnel and any military resistance but without making the country a complete wasteland. Based on my research and conversations with people like Cyrus Harding in Episode 11 of Overcome Babylon, the nuclear fallout from these neutron bombs should only last about two weeks. With buildings still intact, this is the only logical explanation that would still allow Jerusalem to be trampled underfoot by the Gentiles for times, time, and half a time as described both in Daniel 7:25 and Revelation 11:2, assuming that these verses are to be understood literally. There will still be smoke and fire, however; and it is certainly possible that Jerusalem and 1948 Israel could be turned into an uninhabitable wasteland.

Now let's explore the meaning behind Jesus' words when He said, "And pray that your flight may not be in winter or on the Sabbath" (Mat. 24:20). These words are of extreme importance. Now that September 22, 2023 has come and gone and we do not have any other numerology associated with when exactly the abomination of desolation will actually be deployed, we are to rely on these words. Yeshua is telling us of the exact season of the timing. Of course, a Sabbath day is from sunset Friday to sunset Saturday. He is speaking of a literal 24-hour day with bombs going off any time during any Sabbath day moving forward into the future. This reference to the Sabbath could also be speaking of any Holy Day on God's calendar. But what about this idea of *winter?* What most people do not realize is that there are only two seasons in the Bible. There are not four like most people in colder, temperate climates are accustomed to understanding. This truth is established in Genesis 8:22 after the flood:

"While the earth remains,
Seedtime and harvest,
Cold and heat,
Winter and summer,
And day and night
Shall not cease."

God makes this statement right after Noah gets off the ark and sacrifices clean animals on a newly built altar. This verse reveals that the entire prophetic time clock of the Bible is centered around the land of Canaan, and Yeshua's words must therefore be understood in this context. The online Jewish learning platform *Chabad* describes the seasons of Israel as two six-month periods, and they say, "the six months from Nissan to Tishrei are the Season of the Sun, and the Tishrei to Nissan months are our Season of Rains."[35] The Bible itself is also clear that winter begins during the seventh month (known by the Jews as Tishrei) typically around August to September and lasts until February or March, which is around the time Abib begins to usher in the New Year. It has consistently been my position that both conditions—winter and Sabbath— must be met in order for the abomination of desolation to take place. In other words, it won't happen during a Sabbath day in July. Any winter-Sabbath day is fair game for the tribulation period to be ushered in. Even though we don't have any numerology to guide us, we now understand the exact season that we are looking for. It could be the winter of 2024, 2025, 2026, or further out into the future. However, the next chapters will describe why escalation should be anticipated sooner rather than later.

Before moving on, we have to ask the obvious question. Why would Yeshua tell us to "pray" about this event even though there is no stopping what is coming, and it must come to pass on a Sabbath and in the winter? Simply pay attention to what the object of the prayer is supposed to be. His specific words are telling us to pray about our escape, or flight. He is telling us to pray well in advance of this event in order to already be well-positioned for when it takes place. You should already be positioned on higher ground, away from the calamity. You should already be in a place exactly where God wants you to be spiritually, which is the most important aspect of any preparedness plans. And it is only through prayer that the answers and clarity will come from the Throne as to where you need to be physically living and relocated. I have already mentioned Lot escaping Sodom and Gomorrah. I have already mentioned the angel in Revelation telling God's people with ears to hear to come out of Babylon. Many people are going to be caught at the very last minute fleeing for their lives because they didn't pray. Don't be one of them. Have a fruitful prayer life. Exercise diligent prayer regarding this exact topic. Be praying about your escape *right now and not later!* And also share this work with others so they, too, can be positioned to higher ground spiritually. Remember also that everyone's walk with God is a private relationship with public fruit that we must discern. If you have done your best to be ready—whatever that looks like between you and God—and you have warned others, then rest in the promises of God. Comparing yourself to others will only leave you defeated and miserable. The only metric that matters is whether or not an intimate and constant pursuit of the Living God is taking place in your heart and mind during this season. Now, here's what you need to know next (Mat. 24:21,22):

21 "For then there will be great tribulation, such as has not been since the beginning of the world until this time, no, nor ever shall be.
22 "And unless those days were shortened, no flesh would be saved; but for the elect's sake those days will be shortened."

As you can see, Yeshua is quoting Daniel 12:1. These words tell us that the abominations of desolation will actually begin the period of history known as the Great Tribulation that I have been referring to often throughout this book. This will be the topic of a later chapter, but for now, understand that the world will enter the darkest period of history never before seen since the foundation of the world. Physical preparation alone isn't the goal—spiritual preparation is. Now do you see why this book is so important? We need to be spiritually ready for what is coming next because men's hearts will be failing from heart attacks because of the extreme calamity of the Great Tribulation.

MARK 13: TRIBULATION UNPRECEDENTED IN HISTORY

When you compare Mark 13 side-by-side with Matthew 24, they read very similarly. Regarding the tribulation, Mark does give us some more insights and clarity, especially in Mar. 13:19 where he states the following: "For *in* those days there will be tribulation, such as has not been since the beginning of the creation which God created until this time, nor ever shall be." We are being told that these are the darkest hours of mankind and the entire earth itself. Extreme pressure, anxiety, and oppression will take hold of the entire earth, which is what the word *tribulation* means.

To say that Sept. 22, 2023 and every Hebrew winter season afterwards is important to watch is an understatement. The coming desolation will make Pearl Harbor, the terror attacks of September 11, 2001, and all of the most tragic events in all of world history look like a walk in the park by comparison. The only question that remains is concerning those of us who do not actually live in Jerusalem and Judea. What about the rest of the world? Aren't we safe? Isn't this tribulation only for the modern-day land of Israel? You have to pause and think rationally about what is being said here in Mark. Who are the military allies of Israel? Russia, China, and all of its allies understand that in order to successfully capture and trample Jerusalem underfoot in fulfillment of this prophecy, they must successfully eliminate any and all allies of Israel.

That includes the US, UK, and all NATO countries that are either directly or indirectly allies of Israel.

There will very likely be a pre-emptive nuclear strike against the United States and all of its allies shortly after the bombs start going off in Jerusalem. That is why Mark speaks to us with such a dire warning and intense language. All of these things will become even more clear as we examine Luke.

LUKE 21: ARMIES, NEUTRON BOMBS, AND WRATH

Luke's account of Yeshua's words provides an excellent parallel from which to understand all of the nuances, Old Testament connections, and the bigger prophetic picture of what the abomination of desolation is all about. Luke 21:20 tells us this exact sign to be watching for in order to confirm that all of the calculations and understanding put forth within the pages of this book are indeed accurate: "But when you see Jerusalem surrounded by armies, then know that its desolation is near." Consider the nuances here. Is this verse speaking of literal ground troops surrounding Jerusalem? Yes, of course. We have already been witnessing these things in the nightly news. But I think this sign should also be interpreted as any military vessels that are visibly threatening Israel including naval ships, anti-aircraft systems, long-range missile systems, and fighter jets.

The prophetic reality of this verse has now become glaringly obvious with the rise of the aforementioned Axis of Resistance, consisting of Iran, Syria, the Houthis in Yemen, Hezbollah in Lebanon, several Palestinian groups (including Hamas), and an assortment of militias in Iraq along with aid and support coming into the Middle East from Russia and China. The presence of all of these hostile armies in close proximity to the land of Israel is the major sign that confirms all the calculations of this book to be accurate. There should be no doubting or second guessing as to the correct interpretation of Hebrew words like *shabua* at this point in history, and the responsibility of spreading this true understanding should not be taken lightly. I am eternally grateful to Yehovah to have been able to spearhead this correct teaching of the 70 weeks of Daniel when the first edition of this book was published in early 2023. Join me in fulfilling the words of Daniel 11:33 where it says that the wise people who understand shall instruct many. The time to share this urgent message is now!

Going back to the words of Yeshua, He then repeats the absolute necessity to flee to higher ground, stating: "Then let those who are in Judea flee to the mountains, let those who are in the midst of her depart, and let not those who are in the country enter her" (Luke 21:21). What I like about Luke is that unlike Matthew, this gospel writer explicitly makes a distinction between Jerusalem (the "holy place" of Mat. 24) and the surrounding region of Judea. We are again being warned that the literal, physical inhabitants of Judea are supposed to flee. This includes the cities of Tel Aviv, Be'er Sheva, Hebron and all of the West Bank and Gaza Strip.

Of course, the wise virgins that have been either prompted by the Holy Spirit or that have read *this* book well in advance have already made their escape. This is speaking to the unwise virgins who were not able to discern the signs of the times and rightly divide the Truth of the Word of God. They are being told not to go back and enter her (Judea) most likely because of nuclear fallout and radiation. Again, I have already made and will continue to make the case for the use of neutron bombs that release deadly gamma rays in order to destroy biological life but without devastating physical infrastructure. It is my opinion that these bombs could be used to quickly and swiftly destroy any Israeli military opposition to a Russian-Chinese-Islamic alliance and will result in a full ground assault and capture of Jerusalem once the radiation has ceased approximately two weeks after the nuclear abominations are deployed. The armies that will capture Jerusalem may want certain buildings, communications, and even military technologies of the current Israeli establishment to still be intact so that they can more profitably occupy the land of Israel.

This brings me to my next point. Let's skip a few verses and look at what Luke 21:24 says: "And they will fall by the edge of the sword, and be led away captive into all nations. And Jerusalem will be trampled by Gentiles until the times of the Gentiles are fulfilled." Like I already mentioned, these are the times of the Gentiles (Nations) spoken of in Daniel 7:25 and Revelation 11:2. This language of "trampled" is the same exact wording that we have already seen in Daniel regarding captivity and plundering.

But, why?

Why are such awful things going to be taking place? Well, we were already told by Daniel that it is because of transgression (rebellion) against God that these things must happen. This idea is once again confirmed with the use of the word "wrath" in Luk. 21:23. We are also told that the reason these things are happening is because all prophecy must be fulfilled. Just look at what Jesus told us: "For these are the days of vengeance, that all things which are written may be fulfilled" (Luke 21:22). This thought matches exactly what we see at the very beginning of the 70 shabua prophecy (Dan. 9:24). We were told that 70 shabua have been absolutely determined in order to make an end of all types of sins and to make an end of all prophecy. All things that are written are going to be fulfilled because of the events following the abomination(s) of desolation. This is the beginning of the end of various prophetic writings, and I will show you exactly what this looks like on a timeline with the Gog and Magog War alongside other complex prophecies when we discuss the 1,000-year reign of Christ in Chapter 10.

THE ABOMINATION OF DESOLATION COMMANDMENTS

Now that you have an idea of what will happen to the world sometime after September 2023, you need to arm yourself spiritually. Yes, pay attention to your physical needs and the need to make your flight to safety well in advance; but in and of itself, physical prepping is useless. No amount of preparation, strategic relocation, building of underground bunkers, having food stored for decades, living completely off grid, learning every survival skill, and all of these sorts of things is a substitute for intimacy with Almighty God.

No amount of physical preparation will prepare you or anyone else for what is coming.

In and of itself, even trying your absolute best to keep all of the things written in the Torah won't save you.

God wants your heart.

He is looking for worshippers to worship Him in Spirit and Truth. Not just in Spirit, like most Christians boast. Not just Truth, like most Messianics claim. Both must be present. Only this level of spiritual preparation is going to give you the military bearing and battle-hardened mentality to be able to truly experience what the very popular Psalm 91 says:

7 "A thousand may fall at your side,
And ten thousand at your right hand;
But it shall not come near you.
8 "Only with your eyes shall you look,
And see the reward of the wicked.
9 "Because you have made the LORD, *who is* my refuge,
Even the Most High, your dwelling place,"
(Psalm 91:7-9)

With that said, let's take a look at the things that Yeshua commanded us to do in preparation for these events that are about to happen on the earth. This isn't meant to be an all-inclusive list, but let's go through and look at the major things that Yeshua commanded those of us living in the last days.

The first one is to not be deceived (Mat. 24:4) because many false anointed people claiming to know the Messiah and be a true follower of His will be leading people astray with complacency, horrible doctrine, and plans to invest, build, and store up earthly goods but without properly discerning the signs of the times (Luk. 12:20). Their lives will be required of them, and they won't be ready to give a proper account. Don't mix yourself with deception, deceiving spirits, and false prophets.

The second commandment is to not have anxiety or be terrified by the events of the last days (Mat. 24:6). All of the wars and various problems must happen because it is God's will. Rest in His will. He's doing these things and is in full control.

Next we are told to be spiritually prepared for persecution (Mar. 13:10), and we need to prepare ourselves well in advance to be able to discern the voice of the Holy Spirit so that He can work through us and speak His wisdom to our persecutors (Luk. 21:15). In other words, the persecution will be necessary to accomplish the will of the Father. He will choose to magnify Himself through the mouths of the persecuted to create unique opportunities for people to hear the gospel message and also to further condemn the wicked so that the wrath of God can be accomplished. We are commanded to endure until the end, without our love growing cold (Mat. 24:13).

We already discussed the need to pray about your escape well in advance, which is the next commandment. This is obviously true for people living in the land of Israel, specifically Judea. However, it is also true for people living in countries that are military allies of the modern state of Israel. All military targets in ally nations will be devastated in the coming war, and the Russian-Chinese alliance will certainly devastate many major metropolitan targets according to the will of God. Cities and places of deep-rooted spiritual wickedness should be avoided at all cost because they will be judged like Sodom and Gomorrah.

After the great tribulation, Yeshua once again gives us the warning to not be deceived, but this time it is concerning some sort of false visions or demonic hallucinations about the return of Christ to the earth (Mat. 24:23). We are not to believe the lies, and I will describe the essence of this deception in Chapter 13. Our Master also makes it clear that after the cosmic disturbances (powers of the heavens shaken and stars of heaven falling) surrounding these events, we are to lift up our heads and look upwards because He will be returning in the clouds to redeem His people (Luk. 21:27,28).

While we are still able to do so, Yeshua tells us to watch, pray, and provide the spiritual food to His people as these specific events of the last days unfold (Mar. 13:33; Mat. 24:45). That's precisely why sharing *this* book is so important! Let's do our best to spread the word and help God's people truly understand the time of the end. There is also this very profound commandment given to us in Luke 21:35: "Watch therefore, and pray always that you may be counted worthy to escape all these things that will come to pass, and to stand before the Son of Man." The connection of this verse to the selection of the 144,000 in Revelation is unmistakable and truly remarkable. These special people will literally stand before Yeshua in heaven and sing a new song that no one else knows. We will discuss the details of this mysterious prophecy in Chapter 12.

SECRET I: AN OVERVIEW

In summary of the 70 weeks of Daniel prophecy, the correct understanding of the Hebrew word *shabua* together with the true identity of Daniel's people were the first keys to unlocking the entire prophecy. The Feast of Weeks, commonly known as Pentecost, was indeed the code phrase that Daniel used to seal up the numerology of the timeline. The connection of the *shabua* concept to the sabbatical year concept of Leviticus and then the 120 cycles of Moses further revealed the correct sequence of events. It is from the commandment at the burning bush to the birth of King David that the first seven *shabuim* are to be counted, leaving us with 62 weeks afterwards. Counting the years from that time leaves us with the firm conclusion that 1996 to the spring of 2045 is the final and 70th week of Daniel. Rather than being a seven-year period of time as many falsely teach, the "covenant with many" was a 49-year period of time that began in 1972 and ended in 2020.

Regarding the middle of the 70th week and the year 2020, the Covid-19 pandemic was indeed the event that kickstarted the prophetic clock of various chapters of Daniel. The vision of the "2,300 evening-morning" is now complete, since the WHO declared the beginning of the pandemic to be March 11, 2020 and officially declared its end on May 5, 2023—a period of exactly 1150 days, or 2300 total evening-mornings. Therefore, the Daniel 8 prophecy of the little horn trampling underfoot the descendants of Abraham now appears to be fully complete. The remaining prophecies to be fulfilled concern the abomination of desolation and the immense warfare that will commence afterwards. Based on sound logic and the ample evidence presented so far, we know that Iran obtained at least one nuclear weapon on September 22, 2023 that will be used against Israel to usher in the Great Tribulation during any winter-Sabbath day moving forward into the future. The people of the coming prince will likely be an Islamic hoard consisting of various Arab and Islamic-majority nations together with the descendants of Esau taking their share of the spoils of war. The "prince" himself is likely a reference to the prophesied false messiah, or Mahdi, of Islam, though there could easily be collaboration with top Western officials within the World Economic Forum framework to implement the mark of the beast. Finally, we are to expect the total fulfillment of the "anointed will be cut off and have nothing" prophecy of Daniel in which all powers of the West will be subdued and put into slavery in the aftermath of the coming war. The next Secret of this book will further provide undeniable evidence of Iran's role in the abomination of desolation and how key passages of Scripture speak of the use of modern technology in the most remarkable way.

Secret II:

Modern Technology In Ancient Scripture

"But you, Daniel, shut up the words, and seal the book until the time of the end; many shall run to and fro, and knowledge shall increase."

- Daniel 12:4

Chapter 7
Zechariah's Flying Scrolls

At some point in your journey through prophecy you undoubtedly heard a sermon where a preacher has alluded to the Bible's possible descriptions of military technology—be it missiles, bombs, or aircraft—throughout various scriptures. From the rise of early modern warfare in the late 1500s with the widespread use of gunpowder to the present-day development of advanced weaponry systems, the battlefield of the nations has always captivated the minds of men in their interpretations of Daniel, Revelation, and the Prophets. Understanding the generational struggle of geopolitics and warfare is not only essential for investigating all the nuances of Bible prophecy, but our last-days generation now possesses the unique ability to see the Scriptures through such a clear lens at this point in history; so clear, in fact, that it is downright embarrassing for the truths presented in this chapter to have remained so hidden and misunderstood all this time. These truths should have been more widely proclaimed since at least the time of World War II, and alas, here they are. What this chapter will show you using the tried-and-true three laws of interpretation approach is precisely how and where the Scriptures speak of modern warfare along with who the major players are in the fulfillment of various prophecies. This investigation once again begins with Daniel. Speaking of our present day, Daniel 12:4 states:

"But you, Daniel, shut up the words, and seal the book until the time of the end; many shall run to and fro, and knowledge shall increase."

Though everyone knows that knowledge has increased in these last days and with it all the technological breakthroughs of the 21st century, many fail to realize that this reality has been unprecedented in the post-flood world. Military technology had remained stagnant and limited only to the horse and chariot for thousands of years. In fulfillment of various end-times prophecies, however, a sudden shift became apparent within the last five or so centuries. This shift began with several inventions such as Gutenberg's movable type printing press in 1440. Such printing allowed for knowledge to begin spreading far and wide like never before. In terms of warfare, the invention of gunpowder, the earliest known explosive, is credited to the Chinese Taoists in the 9th century who made the discovery while in search of an elixir of immortality.[1] This occult knowledge then spread abroad to the Middle East and Europe in the 1200s and proceeded to revolutionize warfare a little over 300 years later. Because of the simplicity of firearms, the common men and peasants of Europe suddenly possessed the ability to readily organize and show force against governments and nations after the gunpowder revolution. This newly acquired knowledge led to the rise of major wars during the early modern warfare period, beginning with the European wars of religion (1520-1640) and ending with the Napoleonic Wars (1804-1815). This time period also coincided with the rise of the first known iron-cased rockets that were successfully deployed for military use in India. These were the Mysorean rockets that the late 18th century Kingdom of Mysore used for fighting against the British East India Company.[2] Under King Hyder Ali and his son King Tipu Sultan, large caches of tens of thousands of rockets were developed, and the British would describe them as being like a thick and destructive hail in the skies of the battlefield with devastating explosions that would lacerate their victims. These iron-cased Indian rockets proved to be the precursor of the sophisticated projectile technologies that we see today—projectiles that the prophet Zechariah had recorded for us in his book about 2,300 years in advance of their first appearance in the post-flood world.

Figure 7.1: The Mysorean Rockets. (left) An artistic representation of an Indian soldier of Tipu Sultan's army, using his rocket as a flagstaff, by British artist Robert Home. (right) Tipu Sultan used rockets against British forces in the battle of Guntur in 1780 (pictured above) and the battle of Seringapatam in 1792.

THE BOOK OF ZECHARIAH

Our main focus is the fifth chapter of the book of Zechariah, but in order to even hope to understand this particular chapter, a main overview of the history and context surrounding when the entire book was written is necessary. Zechariah was a prophet that wrote his book in the second year of king Darius of the Persians as stated in the first and opening verse. This geopolitical context is paramount. This Darius the Great was a Persian ruler that reigned from 522 to 486 BC, putting the setting of Zechariah's work in approximately 521 BC. At this time, the captives of Judah were already returning back to the land of Canaan from their Babylonian exile. This return is commonly understood to have commenced with a decree from Cyrus the Great, the founder of the Achaemenid (Persian) Empire, that occurred around 538 BC just a few years prior. Though the entire 70 years of captivity had not yet been completed from 586 BC (the fall of Jerusalem) to 516 BC, history records that Judah was allowed to return back in waves near the end of this time period and not all at once as might be imagined. Moreover, Nehemiah's arrival along with Ezra the Scribe took place in the middle of the 5th century BC during the reign of Artaxerxes I of the Persians (465–424 BC). Therefore, the full return of Judah's remnant did not emphatically take place until another six decades after the cutoff date of 516 BC. That being the case, the setting of Zechariah's book still qualifies him as being one of three post-exilic (after the exile) prophets alongside Haggai and Malachi.

Again, this context is of utmost importance for discerning all the words of Zechariah. His book was written about five years before the 516 BC cutoff date of Judah's judgment. Jerusalem was not yet rebuilt and neither was the second temple. Since Israel was fully conquered by the Assyrians in 722 BC, Zechariah's book was written almost exactly 200 years after the fact, which is quite a long time. Therefore, when you open Zechariah and see the name *Israel* being mentioned five times and also the name *Judah* being mentioned twenty-two times, it should be readily obvious that all of the things being described are dealing with future events that have not yet happened. Yehovah's various charges against His people, the extensive judgments involved, and His promises of complete future restoration were of very little relevance to Zechariah's day. All of these prophecies were describing key events to be fulfilled during the 70th week of Daniel. As the book of Zechariah is explored in this chapter and those following, it should be understood that over 90% of this prophet's writings were describing future events rather than historical or contemporary ones.

Book of Zechariah Overview	
Chapter 1	Myrtle Trees vision / What the "former prophets" said
Chapter 2	Four Horns and Four Craftsmen (regathering of Israel & Judah)
Chapter 3	Joshua the earthly High Priest
Chapter 4	The Two Olive Trees and the Menorah
Chapter 5	The Flying Scroll (Nuclear Missile) to judge the whole earth
Chapter 6	Four Chariots (Four Winds) / Charge to rebuild Temple in Jerusalem
Chapter 7	False fasting, refusal to obey Torah, and the scattering of Israel
Chapter 8	Future and Final Restoration of Zion (regathering of all 12 tribes)
Chapter 9	Last days judgment of many nations / Final restoration of Zion
Chapter 10	End times judgment and final regathering of Israel
Chapter 11	Destruction of nations / Two Staffs / Whole earth under judgment
Chapter 12	Future protection of the regathered in Jerusalem
Chapter 13	Final cleansing from sin
Chapter 14	Gog and Magog Part II / Return of Yeshua back to the earth

Figure 7.2: The Book of Zechariah and its Major Themes. Chapters 3 and 6 provide specific details about Zechariah's contemporary time while the remainder are loaded with events—both figurative and literal—pertaining to the 70th week of Daniel.

THE "FLYING SCROLLS" OF ZECHARIAH CHAPTER 5

Herein lies one of the most misunderstood and underappreciated last-days prophecies of the entire Bible with a profound curse that will have consequences for the entire world. It is first important to point out that this vision is a continuation of the same word of Yehovah that came to Zechariah as recorded in the seventh verse of the first chapter.

"On the twenty-fourth day of the eleventh month, which is the month Shebat, in the second year of Darius, the word of the LORD came to Zechariah the son of Berechiah, the son of Iddo the prophet"
(Zec. 1:7)

There is no apparent pause in the narrative nor an obvious break where

Zechariah ceases from prophesying from this point and onward until Zec. 7:1 where a timestamp is once again provided. It should be understood, then, that Zechariah 5 is part of a continuous word from God that was received to initiate his entire book—a word containing direct dictations from the throne of the Most High as well as visions containing critical information about the destiny of scattered Israel and Judah during the last days. By now you should have a clear understanding of the lost tribes of Israel and Judah along with their end-times nations. This prophecy is going to have direct consequences for them both as you will see. Using the King James version due to its more accurate rendering of Zechariah 5, let's begin with the first verse:

"Then I turned, and lifted up mine eyes, and looked, and behold a flying roll." (Zec. 5:1 KJV)

Most translations say flying "scroll" like what you would think of in ancient times as being a book or letter that is rolled up and inserted into a protective sleeve. The underlying Hebrew word (Strong's H4039) can be transliterated as *megillah* and refers to a roll, a volume, or a writing. However, there is a distinction to be made here between a *megillah* and other scrolls like the Torah scroll containing Genesis to Deuteronomy. During the time of Judah's return out of exile, there was a brief revival and recommitment to the God of the Bible under the leadership of both Ezra and Nehemiah. We are told that the following event took place after the rebuilding of Jerusalem's walls and gates was completed:

"Now all the people gathered together as one man in the open square that was in front of the Water Gate; and they told Ezra the scribe to bring the Book of the Law of Moses, which the LORD had commanded Israel." (Neh. 8:1 NKJV)

This is one of the clearest places in Scripture where we see the "Book" of the Torah being described as a "sepher" (Strong's H5612), which is a masculine singular noun often used to refer to books. A Torah scroll in particular has two rollers each having two handles for scrolling through the text. This physical distinction is why Zechariah instead chose the word *megillah* instead of *sepher* to describe what he saw. A megillah, such as the scrolls of Esther, Ecclesiastes, the Song of Solomon, the Book of Ruth, and the Book of Lamentations, is only a single roll instead of being a double roll like the Torah. This conclusion is further reinforced by the exact dimensions provided in the next verse of Zechariah.

Figure 7.3: A Scroll of Esther (Megillat Esther). Unlike a Torah scroll, it has only one roller, or binder.

"And he said unto me, What seest thou? And I answered, 'I see a flying roll; the length thereof is twenty cubits, and the breadth thereof ten cubits.'"
(Zec 5:2 KJV)

The next and primary indication that we are reading about military technology is the fact that Zechariah saw this scroll flying through the air. Such a thing was completely unheard of in his day. A size of 20 cubits long by 10 cubits wide adds further validity to this mysterious object's identity as a ballistic missile of some sort. Of course, the untrained reader has no doubt looked at this verse and imagined a flying rectangle (which I jokingly refer to as a flying carpet) in his mind, as if the scroll were stretched out to be a rectangular 20 x 10 shape. The giveaway that this idea is false is found within the Hebrew word "verakhba" (Strong's H7341) translated as "breadth." Thickness, largeness, and wideness are all meanings ascribed to the Hebrew word. There are two ways of imagining this thickness of the flying scroll. The 10 cubits either describes the circumference of the cylinder or it describes the diameter. We will examine both options. Regarding the cubit itself, this unit of measurement commonly understood as being from the elbow to the tip of the middle finger varies widely from ancient Sumeria to Greece and can be anywhere from about 17 to 22 inches. Though the Bible describes different cubits that were to be employed depending on the context, I will be relying on the BLB description that states the common biblical cubit as being about 18 inches (45.72 cm).[3] The length is therefore:

18"/cubit x 20 cubits = 30', or 9.144 meters

Assuming that Zechariah is referring to the breadth as being diameter rather than circumference, we must divide this diameter (18"/cubit x 10 cubits) in half in order to find the radius, which is 180" divided by two to give us 90". Then we can use the formula for finding circumference:

$$C = 2\pi r$$
$$C = 2 \times 3.14... \times 90"$$
$$C \approx 565" \text{ or } 47' \text{ (14.33 meters)}$$

Because the calculated circumference, or thickness, of 47' far exceeds the actual length of 30', then this interpretation does not make sense just like the "flying carpet" interpretation does not make sense. Zechariah's provided length simply cannot be exceeded by the width. Therefore, the number provided to us for the 10 cubit *breadth* must be referring to the *circumference* of the scroll and nothing else. Therefore, the circumference is: 18"/cubit x 10 cubits = 180" or 15' (4.57m).

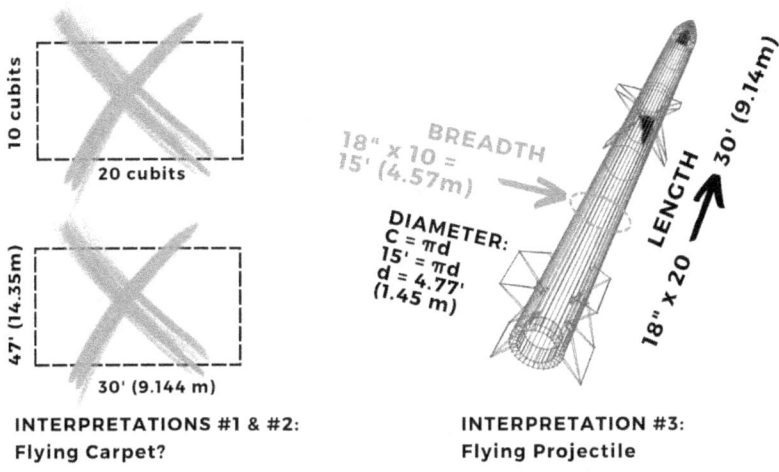

INTERPRETATIONS #1 & #2:
Flying Carpet?

INTERPRETATION #3:
Flying Projectile

Figure 7.4: Visualizing the Flying Scroll's Dimensions. Since we know "breadth" to be circumference, we can calculate the diameter to be 1.45 meters.

What this verse is really telling us is that the flying scroll will have a height of 30', which, assuming that a one-story building is 10-12 feet tall, means that the projectile being described is about three stories tall. The circumference of about 4.57 meters with a diameter of 1.45 meters perfectly matches the specifications for a number of missiles that have currently been developed for Iran's military arsenal. You will see why I am once again focusing on Iran as we move forward in this investigation from a scriptural standpoint, but this is the most hostile country against 1948 Israel that will rise up to fulfill the abomination of desolation prophecy. According to a recent *New York Times* article citing insider knowledge of Iran's military planning, the country's westernmost border with Iraq is now loaded with ballistic missiles that are ready to be used for an eventual clash with Israel and the West.[4] Many of these strategic positions are located within the Zagros Mountains where hardened launch positions and nuclear silos can even be spotted from Google Earth.[5,6] Hundreds of meters beneath the surface, Iran's mountainous terrain is filled with deep underground military bases and manufacturing facilities where missiles, drones, fighter jets, trucks, and various heavy military equipment are located. Declassified video footage of these bases has been released where it appears that the sophisticated tunnel systems stretch for miles within the heart of the country, making Iran extremely difficult for the West to outmaneuver or strike effectively. It has also been reported that Iran's technology has become so advanced that it has now become an exporter, sending hundreds of ballistic missiles to Russia for its fight against Ukraine.[7]

Of all the known missile technologies that Iran currently has at its disposal, there are a few that easily fit the description of the particular missile that Zechariah saw, provided that some elbow room is allowed in the interpretation of a cubit's exact length. Keeping in mind that the distance from Iran's westernmost border to Jerusalem is anywhere from 1,000 to 1,200 km, we are able to clearly discern which missile Iran might use. For example, the Zolfaghar[8] has the appropriate range to strike Israel (1,000 km for Dezful model and 1,400 km for the Qasem model), but it has a diameter of either 0.6 m (Zolfaghar and Dezful) or 0.9 m (Qasem) and therefore falls just short of the missile described by Zechariah at 1.45 m. However, this missile is very close to the specified length at 10.3 m. Next up, the medium-range Khorramshahr ballistic missile has a diameter between 1.5-1.8 m, which is a near-perfect match of Zechariah, but its length of 13 – 13.5 m makes it fall just outside the specifications.[9] Iran's newly developed Fattah class of missiles is particularly interesting in the context of this analysis. Officially unveiled on June 6, 2023, Iran's Fattah is the first domestically-produced hypersonic missile, capable of reaching speeds around Mach 14 (15,000km/h).[10] To put this into perspective, Iran's Sobh-e-Sadegh newspaper purportedly stated that the new Iranian hypersonic missile could reach Israel in 400 seconds, as reported by the *Jerusalem Post*.[11] Oddly enough, 400 seconds happens to be 6.667 minutes. The currently known specifications of the Fattah missile also appear to match the words of Zechariah's 2,500-year-old prophecy. Its length is estimated to be 12 meters and the diameter 0.8 meters;[12] and though these estimates fall outside of Zechariah's measurements, the Fattah's ability to bypass all currently known missile defense systems of the West[13] makes it a very strong candidate for fulfilling the flying scroll prophecy and also the abomination of desolation. Modifications and improvements are a part of any military's routine, and Iran's ability to produce a replica of Zechariah's flying scroll with the exact dimensions provided should be obvious by now. The most important realization at this point in time is that Iran is in the perfect position to fulfill its role in Bible prophecy by using something just like the Fattah that is built to the specifications of Zechariah 5:2.

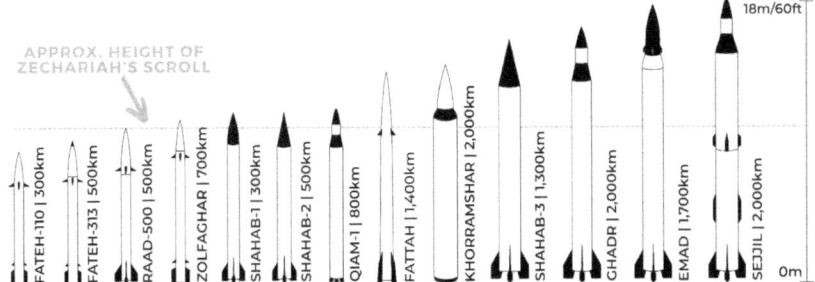

Figure 7.5: The Missiles of Iran and Their Flight Ranges. The dotted line indicates the approximate height of Zechariah's flying scroll. This illustration is based on a 2021 article available at the Missile Threat website[14] but with the addition of the new 2023 Fattah hypersonic missile. The distance from Iran's western border to Jerusalem ranges from just over 1000 km to around 1200 km. Numerous Iranian missiles and their variants fall within the flight range necessary (1000–1200 km) to devastate Jerusalem and fulfill Bible prophecy.

We will now examine the next two verses of Zechariah together because they are part of the same thought. These next words explain *why* the flying scroll is a curse and precisely *why* these scrolls will be raining down upon the whole world:

3 Then said he unto me, This is the curse that goeth forth over the face of the whole earth: for every one that stealeth shall be cut off as on this side according to it; and every one that sweareth shall be cut off as on that side according to it.
4 I will bring it forth, saith the LORD of hosts, and it shall enter into the house of the thief, and into the house of him that sweareth falsely by my name: and it shall remain in the midst of his house, and shall consume it with the timber thereof and the stones thereof.
(Zec. 5:3,4)

The next thing we are being told is that this flying missile is a "curse" from God. This exact same Hebrew word "ha'ala" (Strong's H423, הָאָלָה) is found in Deuteronomy 29:19 where it speaks of the eternal curse of the Torah that applies to all who would walk in rebellion to the most High God. Speaking of such a person, the Word specifically states that "Adonai will be unwilling to forgive him" (Deu. 29:19 TLV). This particular verse of Deuteronomy also happens to perfectly describe what Jesus meant by the unforgivable or "unpardonable" sin in the New Testament. Here is what we read in Matthew 12 (see also Luke 12:10):

"Therefore I say to you, every sin and blasphemy will be forgiven men, but the blasphemy *against* the Spirit will not be forgiven men."
(Mat. 12:31 NKJV)

Time is of the essence, and you must know what this unforgivable sin is that Yeshua describes so that you don't ever become guilty of it. While 1John 1:9 says, "If we confess our sins, He is faithful and just to forgive us our sins and to cleanse us from all unrighteousness", there is in fact a sin that God will not forgive. This is one of those topics that once understood will set you free from the chains of bondage. The shackles of fear, anxiety, and uncertainty will be completely broken off of you. Slowly consider what Jesus is *really* saying here. If "blasphemy against the Spirit" is the sin that is being described by Jesus as being unforgivable, then all you have to do is understand what the Holy Spirit's job is. We are told this fact within the actual context of the "unpardonable sin" in Luke 12:11-12:

11 "Now when they bring you to the synagogues and magistrates and authorities, do not worry about how or what you should answer, or what you should say.
12 For the Holy Spirit will teach you in that very hour what you ought to say."

Speaking of a future persecution, Yeshua explains that the Holy Spirit will provide all of the inspired words and testimony before the accusers of His people so that they might stand blameless. We can plainly see here that the Holy Spirit's job is to teach. The only question is, what does He teach us, exactly? Here is what the Word Made Flesh had to say in John 14:26:

"But the Helper, the Holy Spirit, whom the Father will send in My name, He will teach you all things, and bring to your remembrance all things that I said to you."

The reason I referred to Jesus as the Word Made Flesh is because that is exactly how John describes Him in John 1:1. He had all of the glory of the Father contained within Himself as he tabernacled, or temporary dwelt, among us as John 1:14 also said. The Holy Spirit teaches us all of the Words of the Father that the Word Made Flesh spoke in His name, with His authority, and with all glory. Once you understand these simple connections that I have just presented, you will completely understand the unforgivable sin and its connection to Zechariah's prophecy.

Are you teachable? Are you humbly accepting the leading and guiding of the Holy Spirit in your life? Or, are you rebelling against the Words of God that the Holy Spirit so desperately wants to teach you?

What Jesus taught us is that it is in fact rebellion against the Holy Spirit's teachings, whisperings in our hearts, and bringing to our remembrance all of the Words of God from Genesis to Revelation that will cause us to be unforgiven and suffer the eternal consequences. It is blasphemy of the Holy Spirit when someone does not allow the Holy Spirit to teach them all of the words of the Most High Elohim, specifically His Torah which is now supposed to be written on our hearts through the blood of the Word Made Flesh and the New Covenant that He initiated at the Last Supper. Many churches today teach that God's laws, instructions, precepts, ordinances, and statutes as found in the first five books of the Bible are done away with. Many churches today also teach that God's appointed times were for Jewish people or are now done away with and no longer necessary for us to follow. God says otherwise. For example, He specifically told us that the person that does not rest and "afflict his soul" for the Day of Atonement is supposed to be "cut off" from being a part of His people (Lev. 23:29). One of the biggest false teachings of Western Christianity is that before Jesus came there was no true salvation and there was no true righteousness. Nobody could actually pray to God and be heard because a temple or tabernacle was necessary in order for prayers to be fully accepted. There are variations of these false ideas, but you can see the essence of this prevailing mentality. These popular lies are thoroughly destroyed with a simple understanding of the man, Daniel, and the life he lead. This man was called greatly beloved and was considered one of the three most righteous men of all time alongside Noah and Job (Eze. 14:14). However, there was no temple for Daniel to be able to perform all of the ritualistic things found in Torah. He was not living in the land of Israel. How did he know when to keep Abib and all of the Feasts at the correct time? How did he receive reports of the barley in Israel for the presentation of one omer in order to keep wave sheaf day? He was not able to go to Jerusalem three times a year to present himself for the annual Feasts. He was in exile and living under a government opposed to the Most High just like you and I today. Why was Daniel considered so righteous if he could barely observe God's Torah? Within the answer to this question lies one of the greatest mysteries of the entire Bible—a mystery that most people fail to ever understand in their lifetime. The answer is found in the words of Habbakuk, when he said, "Behold the proud, His soul is not upright in him; But the just shall live by his faith" (Hab. 2:4). Because Daniel understood the helplessness of his spiritual situation in light of the exile and his complete inability to observe the instructions of the Scriptures, he chose to live by his faith.

The Christian world stumbles over this reality due to "dispensational theology," which is a fancy term for "God changes His mind throughout different periods (dispensations) of history." God doesn't change, which is why Daniel's life is so relevant for you and I today. Just like any true follower of Christ, Daniel chose to place 100% of his faith not in his own abilities, knowledge, or performance; but he chose the object of his faith to be God alone. He put his faith in God to justify him and declare him to be righteous. That is what Habakkuk meant by the just living by his faith. It is the object of the faith that makes all the difference in the world. The only real difference between the Old Testament saints and the New Testament saints is that the Hebrews of old only knew Elohim by His name of Yehovah. Today, we understand the more complete revelation of Jesus and His sacrificial fulfillment of numerous Messianic prophecies, though he is the exact same person as Yehovah. We now understand Yehovah, Yeshua, and the Holy Spirit with a more complete understanding than what the Old Testament saints were able to experience.

Keeping in mind the spiritual climate of today, you will notice that all the recipients of Zechariah's flying-scroll curse are guilty of walking in rebellion to God and His instructions as revealed in His Law. They are guilty of committing the unforgivable sin, since they have not been willing to let the Holy Spirit teach them all the words of God. The first sin listed is theft. This may seem like a strange accusation, until these verses from the Torah are carefully weighed out on the scales of justice:

"If you lend money to any of My people who are poor among you, you shall not be like a moneylender to him; you shall not charge him interest."
(Exo. 22:25)

'If one of your brethren becomes poor, and falls into poverty among you, then you shall help him, like a stranger or a sojourner, that he may live with you.

'Take no usury or interest from him; but fear your God, that your brother may live with you.
'You shall not lend him your money for usury, nor lend him your food at a profit.'
(Lev. 25:35-37)

"You shall not charge interest to your brother—interest on money or food or anything that is lent out at interest."
(Deu. 23:19)

The Word of God makes it explicitly clear that there is not to be payable interest amongst God's people. Interest was not something that was supposed to exist between the people of His set-apart nation. In today's world, this law of anti-interest must apply to brethren, or citizens, of the same country and within the same borders. Yet, every single major currency in the world today is a debt-based fiat currency, upon which the payment of interest is an intrinsic part of its value and function. Look up the Hebrew word for *money* in the Scriptures and you will find it referring to *kesef,* or silver. Rather than being backed by a physical commodity such as gold or silver, a fiat currency is a medium of exchange that does not have value in and of itself apart from that which is assigned by a government and agreed to by the consensus of other nations as being a legitimate form of payment. In other words, *paper money* is pieces of paper that, in and of themselves, are not able to be redeemed for something physical with tangible value, since they are backed by nothing. That is why one US dollar in 1920 could buy 3.6 gallons of milk when today the same dollar can only buy 0.3 gallons of milk.[15] Fiat systems are desperately plagued with inflation because they are contrary to the true prosperity described in God's instructions.

In reality, paper money represents meaningless notes of indebtedness due to the fact that the whole fiat system is dependent on interest rates. This complex system of over 30,000 banks worldwide can cause confusion. In simplistic terms, the way the system is *theoretically* supposed to work is that people deposit their money in banks and receive a small amount of interest. The bank then takes this deposited money and lends it out at much higher interest rates, which is a calculated risk that they take on since a certain number of their lenders will default on their debt. This whole process explains how industries and businesses are able to expand and how people take mortgage loans to buy houses. It also explains boom and bust cycles depending on the risky behavior that is enabled by low interest rates. That is why there are direct consequences for borrowers and investors but also indirect consequences for everyone that must participate in a fiat economy. Interest rates, or the amount of interest due in a specific period of time, fluctuate according to the will of the central bank in charge.

The reason I mentioned these principles as being *theoretical* only is because the inner workings are more sinister and complicated. In the US, the whole fiat system is managed by an unelected and unaccountable institution called the Federal Reserve. This establishment makes all the rules on interest rates without the consent of the people. To make matters worse, the US dollar's status as a world reserve currency has allowed it to bully the world through imperialism, the weaponization of economic sanctions (restrictions) upon its enemies, and the printing of money on demand whenever the need arises, be it for stimulus packages like the Covid Rescue Plan or more money for the military industrial complex in Ukraine. The ability of a fiat system to print money out of thin air in order to finance the debt of ongoing operations creates a negative feedback loop of more inflation, resulting in decreased purchasing power for everyday citizens and lifelong servitude to housing loans, for example, that become harder and harder to pay off over time. Fiat money is therefore not *money* in the true sense of the word, but it is an unjust weight and measure of value. Speaking of such a thing, this is what Yehovah told Moses:

13 "You shall not have in your bag differing weights, a heavy and a light.
14 "You shall not have in your house differing measures, a large and a small.
15 "You shall have a perfect and just weight, a perfect and just measure, that your days may be lengthened in the land which the LORD your God is giving you.
16 "For all who do such things, all who behave unrighteously, are an abomination to the LORD your God."
(Deu. 25:13-16)

We are being shown in these words that a standardized unit, or value, of measurement must be used when engaging in righteous business transactions with others. An ever-changing paper note of indebtedness does not maintain a specific value but instead inflates and becomes more worthless over time. This chapter of Deuteronomy is a particular place in the Torah where the specific order of the divine instructions provides deeper insight into what is meant by just weights and measures. The very next verses proclaim the following:

17 "Remember what Amalek did to you on the way as you were coming out of Egypt,

18 "how he met you on the way and attacked your rear ranks, all the stragglers at your rear, when you were tired and weary; and he did not fear God.
19 "Therefore it shall be, when the LORD your God has given you rest from your enemies all around, in the land which the LORD your God is giving you to possess as an inheritance, that you will blot out the remembrance of Amalek from under heaven. You shall not forget."
(Deu. 25:17-19)

The first real war that Israel fought after the Exodus from Egypt was against the Amalekites. The original account provided in Exodus 17 does not mention the details provided here in Deuteronomy about how Amalek acted in cowardice to make a sneak attack against the rear ranks of Israel. In ancient times it was customary to place the men of war at the front of a caravan so as to protect the women and children from conflicts that could arise as the traveling party advanced. Knowing this, Amalek attacked the weakest members of Israel's ranks in the hopes of overwhelming their opponent. Unjust weights and measures such as fiat money are the same as Amalek, which is why Yehovah spoke to Moses in the precise order that He did. The built-in inflation of paper money always hurts the weakest and most vulnerable members of society first. It ruins the livelihoods of those that are less fortunate and that depend on the leadership of others for survival. Inflation destroys women, children, and the needy of society.

The fiat system is a yoke of bondage that is fundamentally tied to the issuing and payment of interest—a thing expressly forbidden by God and therefore considered a form of robbery, extortion, and theft through the lens of Torah. Though we all must participate in such a system in order to carry out our day-to-day lives, it is those people who have whole-heartedly embraced the system, loved it, and wished to see it continue into the future that will bear Zechariah's curse upon their heads. Of course, there are other ways of viewing the concepts of theft and robbery being described by Zechariah, but the whole world's love of gain is fundamentally tied to the exchange of interest-fueled fiat "money."

Zechariah also mentions that the curse is for those that swear and more specifically, those who swear falsely by God's name. While there are many places to search for clarity on this concept, it must once again be repeated that the religious institutions of the West have twisted the Word of God to their own destruction and have claimed to be inspired by the Holy Spirit to speak the truth when in reality they only speak lies. That is why Yeshua will declare to many that He never knew them (Mat. 7:23) on the day of judgment, and they will be forced to depart out of His presence and forbidden to enter the kingdom of heaven. Proverbs 6:16-19 also declares to us what are commonly known as the seven deadly sins. Of these seven abominations that Yehovah hates, two of them are expressly stated as a "lying tongue" and a "false witness who speaks lies." The words of the Proverbs combined with Zechariah's declaration have far-reaching consequences for all inhabitants of the earth, especially those who have led others astray with a false gospel and lawless Christianity.

Regarding the latter part of Zechariah 5:4, it might be obvious to you exactly what this verse is talking about due to the foundation already laid in this book. The question is: What kind of a curse of military technology will remain inside of a home and continue to consume both the dimensional lumber (2x4, 2x6, etc.) and the concrete (stone) foundation even after such a weapon is used? Of course, nuclear weapons with their fallout that remains afterwards perfectly fit this description. To be more specific, nuclear fallout is the leftover radioactive material that is propelled into the atmosphere after a nuclear blast. This radioactive dust and ash "falls out" of the sky after a nuclear weapon explodes and has varying degrees of impact depending on the size of the nuclear warhead that is detonated. The language speaking of nuclear technology will become more evident as the described warhead, or the payload, comes into focus in the next verses. Pay attention to the obvious shift in the narrative.

5 Then the angel that talked with me went forth, and said unto me, "Lift up now thine eyes, and see what is this that goeth forth."
6 And I said, "What is it?" And he said, "This is an ephah that goeth forth." He said moreover, "This is their resemblance through all the earth." (Zec 5:5,6 KJV)

The title of the chapter of this book is "Zechariah's Flying Scrolls" rather than just one singular "Scroll" because we are being told here that there will be numerous such scrolls throughout the face of the earth. Each of them will contain a "basket," which is the most common English rendering of a Hebrew concept that has been "lost in translation," as people say. The KJV's use of the word *ephah* is accurate since this is merely a transliteration of the Hebrew word. Exodus 16:36 tells us that an omer is equal to one tenth of an ephah. Since we understand an omer's measure to be 2 liters, that would make an ephah equal to 20 liters; however, the BLB definition for *ephah* lists the measurement as being either 40 or 20 liters.[16] In other words, Zechariah's ephah is a container between 20-40 liters in volume, and its description as the payload, or warhead, of the weapon will become more clear as the contents are examined in the next two verses. For now, it is important to understand the basic anatomy of a missile because the whole purpose of launching the projectile is to deliver the payload located at the tip of the missile. The entire missile, or flying scroll, itself is composed of mostly fuel. There are different ways to design the cylinder and its fuel system in order to propel the warhead from point A to point B. One typical medium-range design is shown in the next figure.

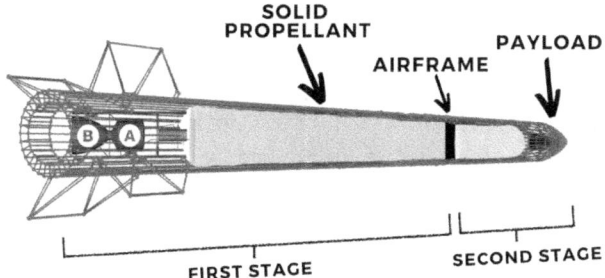

Figure 7.6: The Anatomy of a Ballistic Missile.

The entire missile is encased in the airframe made of a lightweight material that is also as strong as possible. Solid propellants are preferred over liquid for military applications because they are always combat ready whereas liquids require immediate fueling prior to launch. (A) represents the engine while (B) represents the nozzle that directs exhaust gasses to provide thrust. Medium-range missiles like what Iran might use against Israel can consist of a two-step staging process. In such a design, after the propellant of one section is exhausted, the motor and tanks are ejected, and the second segment takes over to allow the payload to reach its final destination.[17] The payload (warhead) can be conventional or nuclear, but Zechariah's description provided in the next verses gives tremendous weight to the latter.

7 And, behold, there was lifted up a talent of lead: and this is a woman that sitteth in the midst of the ephah.
8. And he said, "This is wickedness." And he cast it into the midst of the ephah; and he cast the weight of lead upon the mouth thereof.
(Zec. 5:7,8)

We are being told here that there is a talent of lead inside of the ephah. A talent is simply a unit of weight that varies depending on the material it is associated with. Zechariah's word choice here is not an accident. He could have used a wide variety of different Hebrew words to describe the talent of "lead" such as a talent of iron, copper, brass, gold, or silver. He chose to describe what he saw as being *lead* for a very specific reason, but we must first understand the "woman." The analysis presented so far suddenly falls flat on its face when confronted with the English translation of this key word. Arguably, this is the most difficult concept to comprehend because the false translation of "woman" requires a deep knowledge of the origin of the Masoretic Text itself. This is yet another obstacle similar to what was encountered in Chapter 4 regarding the "mark of the beast" and the original Greek manuscript.

Remember that the Hebrew language is a consonant-heavy language. The "vowelization" of the Hebrew language was not standardized until a group of Hebrews called the Masoretes decided to add the vowel points and dots. This group of Jewish scholars were around from the 5-10th centuries AD and took it upon themselves to standardize the vowel points of the Hebrew language because many people no longer spoke Hebrew in everyday life around that time after the Roman dispersion. The vowelization of Hebrew became necessary because the diaspora was losing the knowledge of their language. The Masoretes helped to produce the oldest Bible in existence, the Aleppo Codex (also called the Masoretic Text), dating to approximately AD 920.[18] This vowel system we see today inside of the Masoretic Hebrew Text of the Bible is therefore not something that Zechariah himself used to write his prophecy in 521 BC. Therein lies the secret of understanding the word "woman" in Zec. 5:7, as depicted in the next figure.

PRE-MASORETIC HEBREW

אשה

VOWELS ADDED

אִשָּׁה   אִשֶּׁה or אִשֶּׁה

"ISHAH"
WOMAN OR WIFE

"ISHEH"
OFFERING MADE BY FIRE

Figure 7.7: Understanding the "Aleph Shin and Heh". Before the Masoretes, the Hebrew language was written as consonants only. This may seem like a strange concept, but if I wrote down "th sky s bl" you would be able to tell that I really meant "the sky is blue" because of your fluency in English. Native and fluent speakers of any language can recognize where the vowels are supposed to be and what they sound like. Hebrew is no exception.

The Masoretes decided to add the vowel sign representing a small "T" below the consonant *shin* so that the word was given the "ah" sound and interpreted as woman, or *ishah*. They chose this vowel sign called the *qamets gadol* because it made the most sense to them when preserving the book of Zechariah. However, the alternate spelling of "offering made by fire" as seen in Exodus 29:18 or Leviticus 1:13 fits the narrative perfectly. There are two ways that the Masoretes write this word with their vowel system. There is the use of the *tsere* which is the two dots below the shin consonant, or there is the use of the *seghol* which is a three-dot sign forming an equilateral triangle below the consonant. Both vowel signs give the "eh" sound as in the word *set* to produce the word *isheh,* or fire offering. When considering the modern technology associated with the payload and the fire of its explosion upon detonation, there is no doubt that the Masoretes chose the incorrect vowel sign when attempting to assign their vowel system to the book of Zechariah. Simply replace the word "woman" with "fire offering" in Zec. 5:7.

Now we must consider Zechariah's word choice of *lead,* which is Strong's H5777 and is pronounced *o-feh'-reth*. What all governments and militaries have been chasing since World War II are fissile materials. These are radioactive elements that can undergo nuclear fission to produce a massive and explosive chain reaction. One such fissile material is an isotope of uranium called uranium-235. When looking at images online of uranium samples containing high percentages of uranium-235, it is hard to distinguish the silvery-gray metal from lead. They look the same. However, plutonium-239 is the preferred fissile isotope for the production of nuclear weapons because it is easier to obtain than uranium-235. Both plutonium-239 and uranium-235 are obtained from natural uranium, which is made up of uranium-238 along with traces of other isotopes of uranium. Uranium-238 itself is also used as a material of choice for surrounding the core fissile material of thermonuclear weapons due to its unique properties. In other words, all roads lead back to uranium-238. Outside of an actual nuclear reaction, uranium-238 is very stable and decays slowly over time. It will first decay into thorium-234, then protactinium-234, and onwards through eleven more decay cycles until the unstable element becomes lead.[19] Lead is the fundamental and stable element from which radioactive uranium is ultimately derived from. It is far beyond the realm of coincidence that Zechariah chose the Hebrew word for *lead* to describe what he saw in his prophecy. This is the final clue given to us that the curse of the flying scrolls is an unmistakable description of modern-day nuclear weapons.

Let's revisit the words of Zechariah 5:8 now that the key words "fire offering" and "uranium" have been decoded. First, we are being told that a certain weight, or talent, of lead is being lifted up. Most likely, this is a direct reference to uranium-238 being some sort of a lid to close the container. This "lead" conceals the fire offering, or fissile material, within the 20-40 liter ephah. The ephah itself is most definitely the inner part of the warhead that is also made up of lead, or uranium. An angelic messenger then spoke with Zechariah and told him that the fire offering inside the container is evil, or wickedness. What is not clear is whether the angel cast the fissile material into the ephah or if he shut the opening of the ephah with the talent of lead that was lifted up at the beginning. Either way, this description perfectly echoes the prophecy of the "abomination" of desolation. The Holy Spirit is telling us that this is an evil device of death and destruction throughout the entire Scriptures.

Finally, the last three verses of Zechariah 5 provide the context of *where* the curse of the flying scrolls will be initiated from in the future.

9 Then lifted I up mine eyes, and looked, and, behold, there came out two women, and the wind was in their wings; for they had wings like the wings of a stork: and they lifted up the ephah between the earth and the heaven.
10 Then said I to the angel that talked with me, Whither do these bear the ephah?
11 And he said unto me, To build it an house in the land of Shinar: and it shall be established, and set there upon her own base.
(Zec. 5:9-11)

Before discussing the nuances of verses nine and ten, it is important to establish the identity of Shinar in these last days. The book of Daniel clearly describes this land along with its geopolitical identity through the reigns of multiple kings. Beginning in the first chapter, we read the following:

1 In the third year of the reign of Jehoiakim king of Judah, Nebuchadnezzar king of Babylon came to Jerusalem and besieged it.
2 And the Lord gave Jehoiakim king of Judah into his hand, with some of the articles of the house of God, **which he carried into the land of Shinar** to the house of his god; and he brought the articles into the treasure house of his god.
(Dan. 1:1,2 NKJV) [emphasis added]

Shinar is described as belonging to the Babylonian king Nebuchadnezzar. It was the primary political and religious location for the kingdom of Babylon during the 6th century BC. This was also the place where the captives of Judah were taken. Regarding this location's identity in our modern context, it is well documented that this area is primarily in and around Iraq. the Baker Encyclopedia of the Bible sheds further light, stating, "The 'Plain of Shinar' comprised the region approximately from modern Baghdad to the Persian Gulf."[20] Based on the descriptions given in other encyclopedias and Bible atlases, modern-day Kuwait also falls into the the general region of Shinar. Sadly, the vast majority of commentaries fail to notice Shinar's obvious connection to modern-day Iran as clearly revealed in the Scriptures. The book of Daniel tells us that after Nebuchadnezzar's death, his successor, Belshazzar, takes the throne of Babylon. This is the same arrogant king that profaned God's holy vessels and consequently received the "writing on the wall" prophecy that Daniel interpreted for him. During the third year of this king Belshazzar and before Darius the Mede conquered Babylon, Daniel received the vision of the goat versus the ram, as stated in the following verses:

1 In the third year of the reign of King Belshazzar a vision appeared to me—to me, Daniel—after the one that appeared to me the first time.
2 I saw in the vision, and it so happened while I was looking, that I was in Shushan, the citadel, which is in the province of Elam; and I saw in the vision that I was by the River Ulai.
(Daniel 8:1,2)

Daniel received the vision in a location that, by implication, was also generally referred to as Shinar in the opening chapter of his book. It was a territory of Babylon. Though the city of Shushan (also called Susa) and the nearby River Ulai are typically only associated with the territory of Elam and the Persians, we are being directly told in these words of Daniel that it belonged to Babylon before this kingdom's fall to the Persians. Again, most atlases and commentaries fail to recognize this simple fact. From a geographical standpoint, Shushan is only a little over 200 miles (360 km) east of the location of ancient Babylon, and it has also been recognized as being part of southern Mesopotamia from antiquity. From a biblical standpoint, we can therefore conclude that Shushan and some of Elam are part of the land of Shinar due to the fact that this location was under the control of Nebuchadnezzar and was one place where his armies rested after the successful conquest of Jerusalem.

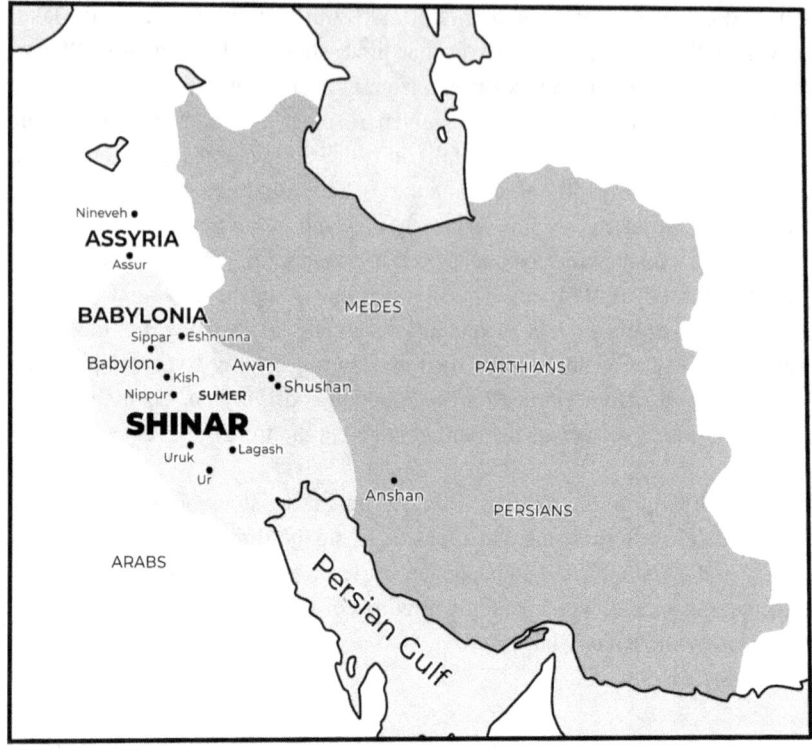

Figure 7.8: The Land of Shinar. The dark gray outline represents modern-day Iran.

Going back to Zechariah's prophecy, the connection is obvious between the biblical land of Shinar and modern-day Iran's westernmost border, which also happens to be where their missiles are armed and ready to be launched against 1948 Israel. If you are still not convinced of Iran's fulfillment of this prophecy, there is a certain chapter of Isaiah speaking of Elam that should completely erase all doubt. We will look at this next. First, there are still a few more ideas from the final words of Zechariah 5 that must be explained. We are told that a "house" will be built for the "ephah", or nuclear warhead, in the land of Shinar. The word *house* (Strong's H1004) is used in the Scriptures to not only describe habitations and dwellings but also prisons and dungeons. For example, after Joseph was falsely accused of wrongdoing by Potiphar's wife, he was thrown into a "house" in Egypt where the king's prisoners were bound. From the descriptions provided in Genesis 39 of this dungeon of political prisoners, we get the impression that this place was most likely underground and certainly a maximum security prison due to the descriptions of the criminals it housed. Both of these ideas can be applied to the hidden tunnel systems and missile bases currently located underneath the surface of Iran's mountainous terrain, especially in the western part of the country. The Hebrew word translated as being the "base" (where the warhead is "set") is only used once in the entire Bible—right here in Zec. 5:11—and we therefore lack context clues to figure out deeper meanings. The English word "base" certainly carries a double meaning that perhaps only a reader of this book could appreciate. Not only is it a military base where the nuclear warhead is housed, but such a weapon would also be placed on a supporting platform, or a base, inside of a missile silo from which it can be launched at a moment's notice.

With the strong evidence now laid forth in this book, we understand that Iran finally obtained their long-anticipated nuclear weapon on September 22, 2023. Simply compare the following two verses side by side:

"And from the time *that* the daily *sacrifice* is taken away, **and the abomination of desolation is set up,** *there shall be* one thousand two hundred and ninety days.
(Dan. 12:11) [emphasis added]

And he said unto me, To build it an house in the land of Shinar: and it shall be established, **and set there upon her own base.**
(Zec. 5:11 KJV) [emphasis added]

The "set up" of Daniel 12:11 is the same thing as the "set there" of Zechariah 5:11. The only question that remains is regarding how the nuclear ephah got to Iran in the first place. This is what Zec. 5:9,10 is attempting to explain to us. Zechariah describes two women with the wings of a stork that lifted up the ephah and brought it to Iran, most likely from a different country. In other words, though Iran has been enriching uranium to weapons-grade purity and has been constantly under condemnation by the West for doing so, there is evidence here in the Bible that the country's first nuclear weapon has already arrived from somewhere else. Clearly, the "wings of a stork" is another reference to military technology and most likely a heavy cargo plane that has brought at least one nuclear warhead to Iran. The wings of a stork are rather long when compared to various birds, and this is a clue given to us that Zechariah was attempting to describe a large aircraft. The two "women" is once again a mistranslation of "fire offerings" but this time in reference to the two jet engines located under the wings that provide the power for the vehicle's flight. There are a handful of countries with mutual interests that could have supplied the specific weapon that will initiate the Great Tribulation. Just imagine any one of the rival powers of the West, and the prophecy will become quite real. Russia, China, and North Korea all possess nuclear weapons but perhaps even India or Pakistan could have provided the weapon. The exact ally is not clear at the moment, but due to the ongoing and regular transfers of weapons between Iran and Russia,[21] President Vladmir Putin appears to be the key player behind the fulfillment of this prophecy. His role as the King of the North will be further explored in Chapter 11.

ISAIAH 22: THE ARCHERS OF ELAM

Just for fun, take a moment and read Isaiah 22:1-14 where this prophecy is located *before* embarking on this commentary. With the "PhD level" of under-standing that you now possess after properly visualizing Zechariah's flying scrolls, these words of Isaiah should be self-evident in their connection to end-times Iran. Let's begin with the first verse:

The burden against the Valley of Vision.
What ails you now, that **you have all gone up to the housetops**
(Isa. 22:1) [emphasis added]

The subject of this judgment is the "Valley of Vision", or the city of Jerusalem. Isaiah makes this obvious throughout the passage when he directly mentions Judah, the city of David, and specific characteristics unique to Jerusalem. The reason why the city is referred to as the Valley of Vision is because this is the place where prophets have received visions from antiquity. It is where God has communicated to His people and where many blessings and curses have been declared. This particular passage describes a curse, or a burden, against end-times Jerusalem. Notice that all Jerusalem—yes, everyone —is on the housetops. The connection of Isaiah's burden to these specific words of Yeshua is immediate and unmistakable:

15 "Therefore when you see the 'abomination of desolation,' spoken of by Daniel the prophet, standing in the holy place" (whoever reads, let him understand),
16 "then let those who are in Judea flee to the mountains.
17 **"Let him who is on the housetop** not go down to take anything out of his house.
18 "And let him who is in the field not go back to get his clothes.
(Mat. 24:15-18) [emphasis added]

Yeshua once again places an emphasis on those people in the "holy place", or Jerusalem itself, standing on the housetops as if He were directly quoting Isaiah 22. As you are about to uncover, He *really was* quoting Isaiah 22. The idea presented in Isaiah is that everyone has suddenly stopped what they were doing and had to go to the highest part of their homes to see what just took place. Armed with smartphones in their hands to grab a video for social media, they stop and look onward like the proverbial deer in the headlights, not realizing that what they are witnessing is the fulfillment of a multitude of scriptures. All Jerusalem is watching explosions and mushroom clouds of smoke going off in and around the city. Isaiah continues to give us a glimpse into this inevitable future, stating:

2 You who are full of noise, A tumultuous city, a joyous city? Your slain men are not slain with the sword, Nor dead in battle.
3 All your rulers have fled together; They are captured by the archers. All who are found in you are bound together; They have fled from afar.
(Isa. 22:2,3)

It is not sword nor battle that is causing everyone to head straight for the housetops. We are told that it is in fact archery that has caused this great slaughter in Jerusalem. While preachers and teachers behind pulpits everywhere have dismissed this prophecy as being merely historical, there is no evidence that Jerusalem was ever conquered at any point in history by an enemy's exclusive use of archery. Nebuchadnezzar, for example, laid siege to Jerusalem, and his soldiers burned it with fire. The Romans used their soldiers against Jerusalem during the siege of AD 70 and also during various events of the Jewish-Roman wars. A historical, or historicist, interpretation makes no sense at all. The only logical explanation, of course, is that the archery being described in this chapter specifically and unequivocally refers to the use of modern ballistic missiles and nuclear weapons. Where these missiles are coming from is the main question that needs answering. Rather than repeating the plain details found in Isaiah 22, I now direct your attention to who is responsible for this doomsday archery attack upon Jerusalem:

Elam bore the quiver
With chariots of men and horsemen,
And Kir uncovered the shield.
(Isa. 22:6)

Let's begin with the end in mind. First, the identity of Kir is up for interpretation. This location can be ascribed to all of Mesopotamia (mostly Iraq) and even upward into the southernmost parts of modern day Turkey. The idea here is that many Axis of Resistance soldiers will be joining themselves to a leading force that is apparently the king of archery in the Middle East. This other and more important identity mentioned in this verse is none other than Elam. The quiver is the place where arrows, or missiles, are kept to then be grabbed and launched by the archer. These archers that are terrorizing end-times Jerusalem and by implication all of the land of Israel belong to a specific people group, and this identity of Elam is once again solidified as being directly responsible for the abomination of desolation prophecy. As mentioned before, the land of Elam has been associated within the people and culture of Persia from antiquity. In describing this territory, Baker says it is an area nearly the size of Denmark and "in a region today that corresponds with southwest Iran."[22] The next figure shows what Elam looks like together with the land of Shinar mentioned in Zechariah and also the borders of modern-day Iran.

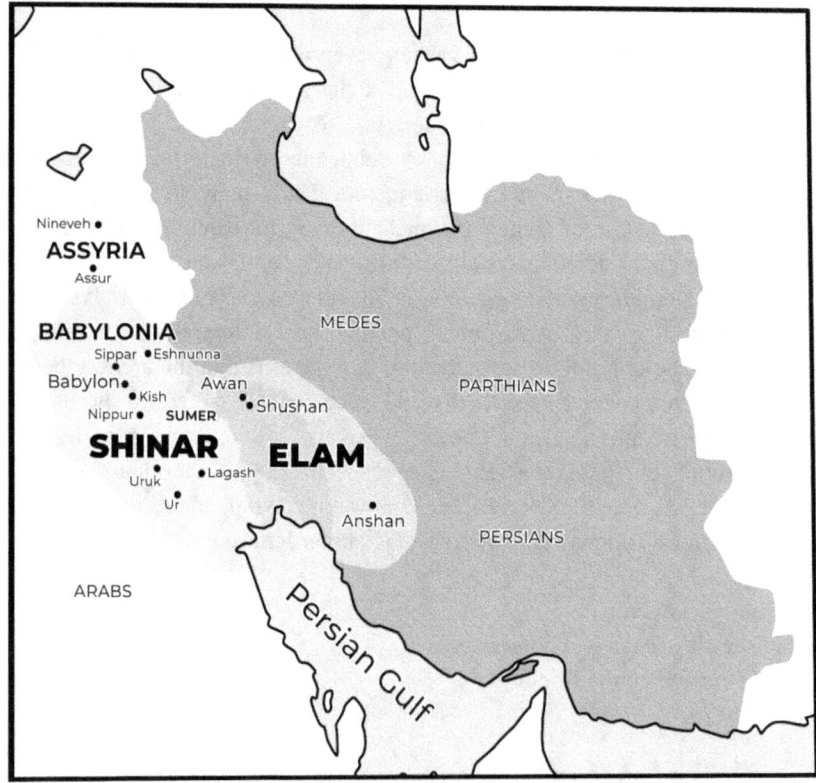

Figure 7.9: Elam (orange), Shinar (green), and Iran (gray).

As you can see from this figure, the prophecies of Zechariah 5 and Isaiah 22 can be overlaid together to reveal critical truths about end-times Iran. The meticulous word choices that both prophets used to describe the lands that they saw leaves us with the firm conclusion that the principal location of focus is the western border of Iran. This is the location responsible for the archery of flying scrolls. This is the location directly connected to the abomination of desolation—both the initial setting up of the device and its eventual deployment against Jerusalem. Somewhere in the region where Shinar and Elam overlap and perhaps in Shushan itself there is a deep underground military base where the prophesied nuclear warhead of Zechariah has already been set up at this moment in history. To my knowledge, this is the only book to properly connect these various scriptures together to paint the complete picture of how the Great Tribulation will unfold and who will be responsible for the initiation of its terror. All of these connections are impossible to be mere chance or coincidence within our timeline of history. The existence of this end-times enemy of the West with the most advanced "archery" capabilities and weaponry that also happens to be perfectly situated in the ancient territory of Elam is living proof that the Bible is the inspired Word of God.

One day, the men responsible for the hell on earth that is yet to come will be held accountable. Yehovah will judge them for their actions, for as Jeremiah said:

Thus says the LORD of hosts:
"Behold, I will break the bow of Elam,
The foremost of their might."
(Jer. 49:35)

Once again we see a clear reference to the archery of Elam, and the bow of his military technology will ultimately be broken. This was a bow that brought terrorism upon the face of the earth and destroyed many. Though Elam's actions were necessary for the fulfillment of Bible prophecy, every man, and nation, must reap what he sows. In describing the inevitable fate of Elam's condemnation inside the Pit, or Sheol, Ezekiel states:

"There is Elam and all her multitude,
All around her grave,
All of them slain, fallen by the sword,
Who have gone down uncircumcised to the lower parts of the earth,
Who caused their terror in the land of the living;
Now they bear their shame with those who go down to the Pit."
(Eze. 32:24)

All those leaders, military personnel, and willing participants in Elam's archery and terrorism will suffer the eternal consequences. Condemned to the lower parts of the earth, or hell, the end result of the abomination of desolation prophecy is that its instigators will be prosecuted by the Living God because of their crimes against humanity. We again see confirmation that Elam's actions were fierce and worthy of great condemnation. Ezekiel gives us perhaps the final supporting evidence that directly ties Elam's acts in these last days to something truly horrendous that must take place for the fulfillment of prophecy.

PALM TREES OF SMOKE

In light of what Zechariah saw and what Isaiah described, the book of Joel must also be weighed out in order to fully picture the coming desolations of World War III described in the 70 weeks prophecy. The book of Joel centers around a particular event called the Day of the LORD (Yehovah). This prophetic day will be fully explored in a later chapter. For now, pay attention to these particular words of Joel because they speak of advanced technology just like what has already been presented:

And I will show wonders in the heavens and in the earth: Blood and fire and pillars of smoke.
The sun shall be turned into darkness, And the moon into blood, Before the coming of the great and awesome day of the LORD.
(Joel 2:30,31)

The words of Yeshua should be coming to mind yet again. After the abomination of desolation is deployed against Jerusalem and the world experiences the Great Tribulation, this is what is what will happen "immediately" afterwards:

"Immediately after the tribulation of those days the sun will be darkened, and

the moon will not give its light; the stars will fall from heaven, and the powers of the heavens will be shaken."
(Mat. 24:29)

Therefore, we should conclude that the abomination of desolation is directly tied to Joel's words. In fact, it is described by the Hebrew language in the most striking way within Joel 2:30. This is one of those verses of the Bible that I had not properly understood for many years. What does the prophet *really* mean by "blood and fire and pillars of smoke"? While the reference to blood seems to be explained in the very next verse speaking of the celestial sign of blood moons, or total lunar eclipses, the phrase "fire and pillars of smoke" had always remained a mystery to me, until now.

Using the three laws of interpretation, a deeper investigation of the word *pillar* is all that is needed. In the English translations, the idea of a pillar first appears in Genesis 19:26 where Lot's wife is turned into a pillar of salt because of her disobedience in looking back at the destruction of Sodom and Gomorrah. This word is "netsib" (Strong's H5333). This is a different type of pillar than the one described later in Genesis 31:13 that describes Jacob's stone pillar, or "matsehbah" (Strong's H4676), that he anointed and dedicated to God at Bethel. The pillar of Lot's wife and the pillar of Jacob's stone are both different from the "pillar of fire" used to describe God's glory in Exodus 13:21. Though the English language here appears to match Joel on the surface, God's glory is described as being an "ammud" (Strong's H5982) of fire, which is different from what Joel wrote down. In other words, Joel had a variety of Hebrew words to describe what he saw, and therefore his word choice in describing the Day of the LORD is extremely deliberate and fully intentional.

The Hebrew word that Joel used for *pillars* is "veh-timarot" (וְתִימֲרוֹת) derived from Strong's H8490 or "timarah" that is used in the Scriptures to speak of columns of smoke that are palm-like and spreading at the top. The root word from which *timarah* is derived is Strong's H8558 (pronounced "tah-mar") and is used twelve times in the Bible to describe palm trees or date palms. The connection of Joel's Hebrew description of pillars to palm trees is why he skipped over using all those other words to describe what he saw. He saw palm trees of fire and smoke that were spreading out at the top in what we would commonly understand today as being mushroom clouds of nuclear explosions. The reason Joel was unable to describe what he saw as being "mushroom clouds" is because the Hebrew language does not actually have a word for *mushroom*. As a matter of fact, no English Bible uses the word *mushroom* anywhere. Perhaps the only reference we see to fungus is within the Torah where instructions are provided for dealing with homes contaminated with mold poisoning. Therefore, the palm tree was Joel's only option for describing the explosions that he witnessed. He was faithful and thoroughly inspired by the Holy Spirit to record a word from God that was far beyond his realm of understanding in ancient times.

Figure 7.10: Palm Trees of Smoke. (left) On November 1, 1951 the first U.S. nuclear field exercise was conducted on the Nevada Test Site, and the troops shown were a mere 6 miles from the blast. This event was known as the Operation Buster-Jangle Dog test. This weapon had a yield of 21 kilotons of TNT, and far more powerful weapons exist today. (right) The Middle Eastern date palm (Phoenix dactylifera) is native to the region. Though similar in appearance, the coconut palm is only found in tropical areas of the Middle East such as Dhofar in Oman, and this type of palm is probably not what Joel saw due to its Asiatic origins. Pictured here are ripening date clusters that are bagged, or covered, to protect them from birds.

Because of the extremely high density of nuclear fuel when compared with conventional or chemical explosives, these weapons have an exponentially greater extent of damage. A fraction of a second after being detonated, the nuclear chain reaction produces immense heat in a series of fireballs that erupt in the form of a column, or pillar. As nature attempts to achieve equilibrium, relatively cool air from the environment rushes into the column and into the hot cloud that is formed at the top, ultimately exiting through the head of the mushroom cloud. This updraft continues while the hot fire and gasses of the explosion circulate at the head of the mushroom cloud. The end product is the pillar of smoke that spreads at the top, just as Joel said. On the ground and around the nuclear explosion there are shockwaves that are produced due to the heat of the fireball. These high-pressure waves move outward in all directions from the blast site and carry with them a force greater than the largest hurricanes imaginable. When the Little Boy nuclear weapon was dropped on the 350,000-person city of Hiroshima during WWII, the initial burst temperature was estimated to be over a million degrees Celsius with eyewitnesses stating that the blast itself was ten times brighter than the sun. The blast waves proceeded to shatter windows from buildings that were ten miles away with the effects of the blast being felt thirty-seven miles away.[23] However, this was only a 14 kiloton weapon. The largest weapon ever tested was the 1961 test of the Russian Tsar bomba with 50 megatons (50,000 kilotons) of yield. Today's most advanced nuclear weapons are likely just as capable and will certainly be involved in carrying out the prophecies of Zechariah, Isaiah, and Joel.

THE FOUR HORSEMEN OF REVELATION

It's now time to look at the four horsemen of the book of Revelation because at least two appear to be describing the consequences of modern technology on a mass scale. Each horseman corresponds to one of four seals that are opened one at a time by Christ the Lamb. For the sake of brevity, I will include only the description of each horseman here.

2 And I looked, and behold, a white horse. He who sat on it had a bow; and a crown was given to him, and he went out conquering and to conquer.
4 Another horse, fiery red, went out. And it was granted to the one who sat on it to take peace from the earth, and that people should kill one another; and there was given to him a great sword.
5 …So I looked, and behold, a black horse, and he who sat on it had a pair of scales in his hand.
6 And I heard a voice in the midst of the four living creatures saying, "A quart of wheat for a denarius, and three quarts of barley for a denarius; and do not harm the oil and the wine."
8 So I looked, and behold, a pale horse. And the name of him who sat on it was Death, and Hades followed with him. And power was given to them over a fourth of the earth, to kill with sword, with hunger, with death, and by the beasts of the earth.
(Rev. 6:2,4-6,8)

Judging from the language of these first four seals of God's scroll, it is evident that there is a lapse of time between the opening of each seal and the

273

unleashing of its judgment within. In other words, they all don't happen at once. The first two seals and the concepts presented are worthy of heavy consideration because it seems that the first seal has now been opened at this point in time with the second seal being an apparent description of nuclear war to follow shortly after. Allow me to explain. The problem with nuclear war is that it will create chaos literally overnight. With the mountains of evidence now presented behind this interpretation of the abomination of desolation, law and order will break down the day after nuclear strikes are carried out first by the Iranians against Israel and later by Russian and Chinese forces on a global scale. Of the four horsemen of the apocalypse, I have been keeping the idea in the back of my mind that the abomination of desolation could very well be the fiery red second horseman that removes peace from the earth and causes men to kill each other (Rev. 6:4). What else could fit the description of "fiery red" except for flying scrolls and bombing campaigns on the face of the earth to destroy the military and economic centers of the nations? This understanding further reinforces the dire language used by Yeshua to describe the Great Tribulation period.

If this interpretation is indeed correct, then the first white horsemen likely symbolized the pandemic of 2020 that conquered the world through fear, pseudo-science, and the use of the internet to effectively deceive the world into complying with this agenda. The latin word *coronavirus* literally means *crown virus,* which fits the description of the crown on the head of the rider. The white symbolizes peace, and the bow without any arrows to shoot symbolizes covert and silent warfare. As already presented, Klaus Schwab and the World Economic Forum successfully conquered the world without firing a single bullet, bomb, or, as is the idea within this metaphor, a single arrow. When you look ahead at the next two horsemen, it becomes obvious that nuclear warfare will lead to the black horse of scarcity on earth, with a day's wage only affording a quart of wheat. Finally, the pale horse of death would logically arrive in the aftermath of this deprivation.

The black horse of scarcity and monetary collapse following a short-lived nuclear war satisfies the pronouncement of judgment that Yehovah makes in Zec. 5:3,4 where the interest-based fiat systems of the world are burned for their organized crimes of theft and hard bondage. This inherently means that the curse of the flying scrolls should be expected to land in all major economic centers of the world, and such locations are indeed primary targets in an all-out nuclear war in order to cripple an enemy nation's morale and its ability to rebuild once the war is over. This unique kind of modern warfare seeks to first decapitate its enemy and then enslave it after the fallout has subsided, usually a two week period or perhaps a little longer.

Regarding the four horsemen, I am not overly dogmatic on these ideas at all, and time will reveal exactly what they represent. Once the flying scrolls prophecy is fulfilled, I think all things will become far more clear than they currently are.

WHITE HORSE:
(OVID-19
MARCH 11TH, 2020

FIERY RED HORSE:
NUCLEAR WAR

BLACK HORSE:
FOOD SCARCITY

PALE HORSE:
CONSEQUENCES OF WAR WITH
SWORD, HUNGER, DEATH, BEASTS

Figure 7.11: A Possible Interpretation of the Four Horsemen. Once again we can visualize how March 11, 2020 was the beginning of several major events on God's prophetic timeline.

NOTHING NEW UNDER THE SUN

With regard to all of these advancements in warfare and technology as a whole, these words of Solomon should be weighed heavily:

That which has been is what will be,
That which is done is what will be done,
And there is nothing new under the sun.
(Ecc. 1:9)

The wisest man who ever lived is telling us here that though the post-flood world has experienced an incredible surge of knowledge and technological prowess, these things are not actually something brand new. The pre-flood world undoubtedly experienced these things already, and without getting lost in the recesses of hidden history and prehistory, evidence does exist of lost civilizations like Atlantis, the megalithic structures of the giants, the lost islands, and the lost continents that likely possessed advanced technology even beyond the capabilities present today. Regarding the Great Pyramid of Giza, it was Nikola Tesla who made it widely known in 1891 that this and other such pyramidal structures were actually the first wireless transmission systems from which to communicate throughout the earth.[24] Regarding the key verse of this chapter, Daniel 12:4, we were told that knowledge would increase, and by implication, this means that the wireless technology systems of today have been resurrected out of the ashes of lost civilizations. Now that the system is in place there is no running from it. There's no hiding from it. The only choice is to hijack the "all-seeing-eye" of the internet grid and modern technology for the good of the Kingdom of Heaven. For as Daniel 11:33a tells us:

"And those of the people who understand shall instruct many..."

These words are recorded two verses after the abomination of desolation is mentioned in the very same chapter. Think about this carefully. Could this mean that even after this event takes place there will still be people instructing others in the Word of God and also people receiving instruction on a large scale? Yes, most likely. The implication of this context appears to confirm that the systems of the internet and wireless communication might remain intact for a short season even after the Great Tribulation begins in Israel. However, there is no guarantee of continued stability and opportunity. It is now time to rise up and proclaim the vastly unknown and unappreciated truth of the 70 weeks of Daniel while there still remains the daylight to do so. For as Jesus also declares:

"I must work the works of Him who sent Me while it is day; the night is coming **when no one can work.**
(John 9:4) [emphasis added]

Secret III:

Navigating Common End Times Deceptions

But evil men and impostors will grow worse and worse, deceiving and being deceived.

- *2Timothy 3:13*

Chapter 8
Surviving the Rapture Fallout and the Coming Flattery Deception

By far one of the most cherished of all currently held end-times doctrines concerns the timing of a "rapture" event whereby millions upon millions of believers will be caught up in the air to meet the Lord Jesus, most likely before anything truly bad like the Great Tribulation should ever take place. This prevailing sentiment is commonly called the pre-trib (pretribulational) rapture theory because the disappearance of millions of "good Christians" is said to take place before the prophesied tribulation occurs on earth. However, there are also two other rapture theories that will be explored in this chapter.

The fundamental problem with this doctrine is that it fails to pass the three laws of interpretation presented in Chapter 1. It does not pass the *law of first mention* because the word "rapture" is never found in any English Bible, leading to intense speculation based on isolated scriptures and their underlying Greek or Hebrew words. These speculations will be investigated in this chapter as we examine them using the *law of definitions*. Doctrines based on words such as *harpadzo* in the Greek (1Th. 4:17) and to a much lesser extent *vaya'al* in the Hebrew (2 Kings 2:11 and Elijah's whirlwind) must be properly tested. Then the final step is to look at the *context* of scriptures that are claimed to be speaking of a future rapture event where millions of people will disappear. It is precisely at this stage where this doctrine falls flat on its face, as you will find out in this chapter.

As clearly and systematically described in the first two Secrets of this book, the abomination of desolation will initiate a period of great distress the likes of which the earth and its inhabitants have never witnessed before. The only plausible interpretation of Yeshua's end-times warnings is made obvious when His words are carefully examined alongside the books of Zechariah, Isaiah, and Joel. The Great Tribulation concerns the recent development of nuclear weapons along with their residual fallout that has lingering effects well after the initial blasts are over. Yet, there is also another kind of lasting consequence to be anticipated in the aftermath of a short-lived thermonuclear war. In the different sense of the word *fallout*, there is indeed going to be an unexpected and incidental byproduct of nuclear war immediately after the dust settles. There is going to be the emotional fallout of believers away from faith in Christ due to their extreme disappointment in the "blessed hope" of the rapture that never arrived at the moment they needed it the most. Millions of formerly Christian survivors will become sorely disenfranchised overnight, leaving them completely vulnerable in the midst of an unfamiliar and war-torn world they thought they would never have to face. This chapter is dedicated to understanding and overcoming this coming fallout, or falling away, from faith in Christ while exposing the erroneous teachings, ignorant assumptions, and false doctrines concerning the three popular theories of the rapture, especially the pre-trib rapture theory. Maintain an open mind, and expect to be heavily challenged in this chapter if you happen to be a diehard rapture adherent. It's now time to rise up and face life victoriously and in the power of the Holy Spirit even after the bombs go off.

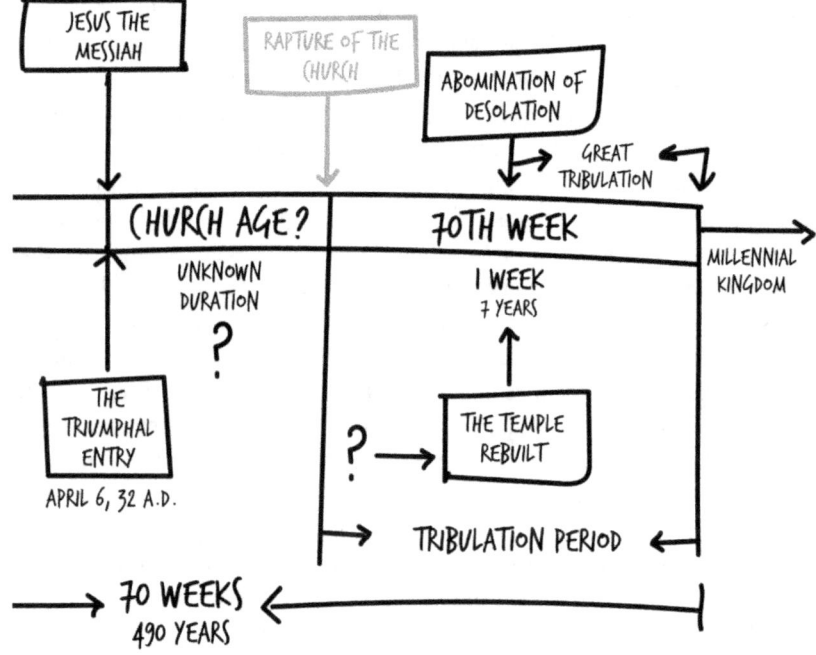

Figure 8.1: The Pre-Trib Rapture Theory Timeline. The rapture is supposed to take place before the 70th week of Daniel, a final 7-year period, ever begins. No rapture ever took place before the 70th week of Daniel from 1996-2045, proving this teaching to be false on its face.

THEORY #1: THE PRE-TRIB RAPTURE

This first figure is the same one from Chapter 1 but zoomed in. To avoid repeating details unnecessarily, it is important only to recognize that the great majority of modern Christians and Messianic Jews believe that we are currently living through the "Church Age." The "church" is said to consist of all believers in Christ who have confessed Him as Lord of their lives and have therefore become part of His church throughout the world. According to the pre-trib point of view, the church's ministry began in the first century, and it will eventually end as soon as the 70th week of Daniel, or tribulation period, begins. This Church Age is said to be an unspecified duration of time. It began around the time of Jesus' triumphal entry into Jerusalem and is supposed to end at a specific, yet random, time in the future when the rapture of the "church" will take place. After the "church" is removed, it is said that all hell can break loose for exactly seven years because there is no way that God's church would ever endure any sort of judgment and certainly not wrath from God, for such things are reserved only for the wicked. Rather than basing these ideas on the teachings of Jesus Himself or the Prophets, pre-trib rapture adherents rely heavily—and oftentimes exclusively—on the words of Paul to back up their doctrinal statements, particularly his second letter to the congregation of Thessalonica in Greece. Due to its tremendous importance in understanding the pre-trib rapture theory, I will include a few verses from the second chapter of this same letter.

1 Now, brethren, concerning **the coming of our Lord Jesus Christ** and **our gathering together to Him,** we ask you,
2 not to be soon shaken in mind or troubled, either by spirit or by word or by letter, as if from us, as though the day of Christ had come.
3 Let no one deceive you by any means; for **that Day will not come unless the falling away comes first,** and the man of sin is revealed, the son of perdition,
4 who opposes and exalts himself above all that is called God or that is worshiped, so that he sits as God in the temple of God, showing himself that he is God.
5 Do you not remember that when I was still with you I told you these things?
6 **And now you know what is restraining,** that he may be revealed in his own time.
7 For the mystery of lawlessness is already at work; only **He who now restrains will do so until He is taken out of the way.**

8 And then the lawless one will be revealed, whom the Lord will consume
with the breath of His mouth and destroy with the brightness of His coming.
9 The coming of the lawless one is according to the working of Satan, with all
power, signs, and lying wonders,
10 and with all unrighteous deception among those who perish, because they
did not receive the love of the truth, that they might be saved.
11 And for this reason God will send them strong delusion, that they should
believe the lie,
12 that they all may be condemned who did not believe the truth but had pleasure in unrighteousness.
(2Th 2:1-12) [emphasis added]

The opening statement of this second chapter describes the "gathering
together" of Christians in the end times—a statement that has fueled much
speculation when in reality the emphasis of this entire passage is on *the Day
that Christ returns*. Paul's words in 2Th. 2:7 are then commonly used as
supporting evidence for claims of a pretribulational rapture because he stated,
"He who now restrains will do so until He is taken out of the way." It is
asserted that by using the pronoun, "He", Paul was referring to the Holy Spirit
and His indwelling within all born-again believers. Once this worldwide
church of believers is "taken out of the way" and with them, the Holy Spirit's
entire ministry on earth, then the 70th week of Daniel can finally begin.
According to this interpretation of Paul's words, it is at this moment in time
after the pre-trib rapture that "then the lawless one will be revealed" so that
the whole world can be deceived by his lying wonders because they are to be
condemned for having pleasure in unrighteousness. In the mind of mainstream
Christianity, it is impossible for "the church" to ever exist in this scenario.
Why would God test his wonderful and set-apart bride by leaving them in
such a world where the "antichrist" reigns? Rather than attempt to corroborate
these claims with the teachings of Jesus, the book of Revelation, or the
Prophets, many Christians close the door of open dialogue here. In essence,
the prevailing pre-trib rapture theory is fundamentally Pauline, or based in the
words of Paul alone, without proper weight or consideration given to the
multitudes of scriptures that came beforehand.

Since this passage of Thessalonians is clearly speaking of the return of
Christ to the earth, then it is of utmost importance to examine these words
alongside what Yeshua actually said about His second coming. For example,
the phrase stating that the "falling away comes first" in 2Th. 2:3 is said to
give further weight to the pre-trib point of view, but this phrase is actually a
specific reference to the words of Jesus. Various commentaries say that the

underlying Greek word for "falling away", or *apostasia,* simply means "departure", and therefore, it is asserted that the day of Christ's return cannot take place until there is first a rapture in which "the church" departs the earth to be with God. This is a gross misunderstanding and ignorant assessment of what the word *apostosia* really means, for this is where the English word *apostasy* is derived. This same word is used in Acts 21:21 where Paul was being falsely accused of "forsaking" the Law of Moses and teaching other men "not to circumcise their children nor to walk according to the customs." In order to make it abundantly clear that he did in fact observe Torah as a born-again follower of Yeshua, Paul proceeded to heed the advice of the elders of Jerusalem and clear his name. This is what they told him:

23 "Therefore do what we tell you: We have four men who have taken a vow.
24 "Take them and be purified with them, and pay their expenses so that they may shave their heads, and that all may know that those things of which they were informed concerning you are nothing, but that you yourself also walk orderly and keep the law.
25 "But concerning the Gentiles who believe, we have written and decided that they should observe no such thing, except that they should keep themselves from things offered to idols, from blood, from things strangled, and from sexual immorality."
26 Then Paul took the men, and the next day, having been purified with them, entered the temple to announce the expiration of the days of purification, at which time an offering should be made for each one of them.
(Acts 21:23-26)

The elders of Jerusalem told Paul that they had four men who had taken the vow of a Nazarite as described in Numbers 6. This was a completely voluntary vow that someone could take. It was not obligatory except for in the rare cases of Samson or Samuel where these men were Nazarites from birth. Here are two important verses from the Torah regarding this vow:

13 And this is the law of the Nazarite, when the days of his separation are fulfilled: he shall be brought unto the door of the tabernacle of the congregation:
18 And the Nazarite shall shave the head of his separation at the door of the tabernacle of the congregation, and shall take the hair of the head of his separation, and put it in the fire which is under the sacrifice of the peace offerings.
(Num. 6:13,18)

In other words, Paul assisted four men in keeping the vow of a Nazarite through to its final act of shaving the head and bringing offerings. He helped them go to the temple and offer sacrificial animal offerings as required by the Law so that the vows of these men could be finished. We also see a clear connection of this account back to the recent event of Acts 18:18 where the following took place:

"So Paul still remained a good while. Then he took leave of the brethren and sailed for Syria, and Priscilla and Aquila were with him. **He had his hair cut off at Cenchrea, for he had taken a vow.**"
[emphasis added]

We are clearly shown here that Paul himself was also under the voluntary act of the Nazaritic vow. This act of cutting his hair off may seem confusing, but Paul did this in order to fulfill these words of Numbers 6:9, where Moses wrote, "And if anyone dies very suddenly beside him, and he defiles his consecrated head, then he shall shave his head on the day of his cleansing; on the seventh day he shall shave it."

Somewhere in the midst of his journey to Syria, Paul must have encountered a dead body, or maybe one of his companions on board his ship suddenly died in the Grecian city of Cenchrea. Because he was defiled by touching a dead body, Paul was forced to cut his hair in order to avoid violating Torah. There is no indication that Paul had ever officially finalized his Nazarite vow after it was first mentioned in Acts 18, leaving us to conclude that he was "purified" in Acts 21 along with the four other men in Jerusalem so that he, too, could finish his vow in the temple, complete with animal sacrifices, grain offerings, and drink offerings. These were the "expenses" that needed to be paid. These "expenses" mentioned in Acts 21 were not money, for money (silver) was never mentioned in Numbers 6 as part of the Nazarite vow. There is an account mentioned in all four gospels regarding Jesus creating a whip of cords from which to drive out the people who were selling sheep, oxen, and doves inside of the temple (John 2:15). The reason He did this is not because He was against the animal offerings themselves but because the temple was not supposed to be the place of buying and selling livestock. The animal offerings were to be acquired somewhere else and then brought to the temple, but the Father's house had been turned into "a house of merchandise" (John 2:16).

Modern Christianity completely ignores these simple facts, and it is commonly taught that offering animal sacrifices after the resurrection of Yeshua is an abomination and "trampling underfoot the blood of Christ" due to butchered interpretations of Paul's letters and the New Testament book of Hebrews. The plain fact is that Paul observed Torah, and there is no way around it. Whatever he may have said in his own letters that is misrepresented and misquoted to say otherwise does not match the actual actions of Paul. He was a Torah-observant man from the tribe of Benjamin that participated in temple-related laws well after the resurrection of Christ. Regarding circumcision, he even took Timothy and circumcised him when he first became his disciple (see Acts 16:3). The only question is why the elders of Jerusalem said that the Nations (Gentiles) should "observe no such thing" in Acts 21:25. The answer should be obvious. The nations of the Lost Tribes were not to be forced to keep the vow of the Nazarite and then subsequently be required to travel long distances to Jerusalem in order to perform the temple ceremonies. Requiring them to do so would place an enormous burden and also confuse the simplicity of grace and new life as presented in the Gospel. Rather than putting such a burden on these other Nations, the Jerusalem elders instead reaffirmed the need to keep the more simple things, such as the dietary laws of never eating blood (Lev. 3:17) nor eating an animal that dies of itself (Deu. 14:21). Therefore, the word *apostasia* is unequivocally referring to the falling away from true faith in Christ and obedience to His commandments as described in the Torah. It has absolutely nothing to do with a rapture, and such extreme ignorance of the word of God is exactly why Paul's prophetic declaration of Thessalonians has now come to pass before our eyes. In fact, Paul was clearly referencing and almost perfectly recounting Yeshua's words when he wrote down the often misquoted passage of 2Th. 2:1-12. Speaking of the end and His return, Yeshua said:

10 "And then many will be offended, will betray one another, and will hate one another.
11 "Then many false prophets will rise up and deceive many.
12 "And because lawlessness will abound, the love of many will grow cold. (Mat. 24:10-12)

Yeshua explicitly told us that lawlessness, or apostasy, would dominate the religious teachings, cultures, and nations of the end times. That is precisely why no "church" of lawless Christians should ever expect to be the recipients of a free ticket to heaven while the rest of the world suffers and burns. God said repeatedly that there is "one law" for His people, whether they are natives or foreigners that have been grafted into the United Kingdom of Israel (Exo. 12:49). Because He is the same yesterday, today and forever, God requires that every one of His followers—Jews or Lost Tribe Gentiles, it makes no difference—must uphold the marriage covenant as first presented on Mount Sinai and once again renewed through the blood of Christ. Based on these self-evident facts of the Bible, lawless Christians would actually be some of the most unlikely candidates to participate in a pre-trib rapture, should such an event even exist.

Another go-to verse that is used as proof that a pre-trib rapture must be true is found within Paul's first letter to the Thessalonians. After recounting some events in his journey and providing a few exhortations, Paul proceeds to offer some end-times insights in chapter four. Once again, the emphasis of his words is on Christ's return to earth in which he states the following:

13 But I do not want you to be ignorant, brethren, concerning those who have fallen asleep, lest you sorrow as others who have no hope.
14 For if we believe that Jesus died and rose again, even so God will bring with Him those who sleep in Jesus.
15 For this we say to you by the word of the Lord, that we who are alive and remain **until the coming of the Lord** will by no means precede those who are asleep.
16 **For the Lord Himself will descend from heaven** with a shout, with the voice of an archangel, and **with the trumpet** of God. And the dead in Christ will rise first.
17 Then we who are alive and remain **shall be caught up** together with them in the clouds to meet the Lord in the air. And thus we shall always be with the Lord.
(1Th 4:13-17) [emphasis added]

The concept of "sleep" will be dissected in a moment, but it is important to first point out that Paul is directly quoting these words of Yeshua:

29 **"Immediately after the tribulation of those days** the sun will be darkened, and the moon will not give its light; the stars will fall from heaven, and the powers of the heavens will be shaken.
30 "Then the sign of the Son of Man will appear in heaven, and then all the tribes of the earth will mourn, and they will see the **Son of Man coming on the clouds of heaven** with power and great glory.
31 "And He will send His angels **with a great sound of a trumpet,** and they will gather together His elect from the four winds, from one end of heaven to the other.
(Mat. 24:29-31) [emphasis added]

Because Paul was directly quoting Yeshua's words, we know the exact context of those who "are alive and remain" when Yeshua comes back; and because of the rock solid foundation laid in the first two Secrets of this book, there should be zero confusion as to what Yeshua meant when He said "immediately after the tribulation of those days." Rather than the tribulation period being the entire 70th week of Daniel and an exact seven-year period of time, you now clearly understand that the tribulation period only begins after the abomination of desolation is unleashed. The tribulation will endure for an unknown but short amount of time and probably not seven years since we are told the man of lawlessness only reigns for 42 months (Rev. 13:5). In reality, Paul was specifically referring to the survivors of the abomination of desolation and the Great Tribulation of worldwide thermonuclear warfare. He was speaking of the *remaining* population of believers that are still *alive* after the great slaughter of the tribulation. These things absolutely must come first before the return of Christ, and there is no escaping this reality. Then, sometime after the flying scrolls are unleashed throughout the face of the earth there will be the appearance of Yeshua on the clouds. This event will occur at a time when no man knows the day or the hour. Of all the Holy Days of Leviticus 23, there is only one that perfectly fits the description of this Hebrew idiom. The Feast of Trumpets is also known as the day of shouting. It is a day of blowing the shofar, or trumpet. However, because this Day always occurs on the first day of the seventh month of the year, its exact timing is never able to be known 100% in advance. We must always wait for the sighted moon to confirm the beginning of this Day. Only then once the crescent new moon is sighted in the evening to begin the first day of the seventh month can the trumpets be blasted. One must watch every year and also wait to see on which Feast of Trumpets Yeshua will be returning. We are not there yet, as I will demonstrate further in this book. There are still too many events that need to happen first. We are very close to the return of Christ, however, and only then can believers be "caught up" (harpadzo), or "regathered", to be with Yeshua as will be discussed in Chapter 13.

Regarding those who "sleep," Paul was once again quoting Jesus. When news arrived from Mary and Martha that Lazarus was sick, Jesus tarried for two days rather than quickly going to the house of Lazarus to heal him. He then told His disciples that Lazarus had fallen asleep, and upon being misunderstood by them, He plainly stated that Lazarus was dead (John 11:14). Yeshua had used the term "sleep" because that is what happens when a born-again believer dies. Within this same chapter of John, He tells Martha, "I am the resurrection and the life. He who believes in Me, though he may die, he shall live. And whoever lives and believes in Me shall never die" (John

11:25,26). In other words, all born-again followers of Christ live even after they depart from their mortal bodies. They are raised up to rule and reign with Christ immediately, which will be the entire subject of Chapter 10. For now, it is only important to understand that Jesus will gather his elect when He returns and that there will also be a supernatural reunification event within the context of these things. Before any of this "catching up" and "regathering" can happen, however, the tribulation must come first. Anyone teaching otherwise has misrepresented the words of our Master, and some of today's biggest churches will be held accountable for leading many astray.

Perhaps the final argument coming from all rapture adherents and especially the pre-trib camp is founded upon the lives of three men in the Old Testament—Enoch, Moses, and Elijah. We read that Enoch never died because "God took him" (Gen. 5:24), and this is cited as evidence of a coming rapture of the church. The same goes for Moses, who God Himself buried but without anyone knowing where his grave was to this day (Deu. 34:6). Moses' later appearance alongside Elijah during Jesus' transfiguration event recorded in Matthew 17 and Mark 9 is cited as evidence that the burial of Moses was likely a supernatural rapture into heaven, and the same thing should be expected to happen to God's church worldwide. Then, of course, Elijah's miraculous disappearance where he "went up by a whirlwind into heaven" (2Ki 2:11) is said to give tremendous weight to all rapture theories in general. When using the three laws of biblical interpretation, particularly *context,* you will find something quite comical that all three of these men have in common. All of them had already completed life-long ministries, and at least two were very old when they were "raptured." Enoch was 365 years old while Moses was 120. Though we are not told the exact age of Elijah, it can be assumed that he was also somewhat advanced in age since he prophesied during the reigns of the northern kings Ahab and Ahaziah—a duration of 24 years. These three were also men of unprecedented righteous character. We are not told specific details about Enoch except that he "walked with God" for 300 years, which is an impressive attribute that is not used to describe any other men in the pre-flood Adamic lineage except Noah. We are later told in Ezekiel 14:14 that Noah, Daniel, and Job are likened to the most righteous men of all time, making the "walked with God" description that was given to both Enoch and Noah of great significance. Moses is described as "very humble, more than all men who were on the face of the earth" in Numbers 12:3. Of course, Elijah follows this pattern of righteousness, performing many miracles such as resurrection and bringing fire down from the sky. When examining the miraculous ascension where Elijah was "caught up" (*vaya'al* in Hebrew) into heaven, no pattern exists in the entire Hebrew Bible where this same word is used to refer to a future rapture event involving millions of people. That being the case, the supernatural departures of Enoch, Moses, and Elijah are three isolated events that span nearly 3,000 years of human history. In their own ways, all of these men were extraordinary. They were extreme outliers on the timeline of history. Anyone claiming to be cut from the same cloth as these most impressive men ever known to us and thereby claiming privilege to receive a similar rapture in their lifetime—such a person has only accomplished one thing. They have exposed the nakedness of their condescending haughtiness, pride, and arrogance in expecting the utmost special treatment from the Most High God. Such special treatment is never the rule but the exception.

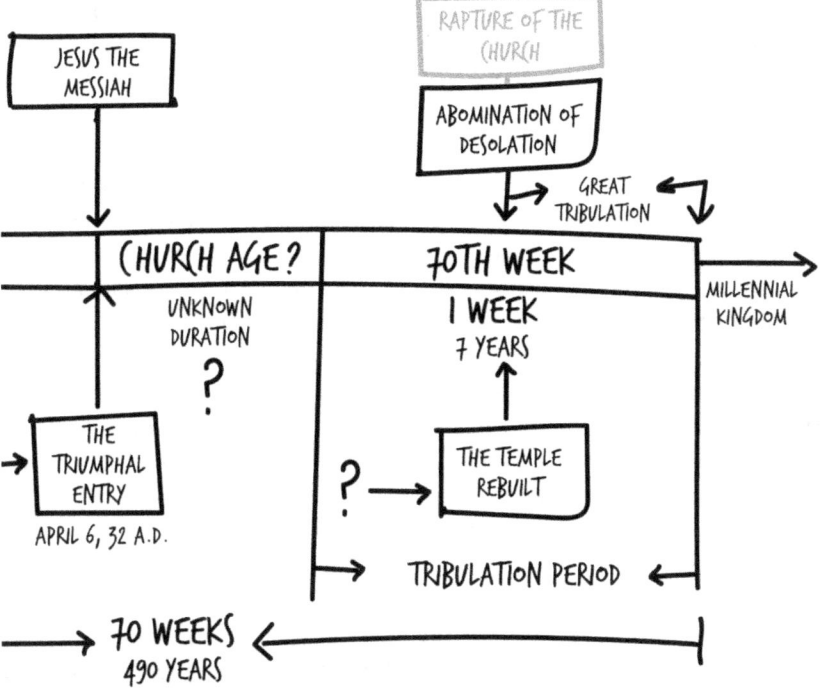

Figure 8.2: The Mid-Trib Rapture Theory Timeline. The rapture is supposed to take place in the middle of the 70th week of Daniel, or exactly 3.5 years into the final 7-year period of history. However, no mid-trib rapture ever took place during the year 2020—the exact middle—of the 70th week of Daniel from 1996-2045, proving this teaching to be false.

THEORY #2: THE MID-TRIB RAPTURE

Another popular rapture theory asserts that at exactly 3.5 years into the final 7-year period, or 70th week of Daniel, there is going to be a life-altering event so horrifying that God's "church" must then be raptured to safety while the very final 3.5 year period of mankind also called the Great Tribulation can consume the entire world. This viewpoint emphasizes that the abomination of desolation is supposed to take place in the exact middle of the 70th week of Daniel, leading to the subsequent rise of the antichrist's reign and intense persecution for 3.5 years of all those who do not take the mark of the beast. This abomination event basically coincides with the exact timing of the mid-trib rapture, since it is presumed that the "church" will not be around during the reign of the antichrist. Instead, those people that are "left behind" to be persecuted are mainly Jews along with all those who have somehow managed to find faith in Christ due to the realization that the Bible was right all along about the horrifying events unfolding before their eyes. Much of these erroneous ideas are also based on the same misunderstood passages from Paul that have already been carefully dissected. Therefore many overlapping ideas can be proven false with the analysis put forth in the last section. However, because of this viewpoint's emphasis on the abomination of desolation in the middle of the 70th week, it is important to take a moment to consider the various opinions surrounding this event.

Like most erroneous end-times teachings, the mid-trib rapture theory strings together isolated scriptures in order to prove that the abomination of desolation must take place in the exact middle of the 70th week of Daniel. In this case, the specific words of Daniel 9:27 and the "middle of the week" are used as authority to assert: (1) the "covenant with many" is a seven-year period of time and the same thing as the 70th week, (2) there will be the end of "sacrifice and offering" in the "middle" of this seven-year period, and (3) this disruption must be directly connected to the abomination of desolation and a literal, sacrificial Jewish temple because of what Jesus said about the "holy place" in Matthew 24. First, we correctly established the "covenant with many" to be a 49-year period from 1972 to 2020, and therefore, this teaching is completely off base. Secondly, the first Secret in this book has clearly demonstrated the importance of the year 2020 in the middle of the final shabua and how "sacrifice and offering" was a code phrase used by Daniel to describe the worldwide lockdowns that "ceased" annual pilgrimage to Jerusalem as a result of the Covid-19 pandemic. That leaves us with point number three of this interpretation where it is assumed that a sacrificial temple in the literal land of 1948 Israel is directly connected to the prophecy of the abomination of desolation. Such an idea is not found in either Zechariah 5 or Isaiah 22 (the latter of which Yeshua directly quoted) proving that use of the word "temple" within the prophecies of the New Testament is to be seen in a figurative sense rather than in the prevailing literal point of view. Again, let me emphasize that Yeshua never used the word "temple" in Matthew 24 or this chapter's parallels including Luke 21 and Mark 13 when speaking of the abomination of desolation. Other references to "temple" such as 2Th. 2:4 and Rev. 11:1 are also used to support the mid-trib theory, but again, both of these scriptures are not to be isolated from either Yeshua's words or the Prophets that came beforehand. The rebuilding of a Jewish third temple will be the entire focus of the next chapter due to widely overlooked scriptures that pertain to this whole idea.

It is widely assumed by mid-trib adherents that the abomination of desolation involves a rebuilt Jewish temple in Israel due to a historical account recorded in the apocryphal book of Maccabees. Originally included as part of the King James Bible, the book of Maccabees begins by detailing the history of the kingdom of Greece and how Alexander the Great had subdued the known world including Israel at the time and reigned for twelve years before succumbing to a terminal illness. After his death, the kingdom was divided, and we are told in 1Macc. 1:10, "And there came out of them a wicked root Antiochus surnamed Epiphanes, son of Antiochus the king, who had been an hostage at Rome, and he reigned in the hundred and thirty and seventh year of the kingdom of the Greeks." Once this wicked ruler asserted power, he sought to change the law of the land and persecute all those who stood in opposition. This is what we read next:

41 Moreover king Antiochus wrote to his whole kingdom, that all should be one people,
42 And every one should leave his laws: so all the heathen agreed according to the commandment of the king.
43 Yea, many also of the Israelites consented to his religion, **and sacrificed unto idols, and profaned the sabbath.**
44 For the king had sent letters by messengers unto Jerusalem and the cities of Juda that they should follow the strange laws of the land,
45 And forbid burnt offerings, and sacrifice, and drink offerings, in the temple; and **that they should profane the sabbaths and festival days:**
46 And pollute the sanctuary and holy people
52 Then many of the people were gathered unto them, to wit every one that forsook the law; and so they committed evils in the land;

53 And drove the Israelites into secret places, even wheresoever they could flee for succour.

54 Now the fifteenth day of the month Casleu, in the hundred forty and fifth year, **they set up the abomination of desolation upon the altar,** and builded idol altars throughout the cities of Juda on every side

57 And whosoever was found with any the book of the testament, or **if any committed to the law,** the king's commandment was, that **they should put him to death.**

(1Macc. 1:41-46, 52-54, 57) [emphasis added]

This account is directly responsible for the generational misunderstanding of the 70 weeks prophecy because it served as the primary lens through which Daniel's words were translated in the 1611 King James Bible. As you can see, the parallels within this chapter of 1Maccabbees to the various prophecies discussed in Secret I of this book are unmistakable when superficially comparing the English words used by the KJV translators. Of course, the proper Hebrew understanding of the abomination of desolation is completely different. Nevertheless, this historical account of the people of Antiochus Epiphanes putting an "abomination of desolation upon the altar" of the Second Temple is often cited as proof that a similar event *must* occur during the 70th week of Daniel. Though it is not clearly stated what the abomination was, the use of the words "meats" and "unclean thing" near the end of this same chapter of Maccabees has led many to speculate that a swine—a biblically unclean animal—was sacrificed on the altar. Widespread death then proceeded to consume all those in the land of Israel who wanted to continue following the Torah, including keeping the sabbath days and the holy feast days. It is fascinating and profoundly ironic how modern Christians cite Antiochus Epiphanes as being the perfect foreshadow of the coming antichrist while then simultaneously and vehemently proclaiming "the law is done away with" and "the law is a yoke of bondage" just as was the law of the land during this wicked ruler's reign. This is mind-numbing foolishness. The way that mainstream Christianity speaks out of both sides of its mouth is perfectly evident here. It is utterly ridiculous how pastors have stood in pulpits to teach these things while then directing everyone to the potluck table after the church service is over to pray over the ham and bacon. If the historical abomination of desolation was a pig, why doesn't everyone stop and consider that maybe— just maybe—it still is an abomination to eat such a thing? For as it is written in Isaiah speaking of the coming judgment:

"Those who sanctify themselves and purify themselves,

To go to the gardens
After an idol in the midst,
Eating swine's flesh and the abomination and the mouse,
Shall be consumed together," says the LORD.
(Isa. 66:17)

The numerous inconsistencies in the mid-trib viewpoint should be apparent by
now. All of the teachings within this theory are loosely based on the underlying Hebrew and Greek words and are disconnected from the actual words of
Yeshua and the Prophets. False connections are fueled by speculation that
does not distinguish between literal or figurative possibilities of the word
"temple." Historical narratives such as that of Antiochus Epiphanes are said to
provide supporting evidence, but this narrative in particular only serves to
condemn the lawless behaviors and ideologies that prevent mid-trib rapture
adherents from ever arriving at the truth of Bible prophecy to begin with.

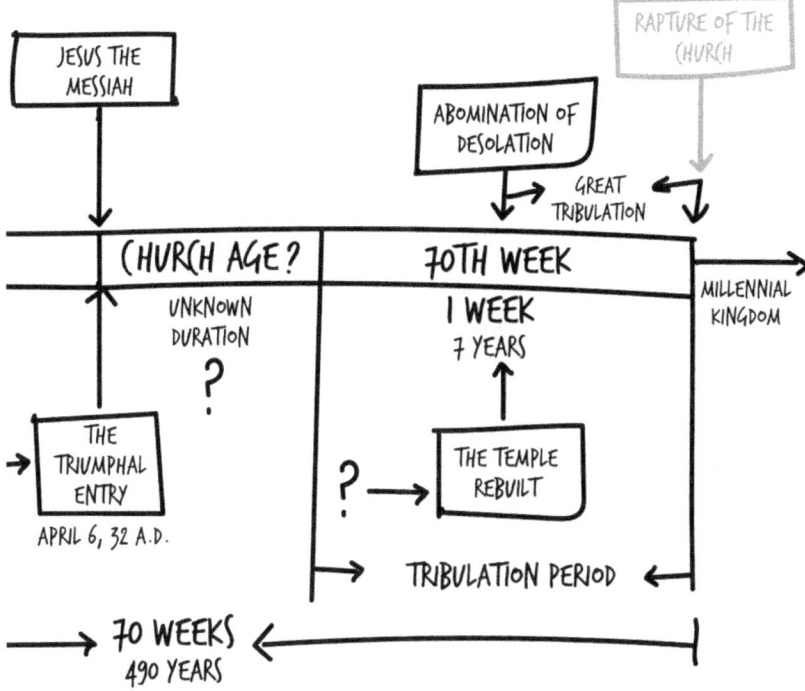

Figure 8.3: The Post-Trib Rapture Theory Timeline. This rapture is
supposed to take place at the end of the 70th week of Daniel, which we
now understand to be the spring of 2045.

THEORY #3: THE POST-TRIB RAPTURE

Of all three theories examined so far, this might be the least popular view-point, but it is one that possesses an intrinsic humility and proper under-standing that even God's people are not immune to suffering in this life. According to this theory, the rapture of the "church" is the same thing as the second coming and the meeting in the air with Jesus before a literal "millen-nial reign" is to take place on the earth. All believers must therefore go through both the abomination of desolation and Great Tribulation events before the conclusion of the 70th week of Daniel. This interpretation is aligned with the words of Christ when He stated, "a servant is not greater than his master" (John 13:16); for as Christ suffered, His people should be ready and willing to suffer for Him also. The post-trib rapture theory also aligns with the exact sequence of events presented in Matthew 24, Mark 13, and Luke 21 where no evidence is provided for a disappearing act of God's people until right when Yeshua calls them by blasting His trumpet. That is why Matthew 24:29-31 is cited as foundational to this doctrine. While this interpre-tation appears to agree with what has been presented in the first two Secrets of this book, the fundamental understanding of this rapture theory is flawed. For example, Yeshua's trumpet blast to call His elect is misunderstood by pre-trib adherents to be a disappearing act into heaven when in reality, it is the fulfill-ment of the trumpet blast of Isaiah 27:13—the trumpet of the Greater Exodus. As will be presented in two upcoming chapters of this book, there are indeed going to be two specific events that might be commonly considered "rapture" type events, though the Bible does not use that sort of language to describe them. Both of them will be occurring before the year 2045, which is, again, why the post-trib view is erroneous. They are (1) the selection of Yeshua's 144,000 firstfruits as described in Revelation 7 and 14 and (2) the regathering of all thirteen tribes of Israel back into the land of Canaan after which the second battle of the Gog and Magog War will commence. These two events will be explored thoroughly in Chapters 12 and 13.

SUMMARY OF THE THREE RAPTURE THEORIES

The prevailing rapture theories fail to examine all of the patterns of Scripture while using the three laws of interpretation to arrive at sound doctrine. When the ten plagues were unleashed upon Egypt in the book of Exodus, the millions of Israelites that were freed from slavery at the conclusion of this judgment did not disappear while all hell broke loose. Instead, they were given a land of their own where they were protected and blessed. They were given the land of Goshen where the plagues of Yehovah did not strike. The whole premise of the ten plagues was built upon making a difference between "My people and your people" (Exo. 8:23). If God had decided to rapture over a million people from the land of Goshen, He would not have been able to make this distinction to Pharaoh and the whole earth. It was only after the ten plagues that God's name became famous once again. After hundreds of years of apparent silence from Noah to Moses, Yehovah was feared once again. This is what we were told in Exodus 9:16, that "indeed for this purpose I have raised you up, that I may show My power in you, and that My name may be declared in all the earth." If the children of Israel had vanished in a great disappearing act, Pharaoh would have had no reason to harden his heart, and there would have been no pretext from which to make Yehovah's name declared in all the earth. For a very similar reason, God will not be rapturing millions of Christians out of the world before the Great Tribulation, as most people suppose. He has specific purposes for leaving his people on the earth to be a witness and a testimony for Him, and this is the clear pattern of Scripture from Genesis to Revelation.

While humility is very much present in the post-trib view, the prideful atti-tude of both the pre-trib and mid-trib rapture theories stands in opposition to the Bible on many levels. Yeshua said that John the Baptist was the greatest man born of women (Mat. 11:11); yet, when John was in his greatest time of need, Yeshua didn't come to his jail cell to rescue him. He left him for dead at the hands of Herod. Yeshua let the forerunner—the greatest man and prophet —have his head cut off and served on a platter. Ponder this. If the greatest man didn't live a comfortable and perfect life, why should we? Bad things happen to followers of God because it is only in the fire that gold, diamonds, or anything precious is crafted to its purest quality. Many of God's people must be tested through the blazing hot fire of the Great Tribulation, and none of us are immune to this reality. It's time to be still and know He is God. The narcissistic and self-centered obsession of escaping the coming tribulation period is going to cause a massive falling away from faith in Christ—the same falling away that Jesus warned about and that Paul simply repeated later.

As alluded to, the fundamental problem is that Western religions view 1948 UN-created Israel as being the "Jews" of the Scriptures, and followers of Christ are the "Church". The "Jews" have scriptures that apply to them, including the curses for disobeying God's Law. The "Church" has separate scriptures that apply to it, including no longer having to obey God's Law because they are suddenly under grace and able to live in disobedience. The "Church" is also able to experience the hope of the rapture while the "Jews" will be left behind to suffer for failing to believe in the promised Messiah. In the mind of the mainstream Christian, a church of gentiles (nations) has currently replaced the biblical Israel in terms of God's favor, and the Scriptures as a whole apply differently to both people groups as a result of this misunderstanding. However, whether someone is a Jew or Christians (it doesn't matter), only those practitioners of God's Torah, Prophets, and Writings who have also believed in Jesus will have the right to the tree of life, as the end of Revelation so clearly states: "Blessed are those who do His commandments, that they may have the right to the tree of life, and may enter through the gates into the city" (Rev. 22:14).

LIFE AFTER THE BOMBS GO OFF

Stick with me. I know there has been a lot of doom and gloom within the pages of this book, and at this point, it might seem like there is no reprieve. Well, the final part of this chapter will shed light on a hidden blessing within the pages of Scripture that will help you tremendously in navigating the flood of judgment ahead. Even as I write this book, there are increasing rumors of wars, nuclear attack strategies, and so much trouble that I can hardly keep up with it all. In fact, I don't want to keep up anymore.

For the longest time, I lived as an Alex Jones junkie and constantly kept up with Steve Quayle's latest doomsday articles or any one of a number of end times blogs and websites in a somewhat misguided attempt to discern the signs of the end times. It all started back in 2013 when I started seeing videos and reports of the Federal Emergency Management Agency (FEMA) purchasing and transporting unusually large amounts of coffins on semi trucks around the US during the Obama administration. Knowing what I know now, they were doing this in anticipation for war with Russia, which is now truly upon us these few years later. Anyways, I remember going to work and putting in my headphones to listen to the Alex Jones Show for the full four-hour transmission and then listening to the whole thing all over again during an entire shift. That was the start of a journey into deep politics, shadow government systems, and bioethics, among various other conspiracy related topics that you never learn in college.

Along the way, I found that a lot of what gets labeled a "conspiracy theory" by the media is just factual information that the government doesn't want people talking about. One of those suppressed conversations circles around suspicious FEMA operations in the event of nuclear war. First, just think of a conspiracy theory as an explanation for something based on the information available but that cannot be fully proven. Iran's possession of nuclear weapons, the coronavirus vaccine's lethal gene therapy properties, the "white replacement" open borders agenda in the West—there are a number of these ideas that have already been carefully presented in this book and backed by the authority of Scripture. They are *conspiracy*—the execution of a secret plan that is criminal and therefore punishable by law—and they are *theoretical* in nature because mountains of evidence are indeed present, but the perpetrators don't come out and plainly admit to their illicit activities and crimes. Going back to the FEMA case study, there has been a theory going around that prison camps have already been built in the US (and all over the West) in preparation for a coming disaster that the government will then use as a pretext to incarcerate and eliminate those opposed to their agenda. We have already witnessed this theory in practice during the last major disaster that the world faced. During the height of the Covid-19 hysteria, healthy Australians with no symptoms were arrested and locked in prison camps because they failed the highly suspicious and inherently flawed PCR tests. In one instance, an old mining camp called Howard Springs was turned into a quarantine camp capable of holding 2,000 people, and Australian police would arrest those who would try to escape, even in the middle of the night.[1] History has taught us that anything tyrannical happening in Australia eventually comes to America. Going back in time a little further, we witnessed the Patriot Act's birth out of the womb of the September 11, 2001 attacks. That was the moment when American citizens officially became potential enemies of the state under the false pretext of preventing terrorism. The next looming disaster of nuclear war, which we *know* is coming, will likely usher in FEMA internment camps offering amenities that average citizens will be begging for. Radiation testing, hot meals, and the lure of shelter will successfully entice many into entering the jurisdiction of FEMA. What they won't realize is that the hot meals are going to be loaded with GMOs and experimental vaccine technologies, and what they thought were shelters are actually going to be interrogation centers, labor camps, or deathbeds, depending on the specific agenda assigned to a given region. This may seem like an outlandish assessment, but I will show you how Daniel 11 seems to support these ideas in a moment. For many years now, the media has been hyping up the "nuclear Iran" narrative, and there is no way they would be doing that for no reason. They are obviously planning on causing some type of event and using it as an excuse for a full-scale FEMA crackdown. This explains why the Biden regime recently unfroze $6 Billion USD in funds for Iran in a supposed prisoner swap deal[2] while simultaneously giving Israel billions in funding and weapons.[3,4] This funding of both sides of the ongoing war is not unique to the Biden administration, of course. This nonsensical activity has been going on for decades. Remember Obama's pallets of cash that were delivered to Iran in 2016?[5] Just follow the money, as they say. You will eventually find out that these payments are not nonsensical after all but part of a well-orchestrated plan to create a totalitarian control grid in all Western countries to usher in a much larger agenda. The Western elites plan to use WW3 to destroy and destabilize the entire world so that all people are ready to submit to a brand new and alien government never before seen on the face of the earth. This same depopulation agenda that was present in the 1972 UNEP documents is simply taking on a new form, yet again. The stage is being set for the final beast power of history under satan's direct control to rise up out of the thermonuclear ashes. The aforementioned FEMA theory speculates that internment camps will likely be set up nationwide and especially at Walmart and Sam's Club locations. These locations are ubiquitous, and many stores have been closing recently due to the economic downturn,[6] leaving behind massive, windowless concrete buildings that can be repurposed by the US government in the event of an emergency.

Regarding nuclear warfare more specifically, most people fail to realize that the prevailing "nuclear winter" narrative is actually a government-promoted conspiracy theory intended to cover up the truth of what will *really* happen in a thermonuclear war. First, the term *nuclear winter* simply refers to the idea that if the world engaged in an all-out nuclear war between the powers of the West and the East, there would be a severe and prolonged climatic cooling due to the blotting out of the sun from all of the smoke in the atmosphere. This period of worldwide cooling is said to last several years, and because of the lack of photosynthesis needed for plants to grow, most of the world's population would die of starvation due to catastrophic crop failures. I was guilty of echoing this same narrative on episode 15 of Overcome Babylon[7] where I cited a 2022 Rutgers University study that claimed that over 5 billion people would die of hunger following a full-scale nuclear war between the U.S. and Russia.[8] Again, this number of deaths is not because of the bombs themselves. Scientists based their findings on the fact that there would be so much soot in the atmosphere from all of the explosions that the sun would be blotted out and crops wouldn't be able to be grow for at least 4-5 years after the war. However, there is a reason why this study is extremely similar to all of the Hollywood nuclear apocalypse movies that have been promoted since around the time of the Cold War. More specifically, the media industrial complex actually began promoting this "nuclear winter" theory in a coordinated fashion around 1983. This was the year that a researcher named Carl Sagan together with a group of scientists known as the TTAPS group published a paper entitled "Global Atmospheric Effects of Nuclear War." Basing their study on volcanic eruption models, they estimated that ambient and land temperatures could reach -15° to -25°C (5 to -13°F), and they further concluded:

"The yield threshold for major optical and climatic consequences may be very low: only about 100 megatons detonated over major urban centers can create average hemispheric smoke optical depths greater than 2 for weeks and, even in summer, subfreezing land temperatures for months. In a 5000-megaton war...long-term exposure to cold, dark, and radioactivity could pose a serious threat to human survivors and to other species."[9]

The idea is that even in a more limited nuclear war scenario (100 megatons of nuclear weapons) many months of freezing temperatures should be expected, and in the case of a larger (5000 megatons) war scenario, several years of freezing is highly likely. These findings ultimately became the foundation of the nuclear winter theory. Just a couple years later on March 14, 1985, Congressman James H. Scheuer led a congressional hearing on the idea of a nuclear winter in which Sagan was permitted to share his findings. Scheuer opened the discussion by asserting that in the years and even decades following a nuclear war, the soot, ash, dust, and smoke released into the atmosphere would cause the world to become a frozen and radiation-filled wasteland with food production virtually eliminated.[10,11] Soon after, the work of the TTAPS scientists was not only adopted by the US Department of Defense, but it also became widely pushed in the media to the point of inspiring popular culture even to this day.

The problem is that the 1983 TTAPS publication was deeply flawed. In a 1986 research report entitled "Nuclear Winter Reappraised", scientists Starley L. Thompson and Stephen H. Schneider point out the major problems with the nuclear winter theory, stating:

"The [TTAPS] model was one-dimensional; that is, it did not take into account north-south and east-west directions, but instead treated the earth as a homogenous all-land sphere having a temperature that depended only on the up-down direction (atmospheric altitude). Thus, the model had no geography, no winds, no seasons, instantaneous spread of smoke to the hemispheric scale, and no feedback of atmospheric circulation changes on the rate of smoke washout by rainfall. ...Let us sum up: despite the continued potential for serious nuclear winter effects, there does not seem to be a real potential for human extinction; nor is there a plausible threshold for severe environmental effects. Thus, the two unique conclusions of the original nuclear winter idea with the most important implications for policy have been removed."[12]

In other words, the original TTAPS model from which modern nuclear winter theories are based was highly simplistic and did not even take into account winds or rainfall—let alone the change in seasons—which would all work together to naturally dissipate and settle the smoke in the atmosphere. The 1986 research, on the other hand, took these things under consideration along with discussing more realistic nuclear attack strategies. That is why the 100 and 5000 megaton scenarios in the original TTAPS report were considered baseless as thresholds from which to make scientific conclusions. Thompson and Schneider were able to present superior findings by taking far more scientific factors into consideration, and in doing so, they found the TTAPS report to be "ignorant at best, or dangerous propaganda at worst,"[13] with its apocalyptic conclusions having a "vanishingly low level of probability."[14] Of course, the government-sanctioned nuclear winter apocalypse theory has continued to be promoted, despite sound evidence to the contrary.

The truth is that the Bible seems to be warning us of a limited nuclear exchange scenario only. Though it could be a complete decapitation strike against the West, it appears that at least Israel will use its "Samson Option" in which it will fire off several nuclear warheads in the Middle East. This conclusion appears supported by Isaiah 17:1 in which all of Damascus in Syria will be wiped out. There is also language in Zechariah 11:1-3 that supports Israel's use of nuclear weapons against Lebanon and Jordan, with northern Israel also getting bombed in return. Ultimately, the flying scrolls will be all over the face of the earth, but the West seems like the primary recipient. This idea will make more sense in Chapter 11 when the coming locust armies of satan are discussed in more detail. Rather than years of smoke and ash, we should really only expect weeks and maybe even two at most. The reality is that nuclear war is very survivable, and most people will be surviving even if they never planned for it. It is the overnight civil unrest, societal collapse, and diminishing resources like food and water that will be causing major problems, especially in urban areas. Western governments have most likely promoted the prevailing nuclear winter theory because they wanted to create a fatalistic culture. Overwhelmed and anxious, most people simply do not want to prepare for the coming nuclear war when they hear that they will likely not survive, anyway. Promoting this falsehood has further enabled the depopulation agenda of the Western secret societies as previously discussed, and this is the likely reason why they have pushed this false narrative.

With all these things considered, it's important to be aware of various conspiratorial developments but not be consumed by them. A lot of people who dig deep into conspiracy theories develop a strange kind of pride. It's a condescending attitude that thinks itself more intelligent than everyone else because of a twisted obsession with hidden knowledge. You see this a lot with the "sacred name" people that believe they are the only ones that know the true pronunciation of the Tetragrammaton (YHVH) name of God while everyone else has been deceived by the Jews and Catholics, who together have colluded to hide the true Name from public view. I've seen too many people develop undiagnosed mental illness over these things, and I am speaking directly from experience. My pursuit of conspiratorial knowledge back in my 2013 days along with my exposure to alternative news media was intense. The truth is, while some of this kind of research can be helpful, it is only the Word of God that tells us the Truth. And it is only the absolute Truth from the Most High that can set us free indeed. Media consumption—whether it was left, right, alternative, or whatever—always left me feeling empty, fearful, and hopeless. Only the Bible can put us in the place where we can experience the peace of God that surpasses all understanding, and my sincere hope is that what I am about to unpack next will help your spirit to settle down in the midst of the noise so that you can discover true rest in the promises of God.

THE 45-DAY BLESSING?

In the original edition of this book, I proposed the idea that Daniel gave us yet another urgent number to work with that is connected to the abomination of desolation. It is found within these words of Dan. 12:11,12:

11 "And from the time *that* the daily *sacrifice* is taken away, and the abomination of desolation is set up, *there shall be* one thousand two hundred and ninety days.
12 "Blessed *is* he who waits, and comes to the one thousand three hundred and thirty-five days.

We already covered the first verse and the 1290 days. In case you need a refresher, here is the math:

March 11, 2020 + 1290 Days = Friday, September 22, 2023

We now know that this was the date when the abomination of desolation was "set up." Now we need to see what is meant by the 1335 days. I originally made the case that because we are given this idea of *waiting* beyond the day of the abomination of desolation, the proper interpretation should be:

1335 Days - 1290 Days = 45 Days

Perhaps Daniel was being told that there is something special about arriving to the 45-day mark after the abomination of desolation. If you do the math, it looks like this:

Friday, September 22, 2023 + 45 Days = Monday, November 6

In other words, if you were to add 1335 days to March 11, 2020, you should also arrive at November 6, 2023. It appeared that we were being told that if we waited until 45 days after the abomination of desolation, we would be blessed. Of course, because September 22, 2023 *was not* the beginning of the Great Tribulation as I had originally proposed, then the 1335 days and its associated blessing must be calculated differently. March 11, 2020 is not the starting point of this time period because there was nothing historically signif-icant about November 6, 2023 in relation to the abomination of desolation or nuclear war. First, let's consider what the actual *blessing* might be in the hope of discerning its timing.

DISSECTING THE HEBREW WORDS

The verse in question is Dan. 12:12, and the first word on our radar is "blessed" (ah'-shree, from the root word "eh-sher" Strong's H835).[15] It simply means *happy*. However, it is a masculine plural noun, which means that we should expect more than one reason to be happy. The first time we see this word appear in the Scriptures is 1Kings 10:8 where the Queen of Sheba describes how happy the nation of Israel is because of the great wisdom of Solomon. She was speechless. Amazed by all of the splendor of Solomon's kingdom, she utters many positive words speaking of great happiness. In other words, Daniel was perhaps hinting at a profound happiness that takes your breath away. As you study this word throughout the Scriptures, it could also mean blessed by God Himself along with the state of blessedness.

There are two more words to look at to completely understand what Daniel is conveying to us. The next word is "waits" (hakah', Strong's H2442), which means to await, wait for, or long for; and it intrinsically carries the meaning of exercising patience.[16] Finally, Daniel used the word "comes" (veh-yah-gee-ah', from the root word Strong's H5060) that carries the meaning of arriving, reaching, or causing to touch.[17]

In other words, Daniel was telling us that blissfully happy is the man that exercises patience and endures hardship in order to touch the 1335-day mark sometime after the abomination of desolation. In other words, sometime after a nuclear war event in Israel itself and likely preemptive strikes against the West (Israel's allies), we are being told that the survivors will be happy as they wait and finally arrive at this 1335-day mark. That being said, I admit that I am currently unsure of what this period of time is supposed to be. Maybe the correct interpretation is to add these 1335 days after the exact date that the abomination of desolation is deployed and the exact day that the Great Tribulation begins in Israel. This interpretation would make sense, though we don't currently know the exact starting point yet. Sometime after the abomination of desolation, the 42-month reign of the man of lawlessness is supposed to begin. Assuming 30-day months, this period of time is 1,260 days long. If we take 1335 and subtract 1260, we get 75 days. Perhaps this prophecy is speaking of those who survive long enough to witness the satanic new world order being judged by God once the 75-day mark is reached. In other words, the 1335-day period might be from the beginning of the 42 months of the antichrist until 75 days after, when it is highly possible for the two witnesses to begin greatly disrupting the reign of the antichrist. As I will present in Chapter 13, the work of the two witnesses immediately follows the 42-month reign of the antichrist. My proposed interpretation of Daniel's 1335 days therefore appears to indicate that God's people will be happy to see the two witnesses doing something quite special for them at the 75-day timestamp. This interpretation makes the most sense at the moment, because we are told in various scriptures that once the 42-month reign is completed, the man of lawlessness will be sorely judged. Just take a look at Daniel 7:

25 Then the saints shall be given into his hand
For a time and times and half a time.
26 But the court shall be seated,
And they shall take away his dominion,
To consume and destroy it forever.
27 Then the kingdom and dominion,
And the greatness of the kingdoms under the whole heaven,
Shall be given to the people, the saints of the Most High.
His kingdom is an everlasting kingdom,
And all dominions shall serve and obey Him.
(Dan. 7:25b-27)

These words should be like gasoline on the blazing fire of hope deep within your soul and consciousness. Those who are alive and remain to inherit the earth with Yeshua as the visible King of the land will certainly be "happy" exactly as described in Daniel 12:12. Not only will they witness the work of the coming two witnesses, but they will be able to see Yeshua returning on the clouds shortly thereafter. Rather than seeing the coming abomination of desolation with deep dread like most people will sadly experience, you should now see that this event begins the countdown of the 42 final months of testing, with a huge blessing waiting at the end of it all. This current evil age is finally almost over!

DANIEL 11: STRONG AND AIDED WITH A LITTLE HELP

We already looked at Dan. 11:31 in Chapter 6 and dissected the words necessary to further understand the abomination of desolation. I purposely did not break down the verses after this one because I was holding back on discussing those secrets until this chapter. There are quite fascinating things written down for us in the following verses of Dan. 11:32-35 (there is also a clear parallel to Revelation 13):

32 Those who do wickedly against the covenant he shall corrupt with flattery; but the people who know their God shall be strong, and carry out great exploits.
33 And those of the people who understand shall instruct many; yet for many days they shall fall by sword and flame, by captivity and plundering.
34 Now when they fall, they shall be aided with a little help; but many shall join with them by intrigue.
35 And some of those of understanding shall fall, to refine them, purify them, and make them white, until the time of the end; because it is still for the appointed time.

We are given a contrast in Dan. 11:32 between the wicked and the righteous during the days after the abomination. It is unclear who the "he" of this verse is referring to by looking at Daniel alone, but it is almost certainly the final beast power that takes over once the nuclear dust settles. This beast is going to use flattery and deceptive language to corrupt the people of the world that do not obey the written covenant (Torah) of God. He will make them take the mark of the beast just as described in Rev. 13:17. However, Daniel shows us that God's people will be strong, even in the midst of these dark days. This word *strong* (yahaziqu, from the root word Strong's H2388) has been translated differently throughout the Bible and can also be used to say to repair (2Ki. 12:5) or to be encouraged (Ps. 64:5).[18] There will most likely be an intervention where God's people are given supernatural provisions of both health (repair) and physical items so that they might be encouraged.

There is a direct parallel between Dan. 11:33 and Rev. 13:7,10. The saints (set-apart people) will be overcome by the final beast power that rules over the earth. They will be killed by captivity, plundering, and sword. However, there is good news. Take a closer look at Daniel 11:34. They are indeed going to "fall" (Strong's H3782) or be brought to injury, overthrown, or ruined;[19] but they will also be "aided" (Strong's H5826) or surrounded and protected with supernatural help.[20] Based on these words it is my understanding that the Most High will be helping his people immediately after the Great Tribulation begins by surrounding them with unique miracles from this point onward. They will be given a little provision, perhaps like Elijah and the widow's house (1Ki. 17:9). They will be given aid to stand through the various trials. They will be helped.

But watch out!

The second part of Daniel 11:34 speaking of "intrigue" is a strong warning for you and I today. We don't have to fall into this snare if we are wise and discerning. To be honest, I have already put myself in somewhat of a compromised position by simply deciding to publish my podcast in early 2022 and also this book. So be it!I knew the stakes were high. I knew that putting myself out there on the internet for all to see would make me somewhat of a target for the enemy. But I also knew that someone needed to rise up and instruct God's people during these last days regarding all these various prophecies. If my cover is blown and I'm first to the slaughter, consider yourself the one that I am now passing the baton to. Run the race in my place.

There is a word in this next line that is only found four times in the Bible, and this is the word translated as "intrigue" in the NKJV or "flatteries" in the KJV. The Hebrew word is Strong's H2519, which is pronounced "khal-ak-lak-kaw'".[21] Wicked people are going to join themselves to the remnant of God's people through the use of flatteries. A closer look at this word reveals the meaning of dark, deceptive tactics of the tongue that employ the use of false promises and seduction (Psa. 35:6, Jer. 23:12, Dan. 11:21).

People will try anything to join the righteous survivors of nuclear war that are being helped by the God Most High through various miracles and provisions. These wicked people will join and deceive God's people with forked tongues of flattery. They will sell you out, they will report you to the authorities on a whim. They will use and abuse you for their own personal gain. They hand you over to the concentration camps both before and after the Muslim-Russian-Chinese invasion of Western countries is successful. Remember, I warned you beforehand!

חֲלַקְלַקּוֹת

Figure 8.4: The Tongues of Flattery - "Khal-ak-lak-kaw".

THE PARABLE OF HEZEKIAH (2 KINGS 20:12-19)

In light of all these truths, you should take heed to the cautionary tale that King Hezekiah's life teaches us. He was the 13th king of the southern Kingdom of Judah, and many significant events happened in his life such as Sennacherib's failed invasion in which 185,000 Assyrians were killed in one night by the Angel of Yehovah (Isa. 37:36). But there is one particular passage from 2Kings that lines up perfectly with what Daniel 11 has been warning us.

Though he was sick about to die, Hezekiah's life was extended by fifteen more years after he prayed and wept to God. It is shortly after this prayer request was answered that the royal messenger, Berodach-Baladan, who was the son of the king of Babylon, came to pay Hezekiah a visit. This is what we read next in 2Ki. 20:13:

"And Hezekiah was attentive to them, and showed them all the house of his treasures—the silver and gold, the spices and precious ointment, and all his armory—all that was found among his treasures. There was nothing in his house or in all his dominion that Hezekiah did not show them."

Hezekiah was boastful. He was proud of his possessions and wanted to show off all of his earthly goods and splendor kind of like King Solomon did with the Queen of Sheba. Why else did he do this except to brag? He showed Berodach-Baladan everything he had and did not conceal anything. Isaiah steps in as a faithful prophet and proclaims these words in light of what Hezekiah just did (2Ki. 20:17):

"'Behold, the days are coming when all that *is* in your house, and what your fathers have accumulated until this day, shall be carried to Babylon; nothing shall be left,' says the LORD."

Everything in which Hezekiah had just found so much boast, comfort, and identity was going to be stripped away. Rather than making his boast in Yehovah, he made his boast in the provisions of Yehovah. Rather than using the spiritual discernment that comes through an intimate relationship with God, Hezekiah allowed his carnal mind to lead his interaction with Berodach-Baladan, and he had successfully planted the seeds of covetousness, jealousy, and sensuality in the heart of Babylon's messenger. All of these seeds would grow into a great harvest only a short time later.

Don't follow in the footsteps of Hezekiah. Make your boast in Yehovah alone and not in the miracles and provisions themselves that He is going to give you. And when the good things do come to pass just as prophesied by Daniel, not everyone needs to know about it.

Yes, there will be a hurt, starving, and dying world around you. You will be tempted to take the good things that God has intended for you and foolishly give them away to those in need that are around you. Simply remember that all of these horrifying events are coming upon the earth because of rebellion. Don't take what God has appointed for you and your family and give it to the rebels. Elijah was indeed only sent to one widow's house during a time of extreme famine when many other widows were also in need (Luk. 4:26).

It's just the way it is.

Don't let your heart of compassion be misguided and misplaced upon those whom it simply does not belong. Failure to use discernment and listen to every whisper of the Holy Spirit during these days will cause many to lose the blessings and happiness that the Most High actually intended them to have. Many will join the righteous through flattery. Don't be deceived.

Chapter 9
The Third Temple in Jerusalem

This chapter will continue to take the rock solid foundation of the 70 shabua of Daniel and lean upon it in order to rise above the noise, distractions, and false prophecies that many are pushing on God's people. This next major topic that must be addressed is the rebuilding of a physical temple in modern-day Israel. Come with an open mind and a level-headed attitude because this chapter will challenge all popular worldviews concerning the Spiritual Israel of God and the 1948 land division of United Nations Resolution 181, commonly called "Israel." We will look past all of the excitement and fanfare surrounding the red heifers that recently arrived in Israel in September 2022 and various other things that Christians and Rabbinic Jews alike are promoting. As alluded to in previous chapters, this topic is of immense importance for three primary reasons: (1) All Christians falsely believe the abomination of desolation to be connected to a literal sacrificial temple in Jerusalem due to extreme ignorance of the Hebrew words in Daniel's prophecies, (2) The majority of believers are currently living in a state of apathy because, according to their views, the rapture, abomination of desolation, and Great Tribulation prophecies are *only* possible if a Jewish temple is present and operational, and (3) Even if the Jewish people do manage to build a temple in Israel, this act will be met with swift retaliation by Muslim forces and will likely not achieve much in terms of Bible prophecy, as will be explored in this chapter.

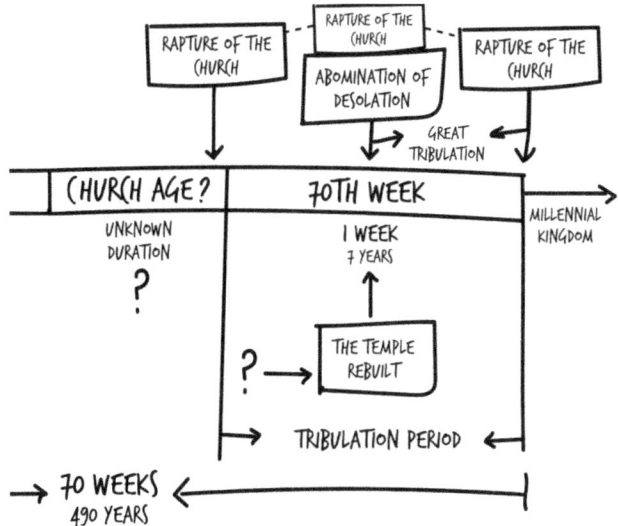

Figure 9.1: The Role of a Jewish Temple in Mainstream Christianity. Of the three rapture theories, the pre- and mid-trib views are heavily dependent on the rebuilding of a new temple in Jerusalem. However, all Christians believe the 70th week of Daniel will only begin once a Jewish temple is at least in the process of being built and certainly once it is fully completed. It is theorized that only then can the antichrist enter into the "holy place" of the temple, declare himself to be God, and unleash the Great Tribulation period by setting up the abomination of desolation that is said to be a sacrificial animal or idol of some sort.

CHRISTIANS & JEWS BECOME UNITED FOR A TEMPLE

The year 2022 was full of fanfare, excitement, and a renewed desire for the building of a literal, physical temple in Israel. Even though this idea of rebuilding the temple is not new and has been in the works for many years now, there were profound and significant events that recently took place that do make it seem as if some sort of physical temple could be built in Israel very soon. Is this structure necessary for end-times prophecy to be fulfilled? As I have already shown you, no.

We already saw how the words *sacrifice, sacrifices,* and *sanctuary* were purposely (and erroneously) inserted within the translation of Daniel's Hebrew words because the translators had a very strong bias concerning the prophecies of the middle of the week and abomination of desolation. They were desperate to push their agenda of a rebuilt temple in Israel for the fulfillment of prophecy. We know better now. We have properly divided the Word of God and have no need to be timid about it. The idea of a temple has been used throughout the New Testament to refer to spiritual and figurative things such as the literal bodies of born again believers. A physical temple was not necessary whatsoever for the prophecies of the year 2020 to be fulfilled, and the same is true for prophecies that have not been fulfilled yet.

Now let's find out what the Word of God *actually* says about the rebuilding of a temple.

You will be shocked if this information is new to you. Make no mistake about it. The Bible is absolutely *not* silent about this desire of both Christians and Jews to see a temple built. Scriptures like Jeremiah 5 and Revelation 18 tell us exactly what to expect concerning this reality, and it's not looking good for those who have already fallen for this deception. Those seeking validation of false end-times teachings such as the timing of the rapture will be sorely disappointed when the temple never arrives the way they thought. Likewise, those who anticipate the temple to be something beneficial, even in the slightest sentiment, to the Jewish and Christian people of the world are going to fall under God's hand of judgment in a terrifying way. All those constantly praying for the peace of the secular state of Israel and wishing God's blessings and prosperity upon this nation and all of its plans, including the blatant idolatry of a temple, are also falling within the crosshairs of divine punishment.

The construction of a temple in Jerusalem along with all of the various articles and vessels used for worship is a plan that has been in the works for many years. Even before 1948 Israel became a nation state, the secretive Freemason fraternal cult was already devising plans to resurrect Solomon's temple, including detailed costs and specific accounting of the personnel needed to complete the project. This information was presented as a major headline within *The Illustrated London News* in an August 28, 1909 newspaper,[1] and it was estimated that back in those days it would cost around 53,248,000 British pounds for only the labor involved in the temple's construction. This figure excluded the various building materials and precious temple items themselves. What makes this 1909 publication all the more intriguing is the statement published at the very top of page 32. It reads:

"There comes, need it be said, from America—in point of fact, from Boston— a suggestion that the Freemasons of the World shall subscribe that the Temple of Solomon may be rebuilt at Jerusalem. With the suggestion comes the remark that the undertaking would be an enormous one, and that it would cost a vast amount of money. This is obviously true, but we wonder whether those with whom the scheme originated have really counted the cost. That some idea of the magnitude of the proposed work may be gained, we print on this page and on the following pages the comparatively few figures that can be given reasonably, and many facts that further emphasise the gigantic sum it would be nesessary to collect before the great building could be re-erected. **The interest of the Freemasons in the Temple is explained by the fact that they believe their order was founded by King Solomon, and that he was the first Grand Master of the Craft.** There is not only the question of ways and means to be considerd. The site originally occupied by the Temple is now filled by the Harem-Esh -Shereef, "the Noble Sanctuary," which to the Moslems is only less sacred than Mecca and Medina, for it is believed to cover the rock that is regarded by them as the centre of the earth, the place from which Mahomet started when he visited Heaven. Therefore, it is obvious that any attempt to interfere with the present condition of things would in all probability **bring about the greatest religious war the world has ever known.** Meantime, it is stated that the Freemasons of Boston have begun operations by applying for the incorporation of a company **to take the matter in hand."[2]** [emphasis added]

So much of the Freemason master plan is revealed right here, front and center. As explained in the second chapter of this book regarding the "star of David" disinformation, King Solomon's descent into witchcraft and paganism fueled a culture within both ancient Israel and Judah that still continues to manifest itself within the most sinister secret societies and cults of today. That is why the hexagram is featured prominently in Masonic lodges and their associated symbolism. The Freemasons view King Solomon as an important Grand Master and patriarch of their secret society. The other key takeaway from this 1909 article's public admission is that building a temple in Jerusalem will bring about the world's greatest religious war ever seen— a war that must take place. The western Freemason groups are one secret society that has been "taking the matter in hand" for over 100 years now through systematic control of governments, the media, and pro-Israel religious institutions. This topic will be explored heavily in Chapter 11, but this 1909 press release once again reveals why both sides of the current war of Iran against Israel have been funded to the tune of billions of dollars by the West. For as Albert Pike (1809–1891)—a 33rd degree Freemason and Grandmaster of the Royal Order of Scotland—is credited as stating: just as the Second World War was necessary for the creation of a Zionist state in Palestine, the Third World War will be necessary for a world divided between Zionism and Islam to destroy itself in order to usher in an age of the "pure doctrine of Lucifer."[3,4] In theory, a new temple would therefore only be a contributing part of a much larger plan to subdue the entire world with nuclear chaos so that the coveted new world order might be ushered in—a world order that the luciferian elites have been seeking for quite a long time.

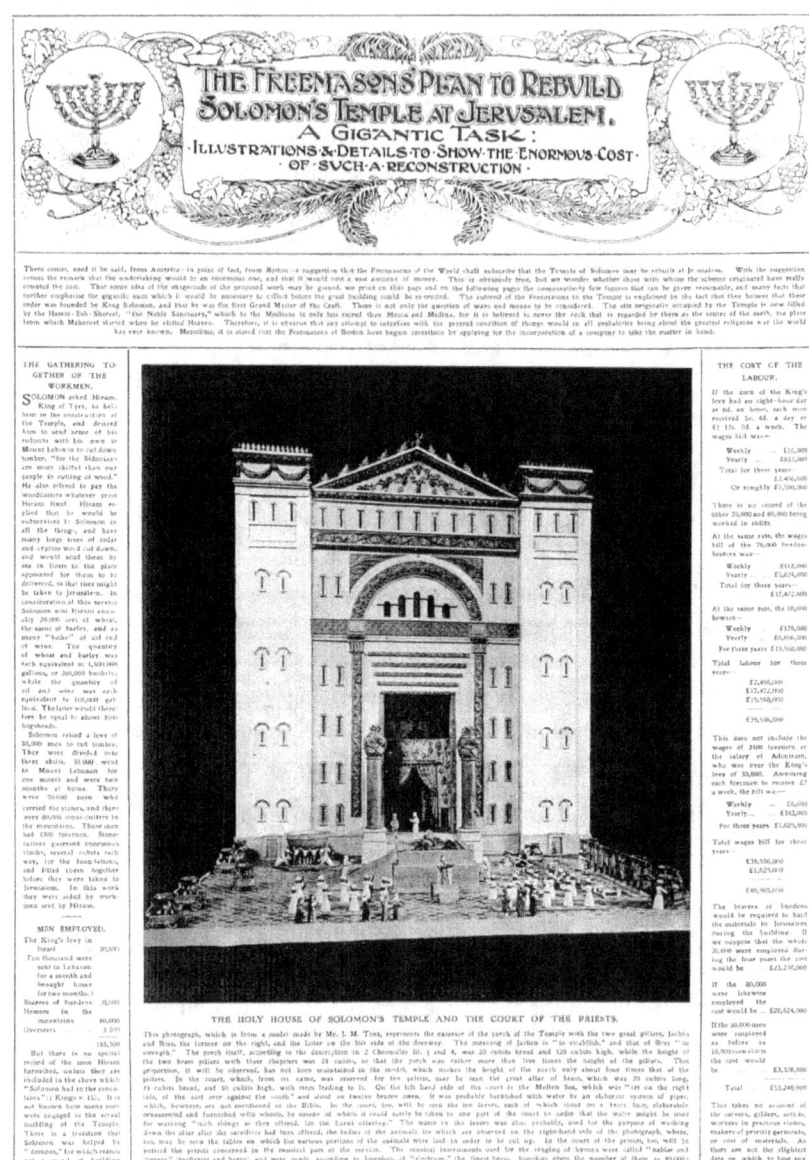

Figure 9.2: The Freemasons' Plan to Rebuild Solomon's Temple at Jerusalem, *The Illustrated London News,* 1909.[5,6]

Going forward in time, the media has continued to push the same desire of the secret societies onto the masses. A 2016 article by the Jewish Telegraphic Agency announced a school for training Levites, and even back in those days the Temple Institute had already completed "…nearly all of the sacred vessels needed to perform the services in a rebuilt Temple, including the High Priest's breastplate featuring the 12 precious stones of the tribes of Israel, the half-ton golden menorah and the musical instruments of the Levitical choir."[7] In addition to these temple items, it was then announced in 2018 that the stone altar for performing sacrifices was now ready to be dedicated by 70 nations in a universalist worship ceremony.[8] Fast forward to September 23, 2022, and five red heifers were flown to Israel from Texas through a coordinated effort so that the Torah requirement for the ashes of water purification could be met in order to begin priestly service (Num. 19).[10] To many watchmen and prophecy students, this single event basically sealed the deal for the anticipated arrival of a physical temple. Nothing else really hinders construction at this moment in history except for diplomatic and political barriers.

In light of these recent events, various campaigns have been accelerated around the rebuilding of a temple. One activist organization, 3rdTemple, reached well over 360,000 people pledging their support for this project; they state on their website, "As our number grows so will our ability to influence the media and on world politics, and thus the project will be realized today."[11] This particular website is backed by many organizations working with the Temple Institute, which is the main organization responsible for rebuilding the Jewish temple.

You might now be wondering why the building of a temple is so important to modern Jews. What is their religious, moral, or legal inspiration for doing this project? Going back to the 3rdTemple website, they state right on their homepage, "Build it today for the benefit of world humanity."[12] Notice the overarching theme of universalism. In their "Statement of Principles," the Temple Institute also makes it abundantly clear that the temple is meant to be for all people; and they go so far as to state that the temple is necessary for "…ushering in a new era of universal harmony and peace unparalleled in the history of man."[13] This emphasis on universalist worship seems harmless at first glance, and to the unsuspecting victim, this seems like good theology, right? I mean, doesn't God want all people to worship Him and come to the saving knowledge of Yeshua the Messiah? Absolutely! But *universalism* and related words like *universal* or *universally* aren't innocent terms to be thrown around lightly in the context of theology. What the Jews are *really* teaching with this temple project is that universal reconciliation can be made available through the temple; and all humans will ultimately receive salvation, regardless of what their religious path is to get to heaven. These teachings are directly opposed to Yeshua's words that no man comes to the Father but through Him alone (Jhn. 14:6). He makes it clear that those who do not believe in Him are already condemned to perish (Jhn. 3:18). The Christians, knowing or unknowingly, are going right along with these universalist teachings by getting excited about the building of a new temple, whether because they are seeking selfish validation for false doctrines or because they are constantly seeking the peace and prosperity of the Jews and 1948 Israel.

This is heresy.

The Jews are teaching the Christians and the rest of the world to commit spiritual sexual immorality, which is the mixing of the truth of the Bible with lies. More specifically, Jewish universalism teaches that "…all paths to the divine are equally Holy and that one's religion is not the sole and exclusive source of truth" because "…all people who follow the dictate to 'love your neighbor as yourself' are 'chosen.'"[14] In other words, they are saying truth is relative and not absolute. The Bible repeatedly warns not to mix the Word of God with doctrines and teachings of men. We are commanded not to add to or take away from the truth of the Word. Sin has consequences, and the Jews and Christians are both committing this sin of casting God's Word behind their backs. Sadly, they will be paying a harsh penalty for this spiritual adultery, as I will reveal in this chapter.

"THIRD" TEMPLE DISINFORMATION

Before unraveling the mystery of the Jewish temple any further, I want to show you just how misleading the narrative is behind this building project. I will touch on this idea only briefly, but there have already been three temples throughout the history of Israel. The first one was Solomon's temple, the second was the Nehemiah and Ezra temple after the return of the captives, and then there was the temple of the Maccabees. What I will do now is walk you through world history from the lens of Daniel chapter 2. Let's take a look at the statue of Nebuchadnezzar's dream so I can show you where these temples all fit into the bigger picture of the empires of the world.

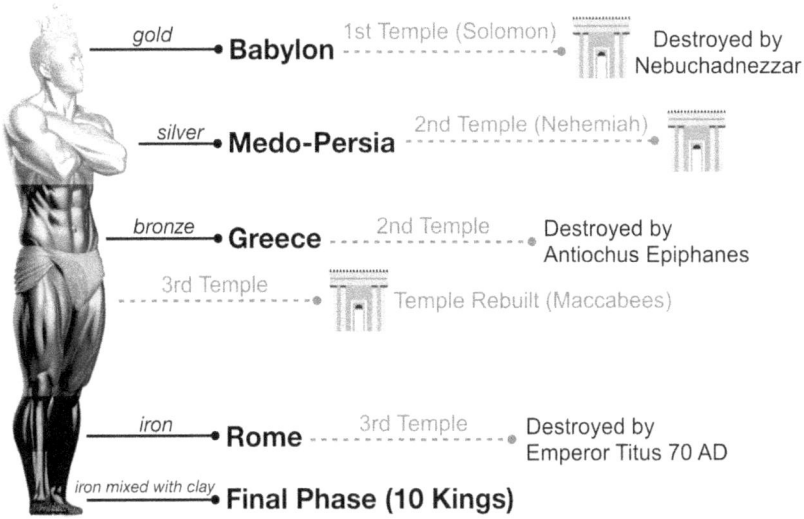

Figure 9.3: The Statue of Daniel Chapter 2

As you can see, Babylon is the golden head; Medo-Persia is the silver arms and chest; Greece is the belly and thighs; Rome is the legs; and finally, there is a final phase of world government in which there are ten kings (toes) that reign and hand over their dominion to the very final beast power of world history. Nebuchadnezzar is the one that destroyed Solomon's temple when Judah was judged for its disobedience to God. After 70 years in captivity, Judah was allowed to return back to their land, and it is during this time period that the second temple was built. However, this temple was not the same temple that Yeshua visited during His time on earth because the second temple was destroyed by Antiochus Epiphanes as recorded in the book of 1Maccabees. Here is what 1Macc. 1:37-39 tells us:

37 "Thus they shed innocent blood on every side of the sanctuary, and defiled it:
38 "Insomuch that the inhabitants of Jerusalem fled because of them: whereupon the city was made an habitation of strangers, and became strange to those that were born in her; and her own children left her.
39 "Her sanctuary was laid waste like a wilderness, her feasts were turned into mourning, her sabbaths into reproach her honour into contempt."[15]

The language here is very exact, and the sanctuary was turned into an ash heap of a wilderness. It doesn't look like the temple of Nehemiah was still standing to me. It was Judas Maccabeus, after whom the book was named, who then stood up and made this declaration to rebuild the temple (1Macc. 4:37):

"Then said Judas and his brethren, Behold, our enemies are discomfited: let us go up to cleanse and dedicate the sanctuary."[16]

They then proceeded to rebuild the temple. The stones of the altar were torn down. There was a massive undertaking to reconstruct the entire temple. This is what 1Macc. 5:1 then tells us:

"Now when the nations round about heard that the altar was built and the sanctuary renewed as before, it displeased them very much."[17]

They made the temple new, and this was the same temple structure that was standing during Yeshua's earthly ministry (Mat. 24:1,2). In other words, it is actually now the fourth temple that the Rabbinic Jews and Christians are so eager to see built during these last days and not the third.

THE SPIRITUAL IDENTITY OF MODERN ISRAEL

Now that the history of this topic has been established, it is easier to see how prophecy might unfold. Let's first take a good, hard look at the role that the physical land of Israel will play during the last days. If you have not already, go back to the "Introduction" of this book to understand the truth of Revelation 11:7-8 and the fact that the Bible tells us that the modern day city of Jerusalem is the "Mystery Babylon" responsible for all the abominations of the earth. But, how did Jerusalem end up becoming the spiritual whore of the world? What went wrong? Let's take a look at a timeline of events to understand the bigger picture.

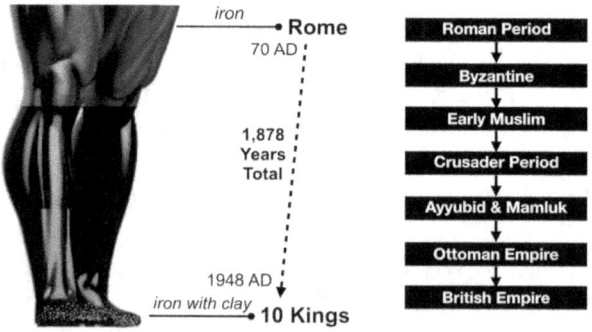

Figure 9.4: The Historical Occupation of Palestine

As you can see, the holy land of Israel has always been under occupation by various governments, from the Romans to the British Empire. Take a look at this verse from Eze. 36:1,2, and this picture will become even more clear:

1 And you, son of man, prophesy to the mountains of Israel, and say, "O mountains of Israel, hear the word of the LORD!"
2 Thus says the Lord GOD: "Because the enemy has said of you, 'Aha! The ancient heights have become our possession'"

Even now, the prophet Ezekiel gives us a timely warning about the fact that the modern Israeli government is considered the "enemy" that has occupied the land. The creation of Israel took place from 1947 to 1948 and was driven by the UN General Assembly Resolution 181 (II) on November 29, 1947, which divided the land into both Jewish and Arab states.[18] The British Empire was the final power to have control of Israel before they negotiated a deal and handed over the land to the United Nations on May 15, 1948 once the British Mandate had ended.[19] The vast majority of people fail to realize that the key events leading up to the creation of Israel involved the organized criminal underworld, billion-dollar backdoor deals, and the illegal smuggling of arms and military equipment that enabled a centuries-long Zionist plan of a Jewish world order to come to pass. Before the Israeli Defense Force (IDF) of today, the formation of the Haganah (literally, "Defense") in 1920 marked a major milestone in the creation of the 1948 state. Zionist groups and figureheads from both Britain and America were directly involved with funding and arming the Haganah. It has been reported that under the leadership of American Zionist activist Rudolf Sonnneborn, "eighteen or so Jewish millionaires and billionaires were recruited into bankrolling the supply effort" of the Haganah well in advance of the 1948 Arab-Israeli War.[20] Surrounding the successful creation of the Israeli state, the financial infrastructure of Swiss Jewish rabbi and businessman Pinchas Tibor Rosenbaum directed the complex flow of dark assets to directly benefit the Zionist cause. Investigative journalist and author Whitney Webb details this intricate movement of illicit money flows out of the criminal underworld and into Israel, stating:

> "With high-level connections secured through his position as a delegate for the World Zionist Congress, Rosenbaum set up his Geneva bank, International Credit Bank (ICB). ICB regularly moved money for Mossad and for Israel's Ministry of Defense. The British *Sunday Times* later reported in 1975 that 'as much as [90%] of the Israeli Defense Ministry's external budget flowed … through Rosenbaum's bank.' It also moved money for organized crime. In

1967, an expose in LIFE magazine fingered ICB as the recipient of large sums of money skimmed off by the mob from the casinos they owned in Las Vegas, the Caribbean, and elsewhere. Overseeing the complex chains of inter-bank relations and transfer chains that enabled this "hot money" to flow around the globe was a series of banking institutions controlled by Meyer Lansky front-men. The set-up was essentially as follows: casino skim (as well as profits generated by the drug trade and other organized crime rackets) was moved into two key offshore banks, the Bank of World Commerce (BWC) and Atlas Bank, the latter of which was a subsidiary of Rosenbaum's ICB. The funds would then be moved to accounts held by ICB in Geneva, where they would be converted into loans and investments to complete the money laundering loop. ... [Some] of these funds may have been used to finance real estate investments that were made by people connected to American and Israeli intel-ligence."[21]

As Webb briefly defined, *hot money* is a term used to describe the esti-mated trillions of dollars worldwide that are directly connected to the illegal activities of prostitution; human and drug trafficking; gambling; and other illicit acts like arms dealings. In order to remain under the radar and away from detection of governments and intelligence agencies, this money tends to flow into places like offshore banks with legal loopholes whereby this dirty capital can be mixed with legitimate capital and then funneled into other banking institutions, real estate investments, the stock market, cryptocurren-cies, and non-profit organizations owned by the same organized crime syndi-cates, to name a few of the many final destinations. The complex series of capital flows that directly benefited Israel in its early days was made possible in part by the aforementioned Meyer Lansky (1902–1983), a prominent figure of the American Jewish mob who was instrumental in the development of the National Crime Syndicate in the United States.

The list of organized crime leaders in connection to the creation of Israel is quite vast, and there is no escaping the reality that the foundation of this 1948 nation state was a direct result of the vast webs of blackmail rings and illegal activities that financed it. This wealth extraction scheme once again cements Jerusalem's identity as the "Mystery Babylon the Great" of Revelation. Consider these words of the ancient prophecy:

9 The kings of the earth who committed fornication and lived luxuriously with her will weep and lament for her, when they see the smoke of her burning,
10 standing at a distance for fear of her torment, saying, 'Alas, alas, that great city Babylon, that mighty city! For in one hour your judgment has come.'

11 And the merchants of the earth will weep and mourn over her, for no one buys their merchandise anymore:

12 merchandise of gold and silver, precious stones and pearls, fine linen and purple, silk and scarlet, every kind of citron wood, every kind of object of ivory, every kind of object of most precious wood, bronze, iron, and marble;

13 and cinnamon and incense, fragrant oil and frankincense, wine and oil, fine flour and wheat, cattle and sheep, horses and chariots, and bodies and souls of men.

(Rev. 18:9-13 NKJV)

The last verse and the "souls of men" is a direct reference to the aforementioned human trafficking of the criminal underworld's initial financing of Israel; but fast forward to today, and Israel's GDP is listed as the 27th greatest economy in the world.[22,23] Despite its geographical size being no larger than the fourth smallest US state of New Jersey, Israel has somehow managed to outpace the vast majority of countries in the world. The uninformed have been deceived into thinking this phenomenon to be "God's blessing" described in the book of Genesis, but the objective truth is far different. As a rite of passage under the watchful eye of Freemasonry, tech companies like Intel, Microsoft, and Apple all built their first overseas research and development facilities in Israel. Of course, "silver" and also "gold" are both integral to the components of technological devices like smartphones and computers. Other mega corporations such as IBM, Google, Motorola, and Facebook all have similar such facilities in the country, further providing an artificial boost to Israel's economy. The Zionist state is also one of the world's top exporters of military arms and weapons, further satisfying the description of "iron" mentioned in Revelation. Because of the current Jewish world order's control over powerful politicians such as Jewish President Claudia Scheinbaum of Mexico, Jewish-converted President Javier Millei of Argentina, Jewish President Volodymyr Zelenskyy of Ukraine, and countless Jewish-born or Jewish-converted leaders in the US and other Western countries, Israel's grip over the world's trade of merchandise is far greater than most people realize. Since Israel's founding in 1948 until 2023, it has "officially" received roughly $318 billion in aid from the US alone, making it the single greatest recipient in history.[24] Considering its illicit origins and the United States' ongoing foreign aid to the tune of billions of dollars annually,[25] there has been much speculation that Israel is in practice a nation whose wealth is in no small way built upon a worldwide money laundering scheme through which the kings of the earth were enabled to live luxuriously at the expense of their citizens.

Interestingly, if you take a look at the charts in Appendix A, Abib 1947-

1948 was the 50th year of Jubilee after the 49th Sabbatical Year from Abib 1946-1947. In the Torah, the 50th year of Jubilee is a time for the return of the captives, the forgiveness of debts, and the return of land ownership back into the hands of the original families and tribes to which the land belonged as a perpetual inheritance. After the events of WWII and the holocaust narrative, this creation of modern day Israel made a lot of sense in the minds of most people. Those claiming Jewish ancestry were allowed to return back to the land on what appears to be God's prophetic time clock. However, we are still not to be deceived as to the true identity of Israel in end-times prophecy. Mainstream Christian thinking has always hailed the 1948 creation of Israel as the fulfillment of all Bible prophecies concerning the return of God's people back to the land of Israel. I have sat in many church services where the pastor taught that the two sticks being joined together as described in Ezekiel 37:21 was already fulfilled in 1948. I have also heard Bible teachers connect prophecies like Jeremiah 16:15 to this event. The list of false teachings goes on and on. The problem is that people are eager to follow what their denominations and organized religions teach about this subject because they care more about the esteem of men than the truth of God's Word. When investigating this future regathering of God's people from all over the world back to the holy land, you will find the Bible to be extremely crystal clear—all Israel will be completely at rest with no one making him afraid (Zep. 3:13, Jer. 30:10, Eze. 34:28, Jer. 46:27, etc.).

Within a few days of Israel's declaration of independence on May 14, 1948, there was an immediate invasion of five Arab countries in what later became known as the War of 1948.[26] We know how the story ended. Israel emerged victorious against these powers, but don't be deceived. This 1948 nation of Israel still does not pass the test of the Scriptures. It was not the true prophetic regathering of all 12 tribes of Israel from the four corners of the earth. Rather than a nation created by God Himself, this modern nation was created by billionaire Zionist oligarchs who ultimately made expedient use of the UN, the latter of which I have repeatedly proven is responsible for many evils of the last days including the covenant made with many.

EZEKIEL 22: THE MYSTERIOUS DOOMSDAY PROPHECY

You understand that Jerusalem is the great city, Mystery Babylon, where our Lord was crucified and where the bodies of the two witnesses will lie on the streets in the future. I revealed to you how Ezekiel further described modern-day Israel as being occupied and controlled by an enemy. This modern nation's origins and financiers have been very briefly discussed. Now we can look at and understand a few key words that Ezekiel the prophet wrote about regarding the coming judgment of end-times Israel in chapter 22. The subject matter of this specific chapter is given to us in the first verse speaking of Jerusalem, the "bloody city." Among God's various accusations against this city, the following should be self-evident by now:

"In you they take bribes to shed blood; you take usury and increase; you have made profit from your neighbors by extortion, and have forgotten Me," says the Lord GOD.
"Behold, therefore, I beat My fists at the dishonest profit which you have made, and at the bloodshed which has been in your midst.
"Can your heart endure, or can your hands remain strong, in the days when I shall deal with you? I, the LORD, have spoken, and will do it."
(Eze. 22:12-14)

We are being clearly shown here that Israel's wealth, its inflated GDP numbers, and its dishonest profits are the direct result of the "extortion" of its neighbors, as described previously. The pronouncement of judgment is rather severe, and we know that this is truly speaking of an end times event because of the language used in the following verses:

17 The word of the LORD came to me, saying,
18 "Son of man, the house of Israel has become dross to Me; they *are* all bronze, tin, iron, and lead, in the midst of a furnace; they have become dross from silver."
19 Therefore thus says the Lord GOD: "Because you have all become dross, therefore behold, I will gather you into the midst of Jerusalem.
20 "*As men* gather silver, bronze, iron, lead, and tin into the midst of a furnace, to blow fire on it, to melt *it;* so I will gather *you* in My anger and in My fury, and I will leave *you there* and melt you.
21 "Yes, I will gather you and blow on you with the fire of My wrath, and you shall be melted in its midst.
22 "As silver is melted in the midst of a furnace, so shall you be melted in its midst; then you shall know that I, the LORD, have poured out My fury on you."
(Eze. 22:17-22)

We must pay close attention to the subject—the House of Israel. As you know, this is very specific wording. Recall that Ezekiel himself was a man from the Southern Kingdom of Judah that was taken captive to Babylon during the destruction of Jerusalem under the second siege of Nebuchadnezzar. Also recall that the House of Israel (Northern Kingdom) had already been conquered by Assyria approximately 150 years beforehand. So, why was Ezekiel speaking of the House of Israel being gathered into Jerusalem to be judged by fire if they had already been conquered 150 years ago? Well, it's because he was prophesying about a future event. In the original edition of this book, I proposed that Ezekiel was prophesying about the abomination of desolation (a nuclear weapon) that would be deployed exactly on Sept. 22, 2023. With this initial interpretation proven to be faulty, let's consider the different possibilities now present.

What we do know is that the House of Israel will be gathered together with the Jews (Judah) in Jerusalem to be judged. I have already explained that modern day Christians are in fact the House of Israel. Christians have that internal desire to worship the Most High God, but they seek to do things according to a broken understanding of God's instructions just as foretold by the prophet Hosea (Hos. 8:12). Even though the House of Israel has lost their identity and has become mixed among all the nations of the earth, they have still retained their desire to worship Jesus and the God of the Bible. However, the House of Israel also generally refers to those nations in which many descendants of Israel have been mixed whether they are practicing Christians or not. One possibility is that so-called "third temple" excitement, festivities, and fanfare could attract Christians, Jews, and religious people from all over the world to visit Jerusalem just in time for the coming abomination of desolation event. Under such circumstances, this verse would then be fulfilled because of the unmistakable and undeniable descriptions of missiles, military technology, and nuclear abominations that will be unleashed upon the land as previously described. In other words, it is possible that universalist temple goers could become melted like silver in a furnace, just like Ezekiel describes, once the bombs start going off. In fact, just look at what happened in Israel in 2022 when all of the pandemic restrictions were finally loosened enough to allow tourism once again. The International Christian Embassy Jerusalem was able to host its annual Feast of Tabernacles from Oct. 9-16, 2022 after two years of being shut down.[27] Many thousands of Christians gathered from every part of the world to listen to live musical performances, worship events, and ceremonies. If for some reason the current tensions between Israel and the Axis of Resistance are miraculously quelled long enough to allow a Jewish temple to be rebuilt, this event could similarly attract thousands of tourists in fulfillment of the "gathering" prophecy of Ezekiel 22. In such a scenario, some sort of grand opening ceremony or "third temple" ritual could rush all of these people to Jerusalem from both houses of Israel so that Ezekiel's prophecy can be accomplished and God's fury spent on the rebels.

With time running out in this final shabua of mankind and regional tensions currently at an all-time high, there is another more likely scenario that is already playing out on the world stage. Ever since October 7, 2023, Israel's tourism industry has been suffering tremendously under the constant threats of missiles and drones from Hamas, Hezbollah, and Iran. Airlines have regularly discontinued flights in and around Israel, various embassies have urged their citizens to evacuate the region, and prominent figures of Israel have been forced into underground bunkers in broad daylight because of the dire situation. Rather than civilians being gathered in Jerusalem, it therefore appears that the Ezekiel 22 prophecy might be referring to the military personnel of Lost Tribes countries being gathered both within and around Jerusalem in an effort to provide protection and assistance. Since the events of Oct. 7th, the US Navy has been deploying multiple carrier strike groups to the Eastern Mediterranean each containing about 7,500 military personnel that are on standby in the event of regional escalation.[28,29] Even before the Oct. 7 attacks, US special forces had been routinely stationed at the embassy in Jerusalem and for joint training purposes.[30] One possible scenario is that Israel might get overrun in the very near future, with ground forces of the Axis of Resistance annexing the border regions of Israel. This might force the deployment of ground forces of the West in significant numbers, culminating with a formidable joint operation of US-led forces in and around Jerusalem. In such a scenario, Iran would be given the prophetic green light for its deployment of "fire offerings" raining down from the sky, the chief of which will be the abomination of desolation. Due to the decently high likelihood of this outcome, the buildup of Western ground forces in Jerusalem could perhaps be the final sign that the desolation of the city is only moments away from taking place.

JEREMIAH 5 AND REVELATION 18

If you are still in need of more proof that 1948 Israel is in fact a deception and a trap, a few key words from Jeremiah should seal the deal. In the final words of Jeremiah 5, there are some parallel verses that shed needed light on the nature of the abomination of desolation prophecy together with the biblical identity of the UN-created state. When you compare these words alongside Revelation 18:1-11, everything becomes clear.

26 For among My people are found wicked men; They lie in wait as one who sets snares; They set a trap; They catch men.

27 As a cage is full of birds, So their houses are full of deceit. Therefore they have become great and grown rich.

28 They have grown fat, they are sleek; Yes, they surpass the deeds of the wicked; They do not plead the cause, The cause of the fatherless; Yet they prosper, And the right of the needy they do not defend.

29 "Shall I not punish them for these things?" says the LORD. "Shall I not avenge Myself on such a nation as this?"

30 "An astonishing and horrible thing Has been committed in the land:

31 The prophets prophesy falsely, And the priests rule by their own power; And My people love to have it so. But what will you do in the end?

(Jer. 5:26-31)

Jeremiah begins by stating that wicked men have mixed themselves with God's people and have been trapping them (Jer. 5:26). These are the exact same words of Rev. 18:9,11 where we receive clarity that the wicked men Jeremiah spoke of are the "kings" and "merchants" of the earth that have gotten rich from immoral relations with Israel. The parallel gets even more striking as Jeremiah talks about the rulers of Israel being like a cage full of birds (Jer. 5:27), which is exactly what Rev. 18:2 says about Babylon (Israel), except John tells us that it is "every unclean and hated bird" that is in the cage. The cage itself most likely represents the land itself being like a trap or a snare of deceitful things. Again, this is just more proof of Israel's true role in these last days.

The next contention Jeremiah makes to Israel is the acquisition of unjust gain and false riches (Jer. 5:28). This same idea is confirmed in Rev. 18:3, as mentioned earlier. Though Jeremiah doesn't explicitly mention the abomination of desolation, he does speak the direct words of Yehovah in stating rhetorically that He will severely "punish" Israel for all of its wickedness (Jer. 5:29). To make matters worse, we are told that this end-times Israel indeed has priests, but they rule according to their own man-made traditions (Jer. 5:31). It's with this understanding that we can then glance back over to Rev. 18:8,10 where we see this profound idea of judgment coming upon Israel in "one day" and then "one hour." Make no mistake about it. This is speaking of the abomination of desolation. Though the rebuilding of a Jewish temple seems unlikely at this point, the "priests" of Judaism have done all of these temple ceremonies, preparations, and various works by the imaginations of their own hearts. They have utterly rejected Yeshua the Messiah as their salvation. Their universal religion has been completely absent of the will of God and of the truth; and they are about to pay the penalty for their transgression.

The Jews are attempting to serve the living God with the deadness of their flesh. They are trying to serve God with the godless traditions of Judaism rather than the newness of the Spirit and instructions of the Torah. Spiritually, they are dead. They are in desperate need of being born again. Meanwhile, most Christians, who claim to be alive and born of the Spirit, are falling into the same snare of religious perversion and universalism due to a twisted desire to see a temple rebuilt so that the second coming of Jesus might be ushered in. They, too, will suffer the consequences because you cannot serve God in Spirit alone. You also cannot serve God by Truth alone. Yehovah is seeking worshippers to worship Him in *both* Spirit and Truth, just like Yeshua told the woman at the well (Jhn. 4:23). In conclusion of all these various end-times deceptions, you must be brutally honest with yourself as time is truly of the essence.

Are *you* worshiping God in Spirit and Truth?

Secret IV:

Using the 70 Shabua Timeline to Understand All Prophecy

"No longer do I call you servants, for a servant does not know what his master is doing; but I have called you friends, for all things that I heard from My Father I have made known to you."

- John 15:15

Chapter 10
The 1,000 Year Reign of Christ

Once this mystery of the 1,000-year reign of Christ is fully unpacked, we will be able to connect even more dots concerning the abomination of desolation, satan being loosed from the bottomless pit, the locusts of Revelation 9, and numerous other prophecies.

Before getting too involved in this topic, be aware that we will be visiting various Scriptures from the book of Revelation where the "thousand year reign" is directly mentioned. This was the final book of the Bible to be written, and it is therefore critically important that we remain faithful to our three laws of biblical interpretation, especially the law of first mention. Many people create all kinds of strange doctrines from Revelation because they are lazy students of the Bible that do not faithfully seek the true meaning of this book from the other writings that came before it. Because we are explicitly told that it was Yeshua Himself that gave John the exact words of Revelation (Rev. 1:1), we will be doing what many people utterly fail to do. We will rely heavily on the words of Yeshua as recorded in the Gospels to completely illuminate some of the greatest mysteries of the book of Revelation. Let's begin this discussion by briefly revisiting what most Christians teach about the 70 weeks of Daniel but with needed emphasis on the 1,000-year reign.

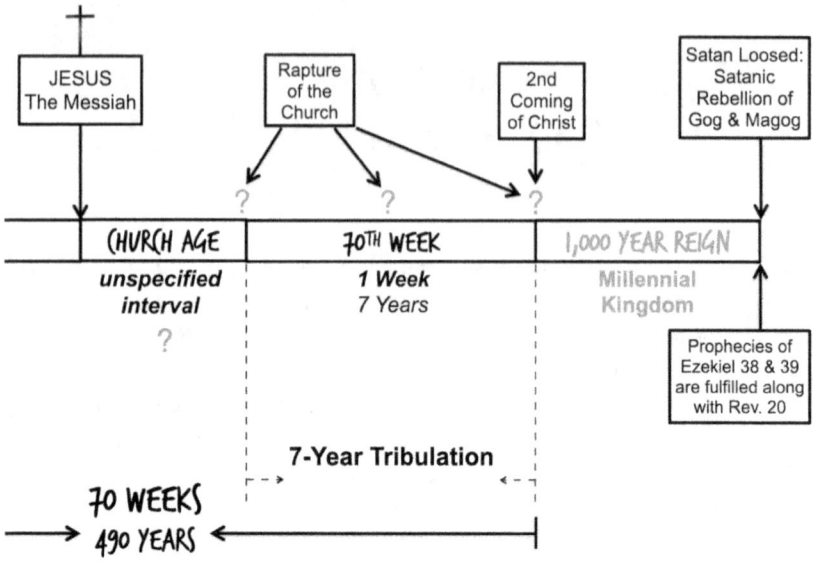

Figure 10.1: How Most Christians View the 1,000-Year Reign

All Mystery Babylon religions without exception interpret the 70 weeks of Daniel in an identical way: 7 x 70 = 490. As already discussed in the first chapter, there are two general disagreements between all religious camps. The apocalyptic cults like SDA and JW believe that all 70 weeks already happened in the past while most Christians and related denominations teach that there is one mysterious week remaining that will unfold at some point in the future but with a rapture taking place before it ever happens. Of course, there is much division concerning the timing of a rapture, but regardless of these disagreements, nearly everyone from all religious circles believes in a millennial reign that will last exactly 1,000 years as soon as the 70th week of Daniel is finished. You are about to find out how man-made and artificial this interpretation of Scripture is because Jesus Himself never taught such a thing. As we uncover this prophecy, it is His words that we will never deviate from neither to the right hand or to the left. His words will keep us on the straight and narrow path and into a place of extreme clarity concerning all secrets of Bible prophecy.

REVELATION 20:1-9 AND THE 1000 YEARS

"And I saw thrones, and they sat on them, and judgment was committed to them. Then I saw the souls of those who had been beheaded for their witness to Jesus and for the word of God, who had not worshiped the beast or his image, and had not received his mark on their foreheads or on their hands. **And they lived and reigned with Christ for a thousand years."** (Rev. 20:4) [emphasis added]

This is the portion of Scripture that serves as the foundation for the vast majority of all end times understanding of the 1,000-year reign. Just like the word "rapture," the words "Millennial" reign, "Millennial" kingdom, or "millennium" are *never* found anywhere in the Bible, neither in the Old or New Testaments. These words are inventions of the imaginations of men's hearts and have suffocated this discussion for many centuries now. Only the phrase *thousand years* is ever used in the actual Text itself.

Nearly every religion teaches that there is a future Kingdom of God on earth that will take place after the 70th week of Daniel is completed. There will then be an unparalleled period of peace on earth and prosperity. The mainstream interpretation then goes on to say that after this so-called millennial reign is finished, satan is to be loosed from the bottomless pit in order to gather up Gog and Magog (Eze. 38; 39) for one last showdown against Israel and God's people who are dwelling in Jerusalem. Satan will be easily defeated by Jesus Himself once and for all, and only then does eternity begin without any more sin, death, or war to exist ever again in the New Jerusalem.

DOCTRINAL ERROR, CONTRADICTIONS, AND INCONSISTENCIES

Daniel 9:24 tells us that 70 weeks are "determined." Like we already discussed, this word in Hebrew is Strong's 2852 and literally means decreed, settled, or to be marked out. It has been settled in Heaven that there will be 70 shabua for Daniel's people (the 12 Tribes of Israel scattered throughout the whole world) and the set apart city of Jerusalem. No more; no less. There will only be 70 shabua. Not only that, but Moses also prophesies to us in Genesis 6:3 that Yehovah will *not* strive with rebellious, sinful, and depraved mankind forever; but man's days are *only* going to be 120 shanah cycles of 49-years each.

It is therefore impossible—utterly and absolutely impossible—for sin, transgression, and depravity of mankind to be present 1,000 years after the 70th week. Nearly every Bible teacher and every pulpit out there is completely ignoring Dan. 9:24 and the end of sins that is going to take place when the 70th shabua is finished. They are teaching that the final satanic rebellion of Gog and Magog is supposed to take place a very long time from now, but a satanic deception and rebellion of many armies from the far north is simply not possible after Abib 2045.

To settle the matter in our minds once and for all, even Yeshua Himself testifies against the teachings and doctrines of men by telling us that during and shortly after the days of the abomination of desolation, "...all things which are written may be fulfilled" (Luk. 21:22). He tells us that all prophecy ever written down within the pages of our Bibles absolutely will be fulfilled shortly after the days of the abomination of desolation. He says this authoritatively because He was quoting Daniel 9:24.

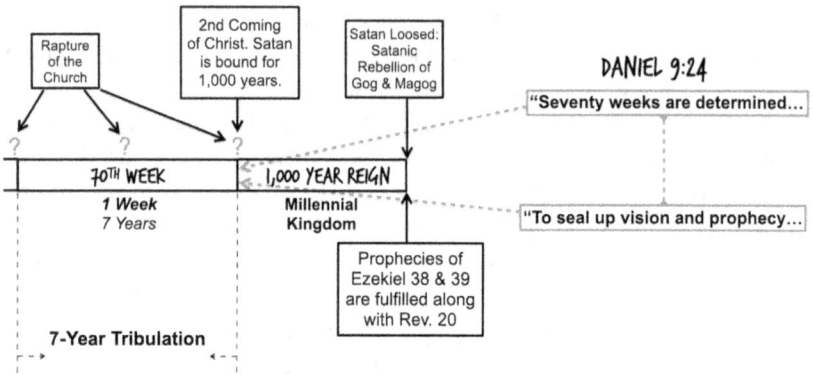

Figure 10.2: Prophecy Will Finish at the End of the 70th Week.

So, there you have it. I have already given you three witnesses—Moses, Daniel, and Yeshua—telling us that a satanic rebellion is *not* possible 1,000 years after the 70th week of Daniel is completed. The Scriptures proclaim that the 70 weeks are a cut-off date for all prophecy and vision because it will be stopped ("ha-tam"; the NKJV translates this word as "to seal up"; Strong's H2856) according to Daniel 9:24.[1] Therefore, Ezekiel 38 and 39 along with the parallel passages of Revelation 19 and 20 that describe the final satanic rebellion and prophecy of Gog and Magog *must* be fulfilled before the 70th week of Daniel is finished.

THE THREE BIG QUESTIONS

In order to understand this mysterious 1,000-year reign, these three questions must be answered:

1. When was satan bound?
...Or is he going to be bound in the future?
2. What is the 1,000-Year Reign?

...Is this a literal or figurative number?
3. When is satan going to be loosed?
...Has he been loosed already?

These questions are what any open-minded scholar and disciple of Yeshua should be asking to properly understand this topic. There should be no reservation, bias, or hanging on for dear life to the words of men that have been taught repeatedly for hundreds of years now. Rather, we should strive to let the Text speak for itself. I will be the first one to admit that it was very difficult to *not* hear the voices of men whispering their interpretations in my head when I seriously studied this material for the very first time. But I urge you to let the Text speak for itself. Let the Holy Spirit show you what is actually being spoken of in the Text.

QUESTION 1: WHEN WAS SATAN BOUND?

The answer to this question is so simple yet absolutely vital for understanding the 1,000-year reign. John 12 tells us that satan was already bound in the 1st century AD. Jesus states this:

"Now is the judgment of this world; now the ruler of this world will be cast out."
(John 12:31)

He specifically said that "now" the ruler of this world would be cast out as He was making His way into Jerusalem in what is commonly referred to as the *Triumphal Entry.* This was the same scene where He was riding a young donkey and people were laying down palm branches before Him and crying out *Hosanna.* Within the context of this event, Jesus spoke repeatedly of His death and work of redeeming mankind through His suffering. He was making it clear that because of the cross and His victory over the grave, satan would be cast out. You can connect the Greek word used for "cast out" in John 12:31 to the word "cast" in Revelation 20:3 (Strong's G1544 and G906, respectively). It's the same thing. In other words, these verses from Rev. 20:1-3 were actually fulfilled in the first century AD:

1 Then I saw an angel coming down from heaven, having the key to the bottomless pit and a great chain in his hand.
2 He laid hold of the dragon, that serpent of old, who is *the* Devil and Satan, and bound him for a thousand years;

3 and he cast him into the bottomless pit, and shut him up, and set a seal on him, so that he should deceive the nations no more till the thousand years were finished. But after these things he must be released for a little while.

That's right! Satan was bound and cast into what John described as a bottomless pit. Going back to the words of Yeshua, the Triumphal Entry wasn't the first time He spoke of victory over satan. There is an important event in the gospels that is recorded three complete times—the unforgivable sin (Mat. 12, Mar. 3, and Luk. 11). The Pharisees had accused Yeshua of casting out demons because of some sort of perverted relationship with Beelzebub, the ruler of demons. Yeshua rebuked them, and warned them that all sins would be forgiven men except blasphemy of the Holy Spirit. I have mentioned this before, but the Holy Spirit's job is to teach you and I all of the words that Yeshua commanded us (Jhn. 14:26). The Holy Spirit's job is to write Moses (the Torah), the prophets, and the Gospels in our hearts in order to observe all the things that the Word Made Flesh commanded us as part of the new covenant in His blood. In other words, Yeshua was telling the Pharisees that because they were unwilling to learn about Him and accept His instruction, they were guilty of committing the unforgivable sin. It is within this context that Yeshua tells us that the strong man (satan) was bound, stating:

"If Satan casts out Satan, he is divided against himself. How then will his kingdom stand?
"Or how can one enter a strong man's house and plunder his goods, unless he first binds the strong man? And then he will plunder his house."
(Mat. 12:26,29)

These words provide the clear reason why Yeshua was able to spoil his (satan's) house, or kingdom. Because the Kingdom of God had arrived, He was able to plunder all demons and evil spirits with great power and authority. Satan had been defeated by someone infinitely stronger, as Luke explains:

"But when a stronger than he comes upon him and overcomes him, he takes from him all his armor in which he trusted, and divides his spoils."
(Luke 11:22)

These clear explanations of satan being bound, overthrown, and cast out are confirmed in other scriptures besides Revelation itself. The entire New Testament offers an abundance of witnesses to what Yeshua said. For example, Col. 2:15 says this:

"Having disarmed principalities and powers, He made a public spectacle of them, triumphing over them in it."

Now do you see why it was called the Triumphal Entry? The ruler of this world was judged because of the cross in the first century, and even now Yeshua has also given us the authority to exercise power and command unclean spirits out of ourselves, our homes, and those around us who are submitting themselves to Jesus. The miracles of the book of Acts weren't just for the first century believers. They are for you and I today. Jesus broke the curse of the Law, and therefore the unclean spirits attached to these various curses can and should be cast out in Jesus' name (Gal. 3:13). John goes on to tell us that Jesus was manifested to expressly destroy the works of the devil (1Jhn. 3:8). Hebrews 2:14 tells us that the devil and the power of death were destroyed by the power of the cross. But I know what you might be thinking at this point:

"Why is the world so full of evil if satan has been bound and cast out?"

Satan was bound not in the way you would think. He is bound not necessarily to a physical, geographical location, though he could be. He is not bound in the sense that he is tied up in a straight jacket like someone in an insane asylum. We are explicitly told that he is bound to the law of Revelation 20:3 in which he can no longer deceive the nations. This connection is easy to make once you understand the word *bound* and how it is used here in Romans 7:2:

"For the woman who has a husband is bound by the law to *her* husband as long as he lives. But if the husband dies, she is released from the law of *her* husband."

Just like the law of marriage is binding, the law of Rev. 20:3 is binding upon satan because he absolutely cannot exercise power and authority to deceive the nations. His power is limited. He has been weakened, and his whole kingdom of darkness is able to be plundered by God's people. Like I mentioned, we are able to cast out demons and give liberty in Jesus' name to people who are hooked on drugs, have porn addictions, think suicidal thoughts, hear voices in their heads, and feel spiritually deadened in their walk with God because of some deceitfulness of sin. We have the authority to destroy demonic strongholds and works of darkness.

If you look at Job chapter one, then everything makes even more sense. Satan's power is on full display in this chapter after Elohim gives him authority over Job, and one of Job's servants speaks to Job, claiming that "fire of God" came down from heaven that caused both people and sheep to be burned alive (Job 1:16). However, this servant was 100% deceived! It was *not* the fire of God! It was fire that came from satan, and it is these kinds of signs and wonders that he simply cannot perform right now. His power is limited!

It is also important to understand that there is much evil present in the world for two major reasons. First, mankind is intrinsically wicked because we inherited our sinful nature from the fall of Adam (Rom. 5:12); and secondly, there is more than one *satan*. This word "satan" in Hebrew (Strong's H7854) simply means *supernatural adversary,* and the law of first mention verse is quite fascinating because it is used to describe the Angel of Yehovah as an "adversary" in Numbers 22:22:

"Then God's anger was aroused because he went, and the Angel of the LORD took His stand in the way as an adversary against him. And he was riding on his donkey, and his two servants *were* with him."

This holy messenger of Almighty God was a *satan* to Balaam, a man who had disobeyed the spoken command to only go with the men of Balak under the condition that they behaved in a hostile or contrary manner towards Balaam. This was the conditional statement that was given by God in Num. 22:20, but you have to look at the Hebrew words carefully in this verse because most translations erroneously use the word "call" or "summon" (Strong's H7121) and do not properly convey the idea of accosting, double-crossing, or hostility. This is why the anger of God was kindled. Balaam was never threatened by Balak's men, and that's why God became his *satan* (adversary). That being the case, here is the short list of supernatural adversaries throughout the Scriptures, but please know that this is *not* an all-inclusive list:

1. The serpent of old, great dragon, devil and satan; this is also Apollyon / Abbadon of the bottomless pit - *Gen. 3:1, Rev. 20:1, Rev. 12:9, Rev. 9:11*
2. Azazel - *Lev. 16:7-10*
3. The demonic princes of nations - *Dan. 10:13,20; Eze. 28:12,14,15; Eze. 38:2; Rev. 16:13,14*
4. Lucifer - the spiritual entity of Babylon - *Isa. 14:4,12*
5. Beelzebub - *Mat. 10:25; 12:24*

Paul made it clear to us in his letter to the church of Ephesus that there are many hosts of wickedness (Eph. 6:11,12), and when you put all these pieces of the puzzle together along with the fact that the heart of man is desperately wicked (Jer. 17:9), then it all starts to make sense. The world is full of wickedness because of fallen angels, demonic spirits, and also because of the fallen nature of mankind.

QUESTION 2: WHAT IS THE 1,000-YEAR REIGN?

Now that we understand that satan has been bound by the law of Revelation 20:3 in that he is unable to deceive the nations, let's consider the true meaning of the 1,000-year reign by starting with the words of Rev. 20:4:

"And I saw thrones, and they sat on them, and judgment was committed to them. Then *I saw* the souls of those who had been beheaded for their witness to Jesus and for the word of God, who had not worshiped the beast or his image, and had not received *his* mark on their foreheads or on their hands. And they lived and reigned with Christ for a thousand years."

When you look at this verse, you should immediately start dissecting the Greek word used for "thousand" years (Strong's G5507). When you do that, the concordance plainly reveals to us that this word can be used figuratively. In fact, this same concept is not only used figuratively in the Greek but also in the Hebrew language as well, which makes perfect sense because the Holy Spirit is the bilingual author of the entire Book. I remember sitting in Bible classes in college where I would regularly hear my professors say something like, "The Koine Greek language of the Bible is much more figurative, descriptive, and many times more eloquent than the Hebrew language of the Old Testament." This is yet another false, totally fake teaching. The Hebrew language has so much figurative, symbolic and poetic usages of words throughout. I guess they forgot about the book of Psalms when they were parroting this nonsense. For figurative usages of *thousand,* please see 2Peter 3:8, Psalm 50:10; 105:8.

Lets now turn our attention to these words of Rev. 20:6 for more clarity on what this reign is all about:

"Blessed and holy *is* he who has part in the first resurrection. Over such the second death has no power, but they shall be priests of God and of Christ, and shall reign with Him a thousand years."

When looking at Rev. 20:6 and the thousand years, it is important to understand that there are two reigns of Yeshua. I will explain these both as they are necessary in properly understanding this topic:

1. The 1000-Year Reign
This reign began with Yeshua's ministry on Earth and this reign ends in Revelation 14:14.

2. The Forever and Ever Reign
This reign begins when He leaves Heaven and returns to Earth to destroy His enemies once and for all at the battle of Gog and Magog in Rev. 20:9.

Let's start by looking at the 1,000-year reign. Both John the Baptist and Yeshua proclaimed the same message (Matt. 3:2; 4:17), and this message is that the Kingdom of Heaven had arrived right then and there in the 1st century AD. Pay attention to this key verse of Luke 16:16:

"The law and the prophets *were* until John. Since that time the kingdom of God has been preached, and everyone is pressing into it."

This verse clearly explains to us that the Kingdom had arrived with John, and this is the reason why he was considered so great by Yeshua in Matt. 11:11. John had the unique opportunity to announce the arrival of Yeshua's 1,000-year reign. Nobody else experienced this distinct honor and ministry. After the resurrection, it is recorded for us many times throughout the New Testament that Yeshua was received into Heaven and seated at the right hand of the Father (Mar. 16:19, Mat. 26:64, Heb. 1:3). This wording is not by mistake but in fact gives us extreme clarity as to the current reign of Jesus. We must make the connection back to Psalm 110:1,2 and what it *really* means that He is at the right hand of the Father; so let's take a careful look at it:

1 A Psalm of David.
The LORD said to my Lord,
"Sit at My right hand,
Till I make Your enemies Your footstool.
2 "The LORD shall send the rod of Your strength out of Zion.
Rule in the midst of Your enemies!"

What this means is that Yeshua is going to reign at the right hand *until* all enemies are completely and utterly subdued under His feet. What nearly everyone teaches about this subject is that Yeshua reigns for 1,000 years in the absence of any and all enemies, that is, until satan is released at the very end of the 1,000 years, or "millennial" reign. This false teaching completely ignores what Psalm 110 so plainly tells us! Yeshua reigns "in the midst" of His enemies. But, why does this reign only last for a figurative 1,000 years?

338

Why did John use figurative language? In John 15:15, Yeshua considers us friends (and no longer simply servants) because He revealed to us all things that the Father wants us to know, except for one specific thing. Ah yes, this is the famous "no man knows the day or the hour" prophecy. So many people use these words of Yeshua as an excuse to be lazy and to completely ignore multitudes of scriptures while living in utter complacency. So many people have twisted these words to their own destruction.

However, when you look at these words very carefully (Matt. 24:36,42; 25:13, etc.), you will begin to understand *why* John wrote "thousand years" throughout Revelation 20. John saw the whole vision. He saw the whole panorama from start to finish. He knew that Yeshua coming on the clouds back to earth to destroy His enemies at Armageddon once and for all would mean that the 1,000-year reign was going to be completed. He knew what he had witnessed in the vision; but he still did not know the exact day or the hour when Yeshua would return to the earth. No man knows. He therefore did not know when the 1,000-year reign would be completed. So, instead of saying "two thousand eleven years" or some specific number, John used figurative language to describe the very long duration of Yeshua's current reign at the right hand of the Father.

It's really that simple.

The 1000-year reign of Yeshua was first announced by John the Baptist according to Luke 16:16, this reign arguably began when Yeshua was seated at the right hand of the Father after His ascension to Heaven, and it will be completed once Yeshua returns back to Earth at a time when no man knows the day or the hour.

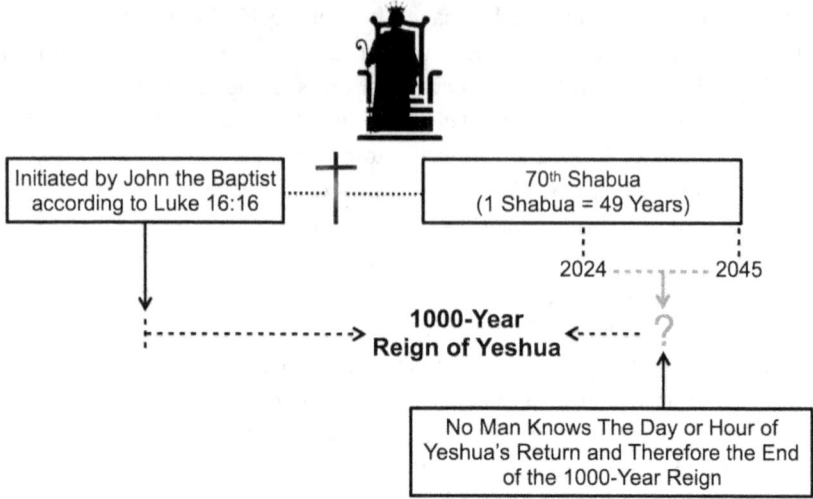

Figure 10.3: An Overview of the 1000-Year Reign

Now that you understand the 1,000-year reign and Psalm 110, I know what you're probably thinking next: *"But wait...Rev. 20:4-6 doesn't really make sense now!"* Let's take a closer look at these verses.

4 And I saw thrones, and they sat on them, and judgment was committed to them. Then I saw the souls of those who had been beheaded for their witness to Jesus and for the word of God, who had not worshiped the beast or his image, and **had not received his mark** on their foreheads or on their hands. And they lived and reigned with Christ for a thousand years.
5 But the rest of the dead did not live again until the thousand years were finished. This is **the first resurrection.**
6 Blessed and holy is he who has part in the first resurrection. Over such **the second death** has no power, but they shall be priests of God and of Christ, and shall reign with Him a thousand years.
(Rev. 20:4-6) [emphasis added]

Because of the complexities of these three verses, we now need to address these three foundational theological concepts:

1. What is the *mark* of Rev. 20:4? Isn't this a future event?
2. What is the first resurrection?
3. What is the second death?

Before we talk more about the *mark* commonly understood as the *mark of the beast,* let's talk about the afterlife.

RESURRECTION AND THE AFTERLIFE - TRUTH VS LIES:

The majority of religions use chapter 20 of Revelation as the foundation for doctrines pertaining to the afterlife. In other words, people have been using this figuratively written, difficult to understand book called *Revelation* that is also written out of order so that they can explain what happens when someone dies. As I have already been showing you repeatedly, the problem that all Mystery Babylon religions have is that they cast aside the words of Yeshua and do not take seriously what He plainly told us in the Gospels.

WHAT 90% OF PEOPLE TEACH:

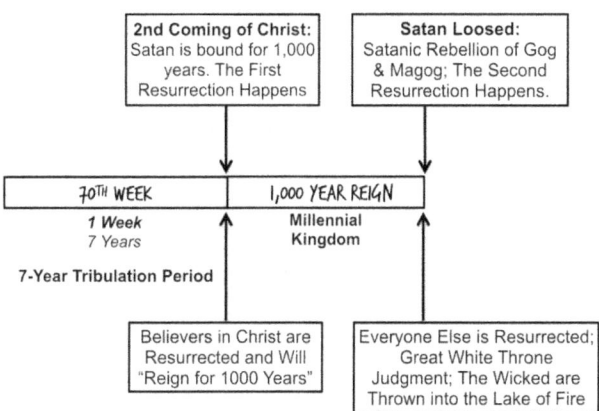

Figure 10.4: The Most Common False Teachings of the Resurrection

What nearly everyone teaches is that at the very end of the 70th week of Daniel, the first resurrection will take place. These resurrected people are the "good Christians" that were somehow righteous enough to be raised up so that they can rule and reign with Christ for 1,000 years. Then, after the 1,000 years are completed, the Gog and Magog prophecy and last satanic rebellion will finally take place. Once this rebellion is crushed, the second resurrection and the Great White Throne judgment of Rev. 20:11 will take place for everyone else who was not raised up during the first resurrection. But remember, I have already shown you that this sequence of events is impossible according to

Moses, Daniel, and Yeshua. All things are to be completed at the end of the 120th shanah, which is the same thing as the end of the 70th week of Daniel.

What John saw is consistent with Yeshua's very own words. In Rev. 20:4, John said that he saw the "souls" of those that were faithful to Yeshua during their time on earth. These souls are given thrones and they execute judgment. They rule and reign with Yeshua during the current 1,000-year reign! Strong's does an excellent job describing this word "psyche" (G5590); it is described as the essence of a person that is different from the physical body and that is *not* dissolved by death.[2]

I will now plainly reveal this mystery of the first resurrection according to Yeshua's own words; *not* the words of men. When we look at the Gospel of John, we get all the clarity we need pertaining to what John saw. John chapter 5:24-29 is so foundational for sound doctrine regarding the afterlife that I will include it right here:

24 "Most assuredly, I say to you, he who hears My word and believes in Him who sent Me has everlasting life, and shall not come into judgment, but has passed from death into life.
25 Most assuredly, I say to you, the hour is coming, and now is, when the dead will hear the voice of the Son of God; and those who hear will live.
26 For as the Father has life in Himself, so He has granted the Son to have life in Himself,
27 and has given Him authority to execute judgment also, because He is the Son of Man.
28 Do not marvel at this; for the hour is coming in which all who are in the graves will hear His voice
29 and come forth—those who have done good, to the resurrection of life, and those who have done evil, to the resurrection of condemnation.
(John 5:24-29)

Pay close attention to John 5:24 and also 25. Those who believe Yeshua's words pass from death to life. They pass from death to life immediately the moment they believe. That's precisely why Yeshua said the hour "now is". He did *not* say "the hour will come at the end of the age when the 1,000-year reign will begin"; but this is precisely what all religions teach. All religions completely cast aside, ignore, and (even worse) misrepresent the words of our Master.

Paul makes it very clear: to be absent from the body is to be present with the Lord (2Cor. 5:6-8). He also says that those who teach against an immediate resurrection as described by Yeshua in John 5:24,25 are considered "false witnesses of God" in 1Cor. 15:15. Make no mistake about it. Paul says that if the dead are not raised immediately after the death of this physical body, then our faith is empty. He makes it clear that such teachings falsely lead someone to believe that those who have fallen asleep in Christ have perished (1Cor. 15:18). The Seventh Day Adventists, Jehovah's Witnesses, and all camps who do not take the words of Yeshua seriously regarding the first resurrection are condemned harshly by Paul, and they should be. Yeshua's words are so clear regarding resurrection. The reason that people do not properly understand these things is because the imaginations of men's hearts have been pushed so systematically upon God's people so as to drown out the simple truth of Yeshua's words.

Now let's investigate the true meaning of the second resurrection. John 5:28 makes it very clear that 100% of the dead are going to hear His voice at the same time in one hour. If you look closely at these words of John 6:39,40 you will then understand this timing to be referred to as the *Last Day* by Yeshua:

39 "This is the will of the Father who sent Me, that of all He has given Me I should lose nothing, but should raise it up at the last day.
40 "And this is the will of Him who sent Me, that everyone who sees the Son and believes in Him may have everlasting life; and I will raise him up at the last day."

This is going to take place near the end of the 70th shabua sometime after Gog and Magog (the BRICS+ Nations of Russia, China, and Iran) are destroyed, and then all of the dead will be raised. Those who have been born again and chose to follow Yeshua and His commandments will not pass into the judgment of condemnation. However, all those who rejected Him will perish in the lake of fire in the "second death." They will burn up like tares while the wheat is gathered into His barn; and the goats will be separated from His sheep. This is what the Scriptures teach. It is at the Last Day that all prophecy is now fulfilled, and the righteous will enter into the New Jerusalem where all things are made new.

Once you take the time to understand these specific words of Yeshua in John chapters 5 and 6, you can then understand verses like Eph. 2:5,6 no problem. We are seated with Christ in the heavenly places, Paul tells us, because he is referring to the fact that as soon as we die, we are present with Him. What Paul also told us is that once the 1,000-year reign is completed and all enemies of God including Gog and Magog are finally destroyed, then the eternal reign of God and His saints can begin.

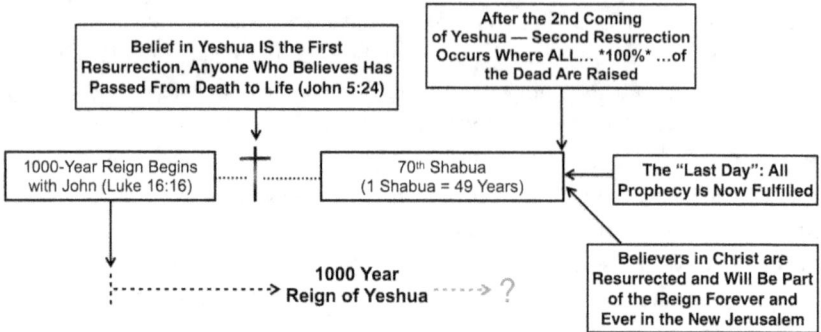

Figure 10.5: Resurrection, According to Yehshua

At the conclusion of the 70th shabua, all of the born again souls will be raised up on the Last Day to receive a new, incorruptible body; for as Paul stated:

50 Now this I say, brethren, that flesh and blood cannot inherit the kingdom of God; nor does corruption inherit incorruption.
51 Behold, I tell you a mystery: We shall not all sleep, but we shall all be changed—
52 in a moment, in the twinkling of an eye, **at the last trumpet.** For the trumpet will sound, and the dead will be raised incorruptible, and we shall be changed.
(1Cor. 15:50-52) [emphasis added]

These things have nothing to do with a rapture event as many suppose. As Paul states, the "mystery" of this Last Day event is preceded by the "last trumpet." Now I will reveal to you the timing of this amazing secret that Paul spoke of within the context of our last days. He was actually making a specific and direct reference to Leviticus 25, where Moses recorded:

8 'And you shall count seven sabbaths of years for yourself, seven times seven years; and the time of the seven sabbaths of years shall be to you **forty-nine years.**
9 Then you shall cause the trumpet of the Jubilee to sound on the tenth day of the seventh month; on the Day of Atonement you shall **make the trumpet to sound** throughout all your land.
10 And you shall consecrate the fiftieth year, and proclaim liberty throughout all the land to all its inhabitants. It shall be a Jubilee for you; and each of you shall return to his possession, and each of you shall return to his family.

(Lev. 25:8-10) [emphasis added]

During the Gregorian year 2044—the 49th year of this final cycle of mankind —and during the Day of Atonement on the tenth day of the seventh month, the very final and last trumpet of this current age will be blasted to announce the arrival of the Jubilee Year that will begin in Abib 2045. It is during this final trumpet blast on the Day of Atonement that we should be expecting Yeshua's prophecy of the Last Day to finally be fulfilled. The Jubilee will then begin where true and lasting liberty will once again return to Earth—a freedom from sin, bondage, and death. All things will be made new, and life will become as it once was in the Garden of Eden. *This* is the true mystery of the very last trumpet.

It is with this essential understanding of Yeshua's direct words about the first and second resurrections that we are now ready to address the next and final question regarding the afterlife.

What is the *mark* of Rev. 20:4? Isn't this a future event?

By continuing to faithfully apply the three laws of interpretation, we can easily understand what is meant by the mark of Rev. 20:4. The first time we ever see the concept of a spiritually significant mark on someone's body is in the account of Cain after he murdered Abel (Gen. 4:15). God placed upon him a mark of protection, but at the same time, it was the mark of an unrepentant murderer. Interesting. The next noteworthy place in Scripture where we see such a concept is in these words of Job 10:14:

"If I sin, then You mark me,
And will not acquit me of my iniquity."

This statement agrees with what we read about the mark of Cain. He sinned, and he received a mark. He did not repent, and therefore he was not forgiven. The flood even made a complete end of his lineage because none of them followed after God like Noah and his descendants. As you are starting to see, the mark of the beast, death, and sin has been around since the very beginning of man; but because people don't faithfully search the Scriptures using the three unwritten laws of correct biblical interpretation, they are hopelessly lost in ever finding the truth of God's Word.

Now that we understand the mark of sin, let's explore the holy mark of God. Ezekiel 9 is another place that shows us that the mark of Yehovah and the mark of the beast have been present since ancient times, well before the

New Testament and book of Revelation were ever written. Consider these verses from this chapter (Eze. 9:4-6):

4 and the LORD said to him, "Go through the midst of the city, through the midst of Jerusalem, and put a mark on the foreheads of the men who sigh and cry over all the abominations that are done within it."
5 To the others He said in my hearing, "Go after him through the city and kill; do not let your eye spare, nor have any pity.
6 "Utterly slay old *and* young men, maidens and little children and women; but do not come near anyone on whom *is* the mark; and begin at My sanctuary." So they began with the elders who *were* before the temple.

Context is key here. We are told that six angelic soldiers of God appear with war axes in their hands, and one had an inkhorn used for writing. It is this angel with the inkhorn that is given the order of Eze. 9:4 to place the mark of Yehovah on the foreheads of the righteous who were grieved and crying over the sins of Israel. We will do a deeper dive into this exact concept when we investigate the 144,000 firstfruits of Revelation. For now, understand that these righteous men of Eze. 9:4 received the mark of protection because they were observing the sabbath day of Yom Kippur (Day of Atonement) at the correct time, and they were therefore not "cut off" as is described in Lev. 23:29 for those that defile this set apart day. In fact, it is in Exodus 31:13 that we receive this extreme clarity about the mark of God:

"Speak also to the children of Israel, saying: 'Surely My Sabbaths you shall keep, for it *is* a sign between Me and you throughout your generations, that *you* may know that I *am* the LORD who sanctifies you."

The "mark" is keeping Yehovah's Sabbaths. This is the sign of both the old and also the renewed covenant in Yeshua's blood, forever. Therefore, the mark of the beast has always been anything (and I mean anything) that keeps someone from observing all of the Sabbaths of Leviticus 23 including the seventh day weekly sabbath. For most people, this mark of the beast is a false religion, but it could also be the idolatry of reporting to a career that will not allow the keeping of the Sabbaths. It could be many things. Of course, in the future I believe Scripture is clear that there will be a short time period (Rev. 17:12 refers to this time as "one hour") in which a literal right hand and forehead mark of the beast will be implemented by the satanic new world order. I have already described this mark's exact appearance in Chapter 4 according to the Greek words used in the original manuscript to portray this coming symbol of death and lawlessness.

THE END OF THE 1,000-YEAR REIGN

The Scriptures tell us that Yeshua must reign at the right hand of the Father *until* all enemies are under His feet (1Cor. 15:25; Psalm 110:1,2; Heb. 1:3). Therefore, as soon as He is no longer seated at the right hand—as soon as He comes on the clouds of heaven and defeats all his enemies—the 1,000-year reign at the right hand will be completed. We begin to see this reign end in Rev. 11:15-19. Just look at these words of Rev. 11:15:

"Then the seventh angel sounded: And there were loud voices in heaven, saying, 'The kingdoms of this world have become *the kingdoms* of our Lord and of His Christ, and He shall reign forever and ever!'"

The proclamation here is that the finality of the 1,000-year reign is about to be realized. All enemies are about to be subdued. The connection here is extremely important to make as we examine these words from Dan. 7:14:

"Then to Him was given dominion and glory and a kingdom,
That all peoples, nations, and languages should serve Him.
His dominion *is* an everlasting dominion,
Which shall not pass away,
And His kingdom *the one*
Which shall not be destroyed."

Again, we see reference to a forever kingdom. Just prior to this verse, Dan. 7:13 speaks of Yeshua returning on the clouds. This is the key concept that must be understood in light of the conclusion of the 1,000-year reign. Now let's go back and look at Rev. 11:19:

"Then the temple of God was opened in heaven, and the ark of His covenant was seen in His temple. And there were lightnings, noises, thunderings, an earthquake, and great hail."

As you examine the words of this verse, you must then make the connection to the words of Hebrews 8:1,2 that explicitly tell us that Yeshua is the High Priest that ministers for His people in the true Sanctuary not made with human hands. In other words, the writer is telling us that Yeshua is in the Temple of Heaven ministering for His people. So, when we see the Temple opened in Revelation 11, this means that Yeshua is leaving behind the role of intercessor, and He is assuming the role of a conquering King, to finish His enemies once and for all. This is the exact moment when the 1,000-year reign ends, and this shift is further revealed to us in Rev. 14:14 when Yeshua is seated on a cloud and no longer at the right hand of the Father.

When examining Revelation 14, there are three harvests that take place in this chapter. The first one is the firstfruits harvest of the 144,000; the second harvest is the harvest of the earth in Rev. 14:14-16; and the third harvest is commonly known as the grapes of wrath. I am of the opinion that the harvest of Rev. 14:14-16 is a good harvest, and I will show you in Chapter 13 that this could be referring to the regathering of all 13 Tribes of Israel out of captivity and back into the Land of Israel. Yeshua will deal with them face to face, bring them under the bond of the covenant, and purge the rebels from them. We will talk more about this later.

The grape harvest of Rev. 14:17-20 is the same event of Ezekiel 38 and 39 along with Rev. 19 and 20. It is also the same event of Joel 3:13 in the valley of Jehoshaphat. Simply compare these scriptures, and the connections will become obvious. This is the Gog and Magog event that will result in a powerful outpouring of Yehovah's wrath upon His enemies that satan will gather up against the regathered people of Israel. Once this event takes place and all the enemies of Yeshua are destroyed, the forever and ever reign then begins.

Now let's look back at Dan. 7 after the final beast power has been destroyed. This is what Daniel 7:12 states:

"As for the rest of the beasts, they had their dominion taken away, yet their lives were prolonged for a season and a time."

Once the final satanic beast power from the bottomless pit is destroyed along with Gog and Magog, the other beasts are still not destroyed just yet. The truth here is very profound if you have not yet carefully considered the proper sequence of these events. Daniel 7:27 completely fills in the gaps for us:

"Then the kingdom and dominion,
And the greatness of the kingdoms under the whole heaven,
Shall be given to the people, the saints of the Most High.
His kingdom *is* an everlasting kingdom,
And all dominions shall serve and obey Him."

348

Once the final satanic rebellion occurs, Yeshua will defeat all His enemies, and the forever reign will begin. All of the kingdoms from one end of the heaven to the other will be given over to the set-apart people of the Most High God. This short season of righteous dominion on earth that occurs starting at an unknown time until Abib 2045 is why we see words like these written in the prophets:

"If the family of Egypt will not come up and enter in, they *shall have* no *rain;* they shall receive the plague with which the LORD strikes the nations who do not come up to keep the Feast of Tabernacles."
(Zec. 14:18)

Take heed to the words of the prophet Zechariah. Not keeping Yehovah's feasts in the Old Testament, New Testament, and even until the end of the age always has been and always will be *sin.* Though it is hard to fathom, the opportunity to rebel and sin against the Most High and His Torah will still be taking place even after the destruction of Gog and Magog. Nations and tribes will still have the opportunity to sin against God, but they will be met with harsh penalties. It is my current understanding that this period of time will be just a short season for God's people to rule here on this present earth, and all of the kingdoms on earth will become vassal states of the United Kingdom of Israel that consists of all thirteen tribes regathered from the four corners. Once this season of history is over at the *Last Day,* eternity will then begin.

John describes for us the New Jerusalem in Rev. 21 coming down out of heaven along with the new heavens and earth. The forever reign that started with the destruction of Gog and Magog will then continue onward into eternity.

Amazing, isn't it?

QUESTION 3: WHEN IS SATAN GOING TO BE LOOSED?

Of the questions presented at the beginning of this chapter, the third and final question can now be fully answered. Though we will look at this topic in greater detail in the next chapter, let's briefly look at Rev. 20:7,8:

7 Now when the thousand years have expired, Satan will be released from his prison
8 and will go out to deceive the nations which are in the four corners of the earth, Gog and Magog, to gather them together to battle, whose number is as the sand of the sea.

Abraham Ojeda

Sometime before the end of the 70th shabua, satan will be loosed from the bottomless pit as described in this verse and also the whole of Revelation chapter 9, particularly Rev. 9:11:

"And they had as king over them the angel of the bottomless pit, whose name in Hebrew *is* Abaddon, but in Greek he has the name Apollyon."

This main satan from Genesis is the angel of the pit that is loosed, also known as Abaddon or Apollyon. These names literally mean *destruction or destroyer*. Revelation 12:12 shows us that once he is loosed, the devil will have great wrath, knowing his time is short. We are shown that the accuser of God's people (Rev. 12:10, Job 1:6) will be violently forbidden from entering heaven to accuse any more. Though it is not 100% clear to me, I am of the opinion that Rev. 17:8 and Rev. 12:10 are describing the same event.

The single most important event that takes place once satan is loosed is the gathering of Gog, Magog, and the northern armies to battle. What I will show you from now and into the next chapter is that the Gog and Magog War is actually a two-part battle. I believe that the first battle begins with the abomination of desolation and further develops into Revelation chapter 9 with the tormenting of men for five months by the locusts; and the second battle occurs when Gog and Magog are destroyed once and for all by Yeshua Himself (Rev. 19:15). Stick with me. I realize what I just said probably went over your head, but I will explain all these things step by step.

THE DAY OF יהוה (THE LORD)

Because all of the Mystery Babylon religions have relentlessly taught that the Day of the LORD (Yehovah) battle will not happen until 1,000 years *after* the 70th week is completed, most people are *not* paying attention to who Gog of the land of Magog is right now along with all of its allies including the people of the far north (the northern army of Joel 2:20). We need to know what their identity is during these last days in order to discern the signs of the times and fully understand the events of Revelation 9 and satan's release from the bottomless pit that will be happening very soon. That is why this prophecy is of utmost importance to this final generation, and in fact, I believe the Day of the LORD is one of the most mentioned prophecies in the entire Bible.

There is a very specific reason why the Holy Spirit repeatedly used the word "Day" to describe this major prophetic event. Night and day are the two separate and distinct parts of any given day, and the Day of the LORD is no different. Two is the number of separation. That is why this Day appears to

350

have many frightening and terrifying aspects to it while at the same time having promises of hope and restoration throughout the Bible. The multitudes of scriptures used to describe this event have left the majority of people confused because they can't seem to make sense of the apparent contradiction of both good and evil being ascribed to this Day. The missing link is that the prophetic "Day of Yehovah" is not a literal 24-hour period of time; but it is instead the description of the two-part battle of Gog and Magog. Just like a Hebrew day, it begins in the thick darkness of the evening with judgment against the West. Gog, Magog, and their entire ten kings alliance will rise up and conquer Jerusalem and all Western nations to begin this pivotal end-times event. The seed of Abraham will be subject to slavery and destruction, just as Daniel had foretold. The takeover will be swift and violent, with a blazing fire going forth from the Russian-Chinese-Islamic alliance of nations. They will conquer the transgressors of God's covenant; and they will be successful.

Thankfully, the dawn of this Day comes next. After extreme punishment and devastation, God's people will finally be declared to have a just cause. Just like the pattern we have seen throughout the Scriptures, God's people will desperately cry out for mercy, and God will raise up a deliverer for them. The bright morning of victory in Yeshua's power will take place as His Israel is regathered back under His direct leadership. Of course, satan won't let go that easily but will gather up Gog and Magog one last time for the final showdown of the Day of the LORD. The second part of this Day is also commonly referred to as Armageddon, which is the physical place where the final Gog-Magog battle will take place according to Rev. 16:16. The prophet Joel told us that this place also goes by the name Valley of Jehoshaphat (Joe. 3:12). Speaking of the second half of the Day of Yehovah and this valley, Zechariah 14 tells us that it is the very feet of Yehovah that will stand on the Mount of Olives; and this glorious appearance will cause the mountain to split in two with all of the enemies of Israel running for their lives through a newly created valley but only to be destroyed.

This is the final battle; and this is where the ten kings will reap the same level of destruction that they had sown during the first part of this day. Look at how Yeshua repays them for their evil deeds, once again indicating that the West will surely be conquered through nuclear means (see also Obadiah 1:15):

"And I will bring him to judgment with pestilence and bloodshed; I will rain down on him, on his troops, and on the many peoples who are with him, flooding rain, great hailstones, fire, and brimstone."
(Ezekiel 38:22)

Abraham Ojeda

WHO ARE THE PEOPLE OF GOG AND MAGOG?

When I first started looking into this subject, I didn't consult modern-day Bible commentaries, DVD presentations, or anything that has been recently published or produced because I wanted to completely avoid the traditions, doctrines, and teachings of men regarding this topic. I went back in history as far as I could to understand what early believers thought of these entities. What I found was fascinating and extremely eye opening.

One of my main resources for this investigation was a book entitled *Gog and Magog in Early Christian and Islamic Sources* that clearly and empirically describes what people of various backgrounds believed about Gog and the people of the far north from antiquity. The authors state:

> "The biblical peoples Gog and Magog, known to Jews, Christians and Muslims alike, were believed to live in the world's extreme north. Moreover, in late Jewish and Early Christian and Islamic tradition they were supposed to have been enclosed behind a barrier (gate, wall) by Alexander the Great—in Islam known as Iskandar 'the two- horned'—until, prior to the Last Days, God would release these apocalyptic hordes to break out from behind their prison."
> 3

Before reading this book, I had no idea that Gog and Magog are spoken about prophetically in the Quran. I also was unaware of the fact that Alexander the Great of Greece was himself aware of the identity of Gog and Magog because of the barrier that he discovered in their territory. This barrier, or rampart, was and still is believed to be the Great Wall of China amongst many students of end-times prophecy. Regarding Rosh and the people of the far north, this is what these same authors state based on accounts of both Alexander and early Eastern Christian sources:

> "According to the ancient geographical tradition, the entire Eastern Caucasus was called the 'Northern land'. The cold and mostly unknown region was understood as being inhabited by uncivilized, warlike and primitive peoples."[4]

It is from these perspectives that we can narrow down our investigation to the region in and around the Caucasus Mountains. When you look at a map, you will see that these mountains are divided into Greater and Lesser Caucasus ranges. To the north we have modern-day Russia; in the center of the ranges we see Georgia and Azerbaijan; and to the south we see Armenia, Turkey, and Iran. All of these nations are going to play central end-times roles, as we have already been seeing on the world stage. Here is what the ancient Islamic sources have to say based on tradition and also the Quran:

> "al-Tabari and al-Baydawi locate the two mountains (mentioned in Koran xvm:93/96): in Armenia, in Azerbaijan or in the most eastern part of the land of the Turks; but the two mountains perhaps are also to be found between Armenia and Azerbaijan or in the farthest North."[5]

Based on all these witnesses along with the current rise of a Russian-Chinese-Islamic alliance, we are now beyond the realm of mere speculation and are indeed witnessing all these prophetic events described in Ezekiel, Revelation, and other Scriptures. However, don't simply take my word for it. Check my sources, and through careful and diligent research, you, too, will find it is easy to conclude that these final enemies of Yeshua will consist of the regions of Russia, Azerbaijan, Georgia, Armenia, Turkey, China, and the surrounding territories. At this moment in history, the overall picture has now become quite clear. This is what 1Chronicles 1:5 says:

"The sons of Japheth *were* Gomer, Magog, Madai, Javan, Tubal, Meshech, and Tiras."

Whereas the physical descendants of the seed of Abraham are from Noah's son Shem, these final enemies of Israel are descendants from the sons of Japeth. These armies will be under the control of satan, which is going to be the major topic of the next chapter that unlocks the mystery of the locusts of Revelation and the great northern army of Joel, among various other secrets.

Chapter 11
Zionism vs. BRICS

You now understand the abomination of desolation. You know that we are supposed to be looking for armies to be rising up against modern day Jerusalem (and its Western allies) right before it happens according to Yeshua's words. You also now know that both the Jews and Lost Tribes of the House of Israel are going to be gathered together in Jerusalem for the judgment that will happen in one hour. You also understand that all of the prophecies concerning Gog, Magog, and the armies of the far north will very soon come to pass. Indeed, the first Gog and Magog battle against Jerusalem and the West is already unfolding on the world stage for everyone to see. This first battle is the same thing as the "night" that begins the Day of the LORD. All of these things had been mysteries since ancient times, but now that we are at the time of the end, all things are able to be understood.

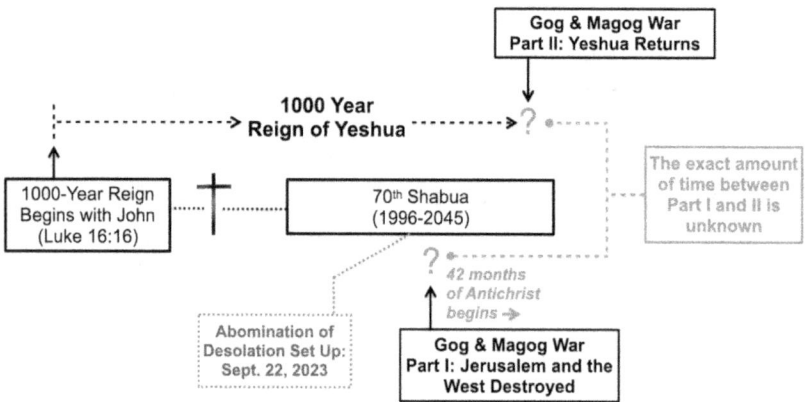

Figure 11.1: The Timeline of the Gog and Magog War.

I am about to give you even more clarity concerning the abomination of desolation and what we should be expecting as we enter this period of history. We must consider the geopolitical climate of the last days, the current Jewish world order, and the often misunderstood prophecy of the Ten Kings that are coming to overthrow Mystery Zionism—the last-days worldwide Jewish movement that resulted in the establishment and ongoing expansion of the

1948 state of Israel in Palestine. By faithfully applying our three laws of interpretation, we will unlock the secrets of all these end times prophecies once
and for all.

THE SUBJECT OF REVELATION

Before uncovering the prophecy of Zionism versus the Ten Kings of BRICS,
always keep in mind that the secret to understanding the book of Revelation is
knowing the subject matter. Just like in Daniel's 70 shabua, the overarching
theme of Revelation is the judgment and redemption of Daniel's people and
the holy city, Jerusalem. I have already described this reality, but you absolutely must recognize that Jerusalem is the woman riding the beast. Jerusalem
is Mystery Babylon the Great. We can easily make this connection because the
phrase *great city* is used ten times in the book of Revelation, and it always,
without fail, explicitly refers to Jerusalem. There is absolutely no way around
this fact. I particularly like Rev. 11:8 where we are told that this *great city* is
where our Lord was crucified, which could never be any other place besides
Jerusalem. It is *not* the Vatican, City of London, Washington DC, or any other
city that many unwise teachers have falsely proclaimed over the many years
now. We need to let the Bible interpret the Bible. Let's allow the Text to speak
for itself. Like I stated, God will redeem Jerusalem after He is done judging it.
Then at the conclusion of the 120 shanah of mankind, John tells us that this
great city coming down out of heaven is the New Jerusalem (Rev. 21:10).
From the judgment of Mystery Babylon to the glorious appearance of the New
Jerusalem, the *great city* plays a vital role in our proper interpretation of all
mysteries.

REVELATION 17: THE MYSTERY OF THE WOMAN RIDING THE BEAST

We will begin our investigation with Revelation chapter 17. An angel takes
John into the wilderness to see a figurative representation of the great city of
Jerusalem. This is what he records for us as he begins to see this "woman":

"So he carried me away in the Spirit into the wilderness. And I saw a woman
sitting on a scarlet beast *which was* full of names of blasphemy, having seven
heads and ten horns."
(Rev. 17:3)

Skipping ahead for a moment, we can see exactly who this "woman" is based on the final words of this same chapter:

"And the woman whom you saw is that great city which reigns over the kings of the earth."
(Rev 17:18)

Now that it is clear who the woman is—the great city—the one and only Jerusalem of the current Jewish world order as described in the previous chapters of this book, it must be considered how John first describes this entity. She has seven heads and ten horns. In addition to this initial description, we are given more clarity about the seven heads of the beast:

"Here is the mind which has wisdom: The seven heads are seven mountains on which the woman sits."
(Rev. 17:9)

Not only is Jerusalem known literally as the city on seven hills, but the "seven heads" is also a figurative reference to the power structure of the beast that this woman currently rests upon. The seven mountains, or hills, of Jerusalem are: (1) Mount Olivet (also called the Mount of Olives) in east Jerusalem, (2) the Mount of Corruption located on the same ridge as Mount Olivet, (3) Mount Scopus located in northeast Jerusalem and the highest point of the city, (4) Mount Ophel located between the City of David and the Temple Mount, (5) the original Mount Zion located just south of the Old City's walls, (6) New Mount Zion situated near the original Mount Zion, and lastly, (7) The Hill of the Antonia Fortress located just north of the Old City walls.

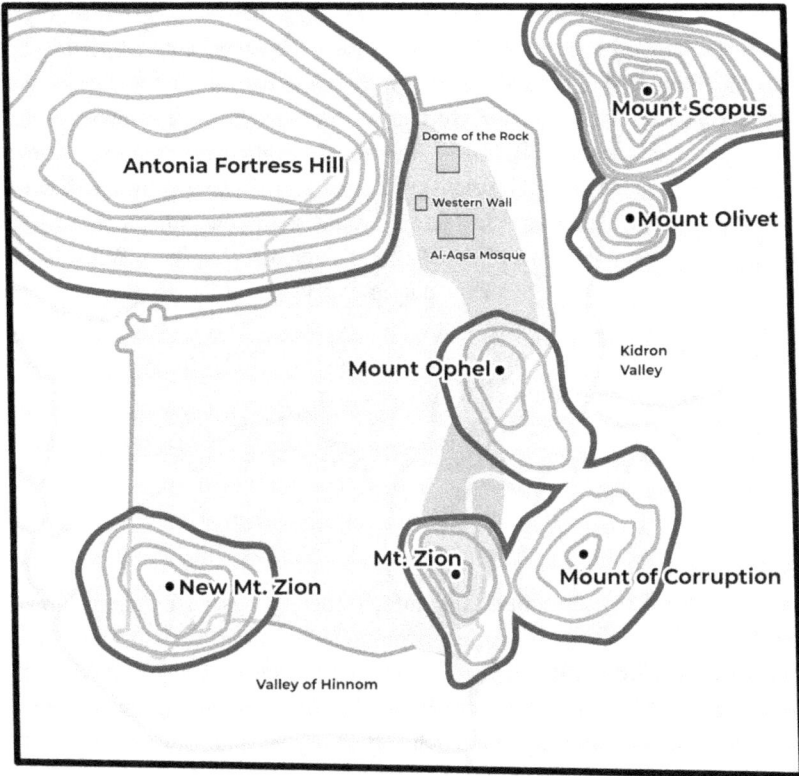

Figure 11.2: The Seven Hills of Jerusalem. The lightly shaded area in the center surrounded by the dark border represents the ancient boundary of Jerusalem. The Dome of the Rock, Western Wall, and Al-Aqsa Mosque are depicted to provide modern context.

We are then simultaneously told that these seven heads, or mountains, also represent seven kings:

"There are also seven kings. Five have fallen, one is, and the other has not yet come. And when he comes, he must continue a short time."
(Rev. 17:10)

Therefore, in addition to the literal understanding of the woman's physical mountains, the Group of Seven (G7) Nations and their respective leaders are the perfect embodiment of the current Zionist world order's power structure. This geopolitical alliance between the Western countries of Japan, France, Canada, Germany, Italy, the United Kingdom, and the United States meets annually in what are called "summit" meetings, which is precisely how you would describe a mountain peak. Representing the seven major International Monetary Fund (IMF) advanced economies in the world,[1] these seven mountains have been instrumental in furthering the agenda of the Jewish world order. For example, the G7's ongoing condemnation of Russia's actions against Ukraine's Jewish-led Zelenskyy regime has placed constant pressure upon the Russian Federation. In fact, this consistent condemnation had been taking place even before Putin's 2022 invasion of Ukraine.[2] What is not entirely clear is the narrative's explanation of "five have fallen, one is, and the other has not yet come", which could be a reference to a variety of historical events pertaining to these nations. However, the G7's identity as the seven mountains seems to be confused by the next verse:

"The beast that was, and is not, is himself also the eighth, and is of the seven, and is going to perdition."
(Rev. 17:11)

If the coming beast—the final antichrist leader possessed by satan himself and "the eighth"—is one "of the seven" as John describes, then this could mean a couple different things. Either the final beast ruler is a Westerner from one of the G7 nations, which would fit the earlier interpretation of someone like German-born Klaus Schwab being the final beast authority (see Chapter 4); or the final beast ruler is someone who has been financed, equipped, and enabled by the West to carry out this role, therefore qualifying as "of" or "out of" the seven. With respect to this latter idea, someone like Iran's supreme leader or a closely related figure would still fit this description. The CIA was directly involved with the overthrow of Iran's ancient monarchy and its Shah along with the subsequent installment of the Islamic Revolutionary Government, which to date has received billions of dollars from the US government as described in Chapter 8. It is a well established fact that the CIA was instrumental in overthrowing what would be Iran's final democratic government under Prime Minister Mohammad Mossadegh from 1951–1953. According to declassified documents, the CIA together with British MI6 overthrew this leader in order to install a pro-western replacement and safeguard the West's oil interests in the region, which they viewed as enabling substantial control of the world.[3] This puppet leader was Fazlollah Zahedi who was Prime Minister from 1953–1955. Not only did US-British spy operations end Iran's sovereign control over its own resources, but it also ended the country's democratic identity on the world stage. As trust slowly eroded under the late leadership of the Shahs from

1953 until its end in 1979, the Iranian people began seeking more radical solutions to Western influence and meddling.[4] Some Iranians look back to the 1979 revolution as a time where the Ayatollah "promised us heaven, but...created a hell on earth" due to the toxic mixture of government and religion.[5] Ultimately, the 1953 coup d'état backfired against the West with severe consequences that have continued to this day. The rise of Iran's Ayatollahs will now have a direct impact on the whole world as we know it, and perhaps a coming Ayatollah or related Mahdi figure of Islam will satisfy the "eighth" horn prophecy—the final "beast" that was first initiated, later enabled, and currently financed out "of the seven", especially America and Britain. Going back to the words of Western Freemason Albert Pike as documented in the 1958 book *Pawns in the Game*:

> "World War Three is to be fomented by using the differences the agentur of the Illuminati stir up between Political Zionists and the leaders of the Moslem world … to be directed in such a manner that Islam (the Arab World including Mohammedanism) and Political Zionism (including the State of Israel) will destroy themselves while at the same time the remaining nations, once more divided against each other on this issue, will be forced to fight themselves into a state of complete exhaustion physically, mentally, spiritually and economically."[6]

Since these words were purportedly penned sometime before Pike's death in 1891, there can be little doubt, if of course the account is true, that the West's 1953 coup d'état and the subsequent rise of the Iranian Ayatollahs was far more orchestrated than the media will ever care to admit. Just follow the money, as they say.

THE MYSTERY OF THE TEN HORNS

The ten horns themselves are also a representation of the current Zionist world order's power structure, but instead of these nations being under Jerusalem's direct control and influence, they are an extension of power only. This conclusion is supported by the reality that these ten horns will organize and successfully revolt against the woman by giving their authority to the very final beast power of history, as described in John's vision:

12 "The ten horns which you saw are ten kings who have received no kingdom as yet, but they receive authority for one hour as kings with the beast.

13 "These are of one mind, and they will give their power and authority to the beast.
(Rev. 17:12,13)

The first thing to notice is that these horns, which could be referring generally to nations or also specifically to leaders of ten nations, have never received a kingdom on the world stage of history. Jerusalem is connected to these ten horns in that she has ruled over them indirectly. This idea will become clear once the ten nations are identified. First, additional information is available within Daniel's vision in the seventh chapter of his book. In fact, Dan. 7:7 describes this same beast having ten horns and being different from all three beasts before it. Daniel 7:24,25 tells us that there is a coming horn from this ten-kings power structure that will reign for "time times and half a time", which can be understood to be "a year, two years, and half a year", or 3.5 years. Going back to Revelation, this 42-month reign is repeated in Rev. 13:5, and we are also shown that the ten kings will rule with the beast for this short-lived reign also referred to metaphorically as "one hour" (Rev. 17:12). Yeshua gives us more details about these ten kings and their nations, stating, "And Jerusalem will be trampled by Gentiles until the times of the Gentiles are fulfilled" (Luke 21:24). After properly identifying the word "gentiles" as simply meaning "nations", it should then be understood that this coming ten kings alliance consists primarily of non-Israelite nations with a different set of cultural values than the West. The coming "times of the nations" will end this current period of dominance that the Lost Tribe Israelite nations have had during the last days, from France, to Britain, and to the USA. Whoever these ten kings are, they are of one mind. As explained in the first edition of this book, we should be looking for a treaty, alliance, or some sort of covenant by which they operate.

As I will now fully reveal within this chapter, this alliance is none other than the BRICS+ nations. Before we seek to identify the ten kings from the Scriptures, we must consider what John wrote when he said that they have no kingdom until the final "beast" shows up. Who is this beast, anyway? This is what John was told regarding this beast that carries the woman, Jerusalem:

"The beast that you saw was, and is not, and will ascend out of the bottomless pit and go to perdition. And those who dwell on the earth will marvel, whose names are not written in the Book of Life from the foundation of the world, when they see the beast that was, and is not, and yet is."
(Rev. 17:8)

In other words, the beast that rules with the ten kings is satan himself who is loosed from the bottomless pit, and he is also known as Apollyon or Abaddon (Rev. 9:11). Now things are starting to become quite clear. We are being shown in Revelation that satan will be granted short-lived authority over every nation on earth (Rev. 13:7). He will implement his mark in order to buy and sell; and just like we saw in the book of Job chapter 1, satan will be able to work signs to deceive the nations such as calling down fire down from heaven (Rev. 13:13). As we enter this discussion regarding the identity of the ten kings themselves, consider these primary verses for meditation from Eze. 38:2-6

2 Son of man, set your face against Gog, of the land of Magog, the prince of Rosh, Meshech, and Tubal, and prophesy against him,
3 and say, "Thus says the Lord GOD: Behold, I *am* against you, O Gog, the prince of Rosh, Meshech, and Tubal.
4 "I will turn you around, put hooks into your jaws, and lead you out, with all your army, horses, and horsemen, all splendidly clothed, a great company *with* bucklers and shields, all of them handling swords.
5 "Persia, Ethiopia, and Libya are with them, all of them *with* shield and helmet;
6 "Gomer and all its troops; the house of Togarmah *from* the far north and all its troops—many people *are* with you."

Even though this passage is speaking of the nations that will be gathered together for the final battle of Armageddon and the Day of Yehovah, what you will find is that ten kings are mentioned. They are Gog, Magog, Rosh, Meshech, Tubal, Persia, Ethiopia, Lybia, Gomer, and Togarmah. These are exactly ten different names. Is this mere coincidence? Absolutely not. I have already described the identity of some of these nations at the conclusion of the last chapter based on historical writings and traditions of Christians, Jews, and Muslims from antiquity. Some of these identities are easy. Modern Iran is Persia. Rosh is Russia. Magog is China, and there is evidence to support that Meshech is Turkey.[7]

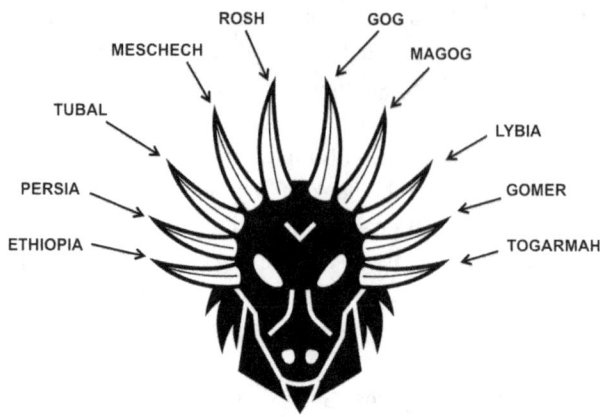

Figure 11.3: The Mystery of the Ten Kings

At this point in history, we have a clear enough picture to see that these ten kings are a Russian-Chinese-Islamic alliance of nations like I have been asserting due to the current political climate and rising conflict between the Western powers and this alliance. Rather than spending too much time identifying them all specifically, let us simply acknowledge that they are prophesied to appear on the world stage in the following manner:

16 "And the ten horns which you saw on the beast, these will hate the harlot, make her desolate and naked, eat her flesh and burn her with fire.
17 "For God has put it into their hearts to fulfill His purpose, to be of one mind, and to give their kingdom to the beast, until the words of God are fulfilled."
(Rev. 17:16,17)

Did you notice the use of the word "desolate"? This should cause alarm bells to go off in your spirit. It is in fact speaking of the abomination of desolation, which, as previously demonstrated, will be carried out exactly as described in numerous chapters from the Prophets and later by Yeshua when He said Jerusalem will be surrounded by armies. These are the armies. They are the armies of the ten kings alliance and the peoples of the far north that will destroy Jerusalem and burn her with fire. The smoke will be visible to all the kings and merchants of the earth through the airwaves of the news media as well as those literally passing through the international trade route of the Suez Canal, insomuch as they cry out the following words:

9 "The kings of the earth who committed fornication and lived luxuriously with her will weep and lament for her, when they see the smoke of her burning,

10 "standing at a distance for fear of her torment, saying, 'Alas, alas, that great city Babylon, that mighty city! For in one hour your judgment has come.'

11 "And the merchants of the earth will weep and mourn over her, for no one buys their merchandise anymore:

(Rev. 18:9-11)

People get very confused when they read these words because the great city of Jerusalem does not strike many people as being a place of luxury and riches like maybe New York City or Dubai. As already explained, Mystery Babylon is a much larger beast than the vast majority of people realize. It is a *mystery* for a reason. The shadow elements of its infrastructure are vast and funded by the most powerful bankers and secret societies on the world stage, and as will be demonstrated next, this reality has been true since the time of Yeshua's birth. Though she is the supreme whore of the earth, she also has many daughters, and the United States is only one of them in these last days. In other words, Mystery Babylon is the geopolitical system of the secret societies, criminal underworld, and blackmail rings through which the kings of the earth and the merchants of Revelation 18 have been enabled to live in luxury.

Figure 11.4: The Coming Smoke of Mystery Babylon's Torment

Abraham Ojeda

THE ANCIENT ORIGINS OF MYSTERY BABYLON

"O Jerusalem, Jerusalem, the one who kills the prophets and stones those who are sent to her! How often I wanted to gather your children together, as a hen gathers her chicks under her wings, but you were not willing!"
(Mat. 23:37)

When Jesus uttered these words in the first century right before the crucifixion, He was also referring back to what almost happened to Him a little over 30 years prior when He first left the womb. Jerusalem had always sought to end His life well before He willingly gave up His Spirit on the cross. The very moment that news began to spread regarding His divine birth from the virgin Mary, this is what took place:

1 Now after Jesus was born in Bethlehem of Judea in the days of Herod the king, behold, wise men from the East came to Jerusalem,
2 saying, "Where is He who has been born King of the Jews? For we have seen His star in the East and have come to worship Him."
3 When Herod the king heard this, he was troubled, and all Jerusalem with him.
(Mat. 2:1-3)

Have you ever wondered why "all Jerusalem" was troubled at the news of Jesus' birth? This key verse contains within it the mystery of modern Zionism and its ancient origins. In fact, the role of the great city Jerusalem from the first century until now is perfectly revealed within this context. Of course, the sinister actions that follow are commonly ascribed only to Herod the Roman tetrarch, but he was not the only one that was "troubled." This is what happened next:

4 And when he had gathered all the chief priests and scribes of the people together, he inquired of them where the Christ was to be born.
5 So they said to him, "In Bethlehem of Judea, for thus it is written by the prophet:
6 'But you, Bethlehem, in the land of Judah, Are not the least among the rulers of Judah; For out of you shall come a Ruler Who will shepherd My people Israel.' "
(Mat. 2:4-6)

King Herod held a secret society meeting with the top leadership of

Jerusalem. We find out that the chief priests and scribes knew full well exactly what was written about the coming Messiah. Yet, we were explicitly told that they were "troubled" just a moment ago, rather than being excited or in a state of rejoicing to see the fulfillment of such a profound event. Shortly after their correct interpretation of Scripture was provided to Herod, he proceeded to put to death all of Bethlehem's male children from two years old and under. Of course, this was not only Herod's desire but also that of all the top occultists disguised as religious leaders within Jerusalem. Judaism and its various sects had already been fully interwoven with pagan mysticism, demonic doctrines, and even the worship of satan himself. That is why Yeshua later spoke with such firm opposition to the scribes and the Pharisees while also exposing who their true master really was:

37 "I know that you are Abraham's descendants, but you seek to kill Me, because **My word has no place in you.**
38 "I speak what I have seen with My Father, and **you do what you have seen with your father.**
44 "You are of your father the devil, and the desires of your father you want to do. He was a murderer from the beginning, and does not stand in the truth, because there is no truth in him. When he speaks a lie, he speaks from his own resources, for he is a liar and the father of it."
(John 8:37,44) [emphasis added]

The key phrase within Yeshua's accusations here is that these leading occultists of His day were doing what they "have seen with your father", that is to say, their father *the devil.* Some manuscripts say "you do what you have seen *from* your father", indicating that the scribes and Pharisees were actively engaging in black magic, seances, and rituals whereby they could make direct contact with satan and receive instructions *from* him. Yeshua reveals that though these people were true Shemitic bloodline descendents of Abraham (and not Hamitic Canaanites as many falsely teach), they fell into the depths of paganism and luciferianism like King Solomon before them. Even though they claimed to be Torah scholars and authorities on the written Word of God, Yeshua openly tells us that His Word had absolutely no place in their hearts, minds, or actions. That is why this same religious order of the first century then proceeded to carry out a "great persecution" in Jerusalem after Christ had ascended to the right hand of the Father. Immediately after the death of Stephen the Martyr in Acts 7, the following event took place:

"... At that time a great persecution arose against the church which was at

Jerusalem; and they were all scattered throughout the regions of Judea and Samaria, except the apostles."
(Acts 8:1)

However, the secret society of Jerusalem failed to successfully carry out the direct orders from their father. Christianity, or *The Way* as it was known, was spreading beyond Jerusalem with an unstoppable force:

"Then the churches throughout all Judea, Galilee, and Samaria had peace and were edified. And walking in the fear of the Lord and in the comfort of the Holy Spirit, they were multiplied."
(Acts 9:31)

In the midst of this often misunderstood spiritual war of the first century, the followers of satan were quickly forced to change tactics. At first they themselves—the practitioners of Judaism—persecuted the believers, but they were getting overwhelmed by doing all the work themselves. Rather than trying to eradicate the churches by force, the synagogue of satan switched to subversion and infiltration tactics that proved to be far more effective. While we see evidence of this approach with the Judiazing cult of circumcision that Paul passionately fought against, there was a greater military strategy at play and one that has had lasting effects till this day. Jerusalem's ruling class decided to join forces with the Romans to carry out their destruction of Christianity and the teachings of Jesus. Not only was this same playbook used in putting Christ to death under the authority of Pontius Pilate, but it continued well after the fact as recorded in Acts:

17 And it came to pass after three days that Paul called the leaders of the Jews together. So when they had come together, he said to them: "Men and brethren, though I have done nothing against our people or the customs of our fathers, yet I was delivered as a prisoner from Jerusalem into the hands of the Romans,
18 "who, when they had examined me, wanted to let me go, because there was no cause for putting me to death.
19 "But when the Jews spoke against it, I was compelled to appeal to Caesar, not that I had anything of which to accuse my nation."
(Acts 28:17-19)

These are some of the final words of the book of Acts, and we see that Paul was contending with the synagogue of satan and their persecution of him.

They had successfully hijacked the Roman governmental infrastructure to oppress one of the leading voices of early Christianity. As mentioned in Chapter 2, Paul ended up dying at the hands of Emperor Nero shortly after this account of his imprisonment. In fact, the Roman persecution of Christians is understood to have begun during the reign of Emperor Nero in AD 64, and it continued for nearly 250 years until the Roman creation of a different kind of Christianity was adopted by Constantine in 313. The mainstream narrative surrounding this period of persecution is that the Roman Empire viewed Christians as a threat to their established order. However, the New Testament plainly disagrees with this lie. When Jesus was examined by the Romans, no fault was found in Him. The same was true in Acts 28:18 with Paul. The Romans found no cause for putting him to death.

Because of these self-evident facts of the Bible, it is not necessary to provide mountains of anecdotal evidence, documents, and events explaining Jerusalem's hijacking of the Roman social and political system in order to carry out its secret society agendas. The New Testament itself clearly reveals this historical pattern from the crucifixion of the Messiah, the imprisonment of Paul, and even the imprisonment of the apostle John—the latter of whom explicitly warned of the "synagogue of satan" in the book of Revelation while saying nothing of the Romans that actually owned the Isle of Patmos. Sadly, the majority of prophecy teachers believe Rome and later its Catholic Church to be the Mystery Babylon of Revelation, but they fail to see who was really pulling the strings the whole time. It was always the synagogue of satan head-quartered in Jerusalem.

As stated before, the Jerusalem order's parasitic use of Rome culminated with a plan to infiltrate and subvert Christianity rather than attempt to destroy it by force. Constantine (AD 306-337), touted as being the first emperor to convert to Christianity, was used to organize the Council of Nicea and its Nicene Creed of faith. Among various things, the Nicene Creed mandated the uniform observance of Easter (instead of Passover), among other man-made traditions that simultaneously excluded the observance of the Holy Days of Leviticus 23. However, it was not until Emperor Theodosius I (AD 379-395) that the Catholic orthodoxy of Nicene Christians was officially recognized as the Roman Empire's state religion. Over time, various other pagan traditions were inserted into the false construct of Roman Christianity such as the abandonment of seventh-day, or Saturday, sabbath observance. The mixing of pagan winter solstice traditions with the birthday of Christ, the incorporation of angel worship, the worship of Mary—the list of false teachings is enormous. Of course, the heresy of Catholic doctrines continued for hundreds of years afterwards and to this very day even amongst all denominations of mainstream Christianity that indirectly adhere to the falsehoods of Catholicism. When Martin Luther arrived on October 1517 with his "Ninety-five Theses" against the Catholic church, he initiated what would become known as a "Protestant Reformation." By definition, this movement sought only to "protest" and "reform" the ways of the Catholic church, and all of the adherents to this movement failed to realize that *separation* rather than *reformation* was what was truly needed in order to walk the ancient path of the first century saints. It cannot be overstated that the Jerusalem order's hijacking of biblical Christianity was carried out by systematically borrowing the infrastructure of the Roman Empire and forever sowing deep-rooted confusion as to what true Christianity *really* is.

Tracing the Jerusalem order's roots from King Solomon and into its present-day operations is not an easy task. This genealogy is an endless web of historical figures, documents, conspiracies, wars, and occultic schools of thought that are all interconnected in what the Bible refers to perfectly as a true *mystery*. That being the case, two historically important occultic groups are relevant for understanding major developments of the last days, and both are described in the Bible. The first one is described in a vision given to the prophet Ezekiel:

15 Then He said to me, "Have you seen this, O son of man? Turn again, you will see greater abominations than these."
16 So He brought me into the inner court of the LORD's house; and there, at the door of the temple of the LORD, between the porch and the altar, were about twenty-five men with their backs toward the temple of the LORD and their faces toward the east, and they were worshiping the sun toward the east.
17 And He said to me, "Have you seen this, O son of man? Is it a trivial thing to the house of Judah to commit the abominations which they commit here? For they have filled the land with violence; then they have returned to provoke Me to anger. Indeed they put the branch to their nose."
(Eze. 8:15-17)

This particular idolatry is credited to the southern kingdom of Judah, and Ezekiel documents the practices of this sun-worshiping mystical Jewish group called the Essenes. Due to the recent discovery of the Qumran archaeological site and its Dead Sea Scrolls, this group's worldview and doctrine has been spreading like cancer because this place is actually an old Essene library. The Essenes based their calendar on the pre-calculated Enochian solar calendar containing exactly 364 days in a year rather than the lunar calendar of the Torah that requires intercalations depending on the season of the barley. This strange love-affair with the book of Enoch and other mystical writings is well documented by author and researcher Gary Wayne. He notes:

> "[The Essenes] unaccountably considered themselves to be an Enochian Judaism sect descending from Enoch (the evil). They unaccountably cherished the serpent/dragon as an ancient symbol of the Essene Therapeutate heritage, the infamous White Snake Brotherhood of Egypt. Essenes further held the book of Jubilees, and anything to do with Enoch, in the highest regard. ... It was their peculiar practice to pray in the morning by turning themselves towards the sun, in defiant contrast and opposition to other Israelite sects, who prayed in the direction of the temple. ... Essenes were a vigorous sun cult that, according to Knight and Lomas, were an alliance of Enochian and Zadokite priests descending from the Melchizidek cult of Canaan. Essenes became known to history and legend as the Zadokites (Zedek the encoded sun god component of Melchizedek), Princes of Jerusalem who escaped to Europe after 70 C.E., forming the families that eventually founded the Knights Templar."[8]

Wayne's description of "Enoch the evil" is a reference to Cain's firstborn son of Genesis 4:17, the same man through whom the remainder of Cain's godless line would be spawned (not to be confused with Enoch the son of Jared of the "good" line of Adam). Even though Cain's lineage was destroyed during the flood, it is common for many occultic groups to claim both physical and spiritual descent from Cain, and in this case, Enoch, within their writings and traditions. For example, the "book of Enoch" found in Essenes' Dead Sea Scrolls library is no doubt a product of Enoch the evil, equipped with the aforementioned sun-based calendar that is in opposition to Moses and the Prophets. The Essenes were an active secret society of Jerusalem from at least the time of Ezekiel the prophet until they were disrupted by the Jewish-Roman wars sometime after AD 70, as Wayne noted. Of course, their legacy didn't end there. The Knights Templar, also called the *Poor Fellow-Soldiers of Christ and of the Temple of Solomon*, was a French military order of the Catholic church that was founded around 1119 under the guise of defending pilgrims on their way to Jerusalem. This European offspring of the Essenes is credited as introducing the first known fiat monetary system that would later inspire the lawless central banking systems of the world today.

The Essenes also held the Kabbalah as a sacred part of their mystical worldview, being inspired by a more Egyptian lineage of paganism.[9] As described in Chapter 2, the writings of the Kabbalah and the practices of its adherents, or Kabbalists, are diametrically opposed to the truth of the Word of

God. However, rather than simply being one book or one belief system, as many assume, the definition of *Kabbalah* varies depending on the sect or society describing it. The overarching theme of the Kabbalah is that it is a secret interpretation of the Hebrew Scriptures, or secret Torah, that with its supernatural knowledge makes it possible for people to access the power of God, thereby transforming themselves and the world around them.[10] One fundamental idea is that the written Hebrew Word of God must be approached exclusively as being metaphorical or allegorical because it was never meant to be understood literally. This doctrine thereby leaves the door wide open for "special" revelations about God, good versus evil, and the nature of the universe. Though Kabbalists falsely claim that their teachings originate with a number of righteous patriarchs including Abraham himself, there is evidence to support that this serpent-inspired lust for secret knowledge spread amongst the Hebrews during the reign of King Solomon. Therefore, though Kabbalah was highly revered by the Essenes, it was not unique to them. They simply played a major part in the dissemination of this occultic knowledge well beyond the first century through their direct influence in Europe after the Jewish dispersion by the Romans.

Depending on the lineage of its teachings, Kabbalah can be divided into three main categories: Judaic Kabbalah, Hermetic Qabalah, and Hollywood Kabbalah[11]—the latter of which has been instrumental in shaping the popular culture of Western countries in these last days. Adherents of Hollywood Kabbalah are often seen wearing a piece of red string around their wrists, which is a type of superstitious talisman that is said to repel misfortune brought about by the so-called *evil eye.* Hollywood Kabbalah was created by former insurance salesman Shraga Feivel Gruberger (1927–2013) who, after leaving his wife and eight children to marry his ex-secretary, changed his name to Philip Berg (Rabbi, or Rav Berg).[12] His system has since been adopted by multitudes of high-profile celebrities such as Madonna, Leonardo DiCaprio, Ashton Kutcher, and Gwyneth Paltrow along with millions of their respective fans.[13] It is not just Hollywood that is in bed with this Kabbalistic philosophy. Even high profile political figures such as Vladmir Putin[14] and celebrity journalists such as Tucker Carlson[15] have been pictured with the red string talisman publicly, though the lineage of their specific Kabbalah adherence is certainly up for debate. In his 2004 book *The Way to the Top,* Donald Trump recounts a specific dialogue with his "Kabbalah teacher" Eitan Yardeni[16]—an ordained rabbi who studied personally with the aforementioned Rav Berg.[17] As you can see, the mystical worldview of the Essenes was not unique to ancient times but has continued to manifest itself amongst the most powerful leaders and influencers within the prophesied Mystery Babylon system of today.

In addition to the Judaic mysticism of the Essenes, the other luciferian force behind the Jerusalem order's worldview can be found within the bull cult of Moloch (Molech), also referred to in the Bible as the star god of Remphan. This important occultic group was already introduced in Chapter 2 within the "star of David" discussion. Like the Essenes, the bull cult of Moloch was inspired from Egyptian paganism as is clearly evident by the actions of Aaron at the base of Mount Sinai where the people pleaded with him to make a golden calf to worship after Moses was assumed to be dead. Going forward in time to King Solomon, we see that this same bull cult of Moloch continued to plague the culture of Israel. Of Jerusalem's seven hills, the Mount of Corruption located east of Jerusalem and on the same ridge as the Mount of Olives bears its name from the idol worship practiced by Solomon. This is where he built altars to the gods of his Moabite and Ammonite wives, thereby desecrating, or corrupting, the mountain range as described in 1 Kings:

7 Then Solomon built a high place for Chemosh the abomination of Moab, on the hill that is east of Jerusalem, and for Molech the abomination of the people of Ammon.
8 And he did likewise for all his foreign wives, who burned incense and sacrificed to their gods.
(1 Kings 11:7,8).

This worship of the bull cult only intensified after Solomon's death and the division of United Israel into northern and southern kingdoms. While the South generally adhered to God's instructions, the North under Jeroboam's leadership immediately created golden calves at Dan and Bethel for the people of his kingdom to worship. Over time, this bull cult took on different names in both kingdoms and is the same god as Milcom, Chemosh, and Baal as described in various scriptures. At its core, the worship of Moloch required the blood of innocents, and especially children. Eventually, the South fell into the same level of idolatry as the North and in fact exceeded their wickedness as recorded by Jeremiah where he refers to Israel as "more righteous" than her sister (Jer. 3:7). At the height of its degeneracy, we read that Judah had become fully overtaken by the bull cult of Moloch, with the abominable practice of child sacrifice a key part of their culture:

"And they built the high places of Baal which are in the Valley of the Son of

Hinnom, to cause their sons and their daughters to pass through the fire to Molech, which I did not command them, nor did it come into My mind that they should do this abomination, to cause Judah to sin."
(Jer. 32:35)

The stronghold of this bull cult is built into the identity of the Valley of Hinnom. This was a place southwest of Jerusalem that was known for its dark history of child sacrifice to the Canaanite and Ammonite god Moloch and also associated with the concepts of Gehenna and hell in the Bible. How this bull cult originated in Jerusalem with its subsequent manifestations in modern Freemasonry is well-documented by Gary Wayne:

> "[There is a] striking similarity between Molech/Baal and the bull of Minos, who designed the legendary Labyrinth on Crete. ...[The] Canaanites actually believed they originally migrated from the island of Crete, likely bringing the bull cult of Atlantis with them that later became manifested in Baal and Molech. The connections become even clearer when you remember that Canaanite builder craftsmen commissioned by Phoenician King Hiram of Tyre to build the first Jerusalem temple believed they were direct blood descendants of (Masonic) craftsmen that built the ancient Mycenaean royal castles and Cretan villa palaces. ...This (Masonic) antediluvian legacy of builder priests survived throughout the epochs, eventually being inherited by the Gnostic Manicheans who worked their way secretly into Christianity as builder priests and architects of the Roman Collegia. The Gnostic Cistercian and Benedictine monks of celtic Christianity then inherited this same legacy, passing it on to the Mason guilds of Europe, which were later dominated by the Benedictine Templars and later passed on the builder priest legacy to Freemasonry."[18]

Wayne connects the Canaanites back to the legends of the bull cult that surround Crete and also the secret megalithic building techniques employed in Mycenaean architecture. According to Greek legend, only a giant had the strength to move the enormous boulders that made up the walls of Mycenae and Tiryns; and this creature is said to be a mythical Cyclopes, which is why this type of architecture is said to be "cyclopean", or of a giant creature with one eye. The Canaanites claimed to be descended from these cyclopean builders, and their boast of this secret knowledge apparently seduced both kingdoms of Israel to participate in the cult of Molech, among other abominable things. Of course, the promotion of Hiram King of Tyre within modern Freemasonry is well documented, and he is viewed as a significant figure in the lineage of the secret society. In other words, though the origins of the bull cult of Molech and child sacrifice can certainly be traced back to Egypt, it was the Canaanite sect that successfully infiltrated Hebrew culture even well after the fall of both kingdoms took place. That is why when we read Stephen the martyr's accusations against the Jerusalem order of the first century, he stated that the "tabernacle of Moloch, and the star of your god Remphan" were both a fundamental identity of those that were persecuting the saints (Acts 7:43). This identity still continues today.

Figure 11.5: "Offering to Molech" in *Bible Pictures and What They Teach Us,* by Charles Foster, 1897. This pagan god is usually depicted as a half-bull, half-man creature often referred to as the *minotaur* in various myths and legends. This cult of child sacrifice continues to manifest itself in the modern abortion clinics and contraceptive practices of Western countries.

In the midst of its bitter hatred and resentment of Christianity, early Judaism sought to memorialize this attitude by updating the teachings of its Talmud to better reflect how its practitioners should view Jesus and His ministry from generation to generation. Unlike the vast majority of non-Christian religions in the world that maintain a simplistic view of Jesus as being a good teacher, or perhaps a prophet, or a man of God, Judaism took a drastically different direction in describing the Son of God. When taking a look at their very own writings in a text called Gittin, an essay in *Seder Nashim* (the "Order of Women," which addresses family law), you will find an account of a man named Onkelos bar Kalonikos who himself wanted to convert to Judaism. It is explicitly described in Gittin that Onkelos used the sorcery of necromancy, or communication with the dead, in order to figure out if Judaism was the religion that he should adopt. The text then proceeds to describe that Onkelos raised three men from the dead: a man named Titus, another named Balaam which was the same one from the Torah that made Israel sin, and lastly, he fictitiously made contact with Jesus through necromancy. Onkelos asks all three men the same question: "Who is most important in that world where you are now?", that is to say, in their afterlife within hell. All three say that the Jewish people are the most important. In his perverted quest to know whether or not Judaism is the correct religion, Onkelos' follow-up question is presented three times: "Should I then attach myself to them here in this world?", that is to say, in the land of the living. Though this blasphemous story is pure fiction, this is what is written about Jesus in Gitten 57a:

> "Onkelos then went and raised Jesus the Nazarene from the grave through necromancy. Onkelos said to him: Who is most important in that world where you are now? Jesus said to him: The Jewish people. Onkelos asked him: Should I then attach myself to them in this world? Jesus said to him: Their welfare you shall seek, their misfortune you shall not seek, for anyone who touches them is regarded as if he were touching the apple of his eye.
>
> Onkelos said to him: What is the punishment of that man, a euphemism for Jesus himself, in the next world? Jesus said to him: **He is punished with boiling excrement.** As the Master said: Anyone who mocks the words of the Sages will be sentenced to boiling excrement. **And this was his sin, as he mocked the words of the Sages.** The Gemara comments: Come and see the difference between the sinners of Israel and the prophets of the nations of the world. As Balaam, who was a prophet, wished Israel harm, **whereas Jesus the Nazarene, who was a Jewish sinner,** sought their well-being."[19] [emphasis added]

The end of this passage includes the "Gemara" (the official "Oral Law" commentary) that poses a rhetorical statement, because both Balaam and Jesus suffered the same fate according to the words of Gitten. Such hatred, scorn, and diabolical ridicule is not found in any other religion like it is within Judaism and its Talmud. To teach that Jesus was (and still is) boiling in hell and covered with hot excrement because of being a sinner that mocked the sages (Jewish scholars and rabbis) of Judaism is a clear example of the culture that followed the first century Jerusalem order and the justification of its barbaric persecution of Christians. The subtle promotion of necromancy, a form of satanic black magic, within this text also shows why Jesus referred to the scribes and Pharisees of His day as having the devil as their father. As I described earlier, they were engaging in dark magic rituals and Kabbalistic teachings during the time of Christ, and the later canonization of this Gitten text demonstrates Judaism's love affair with mystical evil.

Always remember that the Babylonian Talmud is arguably the most revered and widely adhered to text in Judaism. The Torah itself is an afterthought in comparison along with the rest of the Tanakh (Hebrew Bible). That is why it is important to examine a few more thoughts in order to understand how the current Mystery Babylon, or Zionist, system operates and the underlying philosophy that has fueled the many crimes it has committed. In another text of the Talmud called Bava Metzia, and specifically 114a, there is a story of a man ("amora", or scholar) named Rabba bar Avuh that just so happens to stumble across Elijah the Prophet. In this chance meeting, Elijah is standing in a non-Jewish cemetery, and it is within this context that the narrative proceeds:

> The amora proceeded to ask Elijah a different question and said to him: Is not the Master a priest? What is the reason that the Master is standing in a cemetery? Elijah said to him: Has the Master not studied the mishnaic order of Teharot? As it is taught in a baraita: Rabbi Shimon ben Yoḥai says that **the graves of gentiles do not render one impure,** as it is stated: "And you, My sheep, the sheep of My pasture, are man" (Ezekiel 34:31), which teaches that you, i.e., the Jewish people, are called "man," **but gentiles are not called "man."** Since the Torah states with regard to ritual impurity imparted in a tent: "If a man dies in a tent" (Numbers 19:14), evidently **impurity imparted by a tent does not apply to gentiles.**[20] [emphasis added]

This is one of many places in the Talmud that puts Judaism's ethno-religious superiority on full display, referring to non-Jews as subhuman beasts rather than God's chosen sheep. The commentary here takes a verse from Ezekiel out of context to promote a specific agenda while ignoring multitudes of scriptures that came before it such as Exodus 22:21, which states, "You shall neither mistreat a stranger nor oppress him, for you were strangers in the land of Egypt." All cults and false doctrines are guilty of breaking the three laws of biblical interpretation, and this is a case in point. The manner in which

Judaism consistently twists the Bible carries this specific pattern of discrimination, segregation, and apartheid. That is why even before the events of October 7, 2023 and Israel's relentless genocide of the Palestinians, many people including a UN human rights expert had summarized the 1948 state's decades-long occupation of Palestine as being apartheid.[21] Though Israel is a secular state on paper, it is a perfect case study of what the teachings of the Talmud look like in practice when adopted by governmental leadership on a national level. Just look at the words of Sanhedrin 57a that align perfectly with the sentiment of Israel's current leadership, where it states, "With regard to bloodshed, if a gentile murders another gentile, or a gentile murders a Jew, he is liable. If a Jew murders a gentile, he is exempt."[22] In the mind of Judaism and its adherents, premeditated murder is permissible for a Jew to carry out against non-Jews. The Talmud takes this idea further in Yevamot 98a:3 by stating that "the offspring of a male gentile is considered no more related to him than the offspring of donkeys and horses",[23] which is to say that the children of non-Jews are to be compared with animals. It is this same doctrine that paved the way for the rise of atheistic communism together with the worship of government to be used as tools of the Mystery Babylon system to first overthrow and then afterwards control various regions of the world.

FROM ZIONISM TO COMMUNISM: THE ROLE OF KHAZARIA

The number one mass murder weapon in all modern history has been communism. Though difficult to find a reliable source or number, it could be conservatively estimated that well over 100 million people have been murdered since this particular system of government was first ushered in nearly 100 years ago in 1917. The problem is that, whether as a result of public or private schooling —it makes no difference—we have all been force-fed a false narrative of the major events of history and the true nature of Zionism, modern-day Israel, and Jerusalem's mysterious role on the world stage. Yet again, we have an inheritance problem. We have inherited lies about the Bible like I have already explained; but we have also inherited lies about the events of history in general. Hollywood, governments, the media, and institutions have given us Westerners (and indeed, the whole world) a controlled and twisted version of the events of the World Wars, the creation of communism as a form of governance, and the direct role of Zionism within all of history. With the full understanding of Zionist history, philosophy, and symbolism as thoroughly presented at this point of the book, it is now possible to revisit the rise of communism with a far more educated lens.

Let's first go back in history to the eighth century because even the most educated men fail to recognize a specific people group that was instrumental in carrying out modern communism within Russia. Let me stress this point again. If these things were simple to understand, the Bible would not have referred to Jerusalem as a *Mystery*. These things I am about to share with you have been purposely hidden from plain view through deception and trickery. If you decide to go down the rabbit hole even more outside of this book, you will clearly see the link between Mystery Babylon and Zionism but will also suffer a great deal from secular points of view that confuse true biblical Jews and pseudo-Jewish people groups. My biggest fault with much of the information out there on these conspiratorial themes is that people consistently fail to recognize that not everyone who calls themselves a "Jew" is a true Jew from the lineage of Abraham. From a spiritual standpoint, this truth is very clear, and Paul tells us:

28 "For he is not a Jew who *is one* outwardly, nor *is* circumcision that which *is* outward in the flesh;
29 "but *he is* a Jew who *is one* inwardly; and circumcision *is that* of the heart, in the Spirit, not in the letter; whose praise *is* not from men but from God."
(Rom. 2:28,29)

It is with these words from Paul that we can now proceed to uncover the little-known Khazar Kingdom, or Khazar Khanate, which was a major world empire that existed from AD 650–969 and located within the southeastern section of modern European Russia, southern Ukraine, Crimea, and Kazakhstan. Throughout history and to this very day, many self-proclaimed Jews actually originate from this *Judaized* Khazar kingdom and Japeth's son Ashkenaz, which Das, et al. demonstrated through scientific analyses and genomic research to be a people group of Irano-Turko-Slavic origin, rather than true Abrahamic origin.[24] This hidden history of the Khazar kingdom and its pseudo-Jewish identity is a topic that is often misrepresented and also erroneously dismissed as an anti-semitic conspiracy theory. In his recently translated work, *Two Hundred Years Together,* the Nobel Prize winner and Soviet-born author Alexander Solzhenitsyn explains this historical reality particularly well:

"...The Khazars [are an] ancient people of the Turkish race established in the region of the Low Volga since long. In the 6th century they founded a vast empire stretching from the Oural to Dniepr, which fell in the 10th century after their defeat by the prince of Kiev, Sviatoslav...Only the upper class of the

Khazars were of Hebraic descent, the tribe itself consisted of Turcs who converted to Judaism."[25]

Again, Turkish descent can be traced to Japheth rather than Shem. In the Bible, Turkey's identity is distinct from the Israelites, and locations such as Mount Ararat of Eastern Turkey are clearly referenced as belonging to a distinct kingdom and in close association with the kingdom of Ashkenaz as seen in Jeremiah 51:27. The *Jewish Encyclopedia Volume 4* itself also agrees, stating that these "Chazars" were "a people of Turkish origin whose life and history are interwoven with the very beginnings of the history of Jews of Russia."[26] In establishing the origins of these mostly non-Hebraic "Jews", their eventual settlement into Russia, and subsequent rise to political prominence, Solzhenitsyn goes on to explain:

> "The capital city of the Khazarian Khanate rose up starting 724 AD. The tribal princes of the Turkish Khazars (at the time still idol-worshippers), did not want to accept the Muslim faith, lest they should be subordinated to the caliph of Baghdad, nor Christianity, lest they come under vassalage to the Byzantine emperor; and so the clan went over to the Jewish faith in 732."[27]

A "khanate" is a tribal system of government under the rule of a khan, or king, that was unique to the nomadic Turkic and Mongol people groups of the Eurasian Steppe. That is why I referred to the Khazar Khanate as being *Judaized.* This people group mass converted to this form of religion for purely political reasons rather than spiritual; however, most people simply don't recognize the presence of this kingdom as playing a major role in world history nor the role of its descendants in establishing the Zionist state of Israel in modern times. The *Jewish Encyclopedia Volume 4* once again confirms these events as "a historical fact", stating, "From the work 'Kitab al-Buldan,' written about the ninth century…it appears as if all the Chazars were Jews and that they had been converted to Judaism only a short time before that book was written."[28] This people group is where the Yiddish language gets its origins,[29] borrowing a combination of Germanic, Slavic, and Baltic language words that were then phonetically expressed using Hebrew characters.

Figure 11.6: The Kingdom of Khazaria from about AD 650–969.

Before diving into Zionism more specifically, first understand that the historical narrative presented by Solzhenitsyn is not isolated folklore, but this "Khazar hypothesis" as it is commonly called has been fully supported through the empirical findings of genomic research, such as Eran Elhaik's work.[30,31] Recall that Shem is one of the three sons of Noah from which Abraham and the children of Israel originate. Elohim already told us well in advance of Japeth's infiltration into the dwelling places—the tents—of Shem in Gen. 9:27:

"May God enlarge Japheth,
And may he dwell in the tents of Shem;
And may Canaan be his servant."

This was the blessing and prophecy of Noah upon his son, Japeth, and it has now completed its course in these last days. One can be a Jew outwardly in name only but neither in true practice nor in genetic lineage. This is the mystery of Zionism and its entire movement, for it is within the mysterious Khazarian Kingdom that the origins of most of the world's Jewish identity can be traced. Perhaps one the very first and brave attempts at uncovering this truth through a modern academic lens was the work of Abraham N. Polak, a Professor of Medieval Jewish History at Tel Aviv University. His book *Khazaria* was published in 1944 in Tel Aviv and originally written in Hebrew. In

379

the introduction of this work, the Israeli historian explains the importance of Khazaria and his findings, declaring:

> "This book is the first attempt, not only in Hebrew, to comprehensively describe the history of the Kingdom of Khazaria and its Jewish character. In the quarterly 'Zion', devoted to the history of Israel, in the issue of Nisan 57011, I established for the first time the fact that this kingdom was not destroyed by the Rus in the 10th century AD, as previously believed, but only by the Mongols in the 13th century. This means that the period during which Judaism was the official religion of Khazaria lasted not 165-170 years, but about 440 years, and that throughout this time the kingdom was an important power. This fact, in itself, forces us to take a new approach both to the problem of relations between the Jews of Khazaria and other Jewish communities, and to the question to what extent the Khazar Jews should be considered the original source of that large Jewish community that existed in Eastern Europe from the 16th to the 19th century and whose members were commonly called *Ostjuden*. The descendants of this community, those who remained locally, those who emigrated to the United States and other overseas countries, and those who came to Israel, constitute today the overwhelming majority of the followers of Judaism. In any case, the existence of this community should be considered one of the most significant events in the history of the Jewish nation."[32] [translation mine]

As mentioned by Polak, 440 years was a significant amount of time for Judaism to take a firm hold of the culture of Eastern Europe. What this means practically is that while, yes, there are some true bloodline Abrahamic Jews that have been mixed into the overall movement, the origins of modern Zionism began with the sons of Japeth, especially within the regions of the Turks, Ashkenaz, and the Khazars (see Gen. 10:3). The "dwelling" in the tents of Shem component of Noah's prophecy is made obvious when understanding that this underlying Hebrew word means to reside and rest. This fulfillment is apparent in the forceful infiltration of Khazaria's descendants upon the land of Palestine, a land that these Turko-Slavic peoples did not truly originate from.

What does this information have to do with the Bolshevik Revolution (1917) and beginnings of communism worldwide? Well, only a few decades prior to the creation of 1948 Israel, this Judaized Khazar people group had become one of the most powerful commercial and political forces in Russia. As Solzhenitsyn describes:

"...The Jews of Russia at the beginning of the twentieth century still consti-
tuted nearly half of the Jewish population of the planet. This is to be remembered as an important fact in the history of Judaism."[33]

This population became problematic for the Russian Empire under the rule
of the czars. They perceived these so-called Jews to be a disruption to the
commercial and political infrastructure of Russia, so they implemented
various restrictions on how these Jews could engage in commerce and in land
settlement. These restrictions, often cited as the source of *pogroms* or attacks
against Jews, created a cultural dilemma of inequality in Russia. Eventually,
these policies led to the rise of Zionism as the Jewish people of Russia sought
for an identity and political voice in the country. Before this development can
be further dissected, however, we must understand the political and ideological forces that created the perfect atmosphere for the mixing of Zionism and
Communism in the late 1800s going into the twentieth century.

Simply look to the Father of Communism, and you will start to see the
connection. Karl Marx (1818-1883) was born into a non-practicing "Jewish"
household in Germany with rabbis on both his mother's and father's side of
the family.[34] His *Communist Manifesto* along with other works like *Das
Kapital* spelled out the framework and ideological battle plans that were first
used in Russia and later throughout the world. His work was extremely influential, to say the least. He inspired revolutionaries around the world that
aspired to topple existing power structures for their own private agendas while
publicly advocating for the freedoms and rights of the working class. One of
his primary sources of influence was none other than Zionist rabbi Moses
Hess who was also of German Jewish descent and a personal friend and
mentor of Marx. Hess laid the communist framework from which Marx
simply expanded upon. In describing their relationship, historian Tristram
Hunt writes:

"But one German who did associate with [Marx] was the so-called communist
rabbi, or, as Engels would describe him, the 'first Communist of the party':
Moses Hess... He shared with Marx an impressive Semitic heritage, with
rabbis on both parents' sides."[35]

Of course, this author commits the common error of automatically
assuming true Semitic origins simply because of the evidence of rabbinical
Judaism in Moses Hess' lineage. Hess, like Marx, was an atheist; and he
quickly moved on from his childhood upbringing in Judaism later in life,

regarding it as a "cadaver" in light of his discovery of the ethical philosophies that would later become his religion of communism.[36]

Though purposely obscure and mysterious, Zionism can and should be defined as the well-funded and organized political force from which modern communism was able to build and spread worldwide, beginning in Russia, with the chief aim of achieving statehood in the land of Palestine. It is not mere coincidence that Hess, Marx, and numerous prominent figures connected to the Russian Revolution were all of so-called Jewish identity and also pro-Zionist. This is how Solzhenitsyn describes the rise of Zionism less than two decades before the Bolshevik Revolution of 1917:

> "Inevitably, intermediate currents were to emerge. Thus the Zionist party of the left Poalei-Tsion ('Workers of Zion'). It was in Russia that it was founded in 1899; it combined 'socialist ideology with political Zionism.' …In spite of the disagreements that divided the Zionists among themselves, a general shift of Zionism towards socialism took place in Russia, which attracted the attention of the Russian government."[37]

The reason that the existing Russian autocracy at that time was getting nervous about this political force is because rather than seeking identity in Palestine or perhaps assimilation inside Russia, the Zionists were instead seeking autonomy and independent rule within Russia itself.[38] By its own nature, socialism leans towards revolutionary and extreme methodology to achieve its goals. As I mentioned, there were several reasons for this development, and it was not overnight. There was unrest in Russia that had been brewing since the late 1700s because of inequality in how Jews were treated with respect to "Pale of Settlement" laws that restricted them from certain commercial activities.[39] The government under the tsars before communism arrived proved ineffective. Solzhenitsyn recounts this condition of his country to us, stating:

> "The [Pale of Settlement] had only filled the Jews with anti-government bitterness and resentment; it had thrown oil on the fire of social discontent and had struck the Russian government with the seal of infamy in the eyes of the West. But let us be clear: this Russian Empire, with the slowness and sclerosis of its bureaucracy, the mentality of its leaders, where and in what way did it fall behind all through the nineteenth century and decades before the revolution? It had been unable to settle a dozen major problems affecting the life of the country."[40]

Zionism simply took advantage of a bad situation and poor leadership in Russia. Out of this power vacuum, well-financed and organized Zionist factions became united under the doctrines of Karl Marx, a man who himself was directly linked to and inspired by the Zionist movement. As a result, many millions of people died in Russia alone through the brutality of the Red Terror and the genocidal mass starvation brought about under Communism after the execution of Czar Nicholas II and the takeover of the Russian Empire in 1917. This is the kind of information you will never learn in history class. Generally speaking, the mainstream narrative surrounding the events of the early 1900s has always been unnaturally focused on feelings of sadness for the Jews who suffered during the Holocaust of Hitler. However, very few films, books, and media in general have ever paid that same respect for the victims of Communism during the Bolshevik Revolution and furthermore under Joseph Stalin. Tens of millions of civilians were starved, raped, tortured, and destroyed during Russian communism, and past the lies and propaganda that have clouded our judgment is the truth of Zionism's role in the whole orchestrated takeover. Communism in Soviet Russia committed far greater and far more heinous war crimes than Hitler's Germany. Yet, the media never manufactured the same outrage like it did against Nazi Germany.

The evidence for falsely so-called Jews and descendants of Khazaria being behind the rise of communism is overwhelming. The two primary men responsible for organizing and carrying out the Bolshevik Revolution were Leon Trotsky (Lev Bronstein) and Vladmir Lenin. Both were Jews. Trotsky and Lenin also identified as atheist communists like Marx and Hess before them. In his brief article about Trotsky's Jewish upbringing, David Shneer says, "Trotsky's most important biographer, Isaac Deutscher, coined the phrase 'non-Jewish Jew' to describe Trotsky and his generation of universalist thinkers."[41] The true reason that Trotsky and many other revolutionaries and communists are proudly hailed as "Jewish" figures by various rabbis and Jewish organizations is because of their connections to Zionism and the furthering of its agenda. They aren't the only Zionists worth mentioning. Have you ever heard of Genrikh Yagoda, Aaron Solts, Naftaly Frenkel, Yakov Rappoport, Matvei Berman, or Lazar Kogan? These were the commanders in charge of the gulags of Communist Russia according the groundbreaking three-volume series *Gulag Archipelago*.[42] In this work, Solzhenitsyn confirms to us that the aforementioned Genrikh Yagoda was not just a shadow government figure of communist Russia, but he was elevated to the highest position of "worship", with songs sung about him and pictures of him "hung in every barracks."[43] As director of the Soviet Union's security and intelligence agency, Yagoda alone was responsible for the murder of millions of people. Of course, this brutal executioner was born into a "Jewish" family along with all his other aforementioned accomplices. One of these was Aaron Solts, who was known as the conscience of the Communist Party and responsible for Soviet persecution of dissidents. Naftaly Frenkel was a Turkish-born Jew and high-ranking Soviet secret police official who was credited with organizing the structure of the Gulags, or forced labor camps. As a Bolshevik commander, Yakov Rappoport (Yurovsky) was the chief executioner of Emperor Nicholas II of Russia, his family, and four of their servants. He was raised Jewish and studied the Talmud at an early age.[44] In addition, Matvei Davidovich Berman was another Jewish revolutionary who became the head of the Gulag Soviet prison camp system from 1932 to 1937;[45] and finally, Lazar Kogan, the son of a wealthy Jewish merchant, was a high-ranking Soviet secret police official and deputy chief of the Gulag internment camps. Of course, Vladimir Lenin, the founder and first leader of the Soviet Union from 1917-1924, was himself of Jewish descent, having inherited Jewish ancestry through his mother's side.[46] Though this is certainly not an all-inclusive list, it is a well-documented fact of history that the Judaism-practicing descendants of Khazaria played an essential role in the Bolshevik Revolution and the brutality of communism that came afterwards. Jewish Zionists were put into the highest positions of power immediately after the communist revolution was successful in Russia as well as in the surrounding regions that later became incorporated into the Union of Soviet Socialist Republics (USSR). This revolution resulted in massive genocides including the artificial famine called the *Holodomor* from 1932 to 1933 that, according to a 2003 UN report, killed an estimated 7 to 10 million people, most of them Ukrainians.[47]

It is beyond the scope of this work to explain all of the connections of the Zionist movement to the other major events that followed 1917. One scheme worth mentioning was the West's financial backing of the wars that overtook the European continent. For example, the banking behemoth of the Rothschild family simultaneously funded communism in Russia and also fascism in Germany, thereby controlling both sides of the war in a similar fashion to what is taking place today with Iran against the West. Unbeknownst to most people, the Nazi party under Hitler worked closely with the Zionists through the Haavara agreement that allowed for goods and financial assets to be more readily transferred out of Germany and to Jews living in the land of Palestine.[48] Because of this Haavara agreement and other pro-Zionist developments throughout WWII, the Jewish population of the land of Palestine increased from 174,610 in 1931 (Hitler rose to power in 1933) to 449,000 in 1939.[49] In other words, one of the manufactured outcomes of WWII was the planned establishment of a Zionist Jewish homeland in the land of Palestine through the mysterious workings of powerful bankers, elites, and political forces that eventually made use of the UN in 1947-1948 to accomplish the agenda. This planned outcome was precisely what high-level Freemasons like Albert Pike had successfully predicted decades in advance. In more recent times, there have also been unmistakable connections between Zionism and various wars, color revolutions, and also the September 11, 2001 events that led to the invasion of Iraq and Afghanistan—both of which happened to be at war with Israel in the late 1990s. Honestly, a whole book could be dedicated to this topic of Zionism alone. There are so many more articles, reports, and connections that could be expanded upon concerning Jerusalem and its role as Mystery Babylon, but I think you are starting to get the clear picture. From the ancient origins of this woman riding the beast to her modern manifestation primarily through the lineage of Japeth, the antichrist teachings and philosophies of Judaism have had a colossal impact on the events of the world.

REVISITING DANIEL 11: THE KINGS OF THE NORTH AND SOUTH

Only with the true historical account now properly presented can we revisit the eleventh chapter of Daniel with any level of intelligence, for it is within the Khazarian homeland that we see clear connections to the narrative of the North versus the South. Again, this chapter is important to understand because the abomination of desolation is mentioned right in the middle of the events in this entire narrative. Though I once again admit that the details here are difficult to fully piece together, let us begin with this key verse:

"At the appointed time he shall return and go toward the south; but it shall not be like the former or the latter."
(Dan. 11:29)

The pronoun "he" is referring to the King of the North, who is about to enter into wartime hostilities with the King of the South, yet again. This event occurs just two verses prior to the abomination of desolation mentioned in Daniel 11:31, and that is why the identities of both of these kings must be heavily considered. What we are being shown is that in the end times, there will be an ongoing struggle between two geographical areas, their kings, and their armies. Knowing the true history of events leading up to the creation of 1948 Israel together with the recent initiation of Vladmir Putin's "special military operation" in Ukraine on February 24, 2022, the narrative has now become quite clear. The ancient struggle being presented to us is most likely referring to the long history of Khazaria's kings being at war against the kings of Russia.

Though it is difficult to ascertain all the facts in Daniel 11, it does appear to describe a chronology surrounding the rise of communism by the Khazars even to the recent Russian annexation of Crimea in 2014. When Daniel 11:29 says that "he" will go and "return" to the "south", it most likely refers to Putin returning to war against Ukraine and its Jewish President Voldymor Zelenskyy in 2022. Though not literally and geographically "south", Ukraine certainly fits the description since this ancient Khazarian region has always identified with the Judaism of the Southern Kingdom of Judah. Understanding that Daniel wrote his prophecies in code to purposely seal them up, his use of "south" is easily referring to this historical reality. Not only that but the "southern" Jerusalem Empire has been enabling the Zelenskyy regime in the form of billions of dollars in aid, military weapons, endless positive media coverage, and protection via North Atlantic Treaty Organization (NATO) allies. Before diving into more of the specifics, first consider what the passage says next:

30 "For ships from Cyprus shall come against him; therefore he shall be grieved, and return in rage against the holy covenant, and do damage. So he shall return and show regard for those who forsake the holy covenant.
31 "And forces shall be mustered by him, and they shall defile the sanctuary fortress; then they shall take away the daily sacrifices, and place there the abomination of desolation."
(Dan. 11:30,31)

Assuming that this last-days King of the North is unequivocally Vladmir Putin, the passage here is quite clear. Once he returns to go to war with the south at the "appointed time" of the end, there will be the arrival of ships "from Cyprus". What "Cyprus" really means in the Hebrew (Strong's H3794) is all islanders of the Mediterranean Sea located to the west of Israel. This word could therefore be interpreted to mean *western lands,* generally speaking. That being the case, it is obvious how Putin has been deeply enraged and troubled by the West's ongoing provocations in and around the Ukrainian-Russian border. From drone attacks, to naval ship bombardments, oil refinery explosions, various terrorist events inside Moscow, sabotages of the Russian-owned Nord Stream pipeline—the list of Western-backed attacks against Russia has been endless. In fact, Daniel's use of the word "ship" in Hebrew is likely another code word used to generally refer to military vessels and war machines of all kinds. That is exactly what we are witnessing on the world stage as the West continues to relentlessly ship in heavy artillery and weaponry into Ukraine.

One of the more difficult phrases to understand within this context is the "holy covenant." The underlying Hebrew words are exactly what you would imagine: "qodesh berit". Again, understanding that this is just another intentional code phrase used by Daniel, a holy "covenant" can refer to any military alliance that would be deemed as sacred and binding. Any interpretation involving a *religious* alliance would not make any sense here since the context is speaking strictly of wartime activity, with the abomination of desolation being the pinnacle of destruction. That is why I believe that the "qodesh berit" being referred to here is none other than the NATO military alliance of Western nations. Continuing with our interpretation, it says that Putin will do damage against NATO (the holy covenant) and that he will also show regard for those who "forsake" this NATO covenant. This prophecy became all the more apparent after Western media mocked Hungarian Prime Minister Viktor Orban as "auditioning for the role of Kremlin spokesperson"[50] due to his increasing number of peace talks[51] with Putin coupled with Hungary's disruption of NATO expansion,[52] even though it is a NATO member. Putin and Orban no doubt have arranged a closed-door agreement in light of the Prime Minister's forsaking of the "holy covenant" of NATO. Another such country is Turkey, who in spite of being a long-standing member of NATO since 1952, has also deviated from this covenant in recent times under the leadership of President Recep Tayyip Erdoğan. In a recent press release, Erdogan expressed his extreme displeasure regarding Israel's ongoing massacre of the Palestinian people after October 7th, stating that Turkey "must be very strong so that Israel can't do these ridiculous things to Palestine. ...Just like we entered Karabakh, just like we entered Libya, we will do [something] similar exactly to them."[53] Words like these are often disregarded by Western media as empty rhetoric, but they are not to be taken lightly due to the fact that Turkey boasts NATO's second largest military, with 447,000 personnel.[54] Also consider Erdogan's recent meetings with Putin together with the aforementioned prophecies of Kir (Isa. 22:6) and Meschech (Eze. 38:2) that both appear to be describing Turkey and its soldiers invading Israel. It now seems obvious that the Turkish president will continue to work directly with the King of the North in undermining Western power. Erdogan's words are also backed by the recent implementation of a Turkish trade ban on Israel that was announced in May 2024[55]—a ban that has been catastrophic for the small, import-heavy economy of Israel.[56]

Daniel 11:31 has already been interpreted in full detail within Chapter 6; however, we now have a far better understanding. In Chapter 7, I presented evidence from the end of Zechariah 5 that Vladmir Putin was likely involved with an arms transfer of at least one nuclear weapon to Iran in what will initiate the Great Tribulation period. Immediately before this event, Daniel 11:31 shows us that "he", that is to say, the King of the North, shall "muster" up "forces". The underlying Hebrew word for "forces" (Strong's H2220) here has the literal meaning of "arms", or military armaments. The Hebrew word (Strong's H5975) translated as "muster" in the NKJV simply means to set, to stand, or to take a stand. To be more exact, Daniel 11:31 is describing Putin's setting up of military arms, weapons, and equipment in his fight against the South and its Western backers. These words also echo the same idea presented in Chapter 7 and the "set up" of the abomination of desolation, indicating once again that Putin has most likely cut a deal with Iran to successfully defile the "sanctuary fortress" of Jerusalem—the current capital of the Khazarian Kingdom of the South that the Russian people have been at war with for many centuries now. At long last, you are now starting to see how all of the pieces presented in *Bible Prophecy Secrets* have nearly completed the entire prophetic puzzle of the book of Daniel.

It should also be emphasized that Vladmir Putin is currently the chairman of one of the most powerful, yet underrated, organizations in the world. When the scripture says that this King of the North will "show regard" for those who forsake the military alliance of NATO, by implication this also means that all *enemies* of NATO and the West will be allied together with him. Rather than taking time to discern every detail regarding the Kings of the North and South as presented throughout Daniel 11, it is only urgent to now consider the ten kings alliance that will rise up and overthrow the current Zionist world order. This organization is none other than the BRICS nations.

THE BRICS-10 ALLIANCE

Born out of the necessity to challenge the political and economic hegemony created by Jerusalem and her American and European guardians, four Foreign Ministers representing Brazil, Russia, India, and China met informally to discuss a more serious level of cooperation while attending the 2006 UN General Assembly in New York.[57] Due to the successful interaction between these countries, the first formal meeting was initiated just three years later. This event became the first annual BRIC Summit that took place in Yekaterin-burg, Russia, on June 16, 2009. This meeting would prove to be the first of many. Though the original acronym of this four-nation alliance was BRIC, this name was adjusted only a year later to include South Africa who had agreed to join the bloc in 2010. Since then, no other nations had joined the

BRICS alliance, that is, until something quite profound and biblically significant took place in 2023 that perfectly aligned the bloc of nations to Revelation 17 and the ten-kings prophecy.

My first major coverage of the BRICS alliance in relation to Bible prophecy was on an Overcome Babylon video released on Jul 13, 2023 entitled "EVERYTHING Changes September 2023: How Prophecy Unfolds".[58] In this video, I described various aspects of BRICS and predicted that they would be forming the prophesied ten-kings coalition of Revelation 17:16 during the upcoming 15th Annual Summit in Johannesburg, South Africa from August 22-24, 2023. My reason for making this prediction was based on the "time times and half a time" numerology presented in Daniel 7:25 and later repeated in Revelation 13:5. The idea was that, though this period of 3.5 years or 1260 days certainly had a separate context in the Bible, it could be theoretically added to March 11, 2020 as a starting point and then calculated to be August 23, 2023. I proposed that perhaps something should be expected during this date in August which also happened to perfectly coincide with the BRICS Summit that year. This is a good case study of how numerology presented in the Bible can have different outcomes. That is why I stated earlier in Chapter 6 that although the primary interpretation of the "2300 evening-morning" prophecy appears to have been already completed, perhaps we should still expect something to take place on June 28, 2026. Primary interpretations should always adhere to the three laws of interpretation, but sometimes "coincidences" in numerological developments do happen. Going back to the topic at hand, due to the BRICS' lack of expansion since 2010, Western media along with even the most well-versed analysts were quick to downplay the 2023 meeting since it appeared unlikely for anything major to take place. That is, of course, because many people failed to recognize the prophetic time clock of the 70th week of Daniel and the abomination of desolation prophecy. Ultimately, my prediction proved to be correct. Not only did South Africa proceed to invite roughly 70 heads of state to its 2023 Summit,[59] but the BRICS inner circle knew full well that some of these invitees were going to be granted membership during the same event. At the conclusion of this BRICS Summit, a press release on August 24th announced to the world that the bloc of nations had added Saudi Arabia, Iran, Ethiopia, Egypt, Argentina and the UAE to the roster,[60] bringing the total number of BRICS nations to eleven. However, these new nations would not be officially granted membership until the turn of the year on January 1, 2024.[61]

After thirteen years of apparent inactivity, this new BRICS alliance became the most remarkable anti-West geopolitical development ever witnessed in the last days. The fact that no North American, European, or pro-

West countries had ever been invited to BRICS is what made its presence on the world stage so captivating. Suddenly, however, the only thing that became very puzzling about it was the presence of eleven counties rather than ten, as prophesied in Scripture. This apparent contradiction vanished after the results of Argentina's November 2023 presidential election were announced. Javier Milei had successfully defeated the economy minister Sergio Massa on November 19.[62] Only six days later, Milei then visited the traditional *Once* Neighborhood in Buenos Aires, known for its significant population of Orthodox Jews, in order to participate in a *havdalah* ceremony and receive a special blessing from renowned Kabbalist, Rabbi David Pinto.[63] Then, a couple days later on Monday November 27, Milei arrived in New York City in his first official trip abroad as President-elect of Argentina in order to visit the tomb of a famous Jewish orthodox rabbi, Menachem Mendel Schneerson, in Queens while wearing a Jewish kippah and an all black outfit.[64] Milei's adoption of Judaism as a converted (or converso) Jew along with his vocal support for Israel has been very consistent since then. All of these public gestures cemented Argentina's pro-Israel and Zionist posture on the world stage with the arrival of the Milei presidency. It is no surprise then that Argentina withdrew from the BRICS-11 alliance exactly on December 29, 2023 just before the deadline of January 1, 2024 when full membership would have been granted.[65]

The official BRICS-10 alliance now consists of the original five along with Iran, Saudi Arabia, Ethiopia, Egypt, and the UAE. Of course, you now know full well what the presence of Iran within such an alliance truly means from a prophetic standpoint. You can also see how a large portion of this alliance now consists of Islam-adhering nations, further backing the aforementioned interpretation (Chapter 4) of a coming Muslim Mahdi that will destroy the West. Moving into the future, there is no doubt that more nations will continue to be added to the BRICS alliance in probably every annual summit from this point forward. It will eventually become the BRICS-20, BRICS-50, and so on. What is not entirely clear is if the prophecies of the abomination of desolation and destruction of Jerusalem *absolutely must* take place before more nations are added to the BRICS-10. The presence of the "ten horns" could be literally referring to an alliance with a cut off point of no more than ten nations; or, the language used in Revelation 17 could be referring to a figurative representation of power, in which there are ten core nations, or horns, of strength regardless of the exact number within the alliance itself. The latter idea makes sense because the G7 Nations of the West, for example, are currently the core group of Zionist power, though there are far more nations under the feet of the Whore than just these. Time will reveal when exactly the

BRICS will make their military move against Jerusalem. The likelihood that the flying scrolls from Shinar are launched against Israel is very strong before more nations are potentially added on January 1, 2025. Again, there is no accompanying numerology or supporting scripture to proclaim a particular date with any degree of accuracy. We do know that the abomination of desolation is already set up. We know that the ten-kings alliance is here. We know that there is currently a hot war in the Middle East. Nothing else hinders the Great Tribulation from commencing during any Hebrew winter time frame or a sabbath day during the winter from this point in history onward.

It must also be emphasized that the BRICS-10 along with its highest office of Chairman suddenly contains one of the most powerful positions on the world stage. The organization itself represents roughly 30% of the world's land surface and almost half of the world's population at about 45%. The two most populous nations on earth—India and China—along with three of the top five largest economies of Africa are also within this new geopolitical identity. The vast quantities of commodities, oil, and industry represented by the bloc of nations along with their New Development Bank and endless rumors of a coming gold-backed currency have made BRICS a true rival of the West and Jerusalem. The Chairman position itself is rotated on an annual basis, and the President of the country hosting the annual summit has historically been given this leadership role. As of January 1, 2024, the Chairman position has been granted to Vladmir Putin, making him one of the most powerful men during such a pivotal time in history. This King of the North has already been described directly in Daniel 11 with a strong correlation to the final verses of Zechariah 5. Now you will see how this same individual plays a major role in the "locusts" prophecy of the book of Joel, which is later repeated in the ninth chapter of Revelation.

THE LOCUSTS FROM THE SMOKE

It is with great excitement and also with dread that I will now explain to you the mystery of the locusts of Revelation. Most churches have been teaching for a long time that these locusts are literal creatures from the bottomless pit. They might be some sort of nephilim or supernatural creatures, some say, but I want you to pay attention to the first big clue that we are given for understanding this prophecy properly. Do the locusts come out from the bottomless pit? No. They come from the *smoke*. This is what we are told:

1 "Then the fifth angel sounded: And I saw a star fallen from heaven to the earth. To him was given the key to the bottomless pit.

2 "And he opened the bottomless pit, and smoke arose out of the pit like the smoke of a great furnace. So the sun and the air were darkened because of the smoke of the pit.

3 **"Then out of the smoke** locusts came upon the earth. And to them was given power, as the scorpions of the earth have power."

(Rev. 9:1-3) [emphasis added]

We already know that satan is in the bottomless pit. Yeshua made it abundantly clear that satan was bound because of the cross (Jhn. 12:31). When the bottomless pit is finally opened with a spiritual key, only then will satan be loosed exactly as described in this ninth chapter of Revelation. We are later told that satan is king over these locusts in Rev. 9:11. In other words, satan is about to be loosed, and out of the smoke of this event, he will begin to commandeer locust armies. In order to understand what these locusts *really* are it is of utmost importance that we adhere to our three laws of interpretation. Where else in the Bible have such things as this been spoken about? Where else does it speak of locusts like this? Once you answer this question, you will understand the true meaning of what John wrote down for us. Speaking of the destruction of the city of Nineveh in the ancient land of Assyria, this is what Nahum the prophet recorded:

15 "There the fire will devour you,
The sword will cut you off;
It will eat you up like a locust.
Make yourself many—like the locust!
Make yourself many— like the *swarming* locusts!
16 "You have multiplied your merchants more than the stars of heaven. The locust plunders and flies away.
17 "Your commanders *are* like *swarming* locusts,
And your generals like great grasshoppers,
Which camp in the hedges on a cold day;
When the sun rises they flee away,
And the place where they *are* is not known."
(Nah. 3:15-17)

We are being told that locusts are unjust merchants that take advantage of people. We are also being told that locusts are like commanders and generals of war. In other words, the Holy Spirit uses the word "locusts" to describe *people,* not nephilim or anything else. Interesting. Now let's take a look at what Proverbs 30 tells us. There is one particular place that speaks of four very wise creatures—the ant, rock badger, locust, and spider—that can be compared to the characteristics of people. In other words, some people are more like ants in their character while others have character traits that more resemble badgers. This is what Prov. 30:27 says regarding locusts: "The locusts have no king, Yet they all advance in ranks." This is a very interesting concept. Even though locusts do not have an organized central dictator or figurehead, they are able to work together to achieve a common end goal. Keep this idea in mind because as we look at what the prophet Joel tells us, everything will make sense. The entire context of Joel surrounds the coming Day of the LORD and the judgment of end-times Israel, which we know to be the scattered tribes throughout the world and especially in the West. Speaking of a great army of *people* unlike any other, this is what Joel tells us:

3 "A fire devours before them,
And behind them a flame burns;
The land *is* like the Garden of Eden before them,
And behind them a desolate wilderness;
Surely nothing shall escape them.
4 "Their appearance is like the appearance of horses;
And like swift steeds, so they run.
5 "With a noise like chariots
Over mountaintops they leap,
Like the noise of a flaming fire that devours the stubble,
Like a strong people set in battle array.
6 "Before them the people writhe in pain;
All faces are drained of color.
7 "They run like mighty men,
They climb the wall like men of war;
Every one marches in formation,
And they do not break ranks.
8 "They do not push one another;
Every one marches in his own column.
Though they lunge between the weapons,
They are not cut down.
9 "They run to and fro in the city,
They run on the wall;
They climb into the houses,
They enter at the windows like a thief.
10 "The earth quakes before them,
The heavens tremble;

The sun and moon grow dark,
And the stars diminish their brightness.
11 "The LORD gives voice before His army,
For His camp is very great;
For strong *is the One* who executes His word.
For the day of the LORD *is* great and very terrible;
Who can endure it?"
(Joe. 2:3-11)

These verses are describing the first part of the Day of the LORD—the thick darkness of the "evening" judgment. Notice the language speaking of burning with fire. This is exactly what we are told that the ten kings will do to Jerusalem. Notice the parallels between these verses and what we are told in Revelation 9—the noise like chariots, leaping like locusts, advancing in ranks like locusts. Notice the parallels to Matthew 24. Immediately after the abomination of desolation, the sun and moon will not give their light, and this is precisely what we are told here in Joel 2:10. If you are still doubting the connection between Joel and Revelation 9, these words from Joel 2:25 should seal the deal in your mind as Yehovah speaks of restoring His people during the second part of the Day of the LORD (the morning):

"So I will restore to you the years that the swarming locust has eaten,
The crawling locust,
The consuming locust,
And the chewing locust,
My great army which I sent among you."

There should be no doubt in your mind now that Revelation 9 and Joel 2 are speaking of the exact same event. Joel chapter one also has more verses speaking of the locusts and also their appearance having fierce lion's teeth just like Rev. 9:8 says. The only question that might remain is concerning the identity of who these locust armies of men are. I have already stated my case that I believe it is the armies of the ten kings, and especially the King of the North. Now see for yourself what Joel has already testified concerning this truth in Joe. 2:20 where he speaks of the judgment coming to its end:

"But I will remove far from you **the northern *army,***
And will drive him away into a barren and desolate land,
With his face toward the **eastern sea**
And his back toward the **western sea;**

His stench will come up,
And his foul odor will rise,
Because he has done monstrous things."
[emphasis added]

I have now stated and will restate my case that the northern army is in fact speaking of Russia being the head of a Russo-Chinese-Islamic alliance of nations. Of all of these nations, Russia has the most advanced nuclear capabilities and arguably the best trained soldiers. China is the manufacturing arm of this alliance because they have an extremely large and vast economy with countless factories that the West's backstabbing leadership had purposely outsourced to them. The Islamic nations have the oil and other resources needed to make the alliance complete. Overall, it is the northern armies of the Russians that will absolutely crush, devastate, and conduct monstrous crimes against all of the sinners of the Western nations.

More specifically, however, the words "eastern" and "western" sea provide the major clue as to *where* this northern army will be primarily attacking and deploying its ground forces. If this verse were somehow speaking of historical "Israel" (Israel and Judah), then it would not make sense. From a geographical standpoint, the only sea in the ancient land of Israel was the Mediterranean to the west, and therefore this statement cannot somehow be applied to some historical judgment that occurred in ancient Israel's past. The Mediterranean and the Jordan River were always the borders of the land, and even during the peak of expansion under King David, the Euphrates River was the eastern border (1Ch. 18:3). Of course, Joel 2:20 is perfectly embodied in the classic patriotic song "America the Beautiful" by Katherine Lee Bates (1893) where the famous phrase "from sea to shining sea" is used to describe America's glory. That's right. Joel was speaking directly against America and her Atlantic and Pacific Oceans, or seas. Bearing these things in mind, we now have a better idea of the sequence of events after the abomination of desolation. Once Jerusalem is first destroyed, we can expect a sword to be sent to all the nations, especially America; and this is exactly what Jeremiah foretold:

"For behold, I begin to bring calamity on the city which is called by My name, and should you be utterly unpunished? You shall not be unpunished, for I will call for a sword on all the inhabitants of the earth," says the LORD of hosts. (Jer. 25:29)

In addition to this verse from Jeremiah, we can now look back to Daniel 11 to further confirm the King of the North's troop movements after the abomination of desolation. Daniel states:

40 At the time of the end the king of the South shall attack him; and the king of the North shall come against him like a whirlwind, with chariots, horsemen, and with many ships; and he shall enter the countries, overwhelm them, and pass through.
41 He shall also enter the Glorious Land, and many countries shall be overthrown; but these shall escape from his hand: Edom, Moab, and the prominent people of Ammon.
(Dan. 11:40,41)

We are now at the time of the end where the King of the South (Ukraine) has attacked but failed miserably. The King of the North is about to rise up and overthrow "many countries" with his armies, including the "Glorious Land"— a likely reference to end-times America, rather than 1948 Israel as many assume. This concept is repeated in the words of Jeremiah, when he wrote, "Behold, the noise of the report has come, And a great commotion out of the north country, To make the cities of Judah desolate, a den of jackals" (Jer. 10:22). Remember, the King of the North's armies are Yehovah's armies. They are not acting out of their own free will. They are doing our Father's will. That's why the call to action in the book of Joel is to repent, fast, call a sacred assembly and weep for our personal sins and repent of them. As I proposed in the original edition of this book, the words of Joel 2:15 could be a hidden reference to the final Yom Kippur (Day of Atonement) immediately before the abomination of desolation occurs. I will explain this concept more in the next chapter and the 144,000 that are sealed on their foreheads. These will be protected from the armies of Joel's prophecy. For now, the bottom line is that we need to repent for not following Christ with a pure heart and actively observing Yehovah's Torah. Time is absolutely of the essence, and the locusts are now rising up together to take down the West in such an atrocious manner that will never again be witnessed in all of human history.

Satan is about to be loosed from the bottomless pit. He is going to commandeer the armies of the ten kings that are described as swarming, chewing, and devastating locusts. They are going to burn, kill, destroy, and rape everything in their path. This is why Yeshua used the phrase *great tribulation* to describe this time period. It will be a time of extreme devastation. Once they are done with their preemptive, tactical nuclear strikes, the locusts will simply march into all of the major cities and places that they have been commanded by God to go. This is what they are commanded to do in Rev. 9:5:

"And they were not given *authority* to kill them, but to torment them *for* five months. Their torment *was* like the torment of a scorpion when it strikes a man."

It is my understanding that the collective West will be so weakened, caught off guard, betrayed from within, and devastated from tactical nuclear warfare that the Russian alliance will simply walk into these Western nations and take over. They will set up their central command quickly and swiftly; and a completely unorganized and disoriented Western military will be unable to do anything about it. Concentration camps and prisons will be established. Perhaps it is during this five-month period of time that the locusts will inflict their torture upon all civilians and opposition who do not have the mark of protection from the Most High God on their foreheads. Another interpretation could be that the lasting effects of nuclear war could be the torment of the locusts for five months, but based on my research, I doubt this is going to be the case. The "nuclear winter" narrative has been greatly exaggerated by Western media. The torture will most likely be prison camps and concentration camps under the authority of the newly released satan from the pit. He will perform all manner of signs and lying wonders to deceive the nations, and it is during the short period of his reign that the mark of the beast will be implemented in order to buy and sell. All tribes, nations, and tongues will be subjected to this final satanic new world order of the ten kings. Whether through the disguise of a pseudo-alien invasion, or some sort of dark magic ritual, satan will be ushered in as a manifested ruler on the world stage. Always remember that this reign is short. It is described as "one hour" in Rev. 17:12. Its persecution will be enormously intense, but a remnant will survive. The burning question is, who, exactly, is going to be a part of that remnant?

The answer can be discovered in the next two chapters.

Secret V:

How to Overcome These Evil Days with Faith

"Now faith is the substance of things hoped for, the evidence of things not seen."
- *Hebrews 11:1*

Chapter 12
Yeshua's 144,000 Firstfruits and Luke 21:36

The Bible is a book of harvests. Much of the symbolism, idioms, and cultural nuances of the Hebrew men and women of the Scriptures revolve around the practices of agriculture, agricultural products, and the intimate experiences of how the farmland of Israel has been managed from antiquity. Understanding the agricultural cycles of this land is foundational to understanding all secrets of Bible prophecy. This reality is precisely why so many people simply don't understand the deeper meanings of the Word of God. The past hundred years or so since the Industrial Revolution have created a completely unique time in history where people are more disconnected than ever before from farming practices in general. To make matters worse, very few have ever traveled to or taken the time to research how agriculture works in the land of Israel. If that's you, don't worry. It is actually quite simple to understand these things.

This chapter is dedicated to helping you understand why Yeshua referred to His 144,000 chosen people as *firstfruits* of a harvest; and we will also explore exactly what harvest He was speaking of. Once you understand these agricultural nuances, you will be able to see the bigger picture of what prophecy speaks of and precisely what you can do to be ready for all these events that will very shortly come to pass. Get ready to overcome the grave evil of these last days with faith, hope, and unfailing love.

THIS INFORMATION WILL CHANGE YOUR LIFE

I have already demonstrated to you that we are without a doubt living in the last days prophesied about repeatedly in the Scriptures. We are in the 70th shabua of Daniel, and we are running out of time to take action on the information I am about to share with you. Remember, Daniel specifically told us that all vision and prophecy would be "sealed up" or "finished" by Abib 2045. We need to have our eyes and ears open concerning the 144,000 of Revelation chapters 7 and 14. Who are they? Where are they? And what is the criteria by which they will be selected? First, you must consider carefully the words of Yeshua during His discourse about the abomination of desolation:

"Watch therefore, and pray always that you may be counted worthy to escape all these things that will come to pass, and to stand before the Son of Man." (Luke 21:36)

The information in this chapter will allow you to finally obey this commandment from Yeshua with your eyes and ears opened to know what He truly meant. Once you understand the things that I am going to share with you in this chapter, you will understand *why* Yeshua told us to pray that we are "counted" in order to "escape" and "stand" before Him. You will have a very clear idea of what He was actually talking about here because it applies to a select group of believers. However, the opportunity is only available for a very limited time only. The opportunity *will* be expiring extremely soon. Don't forget to share this book with as many people as you can while it is still daylight.

Now that we have completely dissected the prophecy of Daniel's 70 weeks found in chapter 9 of his book, only a couple mysteries remain. Remember that we were told at the end of Daniel 9:24 that one of the final events of the age will be "...to anoint the Most Holy." Seventy shabua have been determined in order for various things to take place and specifically the anointing of the *qodesh qodeshim* as it says it in the Hebrew. We briefly discussed this concept in Chapter 2, and these are in fact the 144,000 Israelites of Revelation.

REVELATION 7

Let's visit this chapter of Revelation to get deeply acquainted with what John recorded for us:

1 "And after these things I saw four angels standing on the four corners of the earth, holding the four winds of the earth, that the wind should not blow on the earth, nor on the sea, nor on any tree.
2 "And I saw another angel ascending from the east, having the seal of the living God: and he cried with a loud voice to the four angels, to whom it was given to hurt the earth and the sea,
3 "Saying, 'Hurt not the earth, neither the sea, nor the trees, till we have sealed the servants of our God in their foreheads.'
4 "And I heard the number of them which were sealed: *and there were* sealed an hundred *and* forty *and* four thousand of all the tribes of the children of Israel."
(Rev. 7:1-4)

This same passage then goes on to number twelve thousand people from the tribes of Israel beginning with Judah and ending with Benjamin. There are a few nuances in Rev. 7:5-8 worth mentioning but not spending too much time on. First, Manasseh is counted and later Joseph is also counted. We can therefore conclude that Joseph is synonymous with Ephraim. Also worth noting is that the tribe of Dan is not mentioned at all. We essentially only have twelve of the thirteen tribes in total (if you count Joseph twice as Ephraim and Manasseh you will get thirteen). Some people cherry pick this verse to come up with strange teachings about Dan, but if you look over at Ezekiel 48:32, Dan is going to have his own gate in the New Jerusalem, thereby indicating that this tribe was never lost or done away with, as some falsely teach.

Before looking at Revelation 14, we need to understand a few key concepts from the first four verses of Revelation 7. First, what is the sealing on the foreheads? We already understood the mark of Yehovah versus the mark of the beast in Chapter 10 within the context of the 1000-Year Reign. I have also alluded to this concept throughout this book. For clarity, all we need to do is search earlier in the book of Revelation for the answer. Recall that the book Revelation was originally sent out as seven letters to seven specific churches from John's prison cell on the Island of Patmos. One of those recipients of this letter was the literal, physical congregation of Philadelphia. Just like all the churches of Revelation, this one represents specific qualities that are the defining characteristics of a group of believers. In other words, the seven churches can be understood as seven different personalities. Throughout my life, I have found myself drifting into each personality type of the seven churches. In my younger days of mainstream Christianity, I was much like Laodicea, thinking I was spiritually rich but not realizing how poverty-stricken I really was. Later in life when I discovered the necessity of obedience to Torah, I found myself identifying with the church of Ephesus. Because of my overemphasis on performance and good works, I had forgotten my first love, Yeshua, and suffered a wide variety of consequences. I can honestly say that I am finding myself identifying more and more with the church of Philadelphia nowadays; and this is the church that every single one of us should be absolutely striving to emulate. Of all the churches, Philadelphia had nothing wrong with it. They were only told to persevere. They were only commanded to keep doing what they were already doing. Let's talk about exactly what made these believers so great. The answer is found in these words of Rev. 3:8:

"I know your works. See, I have set before you an open door, and no one can shut it; for you have a little strength, have kept My word, and have not denied My name."

They had a little strength; they maintained obedience to the Torah and the Gospel; and they were openly proclaiming Yeshua's name before men. This is exactly what I have been presenting throughout this book. Keeping His word is far more than head knowledge; it is practicing all of the words that have been commanded in the Torah, the Prophets, and the Gospel. The one completely mistranslated and overlooked quality of Philadelphia is the fact that they had a little *strength.* This word *strength* is not translated correctly in most Bibles like the NKJV that I have been quoting throughout this book. However, the Tree of Life Version translates it correctly as *power.* A closer look at this word *doo-nam-is* (Strong's G1411) reveals that it has to do with the power for performing miracles, among other things. In other words, these believers were abiding in the Holy Spirit and exercising the miraculous power of God in their lives. They were performing healings, casting out demons, speaking in tongues, and displaying signs and wonders in their lives in order to confirm the message of the Bible to the lost and dying world around them. Notice that this is the very *first* thing that Yeshua said He liked about this church! It was the first thing on His list of positive compliments; and this is the *only* church that He ever mentions exercising His miraculous power. This is the secret of the Great Commission. This is what Yeshua always wanted His people to do, just like it says in Mark 16:15-18; these are the signs that Paul and all the apostles were performing throughout the book of Acts as they traveled around the world.

The power of the Holy Spirit is the sure sign that someone identifies as a member of the church of Philadelphia. Is that you? If it isn't, then pray and ask for your eyes to be opened to the power of the Holy Spirit. So many false teachers have been saying that these kinds of signs were "done away with", and many have taught that these things were only for the first century church so that the Gospel could spread more quickly. These false teachings have castrated the faith and power of so many believers for hundreds of years now. Rise up and claim the miraculous power of God in your life, right now! Don't wait any longer. If you are not familiar with the power to cast out demons and perform healings, you must ask sincerely in prayer. The secret is that you must absolutely abide in Yeshua. Become completely and utterly humble in His sight while renouncing with your lips any and all evil in your life, past and present. Once you renounce sin, thereby canceling any legal access or open doors in your life to the devil, you should proceed to cast out any and all unclean spirits by name. Pride, addiction, lust, greed, procrastination, occultism—these are just some spirits that must be cast out by their name. It is within this position of total submission to God where you will discover the power of the Holy Spirit (James 4:7). Look at the promise that Yeshua gives to believers like Philadelphia in Rev. 3:10:

"Because you have kept My command to persevere, I also will keep you from the hour of trial which shall come upon the whole world, to test those who dwell on the earth."

Doesn't this sound familiar? The *hour* of trial. This is the exact same wording we have been reading over and over again speaking of the destruction of Mystery Babylon when the ten kings finally rise up and burn her with fire. Her destruction will arrive in one hour. What Yeshua is telling us is that those who are members of Philadelphia will be kept from the hour of trial that everyone else will have to go through because they denied God's power. There are only a handful of ministries out there that do practice the Torah and also teach the Gospels, but nearly all of them deny the miraculous power of God. By default, they are going to have to go through the Great Tribulation just like everyone else will. Become a member of the church of Philadelphia! This appears to also be the same group of people that Peter spoke of when he explained the "prophecy" of Jesus' transfiguration, stating, "And so we have the prophetic word confirmed, which you do well to heed as a light that shines in a dark place, until the day dawns and the morning star rises in your hearts" (2Pe. 1:19). The dawn of this prophetic day is coming to pass very soon, and God's glory will rise in the hearts of His 144,000. These will come in the spirit and power of Elijah upon the earth to restore all things (Mat. 17:11). Look what else Yeshua promises to the church of Philadelphia (and *only* to this church) in Rev. 3:12:

"He who overcomes, I will make him a pillar in the temple of My God, and he shall go out no more. **I will write on him the name of My God** and the name of the city of My God, the New Jerusalem, which comes down out of heaven from My God. **And *I will write on him* My new name.**"
[emphasis added]

This is the only church that receives the promise of the name *Yehovah* being written *on them*. Therefore, we can conclude that being kept from the hour of trial and having the imprinted name of *Yehovah* on the forehead are the distinct blessings of the church of Philadelphia. It also just so happens that both of these things are true of the 144,000. They will be protected from the five-month torment of the locusts as stated in Rev. 9:4; and they will not be thrown into the great tribulation of Russian concentration camps and gulags like the rest of the believers who did not get themselves ready in advance. Sadly, most people will suffer tribulation because the whole point of tribulation is to refine God's people like gold and test them through the fire of persecution. The wicked will also be judged severely, of course. With God's judgment arriving soon, one of my regular prayers has been that I am worthy to be counted among the 144,000 Philadelphians, and you should be praying this, too!

The next question we should be considering is the timing of when the sealing will take place. It is going to happen very soon and not on any ordinary day. The way the Greek is translated at the very beginning in Rev. 7:1, it appears to say that *after* the four horseman of the apocalypse and the first six seals—*only then* does John see the vision of the 144,000. This is not the case. The words *And after these things* ("kai meta tauta"; Strong's G2532, G3326, and G5023, respectively) can also be translated to say "And with these things". In fact, the word "meta" is used much more often to say "with" (345 times in NT) than it is "after" or "afterwards" (88 times and 4 times, respectively, in NT);[1] so we can easily say that the sealing of the 144,000 can take place at any time *within* the first six seals of the book of Revelation. Again, the translators simply did not understand the prophetic time clock of Daniel. They were translating these words sort of randomly, without understanding the various secrets of Bible prophecy like you do. Immediately before the sealing takes place, the angels are literally holding back the wind from blowing. Nothing is allowed to be harmed until the 144,000 are sealed. Now that you understand the abomination of desolation prophecy better than 99% of people out there, you know what is taking place here. Why would these believers be sealed *after* the abomination of desolation takes place? Why would they be sealed *after* the great tribulation begins?

They won't.

They will be sealed before nuclear warfare breaks out and before satan is loosed from the bottomless pit.

REVELATION 14

Let's now take a look at Rev. 14:1-5 for additional clarity:

1 "Then I looked, and behold, a Lamb standing on Mount Zion, and with Him

one hundred *and* forty-four thousand, having His Father's name written on their foreheads.

2 "And I heard a voice from heaven, like the voice of many waters, and like the voice of loud thunder. And I heard the sound of harpists playing their harps.

3 "They sang as it were a new song before the throne, before the four living creatures, and the elders; and no one could learn that song except the hundred *and* forty-four thousand who were redeemed from the earth.

4 "These are the ones who were not defiled with women, for they are virgins. These are the ones who follow the Lamb wherever He goes. These were redeemed from *among* men, *being* firstfruits to God and to the Lamb.

5 "And in their mouth was found no deceit, for they are without fault before the throne of God."

The first thing to notice is that the seal on the forehead of these saints is indeed the very name of Yehovah. This unique promise to Philadelphia is once again confirmed here. If you are still skeptical as to whether or not you and I can be qualified or should be praying to be counted as the 144,000 saints, the words of this passage should erase all doubt. Remember what Yeshua told us in Luke 21:36, and notice that these 144,000 are *standing* before the throne singing a new song. Yeshua told us to pray that we would escape and *stand* before Him. The 144,000 are standing in His presence.

At this moment in time, I'm not sure if this could be considered some sort of a *rapture* event. Do these 144,000 people die and go to heaven? Are they "raptured" into heaven like Enoch was to never again come back to Earth? I think I might have the answers to these questions and will explore them with you later in this chapter. For now, understand that it is a blessing to be counted among these saints. We should make it our sincere prayer to be counted among them!

The next concept we will focus on is *redeemed* (Rev. 14:3; Strong's G59), which simply means that these 144,000 already belonged to Yeshua. They have already been purchased. All He is doing is simply redeeming what is already His. Therefore, these 144,000 are not simply genetic, bloodline descendants of Abraham like I was falsely taught in Protestant church circles. These are born-again believers that have made Yeshua the Lord of their lives. I was also falsely taught in mainstream churches that these people are most likely little male children because the word *virgins* (Rev. 14:4) indicates that they have never had literal, physical intercourse with women. The reason people gravitate towards this understanding is because they are trying to examine these words very literally. I am also going to do the exact same thing so that you can see just how foolish this approach is. To unpack the true meaning of Rev. 14:4, you simply have to take a really close look at the word *virgin* in both the Hebrew and Greek languages using our three laws of interpretation. When you do this, you will find that the word *virgin* is always used by the Holy Spirit from cover to cover to refer to a *woman* that has never been married before to any man. It does *not* refer to children whatsoever or even men. It is always referring to a young virgin woman, or maiden, that is of marriageable age and that has not had sex. Therefore, if we make the mistake of interpreting these verses literally, we must conclude that the 144,000 are only and exclusively women in a state of literal virginity. Just for fun, if you then take this literal understanding and translate the Rev. 14:4, this is what it would say: *"...not defiled with women, for they are unmarried women."* This phrase is ridiculous, isn't it? The true meaning of the word *virgin* (Strong's G3933) is explained quite well in the BLB entry under the Outline of Biblical Usage. It states that a *virgin* is anyone "who has abstained from all uncleanness and whoredom attendant on idolatry, and so has kept his chastity."[2] This is a simple matter of common sense. This verse is actually talking about a spiritual condition and *not* a physical one. This verse is speaking of spiritual adultery; spiritual whoring; spiritual fornication. It is those people that have kept themselves from any sort of idolatry that are therefore eligible to be considered one of the 144,000.

But, you might be wondering, "Then why does it say *defiled with women?"*

All you need to do is look up all of the places where women are mentioned in the book of Revelation itself, and you will have the answer. You will find that there are four women total. Two are evil, and two are good. The first one is Jezebel, and she is foundational for understanding the mystery of spiritual virginity. Yeshua says this:

20 "Nevertheless I have a few things against you, because you allow that woman Jezebel, who calls herself a prophetess, to teach and seduce My servants to commit sexual immorality and eat things sacrificed to idols.
21 "And I gave her time to repent of her sexual immorality, and she did not repent.
22 "Indeed I will cast her into a sickbed, and those who commit adultery with her into great tribulation, unless they repent of their deeds."
(Rev. 2:20-22)

Now, let me ask the obvious question. Why would Yeshua take the time to write a letter to this church called Thyatira if they were openly having sex orgies with a false prophetess woman as if it were Sodom and Gomorrah at high noon? Again, Yeshua is not speaking of literal, physical acts of sexual intercourse. He is speaking of spiritually corrupt doctrine that has been mixed with idolatry and paganism. One clear example of this in our modern day context is the doctrine of Ellen G. White and the Seventh Day Adventists. Sure, they keep the seventh-day Sabbath. They also do a few other things that someone could consider biblical and Torah observant, but they don't keep the Feasts of the Most High. White also added numerous restrictions to the Word of God such as having no meat whatsoever, coffee, spices, mustard, wine, and these sorts of things. She falsely predicted that Christ was going to return in the year 1850 and that her followers would only have a few months to prepare for His second coming to earth.[3] They teach that Yeshua is not God in the flesh but that He is Michael the Archangel. They teach this lie because, according to the SDA, since Yeshua has a body, He cannot be omnipresent (present everywhere) like Elohim. In fact, they are extremely anti-Elohim, teaching that the one true plural God of the Bible is actually separate persons and not truly one. The list of doctrinal errors and false prophecies of both the Millerites and Ellen G. White goes on and on. Therefore, just like Yeshua said, eating dinner with folks from the SDA and allowing them to pray over the meal is to eat things sacrificed to another god. If it's not the Jesus of the Bible, then it's an idol. Much of the same anti-trinitarian beliefs also exist in the Mormons, Jehovah's Witnesses, and various Hebrew Roots ministries.

The main point is that though there are some humble and well-meaning people in these churches, they are all still guilty of committing the sexual immorality of mixing God's Word with the doctrine of devils and the Jezebel spirit. That's precisely what Yeshua was speaking about to Thyatira; and that's why He took the time to instruct John to write them a letter. A few members of this church weren't too far gone, and He even mentioned that He liked their last works. They simply needed to repent and get rid of the false doctrine, otherwise "great tribulation" would overcome them (Rev. 2:22). A state of spiritual virginity and purity means that there is no intercourse, or seed, from any outside source that is polluting the Truth of the Word of God. Keep that in mind as we move forward.

The next woman of Revelation is Israel, who is mentioned in Rev. 12:1 as the woman giving birth to the Messianic Savior. Before we talk about the third woman, the fourth woman mentioned is the Bride of the Lamb, who is referred to as Yeshua's "wife" in Rev. 21:9. In fact, all of Revelation 21 provides the amazing conclusion of prophecy where we see the New Jerusalem coming down from heaven and eternal peace being established.

Now, let's take a closer look at the third woman. This is the harlot riding the beast. This is Mystery Babylon. We have already discussed this woman in great detail, but just remember these words from Rev. 17:5:

"And on her forehead a name *was* written:
MYSTERY, BABYLON THE GREAT, THE MOTHER OF HARLOTS AND OF THE ABOMINATIONS OF THE EARTH."

This woman also had a "seal" on her forehead kind of like the mark of Cain—the mark of sin. In other words, every single thing pertaining to idolatry and all spiritually disgusting, despicable things are connected to Jerusalem and its daughters like the United States and the petrodollar. The pride of life, money, sex, big homes, cars, fame, and Hollywood—all of these things originate from the system created by Mystery Babylon. The 144,000 have not mixed themselves in any of the idolatry whatsoever that has been pushed by the system. These 144,000 have rejected the system and all of its mottos, slogans, values, and ideologies. Ideas like *the pursuit of happiness, get rich or die trying,* and *time is money* are dead to these saints. They have rejected the mainstream mentality imposed by the system. They opted for a completely different way of life.

Now you know what it means to be a spiritual virgin. There should be no infiltration in your life at all by the enemy. Whether it's false doctrine about the Bible or strongholds of the enemy, there should be nothing hindering your ability to follow Yeshua wherever He goes. I will add one more thing. Consider these words of Mark, when he writes, "Now when *He* rose early on the first *day* of the week, He appeared first to Mary Magdalene, out of whom He had cast seven demons" (Mark 16:9). Whenever I used to read this verse I would think to myself, "Wow, poor Mary. She must've had a tough life. Seven demons. Man, that's rough." As of the time I am writing this book, I can tell you with Yehovah as my witness that I have casted out over forty demons from myself and over twenty from my wife (but she and I have both lost count). Regarding my wife, she casted many of them out herself. I also "self-casted" demons from my temple but recruited her help for several of them. I have also had the privilege of casting out demons from many other people and have learned tremendous truths of the Bible that many who simply have a form of godliness will never understand (see 2Timothy 3:5). Now, have you ever wondered why it is recorded by Mark that Mary had *seven* demons? How did they know the exact number? As I mentioned before, it is because you must call them out by name. For example: "Spirit of pornography, I cast you out in the name of Yeshua!" We already discussed casting out the Covid-19 demons of fear, infirmity, and death. There are many more. Prayerfully consider which enemy strongholds exist in your life and cast them out by name with authority. There is no such thing as a *stubborn* demon. The only problem that hinders people from experiencing complete deliverance from addictions, anger, sinful behaviors, vices, generational curses, and all compulsive thoughts or behaviors is that they have not fully and completely submitted themselves to God in specific areas. It's really that simple. The apostle James gave us this formula for spiritual victory and entering into a state of complete virginity, when he wrote, "Therefore submit to God. Resist the devil and he will flee from you" (James 4:7).

The formula begins with submitting to God. Confess whatever it is that needs to be confessed. Admit with your mouth to God that you hate the specific sin you are dealing with and that you desire to have a changed heart and renewed mind. Then, as you are prompted by the Holy Spirit, proceed to cancel the enemy's assignment over your life by casting out whatever spirit is attached to the sin in your life, and *call it out by name.* The enemy has no choice but to flee. Demons have no legal right to be in your body, and they only receive this legal access because of sin. Yeshua has broken the curse of the law, which includes diseases, weaknesses of the flesh, and demonic torment. If you haven't had complete freedom in your walk with Yeshua, it's probably because you have not properly asked for it. Rise up and claim victory over all these areas of your life. Experience the little power of Philadelphia.

Now, before talking about what it means to be "firstfruits", we need to discuss the fact that the 144,000 are without deceit and fault according to Rev. 14:5. This seems like an impossible attribute. Who can be *without deceit?* Have these people never told a lie before, ever? Humanly speaking, this seems unachievable. However, by faithfully interpreting the Text, we can understand what is actually being spoken of here. Take a look at these words from John 1:47:

"Jesus saw Nathanael coming toward Him, and said of him, 'Behold, an Israelite indeed, in whom is no deceit!'"

Yeshua sees things much differently than you and I see. He sees the heart. He proclaimed publicly that Nathanael was such a man that perfectly fits the description of the 144,000; and such men exist to this very day. The Greek word used for *deceit* (Strong's G1388) in John 1:47 is the *exact* same word found in Rev. 14:5. This is the secret to being counted worthy to escape judgment. Simply pay attention to what Philip was telling Nathanael immediately before Yeshua met him:

"Philip found Nathanael and said to him, 'We have found Him of whom Moses in the law, and also the prophets, wrote—Jesus of Nazareth, the son of Joseph.'" (John 1:45)

Nathanael was someone kind of like you and me. He was searching the Scriptures to understand prophecy. Sabbath day after Sabbath day, he and Philip were searching the Torah and the Prophets together to understand when the promised Messiah would arrive. When He did arrive in the first century, Nathanael was able to immediately recognize Him and proclaim Him as the Son of God and King of Israel. Nathanael and Philip were diligently seeking the things above and not of this world. They were hungry and thirsty for righteousness. Simply by obtaining a copy of this book you also have demonstrated the same zeal that Nathanael had. You have been searching for a long time to understand the secrets of Bible prophecy. So had I. And the Holy Spirit made known to us the true meaning of the 70 shabua, the importance of keeping Torah, and a profound understanding of all the things that will be shortly coming to pass. We were hungry and thirsty for righteousness, and we have been filled. Take the next steps, and continue to walk out this walk like a true Hebrew, in which there is no deceit from the traditions of men and false doctrines of this world.

REVELATION 14:4 - FIRSTFRUITS TO GOD AND THE LAMB

To be *first* means that something comes later. The very first part will be harvested first, and the greater harvest happens later. This final idea of the 144,000 being *firstfruits* of a greater agricultural harvest is so massive and deeply profound because it reveals to us the *possible* timing of when these firstfruits may be selected. I am not stating that I know for sure when the firstfruits will be gathered, but I am simply stating my case here and letting you do your own homework. You might agree. You might not. Either way, it's important to consider the mysteries of what is being spoken here. It's written down for a reason, after all; but in order to begin to understand this firstfruits harvest, you must understand the seven species of the Torah calendar. They are all found in these words of Deuteronomy 8:8 where Yehovah describes the land of Israel that His people were about to inherit under Joshua as being "a land of wheat and barley, of vines and fig trees and pomegranates, a land of olive oil and honey".

As you can see, there are seven total species listed here. This was recorded on purpose, for it is these seven that reveal to us many otherwise hidden truths about the agricultural cycles of Israel and the prophetic time clock of the Most

High. We have already discussed how the barley is extremely important for beginning the Hebrew New Year at the correct time so that there can be one omer of barley present for Wave Sheaf Day. We also already spoke about Pentecost being the festival where the firstfruits of the wheat harvest are gathered in the third month of any given Hebrew year. Now I want to show you what everything looks like on a timeline.

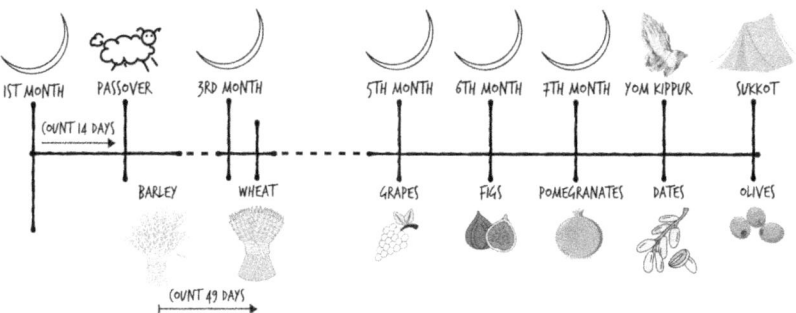

Figure 12.1: The Seven Firstfruits of the Torah Calendar

Based on conversations with Becca Biderman, the founder of In Search of His Ancient Path, and her detailed studies, we can conclude that the first ripe grapes are ready in the fifth month, the figs in the next month, the pomegranates are ready by the seventh new moon, the firstfruit dates are ready at Yom Kippur, and the olives are ready by Sukkot.[4,5] I will describe all of the Feasts in Chapter 14 along with the significance of the seventh new moon. For now, understand that the firstfruits of the ground (barley, wheat) and the firstfruits of the vine and trees were a fundamental part of the Levitical priesthood that Elohim implemented under Moses. This is what Numbers 18:8,12 states:

8 "And the LORD spoke to Aaron: 'Here, I Myself have also given you charge of My heave offerings, all the holy gifts of the children of Israel; I have given them as a portion to you and your sons, as an ordinance forever.
12 "All the best of the oil, all the best of the new wine and the grain, their firstfruits which they offer to the LORD, I have given them to you.'"

The firstfruits offerings were to be set apart to the Levites forever. That's why when the Kingdom of Judah was brought back from Babylonian exile under Nehemiah and the temple was rebuilt in Jerusalem, we read the following words:

Abraham Ojeda

"And *we made ordinances* to bring the firstfruits of our ground and the first-fruits of all fruit of all trees, year by year, to the house of the LORD".
(Neh. 10:35)

Nehemiah made sure that the firstfruits were once again brought into the temple in Jerusalem, year by year, just as required by the commandments of God in the Torah. The reality about the firstfruits is that they are not ready all at once. They are ready in their own season, as I have illustrated in my time-line. It was during the three annual pilgrimage feasts—First Day Unleavened Bread, Pentecost, and First Day of Sukkot—that the firstfruits offerings would be presented to the Levites in Jerusalem. All men are required by the Torah to go and present themselves with their firstfruits offerings and gifts in Jerusalem three times a year. With this understanding, we must now ask this obvious question: Which agricultural product do the 144,000 represent? Should we be looking for the season of figs or grapes? This metaphor of Hosea 9:10 seems to indicate that this is true:

"I found Israel
Like grapes in the wilderness;
I saw your fathers
As the firstfruits on the fig tree in its first season.
But they went to Baal Peor,
And separated themselves *to that* shame;
They became an abomination like the thing they loved."

There are many metaphors like this sprinkled throughout the Scriptures. So, which crop is it we should be examining? The answer is found in the words of Yeshua. Again, we must recognize that Yeshua is the one who really wrote the book of Revelation. People often forget this important fact, which is the reason why they have twisted understandings of major concepts like the 1000-Year Reign. It is in fact Yeshua who already told us exactly what kind of harvest will be taking place at the end of the age. The entire metaphor can be found in Matthew 13. Here are the verses I would like to focus on:

24 "Another parable He put forth to them, saying: 'The kingdom of heaven is like a man who sowed good seed in his field;
25 'but while men slept, his enemy came and sowed tares among the wheat and went his way.'"
(Mat. 13:24,25)

414

Yes, indeed! Yeshua told us of His Kingdom and 1000-Year Reign being like a wheat harvest that He Himself planted. As you know, this period of time is shortly coming to an end. The tares planted by the devil are hard to distinguish from real wheat in the early stages of development, and so they have been left to grow together until the end time harvest, otherwise they might both be plucked up together if the fields were weeded too soon. Here's what happens next:

38 "The field is the world, the good seeds are the sons of the kingdom, but the tares are the sons of the wicked *one.*
39 *"*The enemy who sowed them is the devil, the harvest is the end of the age, and the reapers are the angels.
40 "Therefore as the tares are gathered and burned in the fire, so it will be at the end of this age.
41 "The Son of Man will send out His angels, and they will gather out of His kingdom all things that offend, and those who practice lawlessness,
42 "and will cast them into the furnace of fire. There will be wailing and gnashing of teeth."
(Mat. 13:38-42)

All who practice a lifestyle of breaking Torah (Torah-lessness) are going to be burned with fire. Yeshua has spoken it, and His words are crystal clear. We should now be fully convinced in our minds that there is indeed going to be a wheat harvest at the very end of the age. I will make the case that the wheat harvest will be completely finished at the Last Day in which all believers will be resurrected to receive incorruptible bodies, but the wicked will also be raised up but only to be judged and cast out into the fire to be burned up like tares.

Let me recap what we have been shown. In the Gospel, Yeshua is saying that there is going to be a wheat harvest at the end of the age, which is probably going to happen sometime during the final year of the 70th week from spring 2044 to spring 2045. If it is the "Last Day" spoken of by Paul and Yeshua with the "last trumpet" blast, then it could be the Day of Atonement of 2044 (as mentioned in Chapter 10). In Revelation, Yeshua once again shows us that there will be a firstfruits wheat harvest sometime before the end of the age. You must understand the nature of wild, heirloom wheat that grows in the land of Israel. This kind of wheat is planted by Elohim and not by man. The whole field doesn't become ready all at once like the genetically modified stuff that is uniformly sown and fertilized using modern tractors and implements. No. Some patches of a naturally sown wheat field will be ready first. These are the firstfruits. The other parts will be ready, indeed, but only in stages. A complete harvest of wheat took many weeks in ancient Israel and did not all occur in one day. The rest of the wheat that is not "firstfruits" will have to endure the heat of the sun longer. They will have to endure until the end. Because the abomination of desolation is going to be so horrific and catastrophic, I will now make the case that this firstfruits selection must take place before the Great Tribulation, which is supposed to begin on any winter-sabbath moving forward. Let me show you my theory of the two possible 144,000 firstfruit selections in a graphical format.

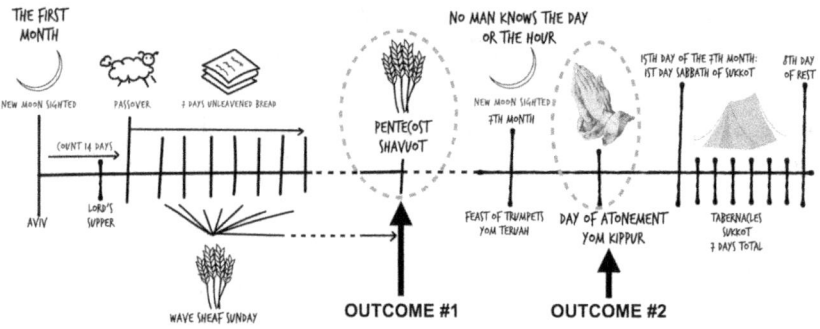

Figure 12.2: Pentecost or Day of Atonement?

At some point in the very near future, God will indeed be selecting his firstfruits on a Holy Day and in accordance with his prophetic timeline. I admit I don't know if the 144,000 have already been selected at this point in time. I was expecting them to be chosen on the Day of Atonement of 2023 due to my misunderstanding of September 22, 2023 as being the start of the Great Tribulation. That being the case, we must watch, wait, and continue to observe these Holy Days. Our eyes are now wide open to see that the hidden 144,000 prophecy could easily be fulfilled on Pentecost. The third month and the Pentecost firstfruits wheat harvest seems to be a perfect match of all the things discussed so far when comparing Revelation 7 and 14 with the words of Yeshua in the Gospels. However, while it seems obvious that Shavuot would be the time that the wheat firstfruits are selected, there is a little *more* evidence to support the idea that they will be selected on Yom Kippur. Since I have already presented the evidence for Shavuot being the day that the 144,000 are selected, let's now discuss why Yom Kippur could also be the day of this event because I think it is more likely based on what various passages of Scripture reveal.

THE EVIDENCE FOR YOM KIPPUR

I already alluded to this possibility when we discussed the undeniable connection of the Joel 2 locusts to the Revelation 9 locusts. After describing all of the devastation that His locust armies will do to the rebellious nations of Israel, Yehovah says this:

12 "Now, therefore," says the LORD,
"Turn to Me with all your heart,
With fasting, with weeping, and with mourning.
14 "Who knows *if* He will turn and relent,
And leave a blessing behind Him—
A grain offering and a drink offering
For the LORD your God?
15 "Blow the trumpet in Zion,
Consecrate a fast,
Call a sacred assembly;
(Joel 2:12,14,15)

The call to action is to call a sacred assembly and legitimately fast, weep, and mourn with the whole heart in order that His people might receive a blessing. Make no mistake about it. Judgment is determined. It is absolutely going to happen. It is my theory that Yehovah is proclaiming that He will in fact bless with a special blessing those people who will be keeping a certain Yom Kippur immediately before the abomination of desolation takes place. The parallels are unmistakable. This blessing could take place in 2024, 2025, 2026 —we simply do not know. Pay attention to the clear overlap between the words of Joel and the instructions for keeping the Day of Atonement:

27 "Also the tenth *day* of this seventh month *shall be* the Day of Atonement.
It shall be a holy convocation for you; you shall afflict your souls, and offer an offering made by fire to the LORD.
28 "And you shall do no work on that same day, for it *is* the Day of Atonement, to make atonement for you before the LORD your God.
29 "For any person who is not afflicted *in soul* on that same day shall be cut off from his people."
(Lev. 23:27-29)

This commandment to observe the Day of Atonement is the same exact language used to describe the sacred assembly of Joel 2. *Afflicting the soul* means that God's people are commanded to fast. Some will argue with me on this point. However, you only need to look into the Text more deeply, and you will see that there is no other interpretation. The only question should really be regarding what the fasting is supposed to look like. For me and my house-hold personally, we don't eat food and we don't drink water. Moses fasted for 40 days and nights, and then he did it again after the sin of the golden calf. Yeshua did it for 40 days and so did Elijah. It's not impossible. Remove the limitations of your mind and the fallen constructs of believing that you require food. You don't require food. You require every single word that comes out of the mouth of Yehovah. *That* is what you really need. Now of course, there are special considerations and accommodations for those with medical conditions and so forth. The Holy Spirit must lead and guide you. Just understand that fasting is indeed an integral part of the Day of Atonement.

The next key place in the Bible where this Holy Day occurs is in the book of Jonah during Nineveh's repentance.

4 "And Jonah began to enter the city on the first day's walk. Then he cried out and said, 'Yet forty days, and Nineveh shall be overthrown!'
5 "So the people of Nineveh believed God, proclaimed a fast, and put on sack-cloth, from the greatest to the least of them.
6 "Then word came to the king of Nineveh; and he arose from his throne and laid aside his robe, covered *himself* with sackcloth and sat in ashes.
7 "And he caused *it* to be proclaimed and published throughout Nineveh by the decree of the king and his nobles, saying, Let neither man nor beast, herd nor flock, taste anything; do not let them eat, or drink water."
(Jonah 3:4-7)

This is again another repetition of the kind of blessing that we see in Joel 2. The people of Nineveh, the ancient capital city of Assyria, fasted and put on sackcloth so that God might turn away from His fierce anger. Just like what will soon be taking place as Joel prophesied, Yehovah did turn away from His anger, and he left behind a blessing for Nineveh. They weren't destroyed. They were spared! Now, you might be challenging me as to whether or not this truly was a Day of Atonement event, but all you have to do is look and see what Jonah does a few days later after he is done preaching. This is what we are told in Jonah 4:5 (KJV):

"So Jonah went out of the city, and sat on the east side of the city, and there made him a booth, and sat under it in the shadow, till he might see what would become of the city."

Notice that Jonah made himself a *booth.* This is a very specific and deliberate word choice. The Hebrew word used here is in fact *sukka* (Strong's H5521), which is a completely different word than *tent* (ohel; Strong's H168). Unlike a tent, a sukka is a structure that is far more flimsy, weak, and thrown together using wood, vegetation, and scrap materials found in the wilderness. The word *ohel* in the Bible used to describe a *tent* is similar to what you most likely imagined in your mind when you have read Jonah in the past. It is something made out of a canvas or strong fabric with wooden poles and a nice, well-planned design so that it can be taken down and erected efficiently. This distinction between Hebrew words is the secret of understanding the entire book of Jonah and the prophecy of Joel. The reason that Jonah made a *sukka* to dwell in is because he was observing the seven-day Feast of Sukkot that happens every year beginning on the 15th day of the seventh month. Yom Kippur is from the evening of the 9th day of the month to the evening of the 10th. Jonah was preaching to Nineveh during the day of the 10th, and this is precisely when the sacred assembly of Yom Kippur is to take place. Not coincidentally, this is also when the people of Nineveh began to repent, weep, fast, and mourn. This was the same day that the news made it all the way to the king's throne. They didn't play games with God. They didn't make excuses for not fasting. They were moved by the Holy Spirit with righteous fear of the Most High and did everything exactly as commanded by the Torah in observance of the Day of Atonement. Remember, this is the Torah of the whole earth. Everyone is held to the standard of the Torah, and Nineveh chose to stop sinning and keep the appointed time of Yehovah so that they would automatically have the blessing come upon them, rather than the curse of destruction. Such is the fate of anyone who will observe Yom Kippur; and those who do not will be *cut off.*

Regarding the literal sign of Jonah that caused Nineveh to repent, this same historical and celestial sign has now appeared to the United States of America in a remarkable way. I am often falsely accused of being some sort of a pagan sign-seeking astrologist when I bring up the significance of celestial events. Most people don't understand the difference between sinful astrological witchcraft practices and pure biblical astronomy as recorded in Genesis 1:14. There is nothing wrong with discerning the signs of God; and in fact, it is the duty of every God-fearing man and woman to see what is being divinely orchestrated through the signs of the heavens. That is why the triple solar eclipse omen over America was of extreme significance. It began in 2017 with a total solar eclipse, continued in 2023 with a partial solar eclipse, and ended with another total solar eclipse in 2024. This seven-year omen was something that Nineveh also happened to see during the reign of Jeroboam II (782–753

BC) when Jonah was a prophet in Israel according to 2 Kings 14:25. Nineveh also received a seven-year solar eclipse omen. For a more in-depth look at what this means for America, read *Bible Prophecy Secrets II* because it is dedicated to exploring this exact topic.

In Chapter 10, we briefly discussed the "sealing" event of Ezekiel 9:4 in which those that were spared from judgment were sighing and crying over the abominations being committed in the land of Israel. I am unsure if this event is an exclusively historical event or if Ezekiel saw a vision of the coming final Day of Atonement just before the Great Tribulation begins. Either way, this chapter of Ezekiel provides an additional witness of a sealing event that is to take place during the weeping, repentance, and intercessory prayers that are an integral part of the Day of Atonement

Finally, there is yet another biblical reference that the Day of Atonement is the correct Holy Day of the selection of the 144,000, and it is found within Isaiah 22 and the archers of Elam prophecy discussed in Chapter 7. Once the flying scrolls come raining down on Jerusalem with everyone heading to the housetops to see what is going on, the city will become devastated and plundered by its enemies in a "day" (Isa. 22:5). There will be a great slaughter. At the end of this passage, God tells us the clear reason *why* the archers of Iran are going to terrorize the land with missiles:

12 And in that day the Lord GOD of hosts Called for weeping and for mourning, For baldness and for girding with sackcloth.
13 But instead, joy and gladness, Slaying oxen and killing sheep, Eating meat and drinking wine: "Let us eat and drink, for tomorrow we die!"
14 Then it was revealed in my hearing by the LORD of hosts, "Surely for this iniquity there will be no atonement for you, Even to your death," says the Lord GOD of hosts.
(Isa. 22:12-14 NKJV)

The connection should be obvious. As is the case with Yom Kippur, there is a call to weep, mourn, and repent of sin. Of course, the people living in Jerusalem won't care. Trusting in their Iron Dome missile defense system, they will have the heart attitude of complacency while being merry with food and drink. Rather than fasting, they will be feasting and carrying on as usual. That is why God said that there will be no "atonement" for them. This inevitable outcome is going to be very obvious to any reader of this book. What may not be so obvious is exactly *why* the people of Jerusalem will have such disregard for the Holy Day of God with no care to observe it. As described at the end of Chapter 3, this sin is due to Judaism's adherence to the false Hillel II calendar system rather than the agricultural and lunar-based calendar of the Torah.

UNDERSTANDING ABIB BARLEY

You cannot keep the Day of Atonement (or any Holy Days) at just any old time. It is not okay to follow the Hillel II Calendar of the Rabbinical Jews, the Karaite Judaism doctrine of harvestable fields, the equinox, or the Enoch and Zadok Dead Sea Scrolls calendars of the Essenes. Many have confronted me and told me that God knows their heart and that they are sincerely trying. However, as I will explain, it *really* does matter that Yom Kippur is observed at exactly the correct time and not even a single day later.

While I have strived to write and publish this book well in advance of the coming Great Tribulation, it has been a very difficult task to accomplish with all of my work responsibilities and managing my homestead. Chances are high that you have not yet been properly exposed to everything that I have been teaching about keeping the Feasts at the correct time versus what most people do in keeping the Feasts a month or two late from the correct timing. It's not too late to begin observing the Feasts no matter where you find yourself. No matter what your circumstances are, it's not too late. As long as you are alive, there is still an opportunity to live your life in a manner that is pleasing to the Most High. Ponder this: Nineveh didn't keep the Spring Feasts the year that Jonah visited them; they only kept Yom Kippur and were spared. I will speak more about the specifics of all the Feasts in Chapter 14. For now, I will present a simple case study of how the first new moon was declared to begin the Hebrew New Year back in the spring of 2023.

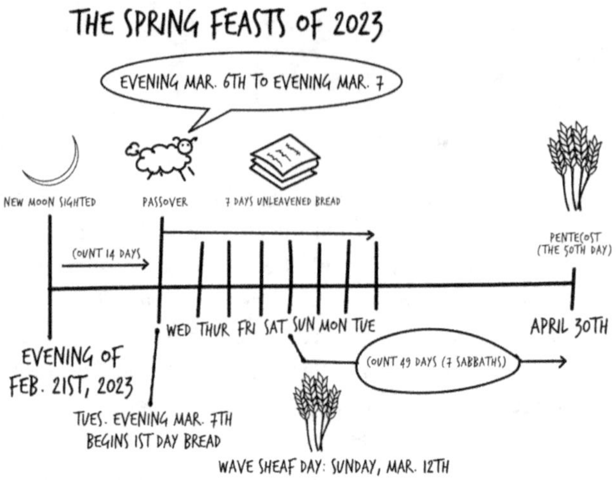

THE SPRING FEASTS OF 2023

Figure 12.3: Determining the Holy Days - A 2023 Case Study

This first month declaration occurred on the evening of February 21, 2023. Why? This month is the beginning of months and is called Abib in the Hebrew (Strong's H24; literally "green ears of barley").[6] There were already firstfruits of barley present at least a week before the new moon of February 21. Again, this barley is required in order to present the one omer offering on Wave Sheaf Day Sunday during the third week of the first month. For help visualizing what abib barley looks like and the various stages of barley plant development, I recommend a video by Norman Willis called "Aviv Barley Simplified" on Youtube;[7] and you can also find this same information in his book, *The Torah Calendar* (available for free on his website).[8] The bottom line is that the biblical calendar is very simple. We look for a moon in the night sky and the very first green barley in the ground to declare the New Year. We don't use advanced calculus, satellites, or the computational power of supercomputers to understand a simple agrarian calendar. I mentioned her already, but Becca Biderman was providing ample evidence of various heirloom barley fields that she was inspecting in the land of Israel in February.

Figure 12.4: Abib Barley in the Land of Israel, 2023

This photo in Figure 12.3 was taken on February 21, 2023 by Becca Bidermann near Tel Te'omim in northern Israel, and she confirmed that there was enough abib barley at this time in order to have one omer ready by Wave Sheaf Day on March 12th.[9] In fact, this happened to be near the same area where the firstfruits abib barley were found in 2022 to begin the year 5858 as confirmed by multiple witnesses.[10] Regarding this photo on Feb. 21, here is what Becca stated in her Facebook group where she posts regular announcements:

> "This is why I hunt for weeks on end. The earth is ever changing here. No one knows when this barley will finish, will it be in time? Only Yah knows but there's a chance. This area needs to be followed this year. Within the field there are a few shattering grains, a few indivisible with the thumbnail, a few soft enough to roll into a ball of dough (bingo!). There's an area that reminds me of last year's firstfruits portion of the field… It's a field of barley. Bigger than last year… The section I took a photo of is enough to make an omer."[11]

Notice she said that she was unsure whether or not the barely would finish in time for Wave Sheaf Day. One thing I really like about Becca's work is that she does not make forecasts or predictions. She only reports her actual find-

423

ings. Notice also that she said that some of the barley was already getting too mature and shattering! This is why I confidently declared the New Year of 5859 to have started during the new moon of February 21. Also, on March 8th, Becca provided drone-enabled video footage of this same field that she had inspected on Feb. 21.[12] The video revealed that some of this barley was again shattering in the 1st month. Why is this concept of *shattering* important? What this term means is that some barley had already become so ripe and golden that it started re-seeding itself back into the ground. Upon slight contact, overly ripe barley will shatter, releasing the hardened seed from the grain head, making it unable to be harvested by hand as in ancient times. Therefore, the *true* firstfruits Abib barley was present as early as the third week of February. That is what Becca meant by soft dough. She was speaking of the stage of abib barley development that is perfect for harvesting so that it can be made into dough. Becca demonstrated this process a couple years ago where she roasted freshly harvested abib barley over fire and turned it into flour for bread.[13]

Again, you must carefully consider exactly how the fields of barley in the land of Israel were harvested manually before the arrival of modern diesel harvesters and equipment. If you try to take your sickle (or scythe) to cut down the standing grain of golden and overly mature barely, it would *shatter* back into the ground, and part of the harvest would be lost as a result of waiting too long. This was financially a big problem and could have even resulted in starvation back in those days. That is precisely why in ancient times the fields were always harvested in phases, as opposed to how it is harvested these days all at once with diesel machinery. Some of the fields would ripen early, and other fields would ripen later, depending on the exact location in the ancient land of Israel. The people would cut down the barley, tie them uprightly in sheaves (bundles) throughout the fields, the sheaves would be given time to dry, and the people would then load these sheaves of barley on the backs of wagons. Once transported back to the homes, these field-dried sheaves would be taken to the threshing floors where the seed was collected for food and the remaining straw, or chaff, was used to feed live-stock. Now, imagine this same process when the barley is too ripe. In such a scenario, the grain falls right out of the head even with the slightest contact when the barley is golden and beyond the state of abib. How would it ever be gathered into bundles and transported along bumpy dirt roads via wooden donkey carts without losing all of the grain from the heads? This is the funda-mental knowledge that has been mostly lost to our current generation of "feast keepers."

Figure 12.5: Sheaves of Barley in a Field. After being cut with a scythe, the stalks of barley used to be bundled and tied into sheaves. Each sheaf contained almost the amount of grain as a Hebrew omer, hence the translation of "sheaf" that is present in many English Bibles in Leviticus 23. The larger upright bundles of sheaves placed upright were called *shocks* and could consist of 12 or more sheaves. This is how the grain would be field dried.

Many people have lost touch with this basic understanding of pre-industrial agriculture. Groups such as the Karaite Jews, Hebrew Roots, Messianics, and related groups also understand the need to look for a sheaf of barley like the Bible states, *but* they only look for large "harvestable fields" because of what the leading group of Karaites teach; and they then falsely claim this barley to be "first" fruits. For this very reason, most groups keep the feasts a month or even two months *late* from the exact timing that we are commanded to honor in the Torah. Rather than looking for green firstfruits, many have been tricked into looking for golden "whole field" fruits of barley. I have also noticed that the mathematically determined Hillel II calendar of Judaism is consistently a month off from the true agriculturally based calendar of the Bible, and the Jews almost always keep the Feasts a month late. However, this mistake has been made for a very long time now. This is an ancient sin.

THE SIN OF JEROBOAM AND THE NORTH

As previously described, the United Kingdom of Israel only existed under three kings—Saul, David, and Solomon. Because of Solomon's sin the kingdom was divided, with Jeroboam, Solomon's personal enemy, receiving the North and Rehoboam, Solomon's son, receiving the South. Ten tribes migrated to the North while only two remained in the South, exactly as prophesied by Ahijah (1Kings 11:30). This means that about 83% of Israelites, or the majority, became Northerners after this split; and they also became blatant idolaters under their first king. In a spirit of fear, pride, and lust for power, this is what Jeroboam does:

26 And Jeroboam said in his heart, "Now the kingdom may return to the house of David:

27 "If these people go up to offer sacrifices in the house of the LORD at Jerusalem, then the heart of this people will turn back to their lord, Rehoboam king of Judah, and they will kill me and go back to Rehoboam king of Judah."

28 Therefore the king asked advice, made two calves of gold, and said to the people, "It is too much for you to go up to Jerusalem. Here are your gods, O Israel, which brought you up from the land of Egypt!"

29 And he set up one in Bethel, and the other he put in Dan.

30 Now this thing became a sin, for the people went *to worship* before the one as far as Dan.

31 He made shrines on the high places, and made priests from every class of people, who were not of the sons of Levi.

32 Jeroboam ordained a feast on the fifteenth day of the eighth month, like the feast that *was* in Judah, and offered sacrifices on the altar. So he did at Bethel, sacrificing to the calves that he had made. And at Bethel he installed the priests of the high places which he had made.

(1Kings 12:26-32)

Remember, all men of Israel are required to appear in Jerusalem three times a year as commanded in the Torah. This singular concept is so pivotal for understanding all manner of prophecy. Jeroboam himself understood the requirement very well. That's why he immediately changes the Torah according to the imagination of his heart (1Ki.12:33) so that the people would *not* go to Jerusalem. He was worried that they would make Rehoboam their king rather than him. Rather than observing the Holy Days at the correct time, he instituted the keeping of the seventh month feasts exactly one month later than the correct time. He made everyone observe the Feast of Trumpets (1st day), the Day of Atonement (10th day), and the Feast of Sukkot (starting the 15th day) a complete month later on the eighth month. He caused 83% of the people to sin by keeping the Feasts a month late. We can safely assume that he also changed the keeping of the rest of the feasts such as Passover and Pentecost to be a month later as well. This same pattern of behavior is precisely what is still going on today but without most people ever being aware of it.

THE JOSHUA AND CALEB REMNANT

Do you understand the dilemma that God's people have always faced? It has always only been a minority of people that have been diligent enough to search the Scriptures and observe the commandments of Elohim exactly as

He intended them to be. I'm boldly telling you that I have done the home-work. I have understood the commandments well and to the best of my ability. I have not added to or subtracted from the keeping of the Torah and the correct time clock of the Most High. You must also do the homework and prove these things for yourself. Back in ancient times, it was 83% of people that were keeping the Feasts a month late. Now it is far greater. My estimate is that at least 95% do not keep the Feasts at the correct time due to willful ignorance, traditions of men, and very misguided interpretations of Scripture. Don't be like the majority. Be like Joshua and Caleb who had a radically different spirit in them than their crooked and perverse genera-tion. These were the two spies out of the twelve that were faithful in reporting that the children of Israel were in fact able to enter into the Promised Land and inherit it, despite the giants that were present (Num. 13). It was only these two that received the blessing of inheriting the promised land—a blessing that not even Moses himself was able to experi-ence. Once again, it was only two out of twelve that were faithful while the rest of the spies were rebellious. This particular sin of the ten spies caused the children of Israel to wander in the wilderness for 40 years until all the men of war died off. Likewise, the sin of not keeping the Feasts and the coming Yom Kippur of the 144,000 at the correct time by the majority of people will also lead to divine punishment. The prophet Isaiah made this truth very clear for all with spiritual eyes and ears that work properly when he said:

"But yet a tenth *will be* in it,
And will return and be for consuming,
As a terebinth tree or as an oak,
Whose stump *remains* when it is cut down.
So the holy seed *shall be* its stump."
(Isa. 6:13)

Whether literal or figurative, Isaiah declares that only ten percent will remain of whatever seed of Abraham is present in the world today. If this verse is to be taken literally, that means that tens of millions of Lost Tribes citizens from Europe to America will perish in the coming events of World War III. The reason that Yehovah is so angry is because His Torah has not been respected. His Torah has been cast behind the backs of the vast majority of so-called feast keepers. Many have regarded the opinions of the Messiah-rejecting Jews over the authority of the Word of God. That is why only 144,000 will be selected as firstfruits. They are the only ones that were able to see past all of the lies, deception, and trickery of men and demons in order to understand the commandments of Elohim without any sexual immorality of false doctrine.

WHAT IF I AM NOT SELECTED AS ONE OF THE 144,000?

This is a question that I often ponder. I really don't know if I will be selected myself. I'm not blinded by arrogance into thinking that because I had a podcast, wrote books, and taught the Torah that I have somehow earned God's favor in this matter. He does whatever He pleases because He is a sovereign ruler. We shouldn't be discouraged no matter what the outcome is because there are still many promises on the table that we should be eagerly looking towards. One of these is regathering of all thirteen tribes of Israel, and this topic will be explored in the next chapter. Even if you die but have made Yeshua the Lord of your life and have turned around from lawlessness and into obedience, there are other promises that should be remembered often. Look at Rev. 14:3, and you will see that it will be a blessing for people to die and be received up into heaven during the coming tribulation period. In fact, this is what John describes to us in Revelation 7:14. Many will be coming out of the Great Tribulation and making themselves holy and acceptable to Elohim through the process of judgment. Remember, that's precisely why judgment must take place. God's people have been extremely lazy and complacent for a long time now. If the current Zionist Mystery Babylon system continued to exist into perpetuity nothing would ever change from a spiritual standpoint. Tribulation is absolutely necessary, and we should sincerely desire all of prophecy to finally come to pass.

The blessing of being selected as one of the 144,000 is something to be desired and genuinely praying for, regardless of the exact outcome. Like I briefly alluded to earlier, these people will not be raptured into heaven to never return again. They will have a specific assignment and a job to do. Based on all my understanding of Scripture, I believe that they will receive the special anointing of the Holy Spirit prophesied at the end of Daniel 9:24. I believe these people are "the most holy." We are told they will sing a new song in heaven. We are told they will stand before Yeshua, just as He said in Luke 21:36. What is overlooked and not considered by most people is that these people could very likely be the two witnesses described in the book of Revelation. Pause and consider this interpretation for a moment. These "two witnesses" of the 144,000 will prophesy and perform incredible miracles. They will be killed by satan while standing in Jerusalem, and they will be resurrected three and a half days later.

Of course, I know what you might be thinking: "The number 144,000 is far greater than the number two, so how could these be the two witnesses?"

The answer is found in the parable of the olive tree that is repeated four times throughout the Scriptures. The first olive tree parable is found in Ezekiel 37 where the prophet takes two olive trees, one in each hand, and joins them together. I know most Bible translations use the word *stick* and *sticks,* but this is a very poor translation of the Hebrew word *tree.* These sticks represent the House of Israel and the House of Judah that are going to be joined together in a two-part prophecy. This idea will be explored in the next chapter. Next, we see this metaphor used in Zechariah 4 where there are two olive trees with a menorah in the middle of them receiving oil from a branch of each of the trees. The correct interpretation of the two olive trees is given in Zec. 4:14 where the messenger tells the prophet, "These are the two anointed ones, who stand beside the Lord of the whole earth" (Zec. 4:14).

Figure 12.6: The Two Olive Trees of Zechariah

The third place we see the metaphor used is found in Romans 11, and this passage will be heavily discussed in the next chapter. The fourth and final place we see the parable of the two olive trees is Revelation 11. Pay attention to these words of Rev. 11:4 where John writes, "These are the two olive trees and the two lampstands standing before the God of the earth." Notice that this is a direct quotation of Zec. 4:14. In the Overcome Babylon podcast, I made the case that these "anointed ones" are two literal people. Most Bible teachers also arrive at this same conclusion and state that they are Moses and Elijah or perhaps Enoch (of the good line of Adam). I have now understood a radically different possibility. I believe these two olive trees are actually a representation of the two houses of Israel, and the 144,000 are the "two witnesses" because they consist of both Judah and Israel. Revelation 11:3 seems to confirm this idea, where John writes, "And I will give *power* to my two witnesses, and they will prophesy one thousand two hundred and sixty days, clothed in sackcloth." Again we see this idea that these people will have the ability to perform great miracles. Why would Yeshua choose any other people for this task than His faithful members of the church of Philadelphia who have already been exercising just a *little* bit of this power in their daily lives? The reason that I also believe that these two witnesses are not a literal number *two* but a conceptual representation of the two houses of the 144,000 is because of these words of Jeremiah 31:36:

"If those ordinances depart
From before Me, says the LORD,
Then the seed of Israel shall also cease
From being a nation before Me forever."

The verse before this stated that the sun, moon, and waves of the sea are governed by ordinances that cannot be nullified. In the same manner as these mathematical ordinances, Israel will never cease from being a nation. That is why the House of Israel and House of Judah are the two olive trees that are always present before Yehovah. They cannot be destroyed. They are established forever and always *standing* before Him. That is why the 144,000 can also be viewed as two witnesses because they represent these same two houses. Regardless of how you may view this topic of the 144,000, it will all shortly come to pass, and we won't need to speculate for much longer. Out of eight billion people in the world today, however, the chances are indeed very low that you will be selected as one of the 144,000. The odds are simply not on your side, nor mine. That is why it is important to properly understand the regathering of Israel as explained in the next chapter. Let your faith continue to be strengthened by the Word of prophecy—a Word that cannot return void but that will accomplish every purpose of the Most High God.

Chapter 13
The Regathering of All 13 Tribes

The regathering of all 13 Tribes of Israel back into their homeland is prophesied everywhere throughout the Scriptures. This topic is massive. In fact, it is the most repeated and talked about prophetic event in the entire Bible, yet hardly anyone understands it. One of the first places that this prophecy is mentioned is near the end of Deuteronomy where Moses warns the people what would happen if they fell away from God. These verses set the very foundation for the coming regathering event:

1 "Now it shall come to pass, when all these things come upon you, the blessing and the curse which I have set before you, and you call them to mind among all the nations where the LORD your God drives you,
2 "and you return to the LORD your God and obey His voice, according to all that I command you today, you and your children, with all your heart and with all your soul,
3 "that the LORD your God will bring you back from captivity, and have compassion on you, and gather you again from all the nations where the LORD your God has scattered you.
4 "If any of you are driven out to the farthest parts under heaven, from there the LORD your God will gather you, and from there He will bring you."
(Deu. 30:1-4)

The scattering of all Israel away from the land of Canaan was already prophesied by Moses thousands of years ago, and the gathering from the "all the nations" and the "farthest parts under heaven" has not yet taken place. If you are not part of the 144,000 and must endure through the tribulation period, you must be praying to be considered part of the regathering of God's people back to the land. Pray that you are counted worthy to be of the "elect", or chosen people, that the angels will be sent to collect with the sound of a trumpet as Yeshua told us in Matthew 24:31. That is what Moses is telling us here. We must return to God with our whole heart and obey His voice. Only then can God's compassion be aroused, and since we are so close to the end of the age, rest assured that your prayers will not be in vain.

This chapter will also address the final part of Daniel's 70 shabua prophecy that was not yet completely uncovered. It is these words here from Daniel 9:24 where he says, "...To make reconciliation for iniquity...". This was a difficult thing for me to comprehend until one day, the Holy Spirit showed me the deeper meaning. Since the time of Yeshua's sacrificial Passover death and the renewed covenant in His blood, we have always had reconciliation for iniquity. This already took place, didn't it? What else could it be talking about? The answer is clearly found inside of the exact prophecy that Yeshua had quoted during the Lord's Supper (Last Supper) the night before He was crucified. He took the cup, and said, "For this is My blood of the new covenant, which is shed for many for the remission of sins" (Mat. 26:28). When He told his disciples to take of the cup of wine that represented the *new covenant* in His blood, He was actually quoting the words of Jeremiah, where he wrote, "Behold, the days are coming, says the LORD, when I will make a new covenant with the house of Israel and with the house of Judah" (Jer. 31:31). Everyone I ever met who calls themself a Christian wants to be a part of this new covenant, yet they do not understand that this covenant was only made with the House of Israel and the House of Judah. It was not made with a "church of gentiles", as people commonly say. It was not made with the "house of pagans" or the "house of nations". The Bible does not say "house of Christians", either. This is the secret, once again, of the subject of the entire 70 weeks prophecy and even the whole Bible itself. Daniel's people not only consist of all those nations with the seed of Abraham within them but also all those who call upon the name of Jesus and want to seek Him and have a relationship with Him.

Anyone who has called upon the name of Jesus for salvation and believed His words while understanding that He is the Son of God (and not just a man or a messenger) has been grafted into the spiritual kingdom of Israel. They have become part of the United Kingdom of Israel. They are no longer of the "lost" tribes, for Jesus came to seek and save that which was "lost". Just like the citizens of any nation, Christ followers must also obey the Law of their nation. They must obey the Constitution and Supreme Law of the land, which of course is the Torah itself together with the Gospel. The Scriptures also make it very clear that through the finished work of the cross, you and I become temples of the living God (1Co. 3:16,17). For the born again believer in the Messiah, the physical body becomes the very dwelling place of the Holy Spirit whose job is to teach us all things that the Word Made Flesh commanded (Jhn. 14:26). Though the Law is not yet perfectly written on our hearts, we are set apart for the glory of the Father. We have been given great authority and power to proclaim the good news of the Kingdom and experience all of the blessings of being a disciple of Yeshua.

As first mentioned in Chapter 2, most people also fail to realize that the new covenant was *initiated* by Yeshua but has not yet been 100% fulfilled. Remember what Jeremiah's prophecy states concerning the entire nation of United Israel under Yeshua's new covenant:

33 "But this *is* the covenant that I will make with the house of Israel after those days, says the LORD: I will put My law in their minds, and write it on their hearts; and I will be their God, and they shall be My people."
34 "No more shall every man teach his neighbor, and every man his brother, saying, 'Know the LORD,' for they all shall know Me, from the least of them to the greatest of them," says the LORD. "For I will forgive their iniquity, and their sin I will remember no more."
(Jer. 31:33,34)

The new covenant has only been partially fulfilled at this point in history because everyone is still teaching their neighbor to know who Yehovah is. That's exactly why this book you hold in your hands was written! The defining characteristic of the new covenant is that the "law" is eventually going to be written on the very hearts of His people. The word in Hebrew that Jeremiah used here is in fact "Torah". Unlike many false teachers today, the Scriptures teach us that God's instructions as revealed through Moses and the Prophets are to be deep within our hearts. One day all of God's people will know Him and have His instructions naturally written within the essence of their being.

Also, notice the language used at the end of this thought. Yehovah says that their iniquity will finally be forgiven, and their sin will be completely forgotten. This is currently not the case. The whole reason that the locusts are coming and satan is about to be released from the bottomless pit is precisely because Yehovah is angry with His people over their stubbornness, rebellion, and refusal to observe His Torah. Their sins have reached to heaven, and He is about to repay all of the sinners of His people very soon along with all those who take the mark of the beast and worship satan. That is why there is a certain sequence of events that will be taking place before the regathering can happen, and I will attempt to describe these things in this chapter. As you will soon discover, before the 70th week of Daniel is over, all of Judah and Israel will be reunited once and for all under the direct leadership of the King of kings, never to be scattered again.

THE OLIVE TREE OF THE SPIRITUAL EXODUS

Before describing the coming literal and physical exodus of God's people out of the nations, it is important to understand that the *spiritual* exodus has already been taking place since the time that the new covenant was initiated by Yeshua. This exodus is described perfectly by Paul in Romans 11 in the olive tree metaphor. Due to the sorely misunderstood language used in this passage, most people fail to recognize the ongoing, modern-day fulfillment of the new covenant and how Paul's skillful word choices connect directly back to the Prophets. Let us begin by examining how Paul describes himself in Acts:

"I am indeed a Jew, born in Tarsus of Cilicia, but brought up in this city at the feet of Gamaliel, taught according to the strictness of our fathers' law, and was zealous toward God as you all are today."
(Acts 22:3)

This topic has already been discussed throughout this book, but Paul was trained in the strictness of the Law but also with the traditions and oral laws of Judaism according to the mentorship of one of the chief rabbis by the name of Gamaliel. This man was Rabban Gamaliel I, a leading authority of the Sanhedrin in the early first century who is also mentioned in the Talmud. Though having this strong background in Judaism, Paul forsakes all of his traditions to become the "apostle to the gentiles (nations)" as he describes himself in Romans 11:

"For I speak to you Gentiles; inasmuch as I am an apostle to the Gentiles, I magnify my ministry"
(Rom. 11:13)

Paul was sent by Yeshua into the nations because of his wealth of knowledge about the Scriptures. These people that he was sent to were not a bunch of random pagans, as people falsely teach. If Paul's primary audience were poly-theists, agnostics, or atheists, it would not have been necessary for Yeshua to call such a well educated and eloquent man. Of course, when the Word says "Gentiles" it is really speaking about "Israelite Gentiles", and to put it more simply, these were the nations where the lost tribes of Israel had been scattered. These nations were the primary focus of Yeshua's calling upon Paul's life. That is why when we open up the book of Acts, we see that Paul's custom was to reason in the synagogues with these scattered Israelites. These people were already trying to keep the Law. They were trying to observe Torah, but they didn't understand who Yeshua was yet. That is why Paul and the apostles were sent out. The lost sheep of the House of Israel is the primary people group being discussed in the olive tree metaphor of Romans, and this context is the key to understanding the future regathering. Before digging further into Romans 11, pay attention to what Paul writes immediately before this chapter:

But to Israel he says: "All day long I have stretched out My hands To a disobedient and contrary people."
(Rom. 10:21)

This verse further provides the exact context of the olive tree metaphor. Paul is quoting Isaiah 65:2, and this is what this chapter says about who these disobedient people are:

2 "I have stretched out My hands all day long to a rebellious people, Who walk in a way that is not good, According to their own thoughts"
8 Thus says the LORD: "As the new wine is found in the cluster, And one says, 'Do not destroy it, For a blessing is in it,' So will I do for My servants' sake, That I may not destroy them all.
9 I will bring forth descendants from Jacob, And from Judah an heir of My mountains; My elect shall inherit it, And My servants shall dwell there."
(Isa. 65:2,8,9)

The "disobedient and contrary people" of Romans 10 is none other than the House of Judah. As recorded in Isaiah 1:1, the prophet Isaiah was sent to "Judah and Jerusalem" since his ministry was to the South. Isaiah 65:9 shows us that Elohim was very angry with Judah because of their constant rejection of Him, but He still promised to bring forth a remnant from the descendants of this kingdom that will eventually be regathered to inherit the land during the Greater Exodus of the end times. When looking back at Romans 10:21, you should understand the use of "Israel" by Paul to be an imprecise description of what Isaiah was really talking about. Though southerners are indeed Israelites, Paul should have said "But to Judah he says:" when beginning his discourse on the olive tree metaphor. When moving forward to Romans 11, the entire discourse will now make much more sense. Here are the key verses from this chapter together with my own annotations to provide needed clarity:

1 I say then, has God cast away His people? Certainly not! For I also am an

Israelite [Judahite], of the seed of Abraham, of the tribe of Benjamin [in the South].

11 I say then, have they stumbled that they should fall? Certainly not! But through their fall, to provoke them to jealousy, salvation has come to the [Israelite] Gentiles.

12 Now if their fall is riches for the world, and their failure riches for the [Israelite] Gentiles, how much more their fullness!

13 For I speak to you [Israelite] Gentiles; inasmuch as I am an apostle to the [Israelite] Gentiles, I magnify my ministry,

14 if by any means I may provoke to jealousy those who are my flesh [of Judah] and save some of them.

15 For if their [Judah's] being cast away is the reconciling of the world, what will their acceptance be but life from the dead?

(Rom. 11:1,11-15)

Remember, Paul was speaking to the scattered Israelites of the North that were living in Rome in this letter. He is attempting to explain a mystery to them, the mystery of why the Jews had rejected Jesus and had consequently fallen from grace. Though the temple was not yet destroyed until AD 70, the House of Judah would eventually be driven out of the land by the Roman Empire in the decades following this event. Paul spoke rather prophetically in this letter, which is why he referred to Judah as being "cast away" for their failure to believe in the Messiah. They had not yet been fully scattered out of Palestine, but Paul saw it coming. As a result of Judah's widespread rejection of the gospel, the message of salvation had spread like wildfire among the Israelites in a mighty way that Paul describes as "riches" to these nations. As described in Chapter 2, one of these primary nations was Britain. The message of Christianity also spread throughout Europe including Spain and would encompass all of the nations we collectively know today as being the West. What Paul masterfully describes next through the inspiration of the Holy Spirit is the same olive tree analogy that was presented in the writings of the Prophets. He states:

16 For if the firstfruit is holy, the lump is also holy; and if the root is holy, so are the branches.

17 And if some of the branches were broken off, and you, being a wild olive tree, were grafted in among them, and with them became a partaker of the root and fatness of the olive tree,

18 do not boast against the branches. But if you do boast, remember that you do not support the root, but the root supports you.

19 You will say then, "Branches were broken off that I might be grafted in."
20 Well said. Because of unbelief they were broken off, and you stand by faith. Do not be haughty, but fear.
21 For if God did not spare the natural branches, He may not spare you either.
22 Therefore consider the goodness and severity of God: on those who fell, severity; but toward you, goodness, if you continue in His goodness. Otherwise you also will be cut off.
23 And they also, if they do not continue in unbelief, will be grafted in, for God is able to graft them in again.
24 For if you were cut out of the olive tree which is wild by nature, and were grafted contrary to nature into a cultivated olive tree, how much more will these, who are natural branches, be grafted into their own olive tree?
(Rom. 11:16-24)

The metaphor presented describes two olive trees. One is the wild olive tree of the Israelite nations. These people were cast away by God and given a certificate of divorce. They were considered "wild" by Paul because they had become mixed among the nations, exactly as the prophets like Hosea had foretold. Though they eventually lost their identity as is the case today, these Israelites still mostly knew who they were in the first century when Paul ministered to them. Through faith in Christ, these branches of the wild olive tree could be grafted into God's holy and cultivated olive tree. This olive tree does not represent the House of Judah itself, but it represents the United Kingdom of Spiritual Israel—the same kingdom of heaven that Jesus proclaimed and that was allowed to reunite through His blood of the new covenant. The act of "grafting" itself is a common horticultural technique that is used in the propagation of orchards. There are different and specific techniques to accomplish a successful graft, but the idea is to cut a certain sized branch, or scion, from one tree and join the exposed tissue to that of the rootstock, which Paul refers to as the "root and fatness" in verse seventeen. Once the vascular tissues are joined together, they must be tied using rope, tape, and sometimes even adhesive in order to ensure that the graft is successful. Over time, the grafted branch will receive nourishment and support from the rootstock and will begin to bud and sprout leaves until it produces unique fruit of its own. This is what Paul meant by Israel being grafted back into the set-apart olive tree of God.

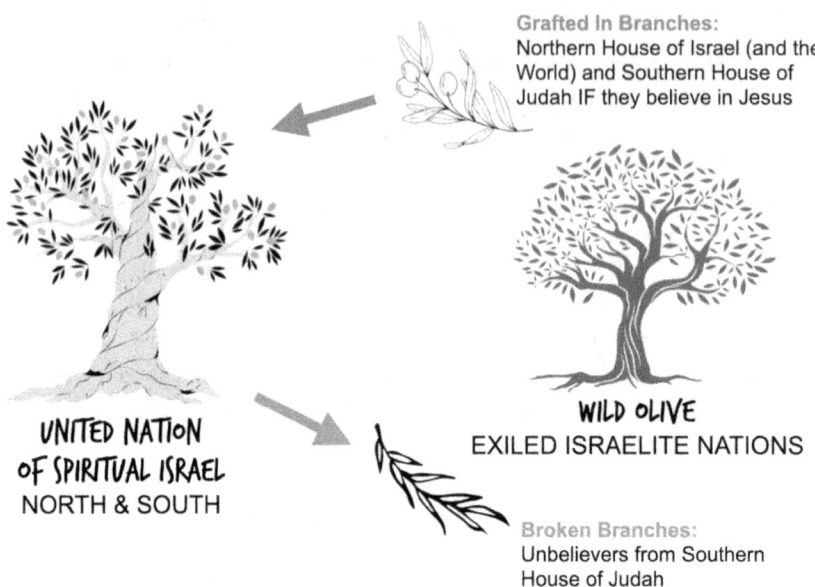

Grafted In Branches:
Northern House of Israel (and the World) and Southern House of Judah IF they believe in Jesus

WILD OLIVE
EXILED ISRAELITE NATIONS

UNITED NATION OF SPIRITUAL ISRAEL
NORTH & SOUTH

Broken Branches:
Unbelievers from Southern House of Judah

Figure 13.1: The Two Olive Trees of Romans

The opposite of this process is also true. Because of unbelief in Christ and stiff-necked adherence to the religion of Judaism, many branches of the House of Judah have been broken off from the olive tree of faith. They have forfeited the inheritance that was rightly theirs, since they were of the cultivated olive tree that returned from Babylonian captivity and once again inherited the land of Canaan. Paul made it clear that both the House of Israel and the House of Judah are able to be grafted back into the holy olive tree through faith in Christ alone. However, they are both also at risk of being cut out and removed from the tree due to unbelief in the finished work of Christ on the cross and disobedience to His commandments. For as Yeshua said, "If anyone does not abide in Me, he is cast out as a branch and is withered; and they gather them and throw them into the fire, and they are burned" (John 15:6). Abiding in Yeshua means taking careful heed to His word and His commandments in order to produce the fruit of repentance. Paul then concludes his dialogue with what has been one of the most confusing Bible verses for most people to understand:

"For I do not desire, brethren, that you should be ignorant of this mystery, lest you should be wise in your own opinion, that blindness in part has happened to [Judah] Israel until the fullness of the [Israelite] Gentiles has come in." (Rom. 11:25)

Without properly understanding the two houses of Israel, this verse will never make sense. Many false teachers have used this verse (along with others) as justification for the idea that a "church of gentiles" has currently replaced "Israel" in terms of God's covenant promises and purposes on the earth. This is one of those key verses where false ideas surrounding the aforementioned "church age" originate from.

The only thing Paul was *really* saying is that the Judaism-adhering South had become blinded by their traditions and oral laws; and as a result, the message of Christianity spread to the other nations outside the land of Canaan. This spread will continue until it reaches its "fullness" at the end of the age, for Jesus said, "And this gospel of the kingdom will be preached in all the world as a witness to all the nations, and then the end will come" (Mat. 24:14). With the rise of the internet and modern technology, this prophecy has now been completed. The world has access to the Bible online for free, and even the most remote places on earth can read the Gospel for themselves through a multitude of translations. That is why the end will now come as described in the first three Secrets of this book.

As alluded to, the olive tree metaphor was not unique to Paul. This same idea was first presented by Ezekiel and later by Zechariah. We also see it mentioned in the book of Revelation within the context of the two witnesses. Since Ezekiel contains the law-of-first-mention passage, let's examine what the prophet wrote.

16 As for you, son of man, take a stick for yourself and write on it: For Judah and for the children of Israel, his companions. Then take another stick and write on it, For Joseph, the stick of Ephraim, and for all the house of Israel, his companions.
17 Then join them one to another for yourself into one stick, and they will become one in your hand.
18 And when the children of your people speak to you, saying, "Will you not show us what you mean by these?"—
19 say to them, "Thus says the Lord GOD: Surely I will take the stick of Joseph, which is in the hand of Ephraim, and the tribes of Israel, his companions; and I will join them with it, with the stick of Judah, and make them one stick, and they will be one in My hand."
21 Then say to them, "Thus says the Lord GOD: "Surely I will take the children of Israel from among the nations, wherever they have gone, and will gather them from every side and bring them into their own land"
(Eze. 37:16-19,21)

As you can see, this passage is describing both the spiritual and physical Greater Exodus. As mentioned at the end of Chapter 12, there is one extremely important yet mistranslated word in this passage. It is the word "stick". The underlying Hebrew word is "עֵץ" (Strong's H6086) and is translated 162 times as "tree" and only 14 times as "stick" in the King James Version. The reason that the translators of most Bibles have made such a fatal mistake here is probably because they could not imagine Ezekiel holding two trees in his hand while joining them together to become one tree. What Ezekiel could have been doing was demonstrating the parable to his audience by somehow grafting the two sticks (scions) together in order to make one tree out of the two. By necessity, this means that one of the "sticks" in his hand acted as the rootstock from which to join the sticks together to become one tree. Another more likely interpretation of this account is that Ezekiel was indeed joining two trees together, but they were young trees still in their pots. Due to their small size, he would have been able to take both trees, one in each hand, and supernaturally join them together using an unconventional grafting technique. The curiosity present in the audience's question seems to indicate a miraculous joining of the two trees rather than the simple use of common grafting techniques. Regardless of the nuances, the point is that Judah and Israel are depicted as two trees, no doubt olives, that became one in the hand of Ezekiel as a representation of a two-part prophecy.

HOUSE OF
ISRAEL

HOUSE OF
JUDAH

ONE NATION

Figure 13.2: The Two Olive Trees of Ezekiel

The *spiritual* component of this metaphor was simply repeated by Jesus and later used by Paul to explain the mystery of the Gospel as it related to both the Judahites and the Israelite nations. The spiritual Greater Exodus is clear. Because of the new covenant, which is really a "renewed" covenant of the Torah, all the Tribes of Israel are able to join themselves to the one holy olive tree containing both kingdoms of the North and South. They have already become one new nation because of the sacrificial death and resurrection of Jesus. We are simply waiting for the complete fulfillment of the *physical* aspect of this prophecy where all of Israel—all thirteen tribes—will be gathered "from among the nations" and "from every side" back into the land of Canaan. This has not yet happened, but as you know, the 1948-Israel deception has completely fooled the vast majority of people into thinking that a Freemason state of the Western luciferian elites was the end-times fulfillment of the regathering. The falsehood of the 1948 state of Israel is far removed from the truth of the Word of God. As you will continue to discover, the physical Greater Exodus is far larger in magnitude than most people realize or care to admit openly for fear of being labeled "antisemitic" by the 1948 religious establishment.

THE COMING GREATER EXODUS

Because this prophecy is almost everywhere in the Bible, only a few key passages will be explored. For further reading, here is a list of references where the end-times exodus of Israel is mentioned (this is not an all-inclusive list):

> Leviticus 26:33-45; Deuteronomy 4:27-31; Deuteronomy 30:4; Isaiah 10:20;
> Isaiah 11:12; Isaiah 14:1,2; Isaiah 19:24; Isaiah 56:7,8; Isaiah 57:13,14; Isaiah
> 58:12-14; Isaiah 59:19-21; Isaiah 60:21 (whole chapter); Isaiah 61:4-6 (whole
> chapter); Isaiah 62:12; Jeremiah 3:18 (whole chapter); Jeremiah 23; Jeremiah
> 30 and 31; Jeremiah 49:39; Ezekiel 6:8,9; Ezekiel 11:16,17; Ezekiel 20:33
> (whole chapter); Ezekiel 22:15; Ezekiel 28:25; Ezekiel 34; Ezekiel 36 starting
> in verse 8; Ezekiel 37 and 38; Ezekiel 43:7 (whole chapter); Psalm 98:3;
> Hosea 3:5 (whole chapter); Joel 3; Amos 9:11 (whole chapter); Habakkuk
> 3:12-13; Zephaniah 3:9-20; Zechariah 7:14; Zechariah 10:6-12; Zechariah
> 13:7-9; Zechariah 14; Micah 2:12-13; Micah 7:14-20; Obadiah 1:17-21;
> Matthew 24:29-31; Mark 13:24-27; and Luke 21:25-28.

Just like the children of Israel experienced the original exodus out of Egyptian captivity, they will once again be freed from a final captivity under the coming satanic new world order. This exodus will be so great and so amazing in every respect that it will bring God a new and lasting level of fame throughout the earth that has never been experienced before.

In fact, just like the children of Israel walked across dry land when crossing the Red Sea, they will be doing this again but this time in a far more significant way. This is what Isaiah records:

15 The LORD will utterly destroy the tongue of the Sea of Egypt; With His mighty wind He will shake His fist over the River, And strike it in the seven streams, And make men cross over dryshod.
16 There will be a highway for the remnant of His people Who will be left from Assyria, As it was for Israel In the day that he came up from the land of Egypt.
(Isa. 11:15,16)

When the Scripture says that the "tongue" of the sea will be destroyed, this is no doubt a reference to the Nile Delta on the Mediterranean Sea. Miraculous winds will transform this entire landscape. It is recorded that the fist of God will then make the Nile River itself split into seven different streams so that a highway for the remnant of Israel can return back to the land of Canaan on dry land. This same description of the regathering is repeated in Zechariah, where he writes, "He shall pass through the sea with affliction, And strike the waves of the sea: All the depths of the River shall dry up. Then the pride of Assyria shall be brought down, And the scepter of Egypt shall depart" (Zec. 10:11). Both of these verses are further corroborated by Isaiah 49:11, where he writes this concerning the Greater Exodus: "I will make each of My mountains a road, And My highways shall be elevated." Standing in agreement, Micah also says, "As in the days when you came out of the land of Egypt, I will show them wonders" (Mic. 7:15). All of these passages together with the multitudes of other descriptions of this coming event paint a picture of immense magnitude. The whole world will see this Greater Exodus and will never be the same again. This is precisely what we are told by Jeremiah:

14 "Therefore behold, the days are coming," says the LORD, "that it shall no more be said, 'The LORD lives who brought up the children of Israel from the land of Egypt,'
15 "but, 'The LORD lives who brought up the children of Israel from the land of the north and from all the lands where He had driven them.' For I will bring them back into their land which I gave to their fathers."
(Jer. 16:14,15)

After this event takes place, Yehovah will forever be remembered as the God of the Greater Exodus. The original Egyptian exodus will pale in comparison. As you can see from Jeremiah's words, the scattered Israelites will be called from every land of the world. Everyone will witness one of the most profound and unprecedented events ever to take place on the stage of history as Israel is brought back to the "land of their fathers" in Canaan. Speaking of this regathering, Ezekiel tells us that God Himself is going to be the one sprinkling His people with clean water in order to properly cleanse them from all filth and idolatry (Eze. 36:25). In other words, not only has Yeshua already fulfilled the cleansing of His people through His blood, but in the future, He is also going to symbolically sprinkle his people with cleansing water. He is going to be the one bringing His people back into a righteous relationship with Him where they are able to serve and worship without any hindrance. Speaking of God's "Holy Mountain", Zephaniah gives us more details on what this Greater Exodus will look like:

9 "For then I will restore to the peoples a pure language, That they all may call on the name of the LORD, To serve Him with one accord.
12 "I will leave in your midst A meek and humble people, And they shall trust in the name of the LORD.
13 "The remnant of Israel shall do no unrighteousness And speak no lies, Nor shall a deceitful tongue be found in their mouth; For they shall feed their flocks and lie down, And no one shall make them afraid."
(Zep. 3:9,12,13)

Just as the languages were first confused by God because of the sin of the Tower of Babel, God will once again restore a pure speech and a pure language for all of His people to speak so that they can have a relationship with Him in unity. It is my speculation that this language will be similar to if not exactly the same as biblical Hebrew. With this fresh outpouring of the breath of life, God will miraculously allow all of His chosen and regathered people to speak this renewed language effortlessly, as if they had been born with the native ability to express this tongue. They will be a meek and humble people, with the Torah of God written on their hearts. Because of this supernatural revival and fresh outpouring of the Holy Spirit, they will not be able to tell lies or act deceitfully towards their neighbors. No one will make them afraid, and they will not require missile defense systems like the Iron Dome or David's Sling as is the case with the current 1948 counterfeit regathering. They will not need nuclear weapons, fighter jets, or tanks to defend themselves. God alone will be their strength and their defense, for as Ezekiel wrote, "Surely with a mighty hand, with an outstretched arm, and with fury poured out, I will rule over you" (Eze. 20:33).

THE COMING REBELLION

Just like during the days of the original Egyptian exodus, the Greater Exodus is not going to be a free ticket to the Promised Land. There will be testing. Sadly, some of these newly regathered people will prove to be ungrateful, stiff-necked, and unworthy. Even after witnessing a host of miracles and literally seeing the face of Jesus, some people will be falling away from grace in the midst of God's camp. This is exactly what we read in these words of Ezekiel:

34 "I will bring you out from the peoples and gather you out of the countries where you are scattered, with a mighty hand, with an outstretched arm, and with fury poured out.
35 "And I will bring you into the wilderness of the peoples, and there I will plead My case with you face to face.
36 "Just as I pleaded My case with your fathers in the wilderness of the land of Egypt, so I will plead My case with you," says the Lord GOD.
37 "I will make you pass under the rod, and I will bring you into the bond of the covenant;
38 "I will purge the rebels from among you, and those who transgress against Me; I will bring them out of the country where they dwell, but they shall not enter the land of Israel. Then you will know that I *am* the LORD."
(Eze. 20:34-38)

God will deal with His regathered people from all nations "face to face" just like He did with the generation of Moses that left Egypt. This is a key phrase. Due to ignorance of the three laws of interpretation, some falsely teach that King David will be resurrected in order to reign over regathered Israel for 1,000 years after the 70th week of Daniel is over. That is not what the Word says. Yeshua will deal with His people "face to face." He will be the King over His people. Much like the original Exodus, his glory will be visible and manifested for all to see. That being the case, we are also told that not everyone who is gathered from the nations will enter into His rest. During the days of Moses, Israel sinned ten times against God and thereby forfeited their opportunity to enter the land of Canaan until 40 years of wandering in the wilderness were completed (Num. 14:22). Once again, there will still be law breakers in the camp. There will still be rebellious sinners in the midst of the righteous, which just goes to show you how merciful Elohim really is. He is truly willing that none perish but that all should come to repentance. His love is unconditional, otherwise no one would be saved at all.

However, also consider the deeper nuances here. He will purposely regather some sinners referred to as *rebels* in this passage in order to test the remainder of the people. Will these people regathered out of harsh captivity follow His Torah and His ways, or not? The rebels will complain, murmur, and groan against Yehovah just like their rebellious fathers did in the original exodus from Egypt. They might be rebelling because of thirst, hunger, or discomfort. God will most likely allow these adverse circumstances to take place so that He can see who really has a heart to follow Him or not. However, we are given a few more clues as to what these rebels will be like. Within the exact context of the Greater Exodus, Ezekiel tells us, "'But as for those whose hearts follow the desire for their detestable things and their abominations, I will recompense their deeds on their own heads,' says the Lord GOD" (Eze. 11:21). The rebels will be desiring the "abominations" of the nations that they were regathered from. This could be a reference to many things, but the first thing that comes to mind is a craving for unclean meats. During the original exodus, we read that one of the main sins of the people was their lust for the meat of Egypt (Numbers 11:6). They eventually despised God's manna. For this reason, many ended up dying as recorded in Numbers 11:34, and something similar will most likely take place again during the coming Greater Exodus.

All these things are to be expected as history repeats itself. Unlike the days of Moses, however, there will not be 40 years of wandering. Instead, the sinners in the camp will be "purged", which really means they will be put to the test, exposed, and quickly removed. Should you be blessed to participate in this coming exodus, these rebels will attempt to drag you down and bring you into their immature spiritual state of mind. Don't let them. Endure to the very end, and you will be saved and inherit the Promised Land just like Joshua and Caleb did in their day. Isaiah 56 tells us that when the outcasts of Israel are gathered it will be "everyone who keeps from defiling the Sabbath, and holds fast My covenant" that will be allowed to dwell at God's holy mountain (Isa. 56:6). Once Israel is regathered, God says, "I will put My Spirit within you and cause you to walk in My statutes, and you will keep My judgments and do them" (Eze. 36:27). It will be a righteous society with mutual love, respect, set-apart living, and the presence of Almighty God within its midst. Such a society has never been witnessed before in history.

THE MATTHEW 24 TIMELINE

Now that you have a clear idea of how the Greater Exodus is described as a miraculous display of God's power, how Yeshua will deal with His people face to face, and how the rebels against God's Torah will be purged, it can be more easily discerned how this event might unfold within a timeline. This information is best presented within Matthew 24, with various Hebrew scriptures filling in the blanks to complete a blurry, yet visible picture of when the Greater Exodus might occur in the future.

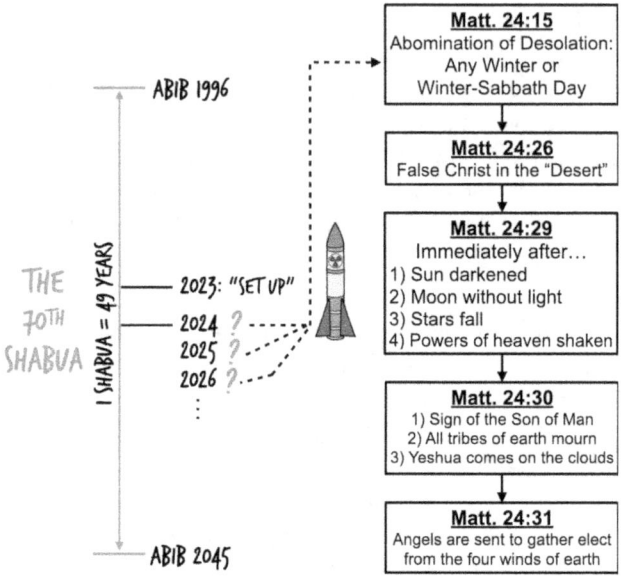

Figure 13.3: The Matthew 24 Timeline

Understanding that the abomination of desolation was set up on September 22, 2023, we can expect the actual deployment of this weapon to take place any winter or winter-sabbath day from that date onward. Maybe it will take place in the winter of 2024, 2025, 2026, or perhaps even beyond; but it is only a matter of time. The archers of Iran will finally make their move against Jerusalem, and all the West will be swarmed by the forces of the BRICS alliance in the aftermath of a short-lived thermonuclear war that Israel and its allies will lose. As demonstrated in Chapter 4, the coming prince and his people will most likely be the prophesied Mahdi of Islam and the Muslim people of the world. After the abomination of desolation is mentioned, Jesus expressly warns us to beware of a false christ that is going to appear in the "desert" in Matthew 24:26, further giving validity to this understanding. We are then told that immediately afterwards, the sun will be darkened, the moon will not give its light, and the powers of the heavens will be shaken. This is most likely a reference to thermonuclear war. Even though the popular "nuclear winter" theory is government-sponsored propaganda, there is no doubt that the sky might be blackened for maybe two weeks due to the immense smoke and ash that will fill the atmosphere from the curse of the flying scrolls worldwide. These events also correspond with the Day of the LORD and Joel's pillars of smoke. Joel 2:2 also told us to expect "A day of darkness and gloominess, A day of clouds and thick darkness", which further parallels the words of Jesus. Yeshua's return has already been described, particularly in Chapter 10. At the conclusion of the 1000-year reign, Yeshua will leave the right hand of the Father and will be seated on a cloud as described in Revelation 14:14-16 where He harvests the earth. I am of the understanding that this "good" harvest is not speaking of judgment, but it is speaking instead of the same exact event as Matthew 24:30,31. With this understanding, it is easy to see how Yeshua sitting on the cloud to perform this harvest will be a visible "sign", and all of the tribes on earth will mourn as they witness Him "coming on the clouds of heaven with power and great glory" (Mat. 24:30). It is precisely at this moment when the trumpet is blasted on the Feast of Trumpets, and the angels are sent out to gather the 13 tribes of Israel out of captivity. In fact, this trumpet blast is the exact same trumpet blast of Isaiah, when he wrote, "So it shall be in that day: The great trumpet will be blown; They will come, who are about to perish in the land of Assyria, And they who are outcasts in the land of Egypt, And shall worship the LORD in the holy mount at Jerusalem" (Isa. 27:13). Notice the strong emphasis of this verse on the territories of Egypt and Assyria. You may have already noticed this wording in several other "regathering" verses that I have presented in this chapter. There is a specific reason for this emphasis on Egypt and Assyria, and I will now attempt to explain it.

Regarding the antichrist from the "desert" of the Middle East, this same figure is going to be awarded the position of Supreme Leader in the BRICS alliance together with all nations of the world. His reign will be 42 months as described in Daniel and Revelation; and now, with the new information I am about to present, I will state my case that this ruler appears to be setting up his headquarters in Egypt, which just became a BRICS-10 member nation in 2023. Just like during the ancient times of Israel's harsh captivity under the Pharaoh, it appears that history might actually repeat itself with a similar captivity being established by a coming Egyptian ruler.

Before I share my findings regarding the antichrist, consider these words of David: "The heavens declare the glory of God; And the firmament shows His handiwork" (Psalm 19:1). Genesis 1:14 further establishes the importance of the sun, moon, and stars as God's witnesses for us to determine the signs and seasons. In addition to these words, Yeshua rebuked the Pharisees, stating,

"Hypocrites! You know how to discern the face of the sky, but you cannot discern the signs of the times" (Mat 16:3). He spoke harshly to them because they knew how to see weather patterns like stormy weather, but they simply did not know how to discern the signs that God had appointed in the heavens. To avoid making the same mistake as the Pharisees, make sure to read *Bible Prophecy Secrets II,* which is book two in this series. In it, I describe in great detail what the "sign of Jonah" over ancient Nineveh was, what it looks like, and what it indicates to the nations that see this celestial sign. The next figures show what this ancient omen looked like in ancient Nineveh and also modern-day America—both of whom were recipients of this divine omen of judgment.

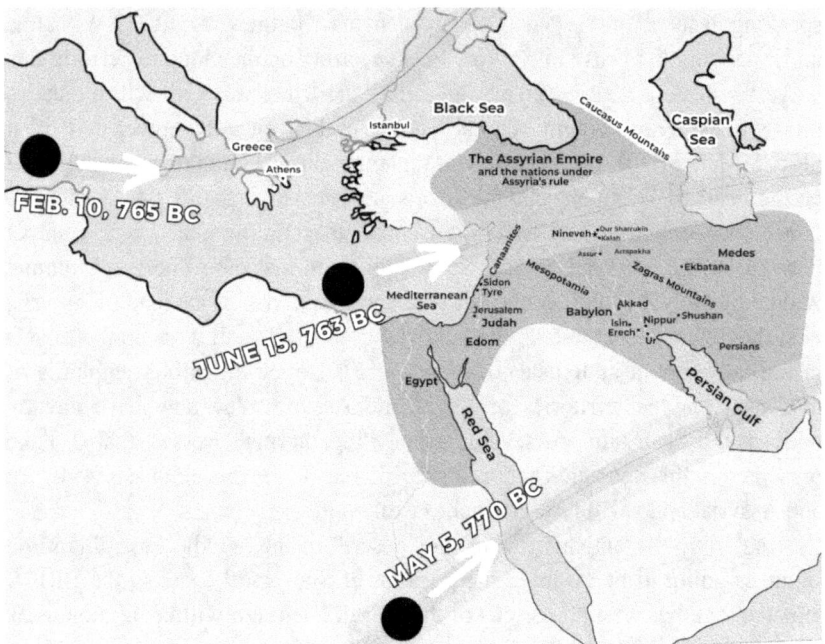

Figure 13.4a: The Sign of Jonah in Nineveh. This was the Assyrian Empire's boundaries at its peak of power during the Neo-Assyrian period (dark purple).

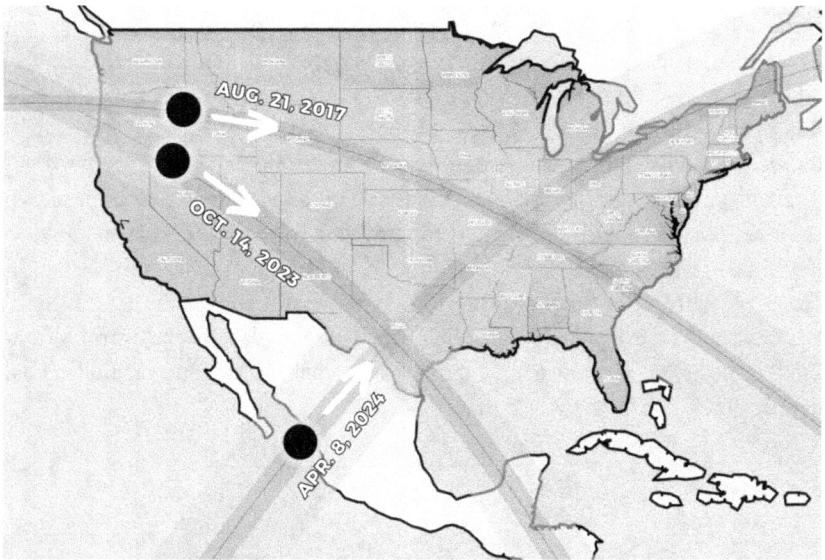

Figure 13.4b: The Sign of Jonah over the United States.

Both ancient Assyria and modern-America received a triple solar eclipse omen over a duration of seven years. In the case of America, the celestial sign began with a total solar eclipse on August 21, 2017 and ended with a total solar eclipse on April 8, 2024. Together, the three solar eclipses covered the four corners of the land in all four cardinal directions. The exact same thing was true of Assyria. The northern and southern extremities of the empire witnessed a total solar eclipse. This original *sign of Jonah* event took place from 770 to 763 BC. During this timeframe, the capital city of Nineveh itself witnessed the two major solar eclipses of 765 and 763 BC. In other words, the sign of Jonah is a total solar eclipse cycle that takes place over a nation. Based on all my research, it is usually a seven-year cycle, though this is not always the case. These specific solar eclipse omens are of extreme importance because they are usually surrounded by natural disasters, war, plagues, and famine, among other catastrophic outcomes.

The reason why the seven-year "sign of Jonah" is so crucial for properly understanding the coming Greater Exodus of the tribes is because there is going to be yet another such event taking place precisely over the land of Egypt and the Red Sea—the same locations that God said He will strike with His fist to create highways in the desert for His remnant to return back to the land of Canaan. According to NASA data, there is going to be a total solar eclipse on August 2, 2027 that will be visible over Africa, Europe, the Middle

East, and Southwest Asia with the path of totality passing directly through Morocco, Spain, Algeria, Libya, Egypt, Saudi Arabia, Yemen, and Somalia.[1] Almost seven years later on March 20, 2034, the final total solar eclipse of this cycle will appear over Africa, Europe, and West Asia with the path of totality through Nigeria, Cameroon, Chad, Sudan, Egypt, Saudi Arabia, Iran, Afghanistan, Pakistan, India, and China.[2] Though the time between these two solar eclipses is roughly 6 years, 7 months, and 18 days, this celestial sign to the Middle East still fits perfectly within the definition of the sign of Jonah. In fact, this will be the final sign of Jonah before the end of the age in 2045 besides another "Aleph" sign of Jonah that will take place over Australia from 2028 to 2037.[3,4] The following figure shows what the upcoming Middle East eclipses look like on the world map.

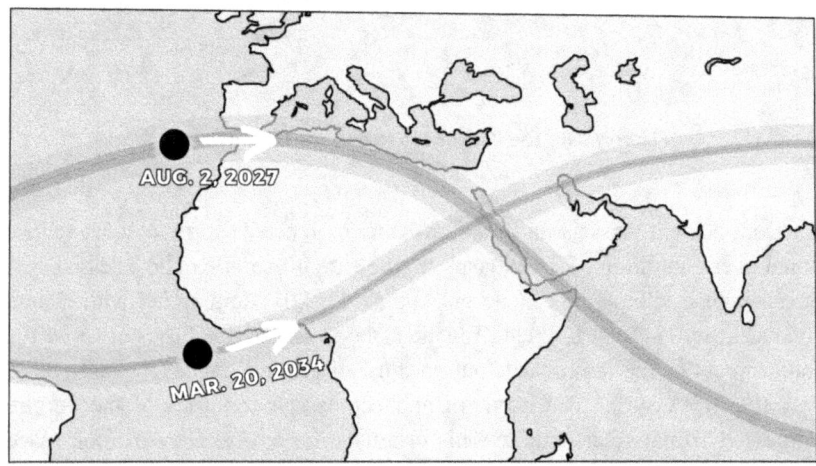

Figure 13.5: The Sign of Jonah to Egypt

These two eclipse events might be considered the most highly visible solar eclipses of all recent history, especially the one in 2034. Nearly all the world's population will be exposed to this celestial event, and its purpose as an omen of judgment against Islam is very obvious. The first eclipse of 2027 will pass through Mecca, Saudi Arabia, which was the birthplace of Muhammed in AD 570. The final eclipse will in like manner pass over Medina, Saudi Arabia— the place where Muhammed died in 623. These two cities are the holiest and second holiest places in all of Islam, respectively. Though no major historical event (besides the eclipse itself) may accompany the beginning of this cycle in 2027, the same cannot be said of the 2034 eclipse. Not only does March 20, 2034 fall within the timeframe of the Hebrew month of Abib, the first month of the year, but there is a strange and overlapping synchronicity between the Hebrew calendar and the calendars of several other major religious systems in 2034. In his detailed analysis of this coming solar eclipse, religious astronomer Dean Coombs states:

"[The eclipse] occurs a few hours before the Muslim (Hijri) New Year, (by the sighting of the first crescent moon). Sunni Muslims observe this day to cele-brate the victory of Moses over the Egyptian Pharaoh. (The Jewish and Muslim calendars overlap in agreement like this only every 12 or 13 years on average because the Muslim calendar employs no leap month or day system to adjust to the solar year.) [It also] occurs a few hours before the Spring Equinox — the Solar New Year! Therefore, it occurs a few hours before the Persian, Kurdish, and Afghan New Years – the same locations where the eclipse also passes over because their calendars are made to coincide with the Spring Equinox. (India's New Year is delayed by one day.) ...Perhaps the most remarkable is that the eclipse passes over Iran, and directly over the city of Shiraz, the home of the Bahá'í faith and its calendar. Their calendar works on 19-year cycles, and the eclipse marks either their New Year's day (in the Middle East), or a few hours before the New Year outside the Middle East. — But amazingly, this day completes the 190th year of their calendar (ten full cycles of 19 years from 1844 AD)![5]

In addition to the Hebrew calendar of the Torah, several other major reli-gious systems will also be experiencing a mathematically improbable meeting point in which a new year will be declared on or immediately around March 20, 2034. Coombs also goes on to state that the Chinese New Year will happen to fall at a later time than usual in 2034. As briefly mentioned, the first day of Nowruz and the Persian New Year always lands on the spring equinox, which is March 20 or 21 depending on the year; and this observance is similar in other nations besides Iran. From the Bible alone, we can see that March of this specific year will be the ushering in of something new and unprecedented. Of course, Abib is completely dependent on the presence of green ears of barley in the land of Israel, but the New Moon to begin the year could easily land on the evening of February 20, 2034, which would result in March 20th still likely falling within the first month, as the next New Moon is expected on the evening of March 20, 2034.[6] Alternatively, the evening of March 20, 2034 could easily be the first new moon of the year. Either way, this eclipse falls right in or around Abib. This sign of Jonah omen to the Middle East, and especially Egypt, also has an exact point of intersection near the southeast border of Egypt and in the Red Sea. As discussed in *Bible Prophecy Secrets II,* this symbol is the ancient Phoenician letter *tav*, which looks like an English "X" or a sideways lowercase "t". The presence of the eclipse intersection here is very reminiscent of the original Exodus when the children of Israel crossed over the Red Sea to go to Mount Sinai. This divinely orchestrated history lesson is no coincidence. As I will now demonstrate, the seven-year eclipse omen from 2027 to 2034 appears to be the climatic sign right before the return of Christ with His judgment upon the Muslim-dominated BRICS alliance and its satan-controlled leader.

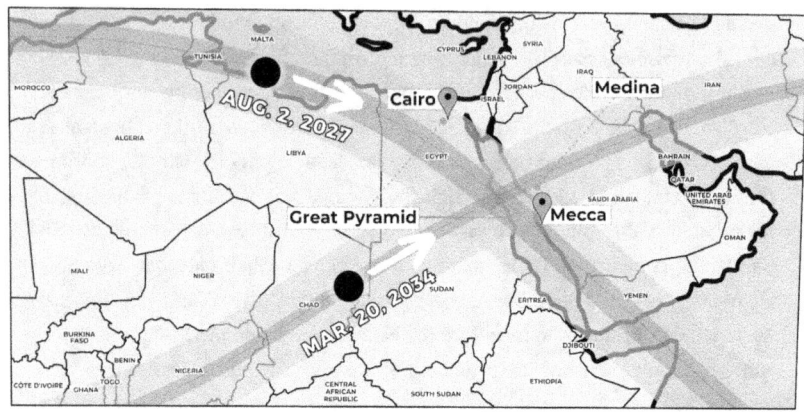

Figure 13.6: The Nations of the Coming Sign of Jonah[7,8]

I will now reveal to you God's judgment within the correct context of the regathering of Israel's tribes and the solar eclipses from 2027 to 2034. It will also become clear as to why Egypt is a key focus of the coming new world order together with its swift destruction. The mystery of this coming sign of Jonah is perfectly described within these words of Isaiah:

1 The burden against Egypt. Behold, the LORD rides on a swift cloud, And will come into Egypt; The idols of Egypt will totter at His presence, And the heart of Egypt will melt in its midst.
2 I will set Egyptians against Egyptians; Everyone will fight against his brother, And everyone against his neighbor, City against city, kingdom against kingdom.
3 The spirit of Egypt will fail in its midst; I will destroy their counsel, And they will consult the idols and the charmers, The mediums and the sorcerers.
4 And the Egyptians I will give Into the hand of a cruel master, And a fierce king will rule over them," Says the Lord, the LORD of hosts.
(Isa. 19:1-4)

The passage opens by reminding us of the triune nature of God, or Elohim, and that Yehovah riding on a cloud is the exact same thing as the "Son of Man coming on the clouds" event that was described in the Matthew 24 timeline. Jesus is God, and this truth is so plainly obvious here. It is at this moment when all tribes mourn when they see the sign of the Son of Man when He returns to both judge the nations and also gather up his elect from the four corners. The Egyptians, as described here, will be among the tribes of the earth that will be greatly mourning at the appearance of Christ. In fact, of all the nations, they receive a special word of righteous indignation from God throughout this chapter of Isaiah. Of special importance are the words describing "a fierce king" ruling over Egypt in verse four. We have already seen the concepts of a "scepter" or "ruler" in the land of Egypt within other verses describing the coming Greater Exodus. Once again, we see here, by implication, that because end-times Egypt dealt so harshly with the nations of the world, God will repay this nation by placing a harsh ruler over it. This wording of Isa. 19:4 is yet another clue that we are to be looking for an antichrist leader from the desert and particularly Egypt, but there are certainly more clues. The third verse indicates an extensive use of sorcery and black magic, which will become more clear when we look at the Great Pyramid of Giza. Regarding the sign of Jonah and the aftermath of the satanic new world order, this is what Isaiah describes next:

5 The waters will fail from the sea, And the river will be wasted and dried up.
6 The rivers will turn foul; The brooks of defense will be emptied and dried up; The reeds and rushes will wither.
7 The papyrus reeds by the River, by the mouth of the River, And everything sown by the River, Will wither, be driven away, and be no more.
8 The fishermen also will mourn; All those will lament who cast hooks into the River, And they will languish who spread nets on the waters.
9 Moreover those who work in fine flax And those who weave fine fabric will be ashamed;
10 And its foundations will be broken. All who make wages will be troubled of soul.
16 In that day Egypt will be like women, and will be afraid and fear because of the waving of the hand of the LORD of hosts, which He waves over it.
(Isa. 19:5-10,16)

This level of catastrophic judgment would by necessity be preceded by the solar eclipses from 2027 to 2034 because this is how God typically judges the nations. He first gives them the sign, and then there is justification for Him to

act swiftly after the warning has been received. In this case, the very foundations of Egypt will be completely broken. Notice that this wording here in
Isaiah 19 perfectly matches the verses from Isaiah 11 and Zechariah 10 that I
presented earlier. Isaiah 11:15 describes Yehovah shaking His "fist" over the
Nile River, and this idea is repeated here in Isaiah 19:16 where it speaks of
the Egyptians being afraid because He will wave His "hand" over the nation.
The waters of the Mediterranean near the Nile Delta will be dried up, which is
exactly what we were told in Zechariah 10:11. Regarding this prophecy about
the Greater Exodus, God tells us that "I will also bring them back from the
land of Egypt, And gather them from Assyria. I will bring them into the land
of Gilead and Lebanon, Until no more room is found for them" (Zec. 10:10).
We see that both Egypt and Assyria will be playing central end-times roles in
the captivity and plundering of the West. I have already discussed Iran's role
in ushering in the Great Tribulation. This nation marks the end of the eastern-
most boundary of the ancient Assyrian empire. Egypt is situated at the westernmost boundary of the Middle East. Together, the modern nations within
the borders of the ancient empires from Egypt to Assyria will be responsible
for carrying out an Islamic jihad against the West in a historical way. Apparently, both of these territories will be housing large numbers of captives from
Israel and Judah, since God will require them to be released sometime after
the sign of Jonah runs its course. Of the two biblical identities, Egypt receives
a far greater judgment than Assyria, as is evident by the location of the
eclipse intersection and all of the natural disasters that are described in the
Prophets. Once the regathering has taken place, this is what Isaiah tells us
next:

17 And the land of Judah will be a terror to Egypt; everyone who makes
mention of it will be afraid in himself, because of the counsel of the LORD of
hosts which He has determined against it.
18 In that day five cities in the land of Egypt will speak the language of
Canaan and swear by the LORD of hosts; one will be called the City of
Destruction.
19 In that day there will be an altar to the LORD in the midst of the land of
Egypt, and a pillar to the LORD at its border.
20 And it will be for a sign and for a witness to the LORD of hosts in the land
of Egypt; for they will cry to the LORD because of the oppressors, and He
will send them a Savior and a Mighty One, and He will deliver them.
21 Then the LORD will be known to Egypt, and the Egyptians will know the
LORD in that day, and will make sacrifice and offering; yes, they will make a
vow to the LORD and perform it.

22 And the LORD will strike Egypt, He will strike and heal it; they will return to the LORD, and He will be entreated by them and heal them.

23 In that day there will be a highway from Egypt to Assyria, and the Assyrian will come into Egypt and the Egyptian into Assyria, and the Egyptians will serve with the Assyrians.

24 In that day Israel will be one of three with Egypt and Assyria—a blessing in the midst of the land,

25 whom the LORD of hosts shall bless, saying, "Blessed is Egypt My people, and Assyria the work of My hands, and Israel My inheritance."

(Isa. 19:17-25)

If anyone tells you that these events all took place at some point in the past, simply bring up verse 25 because clearly, the Middle East from Egypt to Iran has never been at peace like what is being described here. At the conclusion of the sign of Jonah against Egypt, Isaiah states that the newly regathered people of the land of Judah will be a "terror" to the Egyptians. This is most likely referring to Yeshua's punishment of Egypt and how He made a distinction between His people and the people of the antichrist. We again see reference to the words spoken of by Zephaniah 3:9 where the regathered tribes of Israel will be restored with a "pure language", and this language "of Canaan" will also be spoken in five Egyptian cities. As I mentioned earlier, I believe this restored language to be a form of biblical Hebrew. Recall that at the coming of Christ on the clouds, Yehovah said He was going to place a fierce ruler over Egypt. It is here in Isaiah 19:20-22 that we learn why God did this thing. It was to bring Egypt into repentance through hardship, and once this purpose is complete, He will remove the oppression He had appointed over them and allow them to enter into a covenant of peace between the regathered tribes of Israel together with Assyria. At the end of it all, the entire Middle East will finally be at rest and become one people under Yehovah. These words of Isaiah mark the conclusion of the sign of Jonah judgment that will soon take place over end-times Egypt.

Going back to the Matthew 24 timeline, I intentionally left out the last part of the verse when I originally quoted Yeshua's "desert" antichrist warning. Concerning the coming false christ, Jesus actually said, "Therefore if they say to you, 'Look, He is in the desert!' do not go out; or 'Look, He is in the inner rooms!' do not believe it" (Mat. 24:26). Only with the information now presented can we take a look at what He may have meant by the "inner rooms". This word is Strong's G5009 (ταμείοις) and is translated as "secret chambers" in the KJV. It also carries the meaning of a secret room, storehouse, or chamber, especially an inner one. This may come as quite a surprise, but what Jesus was most likely describing to us was none other than the Great Pyramid of Giza located just southwest of Cairo. In a March 2023 article entitled "Hidden Chamber Revealed Inside Great Pyramid of Giza", this is what Smithsonian correspondent Christopher Parker reported:

> "Even at 4,500 years old, the Great Pyramid of Giza is still revealing new secrets. On Thursday, Egyptian officials announced the discovery of a hidden corridor above the pyramid's entrance. Measuring 30 feet long, the passage could serve as a jumping-off point for additional research into the mysterious inner chambers. According to a new study published in the journal *Nature Communications*, the pyramid has been undergoing noninvasive scans since 2015. Through an international partnership known as ScanPyramids, researchers from around the world have been using cosmic-ray imaging and infrared thermography to map out what lies behind the sand-beaten stones of the exterior. These scans have revealed several voids, including the 30-foot passage, which lies just behind a chevron-shaped configuration of stones not far from where today's tourists enter the pyramid. A video released by Scan-Pyramids offers a glimpse into the mapping process and shows where this newly discovered corridor lies. After learning of the void, researchers used an endoscope to collect images of the corridor on February 24. 'The first pictures taken with the endoscope seem to show there is nothing, but we cannot see all the room precisely yet,' Sébastien Procureur [stated]."[9]

Of the seven wonders of the ancient world, the Great Pyramid is the largest of the remaining pyramids of Egypt, most of which lie in ruins. It is still one of the largest stone structures in the world. The Great Pyramid is a solid mass of stone covering just over 13 acres of land and containing 90,000,000 cubic feet of masonry, which is the equivalent of 30 Empire State buildings.[10] The very top triangular piece, or capstone, was never built at the very top of the pyramid, and its absence has been used as a primary logo or insignia of various secret societies and cults from antiquity. This capstone is usually depicted with an *all-seeing eye* such as on the back of the American one dollar bill or the gate of the Catholic Aachen Cathedral in Germany. According to archeologists, there is no evidence that the interior of the Great Pyramid was ever penetrated and explored prior to the year AD 820, which was the year the Caliph of Baghdad, Al Mamoun, sent a crew of workman to find treasure that was assumed to be hidden inside.[11] The pyramid was finally opened as a result of the tremendous effort of the Caliph's men, though they came out empty handed and unable to find secret wealth. What most people don't realize is that within the Great Pyramid, there are multiple chambers, shafts, and passages that have since been discovered in recent times. These are depicted in the next figure.

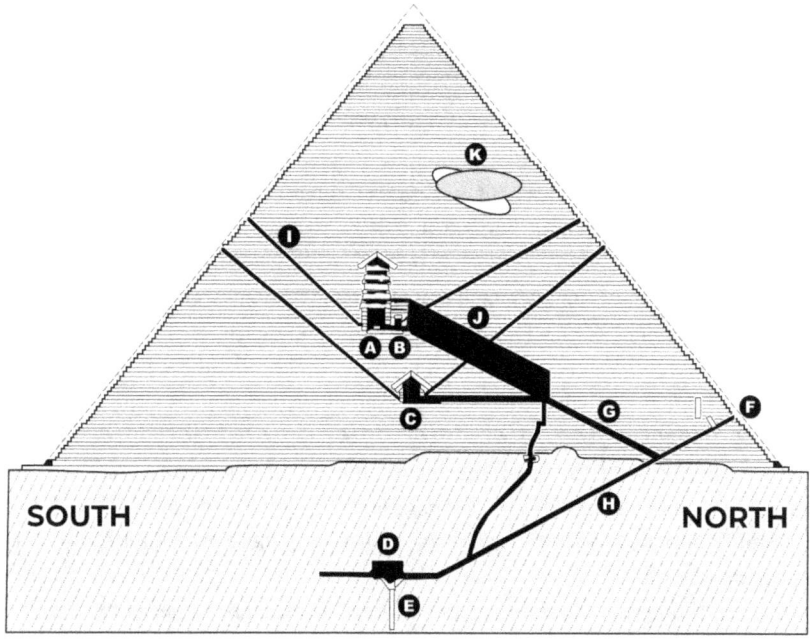

Figure 13.7: Passages and Chambers in the Great Pyramid

The mainstream narrative regarding the pyramid's design and purpose asserts that the structure is no more than a burial site for an ancient Egyptian monarch by the name of Khufu, also known as Cheops (2589–2566 BC). For this reason, the structure called the King's Chamber (A) contains a sarcophagus, or stone coffin, where the monarch was presumed to be buried. The Queen's Chamber (C) also contains a similar sarcophagus. To get inside the structure, the pyramid's true entrance (F) is located on the north side about fifty feet above the base level of the structure. From this point, there are two directions of travel. There is the ascending passage (G) where the King and Queen Chambers can be accessed. On the way to the King's Chamber there is a Grand Gallery (J) with an Ante-Chamber (B) before arriving at the King's Chamber. All of these chambers have air channels (I) so that fresh air can circulate in the structure. One of the greater mysteries of the structure is found when traveling through the descending passage (H) and deep below the pyramid. Notice the large underground cavity called the Subterranean Chamber (D). The purpose of this particular chamber is unknown, however I will provide needed insight when I introduce what the secret society literature has to say about this pyramid. This Subterranean Chamber contains a deep vertical shaft called the Bottomless Pit (E). Of course, this Bottomless Pit is said to simply be a nickname based on a rumor that at some point in the past, this shaft was so deep that a stone could be tossed into but with no sound being made to confirm that there was a bottom. However, this Pit is no longer the same as it once was. It apparently collapsed on itself at some point and is filled with rubble and debris up to about 10 feet down. The presence of this chamber and its bottomless pit has fueled intense speculation, as you can imagine. Some researchers believe that it represents the abode of the dead. However, with the evidence I have presented so far directly from Yeshua's words, the presence of such a deep chamber with a Bottomless Pit gives tremendous weight to the idea that the coming antichrist will in fact ascend within the pyramid and be found in one of its secret chambers just as Yeshua warned. Speaking of such a chamber, researchers recently used an advanced imaging technique to locate what they believe to be two possible configurations of a Big Void (K) near the top of the pyramid's north side.[12,13] This cavity remains to be explored. As mentioned earlier, new research of the Great Pyramid continues to shock scientists, as it seems there are countless secrets to be found within.

Though inherent curiosity of the enormous structure is perfectly normal, the biggest question is why research surrounding the Great Pyramid has been constant and ongoing in modern times. Not only have the Egyptian Ministry of Antiquities and Tourism, UNESCO, and other major organizations provided funding for research and conservation projects related to the Pyramid of Giza, but Western academic institutions and private foundations of all kinds have poured in millions of dollars into studying the secrets of the structure. There are some big red flags present in all of this activity. What have they *really* been looking for all this time? Has this research *really* been a simple and pure pursuit of intellectual discovery, or is there more to the story? All these never-ending research efforts have the fingerprints of the secret societies all over them.

Now that we have looked at the Great Pyramid through the lens of the commonly accepted narrative along with my own commentary, it's time to consider what the secret societies themselves have to say. Recall from Chapter 11 that nearly all secret societies trace their teachings back to Enoch the evil of the lineage of Cain. It is said that this Enoch was directly responsible for preserving and hiding away the ancient knowledge of black magic practices and luciferian knowledge before the flood took place. This coveted knowledge pertains to technology, sciences, and the resurrection of the nephilim (giants), among various things. As was prophesied in Genesis 3:15, God told us that there would be generational warfare between the seed of Adam and the seed of the serpent. It is no surprise, then, that even though the flood destroyed the corruption of the pre-flood world, this corruption would, by necessity, find its way into our world after the flood waters had receded. Based on the writings and traditions of various societies, the original antediluvian knowledge was primarily buried in Egypt beneath the Great Pyramids[14] and hidden within sacred hieroglyphs (Egyptian pictures and symbols) that Enoch used for teaching the original mysticism of the seven sacred sciences, including their secret ceremonies and rituals. Biblical astronomer and pyramidologist Adrian Gilbert credits Enoch with the building of the Great Pyramids,[15] and according to legend, Enoch was the first real builder of cities and the first Master Mason of "the craft."[16] In his research, Gary Wayne notes that within secret storehouses just like the Great Pyramid of Giza, Enoch built nine subterranean vaults containing his mystical knowledge, and these pillars of Enoch were further preserved by Lamech, his grandson, who recorded the precise directions to the location of the nine vaults buried at the foot of the pyramids.[17] Though the tower of Babel and the surrounding region is known as the true birthplace of secret antediluvian knowledge, there is evidence within the lore of the secret societies that Egypt adopted Enochian practices immediately after the confusion of the languages occurred. In explaining the precise origins of Egypt's mysticism, Gary Wayne states:

"Two Craft legends, the Legend of Euclid and The Tower of Babel, both noted that the Seven Liberal Sciences were taught to the Egyptians because Egypt was inundated with so many sons and daughters who had nothing to do. The knowledge of the sciences allowed those unemployed Egyptians to make an honest living. Paul Naudon, author of *The Secret History of Freemasonry* and a noted Freemason, clarifies this legend by noting Abraham and Euclid taught only the Egyptian nobility geometry, for it was the nobility who had produced great numbers with nothing to do. Thus, the Egyptian nobility constructed churches, towers, castles, and all kinds of buildings from stone. The alternative, spurious legend, from the Craft's Anderson Legend and The Cooke Manuscript, states that the Corrupted Sciences were transported to Egypt at an earlier point in time. This occurred almost at the outset of Egyptian colonization. ...Hermes, the discoverer and translator of the Pillars of Lamech, traveled with Ham, Mizraim, and Mizraim's people, the Egyptians, to the land of Egypt, to the antediluvian home of the "first time" Egyptians who built the pyramids, once God confused the languages and dispersed the peoples from Babel."[18]

As you can see from their own writings, Masons believe that Egypt was instrumental in manifesting the knowledge of their craft. According to legend, Hermes was the founder of the ancient Egyptian city Hermopolis, and it would make sense that this mystical figure and ancient Egyptian priest would be responsible for establishing the culture of Egypt, having the knowledge of the "Corrupted Sciences" in the pyramids through the writings of Lamech. Moving forward to modern times, it is obvious why the symbol of the pyramid continues to be so elevated in all of popular culture. Hollywood movies like Stargate, The Mummy trilogy, and countless other works all promote the lore surrounding Egypt's pyramids. The endless scientific and archeological research projects to the tune of millions of dollars are also not accidental. Most likely, the demonic quest for secret antediluvian knowledge has still not been satisfied, and something still remains hidden in Egypt. With these things in mind, there are no other locations in the "desert" of the Middle East that would so perfectly fit Yeshua's warning about the "secret chambers" of a coming antichrist other than the Great Pyramid of Giza itself.

With all these things taken under consideration, we can now have an infinitely more complete understanding of the Matthew 24 timeline when compared to the original edition of this book. Now that the significance of the sign of Jonah over end-times Egypt has been established, it is reasonable to expect the return of Yeshua on the clouds to regather all tribes of Israel immediately before, on, or after the year 2034. If the Great American Eclipse cycle has taught us anything, it is that even the most rare and impressive omens do not necessarily produce immediately visible outcomes. Many were expecting major events to happen right around April 8, 2024 when this seven-year omen came to its end. Though I was partially under this impression, I have always maintained the view that only in the winter or on a sabbath-winter day should any major escalation involving the abomination of desolation be expected. That being the case, the regathering of the tribes could take place exactly within 2034, but it could even take place just before or just after. What we do know with complete certainty is that as soon as the abomination of desolation takes place, we are to expect the appearance of the Muslim antichrist ascending out of the bottomless pit and most likely somehow emerging into one of the secret chambers of Egypt's Great Pyramid. He will assert his rule quickly and reign for 42 months while commandeering the locust armies of BRICS to take down the West. We are also told the following in Revelation 11:3: "And I will give power to my two witnesses, and they will prophesy one thousand two hundred and sixty days, clothed in sackcloth." If we assume the two witnesses to be the same thing as the 144,000 as I proposed in the last chapter, then these "two" witnesses will not be harmed by the locust armies because they will be sealed on their foreheads with the mark of Yehovah. To the best of my current understanding, these "two" witnesses of the 144,000 are therefore also the "woman" in the wilderness described in Revelation 12. Here are the key words John wrote for us regarding this woman within the context of satan being loosed:

12 "Therefore rejoice, O heavens, and you who dwell in them! Woe to the inhabitants of the earth and the sea! For the devil has come down to you, having great wrath, because he knows that he has a short time."
13 Now when the dragon saw that he had been cast to the earth, he persecuted the woman who gave birth to the male Child.
14 But the woman was given two wings of a great eagle, that she might fly into the wilderness to her place, where she is nourished for a time and times and half a time, from the presence of the serpent.
17 And the dragon was enraged with the woman, and he went to make war with the rest of her offspring, who keep the commandments of God and have the testimony of Jesus Christ.
(Rev. 12:12-14,17)

Once again we see the reference to the "time, times, and half a time", or 3.5 years, of the antichrist's reign. Who else would the woman be except for the 144,000 with the seal of God on their foreheads? She represents Israel, who was the nation that gave birth to Christ. Her offspring are the ones who "keep the commandments of God and have the testimony of Jesus Christ" (Rev. 12:17). We are told in this final verse that satan proceeds to make war with the remainder of the offspring of this woman, which happen to be the same people of Daniel's prophecy. More specifically, recall from Chapter 4 that I translated the first part of Daniel 9:26 as follows: "And the Islamic people of a coming Mahdi will destroy Jerusalem along with the Jewish and Christian people." This same thought is being repeated for us in Revelation 12:17. Though the Jewish people claim to keep the commandments of God's Torah and the Christian people claim to have the testimony of Jesus Christ, there are only 144,000 who qualified as being firstfruits that followed God in a manner that was pleasing to Him. That is why the "left behind" Jewish and Christian communities will endure the heat of satan's great wrath in the coming persecution. They simply were not ready in advance.

With the interpretation that I have proposed, there is only one logical and biblical pattern in understanding the 42 months of the 144,000 and the 42 months of the antichrist. Because the 144,000 will be protected during the reign of the antichrist, they will be released to fulfill their calling for "one thousand two hundred and sixty days", or 42 months, as required by Revelation 11:3 only after the first 42 months of the antichrist are fulfilled. Just like Moses and Aaron performed their ministry of judgment upon the first Pharaoh, the "two" witnesses of the 144,000 will perform signs, wonders, and miracles in order to judge the last antichrist Pharaoh. They will turn waters into blood, and they will have the ability to strike the earth with plagues "as often as they desire" (Rev. 11:6). These events will torment the inhabitants of the earth and all those who have accepted the mark of the beast under satan's rule. The newly established Islamic Caliphate will suddenly lose its grip on power and be subject to the judgment of God through the ministry of the 144,000. That is why I stated earlier that these 144,000 are likely not going to be raptured into heaven and disappear to never be seen on the earth again. Instead, I believe they have a clear mission and assignment in fulfilling the same role as Moses and Aaron in these last days. They will be responsible for preparing the way for the return of Christ on the clouds.

If God's plan does unfold like this, then we can expect two periods of 42 months (84 months, or 7 years) to take place immediately after the abomination of desolation is deployed against Jerusalem. With this understanding of the Matthew 24 timeline in Figure 13.3, different outcomes can now be calculated, depending on when the Great Tribulation begins. These are illustrated in the next Figure.

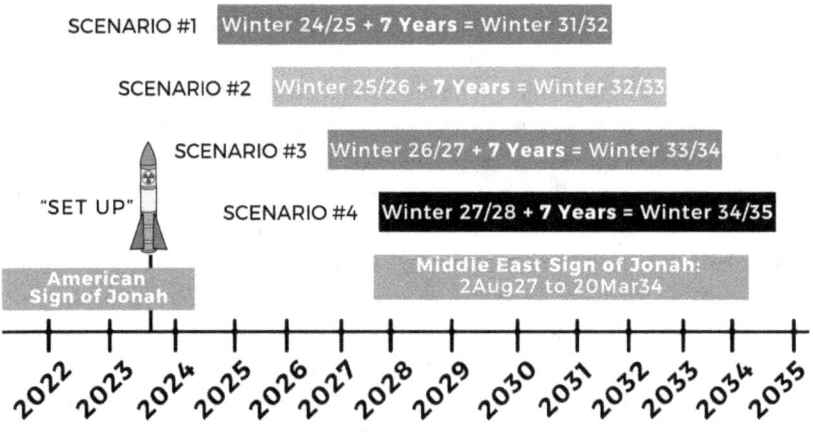

Figure 13.8: The Tribulation Timeline

As you can see, the timeline begins with the setting up of the abomination of desolation on September 22, 2023, which also occurred during the American Sign of Jonah cycle. Four scenarios are then presented depending on when the actual deployment of the nuclear weapon takes place to initiate the Great Tribulation and usher in the antichrist within the smoke of this event. According to the words of Yeshua in the Matthew 24 chronology, this deployment is to take place during the winter time frame. As discussed before, the Hebrew winter begins in what would be considered the North American fall time frame. More specifically, it takes place from about September (once the seventh Hebrew month begins) until March, or six months; the six months of the Hebrew summer then begin with the month of Abib around March to declare the New Year. What we can do is simply add 42 months of the antichrist to the date of the abomination of desolation and then add the 42 months of the two witnesses after the uninterrupted reign of the antichrist is completed to arrive at the point in time right before the regathering. These two 42-month periods are the only exact numbers given to us in the Bible for determining when the regathering of the elect is to take place.

That being the case, there are four assumptions made in this Figure that must be pointed out. First, this timeline assumes that the antichrist immediately asserts his rule no more than a few weeks or perhaps months after the bombs go off in the winter. This idea seems to be presented by Yeshua directly in the Matthew 24 timeline. However, this might not be the case. The antichrist might take longer to appear on the world stage. Because of the language given to us regarding the locust armies being under the direct command of satan in Revelation 9 together with the prophecies of the book of Joel, Daniel 11, and the woman (144,000) of Revelation who is protected in the wilderness, the Word gives us the impression that the antichrist will rise up and rule the nations no more than a few months after the Great Tribulation is initiated. Again, this is an assumption, but one with a solid foundation.

The second assumption is that the reign of the antichrist is immediately followed by the work of the two witnesses who will rise up and begin judging the satanic kingdom. Revelation and Daniel both tell us that the antichrist's reign cannot exceed 42 months, and therefore, this is a safe assumption to make. What the two witnesses will do with their worldwide ministry is disrupt the power of the antichrist, and he will be able to do nothing about it for the next 42 months. What these 144,000 Israelites will most likely be doing is exactly what Moses and Aaron did. They will be teaching the nations about Torah and how to follow the God of the Bible by restoring the ancient path of the Scriptures. At the same time, they might begin gathering up God's remnant into lands of "Goshen" throughout the world. This idea seems to be supported by the original Exodus account along with the "cities of refuge" concept that is recorded in the Torah. These cities were places for the guilty to flee to for safety when charged with accidental manslaughter. The cities were dispersed throughout different tribes such as Ephraim, Naphtali, and Levi as recorded in Joshua 21 and 1Chronicles 6. Perhaps a similar scenario will exist during the ministry of the 144,000 as God begins to prepare a remnant for Himself right after the bitterness of the 42-month antichrist reign is completed. The two witnesses will perform miracles just like the original plagues of Egypt. These plagues upon the satanic new world order and all recipients of the mark of the beast will be extremely severe. In fact, I encourage you to look through the book of Revelation with this understanding and see the parallels to the first Exodus and the ten plagues. Waters turned into blood, massive hailstones, boils on the flesh, darkness—it's all there. Elohim is the same yesterday, today, and forever. Apparently, He is going to use the 144,000 to accomplish these signs as his two witnesses in the end times.

The third assumption also presented in this Figure is that the two witnesses will be finishing their work in the winter time frame due to the necessity of the winter being the correct starting point of the seven-year period as defined by Yeshua in Matthew 24. When examining what happens when the two witnesses are killed by satan, this assumption makes a lot of sense. John declares, "And those who dwell on the earth will rejoice over them, make merry, and send gifts to one another, because these two prophets tormented those who dwell on the earth" (Rev. 11:10). This act of sending gifts and making merry during the winter time perfectly lines up with the pagan holiday of Christmas, or winter solstice, that the world has been celebrating since the time of ancient Egypt. This unbiblical holiday will certainly continue under the reign of the antichrist, and we see a clear description of this festival here. Though this pagan holiday is currently not accepted by Islam, there are two interpretations present in Revelation 11:10. First, it can be assumed that satan's miraculous appearance and reign will be accompanied by modifications to Islamic practice. Because of Christmas and the winter solstice's connection to the rebirth of the sun and worship of a wide variety of false gods, satan might easily demand to be worshiped on this day and institute a new festival of Islam. Secondly, the most holy month of Islam is its ninth month of Ramadan, and this entire month is one in which Muslims attempt to be more generous. The act of giving gifts takes place throughout the month and especially at the end of the month. When examining the upcoming dates for Ramadan as calculated using the Umm al-Qura calendar of Saudi Arabia and most countries of the Gulf, you will find a shocking discovery. The four Ramadan months that correspond with the four scenarios of Figure 13.8 will all be taking place in the Hebrew winter. More specifically, Ramadan will begin on December 15, 2031, December 4, 2032, November 23, 2033, and November 12, 2034.[19] Therefore, the death of the witnesses will take place in the Hebrew winter time frame and just in time for the gift giving activities of either Ramadan or the ancient solstice celebrations. The two witnesses will then be raised up after three and a half days as described in Rev. 11:11. Pay careful attention to what is proclaimed in heaven immediately after the two witnesses complete their testimony and the seventh trumpet is sounded: "Then the seventh angel sounded: And there were loud voices in heaven, saying, 'The kingdoms of this world have become *the kingdoms* of our Lord and of His Christ, and He shall reign forever and ever!'" (Rev. 11:15). This is the exact same language found in Daniel 7:27, indicating that the regathering of Israel will in fact occur immediately after the two witnesses are finished with their work.

The fourth and final assumption implied by Figure 13.8 is that the regathering of all tribes of Israel should take place immediately before or after the total solar eclipse of March 20, 2034. As mentioned earlier, the sign of Jonah gives us a wealth of information about what God is about to orchestrate on the earth, but it does not give us *exact* outcomes that will take place on specific dates. We can therefore speculate that the regathering could happen even before 2034, as is somewhat required by the first two scenarios. Scenario three almost perfectly coincides with the sign of Jonah over the Middle East. In this scenario, Egypt will receive the total solar eclipse in March of 2034, and the tribes would have been regathered only a few months prior during the Feast of Trumpets—the Holy Day of Yeshua's return when no man knows the day or the hour of the event until the new moon is sighted. The close overlap of these events makes scenario three a strong possibility. However, scenario four is also possible since the entire sign of Jonah would be completed at the time that the tribes are regathered during the winter of 2034-2035. It would make sense that only after the sign of Jonah is witnessed that God would then appear in the clouds, gather His people, and strike the land of Egypt to create highways in the desert for His people to come back to Canaan. Though other scenarios are possible beyond scenario four, it seems highly unlikely that the abomination of desolation would be set up in 2023 only to collect dust until its deployment five years later in the winter of 2028-2029, and so on.

With the four assumptions now explained, consider how realistic these different scenarios are. I don't claim to have all the answers, and from a logical standpoint alone, it seems that the Great Tribulation should only begin in the winter of 2026-2027. Having wrestled with this information for a few years now, it just seems wrong for things to tarry that long. In my mind, the first scenario seems to have the highest probability due to the rapidly deteriorating geopolitical situation between BRICS and the West. If the Great Tribulation begins in the winter of 2024-2025 and we simply add seven years to arrive at the winter of 2031-2032, there would be an unexplainable two-year gap until the sign of Jonah is completed in March 2034. Perhaps this two-year period is intended to be a direct replica of Numbers 10:11. As explained in Chapter 3, the Israelites were at the base of Mount Sinai for two years receiving God's Torah and getting trained in His ways before traveling to the promised land actually took place. Perhaps a similar two-year period can be expected in the Greater Exodus where the rebels against God will be purged in the wilderness before the new promised land is inherited. Therefore, because there is no hard rule about the sign of Jonah, the regathering could technically still take place before the Middle Eastern sign of Jonah is complete. In this scenario, the Nile, Mediterranean, and Red Sea would be radically transformed as described in the Prophets to make highways for God's people to return to Canaan right around March 20, 2034.

Recall that the prophecy of Daniel 12:12 and the 1335 days was discussed in Chapter 8. Depending on which scenario proves to be correct, I stated that we need to add the 1335 days of this prophecy to the very day that the antichrist begins his reign. This would bring us to 75 days beyond the 42-month reign of terror. Perhaps it is at this time that the two witnesses will do something quite major on the world stage with regard to "blessing" the remnant of God's people so that they are "happy" to have arrived at that particular day. It will be interesting to see which exact date corresponds with the 75-day prophecy within the timeline of the sign of Jonah, assuming that this interpretation of the 1335 days is correct.

Another consideration is to view the historical events of the American sign of Jonah as having possible future outcomes in the Middle East. As alluded to, the Middle East sign of Jonah will be a period of exactly 2422 days. The exact same thing was true of the American omen—it was *exactly* 2422 days long. The exact midpoint of the American cycle was Monday, December 14, 2020, which also happened to be the month that the first Coronavirus vaccines were ready for the public. In fact, Pfizer was the first company to receive emergency use authorization for its Covid-19 vaccine on December 11, 2020.[20] When adding 1121 days to August 2, 2027, you will arrive at a midpoint date of Monday, November 25, 2030 for the upcoming Middle East omen. There are numerous things to consider with this 2030 date. Assuming that the UN power structure is still around, this could be a date where the end of Agenda 2030 is declared and perhaps something new takes over on the world stage. It might even somehow signal the end of the 42-month reign of the antichrist, assuming that scenario #4 is correct and his reign began during the winter of 2027/28. Another idea worth mentioning is that the entire midpoint year of the

American cycle, 2020, was of extreme significance. Maybe the same will be true of 2030 as a whole.

Time will reveal how the Matthew 24 timeline will unfold, but for now, I believe the analysis presented in this book to be the most complete reckoning of the major prophetic events of the next 10 years with quantifiable outcomes to work with. This information should naturally increase the faith and resilience of all believers worldwide who have taken the time to carefully and methodically dissect the exact sequence of events presented in Matthew 24.

THE DAY OF THE LORD PART II

After the elect are gathered together back into the land of Israel from the four corners of the earth, satan will once again gather up Gog, Magog, Rosh, and all of the armies of the ten kings for battle. Just like in the days of the original Exodus from Egypt, the same events will occur once the people are freed from captivity and returned to the land of Israel. Because of his "success" during part one of the battle of Gog and Magog and the destruction of the seed of Abraham, satan will foolishly think that he can defeat God during part two of the Day of Yehovah. The original Pharaoh did the same thing when he chased Israel up to the waters of the Red Sea. Similarly, the final Pharaoh and his armies will approach Jerusalem and surround the city but only to be totally annihilated. The last time satan tried this his Egyptian armies were destroyed by water. This time it will be by fire, and there will be a great destruction of all the deceived nations under satan's influence. They will finally reap what they have sown. This event begins with the sixth bowl of judgment and the drying of the Euphrates as described in detail here in Revelation 16:13,14 where the three demon frogs are loosed to go deceive the nations:

13 "And I saw three unclean spirits like frogs *coming* out of the mouth of the dragon, out of the mouth of the beast, and out of the mouth of the false prophet.
14 "For they are spirits of demons, performing signs, *which* go out to the kings of the earth and of the whole world, to gather them to the battle of that great day of God Almighty."

I believe the three demonic princes are Rosh, Meshech, and Tubal as described in Eze. 38:2; and the *great day* is a direct reference to what many of the prophets like Isaiah, Jeremiah, and Joel spoke of concerning the Day of the LORD (Yehovah). Speaking of this Day, Ezekiel states, "Son of man, set your face against Gog, of the land of Magog, the prince of Rosh, Meshech, and Tubal, and prophesy against him" (Eze 38:2). Here we see Gog together with Rosh, Meshech, and Tubal that are gathered by the three "frog" spirits. Remember, these verses of Revelation and Ezekiel are describing the destruction of the BRICS nations at the final battle—the battle of Armageddon. Referring to satan's armies at this battle, the prophet Ezekiel writes: "After many days you will be visited. In the latter years you will come into the land of those brought back from the sword *and* gathered from many people on the mountains of Israel, which had long been desolate; they were brought out of the nations, and now all of them dwell safely" (Eze. 38:8). Though I have mentioned this already, we are being shown that they are going to attack the regathered thirteen tribes of Israel that are now dwelling safely in the Land. These words from Ezekiel also support the view that the first harvest of Revelation 14:14-16 is in fact referring to the regathering, or Greater Exodus, of all thirteen tribes from all over the world because the second harvest of this same chapter of Revelation uses the same language used to describe Armageddon.

If you take a moment to compare Ezekiel 39:4-6 with Rev. 14:20, Rev. 19:17, and Rev. 20:7-9, you will notice that these verses are describing the exact same events. The parallels are absolutely unmistakable. All of the language of these passages shows us that a large satanic army will gather itself outside of Jerusalem; fire from God will fall from heaven to destroy these enemies once and for all; and there will be a great supper for the beasts of the field and foul of the air to devour whatever is left. Satan himself will be thrown into the lake of fire when this is all said and done. This event will happen well before the year 2045 because the lives of the ten kings themselves will be prolonged for a short season, for as Daniel states, "...the rest of the beasts, they had their dominion taken away, yet their lives were prolonged for a season and a time" (Dan. 7:12). All of the kingdoms of the earth will become the kingdom of Yeshua our Messiah and His righteous, set apart people. This is the blessed hope of all believers. This is the event we have all been eagerly waiting for, and we are *almost* there!

We can expect these events to unfold any time after March 20, 2034 when (1) the sign of Jonah over the Middle East is complete, (2) the two witnesses are finished doing their work, (3) the regathering of all the scattered tribes of Israel is completed, and (4) Yeshua has dealt with the rebels face to face, with only the righteous being able to enter the land of Canaan. Only once these conditions are met with all Israel back in the land can satan then gather Gog and Magog for the final battle. If satan is finally destroyed and thrown into the lake of fire sometime in the mid- to late 2030s, then that means that there will be less than 10 years of the entire 120 Shanah of mankind remaining before the end of the age in 2045. This is most likely the period of time spoken of by Zechariah the prophet, where he says this in Zec. 14:18,19:

18 "If the family of Egypt will not come up and enter in, they *shall have* no *rain;* they shall receive the plague with which the LORD strikes the nations who do not come up to keep the Feast of Tabernacles.
19 "This shall be the punishment of Egypt and the punishment of all the nations that do not come up to keep the Feast of Tabernacles."

All nations on earth will be required to observe the Torah of Yehovah or face consequences. In other words, sin and rebellion will still exist during this short period of time. We are explicitly told in Daniel 9:24 that 70 Shabua are determined to make a complete end of all manner of sins. What we can conclude is that once the 70th week is finished, something will change. The New Jerusalem will come down from heaven. Mankind will be changed. The new covenant will finally be fulfilled where the Torah is written on the hearts of God's people, and the Last Day spoken of by Yeshua will finally come to pass.

At last, this final secret of the Daniel 9:24 prophecy has now been revealed to you. This is the "reconciliation for iniquity" spoken of by Daniel: when Yeshua finally regathers His people after the work of the two witnesses, He will deal with them face to face and bring them back under the eternal covenant of the Torah, with their sin being completely forgiven forever. This, again, is exactly why this prophecy is referred to as the Greater Exodus. No one will teach anyone anymore about knowing Yehovah at the conclusion of God's miraculous regathering event.

Chapter 14
The Secrets of Living
Righteously

If you have reached the finish line with me, I salute you. I congratulate you. The time is short, and so I will keep this brief.

As you now realize, we were commanded to know and understand all prophecy from Genesis to Revelation. Knowing begins with the head. This is what people commonly refer to as *head knowledge*. Understanding then comes from taking that knowledge to heart. As that understanding is properly applied in your life, it can then become fruitful through the manifestation of intelligence that only comes through experience. As experience is then practiced repeatedly in your life, you can then bear ripe fruit through the acquisition of skill and wisdom. Ultimately, you will strive for a state of mastery in God's Word, where wisdom is effortlessly applied. Mastery is a place of perfect wisdom, and it cannot be achieved in this lifetime with a sinful nature. This entire sequence of events begins with the fear, or respect, of the LORD, Yehovah, as Solomon states:

10 The fear of the LORD is the beginning of wisdom, And the knowledge of the Holy One is understanding.
11 For by me your days will be multiplied, And years of life will be added to you.
12 If you are wise, you are wise for yourself, And if you scoff, you will bear it alone.
(Proverbs 9:10-12)

It is Yehovah that gives wisdom. Only He has the words of eternal life, and there is no other source besides Him. He is also the shield of protection for those who take every single word from His mouth seriously. It is only through the process of first respecting God and then knowing, understanding, applying, experiencing, skillfully practicing, and finally acquiring wisdom that the we can then properly read these words from Psalm 1:1-3:

1 Blessed *is* the man
Who walks not in the counsel of the ungodly,
Nor stands in the path of sinners,
Nor sits in the seat of the scornful;
2 But his delight *is* in the law of the LORD,
And in His law he meditates day and night.
3 He shall be like a tree
Planted by the rivers of water,
That brings forth its fruit in its season,
Whose leaf also shall not wither;
And whatever he does shall prosper.

Is your delight in the Torah of Yehovah, as this Psalm states? Have you made all of the words of Moses your meditation day and night? As you know, this failure on the part of the vast majority of believers is the primary reason why they are hopelessly lost in understanding end times prophecy. They were taught that the Torah is a yoke of bondage, done away with, and nailed to the cross; and they have believed these lies to their own destruction. Make no mistake about it. Judgment is coming upon all those who are breakers of the holy covenant of God that was *never* done away with but that was, in fact, *renewed* through the blood of the Lamb and also the pouring out of the Holy Spirit for newness of life. Let's rise up. Overcome this crooked and perverse generation with me, and let's hide every word from Yehovah's mouth inside our hearts so that we might not sin against Him (Psa. 119:11).

THE SECRETS FOR RIGHTEOUS LIVING

If all this information is new to you, the very first and easiest thing to do is to honor the weekly Sabbath day from Friday at sunset to Saturday at sunset (erev to erev in Hebrew). This commandment was established at the creation week, and Elohim did not take the seventh day of rest because He was fatigued. He did it as an example for mankind to follow. That is why I strongly urge you to be just like your Master. During the creation week, He rested on the seventh day irrespective of the cycle of the moon, which is why "lunar sabbath theory" is fundamentally false. The sabbath days have always been from Friday to Saturday, evening to evening.

Observe His Day because it is a sign of the covenant between you and Him forever (Exo. 31:17). Please don't deceive yourself into thinking that the Sabbath is any time and any day you want it to be. Jesus observed the Sabbath day from Friday night to Saturday night, and so should we. Like John told us, we should practice all of the things that Jesus did if we truly want to abide in Him (1Jo. 2:6). Abiding in Him inherently means that there is a time and place to meet with him regularly. What do you think of when you think of the word *appointment?* That's precisely what these weekly Sabbaths are. Like the most important date with a beautiful significant other; or just like the date of a wedding—this is what the weekly Sabbath is. It's time to meet with God. This is the set-apart time where He wants to hear from you, dine with you, and enjoy fellowship with you. It is His Day. It belongs to Him and to His people forever, and He wants to shower you with His love, presence, and wisdom during these times of rest. If you treat this Day as a common, ordinary, and regular working day just like any other day, how do you think that makes Him feel? We must guard his commands. That also means we must not add to the Torah requirements in keeping the Sabbath. The Torah only states that the physical labor of kindling a fire (Exo. 35:3); the act of gathering sticks (Num. 15:32); work for monetary gain (Exo. 20:10); and plowing and harvesting (Exo. 34:21) are expressly forbidden. The act of harvesting or storing up food is repeated within the commandment to not gather manna on the seventh day (Exo. 16:5). The manna instructions also imply that food preparation for the Sabbath day should take place beforehand and not on the seventh day itself. However, various nuances are certainly up for individual interpretation, and it is best to let the Holy Spirit lead rather than to succumb to the legalistic ideas of anyone else. For example, the disciples of Christ technically "harvested" grain heads on the sabbath day because they were hungry, but Yesuha did not condemn them because they only took a little with no intention of storing up for later use (see Luke 6:1). The whole point is that we are not to "profane" the Sabbath day (Exo. 31:14), which is to pollute or to treat as an ordinary day like any other.

In the book of Acts, it is clear that one of the very first things that all believers also need to focus on is eating like Hebrews. We need to eat like God wants us to eat. Particularly in Acts 15, there were large numbers of Israelite Gentiles turning to the Most High because they understood the good news message that Yeshua had atoned for their sins and allowed them to enter into a renewed covenant in His blood and in the power of the Holy Spirit. The number of nations was so large and diverse that there was a debate over how they should be properly discipled. Where do you begin to train all of these people into the correct keeping of God's holy covenant? This was the question, and the answer was not clear.

There were men influenced by the teachings of the Judaizers stating that these new believers needed to pull their pants down right away and become circumcised according to the exact letter of the Law in order to be considered "saved". However, Paul and Barnabas challenged this position because they understood the spirit of the Law and the need for these new converts to learn Moses little by little with circumcision taking place when they properly understood the commandments. In fact, Paul's letter to the Galatians was written because he was upset with the teachings of the Judaizers that were perverting the simplicity of salvation by faith alone in the finished work of the cross. In Acts 15, Paul and Barnabas were making it clear that salvation comes through faith and that it was a perversion of the truth to force people to immediately become circumcised. This same debate still exists today between those that think immediate water baptism is absolutely necessary in order for a person to be truly saved. The thief on the cross shows us that paradise is inherited through faith. Water baptism is an outward reflection of that faith, and the same is true of circumcision. Both things should be done, just as with the rest of the Torah. That is why Paul took Timothy and circumcised him when he became his disciple (see Acts 16:3). Now, pay very careful attention to these words of the Jerusalem council as they decided how to train up all of the nations in The Way:

19 "Therefore I judge that we should not trouble those from among the Gentiles who are turning to God,
20 "but that we write to them to abstain from things polluted by idols, *from* sexual immorality, *from* things strangled, and *from* blood.
21 "For Moses has had throughout many generations those who preach him in every city, being read in the synagogues every Sabbath."
(Acts 15:19-21)

It was James who declared this final verdict on the matter. The Gentiles were absolutely required to learn, understand, and keep the Torah of Moses, but the most important commandments were these four found in Acts 15:20. We are not to eat food that has been offered to idols like the children of Israel did when they bowed down with the women of Moab to the false god of Baal Peor and were consequently destroyed. We are not to commit sexual immorality, which could be interpreted to mean literal sexual perversion or also spiritual promiscuity. In the Torah, it is clear that any clean animal that dies of itself should not be eaten (Deut. 14:21). Something that dies of itself has perhaps some sort of disease or defect; or maybe old age causes it to die. No matter what the reason, a clean animal must be slaughtered in order to be eligible to be eaten. Notice my use of the word *clean.* Yes, only clean animals are to be eaten (Lev. 11). Finally, we are told many times in the Torah that both blood and animal fat are never to be eaten by God's people (Lev. 3:17).

473

Of these four commandments from Moses, three of them are explicitly dietary laws. The early church was moved by the Holy Spirit to make sure that new believers were guarding the dietary laws because those were the most basic things they needed to do. It says that they can start there because Moses is taught everywhere under heaven in every city on every Sabbath day. In other words, these new believers were going to learn all of the rest of the commandments, so it wasn't necessary to immediately burden them with the commandment to be circumcised, just like we shouldn't immediately burden someone with the commandment to be water baptized (although arguably, baptism is a whole lot easier of a command to keep than circumcising grown men). Again, that's not to say that water baptism is to be taken lightly. It absolutely should be observed, just like all the other commandments from Moses, the Prophets, and the Gospels.

Finally, there are both biblical commandments and extra-biblical traditions that I have adopted in my life over the past eight years since I started observing all of God's commandments. We are told that the words of the Torah are not to depart from our hearts and that we are to teach them regularly (Deut. 6:6). Because of this concept, I read and study the Torah on a yearly cycle beginning with Genesis right at the start of the month of Abib on the Hebrew calendar. Rather than tackling Genesis to Deuteronomy in a random fashion, I go line by line and read each chapter with my wife out loud every Sabbath day. The Tree of Life version of the Bible is nice because it already contains all of the weekly divisions of the Torah, called *Parashat*, of both Messianic and Jewish tradition. You can also go to the Chabad.org website and see the weekly portions of Moses divided up for you so that you can study them on a yearly cycle.[1] As I have practiced this cyclical reading of God's Word in my life, I have noticed a profound impact in how the Holy Spirit is able to bring things to my memory right when I need them. Whether I'm making hard decisions or knowing how to rightly do business with those around me, the reading of the Torah like a Sabbath Hebrew has drastically benefitted my walk of faith in a way that I never experienced as a Sunday Christian.

OBSERVING THE SEVEN SABBATHS OF LEVITICUS 23

As we go through all of the Holy Days, I will show you the Letter of the Law and the Spirit of the Law as these things apply to these commanded days of rest. I can now tell you after eight years into this journey that there is a big difference between *keeping* the Feasts and *observing* them; and I don't want you to be deceived about this reality. First, let me ask a couple of hard questions:

1) Will you be traveling to Jerusalem for the Feasts of Unleavened Bread, Pentecost, or Tabernacles in order to keep the pilgrimage requirement as stated in the Torah?

2) Have you raised a first born year-old lamb, goat, or calf without blemish to be prepared for the Passover meal with its blood applied to the doorposts of your house?

I could ask more questions, but I think you are starting to understand my point here. We cannot actually 100% *keep* the Feasts exactly as described in the pages of the Torah. It's not possible. Some events like Wave Sheaf Day are ceremonial and require you to present an omer of harvested barley from your field to a priest in the literal land of Israel. Don't deceive yourself into thinking you are perfectly keeping these Feast days; rather, you are simply *observing* them as best you can.

With that said, I *do not* attempt to keep these Feasts (like many people sadly do) with a religious spirit of pride, performance, and arrogance because I *know* that I can only *observe* them. I cannot actually keep them to the exact letter of the Torah. Having been around the "Messianic" or "Hebrew Roots" movement now for many years, I truly worry for those that put so much emphasis, trust, and hope in their abilities and rituals pertaining to the observance of these days. The keeping of Torah does not inherently bring salvation. It shows us how imperfect we are.

It condemns us.

Anyone who does not realize how flawed their ability to keep Torah is has fallen from grace and forgotten their first love. That is why I believe the modern Messianic, return-to-Torah movement is the Church of Ephesus in the Book of Revelation—they have forgotten the Master Who bought them; they have forgotten their first Love (Rev. 2:4).

Does that mean that we shrug our shoulders and dismiss these days like so many people do? Absolutely not! We are commanded to observe these days forever, and failure to do so is sinning against the Most High. However, we need to constantly put our trust in Yeshua the Messiah because humbly approaching Him and leaning on Him for grace is the only true way to experience these Holy Days in the exact way that they were meant to be enjoyed; and yes, they are to be enjoyed!

Now, back to how to observe these Sabbaths.

Because the Holy Calendar of Yehovah is based on lunar sightings in the land of Israel with an occasional 13th month intercalation, a Hebrew year can have more than 52 weekly Sabbaths. In addition to these Sabbaths, we are told to guard, proclaim, and observe the other Sabbaths that are commonly under-stood as Feasts, Appointed Times, or Holidays during their seasons.

Colloquially, we know these Feasts as taking place in the spring and then in the fall. However, there are only two seasons in Israel according to Gen. 8:22, so technically these are summer and winter Feasts. The next figure provides an overview of all of these spiritually profound and important days in one chart.

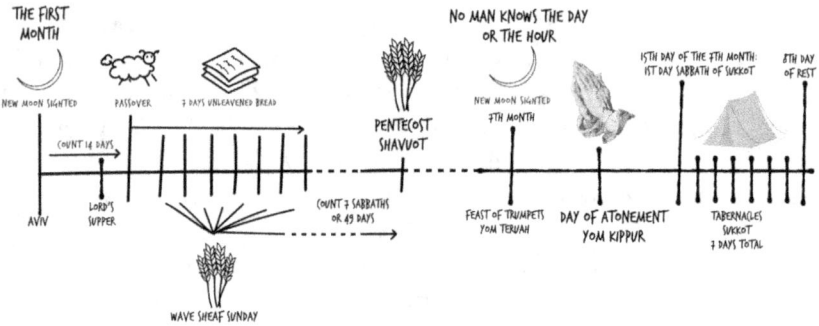

Figure 14.1: The Appointed Times of Elohim

If you would like to download and use the same tool that I use every year to determine when to begin the spring Holy Days, I have included a link in the notes of this chapter.[2] As I have already mentioned, only one omer (two liters, like a bottle of soda pop) of abib barley grains is required to be ready in the land of Israel in order to declare the first month of the year.

It is the sighting of a new crescent moon with the naked eye and without the aid of binoculars or technology that is required to begin the first month and the New Year. Like I have mentioned before, the word *Abib* literally means *green ears of barley;* and therefore this is the firstfruits offering that is required to be waived as an offering on the exact day of Wave Sheaf Day (Lev. 23:11). To make things easier to visualize, make sure to go back to Figure 5.6 in Chapter 5 where I illustrated Covid-19 and the middle of the week with the correct dates for the spring Holy Days of 2020; or you can revisit Figure 12.3 in Chapter 12 for an additional case study. Also keep in mind that the Lord's Supper is the first event in the spring Holy Days timeline, but I couldn't squeeze it into these charts.

LORD'S SUPPER

The first appointment we need to observe on the prophetic time clock happens just before Passover. What many people fail to realize is that the Lord's Supper as instituted in the Gospels is different from Passover itself (see Mat. 26, Mar. 14, Luk. 22). This is the occasion that Jesus said to do "in remembrance of Me" (Luke 22:19).

The Lord's Supper occurred in the late afternoon immediately before the day (sunset to sunset) of Passover was about to begin. In other words, the Lord's Supper is to be observed every single year on the 13th day of the month of Abib in the early evening. Just like Yeshua washed the feet of all His disciples, we observe this day by having a towel, bar of soap, and a basin of water and take turns washing the feet of our friends, family, and loved ones that are believers wanting to observe the day with us. It's best to have women washing the women's feet and men with men. If you are not part of a bigger community, you and your spouse or perhaps your kids can do this ceremonial foot washing and take turns. Prayers acknowledging this day along with Yeshua's distress, shame, and betrayal should be exercised. Because of the seriousness of the events and the betrayal by Judas Iscariot, it is a calm and somber evening of prayer and reflection.

Like Yeshua said to do in remembrance of Him, we also take communion, but with a very careful attitude. Paul further stated that we are to examine ourselves so that we do not partake of this communion in an unworthy manner (1Co. 11:27). If someone is not a believer in the Messiah, they should not be taking part in this ceremonial event. One secret of the New Testament is that whenever you see Paul speaking of communion, he is always referring to the Lord's Supper on the 13th day of the first month. Though many Christian churches like to take communion whenever they want, this 13th day is the one that Yeshua specifically said to keep in remembrance of Him. Thirteen is also the number of Israel's tribes, so it was significant for Yeshua to initiate the renewed covenant with both Houses of Israel during this same day of the first month.

Letter of the Law:

- Have communion on the late afternoon of the 13th day
- Take unleavened bread; eat in remembrance of the body of Yeshua
- Take a cup of wine; drink in remembrance of the blood of the renewed covenant

- After supper, take turns girding yourself with a towel and wash the feet of those in communion with you (Jhn. 13:5)

Spirit of the Law:

- Offer prayers acknowledging Yeshua's betrayal, shame, and redemption
- Read Psalm 41
- Uphold the new commandment to love (Jhn. 13:34) and make a list of ways that you can plan to show love for your friends, family, spouse, and those within your realm of influence so that they can know you are a disciple of Yeshua
- Try watching and praying for one hour this evening (Mat. 26:40)

PASSOVER

The very first Passover reference that we see in the Scriptures is Genesis 4:2-5. Abel brought a firstborn of the flock (either a ram or a male goat) as an offering to Yehovah. Cain brought an offering of the fruit of the ground, but his offering was not respected because it was not Abib barley, as is required for the keeping of Passover. He brought something other than the very first-fruits of the ground, and Yehovah did not respect the offering. This is why it is important to correctly understand the concept of firstfruits that is later repeated in Leviticus 23.

The second time we see Passover observed is in Genesis 18 where Elohim appears to Abraham as three men (Yehovah, Yeshua, and the Holy Spirit)—a clear and perfect picture of the triune nature of God. We are told that Abraham prepares a young and tender calf as a sacrificial meal (Gen. 18:7). Many people fail to realize that this was indeed a Passover event because they do not make the connection to Deuteronomy 16:2 which clearly states that the Passover animal can be taken either from the flock (goats or sheep) or from the herd (cattle). Another noteworthy aspect of the Genesis 18 Passover is the fact that Elohim appeared to Abraham in the heat of the day (Gen. 18:1), which, if we assume this to be high noon, also happens to be the exact middle between the hours of 9:00 am and 3:00 pm when Yeshua was crucified by the Jews (see Mar. 15:25 and Mat. 27:46). Regarding the triune nature, or trinity, of Elohim, it is these words that unlock the mystery of the three men:

20 And the LORD said, "Because the outcry against Sodom and Gomorrah is great, and because their sin is very grave,

21 "I will go down now and see whether they have done altogether according to the outcry against it that has come to Me; and if not, I will know."
22 Then the men turned away from there and went toward Sodom, but Abraham still stood before the LORD.
(Gen. 18:20-22)

The key words are "I will go down", in which Elohim declared that He was taking it upon Himself to physically make an appearance in Sodom and Gomorrah. He did not send messengers; He did it Himself. The narrative clearly states that two of the three men turned and went down to Sodom. Understanding this important distinction unlocks the mystery of the two "angels" that appeared to Lot, as most translations state. These two were not simply angels. It was in fact, God Himself.

Lot was also celebrating the Holy Day of Passover when he invited two— *Yeshua* and the *Holy Spirit*—of the three men into his house while Abraham stayed with *Yehovah* and spoke with Him. It is in the evening when Lot provides the two men with unleavened bread, which is to be eaten in observance of the High Holy Day of the First Day of this seven-day Feast (Gen. 19:3). Then, just as we see in the Passover of Exodus 12:11, Lot eats the meal in haste with the two men and then leaves Sodom and Gomorrah in a hurry, just like the children of Israel left Egypt in a hurry. In other words, Lot was considered "righteous" as is recorded in 2Peter 2:7 because he was observing God's appointed times. It was at this special appointment that God literally met with Lot and took him by the hand to deliver him out of judgment. What a picture of grace perfectly mingled with obedience!

Regarding the Passover requirements, the year-old male of the flock is to be selected on the 10th day of the month (Exo. 12:3). Many people no longer keep the commandment to slaughter a literal yearling (of the flock or herd) because of the Deuteronomy 16:5,6 prohibition that states, "You may not sacrifice the Passover within any of your gates which the LORD your God gives you; but at the place where the LORD your God chooses to make His name abide, there you shall sacrifice the Passover at twilight, at the going down of the sun, at the time you came out of Egypt." Many then interpret this "place" to be 1948 Israel or Jerusalem, and according to this mainstream viewpoint, it is only within this place that such offerings are to be made. However, these arguments are inconsistent with the Bible. Of all places, the children of Israel observed their first Passover within Egypt—a land full of polytheism and lawlessness. God still met with His people in the place where they were. He chose to make His name abide with His people, and this same pattern continued once Israel left Egypt. They stayed at the base of Mount

Sinai for two years (Num. 10:11), which means that they had observed two Passovers outside of Canaan. Then they continued observing 40 more Passovers outside of Canaan as Israel wandered throughout the Sinai Peninsula. Even when Joshua became Moses' successor, they observed another Passover in the plains of Jericho before the conquest of Canaan (Joshua 5:10). That means 44 Passover sacrifices were observed by Israel in numerous different locations, and they were all indeed acceptable in the eyes of God. Therefore, the specific commandment of Deuteronomy 16 most likely had to do with ancient jurisdictions that were established once the children of Israel settled in the land and divided their inherited portions. Rather than families slaughtering the Passover within their gates, there were most likely publicly designated areas throughout the tribes where the sacrifice was to take place in an organized manner, especially since smaller families shared the meal with larger ones (Exo 12:4). Fast forward to today, and no location-specific restrictions apply during this current scattering period. The only restriction is that those participating in the Passover must be circumcised in the heart, for no "stranger" to Christ is to keep the Passover with His people (Exodus 12:48). Only then will God's name abide in the place where you are—the place that He chooses. You must be born again.

Within the Passover instructions, it is not explicitly stated that the year-old animal is to be a firstborn. However, Abel offered a firstborn ram (Gen. 4:4); the Passover of Exodus 12 made a distinction in which all the firstborn of Egypt died who did not observe the Holy Day; and this pattern of the firstborn continues with Yeshua, the ultimate Passover Lamb, being the only begotten of the Father. Exodus 13:12,15 further state that all firstborn male animals of the flock or herd are to be sacrificed to God as a reminder of the Exodus, and this concept is repeated in Numbers 18:17 which makes it clear that firstborn animals are not to be sold for money (redeemed). Moreover, all firstborn males are to be kept with their mothers for seven days and then offered to God sacrificially on the eighth day, as recorded in Exodus 22:29. The only exception to this commandment would be the firstborn of the Passover, which would be raised up to be a yearling specifically for the observance of the Feast. Therefore, it is strongly implied that the yearling for Passover must be a firstborn, and it would be best to adhere to this standard especially since firstborn animals should not be sold, anyways. These instructions also reveal why simply purchasing, for example, ground lamb meat from the supermarket to observe Passover is very disconnected from the Torah. It would be impossible to know if that animal were a male rather than female, and in the case of ground meat, there is likely more than one animal's meat inside the package. In addition, animals sent to the slaughter houses usually have undesirable qualities about them, and the shepherd is likely culling these animals while preserving the best genetics within his flock. Supermarket animals could be sick, maimed, weak, or deformed with their bones broken during any stan-dardized butchering process—all things which are prohibited from an accept-able Passover offering. Only the very best firstborn male of the flock or herd that is also a yearling is to be offered to God with its bones intact.

Regarding preparation, recall that the law of the altar is presented immedi-ately after the "ten commandments" in Exodus 20:22-26. No tool should be used on the altar where the Passover is cooked, which means that no fancy grills or manufactured cooktops can be used to roast the Passover offering over the fire. A great example of a stone altar is given to us in the book of Judges. When Manoah and his wife who were Danites of the land of Zorah had an encounter with the Angel of Yehovah, Manoah said that they had seen God Himself, much like Jacob did when he wrestled with God and saw Him face to face (Gen. 32:20). The Angel of Yehovah proceeded to give Manoah and his wife instructions regarding how they should raise their son, Samson, who would become a judge of Israel to deliver them out of the hand of the Philistines. In accordance with the Torah requirements of an altar made of whole stone, Manoah offered a young goat with a grain offering that was indeed accepted by God in a place well outside of Jerusalem (see Judges 13:19). Of course, this is just one example of an acceptable offering; there are many others.

The New Testament makes it clear that the Holy Spirit abides in us because of the renewed covenant (1Jo. 4:13). Therefore, the place where God makes His name abide is the place where His people dwell, no matter where they have been scattered. That is why I advocate for keeping the command-ment of Passover in a literal sense rather than a figurative one. I believe this is the proper way that this commandment should be observed. Of course, not everyone is in such a position to be a shepherd or cattleman, but the entire act of slaughtering the animal and preparing it for meat is an experience that God commanded His people to observe for a reason. I have learned tremendous life-altering lessons by going through the whole process, and no matter where you currently find yourself in your walk with Christ, take it one step at a time. It took many years for me to firmly establish the convictions I now carry while also having the shepherding experience necessary to follow the letter of the Law; and I have been tremendously blessed.

The 14th day of the month is also known as the Preparation Day. During the daytime, the lambs are being butchered and readied for the Passover meal in the evening of the 14th bleeding into the 15th day. It was during the 14th day beginning in the evening that Yeshua was taken into custody at the garden of Gethsemane and abused by the religious authorities; He was then examined by Pilate early in the morning, subsequently tortured, and crucified beginning at 9:00am. He gave up the ghost in the ninth hour, or 3:00pm, of this 14th day (Mar. 15:34); and this is the precise time that the Passover meal was ready to be observed.

The Passover meal can take on different styles and flavors, but there are requirements. Something bitter must be present. Although many English translations say bitter *herbs,* there is actually no underlying Hebrew word connected to the word *herbs.* It has been inserted by the translators because of tradition. With that said, most people eat parsley as the bitter "herb" requirement. However, I believe bitter wine is just fine, especially during a Sabbatical year when the enjoyment of fresh produce is more limited. Unleavened bread should also be eaten in the evening because the first day of unleavened bread will then begin; and baker's yeast should be removed from the dwelling during this 15th day.

You will commonly hear the word *seder* in reference to the Passover meal. This is a word that simply means *ceremonial guide.* In other words, the seder plate is a meal that is accompanied by offering prayers and worship with various elements of the plate representing different concepts of the Passover. These things are extra-biblical traditions that have been added to the observance of this holiday. As long as the meal itself is eaten in haste as commanded, then these things are perfectly fine to do before the meal, though there should never be any pressure to conform to the traditions of Judaism whatsoever.

Letter of the Law:

- On the 14th day just before sunset: consume the meat of a firstborn yearling male lamb, goat, or calf without blemish; must be roasted over fire and eaten with "bitter" and unleavened bread; none of its bones can be broken during the butchering process, limiting the cuttings of meat to irregular cuts only and not "grocery store" styled delicacies.
- None of the Passover offering can remain until morning; it must be burned in the fire (Exo. 12:10).
- Meal must be eaten in haste with shoes on, your belt on your waist, and a staff in hand (Exo. 12:11)
- Take blood of the animal, apply it using hyssop to the two doorposts and lintel (top central frame) of your main entry door
- Teach your children the Passover story (Exo. 12:27)

Spirit of the Law:

- Read the story of the Exodus account of Passover
- Prepare a special meal in honor of the Passover; make sure that something bitter is present along with unleavened bread; it is common to have wine during this meal. If you do not have shepherding experience or access to a Torah-based community where a firstborn animal can be prepared, putting together a nice meal to honor this Holy Day is still infinitely better than simply dismissing it, like most people do.
- The unleavened bread for this meal and all the days of Unleavened Bread can be crackers commonly known as *matzah;* I personally like to prepare homemade tortillas that are simple, flat, and do not require the use of any yeast
- Eat in haste! Have your belt, shoes, and even your keys ready to go!
- Hang a red banner or red cloth above your door frame and/or on the two sides of the door frame to symbolize the blood
- Either before or after the meal, read the story of Crucifixion (John 18, 19)
- Read Isaiah 53 followed by Psalms of praise
- Worship / Music, song and dance just like Exodus 15:1-21 after the Red Sea crossing
- Maybe try watching the Passion of the Christ or other films that help put you in the spirit of the observance of the day and help you remember the things that Yeshua accomplished on the cross

THE 7-DAY FEAST OF UNLEAVENED BREAD

Like I already mentioned, the first time we see mention of the Feast of Unleavened bread is Gen. 19:3 when Lot prepares a feast for two men of the three (Elohim). In following with the pattern of Scripture, we are told that Lot offered to wash their feet (this is similar to Yeshua during the Lord's Supper, though the timing is off by one day in this Genesis account). Lot then left Sodom in haste shortly after these events, which is exactly how we are told to observe the evening of Passover that bleeds into the evening to begin the first day (sunset to sunset) of Unleavened Bread. He left in haste!

This 15th day of the month is a required Sabbath day. No work is permitted. While many people traditionally start removing leaven (yeast) from their homes much earlier, you must remove all leaven from your home during the

15th day (first day) of Unleavened Bread (Exo. 12:15). The yeast is a picture of sin, particularly hypocrisy and self-righteous pride as made clear by the words of Yeshua (Luk. 12:1).

Just like baker's yeast puffs up dough, the hypocrisy of wrongfully following religious dogmas also puffs up someone's ego and pride. The deeper application is to prayerfully uproot unclean spirits, demonic oppression, and strongholds of the enemy in your life that are also like leaven. These things should be casted out and prayed against with authority using command prayers in Yeshua's mighty name.

The 21st day of the month and the final day of Unleavened Bread is also a required Sabbath day with cooking allowed. Take the day off from work.

Letter of the Law:

- The 15th and 21st days are required days of rest like the weekly Sabbath, but cooking is allowed (Exo. 12:16)
- Eat unleavened bread for seven days
- All males must make their pilgrimage to Jerusalem to present themselves before Yehovah (Exo. 32:14; Deut. 16:16) with their gift offering
- Remove all yeast during the 15th day (Exo. 12:15).
- Nothing leavened is to be eaten during the seven days of Unleavened Bread
- An offering made by fire is to be offered to Yehovah for seven days

Spirit of the Law:

- Take the first and seventh days off from work and monetary gain
- Remove all baker's yeast or sourdough starter from your home. Many use this opportunity for "spring cleaning" by vacuuming out crumbs under the stove, under the couch, in the toaster—wherever leaven or leavened bread may be hiding. Though not necessary, this is a good exercise.
- This is an excellent time for deliverance from strongholds of the enemy in your life. Pray and ask the Father to reveal to you anything wicked like an unclean spirit, demon, or demonic stronghold of the enemy, and cast it out with authority in Yeshua's name as you seek to uncover whatever sin it is attached to.

- Acknowledge that this is one of the three pilgrimage Feasts to be present in Jerusalem. Be like Daniel and pray three times each day (morning, noon, and evening) for all seven days of Unleavened Bread while facing towards Jerusalem in honor of the pilgrimage requirement (Dan. 6:10). This will be your offering made by fire through prayer and worship.

WAVE SHEAF DAY

Wave Sheaf Day occurs on any one of the seven days of Unleavened Bread depending entirely upon which day of the week the new moon was sighted in order to begin the New Year. However, it always occurs on the day after the weekly Sabbath. In other words, it always takes place on Sunday. In terms of observance, Wave Sheaf Day does not have very specific commands attached to it. The lessons that are hidden inside of this day are quite important, however.

Letter of the Law:

- Bring one omer (two liters) of the very firstfruits abib barley from your field to the priest belonging to your jurisdiction in the land of Israel
- No barley grain of the new crop must be eaten until you have brought your offering to Yehovah (Lev. 23:14).
- The priest is to wave the omer, and it will be accepted; the remainder of the harvest can now begin
- A year-old male lamb is to be offered as a burnt offering along with its grain offering and drink offering
- Begin counting seven sabbaths to the Feast of Weeks (Lev. 23:15)

Spirit of the Law:

- (optional) Prepare *unleavened* barley bread and wave some of it while praying in remembrance of Wave Sheaf Day
- Because Yeshua was raised exactly on the first day of the week, Sunday, and therefore revealed to us the mystery of the abib barley and Wave Sheaf Day, take time to read and meditate on Matthew 27:52 (the graves of the saints opened); Matthew 28; and the Great Commission

- Counting is to be done for 49 days until the 50th day of Pentecost Sunday (Shavuot) is reached
- Open with prayer to acknowledge the counting of the seven sabbaths to Pentecost
- Rather than simply counting in your head, physically keep track of the counting by using some sort of paper calendar or chart, day-by-day.
- (optional) Begin Scripture reading with Psalm 119 and the letter Aleph. This is a good psalm to recite in a letter-by-letter fashion of the Hebrew alphabet so that you can learn the language while also confirming your covenant loyalty to God. You will read all of Psalm 119 twice because there are twenty-two letters in the Hebrew language; then read select Psalms for the remaining five days until the Feast of Weeks. Other Scriptures are perfectly fine also. Let the Holy Spirit lead.

PENTECOST - THE FEAST OF WEEKS

This holiday concludes all of the Hebrew summer Holy Days. This is the marriage covenant appointment between God and His people; and we see a clear picture of this event with the 50 days after the Exodus from Egypt when the Torah was given on Mount Sinai (Exo. 19). The mountain was completely set ablaze by the presence of Almighty God. Of course, this is the famous event of the tongues of fire in the book of Acts chapter two. The Comforter arrived and enabled all believers in the Messiah to exercise great power and authority over sin, the enemy, and the weakness of our flesh.

Letter of the Law:

- Proclaim the holy convocation; this is a required day of rest with no regular work allowed (Lev. 23:21)
- Prepare two loaves of wheat bread and wave them in remembrance of Pentecost; they are to be baked with the use of leaven or baker's yeast (Lev. 23:17)
- Several animals along with their grain and drink offerings are to be offered (Lev. 23:18,19)
- You are to be present in Jerusalem with your gift offering (Deut. 16:16)

Spirit of the Law:

486

- Take the day off from work and prepare the two loaves in remembrance of this special day
- Pray three times during this day like Daniel did while facing Jerusalem in honor of this pilgrimage feast
- Read Exodus 19 and Acts 1-2
- Pray for the filling of the fruits of the Spirit (Col. 1:9; Rom. 15:13; Gal. 5:22)
- If you have never asked, pray for the ability to speak in new tongues so that you can edify yourself (Mar. 16:17; 1Co. 14:4)

OBSERVING THE FALL FEASTS OF LEV. 23

Did you notice that the first six chapters of this book focused almost exclusively on the spring Feasts? This book should serve as a testimony of just how critical it is to know and understand the Hebrew summer Feasts, the cycles of 49, and the cycles of agriculture in Israel.

Between Pentecost during the third month of the year and the beginning of the fall, or Hebrew winter Feasts in the seventh month with Yom Teruah, there is a period of time where the land is growing, maturing, and producing the other five firstfruits crops of the land that will be presented during the remaining Holy Days. Now that the barley and wheat have been offered, we are to look to the grapes, figs, pomegranates, dates, and olives for confirmation of the land's timing. Another reason we know that we are keeping the correct calendar each year is because these species will always be ready without fail in the land of Israel according to Yehovah's predetermined agricultural time cycle. Together, they all serve as seven witnesses that are offered to God during each of the three pilgrimage Feasts. Now that we have covered the first Feasts, let's take a look at the next major Holy Days, beginning with Trumpets.

YOM TERUAH - THE DAY OF SHOUTING

Just a few secrets of Bible prophecy remain to be discussed, and the first is the day Yeshua spoke of when He said "no man knows the day or the hour" of His return (Mat. 25:13). Commonly known as the Feast of Trumpets, Yom Teruah (Strong's H8643) literally means the day of shouting, like that of "an alarm of war, war-cry, battle-cry, or shout of joy."[3] This meaning will become more obvious as we take heed to what Yeshua revealed to us about this special day. Lets first look at two Torah passages for a foundational understanding of this day. The first is Leviticus 23:24,25:

24 Speak to the children of Israel, saying: "In the seventh month, on the first *day* of the month, you shall have a sabbath-*rest,* a memorial of blowing of trumpets, a holy convocation.
25 "You shall do no customary work *on it;* and you shall offer an offering made by fire to the LORD."

Now take a look at these words of Num. 29:1 and compare them to Leviticus:

"And in the seventh month, on the first *day* of the month, you shall have a holy convocation. You shall do no customary work. For you it is a day of blowing the trumpets."

This day is on the very first day of the seventh month. It cannot be known in advance *exactly* on which day it will land. Sure, could you estimate the date each year based on when Abib started and arrive within a day or two of the correct date?

Yes!

This reality is precisely why Judaism celebrates Yom Teruah for two days according to their Hillel II calendar. They erroneously practice a two-day feast because you cannot 100% know its timing for sure until the new crescent moon is sighted in the evening sky. Cloud coverage, a dust storm, or perhaps other factors could also hinder the sighting of the new moon. This is precisely why this Day is the one that no one knows. On the holy prophetic time clock, this is the only Feast that cannot be known in advance. For instance, Passover can be known in advance because it is not kept until 14 days after the new moon has already been sighted. The same goes for all the other Holy Days— they occur after a New Moon already proclaims their exact keeping, or, as is the case with Pentecost, they are known based on an exact counting of days. Yom Teruah is simply unique.

Unlike all of the other Holy Days of Yehovah, this is also the only day that does not have a clearly defined and explicit purpose. If you examine the Scriptures pertaining to the other Holy Days, you will see that there is language describing *why* a Day is being observed. For example, the First Day of Unleavened Bread is to be observed because it was the precise day that Israel's armies left Egypt in the Exodus (Exo. 12:17).

Besides the simple fact that He commanded us to do it, there is not an obvious reason why Yom Teruah is observed. However, to the keen student of the Gospels and prophecy, there is much deeper meaning to be found in this day than most realize. The first work to help me clearly understand the deeper significance of this Feast was Joseph Dumond's book *It Was a Riddle Not a Command*. In it, he states:

> "Yom Teruah…is about the day the Messiah was born and it is the announce-
> ment He has arrived. Stop and ask yourself if Yehovah would really send the
> Messiah on just any old day? The answer is a resounding 'No.' …Have you
> ever blown those little party horns on someone's birthday? You are doing the
> very thing that Yehovah commanded to be done when Yeshua was born. This
> day—known as the blowing of Trumpets or Day of Shouting for joy—is
> recorded in the *Gospel of Luke* as the Angels praised God at His birth."[4]

Upon reading through Dumond's claims, I went ahead and decided to conduct serious due diligence on this topic. I mean, could we *really* know that Yom Teruah was the exact day that Yeshua was born? After over twenty hours of study, note-taking, and cross-examination of the evidence, I have proven that the answer is indeed, *yes*. It turns out, not surprisingly, that the Catholic Church pushed the date of December 25th as the birthday of Christ with abso- lutely zero biblical backing, even stating that "the true birthdate of Christ is unknown."[5] Of course, the real reason that Dec. 25th was chosen was in order to accommodate the pagan festivals of winter solstice, saturnalia, and various other rituals that were popular in those days.

I published all of my findings in an hour-long podcast episode that I dedi- cated to this topic entitled "Jesus Was NOT Born on December 25th (HIDDEN End Times Prophecy) [ep.21]".[6] It turns out that there are three bulletproof ways that you can know the exact day in which Yeshua was born, and I will provide a brief overview here:

1. Examining the priestly course of Abijah to calculate a timeline of events during Zechariah the Priest's temple service (Luke 1:5); the nine-month preg- nancy of his wife Elizabeth; and the subsequent birth of John the Baptist.
- We are told that Mary conceived when Elizabeth was already six months pregnant (Luke 1:36)
- Based on Luke 1:36 in conjunction with the priestly courses of temple service (1Chr. 24:1-19; 27:1-15), a timeline can be determined from which to understand that Yeshua was born on the Seventh Month of the year.[7]

2. The reign of Tiberius Caesar of Rome
- We already know Jesus was born in the 7th month of the biblical calendar. John is 6 months older than Jesus. Luke 3:1 tells us that the 15th year of

Tiberius Cesar is when John begins his ministry, and Jesus is baptized at "about thirty years of age" in Luke 3:23.

- Lewin's chronology of the New Testament reveals that August 19th, AD 14 was the first year of Tiberius' reign.[8]

- Therefore, because John begins his ministry during the 15th year of Tiberius' reign, we can know this was sometime from August 19, AD 28 – August 19, AD 29.

- Finally, since Jesus is "about 30 years old" in AD 29, then He must have been born in 3 BC.

3. Understanding the astronomical sign of Virgo and its connection to Revelation 12:1-5—the arrival of a Messianic King born of miraculous conception.

- Now that we know that Jesus was born in the 7th month of 3 BC, we can look to astronomy to confirm if the sign of Revelation 12 was indeed present during that year.

- Not only do numerous witnesses and astronomy experts confirm that September 11, 3 BC was the exact day that the Revelation 12 sign was perfectly visible in Israel,[9,10] we can also use modern technology like the software tool Stellarium in order to go back to this exact point in time to see the sign for ourselves.[11]

I just reviewed numerous hours of research with you in less than two pages. Make sure to investigate this topic properly, and you, too, will understand that the day that Yeshua arrived was indeed the first day of the seventh Hebrew month when the crescent moon was visible on September 11, 3 BC. This is of utmost importance because although we don't know the exact day nor the hour, a future Feast of Trumpets will certainly be the day when Yeshua will return back on the clouds as stated throughout the Gospels. That is why He commanded us to watch and be ready for His return. We should know the season because He was speaking to us in a Hebrew idiom and not in a literal sense. In the Gospels, He used a parable to declare that a particular Yom Teruah yet to take place in the future will be the Day when He returns. Now, let's talk about how to observe this day.

Letter of the Law:

- As you should be doing with every new moon, practice literally waiting outside and seeing the new moon in the evening sky

- Proclaim the holy convocation; this is a required day of rest with no regular work allowed
- There are to be numerous offerings made by fire (one young bull, one ram, seven yearling lambs without blemish, and one kid of the goats as a sin offering to make atonement (Num. 29:2,5)
- Several grain offerings with oil and drink offerings are to be offered with the animals in addition to the regular new moon offerings

Spirit of the Law:

- Take the day off from work and rest in remembrance of this special day
- Have a trumpet, shofar (ram's horn), or some sort of wind instrument that you can blow as soon as you see the new moon in the night sky (yes, even though we use a new moon sighting in the land of Israel to determine new moon day, this is still a good practice)
- Read the accounts of Yeshua's birth as recorded in the Gospels in honor of Him; and also read what He said about his prophetic second coming on the clouds and the Greater Exodus
- You could even make a birthday cake in honor of Yeshua's first coming

THE DAY OF ATONEMENT(S)

This special day occurs on the 10th day of the seventh month. In fact, if it weren't already clear from the creation week of Genesis 1, it is within the context of Yom Kippur that we understand that a biblical day is from evening to evening (sunset to sunset). Look at these words from Lev. 23:27,32:

27 "Also the tenth day of this seventh month shall be the Day of Atonement. It shall be a holy convocation for you; you shall afflict your souls, and offer an offering made by fire to the LORD.
32 "It *shall be* to you a sabbath of *solemn* rest, and you shall afflict your souls; on the ninth *day* of the month at evening, from evening to evening, you shall celebrate your sabbath."

By default, Greco-Roman culture has taught us that a day begins at midnight (12am). However, the Hebrew says otherwise. It is from sunset to sunset. The language here in Leviticus 23 also seems to indicate that just before the tenth day begins and in the late afternoon (or early evening) towards the end of the ninth day, everyone should be well prepared to observe the Day of Atonement.

Regarding the Hebrew name of this Holy Day, you will find that it is actually Yom HaKippurim, or The Day of Atonements, which is plural. Let's examine the Hebrew for deeper meaning:

> "**kipur**—Strong's H3725: expiation (only in plural):—atonement; from H3722: to cover (specifically with bitumen); figuratively, to expiate or condone, to placate or cancel:—appease, make (an atonement, cleanse, disannul, forgive, be merciful, pacify, pardon, purge (away)".[12,13]

This is the day when sins are canceled, forgiven, and pardoned. What an incredibly beautiful day it is! Pay attention to the parallel passage in Isaiah 58 because it is all about the heart. Setting this day apart is useless unless repentance is truly made humbly from the heart. Remain humble and you will be blessed!

This is a day of "afflicting the soul" (Lev. 23:29) and involves fasting for 24 hours, repentance, and prayer. Of all the days on Yehovah's calendar, the Day of the Atonements is arguably the most set-apart day of our year, and we are commanded to proclaim and observe it diligently. This is the one time per year that the high priest would enter into the holy of holies behind the veil of the tabernacle (later, the temple) in order to make atonement for all the children of Israel. Additional information is provided in Leviticus 16 where we see the casting of lots for the two goats—Yehovah and azazel ("scapegoat"; Strong's H5799). The sins of the people were placed on the azazel goat, and it was sent away into the wilderness (Lev. 16:10). However, the Yehovah goat was killed as a sin offering (Lev. 16:9). This is symbolic of Yeshua's sacrificial death on the cross. The sins of the people were placed upon Him, and He was offered up as a sin offering to make all of His bride clean from their sin (Heb. 7:27, 1Peter 1:19).

Yehovah tells us not to do any work at all on this day, and He promises to cut off anyone who does not make this a day of complete rest. As previously discussed, the book of Jonah and the repentance of Nineveh took place on the Day of Atonement; Joel 2 calls for a fast in order to receive a blessing before satan's locust armies come to destroy; and the people who were saved from destruction in Ezekiel 9 were "sighing and crying" on this day, but the rest of the people refusing to honor it were cut off and destroyed. We then discussed Isaiah 22 and the archers of Elam against Jerusalem where another Day of Atonement reference is made at the end of the passage. I strongly believe that on a specific Yom Kippur event at some point, the selection of the 144,000 will be complete. The Old Testament connections are simply overwhelming and numerous. Time will tell, but I would be watching, counting the days, and practicing this Holy Day every single year.

Letter of the Law:

- Proclaim the holy convocation; this is a required day of rest with no regular work allowed
- Afflict your soul! Dry fasting is the standard as seen in the book of Jonah.
- Required offerings: one young bull, one ram, *and* seven yearling lambs; one kid of the goats *as* a sin offering
- Various grain offerings with oil and drink offerings are to be presented with the animals (Num. 29:11)

Spirit of the Law:

- Take the day off from work and rest in remembrance of this special day
- Remember that in the book of Jonah, the king of Nineveh's decree was that man and beast were not to taste food (Jonah 3:7); however, if you don't have that conviction and feel that you must feed animals (livestock) and perform other *essential* responsibilities in order to preserve life, then feel free to do so. Work or responsibilities that are *not* essential should absolutely be rescheduled for another day.
- Fasting for 24 hours (evening to evening) is to be done. Pray for help in this area if it intimidates you, and practice fasting in advance of Yom Kippur so that you are much better equipped to observe this day.
- In the days leading up to the fast, it is helpful to work your way down into the fasting state. Slowly wean yourself off of food as opposed to eating a huge buffet meal the night before so that you are less hungry the next day. Do not engage in gluttony the night before. Do engage in plenty of hydration the days leading up to Yom Kippur. Having raw honey before a day of fasting is also a good idea to help you sustain your energy levels; and adding a little cinnamon could help balance your blood sugar if you feel that this is an area of concern. Simply and eagerly pray about how

Yehovah wants you to observe His day. He understands your situation and wants to instruct you individually as you seek Him in your prayer closet.

- Read Jonah, Isaiah 58, Ezekiel 9, Joel, or Leviticus 16 in honor of this day
- Offer prayers of sincere repentance. Close any doors that you may have opened to the enemy. Renounce (cancel) any sin in your life by confessing it and breaking all curses in Jesus' mighty name. Ask God to reveal your unintentional sins so that you can properly deal with them. Pray the Luke 17:5 prayer so that you can walk in the power of the Holy Spirit and perform all of the signs of the Great Commission as witnessed in the book of Acts.

THE FEAST OF SUKKOT

The next appointed time that comes after Atonements is the Feast of Sukkot, known commonly as the Feast of Tabernacles. The purpose of this day is very clear, for as the Word states:

42 "You shall dwell in booths for seven days. All who are native Israelites shall dwell in booths,
43 "that your generations may know that I made the children of Israel dwell in booths when I brought them out of the land of Egypt: I *am* the LORD your God."
(Lev. 23:42,43)

This Feast is a statement to the world that Elohim's people dwelt in *sukkot* when they left the land of Egypt. The principle is rather profound. A nation of approximately two million people left Egypt in the wilderness and did not have the shelter of a home or even a sturdy tent. They made sukkot to dwell in, which are flimsy structures put together from the scraps, brushes, and branches of the wilderness. Like I mentioned in Chapter 12 speaking of Jonah's booth, a *sukkah* is very different from an *ohel,* which is a well-engineered Hebrew tent. The point is that Elohim's people did not receive protection because of buildings, fortresses, castles, or lavish shelters. They were in sukkot! The whole metaphor demonstrates that it is not the shelter made with human hands that protects an individual from Pharaoh's armies or wild beasts. It is the God of the sukkah that protects. This was and still is an exercise to physically make an outward demonstration that God is our source of protection and strength. We should never put our trust into the things we are able to construct with our own hands. This demonstration is to be done for seven days:

"Also on the fifteenth day of the seventh month, when you have gathered in the fruit of the land, you shall keep the feast of the LORD *for* seven days; on the first day *there shall be* a sabbath-*rest,* and on the eighth day a sabbath-*rest."*
(Lev. 23:39)

This Feast begins on the 15th day and lasts for seven days. This first day is a sabbath, and then there is the eighth-day assembly, which is another set apart sabbath day. These days should be scheduled off from work and non-essential work obligations. Here is what your sukkah is supposed to look like according to Lev. 23:40:

"And you shall take for yourselves on the first day the fruit of beautiful trees, branches of palm trees, the boughs of leafy trees, and willows of the brook; and you shall rejoice before the LORD your God for seven days."

Notice the command to gather both fruit and branches. Traditions from Judaism often confuse the simple truth of the commandment here. Yes, there are very specific species of trees mentioned, but not everyone has the opportunity to live in a place like Hawaii, Southern California, or Israel where palm trees grow. Not everyone has access to the branches of olive trees that the Judahites took in observance of this day as recorded in Nehemiah 8:15. Notice also that the preferred fruit of Judaism—the etrog, or citron—is not explicitly mentioned in the Scriptures. For the majority of us living outside the land of Israel, it is perfectly acceptable to take native tree branches from your local area and use them for your sukkah. The sukkah can take on any shape, height, or size that you want because there are no specific dimensions or number of walls given in the Torah.

Unlike the Lord's Supper or the Day of Atonement, Sukkot is a time of joy, feasting, and family. We see in Nehemiah 8:16-18 that there was great joy during the feast of Sukkot after the exiles had returned from Babylon. Think of it as an annual campout with your loved ones. It's a time to get out in nature more and experience stillness and intimacy with God away from the distractions and noise of everyday life.

Prophetically, Sukkot has some interesting concepts associated with it. In the near future, the nations of the world are required to go to Jerusalem for the Feast of Tabernacles, or they will not have rain according to Zechariah 14:16-

19. It is also important to discern the letter of the Law because we see the saints in heaven before the throne of God having palm branches in their hands (Rev. 7:9), which might be a subtle piece of evidence regarding the timing of the marriage supper of the lamb described in Revelation 19:9 and also the "tabernacle" of God coming down in Revelation 21:3. Yeshua uses the language of marriage and a wedding feast with His people throughout the Gospels; and it is my understanding that Sukkot will be the future and complete fulfillment of Yeshua's renewed marriage covenant with His people.

Regarding the 8th day after Sukkot, there are some important considerations. First, this is not part of Sukkot, so if you want to pack up your sukkah on the 8th day and put it away you technically could (Lev. 23:42). The 8th day is called "Shemini Atzeret" (Strong's H8066 and H6116, respectively) in the Hebrew, and this is what Yeshua proclaimed on this very day during His earthly ministry:

37 "On the last day, that great *day* of the feast, Jesus stood and cried out, saying, 'If anyone thirsts, let him come to Me and drink.
38 "'He who believes in Me, as the Scripture has said, out of his heart will flow rivers of living water.'
39 "But this He spoke concerning the Spirit, whom those believing in Him would receive; for the Holy Spirit was not yet *given,* because Jesus was not yet glorified."
(John 7:37-39)

John interprets the mystery of Yeshua's words. The Holy Spirit is the promise of the living waters, and it is the promise of the 8th Day (Shemini Atzeret). There are many Scriptures that are in alignment with what Yeshua said, but He was most likely quoting these words of Isaiah 44:3:

"For I will pour water on him who is thirsty,
And floods on the dry ground;
I will pour My Spirit on your descendants,
And My blessing on your offspring."

Therefore, it is with this understanding that we should be requesting the anointing of the Holy Spirit during Shemini Atzeret (2Ki. 2:9). This is the day of anointing, which is why the firstfruits of the olive trees in Israel ripen in alignment with Sukkot so that they can be offered during the pilgrimage. The olive oil typically used for anointing symbolizes the Holy Spirit.

Letter of the Law:

- Build a sukkah using the exact species that are listed in Lev. 23:40 and also Neh. 8:15.
- Proclaim the holy convocations: the first and eighth days are required days of rest with no regular work allowed.
- Live in the sukkah for the duration of the entire Feast of Sukkot (seven days).
- Every seventh year in a 49-year cycle, read the entire Torah during the Feast of Sukkot (Deut. 31:10; Neh. 8:18).
- Present yourself in Jerusalem for Sukkot (Exo. 23:17, Deut. 16:16)
- Numerous agricultural offerings are to be offered as described in Numbers 29.

Spirit of the Law:

- Depending on your location, you could build a very primitive sukkah from tree branches just like it is commanded in the Torah; or if it gets too cold during the time of year when you are celebrating Sukkot, you may opt for a more sturdy tent where you can have a propane heater or even a wood stove installed (like some hunting tents do). When the commands were given, the people were living in the mild climate of the Middle East. Sure, it gets cold seasonally, but it gets very cold in the mountains of Montana or Wyoming, for instance. Make preparations in advance.
- Remember, this is a major feast. These are eight days of feasting. I am of the opinion based on Deut. 12:17, Deut. 14:23, and Deut. 15:20 that part of your set-apart tithe should go to the keeping of the three pilgrimage feasts, especially the Feast of Sukkot. Set aside money and enjoy time with your family and Elohim like a true Hebrew. Enjoy whatever good thing your heart desires, just like it states in Deuteronomy 14:26.
- Pray facing Jerusalem (like Daniel did) three times a day for the eight days of this set-apart time in honor of the pilgrimage requirement to appear in Jerusalem
- Read Nehemiah 8 and John 7

OBSERVING THE SABBATICAL YEARS

The next Sabbath years before the end of the age are going to be from Abib 2030–2031, Abib 2037–2038, and Abib 2044–2045, with the Jubilee beginning on Abib 2045, which is also a Sabbath year. As we have explored together throughout this book, this is one of the commandments of the Torah that only takes effect once every 7 years with the 49th and 50th years of a cycle also having special Sabbath year observances. This can be a more advanced and challenging instruction to follow for newcomers. However, yes, we should keep it, and it's actually not that hard! There will always be a special blessing for those who will be observing this commandment moving into the future. Though we do not know what the future holds, I will share the important lessons I learned from observing my first Sabbatical year from 2023–2024.

The Sabbatical Year prohibits us from tilling the soil, planting seed, tending to plants (such as pruning), and harvesting crops from the soil (see Leviticus 25:4). When I say "harvesting" is prohibited by the Torah, what I mean is that storing food away for long periods of time is what is actually prohibited. Just like the children of Israel collected mana in the wilderness, we are also only allowed to harvest crops daily, according to what we can eat each day, from what grows by itself (volunteer crops) from our gardens or our fields. However, the spirit of the Law also implies that it is okay to buy food from the Canaanites, because this is what the Joshua generation did when they entered the Promised Land during the Sabbatical Year of 2500 After Creation (a Jubilee Year) and the manna ceased as recorded in Joshua 5:11,12. Of course, "buying" food is implied, but since Israel had only barely entered the land, it is understood that they were purchasing food from the Canaanites to sustain themselves rather than wild-harvesting their food every single day. Such a thing would be extremely difficult for millions of people to do for survival. Instead, they simply engaged in commerce.

Besides special circumstances like that of the Joshua Sabbatical Year, the fundamental principle of the Sabbath Year is to either grow or purchase enough food to store away before the Sabbath so that the land can rest during the entire year. Usually, one year of food per person in your household is sufficient for meeting the requirements of the Torah. However, because of inevitable wartime scenarios and economic problems, it is wise to have two or even more years of food stored away. Of course, such a thing is always dependent on personal financial circumstances. The keeping of future sabbatical years beginning with 2030-31 will probably look much like the Joshua

Sabbatical Year where the children of Israel did not have much food stored as they traveled.

If future circumstances somehow allow for a more routine observance, however, one of the best foods for storage are wheat berries. These can be ground and turned into flour for making bread, pasta, tortillas, and many other staples. You can even sprout them for wheatgrass that can be juiced. Other excellent foods include beans, lentils, rice, popcorn seeds, barley, and oats. These types of grains and seeds store very well for long periods of time in a root cellar or basement (out of direct sunlight). If you are unfamiliar with making your own bread from wheat berries, there are a wide variety of recipes online, and it would be best to get well acquainted with homemade bread as soon as you can. If you have a root cellar or basement, you might be able to store onions, carrots, potatoes and these sorts of root crops for long periods of time. Don't forget to store plenty of salt, spices, seasonings, and also canned or dehydrated fruits, vegetables, sauces, and more of these types of condiments. Notice that the Sabbatical Year does not prohibit the eating of meat. You can eat as much meat as you'd like. Deer, gazelle, and elk are fine along with other sorts of clean meats such as chicken, chicken eggs, lamb, and beef. Clean meats can be eaten regularly throughout the Sabbatical Year. Just make sure that the meats are prepared according to the Torah (the blood poured out, roasted over fire, and with the fat removed as best you can). There is also no prohibition on dairy products. Butter, milk, cheese and related products should be enjoyed abundantly. Having a couple of dairy goats would supply great quantities of consumable products for one household and alone would bless your home with tremendous resilience in light of the coming storms of the last days. If these concepts are new to you, it's time to become comfortable with being uncomfortable. Your friends and family will no doubt give you strange looks and may even ridicule you as you begin expressing desires to live a more simple life and certainly once you begin acquiring livestock. Always remember these words of the prophet Micah, and you will be just fine:

"He has shown you, O man, what is good;
And what does the LORD require of you
But to do justly,
To love mercy,
And to walk humbly with your God?"
(Mic. 6:8)

SUMMARY

These are the secrets of living righteously. Yes, of course righteousness is given freely through faith in Christ; but faith requires action. Faith without works is dead. Practice all of these things, and little-by-little you will become the Hebrew that Elohim has always desired you to be. As you practice the instructions of God, you will start to become conformed to the image of the Son (Romans 8:29) in a way that the vast majority of religious people will sadly never experience. Consider yourself blessed to be on this journey with me; but also consider the great responsibility we have to educate, inspire, and warn others out of a heart of love.

Conclusion and Next Steps

My number one encouragement if all this information is new to you is not to succumb to a spirit of fear or have unnecessary anxiety regarding end times events. If you are new to Torah, there are many nuances to walking out our faith just as commanded by the spirit and the letter of the Law. Just take it one step at a time. Focus on experiencing intimacy with Yeshua, and try not to take your eyes off of Him. Food price increases, supply chain problems, and war—everything looming on the horizon is looking dreadful; but don't meditate on these things. Instead, learn to hear His voice, walk in obedience, and experience the blessings of Psalm 91. Like I carefully explained to you in the pages of this book, America and the West have sinned against the world by funding, enabling, and unconditionally supporting the Zionist movement that caused the genocide of communism to spread worldwide. Indeed, they have sinned against Yehovah and His Torah. The nations are now rising up against Mystery Babylon and its system of enslavement, lies, and deception. Yehovah is allowing His locust armies to arise because they have a just cause. He has remembered the sins of Mystery Babylon, and she will be repaid double for all her abominations. Millions will die, just like during the early days of communism in Russia.

With that said, I want to invite you to take the next step in this journey. We may only have a brief time of stability after the Great Tribulation begins. Let us all make good use of our time. To get in an accelerated discipleship environment where you can experience a Spirit-filled curriculum that will answer more questions you may still have, consider joining Kingdom Secrets Academy. For more information, go to: https://www.kingdom-secrets.com/academy (make sure to copy this URL into your web browser exactly as it is shown).

Now that you have reached the end of this systematic study of the 70 weeks of Daniel, you can see why the earlier edition of this book along with various Overcome Babylon YouTube videos and podcasts put such a strong emphasis on September 22, 2023. Without knowing exactly what would take place, the only option I had was to get as loud as possible. Like Paul said, "For we know in part and we prophesy in part" (1Co 13:9). My efforts were not in vain. Many have been reached with the fullness of the Gospel and Torah. The proper understanding of God's timeline has also now become freely available to all who are seeking. Still, the prophecies of Daniel concerning the *wise and righteous* of this final generation have yet to be fulfilled. It is implied in Daniel 11:33 that more than one person will be instructing "many" regarding the 70 weeks of Daniel. To the best of my knowledge, I have been the only one properly explaining the 70th week of Daniel from 1996–2045, the cutting off of the Lost Tribes, the setting up of the nuclear abomination of desolation that will be used to begin the Great Tribulation, and how this same abomination is described in Zechariah's flying scroll prophecy. Nearly all men still believe the abomination of desolation to be a statue or idol that is somehow related to a "third temple" in Jerusalem. Many others still believe this prophecy was already fulfilled at some point in the past. We will see how Daniel 11:33 plays out, and I encourage you to take an active role in its fulfillment by teaching the message of this book. Whether you receive honor or ridicule from men, always remember these words of our Lord that were recorded through John the apostle:

"He who is unjust, let him be unjust still; he who is filthy, let him be filthy still; he who is righteous, let him be righteous still; he who is holy, let him be holy still."
(Rev. 22:11)

Yeshua be with you and uphold you with His righteous right hand. Amen.

KINGDOM SECRETS ACADEMY

This Is The Second Part Of The Journey That You Already Started.

"How to...

Walk the Gospel & Torah,
Live the Great Commission,
Fulfill God's calling on your life,

and experience His peace that surpasses all understanding."

Sign Up Today. Be A Part Of The Great Awakening Of The End Times. Equip Yourself; Train Disciples.

https://www.kingdom-secrets.com/academy

Appendix A: 120 Shanah of Mankind Charts

Shanah Cycle #	Year Since Creation	Gregorian Year
1	1 – 49	3836 – 3788 BC
2	50 – 98	3787 – 3739 BC
3	99 –147	3738 – 3690 BC
4	148 – 196	3689 – 3641 BC
5	197 – 245	3640 – 3592 BC
6	246 – 294	3591 – 3543 BC
7	295 – 343	3542 – 3494 BC
8	344 – 392	3493 – 3445 BC
9	393 – 441	3444 – 3396 BC
10	442 – 490	3395 – 3347 BC
11	491 – 539	3346 – 3298 BC
12	540 – 588	3297 – 3249 BC
13	589 – 637	3248 – 3200 BC
14	638 – 686	3119 – 3151 BC
15	687 – 735	3150 – 3102 BC
16	736 – 784	3101 – 3053 BC
17	785 – 833	3052 – 3004 BC
18	834 – 882	3003 – 2955 BC
19	883 – 931	2954 – 2906 BC
20	932 – 980	2856 – 2857 BC
21	981 – 1029	2856 – 2808 BC
22	1030 – 1078	2807 – 2759 BC
23	1079 – 1127	2758 – 2710 BC
24	1128 – 1176	2709 – 2661 BC
25	1177 – 1225	2660 – 2612 BC
26	1226 – 1274	2611 – 2563 BC
27	1275 – 1323	2562 – 2514 BC
28	1324 – 1372	2513 – 2465 BC
29	1373 – 1421	2464 – 2416 BC
30	1422 – 1470	2415 – 2367 BC
31	1471 – 1519	2366 – 2318 BC
32	1520 – 1568	2317 – 2269 BC
33	1569 – 1617	2268 – 2220 BC
34	1618 – 1666	2219 – 2171 BC
35	1667 – 1715	2170 – 2122 BC
36	1716 – 1764	2121 – 2073 BC
37	1765 – 1813	2072 – 2024 BC
38	1814 – 1862	2023 – 1975 BC

			70 Shabua of Daniel
39	1863 – 1911	1974 – 1926 BC	
40	1912 – 1960	1925 – 1877 BC	
41	1961 – 2009	1876 – 1828 BC	
42	2010 – 2058	1827 – 1779 BC	
43	2059 – 2107	1778 – 1730 BC	
44	2108 – 2156	1729 – 1681 BC	
45	2157 – 2205	1680 – 1632 BC	
46	2206 – 2254	1631 – 1583 BC	
47	2255 – 2303	1582 – 1534 BC	
48	2304 – 2352	1533 – 1485 BC	
49	2453 – 2401	1484 – 1436 BC	
50	2402 – 2450	1435 – 1387 BC	**70 Shabua of Daniel**
51	2451 – 2499	1386 – 1338 BC	1
52	2500 – 2548	1337 – 1289 BC	2
53	2549 – 2597	1288 – 1240 BC	3
54	2598 – 2646	1239 – 1191 BC	4
55	2647 – 2695	1190 – 1142 BC	5
56	2696 – 2744	1141 – 1093 BC	6
57	2745 – 2793	1092 – 1044 BC	7
58	2794 – 2842	1043 – 995 BC	8
59	2843 – 2891	994 – 946 BC	9
60	2892 – 2940	945 – 897 BC	10
61	2941 – 2989	896 – 848 BC	11
62	2990 – 3038	847 – 799 BC	12
63	3039 – 3087	798 – 750 BC	13
64	3088 – 3136	749 – 701 BC	14
65	3137 – 3185	700 – 652 BC	15
66	3186 – 3234	651 – 603 BC	16
67	3235 – 3283	602 – 554 BC	17
68	3284 – 3332	553 – 505 BC	18
69	3333 – 3381	504 – 456 BC	19
70	3382 – 3430	455 – 407 BC	20
71	3431 – 3479	406 – 358 BC	21
72	3480 – 3528	357 – 309 BC	22
73	3529 – 3577	308 – 260 BC	23
74	3578 – 3626	259 – 211 BC	24
75	3627 – 3675	210 – 162 BC	25
76	3676 – 3724	161 – 113 BC	26
77	3725 – 3773	112 – 64 BC	27
78	3774 – 3822	63 – 15 BC	28
79	3823 – 3871	14 BC – AD 35	29

80	3872 – 3920	AD 36 – 84	30
81	3921 – 3969	AD 85 – 133	31
82	3970 – 4018	AD 134 – 182	32
83	4019 – 4067	AD 183 – 231	33
84	4068 – 4116	AD 232 – 280	34
85	4117 – 4165	AD 281 – 329	35
86	4166 – 4214	AD 330 – 378	36
87	4215 – 4263	AD 379 – 427	37
88	4264 – 4312	AD 428 – 476	38
89	4313 – 4361	AD 477 – 525	39
90	4362 – 4410	AD 526 – 574	40
91	4411 – 4459	AD 575 – 623	41
92	4460 – 4508	AD 624 – 672	42
93	4509 – 4557	AD 673 – 721	43
94	4558 – 4606	AD 722 – 770	44
95	4607 – 4655	AD 771 – 819	45
96	4656 – 4704	AD 820 – 868	46
97	4705 – 4753	AD 869 – 917	47
98	4754 – 4802	AD 918 – 966	48
99	4803 – 4851	AD 967 – 1015	49
100	4852 – 4900	AD 1016 – 1064	50
101	4901 – 4949	AD 1065 – 1113	51
102	4950 – 4998	AD 1114 – 1162	52
103	4999 – 5047	AD 1163 – 1211	53
104	5048 – 5096	AD 1212 – 1260	54
105	5097 – 5145	AD 1261 – 1309	55
106	5146 – 5194	AD 1310 – 1358	56
107	5195 – 5243	AD 1359 – 1407	57
108	5244 – 5292	AD 1408 – 1456	58
109	5293 – 5341	AD 1457 – 1505	59
110	5342 – 5390	AD 1506 – 1554	60
111	5391 – 5439	AD 1555 – 1603	61
112	5440 – 5488	AD 1604 – 1652	62
113	5489 – 5537	AD 1653 – 1701	63
114	5538 – 5586	AD 1702 – 1750	64
115	5587 – 5635	AD 1751 – 1799	65
116	5636 – 5684	AD 1800 – 1848	66
117	5685 – 5733	AD 1849 – 1897	67
118	5734 – 5782	AD 1898 – 1946	68
119	5783 – 5831	AD 1947 – 1995	69
120	5832 – 5880	AD 1996 – 2045	70

Appendix B: The 70th Shabua of Daniel Charts

The 70th Week of Daniel (Gregorian Years)

First Seven	Second Seven	Third Seven	Fourth Seven	Fifth Seven	Sixth Seven	Seventh Seven
1996	2003	2010	2017	2024	2031	2038
1997	2004	2011	2018	2025	2032	2039
1998	2005	2012	2019	2026	2033	2040
1999	2006	2013	**2020**	2027	2034	2041
2000	2007	2014	2021	2028	2035	2042
2001	2008	2015	2022	2029	2036	2043
2002	2009	2016	2023	2030	2037	2044, Abib 2045

7th Years of Land Rest

The 70th Week of Daniel (Creation Years)

First Seven	Second Seven	Third Seven	Fourth Seven	Fifth Seven	Sixth Seven	Seventh Seven
5832	5839	5846	5853	5860	5867	5874
5833	5840	5847	5854	5861	5868	5875
5834	5841	5848	5855	5862	5869	5876
5835	5842	5849	**5856**	5863	5870	5877
5836	5843	5850	5857	5864	5871	5878
5837	5844	5851	5858	5865	5872	5879
5838	5845	5852	5859	5866	5873	5880

7th Years of Land Rest

Notes

Introduction

1. Carrie Keller-Lynn and ToI Staff, "'The best party': Over 150,000 march in Tel Aviv's 25th annual Pride Parade," *Times of Israel,* June 8, 2023, https://www.timesofisrael.com/the-best-party-tens-of-thousands-march-in-tel-avivs-25th-annual-pride-parade.
2. New York Times, "Dorothy de Rothschild, 93, Supporter of Israel," Obituary, December 13, 1988, https://www.nytimes.com/1988/12/13/obituaries/dorothy-de-rothschild-93-supporter-of-israel.html.
3. The State of Israel, The Judicial Authority Supreme Court, "The Symbols," https://supreme.court.gov.il/sites/en/VirtualTour/Pages/11_icons.aspx.
4. Ibid, "The Gatehouse: The Pyramid and the Library," https://supreme.court.gov.il/sites/en/VirtualTour/Pages/07_gatehouse.aspx.

Chapter 1

1. Joseph Dumond, *2300 Days of Hell,* (Bloomington, US: Xlibris, 2014), 301-302.
2. Robert Anderson, *The Coming Prince: The Marvellous Prophecy of Daniel's Seventy Weeks Concerning the Antichrist,* (Lawton, OK: Trumpet Press, 2014).
3. Jehovah's Witnesses, "How Daniel's Prophecy Foretells the Messiah's Arrival," JW.org, https://www.jw.org/en/library/books/bible-teach/daniels-prophecy-70-weeks-messiah.
4. Francis E. Gigot, "Encyclopedia - Book of Daniel," Catholic Answers, https://www.catholic.com/encyclopedia/book-of-daniel.
5. Seventh-Day Adventist Church, "2023 Annual Statistical Report New Series, Volume 5," ASTR - Office of Archives, Statistics, and Research, March 1, 2022, https://documents.adventistarchives.org/Statistics/ASR/ASR2023A.pdf.
6. Sabbath School Lesson, "The 70 Weeks and the 2300 Days," Sabbath School Net, October 14, 2019, https://ssnet.org/blog/tuesday-the-70-weeks-and-the-2300-days.
7. Julie Tivy Boney, "Prophet or Not," Life Assurance Ministries, November 19, 2019, https://blog.lifeassuranceministries.org/2019/11/19/prophet-or-not.
8. Dudley Marvin Canright, "Origin, History, and Failures of Adventism," Chapter 4, in *Seventh Day Adventism Renounced,* 14th ed. (B.C. Goodpasture, 1961), Accessed online via Life Assurance Ministries:
https://blog.lifeassuranceministries.org/2021/05/13/4-origin-history-and-failures-of-adventism.
9. Blue Letter Bible (BLB). https://www.blueletterbible.org/
10. Blue Letter Bible, "G458 - anomia - Strong's Greek Lexicon (NKJV)," https://www.blueletterbible.org/lexicon/g458/nkjv/tr/0-1.
11. Ibid, "H8451 - tôrâ - Strong's Hebrew Lexicon (NKJV)," https://www.blueletterbible.org/lexicon/h8451/nkjv/wlc/0-1.

Chapter 2

1. Blue Letter Bible, "H2852 - ḥāṯaḵ - Strong's Hebrew Lexicon (NKJV)," https://www.blueletterbible.org/lexicon/h2852/nkjv/wlc/0-1.
2. Ibid, "H7620 - šāḇûaʻ - Strong's Hebrew Lexicon (NKJV)," https://www.blueletterbible.org/lexicon/h7620/nkjv/wlc/0-1.
3. Joseph Dumond, *2300 Days of Hell,* (Bloomington, US: Xlibris, 2014), 246.

Notes

4. Embassy of Israel, "The Twelve Tribes of Israel (ca 1200 BCE)," https://embassies.gov.il/MFA/AboutIsrael/Maps/Pages/The-Twelve-Tribes-of-Israel.aspx.

5. E. Raymond Capt, *Missing Links Discovered in Assyrian Tablets*, (Muskogee, OK: Artisan Publishers, 1985), 140.

6. Blue Letter Bible, "G2078 - eschatos - Strong's Greek Lexicon (KJV)," https://www.blueletterbible.org/kjv/act/1/8/t_conc_1019008.

7. National Records of Scotland, "The Declaration of Arbroath," 700th Anniversary Display (1320–2020), https://www.nrscotland.gov.uk/files/research/NRS_DoA_English_booklet_700_Spreads_WEB.pdf.

8. E. Raymond Capt, *The Lost Chapter of the Acts of the Apostles*, (Muskogee, OK: Artisan Publishers, 1983), 11.

9. Phil Moore, *Straight to the Heart of Acts: 60 Bite-Sized Insights*, (Oxford, England: Monarch Books, 2010), 270.

10. Philip Schaff, *Ante-Nicene Fathers Volume 7, Of the Manner in Which the Persecutors Died*, (Grand Rapids, MI: Christian Classics Ethereal Library, 1885), 691.

11. E. Raymond Capt, *The Lost Chapter of the Acts of the Apostles*, (Muskogee, OK: Artisan Publishers, 1983), 17,18.

12. Ibid, *Missing Links Discovered in Assyrian Tablets*, (Muskogee, OK: Artisan Publishers, 1985), 61.

13. Isabel Hill Elder, *Celt, Druid and Culdee*, 9th Ed., (Muskogee, OK: Artisan Publishers, 2006), 68,69.

14. Ibid, 68.

15. E. Raymond Capt, *The Traditions of Glastonbury*, (Muskogee, OK: Artisan Publishers, 2012).

16. Isabel Hill Elder, *Celt, Druid and Culdee*, 9th Ed., (Muskogee, OK: Artisan Publishers, 2006), 79-81.

17. E. Raymond Capt, *Missing Links Discovered in Assyrian Tablets*, (Muskogee, OK: Artisan Publishers, 1985).

18. Wikipedia contributors, "Jewish population by city," *Wikipedia, The Free Encyclopedia*, https://en.wikipedia.org/w/index.php?title=Jewish_population_by_city&oldid=1148351629.

19. Gutierre Tibón, *Historia del nombre y de la fundación de México*, 3rd Ed., (D.F., México: Fondo De Cultura Económica, 1993), 104.

20. Martha Modzelevich, "Mandragora autumnalis, Mandragora officinarum, Autumn Mandrake" Flowers in Israel, http://flowersinisrael.com/Mandragoraautumnalis_page.htm.

21. Rebecca Biderman, Ancient Path New Moon - Restoring the True Biblical Time, Facebook Group, Post dated February 7, 2018, https://www.facebook.com/share/p/ZWgjfuB7NYUEzcSx.

22. Ashley Jackson, *The British Empire: A Very Short Introduction*. (Oxford, England: Oxford University Press, 2013) 5-9.

23. Alex Rosenson, "The Terms of the Anglo-American Financial Agreement," *The American Economic Review*, 37, No. 1, (1947): 178–187, https://www.jstor.org/stable/1802868.

24. Yair Davidiy, *Hebrew Tribes: The Israelite Tribal Identification of Western Peoples*, (S.l.: Lulu Press, Inc., 2021).

25. Steven M. Collins, *The Origins and Empire of Ancient Israel*, (Royal Oak, MI: Bible Blessings, 1996), 135.

26. Ibid, 138.

27. Jesse David Chariton, "The Mesopotamian Origins of the Hittite Double-Headed Eagle," *UW-L Journal of Undergraduate Research*, XIV (2008):1-13, https://www.researchgate.net/publication/339213501_The_Mesopotamian_Origins_of_the_Hittite_Double-Headed_Eagle.

28. E. Raymond Capt, *Missing Links Discovered in Assyrian Tablets*, (Muskogee, OK: Artisan Publishers, 1985), 210.

29. Steven M. Collins, *Israel's Lost Empires*, (Royal Oak, MI: Bible Blessings, 1996), 100-103.

30. Ibid, *Israel's Tribes Today*, (Royal Oak, MI: Bible Blessings, 2005), 241-243.

31. W.H. Bennett, *Symbols of Our Celto-Saxon Heritage*, (Windsor, Ontario: Covenant Books Publishing, 1976), 25.

32. Ibid, 133-134.

33. House of Names, "Ramos History, Family Crest & Coats of Arms," Swyrich Corporation, https://houseofnames.com/ramos-family-crest.

34. TruthVids, "Heraldry & Symbols of the 12 Tribes of Israel in Europe," YouTube, May 1, 2020. https://www.youtube.com/watch?v=gabcvC2L9mE.

35. UNICEF, "Sweden, Norway, Iceland, Estonia and Portugal rank highest for family-friendly policies in OECD and EU countries," June 12, 2019, https://www.unicef.org/press-releases/sweden-norway-iceland-and-estonia-rank-highest-family-friendly-policies-oecd-and-eu.

36. Government of Sweden, "Parental Leave Act (Föräldraledighetslagen)," Ministry of Employment, 17 November 2016, https://www.government.se/government-policy/labour-law-and-work-environment/1995584-parental-leave-act-foraldraledighetslagen.

37. Megan Mahoney, "How Women Have it All in Sweden: Female Empowerment through Work-Life Balance," The Swedish Program, https://swedishprogram.org/how-women-have-it-all-in-sweden.

38. Steven M. Collins, *Israel's Tribes Today*, (Royal Oak, MI: Bible Blessings, 2005), 211-213.

39. House of Names, Swyrich Corporation, https://www.houseofnames.com.

40. Blue Letter Bible, "H3607 - kālā' - Strong's Hebrew Lexicon (NKJV)," https://www.blueletterbible.org/lexicon/h3607/nkjv/wlc/0-1.

41. Ibid, "H6588 - peša' - Strong's Hebrew Lexicon (NKJV)," https://www.blueletterbible.org/lexicon/h6588/nkjv/wlc/0-1.

42. Ibid, "H2856 - ḥātam - Strong's Hebrew Lexicon (NKJV)," https://www.blueletterbible.org/lexicon/h2856/nkjv/wlc/0-1.

43. Ibid, "H2403 - ḥaṭṭā'āṯ - Strong's Hebrew Lexicon (NKJV)," https://www.blueletterbible.org/lexicon/h2403/nkjv/wlc/0-1.

44. Ibid, "H3722 - kāp̄ar - Strong's Hebrew Lexicon (NKJV)," https://www.blueletterbible.org/lexicon/h3722/nkjv/wlc/0-1.

45. Ibid, "H5771 - 'āôn - Strong's Hebrew Lexicon (NKJV)," https://www.blueletterbible.org/lexicon/h5771/nkjv/wlc/0-1.

46. Ibid, "H5769 - 'ôlām - Strong's Hebrew Lexicon (NKJV)," https://www.blueletterbible.org/lexicon/h5769/nkjv/wlc/0-1.

47. Ibid, "H6664 - ṣeḏeq - Strong's Hebrew Lexicon (NKJV)," https://www.blueletterbible.org/lexicon/h6664/nkjv/wlc/0-1.

48. Ibid, "H2856 - ḥātam - Strong's Hebrew Lexicon (NKJV)," https://www.blueletterbible.org/lexicon/h2856/nkjv/wlc/0-1.

49. Ibid, "H2377 - ḥāzôn - Strong's Hebrew Lexicon (NKJV)," https://www.blueletterbible.org/lexicon/h2377/nkjv/wlc/0-1.

50. Ibid, "H5030 - nāḇî' - Strong's Hebrew Lexicon (NKJV)," https://www.blueletterbible.org/lexicon/h5030/nkjv/wlc/0-1.

51. Ibid, "H4886 - māšaḥ - Strong's Hebrew Lexicon (NKJV)," https://www.blueletterbible.org/lexicon/h4886/nkjv/wlc/0-1.

52. Ibid, "H6944 - qōḏeš - Strong's Hebrew Lexicon (NKJV)," https://www.blueletterbible.org/lexicon/h6944/nkjv/wlc/0-1.

53. Joseph Dumond, *2300 Days of Hell* (Bloomington US: Xlibris, 2014), 375.

Chapter 3

1. Marcia Wendorf, "People routinely live over 100 years in global 'blue zones'. Should you move?", Interesting Engineering, November 4, 2021, https://interestingengineering.com/health/people-routinely-live-beyond-the-age-of-100-in-these-rare-blue-zones.

2. Dan Buettner and Blue Zones, LLC. https://www.bluezones.com.

Notes

3. Gerontology Research Group, "GRG World Supercentenarian Rankings List," https://grg.org/WSRL/TableE.aspx.

4. Ibid.

5. Marcia Wendorf, "People routinely live over 100 years in global 'blue zones'. Should you move?", Interesting Engineering, November 4, 2021, https://interestingengineering.com/health/people-routinely-live-beyond-the-age-of-100-in-these-rare-blue-zones.

6. World Health Organization (WHO), "GHE: Life expectancy and healthy life expectancy," https://www.who.int/data/gho/data/themes/mortality-and-global-health-estimates/ghe-life-expectancy-and-healthy-life-expectancy.

7. Blue Letter Bible, "H8141 - šānâ - Strong's Hebrew Lexicon (NKJV)," https://www.blueletterbible.org/lexicon/h8141/nkjv/wlc/0-1.

8. Wikipedia contributors, "Genealogies of Genesis," *Wikipedia, The Free Encyclopedia,* https://en.wikipedia.org/w/index.php?title=Genealogies_of_Genesis&oldid=1148149977.

9. Joseph Dumond, *Remembering The Sabbatical Years of 2016: Breaking The Curses By Obedience,* (Bloomington, US: Xlibris, 2013),142-145.

10. R. Clover, et al., *The Sabbath and Jubilee Cycle Volume One,* 2nd Ed., (Garden Grove, US: Qadesh La Yahweh Press, 1995), http://www.yahweh.org/publications/sjc/sabjub.pdf.

11. Flavius Josephus, *Antiquities of the Jews,* Available for free at Project Gutenberg: https://www.gutenberg.org/files/2848/2848-h/2848-h.htm.

12. Apocrypha (KJV), Read for free on eBible: https://ebible.org.

13. Joseph Dumond, "45 Sabbatical Year Proofs With Documentation," February 1, 2018, https://sightedmoon.com/45-sabbatical-year-proofs-with-documentation.

14. Joseph Dumond, "30 Tomb Stones of Zoar," November 1, 2018, https://sightedmoon.com/30-tomb-stones-of-zoar.

15. Edwin R. Thiele, *The Mysterious Numbers of the Hebrew Kings,* (Grand Rapids, MI: Kregel, 1994), 174.

16. R. Clover, et al., *The Sabbath and Jubilee Cycle Volume One,* 2nd Ed., (Garden Grove: US Qadesh La Yahweh Press, 1995), http://www.yahweh.org/publications/sjc/sabjub.pdf, 64.

17. Edwin R. Thiele, *The Mysterious Numbers of the Hebrew Kings,* (Grand Rapids, MI: Kregel, 1994), 10-14.

18. Iain W. Provan, V. Philips Long, and Tremper Longman. *A Biblical History of Israel.* (Louisville, KY: Westminster John Knox Press, 2003), 165.

19. Blue Letter Bible, "H4161 - môṣā' - Strong's Hebrew Lexicon (NKJV)," https://www.blueletterbible.org/lexicon/h4161/nkjv/wlc/0-1.

20. Ibid, "H1697 - dāḇār - Strong's Hebrew Lexicon (NKJV)," https://www.blueletterbible.org/lexicon/h1697/nkjv/wlc/0-1.

21. John S. Knox, "Solomon," World History Encyclopedia, January 25, 2017, https://www.worldhistory.org/solomon.

22. Joseph Dumond, *2300 Days of Hell,* (Bloomington US: Xlibris, 2014), 285.

23. Blue Letter Bible, "G1074 - genea - Strong's Greek Lexicon (NKJV)," https://www.blueletterbible.org/lexicon/g1074/nkjv/tr/0-1.

Chapter 4

1. Blue Letter Bible, "WLC Search Results for "וְאֵין", https://www.blueletterbible.org//search/search.cfm?Criteria=%D7%95%D6%B0%D7%90%D6%B5%D7%99%D7%9F&t=WLC#s=s_primary_0_1.

2. Ibid, "WLC Search Results for "לֹּי", https://www.blueletterbible.org//search/search.cfm?Criteria=%D7%9C%D7%95%D6%B9&t=WLC#s=s_primary_0_1.

3. Ibid, "WLC Search Results for "אֵין" AND "לֹּי", https://www.blueletterbible.org//search/search.cfm?Criteria=%D7%95%D6%B0%D7%90%D6%B5%D7%99%D7%9F+%D7%9C%D7%95%D6%B9&t=WLC#s=s_primary_0_1.

4. Ibid, "WLC Search Results for "יַשְׁחִית", https://www.blueletterbible.org//search/search.cfm?

Notes

Criteria=%D7%99%D6%B7%D7%A9%D7%81%D6%B0%D7%97%D6%B4%D7%99%
D7%AA&t=WLC#s=s_primary_0_1.

5. Wikipedia contributors, "Book of Enoch," *Wikipedia, The Free Encyclopedia,* https://en.wiki pedia.org/w/index.php?title=Book_of_Enoch&oldid=1149254159.

6. World Economic Forum, "8 Predictions For The World In 2030," February 7, 2017, Internet Archive, https://archive.org/details/8-predictions-for-the-world-in-2030.

7. Ceri Parker, "8 predictions for the world in 2030," Nov 12, 2016, World Economic Forum, https://www.weforum.org/agenda/2016/11/8-predictions-for-the-world-in-2030.

8. Joseph Mercola, *The Truth About COVID-19,* (London, UK: Chelsea Green Publishing, 2021), iBooks, Foreword.

9. Klaus Schwab, et al. *Covid-19: The Great Reset,* (Cologny/Geneva, Switzerland: World Economic Forum, 2020), 65.

10. Joseph Mercola, *The Truth About COVID-19,* (London, UK Chelsea Green Publishing, 2021), iBooks, Chapter 1.

11. World Economic Forum, "Partners," https://www.weforum.org/partners.

12. Infowars, "Flashback: Great Reset Architect Klaus Schwab Brags WEF 'Penetrates' Cabinets of World Leaders," January 26, 2022, https://www.infowars.com/posts/flashback-great-reset-architect-klaus-schwab-brags-wef-penetrates-cabinets-of-world-leaders.

13. Jamie White, "Video: Canadian MP CENSORED For Pointing Out WEF's Corrupt Influence Over Trudeau's Gov't," Infowars, February 19, 2022, https://www.infowars.com/posts/video-canadian-mp-accused-of-spreading-disinformation-for-pointing-out-wefs-corrupt-influence-over-trudeaus-govt.

14. Tyler Durden, "Bombshell Vax Analysis Finds $147 Billion In Economic Damage, Tens Of Millions Injured Or Disabled", March 28, 2023, *ZeroHedge,* https://www.zerohedge.com/markets/bombshell-vax-analysis-finds-147-billion-economic-damage-tens-millions-injured-or-disabled.

15. Phinance Technologies, "The Vaccine Damage Project - Human Cost," March 2023, https://phinancetechnologies.com/HumanityProjects/The%20VDamage%20Project%20-%20Hu man%20%20Cost.htm.

16. World Economic Forum, "Yuval Noah Harari" https://www.weforum.org/people/yuval-noah-harari

17. World Economic Forum, "Will the Future Be Human? - Yuval Noah Harari," WEF Annual Meeting, YouTube, January 25, 2018, https://youtu.be/hL9uk4hKyg4.

18. Bill Gates, "Does saving more lives lead to overpopulation?", YouTube, February 13, 2018, https://youtu.be/obRG-2jurz0.

19. Bill Gates, "The race for a COVID-19 vaccine, explained," YouTube, April 30, 2020, https://youtu.be/u1AQ5EXcJYc.

20. World Economic Forum, "Preparing for the Next Pandemic with Bill Gates | Davos | #WEF22," YouTube, May 24, 2022, https://youtu.be/NA0Fphx4UMg.

21. Joseph Mercola, *The Truth About COVID-19,* (London, UK: Chelsea Green Publishing, 2021), iBooks, Chapter 8.

22. Ibid.

23. World Economic Forum, "Conversation with Albert Bourla, CEO of Pfizer | Davos | #WEF22," YouTube, May 25, 2022, https://youtu.be/9ccd3LMNMl8.

24. Los Angeles Times, "Despite high vaccination rates, Israel scrambles to curb jump in COVID infections," July 1, 2021, https://www.latimes.com/world-nation/story/2021-07-01/israel-scrambles-curb-covid-infections.

25. NPR, "Israel sets COVID-19 record as rule changes create whiplash," January 5, 2022, https://www.npr.org/2022/01/05/1070478298/israel-sets-covid-19-record-as-rule-changes-create-whiplash.

26. Maryam Rostampour and Marziyeh Amirizadeh, *Captive in Iran: A remarkable true story of hope and triumph amid the horror of Tehran's brutal Evin Prison,* (Atlanta, GA: Tyndale Momentum, 2013), 6.

Notes

27. Britannica, T. Editors of Encyclopaedia, "Mahdi | Definition, Islam, & Eschatology," *Encyclopedia Britannica*, August 13, 2024, https://www.britannica.com/topic/mahdi.
28. Vatican Library, "Codex Vaticanus," Page 1530, https://digi.vatlib.it/view/MSS_Vat.gr.1209#.
29. Walid Shoebat, "Who is Walid? Biography of Walid Shoebat," https://shoebat.com/shoebat-foundation/who-is-walid.
30. Blue Letter Bible, "H7093 - qēṣ - Strong's Hebrew Lexicon (NKJV)," https://www.blueletterbible.org/lexicon/h7093/nkjv/wlc/0-1.
31. Ibid, "H2782 - ḥāraṣ - Strong's Hebrew Lexicon (NKJV)," https://www.blueletterbible.org/lexicon/h2782/nkjv/wlc/0-1.

Chapter 5

1. Wikipedia contributors, "League of Nations," *Wikipedia, The Free Encyclopedia*, https://en.wikipedia.org/w/index.php?title=League_of_Nations&oldid=1148428729.
2. Ibid, "Geneva Conventions," *Wikipedia, The Free Encyclopedia*, https://en.wikipedia.org/w/index.php?title=Geneva_Conventions&oldid=1148116019.
3. Ibid, "Nuremberg Code," *Wikipedia, The Free Encyclopedia*, https://en.wikipedia.org/w/index.php?title=Nuremberg_Code&oldid=1146994155.
4. Ibid, "United Nations," *Wikipedia, The Free Encyclopedia*, https://en.wikipedia.org/w/index.php?title=United_Nations&oldid=1148713682.
5. Mythologian.net, "Laurel Wreath/Crown Symbol, Its Meaning and History," https://mythologian.net/laurel-wreath-crown-symbol-meaning-history.
6. United Nations, *Report of the United Nations Conference on the Human Environment*, A/CONF.48/14/Rev.1 Stockholm, June 5-16, 1972.
7. Meadows, Donella H., Dennis L. Meadows, Jørgen Randers, and William W. Behrens, *The Limits to Growth: A Report for the Club of Rome's Project on the Predicament of Mankind*, (New York: Universe Books, 1972), 183.
8. Nicole Sparks and Darrin J. Rodgers, "John McConnell, Jr. and the Pentecostal Origins of Earth Day," Assemblies of God Heritage, Volume 30, 2010, Page 22, Accessed online via Internet Archive: https://web.archive.org/web/20120331232111/http://ifphc.org/pdf/Heritage/2010.pdf.
9. United Nations, *Report of the United Nations Conference on the Human Environment*, A/CONF.48/14/Rev.1 Stockholm, June 5-16, 1972.
10. Ibid, 4.
11. Ibid, 8.
12. Rosa Koire, *Behind the Green Mask: U.N. Agenda 21*, (Santa Rosa, CA: Post Sustainability Institute Press, 2011), 16.
13. Brian Moonan, *Agenda 21: The Earth Charter, The Ark of Hope, and the New World Order*, 2016, https://vimeo.com/150948709.
(Note: Brian Moonan's website is the following: https://turnfromyouridols.com/. You used to be able to click on the Agenda 21 video from his website and it would take you over to YouTube, but his YouTube video has been banned and deleted. Watch it on Brian's Vimeo and even download it for free, while you still can.)
14. Sally Linder, "Ark of Hope," http://www.arkofhope.org.
15. Earth Charter Commission, "The Earth Charter," page 2, https://earthcharter.org/wp-content/uploads/2020/03/echarter_english.pdf?x95251.
16. Ibid, 3.
17. Blue Letter Bible, "H7673 - šāḇaṯ - Strong's Hebrew Lexicon (NKJV)," https://www.blueletterbible.org/lexicon/h7673/nkjv/wlc/0-1.
18. Ibid, "H2077 - zeḇaḥ - Strong's Hebrew Lexicon (NKJV)," https://www.blueletterbible.org/lexicon/h2077/nkjv/wlc/0-1.
19. Ibid, "H4503 - minḥâ - Strong's Hebrew Lexicon (NKJV)," https://www.blueletterbible.org/lexicon/h4503/nkjv/wlc/0-1.

Notes

20. WebMD, "Pandemics," April 18, 2022, https://www.webmd.com/cold-and-flu/what-are-epidemics-pandemics-outbreaks.
21. Dr. Tedros Adhanom Ghebreyesus, "WHO Director-General's opening remarks at the media briefing on COVID-19 - 11 March 2020," WHO, March 11, 2020. https://www.who.int/direc tor-general/speeches/detail/who-director-general-s-opening-remarks-at-the-media-briefing-on-covid-19---11-march-2020.
22. Devorah Gordon, "New Moon Observation 24 February 2020," Devorah's Date Tree, Email Newsletter, https://mailchi.mp/84e952094079/new-moon-report-24-february-2020.
23. WHO, "Timeline: WHO's COVID-19 response," https://www.who.int/emergencies/diseases/novel-coronavirus-2019/interactive-timeline#.
24. The Gavi Vaccine Alliance, "The COVAX Facility," https://www.gavi.org/covax-facility.
25. WHO, "Boost for global response to COVID-19 as economies worldwide formally sign up to COVAX facility," September 21, 2020, https://www.who.int/news/item/21-09-2020-boost-for-global-response-to-covid-19-as-economies-worldwide-formally-sign-up-to-covax-facility.
26. VOA News, "WHO Says 184 Countries Have Now Joined COVAX Vaccine Program," October 19, 2020, https://www.voanews.com/a/covid-19-pandemic_who-says-184-countries-have-now-joined-covax-vaccine-program/6197326.html.
27. Earth Charter Commission, "The Earth Charter," Pages 3-4, https://earthcharter.org/wp-content/uploads/2020/03/echarter_english.pdf?x95251.
28. Ibid, 2.
29. UN, "Resolution adopted by the General Assembly on 25 September 2015," https://www.un.org/en/development/desa/population/migration/generalassembly/docs/globalcompact/A_RES_70_1_E.pdf.
30. Ibid, "Resolution adopted by the General Assembly on 21 September 2020," https://docu ments.un.org/doc/undoc/gen/n20/248/80/pdf/n2024880.pdf.
31. Thomas Hicks, "The 2030 Mass Migration Agenda," Muckraker, January 21, 2024, https://www.muckraker.com/articles/the-2030-mass-migration-agenda.
32. Eurostat, "Migration and migrant population statistics," March 2024, https://ec.europa.eu/euro stat/statistics-explained/index.php?title=Migration_and_migrant_population_statistics.
33. Interpol, "Europe: Drug trafficking, organized crime increasing by 'an order of magnitude,'" May 8, 2023, https://www.interpol.int/en/News-and-Events/News/2023/Europe-Drug-traffick ing-organized-crime-increasing-by-an-order-of-magnitude.
34. Lizzie Dearden, "Grooming gangs abused more than 700 women and girls around Newcastle after police appeared to punish victims," *The Independent,* February 23, 2018, https://www.independent.co.uk/news/uk/crime/grooming-gangs-uk-britain-newcastle-serious-case-review-operation-sanctuary-shelter-muslim-asian-a8225106.html.
35. Sam Cooper, "PRC narcos in Toronto are 'command and control' for North American money laundering networks used in TD Bank case: US investigator," The Bureau (Substack), August 29, 2024, https://www.thebureau.news/p/prc-narcos-in-toronto-are-command?r=l2dv4&utm_campaign=post&utm_medium=web.

Chapter 6

1. Adam Eliyahu Berkowitz, "The W.E.F has its own police force whose badge resembles Daniel's End-Days prophesy [Watch]," *Israel 365 News,* May 25, 2022, https://www.israel365news.com/269738/the-w-e-f-has-its-own-police-force-whose-badge-resembles-daniels-end-days-prophesy.
2. Blue Letter Bible, "WLC Search Results for "מִן־הַצָּבָא", https://www.blueletterbible.org/search/search.cfm?Criteria=%D7%9E%D6%B4%D7%9F%D6%BE%D7%94%D6%B7%D7%A6%D6%BC%D6%B8%D7%91%D6%B8%D7%90&t=WLC#s=s_primary_0_1.
3. United Nations, "WHO chief declares end to COVID-19 as a global health emergency," UN News, May 5, 2023, https://news.un.org/en/story/2023/05/1136367.
4. Tedros Adhanom Ghebreyesus, Post on X, May 5, 2023, https://x.com/DrTedros/status/

Notes

1654484522358939650?ref_src=twsrc%5Etfw%7Ctwcamp%5Etweetembed%7Ctwterm%
5E1654484522358939650%7Ctwgr%5E123f959b8cb34d1fa57b13308b67244ef18d5b9a%
7Ctwcon%5Es1_&ref_url=https%3A%2F%2Fnews.un.org%2Fen%2Fstory%2F2023%
2F05%2F1136367.

5. BBC, "Covid origin: Why the Wuhan lab-leak theory is so disputed," March 1, 2023, https://www.bbc.com/news/world-asia-china-57268111.

6. NASA, Eclipse map/figure/table/predictions courtesy of Fred Espenak, NASA/Goddard Space Flight Center, from https://eclipse.gsfc.nasa.gov/LEplot/LEplot2001/LE2023May05N.pdf.

7. Asbury University, "What Happened at Asbury University?," https://www.asbury.edu/outpouring.

8. Aaron Mehta, "F-15E Becomes First Aircraft Compatible with New Nuclear Bomb Design," *Defense News,* June 8, 2020, https://www.defensenews.com/smr/nuclear-arsenal/2020/06/08/f-15e-becomes-first-aircraft-certified-for-new-nuclear-bomb-design.

9. Rachel S. Cohen, "The F-35 is One Step Closer to Carrying Nuclear Bombs. What's Next?," *Air Force Times,* October 27, 2021, https://www.airforcetimes.com/news/your-air-force/2021/10/27/the-f-35-is-one-step-closer-to-carrying-nuclear-bombs-whats-next.

10. Aljazeera, "Germany to Buy US-Made F-35s Capable of Carrying Nuclear Weapons," March 15, 2022, https://www.aljazeera.com/news/2022/3/15/germany-to-buy-us-made-f-35s-capable-of-carrying-nuclear-weapons.

11. Alex Jones and Joel Skousen, "Strategic Relocation DVD," Prison Planet TV, December 17, 2012, https://tv.infowars.com/index/display/category/movies/id/4414.

12. NATO, "Defense expenditure of NATO countries (2014-2023)," March 14, 2024, https://www.nato.int/cps/en/natohq/news_223304.htm.

13. Benjamin Fearnow, "NATO Alliance Breaking Up Because Germany 'Not Paying Their Fair Share,' Trump National Security Adviser Says," Newsweek, November 10, 2019, https://www.newsweek.com/nato-alliance-breaking-germany-not-paying-fair-share-trump-national-security-adviser-1470889.

14. Brian Wilson, "Russia Ready To Retaliate Against U.S. With Satan II," Red Pilled TV, June 2, 2022, https://banned.video/watch?id=6298fa3d16f9b23e843f898c.

15. Wikipedia contributors, "List of Israel Defense Forces Bases," *Wikipedia, The Free Encyclopedia,* https://en.wikipedia.org/wiki/List_of_Israel_Defense_Forces_bases.

16. Palestinian Chronicle Staff, "This is How Al-Qassam's Navel Units Stormed Zakim's Fortified Military Base – VIDEO," *The Palestine Chronicle,* October 9, 2023, https://www.palestinechronicle.com/this-is-how-al-qassams-navel-units-stormed-zakims-fortified-military-base-video.

17. Hilo Glazer, "A Handful of Israeli Officers Saved 90 New Recruits From Hamas Terrorists. They Paid With Their Lives," Haaretz, October 20, 2023, https://www.haaretz.com/israel-news/2023-10-20/ty-article-magazine/.premium/a-few-idf-officers-saved-90-trainees-from-hamas-terrorists-they-paid-with-their-lives/0000018b-4da2-dc3c-a5df-ddaadf370000.

18. Ronen Bergman and Adam Goldman, "Israel Knew Hamas's Attack Plan More Than a Year Ago," *New York Times,* November 30, 2023, https://www.nytimes.com/2023/11/30/world/middleeast/israel-hamas-attack-intelligence.html?campaign_id=307&emc=edit_igw b_20231201&instance_id=109019&nl=israel-hamas-war-briefing&regi_id=64680187& segment_id=151409&te=1&user_id=1e9c9142246ac5796beabc2f49486341.

19. Tyler Durden, "Warnings About Alarming Pre-Oct 7 Hamas Activity Ignored, Say Israeli Surveillance Soldiers," *ZeroHedge,* October 28, 2023, https://www.zerohedge.com/geopoliti cal/warnings-about-alarming-pre-oct-7-hamas-activity-ignored-say-israeli-surveillance.

20. Shira Silkoff, "Surveillance soldiers warned of Hamas activity on Gaza border for months before Oct. 7," The Times of Israel, October 26, 2023, https://www.timesofisrael.com/surveillance-soldiers-warned-of-hamas-activity-on-gaza-border-for-months-before-oct-7.

21. The Cradle, "Ben Gvir threatens to implode Israeli govt over concessions to Palestinians," September 23, 2023, https://thecradle.co/articles/ben-gvir-threatens-to-implode-israeli-govt-over-concessions-to-palestinians.

22. Associated Press, "Netanyahu sworn in for unprecedented 6th term in Israel after being ousted last year," *CBC News,* December 29, 2022, https://www.cbc.ca/news/world/netanyahu-israel-prime-minister-1.6699880.

23. Simon Davies and Joshua Hantman, "How Netanyahu and his allies won by a knockout: The data", *Times of Israel,* November 7, 2022, https://www.timesofisrael.com/how-netanyahu-and-his-allies-won-by-a-knockout-the-data.

24. Israel Democracy Institute, "The Elections for the 25th Knesset 1.11.2022," https://en.idi.org.il/israeli-elections-and-parties/elections/2022.

25. Yoav Zitun, "One-fifth of troop fatalities in Gaza due to friendly fire or accidents, IDF reports," Ynet News, December 12, 2023, https://www.ynetnews.com/article/rkjqoobip.

26. Aljazeera, "Gaza toll could exceed 186,000, Lancet study says," July 8, 2024, https://www.aljazeera.com/news/2024/7/8/gaza-toll-could-exceed-186000-lancet-study-says.

27. Rasha Khatiba, Martin McKeec, and Salim Yusufd, "Counting the dead in Gaza: difficult but essential," *The Lancet,* Volume 404, Issue 10449, (July 20, 2024), 237-238, https://www.thelancet.com/journals/lancet/article/PIIS0140-6736(24)01169-3/fulltext.

28. International Criminal Court, "Statement of ICC Prosecutor Karim A.A. Khan KC: Applications for arrest warrants in the situation in the State of Palestine," May 20, 2024, https://www.icc-cpi.int/news/statement-icc-prosecutor-karim-aa-khan-kc-applications-arrest-warrants-situation-state.

29. 118 Congress (2023-2024), "H.Res.559 - Declaring it is the policy of the United States that a nuclear Islamic Republic of Iran is not acceptable," Congress.gov, November 1, 2023, https://www.congress.gov/bill/118th-congress/house-resolution/559/text.

30. Kelsey Davenport, "IAEA Chief Sounds Alarm on Iran Nuclear Progress," Arms Control Association, March 2023, https://www.armscontrol.org/act/2023-03/news/iaea-chief-sounds-alarm-iran-nuclear-progress.

31. Aljazeera, "Iran attacks Israel with over 300 drones, missiles: What you need to know," April 14, 2024, https://www.aljazeera.com/news/2024/4/14/iran-attacks-israel-with-over-300-drones-missiles-what-you-need-to-know.

32. Iran International Newsroom, "Iranian Politician Says Tehran Might Already Have Nukes," Volant Media UK Limited, May 10, 2024, https://www.iranintl.com/en/202405108870.

33. Benjamin Weinthal, "Iranian lawmaker declares Tehran obtained nuclear bombs," Fox News, May 12, 2024, https://www.foxnews.com/world/iranian-lawmaker-declares-tehran-obtained-nuclear-bombs.

34. Wikipedia contributors, "Neutron bomb," *Wikipedia, The Free Encyclopedia,* https://en.wikipedia.org/w/index.php?title=Neutron_bomb&oldid=1149220149.

35. Yanki Tauber, "Winter," Chabad-Lubavitch Media Center, https://www.chabad.org/library/article_cdo/aid/2669/jewish/Winter.htm.

Chapter 7

1. Brenda J. Buchanan, *Gunpowder, Explosives and the State: A Technological History,* (Aldershot, UK: Ashgate, 2006), 42.

2. Frederick C. Durant and John F. Guilmartin, "rocket and missile system | weapons system," Encyclopedia Britannica, January 9, 2024, https://www.britannica.com/technology/rocket-and-missile-system.

3. Blue Letter Bible, "H520 - 'ammâ - Strong's Hebrew Lexicon (KJV)," https://www.blueletterbible.org/lexicon/h520/kjv/wlc/0-1.

4. Farnaz Fassihi, "Iran Tries to Avoid War With U.S. After Stoking Mideast Conflicts," *New York Times,* February 1, 2024, https://www.nytimes.com/2024/02/01/world/middleeast/iran-us-war.html.

5. Jon Gambrell, "An Iranian nuclear facility is so deep underground that US airstrikes likely couldn't reach it," AP News, May 22, 2023, https://apnews.com/article/iran-nuclear-natanz-uranium-enrichment-underground-project-04dae673fc937af04e62b65dd78db2e0.

Notes

6. Joseph Dempsey, "Silo mentality – Iran's Haji Abad missile base," International Institute for Strategic Studies, May 4, 2021, https://www.iiss.org/en/online-analysis/military-balance/2021/04/iran-haji-abad-missile-base.

7. Parisa Hafezi, John Irish, Tom Balmforth, and Jonathan Landay, "Exclusive: Iran sends Russia hundreds of ballistic missiles," Reuters, February 21, 2024, https://www.reuters.com/world/iran-sends-russia-hundreds-ballistic-missiles-sources-say-2024-02-21.

8. Missile Threat, "Zolfaghar (Dezful, Qasem)," The CSIS Missile Defense Project, April 23, 2024, https://missilethreat.csis.org/missile/zolfaghar.

9. Ibid, "Khorramshahr," The CSIS Missile Defense Project, April 23, 2024, https://missilethreat.csis.org/missile/khorramshahr.

10. Al Arabiya News, "Iran unveils its first hypersonic ballistic missile: State media," June 6, 2023, https://english.alarabiya.net/News/middle-east/2023/06/06/Iran-unveils-first-hypersonic-missile-named-Fattah-Report.

11. Tzvi Joffre, "'400 seconds' to Tel Aviv: Iranian media publishes Hebrew hypersonic missile threat," Jerusalem Post, November 14, 2022, https://www.jpost.com/middle-east/iran-news/article-722327.

12. John Pike, "Fattah Hypersonic MRBM," Global Security, https://www.globalsecurity.org/wmd/world/iran/fattah.htm.

13. Jerusalem Post, "Iran issues threat to Israel, US with new hypersonic weapon," November 19, 2023, https://www.jpost.com/middle-east/iran-news/article-774055.

14. Missile Threat, "Missiles of Iran," The CSIS Missile Defense Project, August 10, 2021, https://missilethreat.csis.org/country/iran.

15. Grace Kay, "Watch how the value of a dollar has changed over the past 120 years, from toilet paper to coffee," Business Insider, Dec 21, 2021, https://www.businessinsider.com/see-how-value-of-1-dollar-changed-over-120-years-2021-12.

16. Blue Letter Bible, "H374 - 'ê͞pâ - Strong's Hebrew Lexicon (KJV)," https://www.blueletterbible.org/lexicon/h374/kjv/wlc/0-1.

17. Nuclear Threat Initiative, "Missiles & Other WMD Delivery Systems - Module 2: Understanding Missiles," 2023, https://tutorials.nti.org/delivery-system/understanding-missiles.

18. Anshel Pfeffer, "Fragment of ancient parchment given to Jewish scholars," Haaretz, Archived from the original (http://www.haaretz.com/hasen/spages/920915.html) on July 7, 2009 at: https://web.archive.org/web/20090707031841/http://www.haaretz.com/hasen/spages/920915.html.

19. NASA, "B. The Role of Radioactive Decay," https://imagine.gsfc.nasa.gov/educators/elements/imagine/09.html.

20. Walter A. Elwell, Barry J. Beitzel, et al., "Shinar," entry, in The Baker Encyclopedia of the Bible, Volume 4, (Grand Rapids, MI: Baker Book House, 1997), 1955.

21. Larisa Brown, "Iran sends more than 200 ballistic missiles to Russia," The Times, September 6, 2024, https://www.thetimes.com/uk/defence/article/ballistic-clmpm3d7m.

22. Walter A. Elwell, Barry J. Beitzel, et al., "Elam," entry, in The Baker Encyclopedia of the Bible, Volume 2, (Grand Rapids, MI: Baker Book House, 1997), 676.

23. Joseph M. Siracusa, Nuclear Weapons - A Very Short Introduction, 3rd Ed. (Oxford, UK: Oxford University Press, 2020), Chapter 2.

24. Alan Bellows, "Tesla's Tower of Power," July 2007, Damn Interesting, https://www.damninteresting.com/teslas-tower-of-power.

Chapter 8

1. BBC, "Howard Springs: Australia police arrest quarantine escapees," November 30, 2021, https://www.bbc.com/news/world-australia-59486285.

2. CBS News, "U.S. clears way for release of $6 billion in frozen Iranian funds as part of prisoner swap deal," September 11, 2023, https://www.cbsnews.com/news/iran-prisoner-swap-americans-6-billion-waiver-us-sanctions.

Notes

3. Andrew Stanton, "Fact Check: Did Joe Biden Authorize $8 Billion Aid Package to Israel?" Newsweek, October 7, 2023, https://www.newsweek.com/fact-check-joe-biden-israel-aid-1832895.

4. Natalie Venegas and Jon Jackson, "US Approves $20 Billion Arms Deal for Israel," Newsweek, August 13, 2024, https://www.newsweek.com/us-approves-20-billion-arms-deal-israel-1938806.

5. Richard Lardner, "US payment of $1.7 billion to Iran made entirely in cash," AP News, September 6, 2016, https://apnews.com/united-states-government-fd4113419276444e ba1d2a46d5c29752.

6. Jena Warburton, "Walmart suddenly closing more stores in 2024," The Street, June 24, 2024, https://www.thestreet.com/retail/walmart-suddenly-closing-more-stores-in-2024.

7. Abraham Ojeda, "NEW Nuclear War Research Study Confirms Impending Doomsday Bible Prophecy [ep.15]," Overcome Babylon YouTube Channel, October 18, 2022, https://www.youtube.com/watch?v=fLBZ98PLdBg.

8. Greg Bruno, "Even a nuclear conflict between new nuclear states would decimate crop production and result in widespread starvation," Rutgers Today, August 15, 2022, https://www.rutgers.edu/news/nuclear-war-would-cause-global-famine-and-kill-billions-rutgers-led-study-finds.

9. R. P. Turco et al., "Nuclear Winter: Global Consequences of Multiple Nuclear Explosions," Science, Volume 222, Issue 4630, (December 23, 1983), 1283-1292, https://www.science.org/doi/10.1126/science.222.4630.1283.

10. OSTI, "Nuclear winter. Joint Hearing before the Subcommittee on Natural Resources, Agriculture Research and Environment of the Committee on Science and Technology and the Subcommittee on Energy and the Environment of the Committee on Interior and Insular Affairs, US House of Representatives, Ninety-Ninth Congress, First Session, March 14, 1985," U.S. Department of Energy Office of Scientific and Technical Information, January 1, 1985, https://www.osti.gov/biblio/6433401.

11. Felonious Vendetta, "Mar 14, 1985 Nuclear Winter 1 of 2," Washington, District of Columbia, United States, Date Aired Mar 14, 1985, YouTube, https://www.youtube.com/watch?v=NV_xw_aHpeQ.

12. S. L. Thompson and S. H. Schneider, "Nuclear winter reappraised," Foreign Affairs, Volume 64, Issue 5, (June 6, 1986), 984-985, 991, http://n2t.net/ark:/85065/d7n29wpv.

13. Ibid, 981.

14. Ibid, 983.

15. Blue Letter Bible, "H835 - 'ešer - Strong's Hebrew Lexicon (NKJV)," https://www.blueletter bible.org/lexicon/h835/nkjv/wlc/0-1.

16. Ibid, "H2442 - ḥāḵâ - Strong's Hebrew Lexicon (NKJV)," https://www.blueletterbible.org/lexi con/h2442/nkjv/wlc/0-1.

17. Ibid, "H5060 - nāḡaʿ - Strong's Hebrew Lexicon (NKJV)," https://www.blueletterbible.org/lexicon/h5060/nkjv/wlc/0-1.

18. Ibid, "H2388 - ḥāzaq - Strong's Hebrew Lexicon (NKJV)," https://www.blueletterbible.org/lexicon/h2388/nkjv/wlc/0-1.

19. Ibid, "H3782 - kāšal - Strong's Hebrew Lexicon (NKJV)," https://www.blueletterbible.org/lexi con/h3782/nkjv/wlc/0-1.

20. Ibid, "H5828 - ʿēzer - Strong's Hebrew Lexicon (NKJV)," https://www.blueletterbible.org/lexi con/h5828/nkjv/wlc/0-1.

21. Ibid, "H2519 - ḥălaqlaqqōṯ - Strong's Hebrew Lexicon (NKJV)," https://www.blueletterbible. org/lexicon/h2519/nkjv/wlc/0-1.

Chapter 9

1. Supplement to the Illustrated London News, "The Freemasons' Plan to Rebuild Solomon's Temple at Jerusalem, A Gigantic Task," August 28, 1909.

Notes

2. Grand Lodge of British Columbia and Yukon A.F. & A.M., "Rebuilding the Temple," September 27, 2006, https://freemasonry.bcy.ca/anti-masonry/rebuild_temple03.html.

3. Corey Charlton, "Letter 'written by US Confederate officer 150 years ago predicted first two World Wars and said the third would be between Islamic leaders and the West'... but is it just a hoax?" *Daily Mail,* March 7, 2016, https://www.dailymail.co.uk/news/article-3480720/Letter-written-Confederate-officer-150-years-ago-predicted-two-World-Wars-said-Islamic-leaders-West-just-hoax.html.

4. William Guy Carr, *Pawns in the Game,* a reprint of the 1958 edition, (Willowdale, Ontario: Federation of Christian Laymen, 1958), Introduction, xv-xvi.

5. *Supplement to the Illustrated London News,* "The Freemasons' Plan to Rebuild Solomon's Temple at Jerusalem, A Gigantic Task," August 28, 1909.

6. Thomas R. Horn. *"The rabbis, Donald Trump and the top-secret plan to build the Third Temple: Unveiling the incendiary scheme by religious authorities, government agents, Jewish rabbis to invoke messiah,"* (Crane, MO: Defender, 2019), Chapter 1.

7. Jewish Telegraphic Agency, "Temple Institute announces school to train Levitical priests," August 2, 2016, https://www.jta.org/2016/08/02/israel/temple-institute-announces-school-to-train-levitical-priests.

8. Adam Eliyahu Berkowitz, "Sanhedrin Invites 70 Nations to Dedicate Altar for Third Temple," Israel 365 News, November 29, 2018, https://www.israel365news.com/327422/70-nations-hanukkah-altar-third-temple.

10. Chris Mitchell, "Texas Red Heifers' Arrival Stirs Prophetic Excitement in Israel" CBN News, September 23, 2022, https://www1.cbn.com/cbnnews/israel/2022/september/texas-red-heifers-arrival-stirs-prophetic-excitement.

11. 3rd Temple, "Why Support the Construction," thirdtemple.org, https://thirdtemple.org/en/adhesion-form-complet.

12. Ibid, "Home," thirdtemple.org, https://thirdtemple.org/en.

13. Temple Institute, "Statement of Principles," templeinstitute.org, https://templeinstitute.org/statement-of-principles-2.

14. Jewish Spiritual Leaders Institute, "Jewish Universalism," JSLI, https://jsli.net/jewish-universalism.

15. King James Bible Online™, (2007-2023), https://www.kingjamesbibleonline.org/1-Maccabees-Chapter-1.

16. Ibid, https://www.kingjamesbibleonline.org/1-Maccabees-Chapter-4.

17. Ibid, https://www.kingjamesbibleonline.org/1-Maccabees-Chapter-5.

18. Wikipedia contributors, "United Nations Partition Plan for Palestine," *Wikipedia, The Free Encyclopedia,* https://en.wikipedia.org/w/index.php?title=United_Nations_Partition_Plan_for_Palestine&oldid=1148074278.

19. Avital Ginat, "British Mandate for Palestine," International Encyclopedia of the First World War, December 7, 2018, https://encyclopedia.1914-1918-online.net/article/british_mandate_for_palestine.

20. Whitney Webb, *One Nation Under Blackmail Volume 1,* (Walterville, OR: Trine Day, 2022), 70.

21. Ibid, 75,76.

22. Worldometer, "GDP by Country," 2023, https://www.worldometers.info/gdp/gdp-by-country.

23. International Monetary Fund, "World Economic Outlook - Steady but Slow: Resilience amid Divergence," April 2024, https://www.imf.org/en/Publications/WEO/Issues/2024/04/16/world-economic-outlook-april-2024.

24. Louis Jacobson, "PolitFact FL: What to know about U.S. aid to Israel," PolitiFact - Central Florida Public Media, October 20, 2023, https://www.cfpublic.org/politics/2023-10-20/politfact-florida-united-states-aid-israel-palestine.

25. American-Israeli Cooperative Enterprise, "U.S. Foreign Aid to Israel: Total Aid (1949 - Present)," Jewish Virtual Library, https://www.jewishvirtuallibrary.org/total-u-s-foreign-aid-to-israel-1949-present.

Notes

26. William L. Ochsenwald, et al., "Establishment of Israel," Encyclopedia Britannica, September 12, 2024, https://www.britannica.com/place/Israel/Establishment-of-Israel.
27. Israel365, "First physical Feast since 2019 marks return of Christian tourism to Israel," September 29, 2022, https://www.israel365news.com/355268/first-physical-feast-since-2019-marks-return-of-christian-tourism-to-israel.
28. Tara Corp, "US shifts assault ship to the Mediterranean to deter an escalation of the Israel-Lebanon conflict," Associated Press, June 28, 2024, https://apnews.com/article/navy-warships-lebanon-hezbollah-israel-feec28090bed129618eda05e25a59b09.
29. Melissa Koenig, "US carrier strike group is rushed to the Middle East as new Israeli intelligence suggests Iran attack within days," Daily Mail, August 12, 2024, https://www.dailymail.co.uk/news/article-13734119/US-carrier-strike-group-rushed-Middle-East-Israeli-intelligence-Iran-attack.html.
30. Joe Khalil, Kellie Meyer, Devan Markham, "US special forces already stationed in Israel before attacks: Source," NewsNation, October 11, 2023, https://www.newsnationnow.com/world/war-in-israel/biden-condemns-sheer-evil-of-hamas.

Chapter 10

1. "H2856 - ḥātam - Strong's Hebrew Lexicon (NKJV)." Blue Letter Bible. https://www.blueletterbible.org/lexicon/h2856/nkjv/wlc/0-1/
2. "G5590 - psychē - Strong's Greek Lexicon (NKJV)." Blue Letter Bible. https://www.blueletterbible.org/lexicon/g5590/nkjv/tr/0-1/
3. Emeri van Donzel and Andrea Schmidt, *Gog and Magog in Early Eastern Christian and Islamic Sources: Sallam's Quest for Alexander's Wall,* (Leiden, South Holland: Koninklijke Brill NV, 2009), Preface, xvii.
4. Ibid, 51.
5. Ibid, 81.

Chapter 11

1. International Monetary Fund, "World Economic Outlook Database Groups and Aggregates Information," April 2023, https://www.imf.org/en/Publications/WEO/weo-database/2023/April/groups-and-aggregates#mae.
2. William James and Michael Holden, "G7 Demand Action From Russia on Cybercrimes and Chemical Weapon Use," Reuters, June 13, 2021, https://www.usnews.com/news/world/articles/2021-06-13/g7-demand-action-from-russia-on-cybercrimes-and-chemical-weapon-use.
3. Saeed Kamali Dehghan and Richard Norton-Taylor, "CIA admits role in 1953 Iranian coup," *The Guardian,* August 19, 2013, https://www.theguardian.com/world/2013/aug/19/cia-admits-role-1953-iranian-coup.
4. Mehdi Hasan and Dina Sayedahmed, "Blowback: How a CIA-Backed Coup Led to the Rise of Iran's Ayatollahs," The Intercept, February 5, 2018, https://theintercept.com/2018/02/05/iran-cia-coup-mossadegh-ayatollah.
5. Joan E. Dowlin, "America's Role in Iran's Unrest," HuffPost News, July 18, 2009, https://www.huffpost.com/entry/americas-role-in-irans-un_b_216831.
6. William Guy Carr, *Pawns in the Game,* a reprint of the 1958 edition, (Willowdale, Ontario: Federation of Christian Laymen, 1958), Introduction, xv-xvi.
7. Bible Atlas, "Meshech-Tubal (Meshech)," https://bibleatlas.org/full/meshech-tubal.htm.
8. Gary Wayne, *The Genesis 6 Conspiracy: How Secret Societies and the Descendants of Giants Plan to Enslave Humankind,* (Sisters, OR: Deep River Books, 2014), 591,592.
9. Peter Blake and Paul S. Blezard, *The Arcadian Cipher: The Quest to Crack the Code of Christianity's Greatest Secret,* (London, England: Pan Books, 2001), 104.
10. Walter Martin, et al., *The Kingdom of the Occult,* (Nashville, TN: Thomas Nelson, 2008), 129.
11. Ibid, 130.

Notes

12. Ibid, 151.
13. Ibid, 153.
14. Fitzpatrick Informer, "Putin wears Kabbalah red thread talisman at Eurasian summit (video)," December 19, 2022, https://fitzinfo.net/2022/12/19/putin-wears-kabbalah-red-thread-talisman-video.
15. Ibid, "Tucker Carlson's Kabbalah fetish," March 16, 2023, https://fitzinfo.net/2023/03/16/tucker-carlsons-kabbalah-fetish.
16. Donald J. Trump, *The Way to the Top: The Best Business Advice I Ever Received,* (New York, NY: Crown Business, 2004), 188.
17. The Kabbalah Centre, "Eitan Yardeni," https://www.kabbalah.com/en/people/eitan-yardeni.
18. Gary Wayne, *The Genesis 6 Conspiracy: How Secret Societies and the Descendants of Giants Plan to Enslave Humankind,* (Sisters, OR: Deep River Books, 2014), 586, 588.
19. The William Davidson Talmud (Koren - Steinsaltz), "Gitten 57a," Sefaria, https://www.sefaria.org/Gittin.57a.3?lang=bi&with=all&lang2=en.
20. Ibid, "Bava Metzia 114b:2," Sefaria, https://www.sefaria.org/Bava_Metzia.114b.2?lang=bi.
21. UN News, "Israel's occupation of Palestinian Territory is 'apartheid': UN rights expert," March 25, 2022, https://news.un.org/en/story/2022/03/1114702.
22. The William Davidson Talmud (Koren - Steinsaltz), "Sanhedrin 57a:16," Sefaria, https://www.sefaria.org/Sanhedrin.57a.16?lang=bi&with=all&lang2=en.
23. Ibid, "Yevamot.98a:3," Sefaria, https://www.sefaria.org/Yevamot.98a.3?lang=bi&with=all&lang2=en.
24. Ranajit Das, Paul Wexler, Mehdi Pirooznia and Eran Elhaik, "The Origins of Ashkenaz, Ashkenazic Jews, and Yiddish," *Frontiers in Genetics,* Volume 8, (June 20, 2017), 87, https://www.frontiersin.org/articles/10.3389/fgene.2017.00087/full.
25. Aleksandr Isayevich Solzhenitsyn. *Two Hundred Years Together: On Russian-Jewish Relations, 1795-1995,* 1st English Ed., (The Incorrect Library, 2017), iBooks.
26. Isidore Singer, et al., *The Jewish Encyclopedia,* Volume 4: Chazars–Dreyfus Case, (New York: Funk and Wagnalls Company, 1912), 1, Accessed via: https://archive.org/details/the-jewish-encyclopedia-vol.-4/page/1/mode/2up.
27. Aleksandr Isayevich Solzhenitsyn. *Two Hundred Years Together: On Russian-Jewish Relations, 1795-1995,* 1st English Ed., (The Incorrect Library, 2017), iBooks.
28. Isidore Singer, et al., *The Jewish Encyclopedia,* Volume 4: Chazars–Dreyfus Case, (New York: Funk and Wagnalls Company, 1912), 2, Accessed via: https://archive.org/details/the-jewish-encyclopedia-vol.-4/page/1/mode/2up.
29. Ranajit Das, Paul Wexler, Mehdi Pirooznia and Eran Elhaik, "The Origins of Ashkenaz, Ashkenazic Jews, and Yiddish," *Frontiers in Genetics,* Volume 8, (June 20, 2017), 87, https://www.frontiersin.org/articles/10.3389/fgene.2017.00087/full.
30. Eran Elhaik, "The Missing Link of Jewish European Ancestry: Contrasting the Rhineland and the Khazarian Hypotheses," *Genome Biology and Evolution,* Volume 5, Issue 1, (January 2013), 61–74, https://doi.org/10.1093%2Fgbe%2Fevs119.
31. Ibid, "Ashkenazic Jews' mysterious origins unravelled by scientists thanks to ancient DNA," Phys.org, September 5, 2018, https://phys.org/news/2018-09-ashkenazic-jews-mysterious-unravelled-scientists.html.
32. Abraham Nahum Polak, *Chazaria - Dzieje Krolestwa Żydowskiego W Europie* (Khazaria - The History of the Jewish Kingdom in Europe), Polish Edition, (Przemyśl, Poland: Południowo-Wschodni Instytut Naukowy w Przemyślu, 2015), 29.
33. Aleksandr Isayevich Solzhenitsyn. *Two Hundred Years Together: On Russian-Jewish Relations, 1795-1995,* 1st English Ed., (The Incorrect Library, 2017), iBooks.
34. Wikipedia contributors, "Karl Marx," *Wikipedia, The Free Encyclopedia,* https://en.wikipedia.org/w/index.php?title=Karl_Marx&oldid=1148703430.
35. Tristram Hunt, *Marx's General: The Revolutionary Life of Friedrich Engels,* (New York: Metropolitan Books, 2009), 70.
36. Ibid, 71.

Notes

37. Aleksandr Isayevich Solzhenitsyn. *Two Hundred Years Together: On Russian-Jewish Relations, 1795-1995,* 1st English Ed., (The Incorrect Library, 2017), iBooks.

38. Ibid.

39. Ibid.

40. Ibid.

41. David Shneer, "Modern Jewish History - Leon Trotsky: The Jewish renegade socialist," My Jewish Learning, https://www.myjewishlearning.com/article/leon-trotsky.

42. Aleksandr Isayevich Solzhenitsyn, *The Gulag archipelago, 1918-1956: An Experiment in Literary Investigation,* Volume 2. Translated by Thomas P. Whitney, (London: Collins: Harvill Press, 1974), 79.

43. Ibid, 84.

44. Helen Rappaport, *The Last Days of the Romanovs: Tragedy at Ekaterinburg,* (New York, NY: St. Martin's Press, 2009), 32.

45. Oleg V. Khlevniuk, *The History of the Gulag: From Collectivization to the Great Terror,* Translated by Vadim A. Staklo, (New Haven, CT: Yale University Press, 2004), 346.

46. Yohanan Petrovsky-Shtern, *Lenin's Jewish Question,* (New Haven, CT: Yale University Press, 2010), 66–67.

47. UN, "Joint statement by the delegations of Azerbaijan, Bangladesh, Belarus, Benin, Bosnia and Herzegovina, Canada, Egypt, Georgia, Guatemala, Jamaica, Kazakhstan, Mongolia, Nauru, Pakistan, Qatar, the Republic of Moldova, the Russian Federation, Saudi Arabia, the Sudan, the Syrian Arab Republic, Tajikistan, Timor-Leste, Ukraine, the United Arab Emirates and the United States of America on the 70th anniversary of the Great Famine of 1932-1933 in Ukraine (Holodomor)," November 7, 2003, https://digitallibrary.un.org/record/505743?v=pdf.

48. American-Israeli Cooperative Enterprise, "Haavara," Jewish Virtual Library, https://www.jewishvirtuallibrary.org/haavara.

49. Ibid, "Jewish & Non-Jewish Population of Israel/Palestine (1517 - Present)," Jewish Virtual Library, https://www.jewishvirtuallibrary.org/jewish-and-non-jewish-population-of-israel-palestine-1517-present.

50. Csongor Körömi and Barbara Moens, "Orbán parrots Putin's lines on Ukraine in leaked letter to EU chief" Politico, July 9, 2024, https://www.politico.eu/article/viktor-orban-letter-european-council-charles-michel-vladimir-putin-war-in-ukraine-russia-kremlin.

51. Vladimir Soldatkin and Anita Komuves, "Hungary's Orban talks Ukraine peace with Putin, stirring EU outcry," Reuters, July 5, 2024, https://www.reuters.com/world/europe/hungarys-orban-says-no-position-negotiate-between-ukraine-russia-2024-07-05.

52. Krisztina Than, Alan Charlish, and Angus MacSwan, "Hungary says 'grievances' hold up ratification of Sweden's NATO accession," Reuters, March 29, 2023, https://www.reuters.com/world/europe/hungary-says-grievances-hold-up-ratification-swedens-nato-accession-2023-03-29.

53. Seb Starcevic, "Turkey threatens to 'enter' Israel to protect Palestinians," Politico, July 29, 2024, https://www.politico.eu/article/turkey-nato-tayyip-erdogan-threatens-enter-israel-help-palestinians.

54. Joe Sommerlad, "Nato in numbers: Which members have the biggest armies and how has the military alliance grown?" The Independent, 12 July 2023, https://www.independent.co.uk/news/world/europe/nato-members-countries-map-military-b2373875.html.

55. Ragip Soylu, "War on Gaza: Turkey halts all trade with Israel over war," Middle East Eye, May 2, 2024, https://www.middleeasteye.net/news/war-gaza-turkey-halts-all-trade-israel-over-war.

56. Middle East Eye, "Israeli industry braces for economic damage amid Turkish trade ban," May 3, 2024, https://www.middleeasteye.net/news/israeli-industry-braces-economic-damage-amid-turkish-trade-ban.

57. BRICS Ministry of External Relations, "Information about BRICS, VI BRICS Summit," 2014, https://web.archive.org/web/20150710163822/http://brics6.itamaraty.gov.br/about-brics/

information-about-brics.

58. Abraham Ojeda, "EVERYTHING Changes September 2023: How Prophecy Unfolds," Overcome Babylon YouTube Channel, July 13, 2023, https://www.youtube.com/watch?v= koMH6HuU5I4.

59. Norman Masungwini, "SA invites 70 heads of states to the BRICS summit, but Western leaders excluded," City Press, July 21, 2023, https://www.news24.com/citypress/politics/sa-invites-70-heads-of-states-to-the-brics-summit-but-western-leaders-excluded-20230721.

60. Shweta Sharma, "Brics countries agree historic expansion as six new countries invited to join," The Independent, August 24, 2023, https://www.independent.co.uk/news/world/africa/brics-2023-summit-new-members-saudi-uae-iran-b2398553.html.

61. Carien du Plessis, Anait Miridzhanian, and Bhargav Acharya, "BRICS welcomes new members in push to reshuffle world order," Reuters, August 24, 2023, https://www.reuters.com/world/brics-poised-invite-new-members-join-bloc-sources-2023-08-24.

62. Tom Phillips, Josefina Salomón, and Facundo Iglesia, "Argentina presidential election: far-right libertarian Javier Milei wins after rival concedes," The Guardian, November 19, 2023, https://www.theguardian.com/world/2023/nov/20/argentina-presidential-election-far-right-libertarian-javier-milei-wins-after-rival-concedes.

63. Zvika Klein, "Argentina's Milei wears kippah at havdalah, vows support for Jews and Israel," *Jerusalem Post,* November 26, https://www.jpost.com/international/article-775205.

64. Patrick Gillespie and Manuela Tobias, "Milei's Embrace of Judaism Seals Argentina Pro-Israel Stance," *Bloomberg,* November 27, 2023, https://www.bloomberg.com/news/articles/2023-11-27/milei-s-conversion-to-judaism-seals-pro-israel-push-by-argentina.

65. Cecilia Devanna, "El gobierno de Javier Milei oficializó que la Argentina no entrará a los Brics" December 29, 2023, *La Nación,* https://www.lanacion.com.ar/politica/el-gobierno-de-javier-milei-oficializo-que-la-argentina-no-entrara-a-los-brics-nid29122023.

Chapter 12

1. Blue Letter Bible, "G3326 - meta - Strong's Greek Lexicon (NKJV)," https://www.blueletterbible.org/lexicon/g3326/nkjv/tr/0-1.

2. Ibid, "G3933 - parthenos - Strong's Greek Lexicon (NKJV)," https://www.blueletterbible.org/lexicon/g3933/nkjv/tr/0-1.

3. Julie Tivey Boney, "Prophet or Not," Proclamation Online Magazine, November 19, 2019, https://blog.lifeassuranceministries.org/2019/11/19/prophet-or-not.

4. Rebecca Biderman, In Search of His Ancient Path - Restoring the True Biblical Calendar, https://www.insearchofhisancientpath.com.

5. Abraham Ojeda, "How to Keep God's Feasts at the Correct Time with the 7 Species Witnesses - Becca Biderman [ep.14]," Overcome Babylon, Aug 29, 2022, Bitchute: https://www.bitchute.com/video/QyUnApMvSuAi, See also on YouTube: https://youtu.be/u3QeeUx0C5I.

6. Blue Letter Bible, "H24 - 'āḇîḇ - Strong's Hebrew Lexicon (NKJV)," https://www.blueletterbible.org/lexicon/h24/nkjv/wlc/0-1.

7. Norman B. Willis, "Aviv Barley Simplified," Nazarene Israel YouTube, Apr 24, 2021, https://youtu.be/GDLI_jGGO30.

8. Ibid, The Torah Calendar, (CreateSpace Independent Publishing Platform, 2012), Accessed Online via: https://nazareneisrael.org/books/the-torah-calendar.

9. Rebecca Biderman, Ancient Path New Moon - Restoring the True Biblical Time, Facebook Group, Post dated February 21, 2023, https://www.facebook.com/groups/HisAncientPath/permalink/2060351154161256.

10. Joseph F. Dumond, "The Barley Search March 16, 2022, From Israel," Sighted Moon Newsletter, March 16, 2022, https://sightedmoon.com/the-barley-search-march-16-2022-from-israel.

11. Rebecca Biderman, Ancient Path New Moon - Restoring the True Biblical Time, Facebook

Group, Post dated February 21, 2023, https://www.facebook.com/groups/HisAncientPath/permalink/2060351154161256.

12. Rebecca Biderman, "Another look at the field with a drone Mar 8 2023," Ancient Path New Moon YouTube Channel, Mar. 8, 2023, https://youtu.be/9KfmBwqmqsk.

13. Ibid, "Roasting and grinding the harvested barley into flour," Ancient Path New Moon YouTube Channel, Jan. 29, 2021, https://www.youtube.com/watch?v=Il8Nx6ytrBI.

Chapter 13

1. NASA, Eclipse map/figure/table/predictions courtesy of Fred Espenak, NASA/Goddard Space Flight Center, from https://eclipse.gsfc.nasa.gov/SEplot/SEplot2001/SE2027Aug02T.GIF.

2. Ibid, https://eclipse.gsfc.nasa.gov/SEplot/SEplot2001/SE2034Mar20T.GIF.

3. Ibid, https://eclipse.gsfc.nasa.gov/SEatlas/SEatlas3/SEatlas2021.GIF.

4. Ibid, https://eclipse.gsfc.nasa.gov/SEatlas/SEatlas3/SEatlas2041.GIF.

5. Dean Coombs, "Part Three: 2027 and 2034 Egypt, Mecca, Medina Total Solar Eclipse," August 8, 2017, 1260d, https://1260d.com/2017/08/08/2027-and-2034-egypt-mecca-medina-total-solar-eclipse.

6. Torah Calendar, https://torahcalendar.com/Calendar.asp?YM=Y2033M12.

7. Xavier M. Jubier, "2027 Total Solar Eclipse," Interactive Google Map, http://xjubier.free.fr/en/site_pages/solar_eclipses/xSE_GoogleMap3.php?Ecl=+20270802&Acc=2&Umb=1&Lmt=1&Mag=0.

8. Ibid, "2034 Total Solar Eclipse," Interactive Google Map, http://xjubier.free.fr/en/site_pages/solar_eclipses/xSE_GoogleMap3.php?Ecl=+20340320&Acc=2&Umb=1&Lmt=1&Mag=0.

9. Christopher Parker, "Hidden Chamber Revealed Inside Great Pyramid of Giza," Smithsonian Magazine, March 3, 2023, https://www.smithsonianmag.com/smart-news/hidden-chamber-pyramid-giza-180981745.

10. E. Raymond Capt, *The Great Pyramid Decoded*, (Muskogee, OK: Artisan Publishers, 2005), 15.

11. Ibid, 25.

12. Sébastien Procureur, et al., "Precise characterization of a corridor-shaped structure in Khufu's Pyramid by observation of cosmic-ray muons" *Nature Communications*, Volume 14, Article number 1144, (2023), https://www.nature.com/articles/s41467-023-36351-0.

13. Kamal Tabikha, "'Big Void' at the core of Giza's Great Pyramid continues to baffle scientists," The National, March 19, 2023, https://www.thenationalnews.com/mena/egypt/2023/03/20/big-void-at-the-core-of-gizas-great-pyramid-continues-to-baffle-scientists.

14. Gary Wayne, *The Genesis 6 Conspiracy: How Secret Societies and the Descendants of Giants Plan to Enslave Humankind*, (Sisters, OR: Deep River Books, 2014), 46.

15. Adrian Geoffrey Gilbert, *Signs in the Sky: The Astrological & Archaeological Evidence for the Birth of a New Age*, (New York, NY: Three Rivers Press, 2000), 25.

16. Gary Wayne, *The Genesis 6 Conspiracy: How Secret Societies and the Descendants of Giants Plan to Enslave Humankind*, (Sisters, OR: Deep River Books, 2014), 45.

17. Ibid, 44-45, 63.

18. Ibid, 62,63.

19. Qpp Studio, "The date of Start of Ramadan for the years 2024-2034," Alter Ego Services, https://www.qppstudio.net/global-holidays-observances/start-of-ramadan.htm.

20. Jocelyn Solis-Moreira, "How did we develop a COVID-19 vaccine so quickly?" Medical News Today, November 13, 2021, https://www.medicalnewstoday.com/articles/how-did-we-develop-a-covid-19-vaccine-so-quickly.

Chapter 14

1. Chabad.org, "Weekly Torah Portion - Parshah Archive," https://www.chabad.org/parshah/other parshas_cdo/aid/9175/jewish/All-Parshahs.htm.

Notes

2. Abraham Ojeda, Overcome Babylon, https://overcomebabylon.com/bible-prophecy-secrets-notes.

3. Blue Letter Bible, "H8643 - tᵉrûʿâ - Strong's Hebrew Lexicon (NKJV)," https://www.blueletter bible.org/lexicon/h8643/nkjv/wlc/0-1.

4. Joseph Dumond, *It Was a Riddle Not a Command*, Edited by Joli Darling, (Independently published, 2019), 114-115.

5. Berard L. Marthaler, "Christmas and its cycle," entry, in *New Catholic Encyclopedia*, Volume 3, 2nd Ed., (Farmington Hills, MI: Gale Group, 2002), 551.

6. Abraham Ojeda, "Jesus Was NOT Born on December 25th (HIDDEN End Times Prophecy) [ep.21]," Overcome Babylon YouTube Channel, December 22, 2022, https://youtu.be/kOSv8f P_vMk.

7. William Struse, "The Course of Abija," The 13th Enumeration, 2013, http://www.the13thenu meration.com/Blog13/2012/11/02/the-course-of-abija.

8. Thomas Herbert Lewin, *Fasti Sacri, Or A Key To The Chronology Of The N. T.*, (1875), 53, https://babel.hathitrust.org/cgi/pt?id=yale.39002051303130&view=1up&seq=64&size=125&q1= tiberius.

9. Jack M. Ballinger, "The Birth of Christ Recalculated", Maranatha Church, verseby-verse.org/doctrine/birthofchrist.pdf.

10. Ernest L. Martin, *The Star That Astonished the World*, (Portland, OR: Ask Publications, 1996), Accessed Online via: https://www.askelm.com/star/index.asp.

11. Stellarium app, https://stellarium.org.

12. Blue Letter Bible, "H3725 - kipur - Strong's Hebrew Lexicon (NKJV)," https://www.blueletter bible.org/lexicon/h3725/nkjv/wlc/0-1.

13. Ibid, "H3722 - kāp̄ar - Strong's Hebrew Lexicon (NKJV)," https://www.blueletterbible.org/ lexicon/h3722/nkjv/wlc/0-1.

Bibliography

118 Congress (2023-2024). "H.Res.559 - Declaring it is the policy of the United States that a nuclear Islamic Republic of Iran is not acceptable." Congress.gov, November 1, 2023. https://www.congress.gov/bill/118th-congress/house-resolution/559/text.

3rd Temple, "Home." thirdtemple.org. https://thirdtemple.org/en. ——. "Why Support the Construction." thirdtemple.org. https://thirdtemple.org/en/adhesion-form-complet.

Al Arabiya News. "Iran unveils its first hypersonic ballistic missile: State media." June 6, 2023. https://english.alarabiya.net/News/middle-east/2023/06/06/Iran-unveils-first-hypersonic-missile-named-Fattah-Report.

Aljazeera. "Gaza toll could exceed 186,000, Lancet study says." July 8, 2024. https://www.aljazeera.com/news/2024/7/8/gaza-toll-could-exceed-186000-lancet-study-says.

——. "Germany to Buy US-Made F-35s Capable of Carrying Nuclear Weapons." March 15, 2022. https://www.aljazeera.com/news/2022/3/15/germany-to-buy-us-made-f-35s-capable-of-carrying-nuclear-weapons.

——. "Iran attacks Israel with over 300 drones, missiles: What you need to know." April 14, 2024. https://www.aljazeera.com/news/2024/4/14/iran-attacks-israel-with-over-300-drones-missiles-what-you-need-to-know.

American-Israeli Cooperative Enterprise. "Haavara." Jewish Virtual Library. https://www.jewishvirtuallibrary.org/haavara.

——. "Jewish & Non-Jewish Population of Israel/Palestine (1517 - Present)." Jewish Virtual Library. https://www.jewishvirtuallibrary.org/jewish-and-non-jewish-population-of-israel-palestine-1517-present.

——. "U.S. Foreign Aid to Israel: Total Aid (1949 - Present)." Jewish Virtual Library. https://www.jewishvirtuallibrary.org/total-u-s-foreign-aid-to-israel-1949-present.

Anderson, Robert. *The Coming Prince: The Marvellous Prophecy of Daniel's Seventy Weeks Concerning the Antichrist.* Lawton, OK: Trumpet Press, 2014.

Apocrypha (KJV). Read for free on eBible: https://ebible.org/web.

Asbury University. "What Happened at Asbury University?" https://www.asbury.edu/outpouring.

Associated Press. "Netanyahu sworn in for unprecedented 6th term in Israel after being ousted last year." *CBC News,* December 29, 2022. https://www.cbc.ca/news/world/netanyahu-israel-prime-minister-1.6699880.

Ballinger, Jack M. "The Birth of Christ Recalculated." Maranatha Church. versebyverse.org/doctrine/birthofchrist.pdf.

Bibliography

BBC. "Covid origin: Why the Wuhan lab-leak theory is so disputed." March 1, 2023. https://www.bbc.com/news/world-asia-china-57268111.

—. "Howard Springs: Australia police arrest quarantine escapees." November 30, 2021. https://www.bbc.com/news/world-australia-59486285.

Bellows, Alan. "Tesla's Tower of Power." July 2007, Damn Interesting. https://www.damninteresting.com/teslas-tower-of-power.

Bennett, W.H. *Symbols of Our Celto-Saxon Heritage.* Windsor, Ontario: Covenant Books Publishing, 1976.

Bergman, Ronen and Adam Goldman. "Israel Knew Hamas's Attack Plan More Than a Year Ago." *New York Times,* November 30, 2023. https://www.nytimes.com/2023/11/30/world/middleeast/israel-hamas-attack-intelligence.html?campaign_id=307&emc=edit_igw b_20231201&instance_id=109019&nl=israel-hamas-war-briefing&regi_id=64680187& segment_id=151409&te=1&user_id=1e9c9142246ac5796beabc2f49486341.

Berkowitz, Adam Eliyahu. "Sanhedrin Invites 70 Nations to Dedicate Altar for Third Temple." Israel 365 News, November 29, 2018. https://www.israel365news.com/327422/70-nations-hanukkah-altar-third-temple.

—. "The W.E.F has its own police force whose badge resembles Daniel's End-Days prophesy [Watch]" May 25, 2022. Israel 365 News. https://www.israel365news.com/269738/the-w-e-f-has-its-own-police-force-whose-badge-resembles-daniels-end-days-prophesy/

Bible Atlas. "Meshech-Tubal (Meshech)." https://bibleatlas.org/full/meshech-tubal.htm.

Biderman, Rebecca. Ancient Path New Moon - Restoring the True Biblical Time, Facebook Group. https://www.facebook.com/groups/HisAncientPath.

—. Ancient Path New Moon YouTube Channel. https://www.youtube.com/@ancientpathnewmoon

Blake, Peter and Paul S. Blezard. *The Arcadian Cipher: The Quest to Crack the Code of Christianity's Greatest Secret.* London, England: Pan Books, 2001.

Blue Letter Bible (BLB). https://www.blueletterbible.org.

Boney, Julie T. "Prophet or Not." Life Assurance Ministries, November 19, 2019. https://blog.lifeassuranceministries.org/2019/11/19/prophet-or-not.

BRICS Ministry of External Relations. "Information about BRICS, VI BRICS Summit." 2014. https://web.archive.org/web/20150710163822/http://brics6.itamaraty.gov.br/about-brics/information-about-brics.

Britannica, T. Editors of Encyclopaedia. "Mahdi | Definition, Islam, & Eschatology." *Encyclopedia Britannica,* August 13, 2024. https://www.britannica.com/topic/mahdi.

Brown, Larisa. "Iran sends more than 200 ballistic missiles to Russia." *The Times,* September 6, 2024. https://www.thetimes.com/uk/defence/article/ballistic-clmpm3d7m.

Bibliography

Bruno, Greg. "Even a nuclear conflict between new nuclear states would decimate crop production and result in widespread starvation." Rutgers Today, August 15, 2022. https://www.rutgers.edu/news/nuclear-war-would-cause-global-famine-and-kill-billions-rutgers-led-study-finds.

Buchanan, Brenda J. *Gunpowder, Explosives and the State: A Technological History.* Aldershot, UK: Ashgate, 2006.

Buettner, Dan. Blue Zones, LLC. https://www.bluezones.com.

Canright, D. M. "Origin, History, and Failures of Adventism," Chapter 4, in *Seventh Day Adventism Renounced.* 14th Ed., B.C. Goodpasture, 1961. Accessed online via Life Assurance Ministries: https://blog.lifeassuranceministries.org/2021/05/13/4-origin-history-and-failures-of-adventism.

Capt, E. Raymond. *Missing Links Discovered in Assyrian Tablets.* Muskogee, OK: Artisan Publishers, 1985.

—. *The Great Pyramid Decoded.* Muskogee, OK: Artisan Publishers, 2005.

—. *The Lost Chapter of the Acts of the Apostles.* Muskogee, OK: Artisan Publishers, 1983.

—. *The Traditions of Glastonbury.* Muskogee, OK: Artisan Publishers, 2012.

Carr, William Guy. *Pawns in the Game,* a reprint of the 1958 edition. Willowdale, Ontario: Federation of Christian Laymen, 1958.

CBS News. "U.S. clears way for release of $6 billion in frozen Iranian funds as part of prisoner swap deal." September 11, 2023. https://www.cbsnews.com/news/iran-prisoner-swap-americans-6-billion-waiver-us-sanctions.

Chabad.org. "Weekly Torah Portion - Parshah Archive." https://www.chabad.org/parshah/otherparshas_cdo/aid/9175/jewish/All-Parshahs.htm.

Chariton, Jesse David. "The Mesopotamian Origins of the Hittite Double-Headed Eagle." *UW-L Journal of Undergraduate Research*, XIV (2008):1-13. https://www.researchgate.net/publication/339213501_The_Mesopotamian_Origins_of_the_Hittite_Double-Headed_Eagle.

Charlton, Corey. "Letter 'written by US Confederate officer 150 years ago predicted first two World Wars and said the third would be between Islamic leaders and the West'... but is it just a hoax?" *Daily Mail,* March 7, 2016. https://www.dailymail.co.uk/news/article-3480720/Letter-written-Confederate-officer-150-years-ago-predicted-two-World-Wars-said-Islamic-leaders-West-just-hoax.html.

Clover, R., et al. *The Sabbath and Jubilee Cycle Volume One.* 2nd Ed., Garden Grove: US Qadesh La Yahweh Press, 1995. http://www.yahweh.org/publications/sjc/sabjub.pdf.

Cohen, Rachel S. "The F-35 is One Step Closer to Carrying Nuclear Bombs. What's Next?" Air Force Times, October 27, 2021. https://www.airforcetimes.com/news/your-air-force/2021/10/27/the-f-35-is-one-step-closer-to-carrying-nuclear-bombs-whats-next.

Collins, Steven M. *Israel's Lost Empires.* Royal Oak, MI: Bible Blessings, 1996.

Bibliography

—. *Israel's Tribes Today.* Royal Oak, MI: Bible Blessings, 2005.

—. *The Origins and Empire of Ancient Israel.* Royal Oak, MI: Bible Blessings, 1996.

Coombs, Dean. "Part Three: 2027 and 2034 Egypt, Mecca, Medina Total Solar Eclipse." August 8, 2017, 1260d. https://1260d.com/2017/08/08/2027-and-2034-egypt-mecca-medina-total-solar-eclipse.

Cooper, Sam. "PRC narcos in Toronto are 'command and control' for North American money laundering networks used in TD Bank case: US investigator." The Bureau (Substack), August 29, 2024. https://www.thebureau.news/p/prc-narcos-in-toronto-are-command?r=l2dv4&utm_campaign=post&utm_medium=web.

Corp, Tara. "US shifts assault ship to the Mediterranean to deter an escalation of the Israel-Lebanon conflict." Associated Press, June 28, 2024. https://apnews.com/article/navy-warships-lebanon-hezbollah-israel-feec28090bed129618eda05e25a59b09.

The Cradle, "Ben Gvir threatens to implode Israeli govt over concessions to Palestinians." September 23, 2023. https://thecradle.co/articles/ben-gvir-threatens-to-implode-israeli-govt-over-concessions-to-palestinians.

Davenport, Kelsey. "IAEA Chief Sounds Alarm on Iran Nuclear Progress." Arms Control Association, March 2023. https://www.armscontrol.org/act/2023-03/news/iaea-chief-sounds-alarm-iran-nuclear-progress.

Davidiy, Yair. *Hebrew Tribes: The Israelite Tribal Identification of Western Peoples.* S.l.: Lulu Press, Inc., 2021.

Davies, Simon and Joshua Hantman. "How Netanyahu and his allies won by a knockout: The data." *Times of Israel,* November 7, 2022. https://www.timesofisrael.com/how-netanyahu-and-his-allies-won-by-a-knockout-the-data.

Das, Ranajit, Paul Wexler, Mehdi Pirooznia, and Eran Elhaik. "The Origins of Ashkenaz, Ashkenazic Jews, and Yiddish." *Frontiers in Genetics,* Volume 8, (June 20, 2017), 87. https://www.frontiersin.org/articles/10.3389/fgene.2017.00087/full.

Dearden, Lizzie. "Grooming gangs abused more than 700 women and girls around Newcastle after police appeared to punish victims." *The Independent,* February 23, 2018. https://www.independent.co.uk/news/uk/crime/grooming-gangs-uk-britain-newcastle-serious-case-review-operation-sanctuary-shelter-muslim-asian-a8225106.html.

Dehghan, Saeed Kamali and Richard Norton-Taylor. "CIA admits role in 1953 Iranian coup." *The Guardian,* August 19, 2013. https://www.theguardian.com/world/2013/aug/19/cia-admits-role-1953-iranian-coup.

Dempsey, Joseph. "Silo mentality – Iran's Haji Abad missile base." International Institute for Strategic Studies, May 4, 2021. https://www.iiss.org/en/online-analysis/military-balance/2021/04/iran-haji-abad-missile-base.

Devanna, Cecilia. "El gobierno de Javier Milei oficializó que la Argentina no entrará a los Brics." December 29, 2023, *La Nación.* https://www.lanacion.com.ar/politica/el-gobierno-de-javier-milei-oficializo-que-la-argentina-no-entrara-a-los-brics-nid29122023.

Bibliography

Dowlin, Joan E. "America's Role in Iran's Unrest." HuffPost News, July 18, 2009. https://www.huffpost.com/entry/americas-role-in-irans-un_b_216831.

Du Plessis, Carien, Anait Miridzhanian, and Bhargav Acharya. "BRICS welcomes new members in push to reshuffle world order." Reuters, August 24, 2023. https://www.reuters.com/world/brics-poised-invite-new-members-join-bloc-sources-2023-08-24.

Dumond, Joseph F. *2300 Days of Hell*. Bloomington, US: Xlibris, 2014.

—. *It Was a Riddle Not a Command*. Edited by Joli Darling. Independently published, 2019.

—. *Remembering The Sabbatical Years of 2016: Breaking The Curses By Obedience*. Bloomington US: Xlibris, 2013.

—. Sighted Moon. https://sightedmoon.com.

Durant, Frederick C. and John F. Guilmartin. "rocket and missile system | weapons system." Encyclopedia Britannica, January 9, 2024. https://www.britannica.com/technology/rocket-and-missile-system.

Durden, Tyler. "Bombshell Vax Analysis Finds $147 Billion In Economic Damage, Tens Of Millions Injured Or Disabled." March 28, 2023, Zero Hedge. https://www.zerohedge.com/markets/bombshell-vax-analysis-finds-147-billion-economic-damage-tens-millions-injured-or-disabled.

—. "Warnings About Alarming Pre-Oct 7 Hamas Activity Ignored, Say Israeli Surveillance Soldiers." *ZeroHedge,* October 28, 2023. https://www.zerohedge.com/geopolitical/warnings-about-alarming-pre-oct-7-hamas-activity-ignored-say-israeli-surveillance.

Earth Charter Commission. "The Earth Charter." https://earthcharter.org/wp-content/uploads/2020/03/echarter_english.pdf?x95251.

Elder, Isabel Hill. *Celt, Druid and Culdee*. 9th Ed., Muskogee, OK: Artisan Publishers, 2006.

Elhaik, Eran. "Ashkenazic Jews' mysterious origins unravelled by scientists thanks to ancient DNA." Phys.org, September 5, 2018. https://phys.org/news/2018-09-ashkenazic-jews-mysterious-unravelled-scientists.html.

—. "The Missing Link of Jewish European Ancestry: Contrasting the Rhineland and the Khazarian Hypotheses." *Genome Biology and Evolution,* Volume 5, Issue 1, (January 2013), 61–74. https://doi.org/10.1093%2Fgbe%2Fevs119.

Elwell, Walter A., Barry J. Beitzel, et al. *The Baker Encyclopedia of the Bible*. Volume 2, Grand Rapids, MI: Baker Book House, 1997.

—. *The Baker Encyclopedia of the Bible*. Volume 4, Grand Rapids, MI: Baker Book House, 1997.

Embassy of Israel. "The Twelve Tribes of Israel (ca 1200 BCE)." https://embassies.gov.il/MFA/AboutIsrael/Maps/Pages/The-Twelve-Tribes-of-Israel.aspx.

Encyclopedia Britannica. "Establishment of Israel". https://www.britannica.com/place/Israel/Establishment-of-Israel

Bibliography

Eurostat. "Migration and migrant population statistics." March 2024. https://ec.europa.eu/eurostat/statistics-explained/index.php?title=Migration_and_migrant_population_statistics.

Fassihi, Farnaz. "Iran Tries to Avoid War With U.S. After Stoking Mideast Conflicts." *New York Times*, February 1, 2024. https://www.nytimes.com/2024/02/01/world/middleeast/iran-us-war.html.

Fearnow, Benjamin. "NATO Alliance Breaking Up Because Germany 'Not Paying Their Fair Share,' Trump National Security Adviser Says." Newsweek, November 10, 2019. https://www.newsweek.com/nato-alliance-breaking-germany-not-paying-fair-share-trump-national-security-adviser-1470889.

Felonious Vendetta. "Mar 14, 1985 Nuclear Winter 1 of 2." Washington, District of Columbia, United States, Date Aired Mar 14, 1985, YouTube. https://www.youtube.com/watch?v=NV_xw_aHpeQ.

Fitzpatrick Informer. "Putin wears Kabbalah red thread talisman at Eurasian summit (video)." December 19, 2022. https://fitzinfo.net/2022/12/19/putin-wears-kabbalah-red-thread-talisman-video.

—. "Tucker Carlson's Kabbalah fetish." March 16, 2023. https://fitzinfo.net/2023/03/16/tucker-carlsons-kabbalah-fetish.

Gambrell, Jon. "An Iranian nuclear facility is so deep underground that US airstrikes likely couldn't reach it." AP News, May 22, 2023. https://apnews.com/article/iran-nuclear-natanz-uranium-enrichment-underground-project-04dae673fc937af04e62b65dd78db2e0.

Gates, Bill. "Does saving more lives lead to overpopulation?" Official YouTube Channel, February 13, 2018. https://youtu.be/obRG-2jurz0.

—. "The race for a COVID-19 vaccine, explained" April 30, 2020, Official YouTube Channel. https://youtu.be/u1AQ5EXcJYc.

Gavi Vaccine Alliance. "The COVAX Facility." https://www.gavi.org/covax-facility.

Gerontology Research Group. "GRG World Supercentenarian Rankings List." https://grg.org/WSRL/TableE.aspx.

Ghebreyesus, Tedros Adhanom. "WHO Director-General's opening remarks at the media briefing on COVID-19 - 11 March 2020." WHO, March 11, 2020. https://www.who.int/director-general/speeches/detail/who-director-general-s-opening-remarks-at-the-media-Briefing-on-covid-19---11-march-2020.

—. Post on X, May 5, 2023. https://x.com/DrTedros/status/1654484522358939650?ref_src=twsrc%5Etfw%7Ctwcamp%5Etweetembed%7Ctwterm%5E1654484522358939650%7Ctwgr%5E123f959b8cb34d1fa57b13308b67244ef18d5b9a%7Ctwcon%5Es1_&ref_url=https%3A%2F%2Fnews.un.org%2Fen%2Fstory%2F2023%2F05%2F1136367.

Gigot, Francis E. "Encyclopedia - Book of Daniel." Catholic Answers. https://www.catholic.com/encyclopedia/book-of-daniel.

Gilbert, Adrian Geoffrey, *Signs in the Sky: The Astrological & Archaeological Evidence for the Birth of a New Age*. New York, NY: Three Rivers Press, 2000.

Bibliography

Gillespie, Patrick and Manuela Tobias. "Milei's Embrace of Judaism Seals Argentina Pro-Israel Stance." *Bloomberg,* November 27, 2023. https://www.bloomberg.com/news/articles/2023-11-27/milei-s-conversion-to-judaism-seals-pro-israel-push-by-argentina.

Ginat, Avital. "British Mandate for Palestine." 1914-1918-online, International Encyclopedia of the First World War, December 7, 2018. https://encyclopedia.1914-1918-online.net/article/british_mandate_for_palestine.

Glazer, Hilo. "A Handful of Israeli Officers Saved 90 New Recruits From Hamas Terrorists. They Paid With Their Lives." Haaretz, October 20, 2023. https://www.haaretz.com/israel-news/2023-10-20/ty-article-magazine/.premium/a-few-idf-officers-saved-90-trainees-from-hamas-terrorists-they-paid-with-their-lives/0000018b-4da2-dc3c-a5df-ddaadf370000.

Gordon, Devorah. "New Moon Observation 24 February 2020." Devorah's Date Tree, Email Newsletter. https://mailchi.mp/84e952094079/new-moon-report-24-february-2020.

Government of Sweden. "Parental Leave Act (Föräldraledighetslagen)." Ministry of Employment, 17 November 2016. https://www.government.se/government-policy/labour-law-and-work-environment/1995584-parental-leave-act-foraldraledighetslagen.

Grand Lodge of British Columbia and Yukon A.F. & A.M. "Rebuilding the Temple." September 27, 2006. https://freemasonry.bcy.ca/anti-masonry/rebuild_temple03.html.

Hafezi, Parisa, John Irish, Tom Balmforth, and Jonathan Landay. "Exclusive: Iran sends Russia hundreds of ballistic missiles." Reuters, February 21, 2024. https://www.reuters.com/world/iran-sends-russia-hundreds-ballistic-missiles-sources-say-2024-02-21.

Hasan, Mehdi and Dina Sayedahmed. "Blowback: How a CIA-Backed Coup Led to the Rise of Iran's Ayatollahs." The Intercept, February 5, 2018. https://theintercept.com/2018/02/05/iran-cia-coup-mossadegh-ayatollah.

Hicks, Thomas. "The 2030 Mass Migration Agenda." Muckraker, January 21, 2024. https://www.muckraker.com/articles/the-2030-mass-migration-agenda.

Horn, Thomas R. *The rabbis, Donald Trump and the top-secret plan to build the Third Temple: Unveiling the incendiary scheme by religious authorities, government agents, Jewish rabbis to invoke messiah.* Crane, MO: Defender, 2019.

House of Names. Swyrich Corporation. https://www.houseofnames.com.

—. "Ramos History, Family Crest & Coats of Arms." Swyrich Corporation. https://houseofnames.com/ramos-family-crest.

Hunt, Tristram. Marx's General: The Revolutionary Life of Friedrich Engels. New York: Metropolitan Books, 2009.

(Supplement to the) Illustrated London News. "The Freemasons' Plan to Rebuild Solomon's Temple at Jerusalem, A Gigantic Task." August 28, 1909, Page 32.

Infowars. "Flashback: Great Reset Architect Klaus Schwab Brags WEF 'Penetrates' Cabinets of World Leaders." January 26, 2022. https://www.infowars.com/posts/flashback-great-reset-architect-klaus-schwab-brags-wef-penetrates-cabinets-of-world-leaders.

Bibliography

International Criminal Court. "Statement of ICC Prosecutor Karim A.A. Khan KC: Applications for arrest warrants in the situation in the State of Palestine." May 20, 2024. https://www.icc-cpi.int/news/statement-icc-prosecutor-karim-aa-khan-kc-applications-arrest-warrants-situation-state.

International Monetary Fund, "World Economic Outlook Database Groups and Aggregates Information." April 2023. https://www.imf.org/en/Publications/WEO/weo-database/2023/April/groups-and-aggregates#mae.

—. "World Economic Outlook - Steady but Slow: Resilience amid Divergence." April 2024. https://www.imf.org/en/Publications/WEO/Issues/2024/04/16/world-economic-outlook-april-2024.

Interpol. "Europe: Drug trafficking, organized crime increasing by 'an order of magnitude.'" May 8, 2023. https://www.interpol.int/en/News-and-Events/News/2023/Europe-Drug-trafficking-organized-crime-increasing-by-an-order-of-magnitude.

Iran International Newsroom. "Iranian Politician Says Tehran Might Already Have Nukes." Volant Media UK Limited, May 10, 2024. https://www.iranintl.com/en/202405108870.

Israel365. "First physical Feast since 2019 marks return of Christian tourism to Israel." September 29, 2022. https://www.israel365news.com/355268/first-physical-feast-since-2019-marks-return-of-christian-tourism-to-israel.

Israel Democracy Institute. "The Elections for the 25th Knesset 1.11.2022." https://en.idi.org.il/israeli-elections-and-parties/elections/2022.

Jackson, Ashley. *The British Empire: A Very Short Introduction.* Oxford, England: Oxford University Press, 2013.

Jacobson, Louis. "PolitFact FL: What to know about U.S. aid to Israel." PolitiFact - Central Florida Public Media, October 20, 2023. https://www.cfpublic.org/politics/2023-10-20/politfact-florida-united-states-aid-israel-palestine.

James, William and Michael Holden. "G7 Demand Action From Russia on Cybercrimes and Chemical Weapon Use." Reuters, June 13, 2021. https://www.usnews.com/news/world/articles/2021-06-13/g7-demand-action-from-russia-on-cybercrimes-and-chemical-weapon-use.

Jehovah's Witnesses. "How Daniel's Prophecy Foretells the Messiah's Arrival." JW.org. https://www.jw.org/en/library/books/bible-teach/daniels-prophecy-70-weeks-messiah.

Jerusalem Post. "Iran issues threat to Israel, US with new hypersonic weapon." November 19, 2023. https://www.jpost.com/middle-east/iran-news/article-774055.

Jewish Spiritual Leaders Institute. "Jewish Universalism." JSLI. https://jsli.net/jewish-universalism.

Jewish Telegraphic Agency (JTA). "Temple Institute announces school to train Levitical priests." August 2, 2016. https://www.jta.org/2016/08/02/israel/temple-institute-announces-school-to-train-levitical-priests.

Jubier, Xavier M. "2027 Total Solar Eclipse." Interactive Google Map. http://xjubier.free.fr/en/index_en.html.

Bibliography

Joffre, Tzvi. "'400 seconds' to Tel Aviv: Iranian media publishes Hebrew hypersonic missile threat." *Jerusalem Post,* November 14, 2022. https://www.jpost.com/middle-east/iran-news/article-722327.

Jones, Alex and Joel Skousen. "Strategic Relocation DVD," Prison Planet TV, December 17, 2012. https://tv.infowars.com/index/display/category/movies/id/4414.

Josephus, Flavius. *Antiquities of the Jews.* Read for free at Project Gutenberg: https://www.gutenberg.org/files/2848/2848-h/2848-h.htm.

The Kabbalah Centre. "Eitan Yardeni." https://www.kabbalah.com/en/people/eitan-yardeni.

Kay, Grace. "Watch how the value of a dollar has changed over the past 120 years, from toilet paper to coffee." Business Insider, Dec 21, 2021. https://www.businessinsider.com/see-how-value-of-1-dollar-changed-over-120-years-2021-12.

Keller-Lynn, Carrie and ToI Staff, "'The best party': Over 150,000 march in Tel Aviv's 25th annual Pride Parade." *Times of Israel,* June 8, 2023. https://www.timesofisrael.com/the-best-party-tens-of-thousands-march-in-tel-avivs-25th-annual-pride-parade.

Khalil, Joe, Kellie Meyer, and Devan Markham. "US special forces already stationed in Israel before attacks: Source." NewsNation, October 11, 2023. https://www.newsnationnow.com/world/war-in-israel/biden-condemns-sheer-evil-of-hamas.

Khatiba, Rasha, Martin McKeec, and Salim Yusufd. "Counting the dead in Gaza: difficult but essential." *The Lancet,* Volume 404, Issue 10449, (July 20, 2024), 237-238. https://www.thelancet.com/journals/lancet/article/PIIS0140-6736(24)01169-3/fulltext.

Khlevniuk, Oleg V. *The History of the Gulag: From Collectivization to the Great Terror.* Translated by Vadim A. Staklo. New Haven, CT: Yale University Press, 2004.

King James Bible Online™ (2007-2023). https://www.kingjamesbibleonline.org/1-Maccabees-Chapter-1.

Klein, Zvika. "Argentina's Milei wears kippah at havdalah, vows support for Jews and Israel." *Jerusalem Post,* November 26. https://www.jpost.com/international/article-775205.

Knox, John S. "Solomon." World History Encyclopedia. January 25, 2017. https://www.worldhistory.org/solomon.

Koenig, Melissa. "US carrier strike group is rushed to the Middle East as new Israeli intelligence suggests Iran attack within days." Daily Mail, August 12, 2024. https://www.dailymail.co.uk/news/article-13734119/US-carrier-strike-group-rushed-Middle-East-Israeli-intelligence-Iran-attack.html.

Koire, Rosa. *Behind the Green Mask: U.N. Agenda 21.* Santa Rosa, CA: Post Sustainability Institute Press, 2011.

Körömi, Csongor and Barbara Moens, "Orbán parrots Putin's lines on Ukraine in leaked letter to EU chief." Politico, July 9, 2024. https://www.politico.eu/article/viktor-orban-letter-european-council-charles-michel-vladimir-putin-war-in-ukraine-russia-kremlin.

Bibliography

Lardner, Richard. "US payment of $1.7 billion to Iran made entirely in cash." AP News, September 6, 2016. https://apnews.com/united-states-government-fd4113419276444e ba1d2a46d5c29752.

Lewin, Thomas Herbert. *Fasti Sacri, or a Key to the Chronology of the N.T.* London, 1875. https://babel.hathitrust.org/cgi/pt?id=yale.39002051303130&view=1up&seq=64&size=125& q1=tiberius.

Linder, Sally. "Ark of Hope." http://www.arkofhope.org.

Los Angeles Times. "Despite high vaccination rates, Israel scrambles to curb jump in COVID infections." July 1, 2021. https://www.latimes.com/world-nation/story/2021-07-01/israel-scrambles-curb-jump-covid-infections.

Mahoney, Megan. "How Women Have it All in Sweden: Female Empowerment through Work-Life Balance." The Swedish Program. https://swedishprogram.org/how-women-have-it-all-in-sweden.

Marthaler, Berard L. "Christmas and its cycle," entry, in *New Catholic Encyclopedia*. Volume 3, 2nd Ed. Farmington Hills, MI: Gale Group, 2002.

Martin, Ernest L. *The Star That Astonished the World.* Portland, OR: Ask Publications, 1996.

Martin, Walter, et al. *The Kingdom of the Occult.* Nashville, TN: Thomas Nelson, 2008.

Masungwini, Norman. "SA invites 70 heads of states to the BRICS summit, but Western leaders excluded." City Press, July 21, 2023. https://www.news24.com/citypress/politics/sa-invites-70-heads-of-states-to-the-brics-summit-but-western-leaders-excluded-20230721.

Meadows, Donella H., Dennis L. Meadows, Jørgen Randers, and William W. Behrens. *The Limits to Growth: A Report for the Club of Rome's Project on the Predicament of Mankind.* New York: Universe Books, 1972.

Mehta, Aaron. "F-15E Becomes First Aircraft Compatible with New Nuclear Bomb Design." Defense News, June 8, 2020. https://www.defensenews.com/smr/nuclear-arsenal/2020/06/08/f-15e-becomes-first-aircraft-certified-for-new-nuclear-bomb-design.

Mercola, Joseph. *The Truth About COVID-19.* London, UK: Chelsea Green Publishing, 2021. iBooks.

Middle East Eye. "Israeli industry braces for economic damage amid Turkish trade ban." May 3, 2024. https://www.middleeasteye.net/news/israeli-industry-braces-economic-damage-amid-turkish-trade-ban.

Missile Threat. "Khorramshahr." The CSIS Missile Defense Project, April 23, 2024. https://missilethreat.csis.org/missile/khorramshahr.

—. "Missiles of Iran." The CSIS Missile Defense Project, August 10, 2021. https://missilethreat.csis.org/country/iran.

—. "Zolfaghar (Dezful, Qasem)." The CSIS Missile Defense Project, April 23, 2024. https://missilethreat.csis.org/missile/zolfaghar.

Bibliography

Mitchell, Chris. "Texas Red Heifers' Arrival Stirs Prophetic Excitement in Israel." CBN News, September 23, 2022. https://www1.cbn.com/cbnnews/israel/2022/september/texas-red-heifers-arrival-stirs-prophetic-excitement.

Modzelevich, Martha. "Mandragora autumnalis, Mandragora officinarum, Autumn Mandrake." Flowers in Israel. http://flowersinisrael.com/Mandragoraautumnalis_page.htm.

Moonan, Brian. *Agenda 21: The Earth Charter, The Ark of Hope, and the New World Order.* * 2016. https://vimeo.com/150948709 *Note: Brian Moonan's website is the following: https://turnfromyouridols.com. You used to be able to click on the Agenda 21 video from his website and it would take you over to YouTube, but his YouTube video has been banned and deleted. Watch it on Brian's Vimeo and even download it for free while you still can.

Moore, Phil. *Straight to the Heart of Acts: 60 Bite-Sized Insights*. Oxford, England: Monarch Books, 2010.

Mythologian.net. "Laurel Wreath/Crown Symbol, Its Meaning and History." https://mythologian. net/laurel-wreath-crown-symbol-meaning-history.

NASA. "B. The Role of Radioactive Decay," https://imagine.gsfc.nasa.gov/educators/elements/ imagine/09.html.

—. Eclipse map/figure/table/predictions courtesy of Fred Espenak, NASA/Goddard Space Flight Center Emeritus, from https://eclipse.gsfc.nasa.gov.

National Records of Scotland. "The Declaration of Arbroath." 700th Anniversary Display (1320–2020). https://www.nrscotland.gov.uk/files/research/NRS_DoA_English_booklet_700_Spread s_WEB.pdf.

NATO. "Defense expenditure of NATO countries (2014-2023)." March 14, 2024. https://www. nato.int/cps/en/natohq/news_223304.htm.

New York Times. "Dorothy de Rothschild, 93, Supporter of Israel." Obituary, December 13, 1988. https://www.nytimes.com/1988/12/13/obituaries/dorothy-de-rothschild-93-supporter-of-israel.html.

NPR. "Israel sets COVID-19 record as rule changes create whiplash." January 5, 2022. https://www. npr.org/2022/01/05/1070478298/israel-sets-covid-19-record-as-rule-changes-create-whiplash.

Nuclear Threat Initiative. "Missiles & Other WMD Delivery Systems - Module 2: Understanding Missiles." 2023. https://tutorials.nti.org/delivery-system/understanding-missiles.

Ochsenwald, William L., et al., "Establishment of Israel." Encyclopedia Britannica, September 12, 2024. https://www.britannica.com/place/Israel/Establishment-of-Israel.

Ojeda, Abraham. Overcome Babylon YouTube Channel. https://www.youtube.com/@ overcomebabylon

—. Overcome Babylon. https://overcomebabylon.com/bible-prophecy-secrets-notes.

OSTI. "Nuclear winter. Joint Hearing before the Subcommittee on Natural Resources, Agriculture Research and Environment of the Committee on Science and Technology and the Subcom-

Bibliography

mittee on Energy and the Environment of the Committee on Interior and Insular Affairs, US House of Representatives, Ninety-Ninth Congress, First Session, March 14, 1985." U.S. Department of Energy Office of Scientific and Technical Information, January 1, 1985. https://www.osti.gov/biblio/6433401.

Palestinian Chronicle Staff. "This is How Al-Qassam's Navel Units Stormed Zakim's Fortified Military Base – VIDEO." *The Palestine Chronicle,* October 9, 2023. https://www.palestinechronicle.com/this-is-how-al-qassams-navel-units-stormed-zakims-fortified-military-base-video.

Parker, Ceri. "8 predictions for the world in 2030." Nov 12, 2016. World Economic Forum. https://www.weforum.org/agenda/2016/11/8-predictions-for-the-world-in-2030.

Parker, Christopher. "Hidden Chamber Revealed Inside Great Pyramid of Giza." Smithsonian Magazine, March 3, 2023. https://www.smithsonianmag.com/smart-news/hidden-chamber-pyramid-giza-180981745.

Petrovsky-Shtern, Yohanan. *Lenin's Jewish Question.* New Haven, CT: Yale University Press, 2010.

Pfeffer, Anshel. "Fragment of ancient parchment given to Jewish scholars." Haaretz. Archived from the original (http://www.haaretz.com/hasen/spages/920915.html) on July 7, 2009 at: https://web.archive.org/web/20090707031841/http://www.haaretz.com/hasen/spages/920915.html.

Phillips, Tom, Josefina Salomón, and Facundo Iglesia. "Argentina presidential election: far-right libertarian Javier Milei wins after rival concedes." The Guardian, November 19, 2023. https://www.theguardian.com/world/2023/nov/20/argentina-presidential-election-far-right-libertarian-javier-milei-wins-after-rival-concedes.

Phinance Technologies. "The Vaccine Damage Project - Human Cost." March 2023. https://phinancetechnologies.com/HumanityProjects/The%20VDamage%20Project%20-%20Human%20%20Cost.htm.

Pike, John. "Fattah Hypersonic MRBM." Global Security. https://www.globalsecurity.org/wmd/world/iran/fattah.htm.

Polak, Abraham Nahum. *Chazaria - Dzieje Krolestwa Żydowskiego W Europie* (Khazaria - The History of the Jewish Kingdom in Europe). Polish Edition, Przemyśl, Poland: Południowo-Wschodni Instytut Naukowy w Przemyślu, 2015.

Procureur, Sébastien, et al. "Precise characterization of a corridor-shaped structure in Khufu's Pyramid by observation of cosmic-ray muons." *Nature Communications,* Volume 14, Article number 1144, (2023). https://www.nature.com/articles/s41467-023-36351-0.

Provan, Iain W., V. Philips Long, and Tremper Longman. *A Biblical History of Israel.* Louisville, KY: Westminster John Knox Press, 2003.

Qpp Studio. "The date of Start of Ramadan for the years 2024-2034." Alter Ego Services. https://www.qppstudio.net/global-holidays-observances/start-of-ramadan.htm.

Rappaport, Helen. *The Last Days of the Romanovs: Tragedy at Ekaterinburg.* New York, NY: St. Martin's Press, 2009.

538

Bibliography

Rosenson, Alex. "The Terms of the Anglo-American Financial Agreement." *The American Economic Review*, 37, No. 1, (1947): 178–187. https://www.jstor.org/stable/1802868.

Rostampour, Maryam and Marziyeh Amirizadeh. *Captive in Iran: A remarkable true story of hope and triumph amid the horror of Tehran's brutal Evin Prison.* Atlanta, GA: Tyndale Momentum, 2013.

Sabbath School Lesson. "The 70 Weeks and the 2300 Days." Sabbath School Net, October 14, 2019. https://ssnet.org/blog/tuesday-the-70-weeks-and-the-2300-days.

Schaff, Philip. *Ante-Nicene Fathers Volume 7, Of the Manner in Which the Persecutors Died.* Grand Rapids, MI: Christian Classics Ethereal Library, 1885.

Schwab, Klaus, et al. *Covid-19: The Great Reset.* Cologny/Geneva, Switzerland: World Economic Forum, 2020.

Seventh-Day Adventist Church. "2023 Annual Statistical Report New Series, Volume 5." ASTR - Office of Archives, Statistics, and Research, March 1, 2022. https://documents.adven tistarchives.org/Statistics/ASR/ASR2023A.pdf.

Sharma, Shweta. "Brics countries agree historic expansion as six new countries invited to join." The Independent, August 24, 2023. https://www.independent.co.uk/news/world/africa/brics-2023-summit-new-members-saudi-uae-iran-b2398553.html.

Shneer, David. "Modern Jewish History - Leon Trotsky: The Jewish renegade socialist." My Jewish Learning. https://www.myjewishlearning.com/article/leon-trotsky.

Shoebat, Walid. "Who is Walid? Biography of Walid Shoebat." https://shoebat.com/shoebat-foundation/who-is-walid.

Silkoff, Shira. "Surveillance soldiers warned of Hamas activity on Gaza border for months before Oct. 7." The Times of Israel, October 26, 2023. https://www.timesofisrael.com/surveillance-soldiers-warned-of-hamas-activity-on-gaza-border-for-months-before-oct-7.

Singer, Isidore, et al. *The Jewish Encyclopedia.* Volume 4: Chazars–Dreyfus Case. New York: Funk and Wagnalls Company, 1912. https://archive.org/details/the-jewish-encyclopedia-vol.-4/page/1/mode/2up.

Soldatkin, Vladimir and Anita Komuves. "Hungary's Orban talks Ukraine peace with Putin, stirring EU outcry." Reuters, July 5, 2024. https://www.reuters.com/world/europe/hungarys-orban-says-no-position-negotiate-between-ukraine-russia-2024-07-05.

Solis-Moreira, Jocelyn. "How did we develop a COVID-19 vaccine so quickly?" Medical News Today, November 13, 2021. https://www.medicalnewstoday.com/articles/how-did-we-develop-a-covid-19-vaccine-so-quickly.

Solzhenitsyn, Aleksandr Isayevich. *The Gulag archipelago, 1918-1956: an experiment in literary investigation, Volume 2.* Tran. Thomas P. Whitney. London: Collins: Harvill Press: 1974.

—. *Two Hundred Years Together: On Russian-Jewish Relations, 1795-1995.* 1st English Ed., The Incorrect Library: 2017. iBooks.

Bibliography

Sommerlad, Joe. "Nato in numbers: Which members have the biggest armies and how has the military alliance grown?" The Independent, 12 July 2023. https://www.independent.co.uk/news/world/europe/nato-members-countries-map-military-b2373875.html.

Soylu, Ragip, "War on Gaza: Turkey halts all trade with Israel over war." Middle East Eye, May 2, 2024. https://www.middleeasteye.net/news/war-gaza-turkey-halts-all-trade-israel-over-war.

Sparks, Nicole and Darrin J. Rodgers, "John McConnell, Jr. and the Pentecostal Origins of Earth Day." Assemblies of God Heritage, Volume 30, 2010, Page 22. Accessed online via Internet Archive: https://web.archive.org/web/20120331232111/http://ifphc.org/pdf/Heritage/2010.pdf.

Stanton, Andrew. "Fact Check: Did Joe Biden Authorize $8 Billion Aid Package to Israel?" Newsweek, October 7, 2023. https://www.newsweek.com/fact-check-joe-biden-israel-aid-1832895.

Starcevic, Seb. "Turkey threatens to 'enter' Israel to protect Palestinians." Politico, July 29, 2024. https://www.politico.eu/article/turkey-nato-tayyip-erdogan-threatens-enter-israel-help-palestinians.

State of Israel. The Judicial Authority Supreme Court. "The Gatehouse: The Pyramid and the Library." https://supreme.court.gov.il/sites/en/VirtualTour/Pages/07_gatehouse.aspx.
—. The Judicial Authority Supreme Court. "The Symbols." https://supreme.court.gov.il/sites/en/VirtualTour/Pages/11_icons.aspx.

Stellarium app. https://stellarium.org.

Struse, William. "The Course of Abija." The 13th Enumeration, 2013. http://www.the13thenumeration.com/Blog13/2012/11/02/the-course-of-abija.

Siracusa, Joseph M. Nuclear Weapons - A Very Short Introduction. 3rd Ed., Oxford, UK: Oxford University Press, 2020.

Tabikha, Kamal. "'Big Void' at the core of Giza's Great Pyramid continues to baffle scientists." The National, March 19, 2023. https://www.thenationalnews.com/mena/egypt/2023/03/20/big-void-at-the-core-of-gizas-great-pyramid-continues-to-baffle-scientists.

Tauber, Yanki. "Winter." Chabad-Lubavitch Media Center. https://www.chabad.org/library/article_cdo/aid/2669/jewish/Winter.htm.

Temple Institute. "Statement of Principles." templeinstitute.org. https://templeinstitute.org/statement-of-principles-2.

Than, Krisztina, Alan Charlish, and Angus MacSwan. "Hungary says 'grievances' hold up ratification of Sweden's NATO accession." Reuters, March 29, 2023. https://www.reuters.com/world/europe/hungary-says-grievances-hold-up-ratification-swedens-nato-accession-2023-03-29.

Thiele, Edwin R. The Mysterious Numbers of the Hebrew Kings. Grand Rapids, MI: Kregel, 1994.

Thompson, S. L. and S. H. Schneider. "Nuclear winter reappraised." Foreign Affairs, Volume 64, Issue 5, (June 6, 1986), 981–1005. http://n2t.net/ark:/85065/d7n29wpv.

Bibliography

Tibón, Gutierre. *Historia del nombre y de la fundación de México.* 3rd Ed., D.F., México: Fondo De Cultura Económica, 1993.

Torah Calendar, https://torahcalendar.com/Calendar.asp?YM=Y2033M12.

Trump, Donald J. *The Way to the Top: The Best Business Advice I Ever Received.* New York, NY: Crown Business, 2004.

TruthVids. "Heraldry & Symbols of the 12 Tribes of Israel in Europe." YouTube, May 1, 2020. https://www.youtube.com/watch?v=gabcvC2L9mE.

Turco, R. P., et al. "Nuclear Winter: Global Consequences of Multiple Nuclear Explosions." *Science,* Volume 222, Issue 4630, (December 23, 1983), 1283-1292. https://www.science.org/doi/10.1126/science.222.4630.1283.

United Nations. "Israel's occupation of Palestinian Territory is 'apartheid': UN rights expert." UN News, March 25, 2022. https://news.un.org/en/story/2022/03/1114702.

—. "Joint statement by the delegations of Azerbaijan, Bangladesh, Belarus, Benin, Bosnia and Herzegovina, Canada, Egypt, Georgia, Guatemala, Jamaica, Kazakhstan, Mongolia, Nauru, Pakistan, Qatar, the Republic of Moldova, the Russian Federation, Saudi Arabia, the Sudan, the Syrian Arab Republic, Tajikistan, Timor-Leste, Ukraine, the United Arab Emirates and the United States of America on the 70th anniversary of the Great Famine of 1932-1933 in Ukraine (Holodomor)." November 7, 2003. https://digitallibrary.un.org/record/505743?v=pdf.

—. *Report of the United Nations Conference on the Human Environment.* A/CONF.48/14/Rev.1 Stockholm, June 5-16, 1972. https://documents.un.org/prod/ods.nsf/home.xsp.

—. "Resolution adopted by the General Assembly on 21 September 2020." https://documents.un.org/doc/undoc/gen/n20/248/80/pdf/n2024880.pdf.

—. "Resolution adopted by the General Assembly on 25 September 2015." https://www.un.org/en/development/desa/population/migration/generalassembly/docs/globalcompact/A_RES_70_1_E.pdf.

—. "WHO chief declares end to COVID-19 as a global health emergency." UN News, May 5, 2023. https://news.un.org/en/story/2023/05/1136367.

UNICEF. "Sweden, Norway, Iceland, Estonia and Portugal rank highest for family-friendly policies in OECD and EU countries." June 12, 2019. https://www.unicef.org/press-releases/sweden-norway-iceland-and-estonia-rank-highest-family-friendly-policies-oecd-and-eu.

Van Donzel, Emeri and Andrea Schmidt. *Gog and Magog in Early Eastern Christian and Islamic Sources: Sallam's Quest for Alexander's Wall.* Leiden, South Holland: Koninklijke Brill NV, 2009.

Vatican Library. "Codex Vaticanus." Page 1530. https://digi.vatlib.it/view/MSS_Vat.gr.1209#.

Venegas, Natalie and Jon Jackson, "US Approves $20 Billion Arms Deal for Israel." Newsweek, August 13, 2024. https://www.newsweek.com/us-approves-20-billion-arms-deal-israel-1938806.

Bibliography

VOA News. "WHO Says 184 Countries Have Now Joined COVAX Vaccine Program." October 19, 2020. https://www.voanews.com/a/covid-19-pandemic_who-says-184-countries-have-now-joined-covax-vaccine-program/6197326.html.

Warburton, Jena. "Walmart suddenly closing more stores in 2024." The Street, June 24, 2024. https://www.thestreet.com/retail/walmart-suddenly-closing-more-stores-in-2024.

Wayne, Gary. *The Genesis 6 Conspiracy: How Secret Societies and the Descendants of Giants Plan to Enslave Humankind.* Sisters, OR: Deep River Books, 2014.

Webb, Whitney. *One Nation Under Blackmail Volume 1.* Walterville, OR: Trine Day, 2022.

WebMD. "Pandemics." April 18, 2022. https://www.webmd.com/cold-and-flu/what-are-epidemics-pandemics-outbreaks.

Weinthal, Benjamin. "Iranian lawmaker declares Tehran obtained nuclear bombs." Fox News, May 12, 2024. https://www.foxnews.com/world/iranian-lawmaker-declares-tehran-obtained-nuclear-bombs.

Wendorf, Marcia. "People routinely live over 100 years in global 'blue zones'. Should you move?" Interesting Engineering, November 4, 2021. https://interestingengineering.com/health/people-routinely-live-beyond-the-age-of-100-in-these-rare-blue-zones.

White, Jamie. "Video: Canadian MP CENSORED For Pointing Out WEF's Corrupt Influence Over Trudeau's Gov't." Infowars, February 19, 2022. https://www.infowars.com/posts/video-canadian-mp-accused-of-spreading-disinformation-for-pointing-out-wefs-corrupt-influence-over-trudeaus-govt.

Wikipedia contributors. "Book of Enoch." *Wikipedia, The Free Encyclopedia.* https://en.wikipedia.org/w/index.php?title=Book_of_Enoch&oldid=1149254159.

—. "Genealogies of Genesis." *Wikipedia, The Free Encyclopedia.* https://en.wikipedia.org/w/index.php?title=Genealogies_of_Genesis&oldid=1148149977.

—. "Geneva Conventions." *Wikipedia, The Free Encyclopedia.* https://en.wikipedia.org/w/index.php?title=Geneva_Conventions&oldid=1148116019.

—. "Jewish population by city." *Wikipedia, The Free Encyclopedia.* https://en.wikipedia.org/w/index.php?title=Jewish_population_by_city&oldid=1148351629.

—. "Karl Marx." *Wikipedia, The Free Encyclopedia.* https://en.wikipedia.org/w/index.php?title=Karl_Marx&oldid=1148703430.

—. "League of Nations." *Wikipedia, The Free Encyclopedia.* https://en.wikipedia.org/w/index.php?title=League_of_Nations&oldid=1148428729.

—. "List of Israel Defense Forces Bases." *Wikipedia, The Free Encyclopedia.* https://en.wikipedia.org/wiki/List_of_Israel_Defense_Forces_bases.

—. "Neutron bomb." *Wikipedia, The Free Encyclopedia.* https://en.wikipedia.org/w/index.php?title=Neutron_bomb&oldid=1149220149.

Bibliography

——. "Nuremberg Code." *Wikipedia, The Free Encyclopedia.* https://en.wikipedia.org/w/index.php?title=Nuremberg_Code&oldid=1146994155.

——. "United Nations." *Wikipedia, The Free Encyclopedia.* https://en.wikipedia.org/w/index.php?title=United_Nations&oldid=1148713682.

——. "United Nations Partition Plan for Palestine." *Wikipedia, The Free Encyclopedia.* https://en.wikipedia.org/w/index.php?title=United_Nations_Partition_Plan_for_Palestine&oldid=1148074278.

The William Davidson Talmud (Koren - Steinsaltz). "Bava Metzia 114b:2." Sefaria. https://www.sefaria.org/Bava_Metzia.114b.2?lang=bi.

——. "Gitten 57a." Sefaria. https://www.sefaria.org/Gittin.57a.3?lang=bi&with=all&lang2=en.

——. "Sanhedrin 57a:16." Sefaria. https://www.sefaria.org/Sanhedrin.57a.16?lang=bi&with=all&lang2=en.

——. "Yevamot.98a:3." Sefaria. https://www.sefaria.org/Yevamot.98a.3?lang=bi&with=all&lang2=en.

Willis, Norman B. "Aviv Barley Simplified." Nazarene Israel YouTube, Apr 24, 2021. https://youtu.be/GDLI_jGGO30

——. *The Torah Calendar.* CreateSpace Independent Publishing Platform: April 2, 2012. https://nazareneisrael.org/book/torah-calendar/aviv-barley-the-head-of-the-year.

Wilson, Brian. "Russia Ready To Retaliate Against U.S. With Satan II." Red Pilled TV, June 2, 2022. https://banned.video/watch?id=6298fa3d16f9b23e843f898c.

World Economic Forum, "8 Predictions For The World In 2030." February 7, 2017, Internet Archive. https://archive.org/details/8-predictions-for-the-world-in-2030.

——. "Conversation with Albert Bourla, CEO of Pfizer | Davos | #WEF22." Official YouTube Channel, May 25, 2022. https://youtu.be/9ccd3LMNMl8.

——. "Partners." https://www.weforum.org/partners.

——. "Preparing for the Next Pandemic with Bill Gates | Davos | #WEF22." Official YouTube Channel, May 24, 2022. https://youtu.be/NA0Fphx4UMg.

——. "Will the Future Be Human? - Yuval Noah Harari." Annual Meeting, January 25, 2018, Official YouTube Channel. https://youtu.be/hL9uk4hKyg4.

——. "Yuval Noah Harari." https://www.weforum.org/people/yuval-noah-harari.

World Health Organization (WHO). "Boost for global response to COVID-19 as economies worldwide formally sign up to COVAX facility." September 21, 2020. https://www.who.int/news/item/21-09-2020-boost-for-global-response-to-covid-19-as-economies-worldwide-formally-sign-up-to-covax-facility.

——. "GHE: Life expectancy and healthy life expectancy." https://www.who.int/

Bibliography

data/gho/data/themes/mortality-and-global-health-estimates/ghe-life-expectancy-and-healthy-life-expectancy.

—. "Timeline: WHO's COVID-19 response." https://www.who.int/emergencies/diseases/novel-coronavirus-2019/interactive-timeline#.

Worldometer. "GDP by Country." 2023. https://www.worldometers.info/gdp/gdp-by-country.

Zitun, Yoav. "One-fifth of troop fatalities in Gaza due to friendly fire or accidents, IDF reports." Ynet News, December 12, 2023. https://www.ynetnews.com/article/rkjqoobip.

Abraham's Recommended Reading

Bible Prophecy Secrets II: The Hidden Prophecy of the Phoenicians, Lost Tribes, and America's 3 Solar Eclipse Omens
by Abraham Ojeda

The Origins and Empire of Ancient Israel
by Steven M. Collins

Missing Links Discovered in Assyrian Tablets: Study of Assyrian Tables that Reveal the Fate of the Lost Tribes of Israel
by E. Raymond Capt.

Symbols of Our Celto-Saxon Heritage
by W.H. Bennett

A Game Changing Revelation Volumes 1 and 2: The Hidden Ancestry of America and Great Britain
by Stephen J. Spykerman

The Sabbath and Jubilee Cycle Volume One
by R. Clover and Qadesh La Yahweh Press

Two Hundred Years Together: On Russian-Jewish Relations, 1795-1995
by Alexander Isayevich Solzhenitsyn

The Gulag Archipelago
by Alexander Isayevich Solzhenitsyn

Captive in Iran: A Remarkable True Story of Hope and Triumph Amid the Horror of Tehran's Brutal Evan Prison
by Maryam Rostampour and Marziyeh Amirizadeh

Tortured for Christ
by Richard Wurmbrand

Acknowledgments

No man is an island, as people say; and I am no exception. Many men and women have helped me over the years to help me become the man that I am today. Numerous people could rightfully be mentioned here, and I would barely scratch the surface.

However, nothing "good" in my life would have ever been possible without first saying "yes" to Jesus and accepting Him as the Lord of my life many years ago now. He alone is the one that has made this work possible. While all men will fail, disappoint, and betray eventually, Christ never forsakes His own. His love is perfect. His ways are pure. I'm so happy that I chose to follow His clear calling on my life when I was only a teenager. When I look back on my life and the amazing sequence of events that have taken place, I now realize that saying "yes" to Him meant that I was just along for the ride the whole time. Looking back, there's no other way to describe things. He was, and still is, in sovereign command of my life. I wouldn't have it any other way.

If you still have not called upon the name of Jesus in sincerity and asked Him to reveal Himself to you, there's no reason to delay.

This is the single greatest decision that all men everywhere have to make, and ignoring His voice also means that your decision has already been made.

About the Author

Abraham Ojeda became a born-again Christian at the age of 16 but always struggled with various demonic strongholds, addictions, and anger. After spending a decade in various Christian churches, attending a Christian college, and seeking to walk out his faith within the mainstream paradigm of Western faith, he quit going to church in 2016. Even after attending dozens of churches from all over the US from California to Louisiana, it always felt like something was missing. Why was Passover replaced with Easter? Who decided that Old Testament "tithing" is one of the only laws that still applies to the Church today? What about the other Laws? And what happened to the power of the Holy Spirit that Jesus promised? These questions became a burden.

After a near divorce with his wife in late 2019, Abraham diligently sought Jesus one day early in the morning and full of tears. That was the single moment that changed everything. Jesus made it known that there is true power and authority in His name to uproot and cast out every demonic spirit and spiritual stronghold of wickedness in order to walk exactly as He intended. Jesus clearly revealed the power of the Great Commission that was missing up to this point in Abraham's life.

That singular day was the climax of a great awakening that had already started from a series of unconventional decisions. From being a professional chemist to becoming an off-grid agrarian, Abraham challenged every narrative and religious dogma in order to pursue God's calling in his life. Fast forward to today, and Abraham's marriage has grown stronger than ever, and his walk with Jesus has become transformed through the understanding of both the Spirit and Truth of the Bible.

Kingdom Secrets, an online biblical education platform, was born out of the necessity to show God's people how to experience the fullness of the Gospel and the Instructions (Torah), walk in the miraculous power of the Holy Spirit, and fulfill God's calling on their lives. Kingdom Secrets Academy is dedicated to restoring the faith of 1st century saints and proclaiming the unfiltered truth of end times prophecy during these very last days of mankind.

www.ingramcontent.com/pod-product-compliance
Lightning Source LLC
Chambersburg PA
CBHW071130130626
46553CB00004B/1321